Festschrift in Honor of Peter Schmidt

Robin C. Sickles • William C. Horrace
Editors

Festschrift in Honor of Peter Schmidt

Econometric Methods and Applications

Springer

Editors
Robin C. Sickles
Department of Economics
Rice University
Houston, TX, USA

William C. Horrace
Department of Economics
Syracuse University
Syracuse, NY, USA

ISBN 978-1-4899-8007-6 ISBN 978-1-4899-8008-3 (eBook)
DOI 10.1007/978-1-4899-8008-3
Springer New York Heidelberg Dordrecht London

Library of Congress Control Number: 2013958084

Printed on acid-free paper

Springer is part of Springer Science+Business Media (www.springer.com)

This book is dedicated to Christine.

Demo for Peter-Point© Presentation Software

Contents

Contributors

Seung Chan Ahn Department of Economics, Arizona State University, Tempe, AZ, USA

School of Economics, Sogang University, Seoul, South Korea

Pavlos Almanidis International Tax Services, Ernst and Young LLP, Toronto, ON, Canada

Scott E. Atkinson Department of Economics, Terry College of Business, University of Georgia, Athens, GA, USA

Christopher Cornwell Department of Economics, Terry College of Business, University of Georgia, Athens, GA, USA

Cody P. Dahl Hancock Agricultural Investment Group, Boston, MA, USA

Matthew Greenwood-Nimmo Department of Economics, University of Melbourne, Carlton, Australia

David K. Guilkey Department of Economics and the Carolina Population Center, University of North Carolina at Chapel Hill, Chapel Hill, NC, USA

Kevin Hasker Economics Department, Bilkent University, Bilkent, Ankara, Turkey

William C. Horrace Department of Economics, Syracuse University, Syracuse, NY, USA

Wanling Huang Department of Economics and Finance, College of Business Administration, The University of Texas – Pan American, Edinburg, TX, USA

Kyung So Im Division of Insurance and Research, Federal Deposit Insurance Corporation (FDIC), Washington, DC, USA

Bibo Jiang School of Economics, Fudan University, Shanghai, China

Peter M. Lance Carolina Population Center, University of North Carolina at Chapel Hill, Chapel Hill, NC, USA

Young Hoon Lee Department of Economics, Sogang University, Seoul, South Korea

Junsoo Lee Department of Economics, Finance and Legal Studies, Culverhouse College of Commerce and Business Administration, The University of Alabama, Tuscaloosa, AL, USA

Ming Meng Department of Economics, Temple University, Philadelphia, PA 19122, USA

Hyungsik Roger Moon Department of Economics, University of Southern California, Los Angeles, CA, USA

Department of Economics, Yonsei University, Seoul, South Korea

Charles B. Moss University of Florida, Food and Resource Economics, Gainesville, FL, USA

Artem Prokhorov Department of Economics and CIREQ, Concordia University, Montreal, Canada

School of Economics and Discipline of Business Analytics and MEAFA, University of Sydney, Sydney, Australia

Junhui Qian School of Economics, Shanghai Jiao Tong University, Shanghai, China

Anita Regmi CGIAR Consortium, Montpellier, France

Kurt E. Schnier Department of Economics, Andrew Young School of Policy Studies, Georgia State University, Atlanta, GA, USA

James L. Seale, Jr. University of Florida, Food and Resource Economics, Gainesville, FL, USA

Yongcheol Shin Department of Economics and Related Studies, University of York, York, UK

Jinseok Shin Department of Economics, Sogang University, Seoul, South Korea

Robin C. Sickles Department of Economics, Rice University, Houston, TX, USA

Margie A. Tieslau Department of Economics, University of North Texas, Denton, TX, USA

Byungchul Yu Department of International Trade (BB-1408), School of Management, Dong-A, University, Bumin-Dong, 2 Ga-1 Seo-gu, Busan, South Korea

Chapter 1
Introduction

Robin C. Sickles and William C. Horrace

This volume is dedicated to the remarkable career of Professor Peter Schmidt and the role he has played in mentoring us, his Ph.D. students. Peter's accomplishments are legendary among his students and the profession. Each of the papers in this Festschrift is a research work executed by a former Ph.D. student of Peter, from his days at the University of North Carolina at Chapel Hill to his time at Michigan State University. Most of the papers were presented at *The Conference in Honor of Peter Schmidt*, June 30–July 2, 2011 (http://economics.rice.edu/Content.aspx?id=686). The conference was largely attended by his former students and one current student, who traveled from as far as Europe and Asia to honor Peter. This was a conference to celebrate Peter's contribution to our contributions. By "our contributions" we mean the research papers that make up this Festschrift and the countless others by his students represented and not represented in this volume. Peter's students may have their families to thank for much that is positive in their lives. However, if we think about it, our professional lives would not be the same without the lessons and the approaches to decision making that we learned from Peter.

A brief, and by no means exhaustive, list of those lessons and approaches to decision making we have learned from Peter have filled our collective skill set with attributes that have made our professional successes so much more achievable and inevitable. They are the "Five P's" from Peter. The first is *perfection*. As Peter would remind us, there is no theorem or computer program that can be almost correct. The second is a *positive* attitude. The cup is always half full, not half empty, and if not, then one may wish to get a smaller cup. A third is *perseverance*. Showing up to work every day is not a small part of success. A fourth is to *play* and *play hard*.

R.C. Sickles (✉)
Department of Economics, Rice University, Houston, TX, USA
e-mail: rsickles@rice.edu

W.C. Horrace
Department of Economics, Syracuse University, Syracuse, NY, USA
e-mail: whorrace@syr.edu

R.C. Sickles and W.C. Horrace (eds.), *Festschrift in Honor of Peter Schmidt: Econometric Methods and Applications*, DOI 10.1007/978-1-4899-8008-3_1,

Whether it is on the basketball court, at a professional conference, traveling, etc., in life don't leave anything on the table (or the court). A fifth is that *personal* relationships are crucial in life. No person is an island and one should embrace the possibilities that are opened up by your friendships and collaborations.

We spent our days together at Peter's conference and the months since reminded of these aspects of our personalities and life goals that were enhanced, fostered, and nurtured by the very singular experiences we have had as Peter's students. We recognized in 2011 that it was unlikely we would all be together again to celebrate such a wonderful moment in ours and Peter's lives and pledged then to take full advantage of it. We did then, and we are now in the form of this volume.

Festschrifts often have a topical link, and at first blush the combination of econometric, applied econometric and empirical papers in this volume appear unrelated. However, they are linked in the way that the authors frame and analyze their problems using rigorous econometric techniques, but not for the purpose of showcasing the technical refinements per se. The *applicability* of the techniques are the centerpiece of each paper, with advantages and *disadvantages* of the techniques clearly articulated. Quite frankly, *this* is the remarkable legacy that Peter Schmidt has left to his students and to the profession. We think this volume will be one that graduate students and seasoned scholars alike will find invaluable in their research. We provide a brief overview of the papers below. The names of Peter's students are in boldface.

The contribution of **Guilkey** and Lance is "Estimation of non-random program impact when the program variable and outcome variable are binary indicators." It is the most comprehensive analysis to date of small sample performance of program evaluation models when both outcome and program variables are binary and when the program variable is endogenous. Their focus is the overidentified case, and they consider several estimators that are commonly employed in the literature, including a semiparametric random effects model. Their ambitious Monte Carlo study and application to contraception use in Bangladesh and Tanzania should inform the modelling choices of practitioners, particularly when program assignment is not randomized.

The Almanidis, Qian, and **Sickles** contribution, "Stochastic Frontier Models with Bounded Inefficiency," considers a new parametric specification of the stochastic frontier model where inefficiency is drawn from a double-truncated normal distribution. The new distributional feature achieves two things. First, it places a finite bound on inefficiency in the population. Second, it allows for a richer class of models that includes negatively skewed inefficiency distributions. Both are desirable features of the standard parametric model. They provide simulated evidence and an application to US banking.

In Chap. 4, Hasker, Jiang, and **Sickles** consider the challenges associated with "Estimating Consumer Surplus in eBay Computer Monitor Auctions." Despite the prevalence of studies of eBay auctions, there are very few that consider calculation of consumer surplus, and none that are as comprehensive as this. Using a variety of parametric and non-parametric methodologies, they estimate consumer surplus from eBay auctions of computer monitors and find significant variation in the estimates obtained. They also introduce a new measure of auction competitiveness that does not require estimation of the underlying distribution of bid values. The new measure requires only a mild assumption on bidder homogeneity.

Atkinson and **Cornwell** have contributed "Inference in two-step panel models with time-invariant regressors: Bootstrap versus analytic estimators." The authors consider a commonly employed two-step estimator of time-invariant partial effects in a fixed effect model for panel data. They derive the asymptotic covariance matrix of the estimator and perform a comprehensive Monte Carlo study that compares the finite sample behavior of tests based on the analytic results and the bootstrap. Not surprisingly they find that the bootstrap outperforms tests based on the asymptotic distribution in small samples. However, the bootstrap outperforms up to samples as large as 1,000.

Seale, Dahl, Moss and Regmi have contributed "International evidence on cross-price effects of food and other goods." This paper is a comprehensive empirical study of nine major consumption categories from the 1996 International Comparison Project data across 114 countries. While there are many papers that estimate cross-price elasticities, the scope of this paper is unprecedented.

Lee and Shin's "Comparison of stochastic frontier 'effect' models using Monte Carlo simulation" is a comprehensive simulation study of stochastic frontier models for panel data. The models are differentiated by the way technical inefficiency is specified, both parametrically and semi-parametrically. They find that the semi-parametric fixed effect model is fairly robust to the distribution of technical efficiencies while two parametric models are not. However, the fixed effect estimator produces noisier estimates of the order statistic of ranked efficiency estimates, and this is reflected in rank correlation between estimated and true inefficiency values.

Ahn and Moon consider "Large-N and large-T properties of panel data estimators and the Hausman test." They study asymptotic properties of the "within" and generalized least-squares estimators for panel data that are complicated by cross-sectional heterogeneity and time trends, showing how estimator convergence rates vary with these complications. In doing so, they also consider the finite and asymptotic properties of the Hausman test, and show how the power varies with T and the covariance structure of the regressors. Their paper is important as "big data" (with both large N and T) become increasingly prevalent.

Shin, Yu and Greenwood-Nimmo consider "Modelling asymmetric cointegration and dynamic multipliers in a nonlinear ARDL framework." Their paper develops a simple and flexible nonlinear framework capable of modeling asymmetries in long-run and short-run patterns of time-series adjustment. They use a partial sum decomposition approach to model the negative and non-linear relationship between unemployment and output growth (Okun's Law) in the US, Canada and Japan. Their model uncovers the long- and short-run nonlinearities in the co-integrated series. Their approach is simple but effective, and should prove useful to empiricists into the future.

In "More powerful unit root test with non-normal errors" **Im**, **Lee** and **Tieslau** develop a unit root test statistic for a linearized version of the Residual Augmented Least Squares (RALS) procedure of Im and Schmidt (2008). While the test statistic does not require GMM estimation, they show that the limiting distribution of their static is almost identical to the distribution of the unit root test based on GMM. As such their test is easier to implement. Simulations suggest that their test has improved power over the Dickey-Fuller test. In a follow-up paper "More powerful LM unit root test with non-normal errors" Meng, **Im**, **Lee** and **Tieslau** develop a Lagrange Multiplier unit root test for the RALS procedure. Their LM test also has improved power over the Dickey-Fuller test.

In "Efficiency Selection Procedures for Capacity Utilization Estimation" **Horrace** and Schnier adapt the Multiple Comparison with the Best procedures of Horrace and Schmidt (2000) to the problem of estimating capacity utilization in US fisheries. The data-driven estimator nests the usual capacity estimator, while accounting for uncertainty over a vessel's ability (or inability) to achieve efficiency. The methodology will be useful for policy-makers.

Finally, Huang and **Prokhorov** use Edgeworth expansions to develop a finite sample correction to a general version of the popular Newey-West (1987) distance measure test for competing specifications. Their contribution, "Bartlett-type correction of distance metric test" calculates the asymptotic approximation and provides simulated evidence that the distribution of their test static is surprisingly close to the asymptotic distribution at the 95th percentile. They apply their results to U.S. labor market data.

References

Horrace WC, Schmidt P (2000) Multiple comparisons with the best, with economic applications. J Appl Econom 15:1–26

Im KS, Schmidt P (2008) More efficient estimation under non-normality when higher moments do not depend on the regressors, using residual augmented least squares. J Econometrics 144:219–233

Chapter 2
Program Impact Estimation with Binary Outcome Variables: Monte Carlo Results for Alternative Estimators and Empirical Examples

David K. Guilkey and Peter M. Lance

2.1 Introduction

A common problem in program evaluation is measuring the impact of a binary program indicator on a binary outcome variable. For example, one of the most frequently used methods to promote contraceptive use in less developed countries is multi-media campaigns. Evaluation of such programs is complicated by the fact that, except in a very few cases, an experimental design is not used (Bauman et al. 1993; Mwaikambo et al. 2011) and the program implementers have little control over who is exposed to the campaign. The typical method that has been used to evaluate such programs relies on a cross sectional design where respondents are asked yes/no questions about program exposure and contraceptive use along with questions that solicit information about various other characteristics of the respondents that can serve as control variables in a multivariate analysis. In a systematic review of family planning interventions, Mwaikambo et al. (2011) found that two thirds of the 63 family planning interventions that were evaluated in the published literature between 1995 and 2005 involved this type of demand side intervention, although not all of them only considered binary outcomes.

Statistical methods used to measure program impact with this type of data have ranged from those that ignore the potential endogeneity of program recall, such as simple logit or probit regression (see Mwaikambo et al. 2011; Hutchinson and Wheeler 2006 for reviews) and propensity score matching (Babalola 2005), to

D.K. Guilkey (✉)
Department of Economics and the Carolina Population Center, University of North Carolina at Chapel Hill, Chapel Hill, NC 27514, USA
e-mail: dguilkey@email.unc.edu

P.M. Lance
Carolina Population Center, University of North Carolina at Chapel Hill, Chapel Hill, NC 27516-3997, USA
e-mail: pmlance@email.unc.edu

R.C. Sickles and W.C. Horrace (eds.), *Festschrift in Honor of Peter Schmidt: Econometric Methods and Applications*, DOI 10.1007/978-1-4899-8008-3_2,

estimators that correct for endogenous recall using linear or non-linear instrumental variables methods or some type of full information maximum likelihood method (Guilkey et al. 2006; Chen and Guilkey 2003; Guilkey and Hutchinson 2011). On the surface, it would seem that simple methods that do not correct for the potential endogeneity of program recall should inherently perform worse than those that do. However, it is possible to make a case for these simple approaches since methods that explicitly correct for endogeneity rely on the presence of valid exclusion restrictions – variables that affect program recall directly but only affect contraceptive use indirectly through the recall variable or, in some cases and as a last resort, the nonlinearity provided by parametric assumptions.

Unfortunately, there are typically few variables that are candidates for exclusion from the contraceptive use equation, and this is not a unique complication to the multimedia campaign impact evaluation literature: the paucity of potential credible, strong instruments is a widespread challenge in many other applications with different outcomes and endogenous regressors of interest but a similar behavioral structure. Instrumental variables methods as well as more complicated strategies such as full information maximum likelihood estimation can yield highly unstable results in the face of weak instruments. On the other hand, simple methods, even when inconsistent, could lead to results that capture more reliably true program effects (Bollen et al. 1995). In addition, some of the single and systems of equations estimators rely on the assumption of normally distributed error terms and there is evidence that when that assumption is violated, estimated impacts can be far from the truth (Mroz 1999; Chiburis et al. 2011).

The purpose of this paper is to provide the most comprehensive analysis to date of the finite sample performance of alternative methods to estimate program impact when both the treatment and the outcome variables are binary. We focus primarily on methods that can be implemented in STATA, a widely available statistical package, but we also evaluate a semi-parametric instrumental variables random effects model that is not available in STATA.[1] Much of the work to date has focused on a model in which either the treatment variable or the outcome variable is continuous while the other is binary (Guilkey et al. 1992; Bollen et al. 1995; Mroz 1999). Chiburis et al. (2011) do examine the finite sample performance of the bivariate probit estimator and several linear estimators for our case of interest; however, they focus on a model that is exactly identified case for linear models, which does not allow for the use of tests that require the model, at least in theory, to be overidentified. Further, they do not evaluate the wide range of estimators that are used in this setting, including semi-parametric models that are potentially robust to departures from normality. Our Monte Carlo data generation process is designed to mimic the type of data that has been used to evaluate the impact of program recall on contraceptive use in a developing country and we provide examples of the methods using data from Bangladesh and Tanzania. However, the methods have wide applicability beyond our specific examples given how often the basic behavioral structure behind them

[1] The authors are currently writing STATA commands to implement this estimator.

appears in applied work. In this manuscript we restrict attention to the constant effect case, limiting somewhat the applicability of our findings to instances where, for instance, Local Average Treatment Effects are a concern.

This paper is organized as follows. In the next section, we lay out the statistical model and provide details on the alternative estimation and testing procedures that are evaluated. In Sect. 2.3, we detail the data generating process for the Monte Carlo experiment and the results of the experiment are presented in Sect. 2.4. Section 2.5 presents the empirical example and Sect. 2.6 concludes.

2.2 Model and Estimation Methods

We are concerned with a model of the following form:

$$Y_{i1}^* = X_i' \beta_1 + Z_i' \alpha + \epsilon_{i1} \tag{2.1}$$

$$Y_{i2}^* = X_i' \beta_2 + Y_{i1} \delta + \epsilon_{i2} \tag{2.2}$$

where there are $i = 1, 2, \ldots, N$ observations and the dependent variables are latent variables. The observed dependent variables are binary indicators: $Y_{ij} = 1$ if $Y_{ij}^* > 0$ and $Y_{ij} = 0$ otherwise for $j = 1, 2$. X_i is a $kX1$ vector that represents variables that appear in both Eqs. (2.1) and (2.2) while Z_i is a $k_Z X1$ vector that represents a set of variables that are excluded from Eq. (2.2). The coefficients in the model are column vectors of appropriate dimension.

In our model, the observed binary indicator, Y_{i1}, is the right-hand-side endogenous explanatory variable, as opposed to the latent variable. It is well known for this case that there exist estimators that are technically identified without exclusion restrictions (α could be zero) due to functional form. However, the case that we are interested in this paper is the one in which there are at least two valid exclusion restrictions and so even the linear instrumental variables model would be over-identified. Our primary interest is the outcome in Eq. (2.2) with Eq. (2.1) specifying an endogenous treatment.

Several of the estimation methods that we compare assume that $[\epsilon_{i1}, \epsilon_{i2}]$ follows a bivariate normal distribution. To keep the notation simple, in this manuscript we capture this by assuming that $var(\epsilon_{ij}) = 1$ for $j = 1, 2$ and all i and that $E(\epsilon_{i1}, \epsilon_{i2}) = \rho$. The normalization that the error variances equal 1 means that the parameter estimates are only estimated to scale, as is common when the dependent variable is a binary indicator. However, the scale of the estimated parameters is of little concern in this paper since the most important basis of comparisons will be how well the various estimators approximate the population average treatment effect (ATE) defined as:

$$ATE = E(Y_2|Y_1 = 1) - E(Y_2|Y_1 = 0) \tag{2.3}$$

We now turn to a brief discussion of the estimators we consider in this manuscript.

2.2.1 Linear Probability Model (LPM)

Simple ordinary least squares estimation of Eq. (2.2) ignores the endogeneity of Y_{i1} and the binary nature of the dependent variable Y_{i2}. In this case, the estimated ATE is simply the estimate of δ and it will be a consistent estimator only if $E(Y_{i1}\epsilon_{i2}) = 0$.

2.2.2 Probit

From the class of single equation estimators for Eq. (2.2) that ignore the endogeneity of Y_{i1}, we also consider estimation of Eq. (2.2) by simple probit regression and then note that:

$$\hat{P}\left(Y_{i2} = 1\right) = \Phi\left(X_i\hat{\beta}_2 + Y_{i1}\hat{\delta}\right) \tag{2.4}$$

where $\Phi(\cdot)$ is the cumulative normal distribution function. We can now use (2.4) to obtain an estimate of the ATE:

$$\widehat{ATE} = \frac{1}{N}\sum_{i=1}^{N}\hat{P}\left(Y_{i2} = 1|Y_{i1} = 1\right) - \sum_{i=1}^{N}\hat{P}\left(Y_{i2} = 1|Y_{i1} = 0\right) \tag{2.5}$$

This will be a consistent estimator under the same conditions as presented for the OLS estimator.

2.2.3 Instrumental Variables

We compare three variants of linear instrumental variables: two-stage least squares (TSLS), limited information maximum likelihood (LIML) and generalized method of moments (GMM). In all cases, we use the default options in STATA for estimation per the -ivreg- command. We consider all three because they offer different estimation approaches within the context of linear instrumental variables and allow for different tests for endogeneity and identification. Tests for endogneity are based on the Wu-Hausman (Wu 1974; Hausman 1978) and Durbin (1954) tests for TSLS, the standard Hausman test (Hausman 1978) for LIML, and a test referred to as the C statistic for GMM (Hayashi 2000). The identification tests considered for these estimation methods are: Sargon's test (Sargon 1958) for TSLS; Basmann's test (Bassman 1960) for TSLS (specifically, Basmann's χ^2 test) and LIML (Basmann's F test); the Anderson-Rubin test (Anderson and Rubin 1950) for LIML; and Hansen's test (Hansen 1982) for GMM. Details regarding all tests can be found in the STATA reference manual and the cited references.

For all three estimators, we use the estimated δ as the estimate of the ATE. In general in linear instrumental variables models, what is actually estimated is a local average treatment effect (LATE) (Imbens and Angrist 1994; see Angrist and Pischke 2009 for an excellent and succinct review). However, the design of our experiment precludes the possibility of LATE, though it may be at play in the results from the two applied examples considered in this manuscript.

2.2.4 Linear Predictor and Residual Models

Terza et al. (2008) discuss two basic approaches commonly applied in the face of an endogenous regressor in a non-linear equation of interest and a possibly non-linear first stage for that endogenous regressor: first stage predictor substitution (which is essentially just the extension of linear two-stage least squares estimation to the nonlinear setting) and residual inclusion. The predictor substitution strategy is inconsistent whereas under very general conditions the residual inclusion strategy is consistent (Terza et al. 2008). Previous work has suggested that, in the setting of a second-stage binary dependent variable of interest and endogenous continuous regressor, residual inclusion should be consistent provided that the distribution of the unobservable determinants of the binary outcome and continuous endogenous regressor is jointly normal (Rivers and Vuong 1988; Bollen et al. 1995).

We consider two versions of the residual inclusion approach as adapted to the structure defined by the behavioral model in (2.1) and (2.2).[2] First, for the most obvious potential extension of Terza et al. (2008), Rivers and Vuong (1988) and Bollen et al. (1995) to the present setting, we estimate (2.1) by ordinary least squares (i.e. the linear probability model) and generate predicted residuals that are then included in probit regression of (2.2). In the results tables we refer to this estimator as Residual1. Second, we estimate (2.1) by probit and then calculate the generalized residuals using the following formula (Gourieroux et al. 1987):

$$\frac{\left(Y_{i1} - X_i'\beta_1 - Z_i'\alpha\right)\phi\left(Y_{i1} - X_i'\beta_1 - Z_i'\alpha\right)}{\Phi\left(Y_{i1} - X_i'\beta_1 - Z_i'\alpha\right)\left(1 - \Phi\left(Y_{i1} - X_i'\beta_1 - Z_i'\alpha\right)\right)} \tag{2.6}$$

where $\Phi(\cdot)$ is the cumulative normal distribution function and $\phi(\cdot)$ is the normal density function. These residuals are then included in probit regression of (2.2). In the tables and text we refer to this estimator as Residual2.

[2]We did consider predictor substitution schemes as well but, as expected, they performed poorly and we do not include them in the comparisons.

2.2.5 *Bivariate Probit (BIPROBIT)*

Bivariate probit jointly estimates Eqs. (2.1) and (2.2) by maximum likelihood methods assuming bivariate normality for the error terms. The -biprobit- routine in STATA relies on standard Newton-Raphson estimation using a conventional approximation of the bivariate normal cumulative distribution function based on quadrature. We also considered including the -mvprobit- routine, which is not part of the basic STATA package but available as a user-written program (i.e., an .ado file). This routine is designed to allow for more than two binary outcome equations and uses Geweke-Hajivassilou smooth recursive conditioning simulator to approximate the bivariate cumulative normal density (see Cappellari and Jenkins 2003). In preliminary runs, we found that we needed to use far more than the default number of draws (five) in order to obtain accurate parameter estimates and so we dropped this estimator from consideration.

After the model is estimated, the treatment effect is calculated from the marginal probability distribution for the second outcome – using Eqs. (2.3) and (2.4) but with estimated coefficients obtained from the full information maximum likelihood estimator. An endogeneity test is simply a direct test of the null hypothesis that the error correlation across the two equations is zero. We also report an overidentification test that exploits the fact that this model is identified without exclusion restrictions by including the instruments as explanatory variables in Eq. (2.2) (adding the Z variables) and then performing a likelihood ratio test of the null hypothesis that the coefficients are jointly zero. Support for the null implies that these variables are in fact properly excluded.

2.2.6 *Semi-parametric Maximum Likelihood Estimation (DFM)*

We consider a version of a semi-parametric estimator based on Heckman and Singer (1984) but using a non-linear extension proposed by Mroz (1999). To set up the likelihood function for this model, we adopt an error components approach to the unobservables and re-write Eqs. (2.1) and (2.2) as follows:

$$Y_{i1}^{*} = X_i'\beta_1 + Z_i'\alpha + \mu_{i1} + \epsilon_{i1}^{*} \tag{2.7}$$

$$Y_{i2}^{*} = X_i'\beta_2 + Y_{i1}\delta + \mu_{i2} + \epsilon_{i2}^{*} \tag{2.8}$$

where the correlation in the error terms is between the μ's and $E(\epsilon_{i1}^{*}, \epsilon_{i2}^{*}) = 0$. The approach that we use for this estimator is based on the type-I Extreme Value distribution for the ϵ's (leading to the logit model) instead of the normal distribution. However, the basis of comparison is the ATE as defined in Eq. (2.3) and not the estimated coefficients (which are well known to be different by a scale factor from corresponding probit coefficients). Hence, the shift from the cumulative normal distribution to the logistic function still allows a simple comparison of results. We can then write:

$$P\left(Y_{i1}|\mu_{i1}\right) = \frac{e^{(X_i'\beta_1+Z_i'\alpha+\mu_{i1})}}{1+e^{\left(X_i'\beta_1+Z_i'\alpha+\mu_{i1}\right)}} \tag{2.9}$$

$$P\left(Y_{i2}|\mu_{i2}\right) = \frac{e^{(X_i'\beta_2+Y_{i1}\delta+\mu_{i2})}}{1+e^{\left(X_i'\beta_2+Y_{i1}\delta+\mu_{i2}\right)}} \tag{2.10}$$

The contribution to the likelihood function for observation i, conditional on the μ's is:

$$L_i\left(\mu_{i1},\mu_{i2}\right) = \left[P\left(Y_{i1}=1|\mu_{i1}\right)P\left(Y_{i2}=1|\mu_{i2}\right)\right]^{Y_{i1}Y_{i2}}$$
$$\left[P\left(Y_{i1}=0|\mu_{i1}\right)P\left(Y_{i2}=0|\mu_{i2}\right)\right]^{(1-Y_{i1})(1-Y_{i2})}$$
$$\left[P\left(Y_{i1}=1|\mu_{i1}\right)P\left(Y_{i2}=0|\mu_{i2}\right)\right]^{Y_{i1}(1-Y_{i2})}$$
$$\left[P\left(Y_{i1}=0|\mu_{i1}\right)P\left(Y_{i2}=1|\mu_{i2}\right)\right]^{(1-Y_{i1})Y_{i2}}$$

We assume that the distributions of the μ's can be approximated by a step function with J steps for each of the μ's and probability weights (w_j for $j = 1, 2, \ldots, J$) that sum to one for the J steps. The unconditional contribution to the likelihood function for observation i can then be written:

$$L_i = \sum_{j=1}^{J} w_j L_i\left(\mu_{i1},\mu_{i2}\right) \tag{2.11}$$

The likelihood function is simply the product of (2.11) over the N observations. In addition to the model's coefficients, one searches over $J-1$ weights (since they sum to one) and $J-1$ sets of the μ's (since one of the μ's must be set to zero if there is a constant term in the model). We call this the "discrete factor model" (and, for the sake of brevity, frequently refer to it as the 'DFM' in discussions below); (see Mroz (1999) for additional details). The estimated ATE can be obtained using Eq. (2.10) where the population parameters are replaced with estimates including the estimates for the weights and mass points (the μ's).

In practice, one would add points of support to the heterogeneity distribution until there is no significant improvement in the likelihood function. However, this is not practical in a Monte Carlo experiment and so we simply set the number of points of support for the discrete distribution to four.

2.3 Data Generating Process

The basic logic behind the data generating process is straightforward: within each Monte Carlo experiment data are generated in a fashion that insures that the resulting estimation samples conform to the behavioral parameters of that experiment. Most of these behavioral parameters vary across Monte Carlo experiments (one was fixed across them). It is this variation in these parameters that allows examination of the comparative performance under alternative circumstances of the estimators considered in this study. The behavioral parameters that vary across experiments include the true (i.e. established by the design of the experiment): program effect $(E(Y_2|X, Y_1 = 1) - E(Y_2|X, Y_1 = 0))$; correlation of the errors $\{\epsilon_1, \epsilon_2\}$; average of the program outcome (Y_1) within the sample[3]; average of the outcome of interest (Y_2) within the sample; first stage strength of the instruments Z to explain Y_1 (as reflected in the χ^2 statistic emerging from a test of the joint significance of those instruments); and the bivariate error type (i.e. normal or non-normal errors).

In each experiment, the first step is to draw pseudo-randomly a sample of size N for the exogenous variables X, Z and ϵ (given the error correlation and type specified for that experiment). Given the draws from X and Z and this initial draw from ϵ, we then determine values for the system parameters β_1, β_2, α and δ from Eqs. (2.1) and (2.2) that insure that data generated conditional on those values for the system parameters and X and Z would conform to the remaining behavioral parameters. The experiment itself then involved replications (1,000 replications in the case of experiments involving 1,000 or 5,000 observations and 500 replications in the case of experiments involving 10,000 observations). In each, a new pseudo-random draw was made from the distribution of the error terms ϵ for each of the N observations and, conditional on that new draw, the draw from X and Z and the values for β_1, β_2, α and δ determined in the first step, new values for Y_1 and Y_2 were calculated for each observation. The performance of the various estimators considered in this manuscript was then recorded given "observed" data Y_1, Y_2, X and Z.

2.3.1 *Sample Sizes and Behavioral Parameter Values*

Our various Monte Carlo experiments are distinguished by the values of the behavioral parameters set for them, as well as the sample sizes involved. We consider many alternative combinations of these sample sizes and behavioral parameters. To begin with, three basic sample sizes are considered: 1,000, 5,000 and 10,000. These were selected based on a rough sense of the sort of ranges of sample sizes frequently encountered when estimating systems along the lines of Eqs. (2.1) and (2.2) using real world data.

[3]That is, the program enrollment prevalence within the sample.

For program participation prevalence and outcome prevalence we consider values of 0.5 and 0.25. These capture the cases of programs for which participation is comparatively common and less common, and outcomes of interest for which the same can be said.

For program impact (the true marginal effect of Y_1 on the probability of Y_2) we consider high (0.2) and modest (0.05) impact cases. The program impact levels reflect constant (as opposed to varying with observed or unobserved heterogeneity) effects.

The error terms ϵ are based on two basic bivariate distributions:

1. A bivariate standard normal distribution;
2. A non-normal distribution with a skewness of 1.5 and an excess kurtosis of 3.

The algorithm for drawing the non-normal errors is based on the method proposed by Vale and Maurelli (1983).[4] The Vale and Maurelli (1983) approach involves a combination of Fleishman's (1978) procedure for generating non-normal random variables with a matrix decomposition method typically applied to the task of generating multivariate normal random variables (Kaiser and Dickman 1962). Two levels of error correlation are employed for these bivariate distributions: 0.1 and 0.3, allowing different degrees of endogeneity. Finally, we vary the first stage (Eq. (2.1)) explanatory power of the instruments as manifested by a χ^2 statistic resulting from a test of the joint significance of those instruments based on a probit regression of Y_1 on X and Z. We cover test statistic values of 15, 25, and 50, encompassing a range of instrument strength levels.

Overall explanatory power of Eqs. (2.1) and (2.2), as captured by the R^2 from ordinary least squares regression estimation of them, is fixed at 0.3 in both cases in order to reflect a degree of explanatory power more realistic to regression analyses using micro-level samples. This typically results in pseudo-R^2 values in the 0.15–0.25 range.

2.3.2 Drawing X and Z

The exogenous explanatory variables X and Z are pseudo-randomly drawn from the standard normal distribution. In this manuscript, four exogenous characteristics X (X_1, X_2, X_3 and X_4) and two instruments Z (Z_1 and Z_2) are drawn for each Monte Carlo experiment. Thus, in the terms of the discussion introducing Eqs. (2.1) and (2.2) in Sect. 2.2, $k = 4$ and $k_z = 2$.

---

[4]We are grateful to Stas Kolenikov for generously sharing a STATA .ado file that he wrote implementing that Vale and Maurelli (1983) procedure.

2.3.3 The Mechanics of the Data Generating Process

Each Monte Carlo experiment could be characterized by these behavioral parameters as applied to the system of equations (2.1) and (2.2). To begin with, the Monte Carlo experiments revolve around the latent variable equations

$$Y_{i1}^* = X_i'\beta_1 + Z_i'\alpha + \phi_1\epsilon_{i1} \tag{2.12}$$

$$Y_{i2}^* = X_i'\beta_2 + Y_{i1}\delta + \phi_2\epsilon_{i2} \tag{2.13}$$

which differ from (2.1) and (2.2) primarily by the coefficients ϕ on the error terms ϵ. (As will be seen below, these coefficients are placed on the errors to support the target R^2 of 0.3 in each equation.) Given the dimensionality of X and Z employed in this study, (2.12) and (2.13) are, effectively,

$$Y_{i1}^* = \beta_{10} + X_{1i}\beta_{11} + X_{2i}\beta_{12} + X_{3i}\beta_{13} + X_{4i}\beta_{14} + Z_{1i}\alpha_1 + Z_{2i}\alpha_2 + \phi_1\epsilon_{i1} \tag{2.14}$$

$$Y_{i2}^* = \beta_{20} + X_{1i}\beta_{21} + X_{2i}\beta_{22} + X_{3i}\beta_{23} + X_{4i}\beta_{24} + Y_{i1}\delta + \phi_2\epsilon_{i2} \tag{2.15}$$

These equations are used to generate the variables Y used for each experiment. To do this, specific values need to be assigned to the β's, α's, δ and the ϕ's.

We begin with the β's that served as coefficients for the four exogenous explanatory variables X_1, X_2, X_3 and X_4. The values of these do not vary across experiments. For Eq. (2.1) these (β_{11}, β_{12}, β_{13} and β_{14}, respectively) are set to −0.5, 0.33, 0.57 and −0.2. The corresponding values for Eq. (2.2) are −0.35, 0.33, 0.77 and −0.18. These values were randomly determined at the outset of the study.[5]

The remaining parameters of (2.14) and (2.15) are thus set at the outset of each experiment as follows:

1. N observations for X and Z are pseudo-randomly drawn from the multivariate standard normal distribution with zero correlation across X and Z;
2. For each of these N observations, a pair of errors $\{\epsilon_1, \epsilon_2\}$ was drawn (either the bivariate normal distribution or via the Vale and Maurelli (1983) procedure, with correlation level indicated for that experiment);
3. The values for β_{10}, α_1, α_2 and ϕ_1 were set to guarantee the data generating process conformed to the program participation prevalence and first stage instrument strength indicated for that experiment as well as the explanatory power for Eq. (2.14) of $R^2 = 0.3$. This was done through an iterative search over candidate values for these four parameters as follows:

[5]Experimentation suggests that variation in the values assigned to these coefficient terms had very little impact on the statistics of interest in this study.

(a) Set all four parameters to low initial values;
(b) Find the values for ϕ_1 and β_{10} that yield $R^2 = 0.3$ (from linear regression of Y_{i1}^* on X_i and Z_i) and the target program prevalence (with program participation Y_{1i} determined by whether Y_{i1}^* exceeds zero);
(c) Given these values, determine the χ^2 statistic resulting from a test of the joint significance of Z_1 and Z_2 based on a probit regression of Y_1 on the X's and Z's;
(d) If the χ^2 statistic value matched the target, the parameter value search was concluded. If not the values of α_1 and α_2 were increased incrementally and steps 3(b)–(d) were repeated.

4. Once the values for β_{10}, α_1, α_2 and ϕ_1 had been found, Y_{1i} was determined by whether Y_{i1}^* exceeded zero given the draws for X, Z and ϵ_1 and those parameter values.
5. The focus then shifted to Eq. (2.15), and a similar iterative process was used to find values for β_{20}, δ and ϕ_2. It proceeded as follows:

(a) Set the three parameters to low initial values;
(b) Find values for β_{20} and ϕ_2 that yield $R^2 = 0.3$ (from linear regression of Y_{i2}^* on X_i and Y_{1i}) and the target prevalence for the outcome of interest;
(c) Given these values, determine the program effect according to

$$\Phi\left(\beta_{20} + X_{1i}\beta_{21} + X_{2i}\beta_{22} + X_{3i}\beta_{23} + X_{4i}\beta_{24} + \delta\right)$$
$$-\Phi\left(\beta_{20} + X_{1i}\beta_{21} + X_{2i}\beta_{22} + X_{3i}\beta_{23} + X_{4i}\beta_{24}\right)$$

where $\Phi(\cdot)$ is the cumulative normal distribution function.
(d) If the program impact matched the target parameter value, the search was concluded; if not δ was increased incrementally and steps 5(b)–(d) were repeated.

6. Once appropriate values for β_{20}, δ and ϕ_2 were found, Y_{2i} was determined by whether Y_{2i}^* exceeded zero given the draws for X and ϵ_2 as well as Y_{i1} and those parameter values.

The first phase of each Monte Carlo experiment thusly found values for the equation parameters that conformed to the behavioral parameters of that experiment.

The experiment then shifted to the empirical repetition phase. In each of the repetitions, the same sequence of events occurred:

1. A new draw for $\{\epsilon_1, \epsilon_2\}$ was made[6];

[6]Step 1 was actually slightly more involved. It became apparent in early rounds of experiments that some behavioral parameters, particularly instrument strength, occasionally varied across replications to a degree with which the authors were not comfortable. In particular, the various replications from experiments involving first stage χ^2 statistics with target values of 15 and 25 occasionally produced overlapping ranges for the χ^2 statistic values actually generated across

2. Given the values assigned to β_{10}, β_{11}, β_{12}, β_{13}, β_{14}, α_1, α_2 and ϕ_1, and X_{1i}, X_{2i}, X_{3i}, X_{4i}, Z_{1i}, Z_{2i} and ϵ_{1i}, for each of the N observations Y_{i1} was set to 1 if Y_{i1}^* exceeded 0 and to 0 otherwise;
3. Given the values assigned to β_{20}, β_{21}, β_{22}, β_{23}, β_{24}, δ and ϕ_2, and X_{1i}, X_{2i}, X_{3i}, X_{4i}, Y_{i1} and ϵ_{2i}, for each of the N observations Y_{i2} was set to 1 if Y_{i2}^* exceeded 0 and to 0 otherwise.

The data X, Z, Y_1 and Y_2 so generated thus formed the empirical "observations" over which the performance of each of the estimators was then recorded for that repetition.

2.4 Monte Carlo Results

The results of the Monte Carlo experiments are presented in Tables 2.1–2.25. Tables 2.1–2.8 present mean absolute deviations between estimated and true ATE across either 1,000 (sample sizes 1,000 and 5,000) or 500 (sample size 10,000) replications of the each of the experiments. The experiments differ by their sample sizes or assumed behavioral parameters.[7] Tables 2.9–2.16 present mean estimated ATE. Tables 2.17–2.21 present regression results summarizing the findings regarding ATE estimation. Tables 2.22–2.25 present a restricted set of results for the identification and endogeneity tests. Owing to space constraints, in Tables 2.1–2.16 and 2.22–2.25 we present only results for experiments in which the average frequencies for the two dependent variables Y_{i1} and Y_{i2} were both set to be the same at 0.25 or 0.5.

Most tables presenting Monte Carlo experiment results cover a particular combination of target average treatment effect and error correlation. In all such tables, the columns provide results by the error type applied in the experiment (bivariate normal or bivariate non-normal) and, within each error type, instrument strength in terms of the χ^2 test statistic for the joint significance of the instruments in Eq. (2.1) as estimated by probit (e.g. $\chi^2 = 15$, $\chi^2 = 25$, etc.) for given values of Y_1 and Y_2 (where, for instance, $Y_1 = 0.25$, $Y_2 = 0.25$ indicates results for experiments

---

the replications for the two experiments. This muddied the waters somewhat for the purposes of making inferences about estimator performance differentials as instrument strength varied. To address this, we set tolerance bands for acceptable variation of such χ^2 values around their target for a given experiment. If, on a particular replication, a draw $\{\epsilon_1, \epsilon_2\}$ resulted in a χ^2 value outside of the tolerance range for that experiment, that draw was discarded and a new draw $\{\epsilon_1, \epsilon_2\}$ was made. This was done to insure that the replications within an experiment conformed to an acceptable degree to the parameters of that experiment.

[7] As explained in Sect. 2.3, the behavioral parameters are imposed by the design of the data generating process for each experiment and included the: program effect ($Pr(Y_2|X, Y_1 = 1) - Pr(Y_2|X, Y_1 = 0)$); correlation of the errors $\{\epsilon_1, \epsilon_2\}$; average of the program outcome (Y_1) within the sample; average of the outcome of interest (Y_2) within the sample; first stage strength of the instruments Z to explain Y_1 (as reflected in the χ^2 statistic emerging from a test of the joint significance of those instruments); and bivariate error type (i.e. normal or a non-normal errors).

Table 2.1 Mean absolute deviation of ATE for true ATE = 0.05, error correlation = 0.1, $Y_1 = 0.25$ and $Y_2 = 0.25$

		Normal errors			Non-normal errors		
		$\chi^2 = 15$	$\chi^2 = 25$	$\chi^2 = 50$	$\chi^2 = 15$	$\chi^2 = 25$	$\chi^2 = 50$
N = 1,000							
	LPM	0.0812	0.0805	0.0771	0.0797	0.0776	0.0719
	Probit	0.0597	0.0597	0.0592	0.0662	0.0647	0.0614
	TSLS	0.2099	0.1627	0.1076	0.2123	0.1599	0.1098
	LIML	0.2279	0.1692	0.1096	0.2314	0.1672	0.1121
	GMM	0.2111	0.1632	0.1076	0.2122	0.1600	0.1099
	Residual1	0.2043	0.1674	0.1132	0.1945	0.1572	0.1130
	Residual2	0.1431	0.1235	0.0946	0.1895	0.1564	0.1053
	BIPROBIT	0.1448	0.1251	0.0961	0.2319	0.1927	0.1227
	DFM	0.1175	0.1102	0.0943	0.0938	0.0919	0.0791
N = 5,000							
	LPM	0.0820	0.0824	0.0813	0.0848	0.0838	0.0834
	Probit	0.0588	0.0594	0.0588	0.0691	0.0684	0.0684
	TSLS	0.2208	0.1684	0.1141	0.2009	0.1574	0.1058
	LIML	0.2392	0.1766	0.1163	0.2143	0.1640	0.1081
	GMM	0.2209	0.1684	0.1142	0.2009	0.1574	0.1059
	Residual1	0.2130	0.1730	0.1209	0.1905	0.1576	0.1103
	Residual2	0.0854	0.0832	0.0713	0.3110	0.2591	0.1822
	BIPROBIT	0.0973	0.0900	0.0740	0.2862	0.2648	0.2149
	DFM	0.1198	0.1125	0.1050	0.0643	0.0648	0.0643
N = 10,000							
	LPM	0.0823	0.0808	0.0818	0.0821	0.0810	0.0804
	Probit	0.0594	0.0582	0.0593	0.0664	0.0654	0.0651
	TSLS	0.2054	0.1649	0.1097	0.2066	0.1643	0.1186
	LIML	0.2183	0.1697	0.1117	0.2223	0.1707	0.1205
	GMM	0.2051	0.1649	0.1109	0.2055	0.1643	0.1187
	Residual1	0.1989	0.1635	0.1129	0.2017	0.1650	0.1224
	Residual2	0.0716	0.0644	0.0622	0.3239	0.2951	0.2463
	BIPROBIT	0.0838	0.0771	0.0666	0.2774	0.2675	0.2466
	DFM	0.1310	0.1288	0.1076	0.0597	0.0597	0.0591

for which the average values of the endogenous variable Y_1 and the outcome of interest Y_2 are 0.25). Generally speaking, the rows of these tables provide statistics for the estimators considered in this manuscript at various sample sizes. Finally, to save space, the individual models are referred to in the rows of the tables by shorthand expressions: LPM for linear probability model (i.e. single equation OLS with no control for endogeneity); Probit for single equation probit regression; TSLS for two-stage least squares; LIML for the limited information linear instrumental variables estimator; GMM for the generalized method of moments implementation of the linear instrumental variables estimator; Residual1 and Residual2 for the two variants of the residual inclusion estimators; BIPROBIT for the bivariate probit estimator provided by the STATA -biprobit- command; and DFM for the discrete factor model.

Table 2.2 Mean absolute deviation of ATE for true ATE = 0.05, error correlation = 0.1, $Y_1 = 0.5$ and $Y_2 = 0.5$

		Normal errors			Non-normal errors		
		$\chi^2 = 15$	$\chi^2 = 25$	$\chi^2 = 50$	$\chi^2 = 15$	$\chi^2 = 25$	$\chi^2 = 50$
N = 1,000							
	LPM	0.0832	0.0832	0.0780	0.1001	0.0972	0.0919
	Probit	0.0749	0.0752	0.0712	0.0870	0.0846	0.0816
	TSLS	0.2133	0.1623	0.1109	0.2097	0.1624	0.1138
	LIML	0.2341	0.1688	0.1130	0.2279	0.1693	0.1161
	GMM	0.2136	0.1624	0.1113	0.2099	0.1628	0.1138
	Residual1	0.1986	0.1597	0.1112	0.1937	0.1568	0.1139
	Residual2	0.1666	0.1412	0.1043	0.1572	0.1304	0.1026
	BIPROBIT	0.1773	0.1447	0.1051	0.1269	0.1087	0.0935
	DFM	0.1420	0.1263	0.1045	0.1021	0.0833	0.0669
N = 5,000							
	LPM	0.0815	0.0813	0.0790	0.0998	0.0992	0.0999
	Probit	0.0738	0.0737	0.0718	0.0871	0.0867	0.0877
	TSLS	0.2077	0.1624	0.1116	0.2071	0.1654	0.1128
	LIML	0.2228	0.1688	0.1137	0.2220	0.1713	0.1146
	GMM	0.2079	0.1624	0.1117	0.2071	0.1655	0.1129
	Residual1	0.1906	0.1554	0.1116	0.1900	0.1589	0.1123
	Residual2	0.1286	0.1091	0.0907	0.1771	0.1454	0.0998
	BIPROBIT	0.1399	0.1184	0.0943	0.0983	0.0837	0.0630
	DFM	0.1438	0.1270	0.1043	0.0661	0.0587	0.0511
N = 10,000							
	LPM	0.0820	0.0829	0.0814	0.0993	0.1004	0.0989
	Probit	0.0740	0.0750	0.0737	0.0862	0.0872	0.0859
	TSLS	0.2067	0.1595	0.1077	0.2157	0.1633	0.1206
	LIML	0.2206	0.1663	0.1096	0.2307	0.1699	0.1228
	GMM	0.2049	0.1592	0.1076	0.2150	0.1632	0.1206
	Residual1	0.1861	0.1511	0.1071	0.1975	0.1560	0.1206
	Residual2	0.0997	0.0964	0.0814	0.2287	0.2072	0.1603
	BIPROBIT	0.1202	0.1094	0.0853	0.1081	0.0967	0.0747
	DFM	0.1471	0.1336	0.1127	0.0887	0.0877	0.0810

Before turning to the mean absolute deviation results, it is interesting to note that Tables 2.9–2.16 for mean estimated treatment effect indicate that there is typically, though not always, an upward bias to the estimated treatment effect even for estimators that correct for the endogeneity of the treatment effect. The bias, however, is typically smaller as one moves from a true treatment effect of 0.05–0.2.

The results in Tables 2.1–2.8 on mean absolute deviations are varied and difficult to summarize. A few broad trends seem to emerge. First, the bivariate probit model (BIPROBIT) appears to do well in general when the error terms are indeed jointly normally distributed. However, at sample size 1,000 it is frequently no better than DFM, especially when instrument strength is low and is sometimes

Table 2.3 Mean absolute deviation of ATE for true ATE = 0.05, error correlation = 0.3, $Y_1 = 0.25$ and $Y_2 = 0.25$

		Normal errors			Non-normal errors		
		$\chi^2 = 15$	$\chi^2 = 25$	$\chi^2 = 50$	$\chi^2 = 15$	$\chi^2 = 25$	$\chi^2 = 50$
N = 1,000							
	LPM	0.1945	0.1923	0.1835	0.2124	0.2084	0.1968
	Probit	0.1678	0.1658	0.1598	0.1929	0.1896	0.1814
	TSLS	0.2149	0.1612	0.1118	0.2146	0.1625	0.1061
	LIML	0.3353	0.1668	0.1136	0.2378	0.1686	0.1083
	GMM	0.2154	0.1617	0.1119	0.2144	0.1625	0.1065
	Residual1	0.2057	0.1605	0.1134	0.2020	0.1586	0.1099
	Residual2	0.1473	0.1281	0.0942	0.2115	0.1553	0.0980
	BIPROBIT	0.1540	0.1295	0.0923	0.2308	0.1696	0.0994
	DFM	0.1164	0.1155	0.0981	0.1125	0.1004	0.0742
N = 5,000							
	LPM	0.1986	0.1991	0.1977	0.2018	0.2012	0.1991
	Probit	0.1713	0.1720	0.1710	0.1854	0.1848	0.1831
	TSLS	0.2246	0.1673	0.1238	0.1969	0.1489	0.1021
	LIML	0.2421	0.1718	0.1255	0.2114	0.1558	0.1042
	GMM	0.2248	0.1675	0.1240	0.1970	0.1490	0.1020
	Residual1	0.2182	0.1695	0.1268	0.1801	0.1485	0.1064
	Residual2	0.0897	0.0899	0.0758	0.2005	0.1686	0.1173
	BIPROBIT	0.1051	0.0963	0.0782	0.2130	0.1777	0.1232
	DFM	0.1506	0.1443	0.1240	0.1207	0.1066	0.0924
N = 10,000							
	LPM	0.1948	0.1951	0.1942	0.2081	0.2085	0.2075
	Probit	0.1675	0.1678	0.1672	0.1909	0.1914	0.1903
	TSLS	0.1938	0.1598	0.1113	0.2015	0.1549	0.1068
	LIML	0.2100	0.1650	0.1134	0.2194	0.1621	0.1088
	GMM	0.1954	0.1598	0.1112	0.2013	0.1549	0.1066
	Residual1	0.1850	0.1566	0.1129	0.1891	0.1488	0.1114
	Residual2	0.0698	0.0658	0.0613	0.2661	0.2407	0.1901
	BIPROBIT	0.0956	0.0830	0.0684	0.2665	0.2428	0.1862
	DFM	0.1562	0.1447	0.1083	0.1053	0.1080	0.0881

worse than LPM and Probit when sample size is small and error correlation is low. In addition, the Residual2 estimator which uses a first stage probit regression to generate generalized residuals frequently has lower mean absolute deviation (MAD) than BIPROBIT. Whatever advantage BIPROBIT has when the true errors are normal disappears for non-normal errors. For non-normal errors, the DFM model typically performs the best. The linear instrumental variables estimators' performance increases significantly as instrument strength and sample size increases regardless of whether or not the true error distribution is normal or non-normal. That said, it is understandably difficult to grasp general patterns from the many cells of these tables.

Table 2.4 Mean absolute deviation of ATE for true ATE = 0.05, error correlation = 0.3, $Y_1 = 0.5$ and $Y_2 = 0.5$

		Normal errors			Non-normal errors		
		$\chi^2 = 15$	$\chi^2 = 25$	$\chi^2 = 50$	$\chi^2 = 15$	$\chi^2 = 25$	$\chi^2 = 50$
N = 1,000							
	LPM	0.2033	0.1994	0.1946	0.2308	0.2293	0.2211
	Probit	0.1948	0.1913	0.1871	0.2089	0.2076	0.2010
	TSLS	0.2192	0.1680	0.1162	0.2135	0.1633	0.1180
	LIML	0.2345	0.1726	0.1174	0.2305	0.1702	0.1188
	GMM	0.2193	0.1684	0.1166	0.2138	0.1643	0.1189
	Residual1	0.2047	0.1633	0.1162	0.1975	0.1576	0.1141
	Residual2	0.1805	0.1495	0.1093	0.1525	0.1263	0.0968
	BIPROBIT	0.1854	0.1494	0.1068	0.1331	0.1132	0.0909
	DFM	0.1411	0.1170	0.0969	0.1107	0.0933	0.0775
N = 5,000							
	LPM	0.2031	0.2020	0.2015	0.2269	0.2255	0.2249
	Probit	0.1953	0.1942	0.1939	0.2115	0.2101	0.2099
	TSLS	0.2092	0.1600	0.1139	0.2156	0.1706	0.1244
	LIML	0.2347	0.1657	0.1157	0.2288	0.1751	0.1250
	GMM	0.2092	0.1601	0.1140	0.2158	0.1707	0.1245
	Residual1	0.1893	0.1539	0.1132	0.1977	0.1638	0.1193
	Residual2	0.1248	0.1080	0.0934	0.2125	0.1742	0.1203
	BIPROBIT	0.1480	0.1180	0.0946	0.1177	0.0873	0.0657
	DFM	0.1491	0.1380	0.1070	0.0516	0.0454	0.0468
N = 10,000							
	LPM	0.2039	0.2024	0.2029	0.2316	0.2309	0.2297
	Probit	0.1956	0.1941	0.1947	0.2136	0.2130	0.2120
	TSLS	0.2186	0.1673	0.1142	0.2117	0.1599	0.1102
	LIML	0.2392	0.1768	0.1166	0.2273	0.1668	0.1116
	GMM	0.2184	0.1649	0.1138	0.2146	0.1606	0.1103
	Residual1	0.1869	0.1540	0.1127	0.1959	0.1547	0.1103
	Residual2	0.1077	0.0968	0.0746	0.1922	0.1683	0.1265
	BIPROBIT	0.1413	0.1186	0.0837	0.0725	0.0627	0.0516
	DFM	0.1557	0.1322	0.1102	0.0761	0.0689	0.0678

To perhaps provide a somewhat clearer overall picture, we consider a series of simple regression results. Tables 2.17–2.21 provide results for these regression analyses. These involve regressing mean absolute deviation estimates across the replications of our Monte Carlo experiments on dummy variables capturing the models that generated those mean absolute deviation estimates. The regression relies on a sample that has an observation for each mean absolute deviation estimate generated by each model considered in each Monte Carlo experiment (for instance, the typical Monte Carlo experiment will yield nine observations in the regression sample corresponding to the mean absolute deviation estimates generated by the various models). In Table 2.17, we present results across all experiments and a

Table 2.5 Mean absolute deviation of ATE for true ATE = 0.2, error correlation = 0.1, $Y_1 = 0.25$ and $Y_2 = 0.25$

		Normal errors			Non-normal errors		
		$\chi^2 = 15$	$\chi^2 = 25$	$\chi^2 = 50$	$\chi^2 = 15$	$\chi^2 = 25$	$\chi^2 = 50$
N = 1,000							
	LPM	0.0972	0.0976	0.0939	0.0577	0.0569	0.0565
	Probit	0.0711	0.0715	0.0700	0.0426	0.0424	0.0432
	TSLS	0.2150	0.1650	0.1145	0.2036	0.1595	0.1051
	LIML	0.2350	0.1711	0.1167	0.2204	0.1663	0.1071
	GMM	0.2160	0.1652	0.1148	0.2044	0.1603	0.1053
	Residual1	0.2312	0.1897	0.1372	0.2173	0.1820	0.1270
	Residual2	0.1684	0.1457	0.1112	0.1974	0.1690	0.1093
	BIPROBIT	0.1741	0.1500	0.1111	0.2482	0.2076	0.1318
	DFM	0.1324	0.1264	0.1143	0.1332	0.1328	0.1250
N = 5,000							
	LPM	0.0919	0.0919	0.0906	0.0734	0.0735	0.0706
	Probit	0.0639	0.0639	0.0633	0.0555	0.0558	0.0536
	TSLS	0.2245	0.1621	0.1155	0.2026	0.1485	0.1078
	LIML	0.2446	0.1690	0.1172	0.2175	0.1539	0.1097
	GMM	0.2246	0.1621	0.1157	0.2027	0.1484	0.1077
	Residual1	0.2385	0.1892	0.1375	0.2161	0.1714	0.1312
	Residual2	0.0950	0.0929	0.0825	0.3361	0.2919	0.2127
	BIPROBIT	0.1071	0.1004	0.0849	0.3154	0.2988	0.2520
	DFM	0.0977	0.0933	0.0924	0.0616	0.0576	0.0542
N = 10,000							
	LPM	0.0960	0.0962	0.0958	0.0577	0.0584	0.0577
	Probit	0.0673	0.0676	0.0673	0.0405	0.0411	0.0407
	TSLS	0.1935	0.1508	0.1062	0.1974	0.1516	0.1093
	LIML	0.2066	0.1571	0.1081	0.2147	0.1572	0.1116
	GMM	0.1933	0.1507	0.1064	0.1968	0.1518	0.1093
	Residual1	0.2190	0.1793	0.1293	0.2154	0.1741	0.1292
	Residual2	0.0746	0.0790	0.0663	0.3123	0.2908	0.2362
	BIPROBIT	0.0869	0.0902	0.0725	0.2798	0.2707	0.2444
	DFM	0.1351	0.1341	0.1157	0.0414	0.0433	0.0412

stratification by error type (bivariate normal versus bivariate non-normal). The omitted category among the regressors (which are dummy variables indicating the model behind the mean absolute deviation estimate in a particular observation) is the linear probability model (LPM). Thus, a negative number means that the model outperforms the omitted category model (the LPM) while a positive number means that it performed more poorly than that omitted category model. For these tables we used all of the experiments (i.e. we did not confine ourselves to cases where program participation prevalence and outcome prevalence were both 0.25 or 0.5).

From Table 2.17 it is clear that, across all Monte Carlo experiments, only simple Probit and DFM perform slightly better than LPM while all other estimators perform

Table 2.6 Mean absolute deviation of ATE for true ATE = 0.2, error correlation = 0.1, $Y_1 = 0.5$ and $Y_2 = 0.5$

		Normal errors			Non-normal errors		
		$\chi^2 = 15$	$\chi^2 = 25$	$\chi^2 = 50$	$\chi^2 = 15$	$\chi^2 = 25$	$\chi^2 = 50$
N = 1,000							
	LPM	0.0809	0.0814	0.0816	0.1071	0.1062	0.1035
	Probit	0.0728	0.0737	0.0746	0.0888	0.0886	0.0891
	TSLS	0.2147	0.1704	0.1173	0.2233	0.1676	0.1193
	LIML	0.2328	0.1780	0.1192	0.2447	0.1739	0.1209
	GMM	0.2157	0.1706	0.1175	0.2240	0.1684	0.1197
	Residual1	0.2080	0.1752	0.1259	0.2210	0.1732	0.1263
	Residual2	0.1801	0.1548	0.1137	0.1859	0.1450	0.1100
	BIPROBIT	0.1879	0.1591	0.1144	0.1362	0.1126	0.0962
	DFM	0.1430	0.1405	0.1216	0.1671	0.1634	0.1555
N = 5,000							
	LPM	0.0759	0.0747	0.0756	0.1003	0.0997	0.1006
	Probit	0.0681	0.0670	0.0680	0.0831	0.0829	0.0841
	TSLS	0.2017	0.1592	0.1176	0.2119	0.1647	0.1208
	LIML	0.2182	0.1654	0.1195	0.2243	0.1708	0.1225
	GMM	0.2018	0.1592	0.1177	0.2121	0.1648	0.1209
	Residual1	0.2001	0.1641	0.1252	0.2091	0.1713	0.1283
	Residual2	0.1307	0.1164	0.1000	0.2655	0.2196	0.1481
	BIPROBIT	0.1443	0.1252	0.1023	0.1519	0.1224	0.0851
	DFM	0.1273	0.1185	0.1060	0.1026	0.1046	0.0983
N = 10,000							
	LPM	0.0826	0.0816	0.0809	0.0939	0.0930	0.0921
	Probit	0.0744	0.0734	0.0728	0.0764	0.0756	0.0748
	TSLS	0.2023	0.1590	0.1140	0.2204	0.1684	0.1187
	LIML	0.2173	0.1645	0.1159	0.2361	0.1764	0.1209
	GMM	0.2034	0.1606	0.1143	0.2205	0.1673	0.1192
	Residual1	0.2010	0.1649	0.1231	0.2178	0.1740	0.1298
	Residual2	0.1051	0.0998	0.0880	0.3435	0.3172	0.2567
	BIPROBIT	0.1227	0.1102	0.0946	0.2020	0.1792	0.1398
	DFM	0.1462	0.1352	0.1160	0.0693	0.0676	0.0694

slightly worse. For Monte Carlo experiments involving normal errors, BIPROBIT and Residual2 perform slightly better than LPM while DFM and Probit perform about the same as LPM. This result for BIPROBIT is not surprising since it is the asymptotically efficient estimator, given that it is based on a joint distributional assumption for the errors that happens to exactly match the actual error distribution behind the data generating process. The other four estimators perform worse. Although their point estimates are small, they are significantly different from zero in all four cases. For non-normal errors, no estimator performs better than LPM except for DFM and the two worst performing estimators are Residual2 and BIPROBIT. This is not surprising since these two estimators rely heavily on a normality assumption for the error term.

Table 2.7 Mean absolute deviation of ATE for true ATE = 0.2, error correlation = 0.3, $Y_1 = 0.25$ and $Y_2 = 0.25$

		Normal errors			Non-normal errors		
		$\chi^2 = 15$	$\chi^2 = 25$	$\chi^2 = 50$	$\chi^2 = 15$	$\chi^2 = 25$	$\chi^2 = 50$
N = 1,000							
	LPM	0.1985	0.2020	0.1918	0.1951	0.1883	0.1747
	Probit	0.1779	0.1820	0.1718	0.1806	0.1741	0.1630
	TSLS	0.2144	0.1643	0.1098	0.2126	0.1599	0.1116
	LIML	0.2295	0.1701	0.1108	0.2302	0.1658	0.1137
	GMM	0.2157	0.1648	0.1100	0.2134	0.1602	0.1116
	Residual1	0.2322	0.1898	0.1348	0.2290	0.1894	0.1419
	Residual2	0.1565	0.1472	0.1130	0.2076	0.1661	0.1137
	BIPROBIT	0.1647	0.1469	0.1086	0.2401	0.1867	0.1180
	DFM	0.1432	0.1415	0.1208	0.1757	0.1546	0.1407
N = 5,000							
	LPM	0.1957	0.1955	0.1936	0.1602	0.1606	0.1575
	Probit	0.1749	0.1748	0.1733	0.1487	0.1490	0.1461
	TSLS	0.2196	0.1737	0.1211	0.2033	0.1526	0.1068
	LIML	0.2346	0.1788	0.1224	0.2197	0.1598	0.1094
	GMM	0.2198	0.1739	0.1212	0.2034	0.1526	0.1067
	Residual1	0.2381	0.2004	0.1422	0.2208	0.1829	0.1471
	Residual2	0.0962	0.0928	0.0853	0.1612	0.1429	0.0988
	BIPROBIT	0.1144	0.1041	0.0883	0.1907	0.1648	0.1160
	DFM	0.1093	0.1098	0.0978	0.0966	0.0925	0.0782
N = 10,000							
	LPM	0.1963	0.1969	0.1960	0.1694	0.1692	0.1701
	Probit	0.1748	0.1754	0.1747	0.1571	0.1570	0.1577
	TSLS	0.1784	0.1465	0.1072	0.1987	0.1503	0.1087
	LIML	0.1895	0.1517	0.1083	0.2153	0.1581	0.1115
	GMM	0.1791	0.1452	0.1085	0.1989	0.1505	0.1087
	Residual1	0.2090	0.1787	0.1380	0.2216	0.1827	0.1484
	Residual2	0.0809	0.0692	0.0680	0.1978	0.1720	0.1366
	BIPROBIT	0.1051	0.0869	0.0793	0.2025	0.1780	0.1439
	DFM	0.1381	0.1244	0.1060	0.1056	0.0916	0.0727

The results presented above likely mask some important variations in the performance of the estimators for different configurations of the data generating process. In Table 2.18 we present results based on further stratification of the simple regression by error correlation. For normal errors and the lower error correlation level of 0.1, no estimator has a lower MAD than LPM but the Probit estimator's MAD is not significantly different from that for the LPM. However, it is interesting to note that the relative performance of the estimators is completely different with normal errors and error correlation 0.3. Now Residual2 and BIPROBIT are the dominant estimators followed closely by DFM while the other estimators are not much different in terms of MAD from LPM. For non-normal errors, the results

Table 2.8 Mean absolute deviation of ATE for true ATE = 0.2, error correlation = 0.3, $Y_1 = 0.5$ and $Y_2 = 0.5$

		Normal errors			Non-normal errors		
		$\chi^2 = 15$	$\chi^2 = 25$	$\chi^2 = 50$	$\chi^2 = 15$	$\chi^2 = 25$	$\chi^2 = 50$
N = 1,000							
	LPM	0.1757	0.1706	0.1712	0.2202	0.2199	0.2151
	Probit	0.1715	0.1662	0.1669	0.2027	0.2025	0.1990
	TSLS	0.2177	0.1627	0.1134	0.2101	0.1670	0.1324
	LIML	0.2342	0.1698	0.1156	0.2252	0.1712	0.1335
	GMM	0.2182	0.1636	0.1138	0.2105	0.1679	0.1334
	Residual1	0.2162	0.1728	0.1258	0.2183	0.1787	0.1372
	Residual2	0.1862	0.1549	0.1172	0.1891	0.1507	0.1195
	BIPROBIT	0.1920	0.1535	0.1125	0.1487	0.1226	0.1049
	DFM	0.1428	0.1385	0.1199	0.1607	0.1634	0.1512
N = 5,000							
	LPM	0.1750	0.1745	0.1732	0.1934	0.1932	0.1926
	Probit	0.1707	0.1703	0.1691	0.1835	0.1832	0.1830
	TSLS	0.2058	0.1630	0.1143	0.2038	0.1582	0.1135
	LIML	0.2201	0.1700	0.1166	0.2188	0.1641	0.1150
	GMM	0.2059	0.1631	0.1144	0.2037	0.1583	0.1136
	Residual1	0.2074	0.1777	0.1292	0.2130	0.1738	0.1272
	Residual2	0.1324	0.1179	0.0992	0.3206	0.2778	0.2028
	BIPROBIT	0.1526	0.1310	0.1020	0.2706	0.2052	0.1334
	DFM	0.1211	0.1090	0.0992	0.0905	0.0924	0.0889
N = 10,000							
	LPM	0.1799	0.1797	0.1793	0.2073	0.2063	0.2068
	Probit	0.1753	0.1751	0.1748	0.1939	0.1930	0.1936
	TSLS	0.2101	0.1485	0.1133	0.2052	0.1657	0.1058
	LIML	0.2290	0.1549	0.1154	0.2200	0.1721	0.1076
	GMM	0.2116	0.1483	0.1132	0.2052	0.1657	0.1085
	Residual1	0.2166	0.1623	0.1305	0.2141	0.1792	0.1249
	Residual2	0.1065	0.1052	0.0907	0.3346	0.3080	0.2551
	BIPROBIT	0.1393	0.1226	0.0991	0.2238	0.1890	0.1397
	DFM	0.1349	0.1364	0.1157	0.0504	0.0521	0.0485

are quite different. We see that for error correlation 0.1, only PROBIT and DFM perform as well as LPM, with all other methods performing significantly worse. At the error correlation level of 0.3, DFM dominates all other estimators.

We also consider stratification of the summary regression by instrument strength. Results for this are presented in Tables 2.19 and 2.20. We consider only two instrument strength levels (as manifested by the size of the χ^2 statistic obtained from a test of the joint significance of the instruments in a probit regression with Y_2 as the dependent variable): $\chi^2 = 15$ and $\chi^2 = 50$. Not surprisingly, the estimators most affected by instrument strength are the linear instrumental variables methods. They perform quite poorly compared with the LPM at instrument strength $\chi^2 = 15$.

Table 2.9 Mean ATE for true ATE = 0.05, error correlation = 0.1, $Y_1 = 0.25$ and $Y_2 = 0.25$

		Normal errors			Non-normal errors		
		$\chi^2 = 15$	$\chi^2 = 25$	$\chi^2 = 50$	$\chi^2 = 15$	$\chi^2 = 25$	$\chi^2 = 50$
Obs = 1,000							
	LPM	0.1306	0.1299	0.1261	0.1291	0.1269	0.1212
	Probit	0.1084	0.1086	0.1077	0.1155	0.1139	0.1106
	TSLS	0.0755	0.0770	0.0654	0.0184	0.0444	0.0486
	LIML	0.0739	0.0745	0.0642	0.0074	0.0400	0.0469
	GMM	0.0761	0.0773	0.0657	0.0181	0.0443	0.0488
	Residual1	0.1089	0.0980	0.0677	0.0527	0.0613	0.0516
	Residual2	0.0896	0.0852	0.0701	0.1755	0.1410	0.0913
	BIPROBIT	0.0811	0.0808	0.0735	0.1675	0.1465	0.0943
	DFM	0.1175	0.1076	0.0952	0.1076	0.1045	0.0819
Obs = 5,000							
	LPM	0.1315	0.1319	0.1309	0.1343	0.1334	0.1329
	Probit	0.1083	0.1089	0.1083	0.1186	0.1179	0.1179
	TSLS	0.0948	0.0880	0.0821	0.0477	0.0480	0.0545
	LIML	0.0913	0.0858	0.0810	0.0424	0.0443	0.0530
	GMM	0.0949	0.0883	0.0823	0.0481	0.0481	0.0547
	Residual1	0.1122	0.0967	0.0793	0.0655	0.0532	0.0483
	Residual2	0.0705	0.0726	0.0699	0.3602	0.3070	0.2279
	BIPROBIT	0.0524	0.0596	0.0640	0.3292	0.3034	0.2495
	DFM	0.1186	0.1082	0.1105	0.1105	0.1097	0.1096
Obs = 10,000							
	LPM	0.1318	0.1303	0.1313	0.1316	0.1305	0.1300
	Probit	0.1089	0.1077	0.1088	0.1159	0.1149	0.1146
	TSLS	0.0837	0.0663	0.0727	0.1136	0.0944	0.0981
	LIML	0.0813	0.0647	0.0719	0.1125	0.0927	0.0979
	GMM	0.0837	0.0664	0.0801	0.1158	0.0941	0.0982
	Residual1	0.0878	0.0656	0.0669	0.1160	0.0915	0.0883
	Residual2	0.0708	0.0560	0.0730	0.3734	0.3446	0.2958
	BIPROBIT	0.0532	0.0399	0.0613	0.3269	0.3171	0.2940
	DFM	0.1227	0.1229	0.1007	0.1088	0.1085	0.1079

However, even at instrument strength $\chi^2 = 50$, they do not perform any better than the LPM model (or at least they do not do so to a statistically significant degree). For BIPROBIT and Residual2, we see improved performance as instrument strength increases for both normal and non-normal errors. Finally, DFM improves with increasing instrument strength for normal errors but does roughly equally well at the two instrument strengths when the errors are non-normal.

In Table 2.20, rather than stratifying by error distribution, we stratify by error correlation and then instrument strength. This table clearly isolates the cases in which the linear instrumental variables estimators perform relatively well. We see that all three linear instrumental variables estimators are inferior to LPM when the error correlation is low regardless of instrument strength. At the lower value

Table 2.10 Mean ATE for true ATE = 0.05, error correlation = 0.1, $Y_1 = 0.5$ and $Y_2 = 0.5$

		Normal errors			Non-normal errors		
		$\chi^2 = 15$	$\chi^2 = 25$	$\chi^2 = 50$	$\chi^2 = 15$	$\chi^2 = 25$	$\chi^2 = 50$
Obs = 1,000							
	LPM	0.1327	0.1326	0.1273	0.1496	0.1467	0.1414
	Probit	0.1243	0.1245	0.1204	0.1365	0.1341	0.1310
	TSLS	0.0826	0.0818	0.0773	0.0923	0.0874	0.0812
	LIML	0.0743	0.0804	0.0763	0.0884	0.0843	0.0800
	GMM	0.0832	0.0819	0.0778	0.0926	0.0881	0.0817
	Residual1	0.0823	0.0787	0.0719	0.0813	0.0760	0.0707
	Residual2	0.0804	0.0783	0.0746	0.0100	0.0290	0.0589
	BIPROBIT	0.0703	0.0779	0.0761	0.0271	0.0420	0.0654
	DFM	0.1224	0.1131	0.0922	0.1215	0.0982	0.0808
Obs = 5,000							
	LPM	0.1310	0.1308	0.1285	0.1493	0.1487	0.1494
	Probit	0.1233	0.1232	0.1213	0.1366	0.1362	0.1372
	TSLS	0.0770	0.0680	0.0639	0.1066	0.0896	0.0906
	LIML	0.0724	0.0653	0.0626	0.1054	0.0872	0.0895
	GMM	0.0771	0.0680	0.0639	0.1068	0.0897	0.0908
	Residual1	0.0751	0.0631	0.0568	0.1032	0.0835	0.0818
	Residual2	0.0745	0.0689	0.0613	−0.1167	−0.0774	−0.0217
	BIPROBIT	0.0538	0.0563	0.0567	−0.0320	−0.0098	0.0230
	DFM	0.1315	0.1148	0.0978	0.1074	0.0998	0.0918
Obs = 10,000							
	LPM	0.1315	0.1324	0.1309	0.1488	0.1499	0.1484
	Probit	0.1235	0.1245	0.1232	0.1357	0.1367	0.1354
	TSLS	0.0293	0.0377	0.0518	0.0605	0.0592	0.0721
	LIML	0.0242	0.0347	0.0503	0.0544	0.0562	0.0705
	GMM	0.0314	0.0362	0.0519	0.0575	0.0562	0.0726
	Residual1	0.0569	0.0494	0.0568	0.0905	0.0799	0.0830
	Residual2	0.0742	0.0652	0.0580	−0.1792	−0.1570	−0.1088
	BIPROBIT	0.0454	0.0486	0.0525	−0.0566	−0.0451	−0.0186
	DFM	0.1296	0.1185	0.1045	0.1360	0.1348	0.1285

for instrument strength, the linear instrumental variables estimators still offer no improvement over LPM when error correlation is 0.1. However, they offer substantial improvement over LPM when error correlation is 0.3 and instrument strength is high. We do not display results for instrument strength 25 but in this case, the linear instrumental variables estimators offer slight improvement over LPM with the higher error correlation. This relatively strong performance for the linear instrumental variables methods is robust to a further stratification by error distribution (results not displayed). When error correlation is 0.3 and instrument strength is 50, there is no difference in the level of improvement over LPM for normal or non-normal errors. This is reassuring given that the linear instrumental approach has been recommended in this setting (e.g. Angrist and Krueger 2001).

Table 2.11 Mean ATE for true ATE = 0.05, error correlation = 0.3, $Y_1 = 0.25$ and $Y_2 = 0.25$

		Normal errors			Non-normal errors		
		$\chi^2 = 15$	$\chi^2 = 25$	$\chi^2 = 50$	$\chi^2 = 15$	$\chi^2 = 25$	$\chi^2 = 50$
Obs = 1,000							
	LPM	0.2440	0.2418	0.2330	0.2619	0.2579	0.2463
	Probit	0.2173	0.2153	0.2093	0.2424	0.2391	0.2309
	TSLS	0.0965	0.0886	0.0742	0.0768	0.0613	0.0538
	LIML	−0.0203	0.0812	0.0706	0.0683	0.0533	0.0499
	GMM	0.0960	0.0889	0.0745	0.0765	0.0610	0.0537
	Residual1	0.1086	0.0827	0.0531	0.0856	0.0543	0.0302
	Residual2	0.1071	0.0983	0.0728	0.2143	0.1460	0.0825
	BIPROBIT	0.0969	0.0955	0.0751	0.1886	0.1280	0.0722
	DFM	0.1306	0.1298	0.1059	0.1380	0.1230	0.0835
Obs = 5,000							
	LPM	0.2481	0.2486	0.2472	0.2513	0.2507	0.2486
	Probit	0.2209	0.2215	0.2205	0.2349	0.2343	0.2326
	TSLS	0.1234	0.1226	0.1071	0.0254	0.0442	0.0453
	LIML	0.1148	0.1168	0.1040	0.0109	0.0359	0.0414
	GMM	0.1242	0.1232	0.1076	0.0256	0.0446	0.0455
	Residual1	0.1229	0.1076	0.0802	0.0303	0.0298	0.0152
	Residual2	0.0907	0.0970	0.0866	0.2387	0.2068	0.1512
	BIPROBIT	0.0638	0.0810	0.0770	0.1984	0.1731	0.1202
	DFM	0.1742	0.1675	0.1497	0.1665	0.1511	0.1353
Obs = 10,000							
	LPM	0.2444	0.2446	0.2438	0.2576	0.2580	0.2570
	Probit	0.2170	0.2173	0.2167	0.2404	0.2409	0.2398
	TSLS	0.0552	0.0694	0.0730	0.0571	0.0566	0.0566
	LIML	0.0401	0.0635	0.0694	0.0409	0.0480	0.0519
	GMM	0.0532	0.0697	0.0732	0.0568	0.0561	0.0563
	Residual1	0.0459	0.0485	0.0376	0.0495	0.0364	0.0210
	Residual2	0.0839	0.0803	0.0748	0.3151	0.2896	0.2390
	BIPROBIT	0.0410	0.0465	0.0530	0.2984	0.2745	0.2219
	DFM	0.1764	0.1647	0.1309	0.1546	0.1571	0.1361

However, the linear instrumental variables estimator never performs as well as DFM for any of these stratifications.

Finally, in Table 2.21 we add to the basic summary models presented in Table 2.17 controls for the behavioral parameters of the Monte Carlo experiment. Among the sample size regressors, the omitted category is experiments with 1,000 observations. The omitted instrument strength is $\chi^2 = 15$ (the lowest). The comparison values for error correlation and treatment effect are 0.1 and 0.05, respectively. Finally, for both program (i.e. program enrollment) and treatment prevalence the comparison value is 0.5.

There appears to be a clear performance improvement at the larger sample sizes with normal errors but performance actually deteriorates as sample size

Table 2.12 Mean ATE for true ATE = 0.05, error correlation = 0.3, $Y_1 = 0.5$ and $Y_2 = 0.5$

		Normal errors			Non-normal errors		
		$\chi^2 = 15$	$\chi^2 = 25$	$\chi^2 = 50$	$\chi^2 = 15$	$\chi^2 = 25$	$\chi^2 = 50$
Obs = 1,000							
	LPM	0.2528	0.2489	0.2441	0.2803	0.2788	0.2706
	Probit	0.2444	0.2408	0.2366	0.2584	0.2571	0.2505
	TSLS	0.1183	0.0991	0.0997	0.1100	0.0998	0.1123
	LIML	0.1084	0.0932	0.0970	0.0932	0.0902	0.1085
	GMM	0.1185	0.0996	0.1001	0.1119	0.1013	0.1142
	Residual1	0.1108	0.0890	0.0839	0.0851	0.0695	0.0784
	Residual2	0.1138	0.0948	0.0903	0.0251	0.0368	0.0717
	BIPROBIT	0.1087	0.0956	0.0933	0.0531	0.0624	0.0896
	DFM	0.1471	0.1224	0.1006	0.1382	0.1168	0.1035
Obs = 5,000							
	LPM	0.2526	0.2515	0.2510	0.2765	0.2750	0.2744
	Probit	0.2448	0.2437	0.2434	0.2610	0.2596	0.2594
	TSLS	0.0375	0.0667	0.0735	0.1199	0.1332	0.1153
	LIML	0.0131	0.0597	0.0700	0.1091	0.1278	0.1122
	GMM	0.0374	0.0668	0.0734	0.1202	0.1333	0.1154
	Residual1	0.0402	0.0577	0.0565	0.1069	0.1115	0.0892
	Residual2	0.0729	0.0737	0.0712	−0.1611	−0.1201	−0.0576
	BIPROBIT	0.0380	0.0548	0.0644	−0.0585	−0.0189	0.0212
	DFM	0.1577	0.1424	0.1145	0.0952	0.0890	0.0909
Obs = 10,000							
	LPM	0.2534	0.2519	0.2524	0.2811	0.2804	0.2792
	Probit	0.2451	0.2436	0.2442	0.2631	0.2625	0.2615
	TSLS	−0.0107	−0.0095	0.0325	0.0611	0.0701	0.0788
	LIML	−0.0313	−0.0211	0.0285	0.0445	0.0602	0.0742
	GMM	−0.0105	−0.0080	0.0329	0.0641	0.0685	0.0803
	Residual1	0.0166	−0.0015	0.0261	0.0818	0.0742	0.0712
	Residual2	0.0694	0.0526	0.0601	−0.1421	−0.1172	−0.0732
	BIPROBIT	0.0161	0.0156	0.0394	−0.0086	0.0083	0.0318
	DFM	0.1674	0.1426	0.1111	0.1253	0.1183	0.1172

increases for non-normal errors. Interestingly, however, the effects of instrument strength and error correlation do not differ substantially by error type. Increasing the instrument strength always reduces MAD while increasing the error correlation always increases it. The true treatment effect has a small but significant effect on performance (with performance deteriorating as true treatment effect increases). Program participation and outcome prevalence have substantial, highly significant effects, but in opposite directions. Performance clearly worsens with non-normal errors.

Before proceeding, it is worth reflecting on the generally poor performance of several estimators in the case of non-normal errors. This is very concerning when one considers that, in many respects, the non-normal error distribution considered in

Table 2.13 Mean ATE for true ATE = 0.2, error correlation = 0.1, $Y_1 = 0.25$ and $Y_2 = 0.25$

		Normal errors			Non-normal errors		
		$\chi^2 = 15$	$\chi^2 = 25$	$\chi^2 = 50$	$\chi^2 = 15$	$\chi^2 = 25$	$\chi^2 = 50$
Obs = 1,000							
	LPM	0.2965	0.2970	0.2933	0.2564	0.2559	0.2556
	Probit	0.2694	0.2704	0.2691	0.2395	0.2399	0.2410
	TSLS	0.2403	0.2468	0.2399	0.1717	0.2068	0.1941
	LIML	0.2315	0.2437	0.2387	0.1624	0.2043	0.1928
	GMM	0.2404	0.2469	0.2402	0.1714	0.2066	0.1941
	Residual1	0.2336	0.2325	0.2209	0.1688	0.1966	0.1766
	Residual2	0.2223	0.2349	0.2228	0.3155	0.2953	0.2319
	BIPROBIT	0.2115	0.2326	0.2246	0.3170	0.3030	0.2375
	DFM	0.1704	0.1715	0.1846	0.1981	0.1949	0.1900
Obs = 5,000							
	LPM	0.2914	0.2914	0.2901	0.2730	0.2730	0.2701
	Probit	0.2634	0.2634	0.2628	0.2550	0.2553	0.2531
	TSLS	0.2522	0.2404	0.2507	0.2097	0.2061	0.2032
	LIML	0.2504	0.2377	0.2502	0.2043	0.2039	0.2021
	GMM	0.2527	0.2406	0.2510	0.2102	0.2061	0.2033
	Residual1	0.2378	0.2237	0.2293	0.1968	0.1870	0.1761
	Residual2	0.2167	0.2147	0.2208	0.5348	0.4901	0.4086
	BIPROBIT	0.1996	0.2035	0.2167	0.5092	0.4914	0.4409
	DFM	0.2120	0.2024	0.2199	0.2074	0.2053	0.2033
Obs = 10,000							
	LPM	0.2956	0.2957	0.2953	0.2572	0.2579	0.2572
	Probit	0.2668	0.2671	0.2668	0.2400	0.2406	0.2402
	TSLS	0.2417	0.2283	0.2309	0.2236	0.2338	0.2192
	LIML	0.2380	0.2254	0.2295	0.2231	0.2333	0.2182
	GMM	0.2419	0.2283	0.2310	0.2183	0.2338	0.2192
	Residual1	0.2124	0.1928	0.1942	0.1981	0.2105	0.1939
	Residual2	0.2133	0.2122	0.2092	0.5118	0.4902	0.4354
	BIPROBIT	0.1977	0.1975	0.2006	0.4792	0.4698	0.4432
	DFM	0.2560	0.2504	0.2378	0.2165	0.2164	0.2136

this study represents a rather forgiving departure from joint normality. For instance, it still involves unimodal marginal distributions for the errors and a unimodal surface for the joint density of the errors in $\mathbf{R}^3$. This may indeed be too generous from the standpoint of accurately reflecting conditions likely to be encountered in actual applied microeconometric settings.

For instance, in the real world the joint distribution of the error term from a particular application involving a system along the lines of Eqs. (2.1) and (2.2) is likely often to involve multi-modality: the joint distribution of the unobservables for the error term in many settings is likely to reflect substantial mass for extreme (in terms of behavior) types of individuals that would be difficult to accommodate accurately with unimodal joint distributions under which such varied and extreme

Table 2.14 Mean ATE for true ATE = 0.2, error correlation = 0.1, $Y_1 = 0.5$ and $Y_2 = 0.5$

		Normal errors			Non-normal errors		
		$\chi^2 = 15$	$\chi^2 = 25$	$\chi^2 = 50$	$\chi^2 = 15$	$\chi^2 = 25$	$\chi^2 = 50$
Obs = 1,000							
	LPM	0.2803	0.2809	0.2809	0.3066	0.3057	0.3030
	Probit	0.2722	0.2731	0.2737	0.2883	0.2880	0.2886
	TSLS	0.2511	0.2310	0.2291	0.2714	0.2665	0.2611
	LIML	0.2471	0.2289	0.2279	0.2646	0.2642	0.2601
	GMM	0.2525	0.2316	0.2297	0.2729	0.2676	0.2618
	Residual1	0.2305	0.2154	0.2147	0.2383	0.2410	0.2459
	Residual2	0.2307	0.2167	0.2183	0.1206	0.1569	0.2122
	BIPROBIT	0.2262	0.2162	0.2197	0.1575	0.1826	0.2237
	DFM	0.1932	0.1802	0.1781	0.2455	0.2402	0.2563
Obs = 5,000							
	LPM	0.2754	0.2742	0.2751	0.2998	0.2992	0.3001
	Probit	0.2676	0.2665	0.2676	0.2826	0.2824	0.2836
	TSLS	0.2061	0.2139	0.2202	0.2811	0.2649	0.2628
	LIML	0.2016	0.2116	0.2192	0.2799	0.2633	0.2621
	GMM	0.2063	0.2140	0.2203	0.2814	0.2649	0.2630
	Residual1	0.1858	0.1968	0.2044	0.2575	0.2433	0.2437
	Residual2	0.2070	0.2054	0.2061	−0.0613	−0.0140	0.0676
	BIPROBIT	0.1901	0.1941	0.2026	0.0547	0.0859	0.1351
	DFM	0.2132	0.2075	0.2031	0.1920	0.1947	0.2053
Obs = 10,000							
	LPM	0.2821	0.2811	0.2804	0.2934	0.2925	0.2916
	Probit	0.2739	0.2729	0.2723	0.2759	0.2751	0.2743
	TSLS	0.1942	0.2002	0.2089	0.2346	0.2432	0.2289
	LIML	0.1878	0.1977	0.2076	0.2294	0.2404	0.2273
	GMM	0.1937	0.2000	0.2103	0.2348	0.2418	0.2289
	Residual1	0.1869	0.1938	0.2013	0.2339	0.2372	0.2224
	Residual2	0.2126	0.2031	0.2041	−0.1440	−0.1177	−0.0572
	BIPROBIT	0.1898	0.1888	0.1984	−0.0025	0.0203	0.0598
	DFM	0.2488	0.2482	0.2307	0.1748	0.1718	0.1780

combinations are typically found only with much lower probability. If Y_1 were smoking and Y_2 were obesity, for example, one could easily imagine a significant proportion of the population with combinations of strong unobserved tendencies toward and away from smoking and obesity that are hard to accommodate with unimodal (in terms of marginal errors or density surface in $\mathbf{R}^3$) errors, let alone joint normality. However, it also hard to believe that the performance of many models (such as those based on joint normality) would improve from what is presented in this manuscript once the departure from joint normality involved relaxing the assumption of unimodality.

In Tables 2.22–2.25, we examine a limited set of results for the endogeneity tests and the identification tests considered in our Monte Carlo experiments. To begin

Table 2.15 Mean ATE for true ATE = 0.2, error correlation = 0.3, $Y_1 = 0.25$ and $Y_2 = 0.25$

		Normal errors			Non-normal errors		
		$\chi^2 = 15$	$\chi^2 = 25$	$\chi^2 = 50$	$\chi^2 = 15$	$\chi^2 = 25$	$\chi^2 = 50$
Obs = 1,000							
	LPM	0.3981	0.4015	0.3913	0.3946	0.3878	0.3742
	Probit	0.3774	0.3815	0.3713	0.3801	0.3736	0.3625
	TSLS	0.2668	0.2543	0.2463	0.2156	0.2264	0.1967
	LIML	0.2561	0.2474	0.2431	0.2005	0.2190	0.1930
	GMM	0.2676	0.2549	0.2468	0.2154	0.2267	0.1970
	Residual1	0.2317	0.2095	0.1909	0.1826	0.1830	0.1460
	Residual2	0.2301	0.2257	0.2129	0.3335	0.2908	0.2075
	BIPROBIT	0.2189	0.2221	0.2173	0.3056	0.2755	0.1984
	DFM	0.1947	0.1892	0.1794	0.2499	0.2228	0.1860
Obs = 5,000							
	LPM	0.3952	0.3950	0.3931	0.3597	0.3601	0.3570
	Probit	0.3744	0.3743	0.3728	0.3482	0.3485	0.3456
	TSLS	0.2850	0.2826	0.2625	0.1494	0.1651	0.1624
	LIML	0.2770	0.2779	0.2590	0.1358	0.1573	0.1587
	GMM	0.2855	0.2832	0.2629	0.1498	0.1655	0.1625
	Residual1	0.2464	0.2408	0.2081	0.1246	0.1236	0.1066
	Residual2	0.2164	0.2219	0.2175	0.3340	0.3097	0.2487
	BIPROBIT	0.1905	0.2048	0.2092	0.2971	0.2809	0.2194
	DFM	0.2483	0.2534	0.2409	0.2604	0.2486	0.2191
Obs = 10,000							
	LPM	0.3958	0.3964	0.3955	0.3689	0.3687	0.3696
	Probit	0.3743	0.3749	0.3742	0.3566	0.3565	0.3572
	TSLS	0.2316	0.2282	0.2297	0.1636	0.1702	0.1713
	LIML	0.2227	0.2211	0.2260	0.1480	0.1609	0.1670
	GMM	0.2306	0.2265	0.2288	0.1630	0.1699	0.1712
	Residual1	0.1730	0.1621	0.1588	0.1274	0.1185	0.1098
	Residual2	0.2176	0.2123	0.2032	0.3943	0.3681	0.3288
	BIPROBIT	0.1836	0.1817	0.1827	0.3824	0.3548	0.3092
	DFM	0.2762	0.2559	0.2367	0.2920	0.2794	0.2546

with, in each of these tables we list models with the specific test associated with that model in parentheses. In both tables we present proportions of p-values that exceed or fall below some important threshold. We begin with the overidentification tests in Tables 2.22 and 2.23, for which the null is that the overidentifying restrictions are valid (i.e. that the specification considered is valid).[8] Since the identifying

[8]Recall that the overidentification test statistic for the bivariate probit model is simply the χ^2 statistic for a test of the joint significance of the instruments in the marginal probit equation for Y_2 under the "just identified" specification under which the instruments appear in both marginal probit equations and identification rests on nonlinearity from functional form (i.e. joint normality) alone. The null hypothesis of such a test is that the instruments are not jointly significant regressors

Table 2.16 Mean ATE for true ATE = 0.2, error correlation = 0.3, $Y_1 = 0.5$ and $Y_2 = 0.5$

		Normal errors			Non-normal errors		
		$\chi^2 = 15$	$\chi^2 = 25$	$\chi^2 = 50$	$\chi^2 = 15$	$\chi^2 = 25$	$\chi^2 = 50$
Obs = 1,000							
	LPM	0.3752	0.3701	0.3707	0.4197	0.4194	0.4146
	Probit	0.3710	0.3657	0.3665	0.4022	0.4020	0.3985
	TSLS	0.2350	0.2126	0.2262	0.2729	0.2709	0.2804
	LIML	0.2255	0.2051	0.2229	0.2584	0.2639	0.2769
	GMM	0.2357	0.2135	0.2269	0.2747	0.2729	0.2823
	Residual1	0.2155	0.1894	0.2006	0.2235	0.2195	0.2345
	Residual2	0.2185	0.1941	0.2034	0.0842	0.1343	0.1948
	BIPROBIT	0.2140	0.1949	0.2085	0.1373	0.1765	0.2229
	DFM	0.1853	0.1671	0.1668	0.2149	0.2113	0.2298
Obs = 5,000							
	LPM	0.3745	0.3740	0.3727	0.3929	0.3927	0.3921
	Probit	0.3702	0.3698	0.3686	0.3830	0.3827	0.3825
	TSLS	0.1848	0.1780	0.2060	0.2153	0.2274	0.2348
	LIML	0.1716	0.1707	0.2026	0.2031	0.2206	0.2317
	GMM	0.1849	0.1780	0.2059	0.2151	0.2277	0.2350
	Residual1	0.1651	0.1532	0.1786	0.1800	0.1896	0.1963
	Residual2	0.1855	0.1813	0.1892	−0.1205	−0.0773	0.0004
	BIPROBIT	0.1597	0.1647	0.1842	−0.0701	−0.0033	0.0731
	DFM	0.2231	0.2071	0.1977	0.1265	0.1244	0.1334
Obs = 10,000							
	LPM	0.3794	0.3792	0.3788	0.4068	0.4058	0.4063
	Probit	0.3748	0.3746	0.3743	0.3934	0.3925	0.3931
	TSLS	0.1182	0.1547	0.1773	0.2124	0.2121	0.2165
	LIML	0.1038	0.1462	0.1734	0.1984	0.2039	0.2125
	GMM	0.1193	0.1534	0.1773	0.2125	0.2123	0.2175
	Residual1	0.1069	0.1300	0.1491	0.1916	0.1857	0.1810
	Residual2	0.1804	0.1819	0.1804	−0.1350	−0.1085	−0.0555
	BIPROBIT	0.1377	0.1580	0.1664	−0.0241	0.0108	0.0610
	DFM	0.2372	0.2437	0.2148	0.1561	0.1563	0.1609

restrictions in our Monte Carlo experiments are indeed valid by construction, large test statistics (and accompanying low p-values) would be cause for concern. Tables 2.22 and 2.23 thus present the percentage of p-values that are in the concerning range (i.e. below the conventional cutoff level of 0.1). Interestingly, here all three linear instrumental variables models appear to do quite well.

The same cannot be said for the bivariate probit model, which produces large test statistics (as evidenced by low p-values) alarmingly often. Its performance appears

in marginal probit equation for Y_2 (i.e. that they are legitimately excluded from the marginal probit equation for Y_2).

Table 2.17 Basic summary regressions

	All models		Normal errors		Non-normal errors	
Method	Coeff.	T-statistic	Coeff.	T-statistic	Coeff.	T-statistic
Probit	−0.0038	−0.71	−0.0054	−1.05	−0.0023	−0.28
TSLS	0.0361	6.76	0.0397	7.81	0.0325	4.03
LIML	0.0450	8.42	0.0490	9.64	0.0410	5.07
GMM	0.0363	6.79	0.0399	7.85	0.0326	4.04
Residual1	0.0361	6.76	0.0393	7.72	0.0330	4.08
Residual2	0.0409	7.64	−0.0201	−3.96	0.1018	12.6
BIPROBIT	0.0402	7.52	−0.0128	−2.52	0.0933	11.54
DFM	−0.0242	−4.52	−0.0041	−0.81	−0.0442	−5.47
N	2,592		1,296		1,296	

to improve considerably with larger sample sizes and joint normality of errors. On the whole, however, using an overidentification test which relies on the non-linearity of the bivariate probit model is of limited usefulness.

Turning to Tables 2.24 and 2.25 and the endogeneity test results, we now consider the proportion of the time that the test statistic yields a large p-value. This is once again natural and fitting since the null hypothesis in these tests is exogeneity. A small test statistic (and accompanying large p-value) would thus be cause for concern since endogeneity is present in our models by design (and therefore the null should be rejected). We consider the proportion of p-values that exceed 0.1. Here the results are generally far less reassuring. The performance of endogeneity tests in the linear instrumental variables models is poor,[9] with particularly misleading results in the case of the Hausman test. The performance of the bivariate probit model, Residual1 and Residual2 are not much better. In general, these results suggest that conventional endogeneity tests are more or less completely unreliable, at least in terms of conventional benchmark p-value thresholds when both dependent variables are binary.

2.5 Empirical Examples

We present two empirical examples based on data sets from Bangladesh and Tanzania that have been previously analyzed by Chen and Guilkey (2003) and Guilkey and Hutchinson (2011). The models that we use in this paper are highly simplified compared to those presented in the original papers. However, they are sufficiently detailed to provide a good comparison of the methods and to demonstrate the pitfalls that one might encounter in analyzing similar problems.

[9]We refer to the Wu-Hausman test (Wu 1974; Hausman 1978) simply as "Wu" in Tables 2.24 and 2.25.

Table 2.18 Summary regressions stratified by error correlation

	Normal errors				Non-normal errors			
	Error correlation 0.1		Error correlation 0.3		Error correlation 0.1		Error correlation 0.3	
Method	Coeff.	T-statistic	Coeff.	T-statistic	Coeff.	T-statistic	Coeff.	T-statistic
Probit	−0.0063	−1.1	−0.0044	−0.72	−0.0029	−0.29	−0.0016	−0.15
TSLS	0.0906	15.77	−0.0111	−1.81	0.0867	8.55	−0.0216	−1.96
LIML	0.0992	17.28	−0.0012	−0.19	0.0950	9.37	−0.0131	−1.19
GMM	0.0908	15.8	−0.0109	−1.78	0.0867	8.54	−0.0214	−1.94
Residual1	0.0895	15.58	−0.0109	−1.79	0.0856	8.44	−0.0197	−1.79
Residual2	0.0304	5.3	−0.0707	−11.58	0.1711	16.87	0.0326	2.96
BIPROBIT	0.0372	6.47	−0.0628	−10.29	0.1623	16	0.0242	2.2
DFM	0.0453	7.89	−0.0536	−8.77	0.0034	0.33	−0.0918	−8.34
N	648		648		648		648	

Table 2.19 Summary regressions stratified by instrument strength

	Normal errors				Non-normal errors			
	Instrument strength 15		Instrument strength 50		Instrument strength 15		Instrument strength 50	
Method	Coeff.	T-statistic	Coeff.	T-statistic	Coeff.	T-statistic	Coeff.	T-statistic
Probit	−0.0055	−0.73	−0.0052	−0.88	−0.0023	−0.18	−0.0021	−0.17
TSLS	0.0878	11.64	−0.0085	−1.44	0.0792	6.16	−0.0131	−1.06
LIML	0.1070	14.19	−0.0065	−1.11	0.0958	7.45	−0.0110	−0.89
GMM	0.0881	11.68	−0.0084	−1.42	0.0792	6.16	−0.0129	−1.04
Residual1	0.0788	10.45	−0.0028	−0.47	0.0707	5.5	−0.0057	−0.46
Residual2	−0.0073	−0.97	−0.0352	−5.96	0.1377	10.71	0.0599	4.84
BIPROBIT	0.0046	0.61	−0.0328	−5.55	0.1250	9.72	0.0562	4.54
DFM	0.0059	0.79	−0.0168	−2.84	−0.0406	−3.16	−0.0486	−3.93
N	432		432		432		432	

Table 2.20 Summary regressions by error correlation and instrument strength

	Error correlation 0.1				Error correlation 0.3			
	Instrument strength 15		Instrument strength 50		Instrument strength 15		Instrument strength 50	
Method	Coeff.	T-statistic	Coeff.	T-statistic	Coeff.	T-statistic	Coeff.	T-statistic
Probit	−0.0048	−0.42	−0.0044	−0.45	−0.0030	−0.27	−0.0029	−0.31
TSLS	0.1362	11.84	0.0414	4.23	0.0309	2.69	−0.0630	−6.77
LIML	0.1530	13.3	0.0434	4.44	0.0498	4.35	−0.0609	−6.56
GMM	0.1361	11.84	0.0415	4.24	0.0312	2.72	−0.0627	−6.75
Residual1	0.1263	10.98	0.0468	4.78	0.0232	2.03	−0.0553	−5.95
Residual2	0.1259	10.95	0.0711	7.27	0.0044	0.39	−0.0464	−4.99
BIPROBIT	0.1227	10.67	0.0724	7.39	0.0068	0.6	−0.0489	−5.26
DFM	0.0301	2.61	0.0168	1.71	−0.0647	−5.65	−0.0822	−8.84
N	432		432		432		432	

Table 2.21 Summary regressions with controls for all experimental features

	All models		Normal errors		Non-normal errors	
Method	Coeff.	T statistic	Coeff.	T statistic	Coeff.	T statistic
Probit	−0.0038	−0.84	−0.0054	−1.39	−0.0023	−0.33
TSLS	0.0361	7.95	0.0397	10.32	0.0325	4.82
LIML	0.0450	9.9	0.0490	12.73	0.0410	6.07
GMM	0.0363	7.99	0.0399	10.37	0.0326	4.84
Residual1	0.0361	7.95	0.0393	10.2	0.0330	4.89
Residual2	0.0409	8.99	−0.0201	−5.23	0.1018	15.1
BIPROBIT	0.0402	8.85	−0.0128	−3.33	0.0933	13.82
DFM	−0.0242	−5.32	−0.0041	−1.07	−0.0442	−6.55
Sample size 5,000	−0.0019	−0.74	−0.0099	−4.47	0.0061	1.55
Sample size 10,000	−0.0013	−0.48	−0.0154	−6.93	0.0129	3.31
Instrument strength 25	−0.0271	−10.31	−0.0257	−11.55	−0.0284	−7.3
Instrument strength 50	−0.0577	−21.98	−0.0546	−24.55	−0.0607	−15.59
Error correlation 0.3	0.0213	9.93	0.0252	13.86	0.0174	5.47
Treatment effect 0.2	0.0038	1.75	0.0001	0.04	0.0074	2.34
Program prevalence 0.25	0.0251	11.7	0.0115	6.35	0.0386	12.14
Outcome prevalence 0.25	−0.0265	−12.35	−0.0164	−9.02	−0.0365	−11.49
Non-normal errors	0.0239	11.14				
N	2,592		1,296		1,296	

That said, an important consideration to remember now that we have moved from simulations (for which we control all parameters) to applications with real world samples is that heterogeneous treatment effects (which were not considered in the simulations) may be at play and driving differences in estimates.

In Bangladesh, we use data that was gathered to examine how self-exposure to the Smiling Sun multimedia communication campaign in rural Bangladesh impacted women's use of modern contraception (more details and more extensive models are to be found in Guilkey and Hutchinson (2011)). The Smiling Sun communication program, launched in Bangladesh in 2001, was a multi-channel campaign with the objectives of establishing the Smiling Sun symbol, disseminating important health-related messages, and promoting health services in urban and rural areas at Paribarik Shastha Clinics (Family Health Clinics) operated by the NGO Service Delivery Program (for which the Smiling Sun served as a logo). The campaign involved a 26-episode television drama serial 'Eyi Megh Eyi Roudro' ("Now cloud, now sunshine"), television advertisements, radio spots, posters, billboards, press ads in daily newspapers and local publicity efforts.

The data were collected roughly at the beginning of the Smiling Sun campaign in 2001 and then again 2 years later. Questions were asked of women of reproductive age about whether they had seen the Smiling Sun logo and, if so, whether they had seen it in a television drama, in a television advertisement, on the radio, on a billboard, at a signboard at a clinic, or elsewhere. In the original paper, we examined the impact of recall for each source separately. In the simplified model used here, all sources are combined into a single binary indicator for exposure to the program.

Table 2.22 Identification tests for true ATE = 0.2, error correlation = 0.3, $Y_1 = 0.25$ and $Y_2 = 0.25$: proportion of times that the p-value for the test statistic is less than 0.1

		Normal errors			Non-normal errors		
		$\chi^2 = 15$	$\chi^2 = 25$	$\chi^2 = 50$	$\chi^2 = 15$	$\chi^2 = 25$	$\chi^2 = 50$
N = 1,000							
	TSLS_Sargan	0.0900	0.1010	0.0980	0.1010	0.0950	0.0940
	TSLS_Basmann	0.0900	0.1000	0.0980	0.1010	0.0950	0.0930
	LIML_AndersonRubin	0.0880	0.0990	0.0980	0.1010	0.0950	0.0950
	LIML_Basmann	0.0880	0.0970	0.0980	0.0950	0.0930	0.0920
	GMM_Hansen	0.0840	0.1000	0.0980	0.0990	0.0920	0.0880
	BIPROBIT	0.2748	0.2890	0.2821	0.2624	0.3361	0.3810
N = 5,000							
	TSLS_Sargan	0.1080	0.0910	0.1190	0.0930	0.1040	0.0990
	TSLS_Basmann	0.1080	0.0910	0.1190	0.0930	0.1040	0.0990
	LIML_AndersonRubin	0.1030	0.0910	0.1190	0.0910	0.1020	0.0990
	LIML_Basmann	0.1010	0.0910	0.1180	0.0910	0.1020	0.0990
	GMM_Hansen	0.1070	0.0890	0.1200	0.0930	0.1030	0.0970
	BIPROBIT	0.1416	0.1249	0.1263	0.2385	0.2613	0.3340
N = 10,000							
	TSLS_Sargan	0.1100	0.1080	0.1180	0.1000	0.1240	0.1200
	TSLS_Basmann	0.1100	0.1080	0.1180	0.1000	0.1240	0.1200
	LIML_AndersonRubin	0.1080	0.1060	0.1180	0.0980	0.1200	0.1200
	LIML_Basmann	0.1080	0.1060	0.1180	0.0980	0.1200	0.1200
	GMM_Hansen	0.1080	0.0960	0.1200	0.1000	0.1240	0.1180
	BIPROBIT	0.1172	0.0984	0.1240	0.2360	0.3026	0.4140

We pool the data from 2001 and 2003 in the analysis. Descriptive statistics and variable definitions are presented in Table 2.26. There are three exclusion restrictions in the current use of contraception equation: the last three variables that indicate the number of Smiling Sun posters in clinics that are within 1 km of the sample cluster and whether or not the household owns a TV and radio (two separate indicators).

In Tanzania, we use data gathered over a 9-year period for the purpose of evaluating that nation's National Population Policy (NPP). The NPP began in 1992 and was developed to address a very high total fertility rate of about 6.3 children (Ngallaba et al. 1993) and an under five mortality rate of 141 per 1,000 live births. The NPP had substantial funding from donor agencies including the United States Agency for International Development (USAID).

The main USAID program in Tanzania for family planning was the Family Planning Support System (FPSS) project. The major components of the program were to train health providers in the provision of family planning, to provide logistical support for the provision of family planning supplies and to develop an information, education and communication (IEC) program to promote family planning. This program ended in 1999 and cross sectional data were gathered in 1991, 1994, 1996, and 1999 to evaluate its impact. Chen and Guilkey (2003)

Table 2.23 Identification tests for true ATE = 0.2, error correlation = 0.3, Y_1 = 0.5 and Y_2 = 0.5: proportion of times that the p-value for the test statistic is less than 0.1

		Normal errors			Non-normal errors		
		$\chi^2 = 15$	$\chi^2 = 25$	$\chi^2 = 50$	$\chi^2 = 15$	$\chi^2 = 25$	$\chi^2 = 50$
N = 1,000							
	TSLS_Sargan	0.0880	0.1000	0.0900	0.0910	0.1070	0.1210
	TSLS_Basmann	0.0860	0.1000	0.0890	0.0910	0.1070	0.1200
	LIML_AndersonRubin	0.0840	0.1000	0.0900	0.0910	0.1070	0.1210
	LIML_Basmann	0.0820	0.0990	0.0880	0.0900	0.1060	0.1200
	GMM_Hansen	0.0900	0.0970	0.0890	0.0950	0.1050	0.1190
	BIPROBIT	0.2791	0.3252	0.3439	0.3141	0.3033	0.2464
N = 5,000							
	TSLS_Sargan	0.0970	0.0890	0.0990	0.0790	0.0820	0.0900
	TSLS_Basmann	0.0970	0.0890	0.0990	0.0790	0.0810	0.0900
	LIML_AndersonRubin	0.0930	0.0890	0.0990	0.0780	0.0800	0.0900
	LIML_Basmann	0.0920	0.0870	0.0990	0.0780	0.0800	0.0880
	GMM_Hansen	0.0990	0.0900	0.1010	0.0790	0.0840	0.0920
	BIPROBIT	0.1518	0.1436	0.1506	0.4598	0.5172	0.5518
N = 10,000							
	TSLS_Sargan	0.0960	0.0980	0.1060	0.0860	0.1040	0.0900
	TSLS_Basmann	0.0960	0.0980	0.1060	0.0860	0.1040	0.0900
	LIML_AndersonRubin	0.0940	0.0980	0.1040	0.0860	0.1040	0.0900
	LIML_Basmann	0.0940	0.0980	0.1040	0.0860	0.1040	0.0900
	GMM_Hansen	0.1000	0.1000	0.1020	0.0860	0.1040	0.1060
	BIPROBIT	0.1443	0.1403	0.1506	0.2385	0.2780	0.3560

provide a comprehensive evaluation of the program's impact. In this example, we estimate the impact of having heard a family message from any source on current contraceptive use. The summary statistics for the sample are found in Table 2.27.

We estimated the two equation models, one for self-reported exposure to a message and one for current contraceptive use, using all nine methods that were evaluated in the Monte Carlo experiments. The results of the Monte Carlo experiments suggest that the overidentification tests were reasonably reassuring while the endogeneity tests were highly inaccurate. The overidentification tests in Bangladesh for 2SLS, LIML, GMM all fail to reject the null hypothesis that the exclusion restrictions are valid, the desired result. The results for these tests for Tanzania were mixed: the p-values were 0.09, 0.09, and 0.21 for 2SLS, LIML, and GMM respectively and so there is weak evidence to support the null. When we included the excluded variables in the BIPROBIT models and tested to see if these variables had direct effects on contraceptive use, we found that two of three exclusion restrictions were valid for Bangladesh while both exclusion restrictions were valid for Tanzania. Since the DFM is also identified without exclusion restrictions, we performed the same test using DFM and found that none of the excluded variables had direct effects on contraceptive use. Thus, the evidence seems to suggest that the models are identified.

Table 2.24 Endogeneity tests for true ATE = 0.2, error correlation = 0.3, $Y_1 = 0.25$ and $Y_2 = 0.25$: proportion of times that the p-value for the test statistic is greater than 0.1

		Normal errors			Non-normal errors		
		$\chi^2 = 15$	$\chi^2 = 25$	$\chi^2 = 50$	$\chi^2 = 15$	$\chi^2 = 25$	$\chi^2 = 50$
N = 1,000							
	TSLS_Durban	0.8630	0.8010	0.7140	0.8180	0.7930	0.6280
	TSLS_Wu	0.8630	0.8020	0.7160	0.8180	0.7950	0.6280
	LIML_Hausman	1.0000	1.0000	0.9900	1.0000	1.0000	0.9810
	GMM_Hayashi	0.8610	0.8000	0.7060	0.8180	0.7880	0.6240
	Residual1	0.8710	0.8180	0.7300	0.8230	0.8000	0.6440
	Residual2	0.8330	0.7770	0.6860	0.8970	0.8740	0.7180
	BIPROBIT	0.8499	0.7658	0.6690	0.7886	0.8006	0.6640
N = 5,000							
	TSLS_Durban	0.8750	0.8420	0.7490	0.7860	0.7290	0.5740
	TSLS_Wu	0.8750	0.8430	0.7510	0.7860	0.7290	0.5740
	LIML_Hausman	1.0000	1.0000	0.9940	1.0000	0.9970	0.9750
	GMM_Hayashi	0.8780	0.8390	0.7490	0.7830	0.7280	0.5720
	Residual1	0.8770	0.8410	0.7690	0.7910	0.7280	0.5820
	Residual2	0.6410	0.6140	0.5590	0.9010	0.8840	0.7870
	BIPROBIT	0.7570	0.7090	0.6020	0.8400	0.8220	0.7230
N = 10,000							
	TSLS_Durban	0.8500	0.7680	0.6740	0.7780	0.7280	0.5860
	TSLS_Wu	0.8500	0.7680	0.6740	0.7780	0.7300	0.5860
	LIML_Hausman	1.0000	0.9980	0.9780	1.0000	0.9920	0.9620
	GMM_Hayashi	0.8460	0.7600	0.6660	0.7720	0.7220	0.5840
	Residual1	0.8460	0.7780	0.6780	0.7740	0.7260	0.6020
	Residual2	0.4940	0.4660	0.3600	0.8720	0.8940	0.8980
	BIPROBIT	0.6300	0.5680	0.4300	0.8040	0.8540	0.8480

We also performed tests of the null hypothesis that having heard a family planning message is exogenous. The results across the two data sets were consistent for 2SLS, GMM, Residual1, Residual2, and BIPROBIT: the null hypothesis was strongly rejected for Tanzania and the tests failed to reject the null hypothesis in Bangladesh. We did not perform a formal endogeneity test for DFM. However, for both data sets, the DFM yielded highly significant heterogeneity parameters using a four point of support model (the same number of points of support employed in the Monte Carlo experiments) and, as can be seen in the tables below, in both samples the point estimate of the ATE is quite different for the DFM and models that do not correct for endogeneity.

Table 2.28 presents the estimated ATE's across all nine methods along with standard errors. The ATE's and standard errors are drawn directly from the regression results for the linear models while the STATA margins command was used to obtain the ATE and standard errors for all non-linear models except DFM. The standard errors for the DFM model were obtained by using a parametric bootstrap procedure with 10,000 replications using a FORTRAN program.

Table 2.25 Endogeneity tests for true ATE = 0.2, error correlation = 0.3, $Y_1 = 0.5$ and $Y_2 = 0.5$: proportion of times that the p-value for the test statistic is greater than 0.1

		Normal errors			Non-normal errors		
		$\chi^2 = 15$	$\chi^2 = 25$	$\chi^2 = 50$	$\chi^2 = 15$	$\chi^2 = 25$	$\chi^2 = 50$
N = 1,000							
	TSLS_Durban	0.8500	0.7980	0.7040	0.8620	0.8110	0.7330
	TSLS_Wu	0.8510	0.8040	0.7060	0.8630	0.8130	0.7340
	LIML_Hausman	1.0000	0.9980	0.9920	1.0000	0.9980	0.9900
	GMM_Hayashi	0.8430	0.8020	0.7080	0.8600	0.8080	0.7300
	Residual1	0.8440	0.7980	0.7080	0.8510	0.8090	0.7380
	Residual2	0.8410	0.7820	0.6870	0.5760	0.5860	0.5680
	BIPROBIT	0.8510	0.7800	0.6680	0.7287	0.6740	0.6210
N = 5,000							
	TSLS_Durban	0.8010	0.7340	0.6510	0.8240	0.7850	0.6910
	TSLS_Wu	0.8010	0.7350	0.6510	0.8240	0.7850	0.6920
	LIML_Hausman	1.0000	0.9960	0.9840	1.0000	1.0000	0.9820
	GMM_Hayashi	0.8000	0.7280	0.6540	0.8250	0.7840	0.6870
	Residual1	0.8020	0.7350	0.6510	0.8220	0.7790	0.6930
	Residual2	0.6870	0.6450	0.5670	0.0110	0.0230	0.0350
	BIPROBIT	0.7400	0.6760	0.5760	0.0864	0.0590	0.0720
N = 10,000							
	TSL_Durban	0.6960	0.7080	0.5680	0.8040	0.7220	0.6060
	TSLS_Wu	0.6960	0.7080	0.5680	0.8040	0.7240	0.6060
	LIML_Hausman	1.0000	0.9960	0.9680	1.0000	0.9940	0.9720
	GMM_Hayashi	0.7000	0.7080	0.5640	0.8060	0.7240	0.6140
	Residual1	0.6980	0.7280	0.5740	0.8340	0.7440	0.6380
	Residual2	0.6060	0.5280	0.4280	0.0000	0.0000	0.0020
	BIPROBIT	0.6640	0.5960	0.4540	0.0020	0.0040	0.0040

There is a fairly wide range in estimated ATEs across methods. For Bangladesh, the DFM has the largest estimated ATE but also the largest standard error. We also see that LPM and all the methods that assume normality give similar estimated ATE's while the three instrumental variables methods give results between these methods and DFM. For Tanzania, DFM and the three instrumental variables methods give very consistent results with estimated ATE's approximately double what is found for the two methods that do not correct for endogeneity (LPM and Probit). The residual inclusion methods yield similar point estimates for the ATE as BIPROBIT which falls above the methods that do not correct for endogeneity and below the DFM and the instrumental variables methods.

Given the results of the Monte Carlo experiments, one would probably place the most confidence in the results obtained for the DFM followed by the instrumental variables methods. None of these methods rely on the assumption of normality for the error distributions in models and the results of these methods are highly consistent for Tanzania and least somewhat consistent for Bangladesh.

Table 2.26 Descriptive statistics for Bangladesh ($N = 21{,}472$)

Variable	Mean	Standard dev.
Endogenous variables		
Current user of contraception	0.458	0.498
Recall smiling sun message	0.223	0.417
Exogenous variables		
Woman age 20–24	0.179	0.383
Woman age 25–29	0.178	0.383
Woman age 30–34	0.169	0.375
Woman age 35–39	0.140	0.347
Woman age 40–44	0.111	0.314
Woman age 45–49	0.072	0.259
Woman has primary education	0.248	0.432
Woman has secondary education	0.180	0.385
Husband has primary education	0.190	0.392
Husband has secondary education	0.243	0.429
Husband has college education	0.020	0.141
Sum of the number of contraceptive methods available within 1 km	1.318	2.333
Indicator for 2003 survey	0.406	0.491
Number of facilities within 1 km with smiling sun posters	0.305	0.542
Household has a radio	0.305	0.461
Household has a television	0.142	0.349

2.6 Conclusion

We conclude with some thoughts regarding the pattern of results presented in Sect. 2.4. We first note that, when error correlation and instrument strength are low, the models that we consider that attempt explicitly to correct for the endogeneity of a binary regressor do not seem to perform as well as alternatives that simply ignore potential endogeneity. Even BIPROBIT, for which identification ultimately rests on the assumption of jointly normal errors in Eqs. (2.1) and (2.2) does not perform as well as LPM under circumstances of weak error correlation and weak instruments, even when the true error distribution is bivariate normal.

As either instrument strength or error correlation increases, our findings suggest that the researcher has attractive options relative to the simple methods. As expected, BIPROBIT performs well under these circumstances when the true error distribution is bivariate normal. However, Residual2 performs as well or is even slightly better than BIPROBIT. In addition, even when the true error distribution is bivariate normal, DFM represents a significant improvement over LPM and performs only slightly worse than Residual2 and BIPROBIT. When the true error distribution is non-normal, DFM dominates all other estimators. The only estimation methods that come close are the linear instrumental variables estimators, which are also robust to non-normal errors. However, these estimators only approach but do not equal the

Table 2.27 Descriptive statistics for Tanzania ($N = 17{,}724$)

Variable	Mean	Standard dev.
Endogenous variables		
Current user of contraception	0.115	0.319
Recall family planning message	0.387	0.487
Exogenous variables		
Woman age 15–19	0.221	0.415
Woman age 20–24	0.196	0.397
Woman age 25–29	0.174	0.379
Woman age 30–34	0.132	0.338
Woman age 35–39	0.113	0.317
Woman age 40–44	0.086	0.280
Woman 1–6 years of education	0.219	0.413
Woman 7 years of education	0.411	0.492
Woman 8 or more years of education	0.017	0.128
Partner 1–6 years of education	0.170	0.376
Partner 7 years of education	0.274	0.446
Partner 8 or more years of education	0.042	0.201
Number of contraceptive methods seen in stock in facilities within 5 km	1.229	1.702
Household owns a radio	0.347	0.476
Household owns a television	0.002	0.044

Table 2.28 Estimated average treatment effects and standard errors for the two empirical examples

	Bangladesh		Tanzania	
Method	ATE	SE	ATE	SE
LPM	0.0669	0.0082	0.0700	0.0050
Probit	0.0699	0.0082	0.0676	0.0050
TSLS	0.0843	0.0376	0.1327	0.0224
LIML	0.0843	0.0376	0.1329	0.0224
GMM	0.0841	0.0377	0.1320	0.0236
Residual1	0.0840	0.0375	0.1231	0.0243
Residual2	0.0508	0.0358	0.1181	0.0236
BIPROBIT	0.0508	0.0358	0.1178	0.0229
DFM	0.1188	0.0545	0.1361	0.0440
N	21,472		17,724	

performance of DFM when both error correlation and instrument strength are high. Nonetheless, they are a reasonable option for researchers using standard statistical packages (at least until an implementation of the DFM becomes available within one of these packages, a project on which the authors have now embarked with STATA).

The superior performance of the DFM and, to some extent, the linear instrumental variables estimators when the true error distribution is non-normal is even more impressive when one considers that the design of our experiments involving non-normal errors was likely comparatively favorable to models that assume normality compared with real world circumstances: our approach to non normal errors still retained the unimodality of the joint distribution of the errors and of the surface of its joint distribution in $\mathbf{R}^3$. In some sense this likely gave even those models explicitly motivated by joint normality some fighting chance for reasonable fit to the data. Real world circumstances will likely involve multi-modal distributions, reflecting the presence of combinations of pronounced "types" within the population. Nonetheless, our results suggest that methods that rely on the assumption of normally distributed errors are a poor choice relative to the more robust methods considered in this paper even in the unimodal case. In that sense they echo the concerns about the fragility of identification by functional form that have been in the literature in various contexts for nearly three decades (e.g. LaLonde 1986; Manning et al. 1987).

In terms of practical advice for applied researchers, our results thus do suggest some guidelines. First, less parametric methods, including linear instrumental variables models if not the DFM itself (the estimation of which is, for the moment, impractical for most) are preferable to methods that rely on more parametric assumptions for the joint error distribution: joint normality assumptions work out particularly well only when the errors are indeed jointly normal (and even then only when instrument strength and error correlation were high), and this is likely a heroic assumption in many applied microeconometric applications. Even when the bivariate probit performs well, it does not necessarily significantly outperform simpler methods (such as Residual2) that also implicitly rely on joint normality. Put slightly differently, it is not clear that the explicit functional form assumption of the bivariate probit model is buying the user much in terms of performance, even under ideal circumstances.

Second, and perhaps intuitively unsurprisingly in light of the evidence regarding weak instruments in the setting of continuous outcomes of interest and endogenous variables (e.g. Stock and Staiger 1997; Bound et al. 1995), instrument strength matters. Indeed, even in the case of models relying on joint normality assumptions for the errors when the errors are actually jointly non-normal, increases in instrument strength yield performance benefits. Moreover, it is straightforward to assess instrument strength.

Overidentification tests proved reasonably reliable in the binary outcome and binary endogenous variable setting even with linear instrumental variables based tests. We can offer far less guidance regarding the other key indicator of likely model performance, tests of endogeneity. Unfortunately, we cannot even say with any confidence that formal endogeneity tests are, in this setting and with the currently available set of conventional tests, necessarily any more reliable than informed theoretical assumptions by applied researchers.

As for future work in the methodological arena, it is clear that nonparametric full-information maximum likelihood approaches hold great potential promise. Much remains to be done in this area, including the introduction of routines for estimating these models as part of standard statistical packages such as STATA, continued improvement of estimation methodology and the development and refinement of tests (such as a formal endogeneity test). Finally, model performance in circumstances of heterogeneous treatment effects is now under consideration by the authors in a follow-up to this manuscript.

References

Anderson T, Rubin H (1950) The asymptotic properties of estimates of the parameters of a single equation in a complete system of stochastic equations. Ann Math Stat 21:570–582

Angrist J, Krueger A (2001) Instrumental variables and the search for identification: from supply and demand to natural experiments. J Econ Perspect 15:69–85

Angrist J, Pischke J (2009) Mostly harmless econometrics: an empiricist's companion. Princeton University Press, Princeton

Babalola S (2005) Communication, ideation and contraceptive use in Burkina Faso: an application of the propensity score matching method. J Fam Plan Reprod Health Care 31:207–212

Bassman R (1960) On finite sample distributions of generalized classical linear identifiability test statistics. J Am Stat Assoc 55:650–659

Bauman K, Viadro C, Tsui A (1993) Family planning program effects in developing countries: conclusions and related considerations. The evaluation project working paper IM-03-03

Bollen K, Guilkey D, Mroz T (1995) Binary outcomes and endogenous explanatory variables: tests and solutions with an application to the demand for contraceptive use in Tunisia. Demography 32:111–131

Bound J, Jaeger D, Baker R (1995) Problems with instrumental variables estimation when the correlation between the instruments and the endogenous explanatory variable is weak. J Am Stat Assoc 90:443–450

Cappellari L, Jenkins S (2003) Multivariate probit regression using simulated maximum likelihood. STATA J 3:278–294

Chen S, Guilkey D (2003) Determinants of contraceptive method choice in rural Tanzania between 1991 and 1999. Stud Fam Plan 34:263–276

Chiburis RC, Das J, Lokshin M (2011) A practical comparison of the bivariate probit and linear IV estimators. The World Bank Policy research working paper 5601

Durbin J (1954) Errors in variables. Rev Int Stat Inst 22:23–32

Fleishman A (1978) A method for simulating nonnormal distributions. Psychometrika 43:521–532

Gourieroux C, Monfort A, Renault E, Trognon A (1987) Generalized residuals. J Econom 34:5–32

Guilkey D, Hutchinson P (2011) Overcoming methodological challenges in evaluating health communication campaigns: evidence from rural Bangladesh. Stud Fam Plan 42:93–106

Guilkey D, Mroz T, Taylor L (1992) Estimation and testing in simultaneous equations models with discrete outcomes using cross section data. UNC-CH Department of Economics working paper

Guilkey D, Hutchinson P, Lance P (2006) Cost effectiveness analysis for health communications programs. J Health Commun 11:47–67

Hansen L (1982) Large sample properties of generalized method of moments estimators. Econometrica 50:1029–1054

Hausman J (1978) Specification tests in econometrics. Econometrica 46:1251–1271

Hayashi F (2000) Econometrics. Princeton University Press, Princeton

Heckman J, Singer B (1984) A method for minimizing the impact of distributional assumptions in econometric models for duration data. Econometrica 52:271–320

Hutchinson P, Wheeler J (2006). The cost effectiveness of health communication programs: what do we know? J Health Commun 11:7–45

Imbens G, Angrist J (1994) Indentification and estimation of local average treatment effects. Econometrica 62:467–475

Kaiser H, Dickman K (1962) Sample and population score matrices and sample correlation matrices from an arbitrary population correlation matrix. Psychometrika 27:179–182

LaLonde R (1986) Evaluating the econometric evaluations of training programs with experimental data. Am Econ Rev 76:604–620

Manning W, Duan N, Rogers W (1987) Monte Carlo evidence on the choice between sample selection and two-part models. J Econom 35:59–82

Mwaikambo L, Speizer I, Schurmann A, Morgan G, Fikree F (2011) What works in family planning interventions: a systematic review. Stud Fam Plan 42:67–82

Mroz T (1999) Discrete factor approximations in simultaneous equations models: estimating the impact of a dummy endogenous variable on a continuous outcome. J Econom 92:233–274

Ngallaba S, Kapiga S, Ruyoba I, Boerma J (1993) Tanzania demographic and health survey 1991/1992. Macro International Inc., Columbia

Rivers D, Vuong Q (1988) Limited information estimators and exogeneity tests for simultaneous probit models. J Econom 39:347–366

Sargon J (1958) The estimation of economic relationships using instrumental variables. Econometrica 26:393–415

Stock J, Staiger D (1997) Instrumental variables regression with weak instruments. Econometrica 65:557–586

Terza J, Basu A, Rathouz P (2008) Two-stage residual inclusion estimation: addressing endogeneity in health econometric modelling. J Health Econ 27:531–543

Vale C, Maurelli V (1983) Simulating multivariate nonnormal distributions. Psychometrika 48:465–471

Wu D (1974) Alternative tests of independence between stochastic regressors and disturbances: finite sample results. Econometrica 42:529–546

Chapter 3
Stochastic Frontier Models with Bounded Inefficiency

Pavlos Almanidis, Junhui Qian, and Robin C. Sickles

JEL Classification: C13, C21, C23, D24, G21

3.1 Introduction

The parametric approach to estimate stochastic production frontiers was introduced by Aigner et al. (1977), Meeusen and van den Broeck (1977), and Battese and Corra (1977). These approaches specified a parametric production function and a two-component error term. One component, reflecting the influence of many unaccountable factors on production as well as measurement error, is considered "noise" and is usually assumed to be normally distributed. The other component describes inefficiency and is assumed to have a one-sided distribution, of which the conventional candidates include the half normal (Aigner et al. 1977), truncated normal (Stevenson 1980), exponential (Meeusen and van den Broeck 1977) and gamma (Greene 1980a,b, 1990; Stevenson 1980). This stochastic frontier production function has become an iconic modeling paradigm in econometric research, rate making

P. Almanidis (✉)
International Tax Services, Ernst & Young LLP, 222 Bay Street, P.O. Box 251, Toronto, ON, M5K 1J7, Canada
e-mail: pavlos.almanidis@ca.ey.com

J. Qian
School of Economics, Shanghai Jiao Tong University, 535 Fa Hua Zhen Road, Shanghai 200052, China
e-mail: jhqian@sjtu.edu.cn

R.C. Sickles
Department of Economics, Rice University, 6100 South Main Street, Houston, TX 77005-1892, USA
e-mail: rsickles@rice.edu

R.C. Sickles and W.C. Horrace (eds.), *Festschrift in Honor of Peter Schmidt: Econometric Methods and Applications*, DOI 10.1007/978-1-4899-8008-3_3,

decisions in regulated industries across the world, in evaluating outcomes of market reforms in transition economies, and in establishing performance benchmarks for local, state, and federal governmental activities.

In this paper we propose a new class of parametric stochastic frontier models with a more flexible specification of the inefficiency term, which we view as improvement on the basic iconic stochastic frontier production model. Instead of allowing unbounded support for the distribution of productive (cost) inefficiency term in the right (left) tail, we introduce an unobservable upper bound to inefficiencies or a lower bound to the efficiencies, which we call the *inefficiency bound*. The introduction of the inefficiency bound makes the parametric stochastic frontier model more appealing for empirical studies in at least two aspects. First, it is plausible to allow only bounded support in many applications of stochastic frontier models wherein the extremely inefficient firms in a competitive industry of market are eliminated by competition. Bounded inefficiency makes sense in this setting since the extremely inefficient stores will be forced to close and thus individual production units constitute a truncated sample.[1] This is consistent with the arguments of Alchian (1950) and Stigler (1958) wherein firms are at any point in time not in a static long run equilibrium, but rather are tending to that situation as they are buffeted by demand and cost shocks. As a consequence, even if we correctly specify a family of distributions for the inefficiency term, the stochastic frontier model may still be misspecified. This particular setting is one in which the inefficiency bound is informative as an indicator of competitive pressures and/or the extent of supervisory oversight by direct management or by corporate boards. In settings in which firms can successfully differentiate their product, which is the typical market structure and not the exception, or where there are market concentrations that may reflect collusive behavior or conditions for a natural monopoly and regulatory oversight, incentives to fully exploit market power or to instead make satisficing decision are both possible outcomes. Much more likely is that it is not one or the other but some middle ground between the two extremes that would be found empirically.[2]

[1] In addition, the frequent use of balanced panels in empirical studies would in effect eliminate those failing firms from the sample and thus would provide more merit to the bounded inefficiency model.

[2] "The quiet life hypothesis" (QLH) by Hicks (1935) argues that, due to management's subjective cost of reaching the optimal profits, firms use their market power to allow inefficient allocation of resources. Increasing competitive pressure is likely to force management to work harder to reach optimal profits. Another hypothesis that relates market power and efficiency is "the efficient structure hypothesis" (ESH) by Demsetz (1973). ESH argues that firms with superior efficiencies or technologies have lower costs and therefore higher profits. These firms are assumed to gain larger market shares which lead to higher concentration. Recently Kutlu and Sickles (2012) have constructed a model in which the dynamic game is played out and have tested for the alternative outcomes, finding support for the QLH in certain airlines city-pair markets and the ESH in others. Orea and Steinbuks (2012) have also explored the use of such a lower bound in their analysis of market power in the California wholesale electricity market.

A second justification for our introduction of the inefficiency bound into the classical stochastic production frontier model is that our model points to an explanation for the finding of positive skewness in many applied studies using the traditional stochastic frontier, and thus to the potential of our bounded inefficiency model to explain these positive ("wrong") skewness findings.[3] Researchers have often found positive instead of negative skewness in many samples examined in applied work, which may point to the stochastic frontier being incorrectly specified. However, we conjecture that the distribution of the inefficiency term may itself be negatively skewed, which may happen if there is an additional truncation on the right tail of the distribution. One such specification in which this is a natural consequence is when the distribution of the inefficiency term is doubly truncated normal, that is, a normal distribution truncated at a point on the right tail as well as at zero. As normal distributions are symmetric, the doubly truncated normal distribution may exhibit negative skewness if the truncation on the right is closer to the mode than that on the left. We also consider the truncated half normal distribution, which is a special case of the former, and the truncated exponential distribution. Although these two distributions are always positively skewed, the fact that there is a truncation on the right tail makes the skewness very hard to identify empirically. That is to say, when the true distribution of the one-sided inefficiency error is bounded (truncated), the extent to which skewness is present in any finite sample may be substantially reduced, often to the extent that negative sample skewness for the composite error is not statistically significant. Thus the finding of positive skewness may speak to the weak identifiability of skewness properties in a bounded frontier model.

In addition to proposing new parametric forms for the classical stochastic production frontier model, we also show that our models are identifiable, and in which cases the identification is local or global. Initial consistent estimates are based on method of moments estimates, based on explicit analytic expressions which we derive, and which either can be used in a two-step method of scoring or as starting values in solving the normal equations for the relevant sample likelihood, based on the parametric density functions whose expressions we also provide. As the regulatory conditions for maximum likelihood estimation method are satisfied, we employ it in order to obtain consistent and asymptotically efficient estimates of the model parameters, including this of the inefficiency bound. We conduct Monte Carlo experiments to study the finite sample behavior of our estimators. We also extend the model to the panel data setting and allow for a time-varying inefficiency bound. By allowing the inefficiency bound to be time-varying, we contribute another time-varying technical efficiency model to the efficiency literature. Our model differs from those most commonly used in the literature, e.g., Cornwell et al. (1990), Kumbhakar (1990), Battese and Coelli (1992), and Lee and Schmidt (1993) in

[3]The term wrong is set in quotes to point out that the conventional wisdom that positive skewness is inconsistent with the standard stochastic frontier production model errors skewness is not necessarily the correct wisdom.

that, while previous time-varying efficiency models are time-varying in the mean or intercept of individual effects, our model is time-varying in the lower support of the distribution of individual effects.

The outline of this paper is as follows. In Sect. 3.2 we present the new models and derive analytic formula for density functions and expressions that allow us to evaluate inefficiencies. Section 3.3 deals with the positive skewness issue inherent in the traditional stochastic frontier model. Section 3.4 discusses the identification of the new models and the methods of estimation. Section 3.5 presents Monte Carlo results on the finite sample performance of the bounded inefficiency model vis-a-vis classical stochastic frontier estimators. The extension of the new models to panel data settings and specification of the time-varying bound is presented in Sect. 3.6. In Sect. 3.7 we give an illustrative study of the efficiency of US banking industry in 1984–2009. Section 3.8 concludes.

3.2 The Model

We consider the following Cobb-Douglas production model,

$$y_i = \alpha_0 + \sum_{k=1}^{K} \alpha_k x_{i,k} + \varepsilon_i \tag{3.1}$$

where

$$\varepsilon_i = v_i - u_i. \tag{3.2}$$

For every production unit i, y_i is the log output, x_{ik} the k-th log input, v_i the noise component, and u_i the (nonnegative) inefficiency component. We maintain the usual assumption that v_i is iid $N(0, \sigma_v^2)$, u_i is iid, and v_i and u_i are independent from each other and from regressors. Clearly we can consider other more flexible functional forms for production (or cost) that are linear or linear in logarithms, such as the generalized Leontief or the transcendental logarithmic, or ones that are nonlinear. The only necessary assumption is that the error process ε_i is additively separable from the functional forms we employ in the stochastic production (cost) frontier.

As described in the introduction, our model differs from the traditional stochastic frontier model in that u_i is of bounded support. Additional to the lower bound, which is zero and which is the frontier, we specify an upper bound to the distribution of u_i (in the case of the cost frontier $\varepsilon_i = v_i + u_i$). In particular, we assume that u_i is distributed as doubly truncated normal, the density of which is given by

$$f(u) = \frac{\frac{1}{\sigma_u}\phi(\frac{u-\mu}{\sigma_u})}{\Phi(\frac{B-\mu}{\sigma_u}) - \Phi(\frac{-\mu}{\sigma_u})} \mathbf{1}_{[0,B]}(u),\ \sigma_u > 0, B > 0 \tag{3.3}$$

where $\Phi(\cdot)$ and $\phi(\cdot)$ are the cdf and pdf of the standard normal distribution, respectively, and $1_{[0,B]}$ is an indicator function. It is a distribution obtained by truncating $N(\mu, \sigma_u^2)$ at zero and $B > 0$. The parameter B is the upper bound of the distribution of u_i and we may call it the inefficiency bound. The inefficiency bound may be a useful index of competitiveness of a market or an industry.[4] In the banking industry, which we examine in Sect. 3.7, the inefficiency bound may also represent factors that influence the financial health of the industry. It may be natural to extend this specification and treat the bound as a function of individual specific covariates z_i, such as $\exp(\delta' z_i)$, which would allow identification of bank-specific measures of financial health.

Using the usual nomenclature of stochastic frontier models, we may call the model described above the normal-doubly truncated normal model, or simply, the doubly truncated normal model. The doubly truncated normal model is rather flexible. It nests the truncated normal ($B \to \infty$), half normal ($\mu = 0$ and $B \to \infty$), and truncated half normal models ($\mu = 0$). One desirable feature of our model is that the doubly truncated normal distribution may be positively or negatively skewed, depending on the truncation parameter B. This feature provides us with an alternative explanation for the positive skewness problem prevalent in empirical stochastic frontier studies. This will be made more clear later in the paper. Another desirable feature of our model is that, like the truncated normal model, it can describe the scenario that only a few firms in the sector are efficient, a phenomenon that is described in the business press as "few stars, most dogs", while in the truncated half normal model and the truncated exponential model (in which the distribution of u_i is truncated exponential), most firms are implicitly assumed to be relatively efficient.[5]

In Table 3.1 we provide detailed properties of our model. In particular, we present the density functions for the error term ε_i, which is necessary for maximum likelihood estimation, and the analytic form for $E[u_i|\varepsilon_i]$, which is the best predictor of the inefficiency term u_i under our assumptions, and the conditional distribution of u_i given ε_i, which is useful for making inferences on u_i. The results for the truncated half normal model, a special case of the doubly truncated normal model ($\mu = 0$), are also presented. Finally, we also provide results for the truncated exponential model, in which the inefficiency term u_i is distributed according to the following density function,

$$f(u) = \frac{1}{\sigma_u(1 - e^{-B/\sigma_u})} e^{-\frac{u}{\sigma_u}} \mathbf{1}_{[0,B]}(u), \sigma_u > 0, B > 0 \tag{3.4}$$

The truncated exponential distribution can be further generalized to the truncated gamma distribution, which shares the nice property with the doubly truncated normal distribution that it may be positively or negatively skewed.

---

[4]The inefficiency bound has a natural role in gauging the tolerance for or ruthlessness against inefficient firms. It is also worth mentioning that, using this bound as the "inefficient frontier," we may define "inverted" efficiency scores in the same spirit of "Inverted DEA" described in Entani et al. (2002).

[5]We thank C. A. K. Lovell for providing us this link between our econometric methodology and the business press.

Table 3.1 Key results. $f(\varepsilon)$ is the density of $\varepsilon = v - u$, $\mathbb{E}(u|\varepsilon)$ is the conditional mean of u given ε, and $f(u|\varepsilon)$ is the conditional density of u given ε. $\phi(\cdot)$ and $\Phi(\cdot)$ are the pdf and cdf of the standard normal distribution, respectively. And $\mathbf{1}_{[0,B]}(\cdot)$ is an indicator function

Model	$f(\varepsilon)$	$\mathbb{E}(u\|\varepsilon)$	$f(u\|\varepsilon)$
Doubly truncated normal	$\left[\Phi(\frac{B-\mu}{\sigma_u}) - \Phi(\frac{-\mu}{\sigma_u})\right]^{-1} \cdot \left[\frac{1}{\sigma}\phi(\frac{\varepsilon+\mu}{\sigma})\right] \cdot \left[\Phi(\frac{(B+\varepsilon)\lambda+(B-\mu)\lambda^{-1}}{\sigma}) - \Phi(\frac{\varepsilon\lambda-\mu\lambda^{-1}}{\sigma})\right]$	$\mu_* + \sigma_* \frac{\phi(-\frac{\mu_*}{\sigma_*})-\phi(\frac{B-\mu_*}{\sigma_*})}{\Phi(\frac{B-\mu_*}{\sigma_*})-\Phi(-\frac{\mu_*}{\sigma_*})}$	$\frac{\frac{1}{\sigma_*}\phi(\frac{u-\mu_*}{\sigma_*})}{\Phi(\frac{B-\mu_*}{\sigma_*})-\Phi(-\frac{\mu_*}{\sigma_*})}\mathbf{1}_{[0,B]}(u)$
Truncated half normal	$\sigma = \sqrt{\sigma_u^2 + \sigma_v^2}$, $\lambda = \sigma_u/\sigma_v$	$\mu_* = \frac{\mu\sigma_v^2 - \varepsilon\sigma_u^2}{\sigma^2}$, $\sigma_* = \frac{\sigma_u\sigma_v}{\sigma}$	
	$[\Phi(\frac{B}{\sigma_u}) - 1/2]^{-1} \cdot \frac{1}{\sigma}\phi(\frac{\varepsilon}{\sigma}) \cdot [\Phi(\frac{(B+\varepsilon)\lambda+B\lambda^{-1}}{\sigma}) - \Phi(\frac{\varepsilon\lambda}{\sigma})]$	$\mu_* + \sigma_* \frac{\phi(-\frac{\mu_*}{\sigma_*})-\phi(\frac{B-\mu_*}{\sigma_*})}{\Phi(\frac{B-\mu_*}{\sigma_*})-\Phi(-\frac{\mu_*}{\sigma_*})}$	$\frac{\frac{1}{\sigma_*}\phi(\frac{u-\mu_*}{\sigma_*})}{\Phi(\frac{B-\mu_*}{\sigma_*})-\Phi(-\frac{\mu_*}{\sigma_*})}\mathbf{1}_{[0,B]}(u)$
		$\mu_* = -\frac{\varepsilon\sigma_u^2}{\sigma^2}$, $\sigma_* = \frac{\sigma_u\sigma_v}{\sigma}$	
Truncated exponential	$\frac{e^{\frac{\varepsilon}{\sigma_u}+\frac{\sigma_v^2}{2\sigma_u^2}}[\Phi(\frac{B+\varepsilon}{\sigma_v}+\frac{\sigma_v}{\sigma_u})-\Phi(\frac{\varepsilon}{\sigma_v}+\frac{\sigma_v}{\sigma_u})]}{\sigma_u(1-e^{-B/\sigma_u})}$	$\mu_* + \sigma_v \frac{\phi(-\frac{\mu_*}{\sigma_v})-\phi(\frac{B-\mu_*}{\sigma_v})}{\Phi(\frac{B-\mu_*}{\sigma_v})-\Phi(-\frac{\mu_*}{\sigma_v})}$	$\frac{\frac{1}{\sigma_v}\phi(\frac{u-\mu_*}{\sigma_v})}{\Phi(\frac{B-\mu_*}{\sigma_v})-\Phi(-\frac{\mu_*}{\sigma_v})}\mathbf{1}_{[0,B]}(u)$
		$\mu_* = -\varepsilon - \frac{\sigma_v^2}{\sigma_u}$	

For the doubly truncated normal model and the truncated half normal model, the analytic forms of our results use the so-called γ-parametrization, which specifies

$$\sigma = \sqrt{\sigma_u^2 + \sigma_v^2}, \quad \gamma = \sigma_u^2/\sigma^2. \tag{3.5}$$

By definition $\gamma \in [0, 1]$, a compact support, which is desirable for the numerical procedure of maximum likelihood estimation. Another parametrization initially employed by Aigner et al. (1977) is the λ-parametrization

$$\sigma = \sqrt{\sigma_u^2 + \sigma_v^2}, \quad \lambda = \sigma_u/\sigma_v. \tag{3.6}$$

We may check that when $B \to \infty$, the density function for ε_i in the doubly truncated normal model reduces to that of the truncated normal model introduced by Stevenson (1980). Furthermore, if $\mu = 0$, it reduces to the likelihood function for the half normal model introduced by Aigner et al. (1977). Similarly, the truncated exponential model reduces to the exponential model introduced by Meeusen and van den Broeck (1977).

3.3 The Skewness Issue

A common and important methodological problem encountered when dealing with empirical implementation of the stochastic frontier model is that the residuals may be skewed in the wrong direction. In particular, the ordinary least squares (OLS) residuals may show positive skewness even though the composed error term $v - u$ should display negative skewness, in keeping with $u's$ positive skewness. This problem has important consequences for the interpretation of the skewness of the error term as a measure of technological inefficiency. It may imply that a nonrepresentative random sample had been drawn from an inefficiency distribution possessing the correct population skewness (see Carree 2002; Greene 2007; Simar and Wilson 2010; Almanidis and Sickles 2011[6]; Feng et al. 2012). This is considered a finite sample "artifact" and the usual suggestion in the literature and by programs

[6]This paper goes far beyond the topics covered in Almanidis and Sickles (2011). In this paper we are concerned with the set identification of the bounded inefficiency model as well as in its use to better understand the behavior of this lower bound as the banking industry moved towards and through the financial meltdown. Such a pattern of a lower bound for inefficiency during the period prior to the meltdown speaks to the industry becoming lax in its allowance of banks that are not efficient in their provision of intermediation services as they appeared to focus instead on other off-balance sheet activities for which of course we do not have much credible information, as they are off-balance sheet operations. Our paper also shows the advantages of specifying a lower bound and estimating it, along with the other parameters of the model. Our paper is based on substantial efforts in data construction and uses data that has not appeared yet in the literature. Our paper also carries out a much more detailed set of MC experiments.

implementing stochastic frontier models is to treat all firms in the sample as fully efficient and proceed with straightforward OLS based on the results of Olson et al. (1980) and Waldman (1982). As this would suggest setting the variance of the inefficiency term to zero, it would have problematic impacts on estimation and on inference. Simar and Wilson (2010) suggest a bagging method to overcome the inferential problems when a half-normal distribution for inefficiencies is specified. However, a finding of positive skewness in a sample may also indicate that inefficiencies are in fact drawn from a distribution which has positive skewness.[7] Carree (2002) considers one-sided distributions of inefficiencies (u_i) that can have negative or positive skewness. However, Carree (2002) uses the binomial distribution, which is a discrete distribution wherein continuous inefficiencies fall into discrete "inefficiency categories" and which implicitly assumes that only a very small fraction of the firms attain a level of productivity close to the frontier, especially when u_i is negatively skewed.[8]

Our model addresses the positive skewness problem in the spirit of Carree (2002), but with a more appealing distributional specification on the efficiency term. For the doubly truncated normal model, let $\xi_1 = \frac{-\mu}{\sigma_u}$, $\xi_2 = \frac{B-\mu}{\sigma_u}$, and $\eta_k \equiv \frac{\xi_1^k \phi(\xi_1) - \xi_2^k \phi(\xi_2)}{\Phi(\xi_2) - \Phi(\xi_1)}$, $k = 0, 1, \ldots, 4$. Note that η_0 is the inverse Mill's ratio and it is equal to $\sqrt{2/\pi}$ in the half normal model, and that ξ_1 and ξ_2 are the lower and upper truncation points of the standard normal density, respectively. The skewness of the doubly truncated normal distribution is given by

$$S_u = \frac{2\eta_0^3 - \eta_0(3\eta_1 + 1) + \eta_2}{\left(1 - \eta_0^2 + \eta_1\right)^{3/2}}. \tag{3.7}$$

It can be checked that when $B > 2\mu$, S_u is positive and when $B < 2\mu$, S_u is negative. Since $B > 0$ by definition, it is obvious that only when $\mu > 0$ is it possible for u_i to be negatively skewed. The larger μ is, the larger range of values B may take such that u_i is negatively skewed. Consider the limiting case where a normal distribution with $\mu \to \infty$ is truncated at zero and $B > 0$. An infinitely

[7] Simar and Wilson (2010) consider inferences on efficiency conditional on composite error. They propose a bagging method and a bootstrap procedure for interval prediction and show that they are superior over the conventional methods that are based on the estimated conditional distribution. The relation of theirs to our paper is that they show that their methods work even when "wrong skewness" appears, while traditional MLE-based procedures do not. When the latter discovers a "wrong skewness", either (i) obtain a new sample, or (ii) re-specify the model (but not like what we do). What is common between our paper and SW is that both address the skewness problem. But "wrong skewness" in SW is due to finite sample bad luck, while we argue that it may be due to model specification. Larger samples would correct finite sample bad luck, but not if the underlying DGP is doubly truncated as we propose. The skewness problem is not the main issue in SW but their paper does have implications for it. The SW paper focuses on computational matters, while our paper concerns econometric specification and estimation.

[8] A negatively skewed doubly truncated normal inefficiency distribution does not necessarily imply that there are only few units in the population that operate close to the frontier.

large μ means that there is effectively no truncation on the left at all and that any finite truncation on the right gives rise to a negative skewness. Finally, for both the truncated half normal model ($\mu = 0$) and the truncated exponential model, the skewness of u_i is always positive.

Consequently, the doubly truncated normal model has a residual that has an ambiguous sign of the skewness, which depends on an unobservable relationship between the truncation parameter B and μ. We argue that this ambiguity theoretically could explain the prevalence of the positive skewness problem in applied stochastic frontier research. When the underlying data generating process for u_i is based on the doubly truncated normal distribution, increasing sample size does not solve the positive skewness problem. The skewness of the OLS residual ε may be positively skewed even when sample size goes to infinity. Hence the positive skewness problem also may be a large sample problem.[9]

Based on the above discussion, it is clear that the doubly truncated normal model generalizes the stochastic frontier model in a way that allows for positive as well as negative skewness for the residual. In addition, although the truncated half normal and the truncated exponential models have negative (correct) skewness in large samples, the existence of the inefficiency bound reduces the identifiability of negative skewness in finite sample, often to the extent that positive skewness appears. This implies that finding a positive skewness does not necessarily mean that the stochastic frontier model is inapplicable. It may be due to a finite sample "artifact" (Simar and Wilson 2010) or it may be that we are studying a market or an industry in which firms do not fall below some minimal level of efficiency in order to remain in the market or industry. In the latter case, the traditional unbounded support for the inefficiency term would be misspecified and should be substituted with the model of bounded inefficiency.

3.4 Identification and Estimation

3.4.1 Identification

We utilize the set or partial identification concepts that have been revisited (see, for example, Tamer 2010) and that were enunciated early in the production setting by Marschak and Andrews (1944) (see also the critique by Nerlove (1965)). That this has been the relatively recent interest of many econometricians speaks to a cycle of classical econometric study that has defined the production frontier portion of

[9] See Almanidis and Sickles (2011) for more discussion and simulation study on positive skewness issue in parametric stochastic frontier models.

Peter Schmidt's research that our paper develops. We can put it into a historical perspective by looking at the intellectual development of the production function by Paul Samuelson (see his 1979 review of his professor Paul Douglas), his student Lawrence Klein whose classic Textbook of Econometrics (1953) sold at the unheard price of $6.00 and which provides insights today for those interested in production econometrics, his student Arthur Goldberger (see, for example, "The Interpretation and Estimation of Cobb-Douglas Functions", 1968), his student Jan Kmenta (see, for example, Zellner et al. 1966), and his student Peter Schmidt, whose work on the stochastic frontier production function with Dennis Aigner and C. A. Knox Lovell (1977) is regarded as the seminal research contribution to the field of productive efficiency econometrics. In turn, each of these legacies arguably can be viewed as the most successful student of their respective professor. Our contribution is leveraged by these seminal contributions as well as the selective constraints that economic theory has imposed on their contributions, which we try to address in our stochastic frontier model with bounded inefficiency.

Identification using first and second order moments is a well-accepted methodology. Our models are not identified by such moments alone and require higher order moments. The use of higher order moments to identify and estimate econometric models is well-known and has proven quite important in parametric econometric modeling (see, for example, Cragg 1997; Dagenais and Dagenais 1997). Identification strategies that utilize the properties of the underlying joint distribution function for the exponential class, requiring the identification of distributions defined by third and forth order moments, have been the mainstay of recent work in nonparametric identification (Newey and Powell 2003; Matzkin 2012). Alternative approaches have also been introduced to utilize other types of information, such as heteroskedastic covariance restrictions to obtain point and set identification for parametric and semiparametric models (Lewbel 2012). We explore the sensitivity of the use of such higher order moments restrictions in our Monte Carlo experiments.

Identification of our model may be done in two parts. The first part is concerned with the parameters describing the technology, and the second part identifies the distributional parameters using the information contained in the distribution of the residual. For models without an intercept term the identification conditions for the first part are well known and are satisfied in most of the cases. The structural parameters can be consistently obtained by applying straightforward OLS. However, for models containing an intercept term there is a need to bias correction it using the distributional parameters since $E[\varepsilon] = -E[u] \neq 0$ (see Afriat 1972; Richmond 1974). Therefore, the identification of the second part, which is based on method-of-moments requires a closer examination. Table 3.2 lists the population (central) moments of (ε_i) for the doubly truncated normal model and the truncated exponential model. The moments of the truncated half normal model can be obtained by setting $\mu = 0$ in the doubly truncated normal model. These results are essential for the discussion of identification and the method of moments estimation.

Table 3.2 Central moments of ε

Moment	Doubly-truncated-normal
ψ_1	$-\mu - \sigma_u \eta_0$
ψ_2	$\sigma_u^2 \left(1 - \eta_0^2 + \eta_1\right) + \sigma_v^2$
ψ_3	$-\sigma_u^3 \left(2\eta_0^3 - 3\eta_1\eta_0 - \eta_0 + \eta_2\right)$
ψ_4	$\sigma_u^4 \left(3 + 3\eta_1 + \eta_3 - 2\eta_0^2 - 4\eta_0\eta_2 + 6\eta_0^2\eta_1 - 3\eta_0^4\right) + 6\sigma_u^2\sigma_v^2 \left(1 - \eta_0^2 + \eta_1\right) + 3\sigma_v^4$
ψ_5	$-10\sigma_v^2\sigma_u^3 \left(2\eta_0^3 - 3\eta_1\eta_0 - \eta_0 + \eta_2\right)$
	$-\sigma_u^5 \left(\eta_4 + 4\eta_2 - 5\eta_0\eta_3 + 10\eta_0^2\eta_2 - 10\eta_0^3\eta_1 + 10\eta_0^3 - 15\eta_0\eta_1 + 4\eta_0^5 - 7\eta_0\right)$
	See the text for the definitions of $\eta_k, k = 0, \ldots, 4$
	Truncated-exp.
ψ_1	$-\sigma_u \left(1 - \frac{\kappa}{e^\kappa - 1}\right)$
ψ_2	$\sigma_v^2 + \sigma_u^2 \frac{e^{2\kappa} - (\kappa^2+2)e^\kappa + 1}{e^{2\kappa} - 2e^\kappa + 1}$
ψ_3	$-\sigma_u^3 \frac{2e^{3\kappa} - (\kappa^3+6)e^{2\kappa} + (6-\kappa^3)e^\kappa - 2}{e^{3\kappa} - 3e^{2\kappa} + 3e^\kappa - 1}$
ψ_4	$\sigma_u^4 \frac{-9e^{4\kappa} + 36e^{3\kappa} - 54e^{2\kappa} + 36e^\kappa - 9 + 6\kappa^2 e^\kappa (e^{2\kappa} - 2e^\kappa + 1) + \kappa^4 e^\kappa (e^{2\kappa} + e^\kappa + 1)}{-e^{4\kappa} + 4e^{3\kappa} - 6e^{2\kappa} + 4e^\kappa - 1}$
	$+6\sigma_v^2\sigma_u^2 \frac{e^{2\kappa} - (\kappa^2+2)e^\kappa + 1}{e^{2\kappa} - 2e^\kappa + 1} + 3\sigma_v^4, \quad \kappa = B/\sigma_u$

To examine the identification of the second part we note that under the assumption of independence of the noise and inefficiency term the following equality holds

$$
\begin{aligned}
& E\left[(\varepsilon - E(\varepsilon))^4\right] - 3\left(E\left[(\varepsilon - E(\varepsilon))^2\right]\right)^2 \\
& = \psi_4 - 3\psi_2^2 = E\left[(u - E(u))^4\right] - 3\left(E\left[(u - E(u))^2\right]\right)^2
\end{aligned} \tag{3.8}
$$

This is a measure of excess kurtosis and for the truncated half-normal model is derived as

$$
\psi_4 - 3\psi_2^2 = \sigma_u^4(-\xi^3\tilde{\eta}_0 + 3\xi\tilde{\eta}_0 - 4\xi^2\tilde{\eta}_0^2 - 4\tilde{\eta}_0^2 - 3\xi^2\tilde{\eta}_0^2 - 12\xi\tilde{\eta}_0^3) \tag{3.9}
$$

where $\tilde{\eta}_0 = \frac{(2\pi)^{-1/2} - \xi\phi(\xi)}{\Phi(\xi) - \frac{1}{2}}$. Notice that for normal distribution $\tilde{\eta}_0 = 0$ and thus the excess kurtosis is also zero.

After multiplying (3.9) by $\psi_3^{-4/3}$ we eliminate σ_u and the resulting function, which we denote by g has only one argument ξ

$$
g(\xi) = \frac{-\xi^3\tilde{\eta}_0 + 3\xi\tilde{\eta}_0 - 4\xi^2\tilde{\eta}_0^2 - 4\tilde{\eta}_0^2 - 3\xi^2\tilde{\eta}_0^2 - 12\xi\tilde{\eta}_0^3}{\left(2\tilde{\eta}_0^3 - 3\xi\tilde{\eta}_0^2 - \tilde{\eta}_0 + \xi^2\tilde{\eta}_0\right)^{-4/3}} \tag{3.10}
$$

The weak law of large numbers implies that

$$\operatorname{plim}\frac{1}{n}\sum_i \hat{\varepsilon}_i^k = m_k = \psi_k \tag{3.11}$$

The first order moment is zero by definition and thus is not useful for identification purposes. By employing the Slutsky theorem we can specify the following function G

$$\begin{aligned} g(\xi) &= \frac{m_4 - 3m_2^2}{m^{4/3}} \\ &\Longrightarrow \\ G(\xi) &= g(\xi) - \frac{m_4 - 3m_2^2}{m^{4/3}} \end{aligned}$$

Similarly, we can derive the function G for the normal-truncated exponential model with function g expressed by

$$g(\xi) = \frac{36e^{2\xi} - 24e^{\xi} - 24e^{3\xi} + 6e^{4\xi} - \xi^4 e^{\xi} - 4\xi^4 e^{2\xi} - \xi^4 e^{3\xi} + 6}{(6e^{2\xi} - 4e^{\xi} - 4e^{3\xi} + e^{4\xi} + 1)(-\frac{2e^{3\xi} - (\xi^3+6)e^{2\xi} + (6-\xi^3)e^{\xi} - 2}{e^{3\xi} - 3e^{2\xi} + 3e^{\xi} - 1})^{4/3}} \tag{3.12}$$

Both the truncated half normal model and the truncated exponential model are globally identified. To see this, we can examine the monotonicity of the function G with respect to the parameter ξ which will allow us to express this parameter (implicitly) as a function of sample moments and data. This condition provides the necessary and sufficient condition for global identification ala Rothenberg (1971). For the truncated half normal model, G is monotonically decreasing and for the truncated exponential model, G is monotonically increasing. Hence, in both cases, G is invertible and ξ can be identified. The identification of other parameters then follows from the third order moment of least squares residuals. Note, however, that for large values of ξ (e.g., $\xi > 5$ for the normal-truncated half-normal model and $\xi > 20$ for the normal-truncated exponential model), the curve $g(\xi)$ is nearly flat and gives poor identification. ξ can be large for two reasons: either σ_u goes to zero or the bound parameter is large. In the first case the distribution of the inefficiency process approaches the Dirac-delta distribution which makes it very hard for the distributional parameters to be identified. This limiting case is discussed in Wang and Schmidt (2008). In the second case the distribution of the inefficiency term becomes unbounded as in the standard stochastic frontier models for which it is straightforward to show that the model is globally identified (see Aigner et al. 1977; Olson et al. 1980).

It is not clear, however, that the doubly truncated normal model is globally identifiable. However, local identification can be verified. We may examine $\psi_3^{-4/3}(\psi_4 - 3\psi_2^2)$ and $\psi_3^{-5/3}(\psi_5 - 10\psi_2\psi_3)$, both of which are functions of ξ_1 and ξ_2 only and we denote them as $g_1(\xi_1, \xi_2)$ and $g_2(\xi_1, \xi_2)$, respectively. Let $\hat{g}_1$ and $\hat{g}_2$ be the sample versions of g_1 and g_2, respectively, we have the following system of identification equations,

$$\begin{aligned} G_1(\xi_1, \xi_2) &\equiv g_1(\xi_1, \xi_2) - \hat{g}_1 = 0 \\ G_2(\xi_1, \xi_2) &\equiv g_2(\xi_1, \xi_2) - \hat{g}_2 = 0. \end{aligned}$$

By the implicit function theorem (or Rothenberg 1971), the identification of ξ_1 and ξ_2 depends on the rank of the matrix

$$H = \begin{pmatrix} \frac{\partial g_1}{\partial \xi_1} & \frac{\partial g_1}{\partial \xi_2} \\ \frac{\partial g_2}{\partial \xi_1} & \frac{\partial g_2}{\partial \xi_2} \end{pmatrix}.$$

If H is of full rank, then ξ_1 and ξ_2 can be written as functions of $\hat{g}_1$ and $\hat{g}_2$; the identification of the model then follows. The analytic form of H is very complicated, but we may examine the invertibility of H by numerically evaluating g_1 and g_2 and inferring the sign of each element in H. It can be verified that the determinant of H is nonzero in neighborhoods within I_1, I_2, and I_4, the definitions of which are given as follows,

(i) $I_1 \equiv \{(\mu, B) | \mu \leq 0, B > 0\}$
(ii) $I_2 \equiv \{(\mu, B) | \mu > 0, B \in (0, 2\mu)\}$
(iii) $I_3 \equiv \{(\mu, B) | B = 2\mu > 0\}$
(iv) $I_4 \equiv \{(\mu, B) | \mu > 0, B > 2\mu\}$.

The line $I_3 \equiv \{(\mu, B) | B = 2\mu > 0\}$ corresponds to the case where $B = 2\mu$ and $\psi_3 = 0$, hence the functions g_1 and g_2 are not continuous and the implicit function theorem is not applicable. Nonetheless, simulation results in the next section show that when the true values of B and μ satisfy $B = 2\mu$, both B and μ are consistently estimated. This may indicate that the restricted ($B = 2\mu$) model may be nested in the unrestricted model and the model is locally identifiable on $I_2 \bigcup I_3 \bigcup I_4$.

We may treat the doubly truncated normal model as a collection of different sub-models corresponding to the different domains of parameters. Treated separately, each of the sub-models is globally identified. In maximum likelihood estimation, the separate treatment is easily achieved by constrained optimization on each parameter subset. For example, on the line of $\{(\mu, B) | \mu = 0, B > 0\} \subset I_1$, the doubly truncated normal model reduces to the truncated half normal model. As another useful example, the line I_2 corresponds to a sub-model that has positive skewness even asymptotically.

3.4.2 *Method of Moment Estimation*

The method-of-moments (Olson et al. 1980) may be employed to estimate our model or to obtain initial values for maximum likelihood estimation. In the first step of this approach, OLS is used to obtain consistent estimates of the parameters describing the technology, apart from the intercept. In the second step, using the distributional assumptions on the residual, equations of moment conditions are solved to obtain estimates of the parameters describing the distribution of the residual.

More specifically, we may rewrite the production frontier model in (3.1) and (3.2) as

$$y_i = (\alpha_0 - \mathbb{E}u_i) + \sum_{k=1}^{K} \alpha_k x_{i,k} + \varepsilon_i^*,$$

where $\varepsilon_i^* = \varepsilon_i + (\mathbb{E}u_i)$ has zero mean and constant variance σ_ε^2. Hence OLS yields consistent estimates for ε_i^* and α_k, $k = 1, \ldots, K$. Equating the sample moments of estimated residuals $(\hat{\varepsilon}_i^*)$ to the population moments, one can solve for the parameters associated with the distribution of (ε_i^*).

3.4.3 Maximum Likelihood Estimation

For more efficient estimation, we may use maximum likelihood estimation (MLE). Note that with the presence of a noise term v_i, the range of residual is unbounded and does not depend on the parameter. No other standard regularity conditions might be questioned. In the remainder of this section we provide the log-likelihood functions for the bounded inefficiency model for the three parametric distributions we have considered. Note that in practice we may also need the gradients of the log likelihood function. The gradients are complicated in form but straightforward to derive. These are provided in the appendix.

In addition to the γ-parametrization discussed earlier, we re-parametrize the bound parameter with another parameter $\tilde{B} = \exp(-B)$. Unlike the bound, $\tilde{B}$ takes values in compact unit interval which facilitates the numerical procedure of maximum likelihood estimation as well as establishing the asymptotic normality of this parameter. When $\tilde{B}$ lies in the interior of parameter space, the MLE estimator is asymptotically normal (see Rao 1973; Davidson and MacKinnon 1993 among others).

The log-likelihood function for the doubly truncated normal model with γ-parameterization is given by

$$\ln L = -n \ln \left[\Phi\left(\frac{-\ln \tilde{B} - \mu}{\sigma_u(\sigma, \gamma)}\right) - \Phi\left(\frac{-\mu}{\sigma_u(\sigma, \gamma)}\right) \right]$$

$$-n \ln \sigma - \frac{n}{2} \ln(2\pi) - \sum_{i=1}^{n} \frac{(\varepsilon_i + \mu)^2}{2\sigma^2}$$

$$+\sum_{i=1}^{n} \ln \left\{ \Phi\left(\frac{(-\ln \tilde{B} + \varepsilon_i)\sqrt{\gamma/(1-\gamma)} - (\ln \tilde{B} + \mu)\sqrt{(1-\gamma)/\gamma}}{\sigma}\right) \right.$$

$$\left. -\Phi\left(\frac{\varepsilon_i \sqrt{\gamma/(1-\gamma)} - \mu\sqrt{(1-\gamma)/\gamma}}{\sigma}\right)\right\}, \tag{3.13}$$

where $\varepsilon_i = y_i - x_i\alpha$, $x_i = (1, x_{ik})$, and $\alpha = (\alpha_0, \alpha_k)'$.

$$\sigma_u(\sigma, \gamma) = \sigma\sqrt{\gamma}. \tag{3.14}$$

This can be expressed in terms of the λ-parametrization as in Aigner et al. (1977) by substituting γ in (3.13) with

$$\gamma(\lambda) = \frac{\lambda^2}{1+\lambda^2}. \tag{3.15}$$

The log-likelihood function for the truncated half normal model is

$$\ln L = -n \ln\left(\Phi\left(\frac{-\ln \tilde{B}}{\sigma_u(\sigma,\gamma)}\right) - \frac{1}{2}\right) - n\ln\sigma - \frac{n}{2}\ln(2\pi)$$

$$-\sum_{i=1}^{n} \frac{\varepsilon_i^2}{2\sigma^2} + \sum_{i=1}^{n} \ln\left\{\Phi\left(\frac{(-\ln \tilde{B} + \varepsilon_i)\sqrt{\gamma/(1-\gamma)} - \ln \tilde{B}\sqrt{(1-\gamma)/\gamma}}{\sigma}\right)\right.$$

$$\left. -\Phi\left(\frac{\varepsilon_i\sqrt{\gamma/(1-\gamma)}}{\sigma}\right)\right\}, \tag{3.16}$$

Again, substituting γ into (3.16) with $\gamma(\lambda)$ in (3.15), we get the $\log L$ with λ-parametrization.

Finally, the log-likelihood function for the truncated exponential model with γ-parametrization is given by

$$\ln L = -\frac{n}{2}\ln\gamma - n\ln\sigma - n\ln\left(1 - e^{\frac{\ln \tilde{B}\gamma^{-1/2}}{\sigma}}\right) + \frac{n}{2}\frac{1-\gamma}{\gamma} + \frac{\gamma^{-1/2}}{\sigma}\sum_{i=1}^{n}\varepsilon_i$$

$$+\sum_{i=1}^{n}\ln\left[\Phi\left(\frac{(-\ln \tilde{B} + \varepsilon_i)(1-\gamma)^{-1/2}}{\sigma} + \sqrt{\frac{1-\gamma}{\gamma}}\right)\right.$$

$$\left. -\Phi\left(\frac{\varepsilon_i(1-\gamma)^{-1/2}}{\sigma} + \sqrt{\frac{1-\gamma}{\gamma}}\right)\right], \tag{3.17}$$

where $\varepsilon_i = y - x_i\alpha$.

After estimating the model, we can estimate the composed error term ε_i:

$$\hat{\varepsilon}_i = y_i - \hat{\alpha}_0 - \sum x_{i,k}\hat{\alpha}_k, i = 1, \cdots, n. \tag{3.18}$$

From this we can estimate the inefficiency term u_i using the formula for $E(u_i|\varepsilon_i)$ in Table 3.1.

One reasonable question is whether or not one can test for the absence or the presence of the bound ($H_0 : \tilde{B} = 0$ vs. $H_1 : \tilde{B} > 0$), which one may wish to test since this would suggest that the proper specification would be the standard SF model which assumes no bound as a special case of our more general bounded SF model. The test procedure is slightly complicated but still feasible. The first complication arises from the fact that $\tilde{B}$ lies on the boundary of the parameter space under the null. Second, it is obvious from the log-likelihood functions provided above that the bound is not identified in this case and it can be shown that any finite order derivative of the log-likelihood function with respect to $\tilde{B}$ is zero. Thus the conventional Wald and Lagrange Multiplier (LM) statistics are not defined and the Likelihood Ratio (LR) statistic has a nonstandard asymptotic distribution that strictly would dominate the $\chi^2_{(1)}$ distribution. Lee (1993) derives the asymptotic distribution of such an estimate as a mixture of χ^2 distributions under the null that its value is zero, focusing in particular on the SF model under the assumption of half-normally distributed inefficiencies. Here λ is globally identified, which can also be seen using the method-of-moments estimator provided in Aigner et al. (1977). Lee (1993) provides useful one-to-one reparametrization which transform the singular information matrix into a nonsingular one. However, since the bound in our model case is not identified in this situation, there is no such re-parametrization and hence this procedure cannot be used. An alternative is to apply the bootstrap procedure proposed by Hansen (1996, 1999) to construct asymptotically equivalent p-values to make an inference. To implement the test we treat the $\hat{\varepsilon}_i$ $(i = 1, \ldots, n)$ as a sample from which the bootstrap samples $\hat{\varepsilon}_i^{(m)}$ $(i = 1, \ldots, n; m = 1, \ldots, M)$ are drawn with replacement. Using the bootstrap sample we estimate the model under the null and the alternative of bounded inefficiency and construct the corresponding LR statistic. We repeat this procedure M times and calculate the percentage of times the bootstrap LR exceeds the actual one. This provides us with the bootstrap estimate of the asymptotic p-value of LR under the null.

3.5 Panel Data

In the same spirit as Schmidt and Sickles (1984) and Cornwell et al. (1990), we may specify a panel data model of bounded inefficiencies:

$$y_{it} = \alpha_0 + \sum_{k=1}^{K} \alpha_k x_{it,k} + \varepsilon_{it} \tag{3.19}$$

where

$$\varepsilon_{it} = v_{it} - u_{it}. \tag{3.20}$$

We assume that the inefficiency components (u_{it}) are positive, independent from the regressors, and are independently drawn from a time-varying distribution with upper bound B_t. We may set B_t to be time-invariant. However, it is certainly more plausible to assume otherwise, as the market or industry may well become more or less forgiving as time goes by, especially in settings in which market reforms are being introduced or firms are adjusting to a phased transition from regulation to deregulation.

Note that since u_{it} is time-varying, the above panel data model is in effect a time-varying technical efficiency model. Our model differs from the existing literature in that, while previous time-varying efficiency models, notably Cornwell et al. (1990), Kumbhakar (1990), Battese and Coelli (1992), and Lee and Schmidt (1993), are time-varying in the mean or intercept of individual effects, our model is time-varying in the upper support of the distribution of inefficiency term u_i.

The assumption that u_{it} is independent over time simplifies estimation and analysis considerably. In particular, the covariance matrix of $\varepsilon_i \equiv (\varepsilon_{i1}, \ldots, \varepsilon_{iT})'$ is diagonal. This enables us to treat the panel model as a collection of cross-section models in the chronological order. We may certainly impose more structure on the sample path of the upper bound of u_{it}, B_t, without incurring heavy costs in terms of analytic difficulty. For example, we may impose smoothness conditions on B_t. This is empirically plausible, indeed, since changes in the market competitive conditions may come gradually. And it is also technically desirable, since imposing smoothness conditions gives us more degree of freedom in estimation, hence better estimators of model parameters. A natural way of doing this is to let B_t be a sum of weighted polynomials,

$$B_t = \sum_{i=0}^{K} b_i (t/T)^i, \quad t = 1, \ldots, T, \tag{3.21}$$

where (b_i) are constants. We may also use trigonometric series, splines, among others, in the modeling of B_t. For an extensive survey of efforts to generalize such heterogeneities in efficiencies see Sickles et al. (2013).

3.6 Simulations

To examine the finite sample performance of the MLE estimator of the doubly truncated normal model,[10] we run a series of Monte Carlo experiments in the standard cross-sectional setting. The data generating process is (3.1) and (3.2) with

[10]The results for the truncated half-normal and truncated exponential models are available upon the request.

one regressor x and no constant term and is based on the data generating process utilized in study 2 of Aigner, Lovell, and Schmidt. We maintain the assumption that v_i is iid $N(0, \sigma_v^2)$, u_i is iid, and v_i and u_i are independent from each other and from regressors. The number of repetitions is 1,000. Throughout we keep the coefficient α on the single regressor technology parameter set at 0.6 and examine performances in terms of bias and mean absolute error as we change in each of the distributional parameters (σ, γ, μ, and B). As the SF benchmark we use the singly truncated normal model (Stevenson 1980) on the simulated data. We report average estimates and mean absolute errors (MAE) in Tables 3.3–3.6. Each of these sets of experiments selectively change the distributional parameters. We draw the following conclusions from these experiments.[11]

First, all parameters in the doubly truncated normal model appear to be well-estimated, with biases and MAE's that fall as sample sizes rise. The biases are generally small, and the MAE's of almost all estimates decrease at $\sqrt{N}$ rate as N increases, except that of $\hat{\mu}$ in a couple of particular cases. More specifically, when σ is small (i.e., the variation in the composite error is small), $\hat{\mu}$ does not converge at the optimal rate as N increases (see Table 3.3). The same happens when B is large (see Table 3.5). This observation is connected with the well-known difficulty of identifying μ in the singly truncated model ($B \to \infty$) from finite sample. As is well known, the technological parameter α in the singly truncated normal model is consistently estimated. However, estimates of distributional parameters in the singly truncated model are not well-defined and thus we do not calculate the corresponding MAE's.

Second, Table 3.3 shows that as σ becomes smaller, the MAE of $\hat{\alpha}$ is monotone decreasing, while the MAE's of $\hat{\sigma}$, $\hat{\gamma}$, and $\hat{\mu}$ is monotone increasing. To reconcile the apparent divergence, note that the composite error ε is noise for the technological parameters, but signal for distributional parameters. The effect of σ on the MAE of $\hat{B}$ is ambiguous, which decreases at first and then increases as σ becomes smaller.

Third, if we mistakenly estimate a singly truncated model on a DGP with double truncation, we tend to underestimate the average technical efficiency (ATE). This is understandable since the singly truncated model may treat some extreme (negative) measurement errors as inefficiencies. Within the doubly truncated model, it is also clear that as B becomes larger, the ATE decreases (See Table 3.5). However, our simulation results show that the efficiency ranking would not be affected if we estimate a misspecified model.

Finally, as is expected, MLE correctly estimates the doubly truncated normal model when the composite error has positive population skewness. This is evident in Table 3.6, where the third case ($\mu = 0.3$, $B = 0.5$) corresponds to negative (positive) skewness in u (ε). In all cases, the double truncation in the DGP of u makes finite-sample positive skewness more probable, resulting in many zero $\hat{\gamma}$'s (super-efficiency) from the misspecified (singly truncated) model. Hence the average $\hat{\gamma}$'s in the misspecified model are generally much lower than the true value.

[11]We have similar limited Monte Carlo results based on two regressors with varying correlations and our results are qualitatively similar. Results are available on request.

Table 3.3 Monte Carlo simulation of the doubly truncated normal model: on the dimension of σ. $\gamma = 0.95$, $\mu = 0$, $B = 0.5$. The number of repetitions is 1,000. Mean absolute errors (MAE) are given in parentheses

		Doubly truncated						Singly truncated				
σ	N	$\hat{\alpha}$	$\hat{\sigma}$	$\hat{\gamma}$	$\hat{\mu}$	$\hat{B}$	ATE	$\hat{\alpha}$	$\hat{\sigma}$	$\hat{\gamma}$	$\hat{\mu}$	ATE
2	500	0.599(0.0170)	1.993(0.0099)	0.950(0.0025)	0.00371(0.1720)	0.500(0.0351)	0.887	0.599(0.0170)	0.515	0.208	0.0446	0.826
	1,000	0.600(0.0124)	1.995(0.0069)	0.950(0.0017)	0.000001(0.1250)	0.501(0.0239)	0.882	0.600(0.0125)	0.504	0.188	0.0980	0.825
	5,000	0.600(0.0054)	1.998(0.0029)	0.950(0.00078)	0.006(0.0585)	0.500(0.0111)	0.873	0.600(0.0054)	0.488	0.147	0.175	0.824
$\sqrt{2}$	500	0.600(0.0124)	1.405(0.0111)	0.950(0.0029)	−0.0253(0.3380)	0.502(0.0273)	0.860	0.600(0.0124)	0.369	0.205	0.177	0.842
	1,000	0.600(0.0092)	1.409(0.0071)	0.950(0.0019)	−0.00600(0.2850)	0.500(0.0189)	0.857	0.600(0.0092)	0.362	0.176	0.203	0.849
	5,000	0.600(0.0037)	1.412(0.0030)	0.950(0.0009)	0.0129(0.1280)	0.500(0.0094)	0.848	0.600(0.0037)	0.354	0.138	0.229	0.856
1	500	0.600(0.0093)	0.884(0.1180)	0.929(0.0220)	0.0120(0.4170)	0.532(0.0545)	0.820	0.600(0.0093)	0.276	0.227	0.219	0.853
	1,000	0.600(0.0071)	0.917(0.0844)	0.938(0.0127)	−0.013(0.4070)	0.519(0.0386)	0.822	0.600(0.0071)	0.274	0.221	0.225	0.845
	5,000	0.600(0.0029)	0.984(0.0171)	0.948(0.0022)	−0.00413(0.2990)	0.504(0.0172)	0.826	0.600(0.0029)	0.271	0.198	0.234	0.839

Table 3.4 Monte Carlo simulation of the doubly truncated normal model: on the dimension of γ. $\sigma = \sqrt{2}$, $\mu = 0$, $B = 0.5$. The number of repetitions is 1,000. Mean absolute errors (MAE) are given in parentheses

		Doubly truncated						Singly truncated				
γ	N	$\hat{\alpha}$	$\hat{\sigma}$	$\hat{\gamma}$	$\hat{\mu}$	$\hat{B}$	ATE	$\hat{\alpha}$	$\hat{\sigma}$	$\hat{\gamma}$	$\hat{\mu}$	ATE
0.8	500	0.600(0.0170)	1.409(0.0099)	0.799(0.0025)	0.00540(0.1720)	0.500(0.0351)	0.912	0.600(0.0232)	0.729	0.234	−0.238	0.806
	1,000	0.599(0.0124)	1.411(0.0069)	0.799(0.0017)	0.0154(0.1250)	0.500(0.0239)	0.908	0.599(0.0162)	0.723	0.223	−0.194	0.798
	5,000	0.600(0.0054)	1.413(0.0029)	0.800(0.0008)	−0.00171(0.0585)	0.500(0.0111)	0.898	0.600(0.0073)	0.726	0.245	−0.203	0.737
0.5	500	0.602(0.0379)	1.411(0.0190)	0.500(0.0127)	−0.00521(0.0887)	0.495(0.0731)	0.941	0.602(0.0378)	1.124	0.225	−0.797	0.822
	1,000	0.600(0.0268)	1.412(0.0139)	0.500(0.0093)	0.00735(0.0709)	0.503(0.0536)	0.936	0.600(0.0268)	1.133	0.242	−0.846	0.793
	5,000	0.600(0.0112)	1.414(0.0060)	0.500(0.0042)	−0.00347(0.0243)	0.500(0.0234)	0.930	0.600(0.0112)	1.138	0.247	−0.878	0.748
0.3	500	0.601(0.0382)	1.410(0.0225)	0.303(0.0152)	0.0231(0.0935)	0.500(0.0906)	0.947	0.601(0.0382)	1.293	0.182	−0.877	0.847
	1,000	0.600(0.0301)	1.413(0.0149)	0.301(0.0101)	0.0100(0.0693)	0.498(0.0658)	0.946	0.600(0.0301)	1.303	0.191	−0.928	0.832
	5,000	0.600(0.0130)	1.414(0.0067)	0.301(0.0046)	−0.00432(0.0268)	0.501(0.0288)	0.939	0.600(0.0131)	1.309	0.200	−0.984	0.795

Table 3.5 Monte Carlo simulation of the doubly truncated normal model: on the dimension of B. $\sigma = \sqrt{2}, \gamma = 0.95, \mu = 0$. The number of repetitions is 1,000. Mean absolute errors (MAE) are given in parentheses

		Doubly truncated						Singly truncated				
B	N	$\hat{\alpha}$	$\hat{\sigma}$	$\hat{\gamma}$	$\hat{\mu}$	$\hat{B}$	ATE	$\hat{\alpha}$	$\hat{\sigma}$	$\hat{\gamma}$	$\hat{\mu}$	ATE
0.3	500	0.599(0.0111)	1.409(0.0077)	0.950(0.0022)	0.000963(0.0910)	0.298(0.0251)	0.939	0.599(0.0111)	0.370	0.222	−0.0808	0.882
	1,000	0.600(0.0078)	1.411(0.0051)	0.950(0.0015)	0.0110(0.0744)	0.300(0.0169)	0.935	0.600(0.0078)	0.359	0.191	−0.0113	0.884
	5,000	0.600(0.0037)	1.413(0.0022)	0.950(0.0007)	−0.00142(0.0311)	0.300(0.0076)	0.929	0.600(0.0037)	0.345	0.149	0.0688	0.883
0.5	500	0.600(0.0126)	1.405(0.0120)	0.949(0.0030)	−0.0248(0.3440)	0.503(0.0280)	0.860	0.600(0.0126)	0.370	0.206	0.176	0.842
	1,000	0.600(0.0090)	1.408(0.0074)	0.950(0.0019)	−0.0177(0.2870)	0.502(0.0202)	0.856	0.600(0.0090)	0.362	0.181	0.201	0.846
	5,000	0.600(0.0037)	1.412(0.0031)	0.950(0.0009)	0.00974(0.1370)	0.500(0.0093)	0.848	0.600(0.0037)	0.354	0.137	0.229	0.857
0.7	500	0.600(0.0129)	1.316(0.1010)	0.940(0.01230)	−0.0184(0.5450)	0.732(0.0633)	0.766	0.600(0.0129)	0.392	0.244	0.299	0.791
	1,000	0.600(0.0097)	1.364(0.0524)	0.946(0.0060)	−0.00766(0.5040)	0.715(0.0401)	0.770	0.600(0.0097)	0.387	0.218	0.312	0.797
	5,000	0.600(0.0043)	1.407(0.0091)	0.950(0.0011)	0.00365(0.3010)	0.702(0.0178)	0.769	0.600(0.0044)	0.382	0.202	0.326	0.779

Table 3.6 Monte Carlo simulation of the doubly truncated normal model: On the dimension of μ. $\sigma = \sqrt{2}$, $\gamma = 0.95$, $B = 0.5$. The number of repetitions is 1,000. Mean absolute errors (MAE) are given in parentheses

		Doubly truncated						Singly truncated				
μ	N	$\hat{\alpha}$	$\hat{\sigma}$	$\hat{\gamma}$	$\hat{\mu}$	$\hat{B}$	ATE	$\hat{\alpha}$	$\hat{\sigma}$	$\hat{\gamma}$	$\hat{\mu}$	ATE
−0.2	500	0.601(0.0128)	1.405(0.0117)	0.949(0.0029)	−0.0903(0.3320)	0.498(0.0277)	0.862	0.601(0.0128)	0.370	0.211	0.168	0.839
	1,000	0.600(0.0089)	1.409(0.0068)	0.950(0.0018)	−0.0941(0.2710)	0.498(0.0190)	0.857	0.600(0.0089)	0.362	0.184	0.198	0.842
	5,000	0.600(0.0040)	1.412(0.0031)	0.950(0.0009)	−0.122(0.1490)	0.499(0.0094)	0.848	0.600(0.0040)	0.354	0.138	0.226	0.856
0.2	500	0.599(0.0128)	1.405(0.0117)	0.950(0.0029)	0.0386(0.3480)	0.506(0.0271)	0.859	0.599(0.0127)	0.368	0.206	0.183	0.840
	1,000	0.600(0.0088)	1.409(0.0070)	0.950(0.0019)	0.0626(0.2820)	0.503(0.0193)	0.856	0.600(0.0088)	0.361	0.176	0.208	0.849
	5,000	0.600(0.0038)	1.412(0.0028)	0.950(0.0008)	0.156(0.1070)	0.501(0.0088)	0.849	0.600(0.0038)	0.353	0.133	0.233	0.860
0.3	500	0.600(0.01270)	1.407(0.0095)	0.950(0.0025)	0.0658(0.3550)	0.505(0.0263)	0.859	0.600(0.0127)	0.368	0.206	0.184	0.840
	1,000	0.600(0.0081)	1.409(0.0071)	0.950(0.0019)	0.121(0.2790)	0.504(0.0201)	0.856	0.600(0.0081)	0.361	0.182	0.207	0.844
	5,000	0.600(0.0041)	1.412(0.0033)	0.950(0.00084)	0.215(0.1310)	0.502(0.0095)	0.848	0.600(0.0041)	0.353	0.134	0.233	0.860

3.7 An Empirical Illustration to Analyze US Banking Industry Dynamics

3.7.1 Empirical Model and Data

We now apply the bounded inefficiency (BIE) model to an analysis of the US banking industry, which underwent a series of deregulatory reforms in the early 1980s and 1990s, and experienced an adverse economic environment in the last few turbulent years of 2000s.[12] Our analysis covers a lengthy period between 1984 and 2009 and our illustration aims to use the panel variant of our BIE model to capture efficiency trends of the US banking sector during these years as well as how the lower bound of inefficiency also changed as the market became more or less competitive vis-a-vis inefficient firms.

Following Adams et al. (1999) and Kneip et al. (2012), we specify a multi-output/multi-input stochastic output distance frontier model as[13]

$$Y_{it} = Y_{it}^{*\prime}\gamma + X_{it}^{\prime}\beta + v_{it} - u_{it}, \tag{3.22}$$

where Y_{it} is the log of real estate loans; X_{it} is the negative of log of inputs, which include demand deposit (dd), time and savings deposit (dep), labor (lab), capital (cap), and purchased funds (purf).[14] Y_{it}^{*} includes the log of commercial and industrial loans/real estate loans (ciln) and installment loans/real estate loans (inln). In order to account for the riskiness and heterogeneity of the banks we include the log of the ratio of equity to total assets ($eqrt$) which usually measures the risk of insolvency of the banks in banking literature.[15] The lower the ratio the more riskier a bank is considered. We assume the v_{it} are iid across i and t, and for each t, u_{it} has a upper bound B_t. Then we can treat this model as a generic panel data bounded inefficiency model as discussed in Sect. 3.5. Once the individual effects u_{it} are estimated, technical efficiency for a particular firm at time t is calculated as $TE = \exp(u_{it} - \max_{1\leq j\leq N} u_{jt})$.

The output distance function is known as a Young index (ratio of the geometric mean of the outputs to the geometric mean of the inputs) described in Balk (2008), which leads to the Cobb-Douglas specification of the distance function

---

[12]These deregulations gradually allowed banks in different states to merge with other banks across the state borders. The Reigle-Neal Act that was passed by the Congress in 1994 also allowed the branching by banks across the state lines.

[13]For more discussion on stochastic distance frontiers see Lovell et al. (1994).

[14]Purchased funds include federal funds purchased and securities sold under agreements to repurchase, time deposits in \$100,000 denominations, mortgage debt, bank's liability on acceptances, and other liabilities that are not demand deposits and retail time and savings deposits.

[15]We exclude from the sample banks with $eqrt$ less that 0.02. Typically, these banks are close to failure and estimation of their efficiency scores require special treatments (see Wheelock and Wilson 2000; Almanidis 2013 for more discussion).

introduced by Klein (1953). Although this functional form has been criticized for its separability and curvature properties it remains a reasonable and parsimonious first-order local approximation to the true function (Coelli 2000) and we use it in our limited empirical illustration of the bounded stochastic frontier model. We use the parsimonious Cobb-Douglas model as well to allow comparisons with the results from our Monte Carlo simulations, which due to the need to estimate highly nonlinear models, have been somewhat limited by computational and time constraints to a relatively simple linear in logs specification.[16] Translog distance function estimates, which one may view as more general, have their own attendant problems due to multicollinearity in the second order terms of the four-output/five-input technology. This typically is addressed by utilizing additional restrictions, such as those imposed by cost minimization or profit maximization, in order to be empirically identify the translog parameters.[17] We do not use these side conditions to empirically identify the parameters due to our use of a stochastic frontier model that admits to technical inefficiency but does not attempt to trace this inefficiency to its logical implication in the first order conditions of cost minimization or profit maximization (the so-called "Greene problem", Kutlu 2013). Utilization of side conditions to address errors in the optimization of allocations is beyond the scope of this paper. That said, our translog estimates have provided qualitatively similar results, which are available on request.

We use US commercial banking data from 1984 first quarter through 2009 third quarter. There are several ways in which data can be merged or deleted depending on whether or not banks continued as independent entities during the sample period we consider in our illustration of the insights gained by the bounded inefficiency model.

---

[16]The empirical illustration is used in part to link the use of the Cobb–Douglas functional form in expressing the provision of banking intermediation services to Peter Schmidt's intellectual predecessors, whom we have discussed above, and who used the Cobb-Douglas functional form substantially. It also has been the predominate functional form used by the NBER's Productivity Program in their seminal work on productivity and growth. We understand the limitations of the Cobb–Douglas functional form. Indeed, one of the authors has been writing on the topic for 30 years (Guilkey et al. 1983). Recent work on banking efficiency and returns to scale by Wheelock and Wilson (2012) have fitted local linear and local quadratic estimator with on the order of one million parameters to a cost relationship and use duality theory to link the cost estimates to the returns to scale in the banking industry and utilize multi-step bootstrapping methods to assess significance. It is unclear what has been estimated in such an exercise as standard regularity conditions for the function to indeed be a cost function have not been checked, nor it is clear how such a test would be conducted. Obviously, with such an overparameterized model, they overwhelmingly reject generalizations of the Cobb–Douglas, such as second-order Taylor series expansions in logs, such as the translog functional form. Without the regularity conditions met by at least some of the observations their results are meaningless. Moreover, it is not even clear that their use of the bootstrap in the multi-step algorithms they use is even valid. We find that regularity conditions are met by a substantial portion of the data we use and do find little qualitative difference in terms of the efficiency patterns, which is of course what the paper focuses on, between those generated by the Cobb–Douglas and the translog.

[17]For an example of the use of such side conditions and with just such justifications in the multi-output cost function setting see Hughes and Mester (1993).

One approach is to express the data for a bank on a pro-forma basis that goes back in time to account for mergers. For example, if a bank in 2008 is the result of a merger in 2008 then the pre-2008 data is merged on a pro-forma basis wherein the non-surviving bank's data is viewed as part of the surviving bank in earlier time periods. The Federal Reserve uses this approach in estimating risk measurement models, such as the Charge-off at Risk Model (Frye and Pelz 2008), which is the basis of risk dashboards used for centralized bank supervision. This sample design reflects methodologies used by banks in calibrating credit risk models, such as those used for Basel III and for Comprehensive Capital Analysis and Review (CCAR).[18] An alternative to the retroactive merging in of legacy banks is to utilize an unbalanced design wherein banks simply attrit from the sample when their ownership changes. Although at first blush this would seem to address the problem of selection in cases when weaker banks get taken over, there are also many cases of mergers-of-equals as well (e.g., JP Morgan and Bank One merger). Roughly 84 % of banks in our sample ceased their operation due to reasons other than failure, such as merger or voluntary liquidation, or remained inactive, or were no longer regulated by the Federal Reserve. Almanidis and Sickles (2012) have proposed a general model that combines the mixture hazard model with the canonical stochastic frontier model to investigate the main determinants of the probability and time to failure of a panel of US commercial banks during the financial distress that began in August of 2007. In their analysis they focused on banks failures, not on ownership changes or changes in regulatory oversight that were not due to liquidation due to financial distress. Unlike the standard hazard model, which would assume that all banks in the sample eventually experience the event (failure), the mixture hazard model distinguishes between healthy (long-term survivors) and at-risk banks. Almanidis and Sickles did not find that selection on banks per se impacted their estimates in any significant way. Moreover, their formal mixture hazard framework is far removed from the basic modeling issues addressed in this paper, namely the introduction of a different stochastic frontier paradigm that acknowledges a lower bound to inefficient firm operating practices. In order to maintain comparability between our results and those from many other studies using stochastic frontier analysis and to find some middle ground between the pro-forma merging algorithm practiced by the Federal Reserve and the deletion of firms from the sample that attrit and the potential misspecification due to the many potential ways (unobserved in our sample) in which such attrition may have occurred, we utilize a balanced panel and study only firms that have remained in business during our sample period.

The data is a balanced panel of 4,193 commercial banks and was compiled from the Consolidated Reports of Condition and Income (Call Report) and the FDIC Summary of Deposits. The data set includes 431,879 observations for 103 quarterly periods. This is a fairly long panel and thus the assumption of time-invariant inefficiencies does not seem tenable. For this reason we compare the estimates from our BIE model to the estimates from other time-varying effects

[18]For more discussion of this issue and the use of similar data in models of risk aggregation see Inanoglu and Jacobs (2009).

Table 3.7 Descriptive statistics for bank-specific variables

Variable name	Mean	Median	Standard deviation	Min	Max
Real estate loans	212,968	17,549	4,341,501	145	4.61E+08
Commercial and industrial loans	103,272	4,908	2,143,974	46	1.82E+08
Installment loans	58,869	4,360	1,417,908	86	1.51E+08
Demand deposits	54,913	7,282	912,761	186	1.03E+08
Time and savings deposits	449,003	46,954	1.00E+07	1,446	9.93E+08
Labor	186	29	2,960	4	215,670
Capital	8,196	913	129,778	9	1.16E+07
Purchased funds	163,785	13,698	3,322,838	286	3.37E+08
Ratio of equity to total assets	0.1007	0.0936	0.0312	0.0210	0.7459

models such as CSSW (the within variant of Cornwell et al. (1990)) and BC (Battese and Coelli 1992) models, along with the baseline fixed effect estimator (FIX) of Schmidt and Sickles (1984). Descriptive statistics for the bank-level variables are given in Table 3.7, where all nominal values are converted to reflect 2000 year values.

3.7.2 *Results*

Table 3.8 compares the parameter estimates of the bounded inefficiency (BIE) model with that of FIX, CSSW, and BC.[19] The structural parameters are statistically significant at the 1 % level and have the expected sign for all four models. The adjusted Bera and Premaratne (2001) skewness test statistic is calculated to be 990.26, leading to rejection of the null hypothesis of symmetry at any conventional significance level. The asymmetry of the least squares residuals is also verified by quantile-quantile plot representation in Fig. 3.1. The technology parameters from BIE model are somewhat different from those obtained from other models. The negative value of the coefficient of the $eqrt$ implies that riskier firms tend to produce more loans, and especially real estate loans that are considered of high risk. The positive sign of the estimate of the time trend shows technological progress on average. There is a slight difference between the distributional parameters of BIE and BC model which are also statistically significant at any conventional significance level. We also tested (not reported here) other distributional specifications for BIE discussed above. The distributional parameters obtained from normal-truncated half-normal model did not differ very much from that reported in the table, but those obtained from normal-truncated exponential model did. However, this is not a specific to bounded inefficiency models. Similar differences have been documented in unbounded SF models as well.

[19]We estimate the normal-doubly truncated normal model in order to be able to compare it with the BC model which specifies the inefficiencies to follow the truncated normal distribution.

Table 3.8 Comparisons of various estimators. Estimates and standard errors (in parentheses) for each model parameters from competing models (FIX, CSSW, BC, BIE)

	FIX	CSSW	BC	BIE
ciln	0.2407(0.0015)	0.2971(0.0014)	0.2284(0.0013)	0.2838(0.0012)
inln	0.2206(0.0013)	0.1715(0.0012)	0.2043(0.0013)	0.2609(0.0013)
dd	−0.0940(0.0024)	−0.0935(0.0020)	−0.1197(0.0024)	−0.0996(0.0020)
dep	−0.3999(0.0048)	−0.4037(0.0051)	−0.4368(0.0048)	−0.4053(0.0034)
lab	−0.3104(0.0046)	−0.2219(0.0042)	−0.1610(0.0044)	−0.1892(0.0020)
cap	−0.0460(0.0016)	−0.0464(0.0014)	−0.0510(0.0015)	−0.0965(0.0015)
purf	−0.1507(0.0034)	−0.1658(0.0029)	−0.1627(0.0034)	−0.1665(0.0031)
time	0.0057(0.0001)	–	0.0020(0.0001)	0.0021(0.0001)
eqrt	−0.1369(0.0045)	−0.1189(0.0041)	−0.0975(0.0044)	−0.1088(0.0039)
γ	0	0	0.7980(0.0115)	0.7690(0.0058)
σ	0.2210(0.0034)	0.2070(0.0020)	0.2733(0.0045)	0.2712(0.0022)
μ	–	–	0.3240(0.0139)	0.3518(0.0630)
B	–	–	–	1.5186
ATE	0.5853	0.6470	0.6410	0.6998

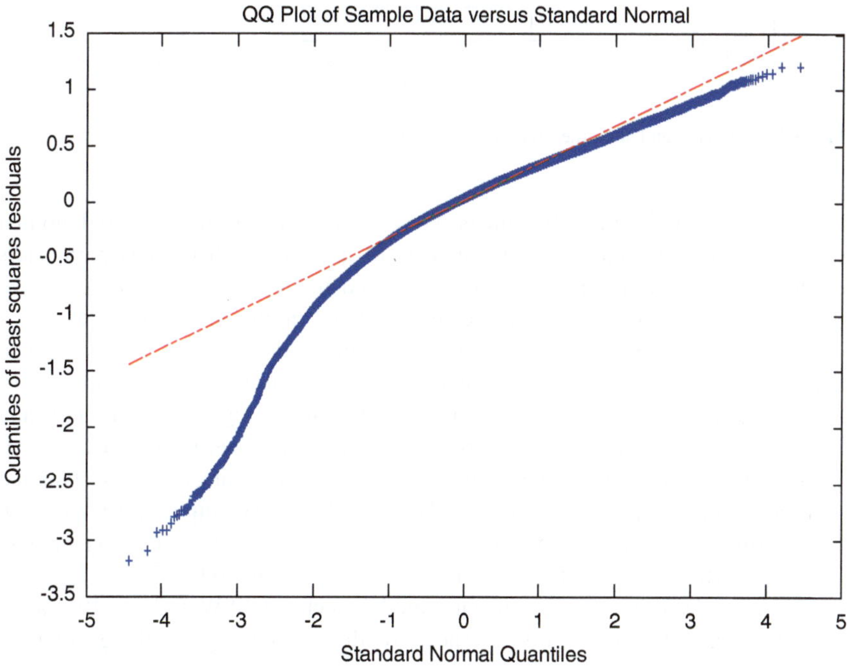

Fig. 3.1 Quantile-quantile plot

We also estimate the time-varying inefficiency bound, B, using two approaches. First we estimate the bound for the panel data model without imposing any restriction on its sample path. In the second approach we specify the bound as

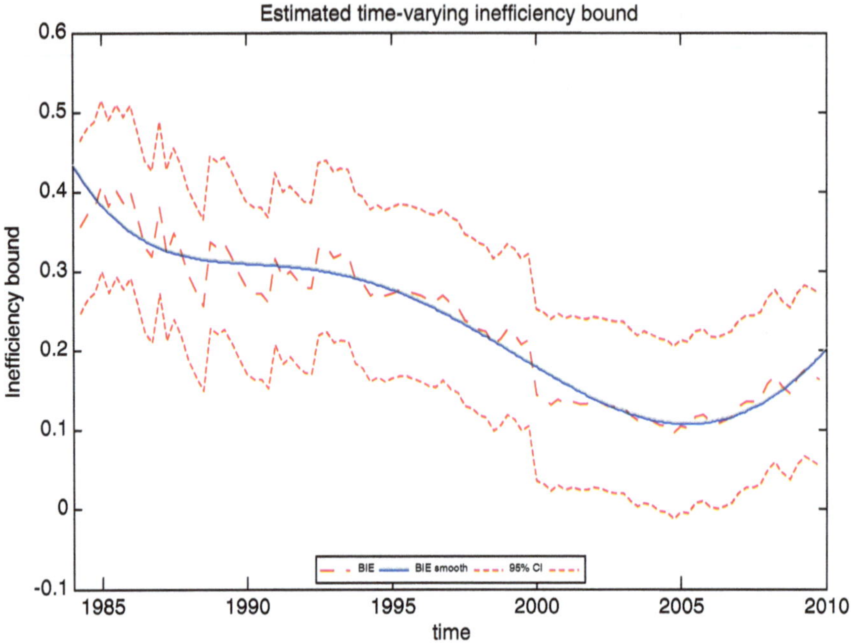

Fig. 3.2 Estimated and smoothed inefficiency bound

a sum of weighted time polynomials. We choose to fit a fifth degree polynomial the coefficients of which are estimated by MLE along with the rest parameters of the model.[20] Both approaches are illustrated in Fig. 3.2 with their respective 95 % confidence intervals. It can be seen that the inefficiency bound has had a decreasing trend up to year 2005, when the financial crisis (informally) began, and then it is increasing for the remaining periods through the third quarter of 2009. One interpretation of this trend can be that the deregulations in 1980s and 1990s increased competitive pressures and forced many inefficient banks to exit the industry, reducing the upper limit of inefficiency that banks could sustain and still remain in their particular niche market in the larger banking industry. The new upward trend can be attributed to the adverse economic environment and an increase in the proportion of banks that are characterized as "too big to fail."

Of course, for time-varying efficiency models such as CSSW, BC, and BIE, average efficiencies change over time.[21] These are illustrated in Fig. 3.3 along with their

[20]The choice of degrees of the time polynomial was based on a simple likelihood-ratio (LR) test and degrees of the polynomial ranging from 1 to 10. The maximum likelihood estimates of coefficients for this polynomial are given by

$b_0 = -3.9477e-007$, $b_1 = 0.0039509^{**}$, $b_2 = -15.816^{***}$, $b_3 = 31656^{**}$, $b_4 = -3.168e+007^{*}$, $b_5 = 1.2682e+010$.

[21]We trimmed the top and bottom 5 % of inefficiencies to remove the effects of outliers.

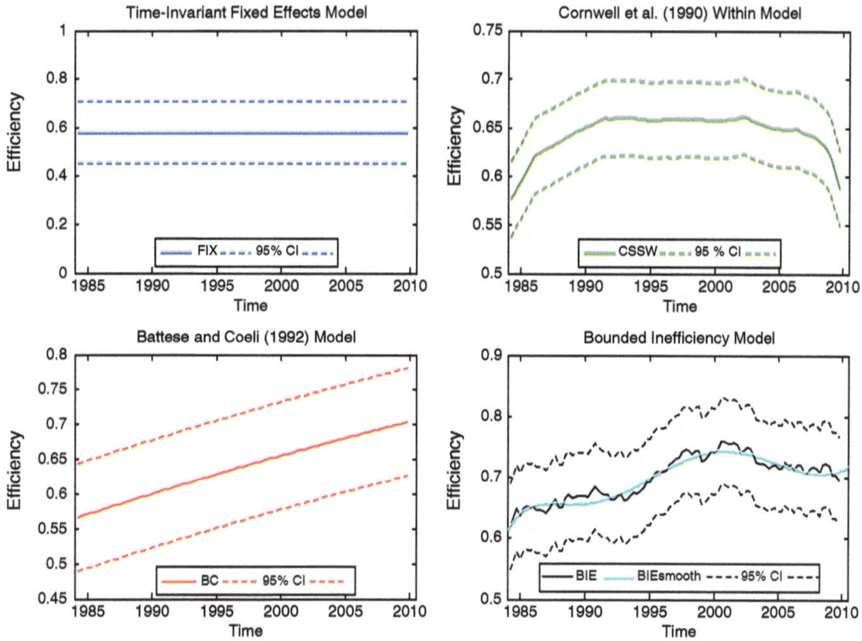

Fig. 3.3 Averaged efficiencies from each estimator

95 % confidence bounds. The BIE averaged efficiencies (panel 4) are significantly higher than those obtained from the fixed effect time-invariant model. However, the differences are small compared to BC and CSSW models. These small differences are not unexpected, however, since the existence of the inefficiency bound implies that the mean conditional distribution of inefficiencies is also bounded from above, resulting in higher average efficiencies. Failing to take the bound into account could possibly yield underestimated mean and individual efficiency scores (see Table 3.1). We smooth the BIE averaged efficiencies by fitting ninth degree polynomial of time in order to capture their trend and also to be able to compare them with other two time-varying averaged efficiency estimates. These are represented by a curve labeled BIEsmooth. It can be seen that the efficiency trend for the BIE model is in close agreement with the CSSW model and better reflects the deregulatory reforms and consolidation of the US commercial banking industry. It is increasing initially and then falls soon after the saving and loans (S&L) crisis of early 1990s began. It has the decreasing pace and reaches its minimum in 1993 a year before Congress passed the Reigle-Neal Act which allowed commercial banks to merge with and acquire banks across the state lines. This spurred a new era of interstate banking and branching, which along with the Gramm-Leach-Billey Act that granted broad-based securities and insurance power to commercial banks, substantially decreased the number of banks operated in the US from 10,453 in 1994 to 8,315 by the end of the millennium. After 1994 the banking industry witnessed a rapid increase in

averaged efficiencies of its institutions due in part to the disappearance of inefficient banks previously sheltered from competitive pressure and due to the expansion of large banks that both financially and geographically diversified their products. The increasing trend continues until the new recessionary period of 2001 and then steadily falls thereafter until the rapid decline illustrating the effects of the 2007–2009 crisis. The CSSW model is able to show the weakness of the banking industry as early as 2005. This weakness is illustrated by the estimated inefficiency bound from the BIE model. On the other hand, the BC model shows a slight, statistically non-significant, upward efficiency trend for all these periods ($\eta = 0.0066$).

In sum, Figs. 3.2 and 3.3 display an interesting findings: on one hand, an upward trend is observed for the average efficiency of the industry, presumably benefiting from the deregulations in the 1980s and 1990s; on the other hand, the industry appears to be more "tolerant" of less efficient banks in the last decade. Possibly, these banks have a characteristic that we have not properly controlled for and we are currently examining this issue. Given the recent experiences in the credit markets due in part to the poor oversight lending authorities gave in their mortgage and other lending activities, our results also may be indicative of a backsliding in the toleration of inefficiency that could have contributed to the problems the financial services industry faces today.

3.8 Conclusions

In this paper we have introduced a series of parametric stochastic frontier models that have upper (lower) bounds on the inefficiency (efficiency). The model parameters can be estimated by maximum likelihood, including the inefficiency bound. The models are easily applicable for both cross-section and panel data settings. In the panel data setting, we set the inefficiency bound to be varying over time, hence contributing another time-varying efficiency model to the literature. We have examined the finite sample performance of the maximum likelihood estimator in the cross-sectional setting. We also have showed how the positive skewness problem inherent in traditional stochastic frontier model can be avoided when the bound is taken into account. An empirical illustration focusing on the US banking industry using the new model revealed intuitive and revealing trends in efficiency scores.

Acknowledgements The idea of addressing the skewness problem in stochastic frontier models via the use of our new Bounded Stochastic Frontier was conjectured by C. A. Knox Lovell in discussions at the presentation of a very preliminary draft of this paper at the Tenth European Workshop on Efficiency and Productivity, Lille, France, June, 2007. Subsequent versions have been presented at the Texas Econometrics Camp XV, Montgomery, Texas, February, 2010; the Efficiency and Productivity Workshop, University of Auckland, New Zealand, February, 2010; the North American Productivity Workshop, Houston, Texas, June 2010; the International Econometrics Workshop, Guanghua Campus (SWUFE), Chengdu, August 12, 2010; and the 10th World Congress of the Econometric Society, Shanghai, August 21, 2010. We would like to thank participants of those conferences and workshops for their helpful comments and insights. We thank Carlos Martins-Filho for his helpful suggestions and criticism. We would especially like to thank

Robert Adams at the Board of Governors of the Federal Reserve System for his guidance and Rob Kuvinka for his excellent research assistance that was essential in our development of the banking data set that we analyze in our empirical illustration. The views expressed by the first author are independent of those of Ernst&Young LLP. The usual caveat applies.

Appendix

First-Order Derivatives of Log-Likelihood Function

The scores for the normal-doubly-truncated normal model that can either be used in a generalized method of moments estimation or in standard mle (3.13) under the γ-parametrization and the $\tilde{B}$-parametrization are:

$$\frac{\partial \ln L}{\partial a} = \sum_{i=1}^{n} \frac{(\varepsilon_i + \mu)x_i}{\sigma^2} + \frac{\sqrt{\gamma/(1-\gamma)}}{\sigma} \sum_{i=1}^{n} x_i \frac{\phi(z_{4i}) - \phi(z_{3i})}{\Phi(z_{3i}) - \Phi(z_{4i})}$$

$$\frac{\partial \ln L}{\partial \gtrapprox^2} = \frac{n}{2\sigma^2} \frac{[(z_1\phi(z_1) - z_2\phi(z_2)]}{\Phi(z_1) - \Phi(z_2)} - \frac{n}{2\sigma^2} + \sum_{i=1}^{n} \frac{(\varepsilon_i + \mu)^2}{2\sigma^4}$$
$$+\frac{1}{2\sigma^2} \sum_{i=1}^{n} \frac{[z_{4i}\phi(z_{4i}) - z_{3i}\varphi(z_{3i})]}{\Phi(z_{3i}) - \Phi(z_{4i})}$$

$$\frac{\partial \ln L}{\partial \lambda} = \frac{n}{\gtrsim} \frac{[(z_1\phi(z_1) - z_2\phi(z_2)]}{\Phi(z_1) - \Phi(z_2)}$$
$$+\frac{1}{\sigma} \sum_{i=1}^{n} \frac{1}{\Phi(z_{3i}) - \Phi(z_{4i})} \Big\{ ((-\ln(\tilde{B}) + \varepsilon_i) \frac{1}{(1-\gamma)^2} \sqrt{(1-\gamma)/\gamma}$$
$$+(\ln(\tilde{B}) + \mu) \frac{1}{\gamma^2} \sqrt{\gamma/(1-\gamma)}) \phi(z_{3i})$$
$$-(\varepsilon_i \frac{1}{(1-\gamma)^2} \sqrt{(1-\gamma)/\gamma} - \mu\lambda \frac{1}{\gamma^2} \sqrt{\gamma/(1-\gamma)}) \phi(z_{4i}) \Big\}$$

$$\frac{\partial \ln(L)}{\partial \mu} = \frac{n}{\sigma\sqrt{\gamma}} \frac{\phi(z_1) - \phi(z_2)}{\Phi(z_1) - \Phi(z_2)} - \sum_{i=1}^{n} \frac{(\varepsilon_i + \mu)}{\sigma^2} + \frac{\sqrt{(1-\gamma)/\gamma}}{\sigma} \sum_{i=1}^{n} \frac{\phi(z_{4i}) - \varphi(z_{3i})}{\Phi(z_{3i}) - \Phi(z_{4i})}$$

$$\frac{\partial \ln(L)}{\partial \tilde{B}} = \frac{n}{\tilde{B}\sigma\sqrt{\gamma}} \frac{\phi(z_1)}{\Phi(z_1) - \Phi(z_2)} - \frac{1}{\tilde{B}\sigma\sqrt{(1-\gamma)\gamma}} \sum_{i=1}^{n} \frac{\phi(z_{3i})}{\Phi(z_{3i}) - \Phi(z_{3i})}$$

where $z_1 = -\frac{(\ln(\tilde{B})+\mu)}{\sigma\sqrt{\gamma}}$, $z_2 = \frac{-\mu}{\sigma\sqrt{\gamma}}$, $z_{3i} = -\frac{(\ln(\tilde{B})-\varepsilon_i)\sqrt{\gamma/(1-\gamma)}+(\ln(\tilde{B})+\mu)\sqrt{(1-\gamma)/\gamma}}{\sigma}$, and $z_{4i} = \frac{\varepsilon_i\sqrt{\gamma/(1-\gamma)}-\mu\sqrt{(1-\gamma)/\gamma}}{\sigma}$. The scores for the normal-truncated half-normal model are obtained after substituting $\mu = 0$ in the above expressions.

The scores for normal-truncated exponential model are derived from (3.17) as

$$\frac{\partial \ln L}{\partial a} = -\frac{\gamma^{-1/2}}{\sigma}\sum_{i=1}^{n} x_i + \frac{(1-\gamma)^{-1/2}}{\sigma}\sum_{i=1}^{n}\frac{\phi(\tilde{z}_{2i})-\phi(\tilde{z}_{1i})}{\Phi(\tilde{z}_{1i})-\Phi(\tilde{z}_{2i})}x_i$$

$$\frac{\partial \ln L}{\partial \sigma} = -\frac{n}{\sigma} - \frac{n\ln\tilde{B}\gamma^{-1/2}}{\sigma^2}\frac{e^{\frac{\ln\tilde{B}\gamma^{-1/2}}{\sigma}}}{1-e^{\frac{\ln\tilde{B}\gamma^{-1/2}}{\sigma}}} + \frac{(1-\gamma)^{-1/2}}{\sigma^2}\sum_{i=1}^{n}\left\{\frac{\phi(\tilde{z}_{2i})-\phi(\tilde{z}_{1i})}{\Phi(\tilde{z}_{1i})-\Phi(\tilde{z}_{2i})}\varepsilon_i + \frac{\phi(\tilde{z}_{1i})}{\Phi(\tilde{z}_{1i})-\Phi(\tilde{z}_{2i})}\ln\tilde{B}\right\}$$

$$\frac{\partial \ln L}{\partial \sigma} = -\frac{n}{2\gamma} - \frac{n\ln\tilde{B}}{2\gamma^{3/2}}\frac{e^{\frac{\ln\tilde{B}\gamma^{-1/2}}{\sigma}}}{1-e^{\frac{\ln\tilde{B}\gamma^{-1/2}}{\sigma}}} - \frac{n}{2\gamma^2} - \frac{1}{2\gamma^{3/2}}\sum_{i=1}^{n}\varepsilon_i - \frac{1}{2}\sum_{i=1}^{n}\left\{\frac{\phi(\tilde{z}_{2i})-\phi(\tilde{z}_{1i})}{\Phi(\tilde{z}_{1i})-\Phi(\tilde{z}_{2i})}\left(\frac{\varepsilon_i}{\sigma(1-\gamma)^{3/2}} - \frac{1}{\gamma^2}\sqrt{\frac{\gamma}{1-\gamma}}\right) - \frac{\ln\tilde{B}}{\sigma(1-\gamma)^{3/2}}\frac{\phi(\tilde{z}_{1i})}{\Phi(\tilde{z}_{1i})-\Phi(\tilde{z}_{2i})}\right\}$$

$$\frac{\partial \ln L}{\partial \tilde{B}} = \frac{n\gamma^{-1/2}}{\sigma\tilde{B}}\frac{e^{\frac{\ln\tilde{B}\gamma^{-1/2}}{\sigma}}}{1-e^{\frac{\ln\tilde{B}\gamma^{-1/2}}{\sigma}}} - \frac{(1-\gamma)^{-1/2}}{\tilde{B}\sigma}\sum_{i=1}^{n}\frac{\phi(\tilde{z}_{1i})}{\Phi(\tilde{z}_{1i})-\Phi(\tilde{z}_{2i})}$$

where $\tilde{z}_{1i} = \frac{(-\ln\tilde{B}+\varepsilon_i)(1-\gamma)^{-1/2}}{\sigma} + \sqrt{\frac{1-\gamma}{\gamma}}$ and $\tilde{z}_{1i} = \frac{\varepsilon_i(1-\gamma)^{-1/2}}{\sigma} + \sqrt{\frac{1-\gamma}{\gamma}}$.

References

Adams RM, Berger AN, Sickles RC (1999) Semiparametric approaches to stochastic panel frontiers with applications in the banking industry. J Bus Econ Stat 17:349–358

Afriat SN (1972) Efficiency estimation of production functions. Int Econ Rev 13:568–598

Aigner D, Lovell CAK, Schmidt P (1977) Formulation and estimation of stochastic frontier production function models. J Econom 6:21–37

Alchian AA (1950) Uncertainty, evolution, and economic theory. J Political Econom 58:211–221

Almanidis P (2013) Accounting for heterogeneous technologies in the banking industry: a time-varying stochastic frontier model with threshold effects. J Product Anal 39(2):191–205
Almanidis P, Sickles RC (2011) Skewness problem in stochastic frontier models: fact or fiction? In: Van Keilegom I, Wilson P (eds) Exploring research frontiers in contemporary statistics and econometrics: a festschrift in Honor of Leopold Simar. Springer, New York
Almanidis P, Sickles RC (2012) Banking crises, early warning models, and efficiency, Mimeo, Rice University
Balk BM (2008) Price and quantity index numbers: models for measuring aggregate change and difference. Cambridge University, New York
Battese GE, Coelli TJ (1992) Frontier production functions, technical efficiency and panel data, with application to paddy farmers in India. J Product Anal 3:153–169
Battese GE, Corra G (1977) Estimation of a production frontier model: with application to the pastoral zone of eastern Australia. Aust J Agric Econ 21:167–179
Bera AK, Premaratne G (2001) Adjusting the tests for skewness and kurtosis for distributional misspecifications. UIUC-CBA Research Working Paper No. 01-0116
Carree MA (2002) Technological inefficiency and the skewness of the error component in stochastic frontier analysis. Econ Lett 77:101–107
Coelli T (2000) On the econometric estimation of the distance function representation of a production technology. Center for Operations Research & Econometrics, Universite Catholique de Louvain
Cornwell C, Schmidt P, Sickles RC (1990) Production frontiers with cross-sectional and time series variation in efficiency levels. J Econom 46:185–200
Cragg JG (1997) Using higher moments to estimate the simple errors-in-variables model. RAND J Econ 28(Special Issue in Honor of Richard E. Quandt):S71–S91
Dagenais M, Dagenais D (1997) Higher moment estimators for linear regression models with errors in the variables. J Econom 76:193–221
Davidson R, MacKinnon JG (1993) Estimation and inference in econometrics. Oxford University Press, New York
Demsetz H (1973) Industry structure, market rivalry, and public policy. J Law Econ 16:1–9
Entani T, Maeda Y, Tanaka H (2002) Dual models of interval DEA and its extension to interval data. Eur J Oper Res 136:32–45
Feng Q, Horrace W, Wu GL (2012) Wrong skewness and finite sample correction in parametric stochastic frontier models. Mimeo
Frye J, Pelz E (2008) BankCaR (bank capital-at-risk): US commercial bank chargeoffs. Working paper # 3, Federal Reserve Bank of Chicago
Goldberger A (1968) The interpretation and estimation of Cobb-Douglas functions. Econometrica 35:464–472
Greene WH (1980a) Maximum likelihood estimation of econometric frontier functions. J Econom 13:27–56
Greene WH (1980b) On the estimation of a flexible frontier production model. J Econom 13: 101–115
Greene WH (1990) A gamma distributed stochastic frontier model. J Econom 46:141–164
Greene WH (2007) The econometric approach to efficiency analysis In: Fried HO, Lovell CAK, Schmidt SS (eds) The measurement of productive efficiency: techniques and applications. Oxford University Press, New York
Guilkey DK, Lovell CAK, Sickles RC (1983) A comparison of the performance of three flexible functional forms. Int Econ Rev 24:591–616
Hansen BE (1996) Inference when a nuisance parameter is not identified under the null hypothesis. Econometrica 64:413–430
Hansen BE (1999) Threshold effects in non-dynamic panels: estimation, testing, and inference. J Econom 93:345–368
Hicks JR (1935) Annual survey of economic theory: the theory of monopoly. Econometrica 3:1–20
Hughes JP, Mester LJ (1993) A quality and risk-adjusted cost function for banks: evidence on the "too-big-to-fail" doctrine. J Product Anal 4:293–315

Inanoglu H, Jacobs M Jr (2009) Models for risk aggregation and sensitivity analysis: an application to bank economic capital. J Risk Financ Manag 2:118–189
Klein L (1953) Textbook of econometrics. Row, Peterson and Company, New York
Kneip A, Sickles RC, Song W (2012) A new panel data treatment for heterogeneity in time trends. Econom Theory 28:590–628
Kumbhakar SC (1990) Production frontiers, panel data, and time-varying technical efficiency. J Econom 46:201–212
Kutlu L (2013) Misspecification in allocative efficiency: a simulation study. Econ Lett 118: 151–154
Kutlu L, Sickles RC (2012) Estimation of market power in the presence of firm level inefficiencies. J Econom 168:141–155
Lee L (1993) Asymptotic distribution of the maximum likelihood estimator for a stochastic frontier function model with a singular information matrix. Econom Theory 9:413–430
Lee YH, Schmidt P (1993) A production frontier model with flexible temporal variation in technical efficiency. In: Fried HO, Lovell CAK, Schmidt P (eds) The measurement of productive efficiency: techniques and applications. Oxford University Press, New York
Lewbel A (2012) Using heteroskedasticity to identify and estimate mismeasured and endogenous regressor models. J Bus Econ Stat 30:67–80
Lovell CAK, Richardson S, Travers P, Wood L (1994) Resources and functionings: a new view of inequality in Australia. In: Eichhorn W (ed) Models and measurements of welfare and inequality. Springer, Berlin
Marschak J, Andrews WH (1944) Random simultaneous equations and the theory of production. Econometrica 12:143–203
Matzkin R (2012) Nonparametric identification, Mimeo, UCLA Department of Economics
Meeusen W, van den Broeck J (1977) Efficiency estimation from Cobb-Douglas production function with composed error. Int Econ Rev 18:435–444
Nerlove M (1965) Estimation and identification of Cobb-Douglas production functions. Rand McNally, Chicago
Newey WK, Powell JL (2003) Instrumental variable estimation of nonparametric models. Econometrica 71:1565–1578
Olson JA, Schmidt P, Waldman DM (1980) A Monte Carlo study of estimators of the stochastic frontier production function. J Econom 13:67–82
Orea L, Steinbuks J (2012) Estimating market power in homogenous product markets using a composed error model: application to the California electricity market. EPRG Working Paper 1210, CWPE Working Paper 1220
Rao CR (1973) Linear statistical inference and its applications, 2nd edn. Wiley, New York
Richmond J (1974) Estimating the efficiency of production. Int Econ Rev 15:515–521
Rothenberg TJ (1971) Identification in parametric models. Econometrica 39(3):577–591
Samuelson PA (1979) Paul Douglas's measurement of production functions and marginal productivities. J Political Econ 87(Part 1):923–939
Schmidt P, Sickles RC (1984) Production frontiers and panel data. J Bus Econ Stat 2:367–374
Sickles RC, Hao J, Shang C (2013) Productivity and panel data. In: Baltagi B (ed) Chapter 17 of Oxford handbook of panel data. Oxford University Press, New York (forthcoming)
Simar L, Wilson PW (2010) Estimation and inference in cross-sectional, stochastic frontier models. Econom Rev 29:62–98
Stevenson RE (1980) Likelihood functions for generalized stochastic frontier estimation. J Econom 13:57–66
Stigler GS (1958) The economies of scale. J Law Econ 1:54–71
Tamer E (2010) Partial identification in econometrics. Annu Rev Econ 2:167–195
Waldman DM (1982) A stationary point for the stochastic frontier likelihood. J Econom 18: 275–279
Wang WS, Schmidt P (2008) On the distribution of estimated technical efficiency in stochastic frontier models. J Econom 148:36–45

Wheelock D, Wilson P (2000) Why do banks disappear? The determinants of US bank failures and acquisitions. Rev Econ Stat 82(1):127–138

Wheelock DC, Wilson PW (2012) Do large banks have lower costs? New estimates of returns to scale for US banks. J Money Credit Bank 44:171–199

Zellner A, Kmenta J, Dreze J (1966) Specification and estimation of Cobb-Douglas production function models. Econometrica 34:784–795

Chapter 4
Estimating Consumer Surplus in eBay Computer Monitor Auctions

Kevin Hasker, Bibo Jiang, and Robin C. Sickles

JEL Classification: C22, C51

4.1 Introduction and Brief Discussion of the Consumer Surplus Auction Literature

It is well established that eBay is a significant economic marketplace. Economists have long hailed the price discovery power of auctions, but unfortunately the cost of establishing a cohesive market place prevented their widespread usage. eBay overcame this problem by allowing people to auction items over the Internet. Because of this eBay has become a significant marketplace, and due to the economies of the marketplace it is likely to remain one in the future. It is still unclear, however, the degree to which eBay benefits the economy. One measure of this benefit is the consumer surplus that eBay generates. Our paper measures this important economic fundamental in the market for computer monitors.

There are, however, important methodological issues that must be addressed in any empirical study of auctions. As has been shown for second price private-value

K. Hasker (✉)
Economics Department, Bilkent University, 06800 Bilkent, Ankara, Turkey
e-mail: hasker@bilkent.edu.tr

B. Jiang
School of Economics, Fudan University, 600 Guoquan Road, Shanghai 200433, China
e-mail: jiangbibo@fudan.edu.cn

R.C. Sickles
Department of Economics, Rice University, 6100 South Main Street,
Houston, TX 77005-1892, USA
e-mail: rsickles@rice.edu

R.C. Sickles and W.C. Horrace (eds.), *Festschrift in Honor of Peter Schmidt: Econometric Methods and Applications*, DOI 10.1007/978-1-4899-8008-3_4,

auctions considered in this paper, the standard model is nonparametrically identified and nonparametric methods can be employed. Our paper employs the technique proposed in Song (2004) with some adjustments to allow for the semi-nonparametric estimation of consumer surplus. Estimates of consumer surplus based on semi-nonparametric estimation of the bidding function also can be analyzed along with estimates generated from parametric analysis with the same data. Such parametric models of the bidding function, although not nonparametrically identified, can utilize a much larger set of our data and they provide a useful robustness check for our semi-nonparametric results. Fully nonparametric estimates of consumer surplus also can be derived and yield yet another method of comparison.

Our research also provides a new methodology for estimating consumer surplus. This methodology relies on a strong assumption of homogeneity in the pool of potential bidders as new auctions for the same generic product are conducted. This method is robust to tail probability properties of the underlying and nonparametrically specified distribution of private values. Essentially this methodology considers a counter factual wherein, if the price setting bidder in auction t' won auction t, then the consumer surplus would be the average over the t' that could have won the given auction. In distribution free estimations this would be the only feasible manner to estimate consumer surplus. In our paper it provides yet another set of robustness checks on our estimates.

We thus consider six different methods to calculate the consumer surplus and consumer share of the total surplus in our auction data. Although there is significant variation among these estimates, they do provide relatively tight bound for the consumer surplus for the auctioned good we analyze, computer monitors. According to our semi-nonparametric analysis, the median consumer surplus per computer monitor may be as high as \$51 or as low as \$17 with a median value of \$28. The median lower bound on the consumer share of surplus may be as high as 62.9 % or as low as 9.5 % with a median value of 19.0 %.

Using a spider program we collected data on over 9,000 computer monitors auctioned on eBay between February 23, 2000 and June 11, 2000 (Gonzalez 2002; Gonzalez et al. 2009). Lucking-Reiley et al. (2007) utilized a spider program to collect eBay data on 461 "U.S. Cent" category auctions held at eBay over a 30-day period during July and August of 1999.[1] Recent methods for accessing data via "spider" programs have become commonplace.[2] We also discuss the data collection techniques that allowed us to construct our relatively large set of auction data.

Relatively few attempts have been made to estimate consumer surplus in auction models, although this is presumably one of the arguments in favor of such mechanisms. Song (2004) constructs an innovative methodology using the second

[1]Specifically, Lucking-Reiley et al. (2007) focused on U.S. Indian Head pennies minted between 1859 and 1909, auctions in which only one coin was for sale, and the coin was in mint state (MS) with grades of between 60 and 66 on a 70-point scale.

[2]See, for example, the website at http://www.baywotch.de/. We thank Rouwen Hahn from the University of Münster, Germany for this information.

and third highest bids and estimates the median consumer surplus in university yearbook auctions at \$25.54. With a median price in her study of \$22.50, the median consumer share of the surplus is 53 %. Bapna et al. (2008) also estimates consumer surplus, utilizing an innovative data collection technique that allows them to directly observe a bidder's stated value. With their rather heterogenous data, however, they cannot estimate a structural bidding function. They do, however, find that consumers capture around 18.3 % of the total surplus. Several other articles estimate consumer surplus in multi-unit auctions—Carare (2001), Bapna et al. (2003a,b) and Bapna et al. (2004)—but these papers primarily focus on mechanism design issues and tend to use ad hoc techniques since the equilibrium bidding function in general multi-unit auctions is unknown.

eBay has two different auction formats. The common format is an English auction with a hard stop time. This is the type of auction used in 87 % of our original data set and the type of auctions on which we focus. When our data was collected, bidding went from 3 to 10 days and then stopped at a preset time.

Our estimation techniques are based on a modification of the methods developed in Song (2004). As discussed in Bulbul Toklu (2010), there have been several techniques identified for estimating bidders' values in online auctions. In order to nonparametrically identify his model, Adams (2007) assumes exogenous entry and that entry is not affected by any variables that affect bidders values. Parametric structural analysis of the bidding function and the entry rule can relax these assumptions, albeit at the cost of not being nonparametrically identified. Such structural analysis rejects these assumptions with our data but relies on the strong assumption that the pool of potential entrants is quite large. Nekipelov (2007) introduces an endogenous entry rule, wherein a rise in the auction price is assumed to decrease the probability of entry but increase the average bid conditional on entry. However, his model relies on the explicit calculation of the equilibrium bidding function at all parameter values and thus limits the computational appeal of his approach when there are a reasonable number of covariates. His model also requires the assumption that all bidders use the nonparametrically identified but rather opaque and complex equilibrium bidding functions. Nekipelov's model can explain both squat bidding (bid early to deter others from bidding: Ely and Hossain 2009) and snipe bidding (bid at the last second to deter counter bidding: Roth and Ockenfels 2002). In contrast to the complex equilibrium bidding functions used by Nekipelov (2007) Song (2004) only assumes that the second, some of the third highest bidders bid their true value. It is known that not all the third bidders will bid their true value, but her methodology allows one to test which bids should not be used. Her model also allows for exogenous entry, endogenous entry (for a range of models), and heterogeneous entry decisions and utilizes a relatively straightforward rule to determine how much to bid. One weakness of all these models is that they do not take into consideration the exit value of bidders. In an eBay auction this value may be significant. The only paper currently in the literature that takes this into consideration is Sailer (2006). Formally these models must rely on the *steady state hypothesis* (Hasker and Sickles 2010) and the distribution is only identified up to a shift parameter.

There also several parametric techniques that deserve special mention, though currently none of these techniques are nonparametrically identified. Bajari and Hortaçsu (2003) develop a Bayesian methodology, but require that the bidding functions be linearly scalable. Non-linear simulated least squares, developed by Laffont et al. (1995) and used in Gonzalez et al. (2009), is another estimation methodology. This approach overcomes the complexity of calculating the likelihood function by simulating the auctions, and it is a flexible methodology that can be used for any bidding model in which revenue equivalence holds.

We organize our discussion of methods to analyze consumer surplus in eBay auction in the following way. Section 4.2 reviews our econometric methodology. Section 4.3 describes the data used in our estimation. Section 4.4 discusses our results. Sections 4.5 and 4.6 develop various measures of Consumer Surplus and Consumer Share of Surplus generated in our auctions and provides estimates of these measures. Section 4.7 concludes.

4.2 Econometric Methodology

Athey and Haile (2002, 2005) show that the underlying distribution of private values is uniquely determined if the distribution of any order statistic with a known number of bidders is identified. However, in eBay auctions, the number of potential bidders is generally not observable. Song (2004) addressed this issue by proving that, within the symmetric independent private values model, observations of any two valuations whose ranking is known can nonparametrically identify the bidders' underlying value distribution. Song goes on to point out that one can use the second and third highest bids to identify the distribution of bidders' private values. This approach is not without attendant problems, however, since whether or not the third highest bids reflect the third highest bidders' true private valuations can be questioned. To deal with this issue, Song suggests that one should use data wherein either the third highest bidder had a good reason to believe she could win the auction or the higher bids were submitted late. She develops an econometric test to discover which third highest bids can be used. We will adopt her methodology to pursue our nonparametric estimation of consumer surplus from eBay auctions. We also follow Haile and Tamer (2003) by first assuming that bidders adhere to two intuitive rules:

1. No bidder ever bids more than he is willing to pay.
2. No bidder allows opponents to win at a price he is willing to pay.
   These rules are transparent and appealing, and guarantee that the second highest bidder will bid his value. Unfortunately the conditions are not sufficient for identification. As Haile and Tamer (2003) show, there are equilibria in second price auctions (and eBay auctions) in which these rules do not imply that the third highest bidder bids his true value. Thus we make a third assumption

3. A finite number of bids from the third highest bidder reflect the bidders' true value.
4. We will thus need to examine which bids are the third highest bidders true value. We should mention that this is not only a theoretical problem. Empirical evidence also shows that bidders do not bid their true value on eBay. To give an example to illustrate, assume that a bidder bids \$50 for an item which he values at \$80, and two other bidders immediately bid \$100. After observing the higher bid of \$100, this bidder will not update his bid and his final bid will be less than his value. On the other hand if only one bidder makes a bid higher than \$80, and another bidder bids between \$50 and \$80, the given bidder will update his bid to his value \$80. In this case the bidder bids more than once. This would not occur were bidders to bid their values. In other words, the existence of multiple bids is evidence that bidders are not bidding their value, and in fact there frequently are multiple bids per active bidder on eBay. Song (2004) points out that if the two highest bids are submitted right before the end of the auction (for example, within the last minute of the auction) then the third highest bid will almost certainly be that bidder's true value. In this case the third highest bidder must know that if he raises his bid then he might win the auction and thus his final bid must be his true value. This approach therefore requires that the third highest bidders who outbid in the last minute are bidding their value. One then tests whether or not bidders outbid at earlier times are using the same bidding rule. We also make a relatively standard assumption about the bidder's values in our next condition.
5. Bidders' values are private, independent, and log-linear in a set of auction specific characteristics. Private values are given by:

$$\ln V_{m|i} = x_m^{'}\beta + v_{m|i}, \tag{4.1}$$

with $m = 1, \ldots, M$, where M is the number of auctions and $i = 1, 2 \ldots, N_m$, where N_m is the number of potential bidders in auction m. For the estimation procedure we outline below, we require the potential number of bidders in any auction to be greater or equal to 3. We note that the standard assumption of private values is proscribed for the good under consideration. At the time of data collection computer monitors were subject to rapid technological development, thus anyone considering buying a monitor would know that the value of the monitor would decrease sharply in as little time as 6 months. It is also a relatively standard good, thus there would not be much information discovery from bids.

$V_{m|2}$ and $V_{m|3}$ represent the second and third highest bidders' valuations in auction m, respectively. We use the second and third highest bids as estimates of these two valuations. $v_{m|2}$, and $v_{m|3}$ are the corresponding error terms. x_m is the control variable including 7 auction specific characteristics that we specify below, $\beta = [\beta_1, \cdots, \beta_7]$ is the corresponding vector of coefficients. We consider the sample counterpart of conditional likelihood function $f\left(v_{m|2} \mid v_{m|3}\right)$ specified by Song (2004), since the full likelihood (the joint density of $\left(v_{m|2}, v_{m|3}\right)$) requires the unknown number of potential bidders. According to the basic theory of order statistics, the sample likelihood function can be written as:

$$L_M\left(\hat{f}\right) = \frac{1}{M}\sum_{m=1}^{M} \ln \frac{2\left[1-\hat{F}\left(v_{m|2}\right)\right]\hat{f}\left(v_{m|2}\right)}{\left[1-\hat{F}\left(v_{m|3}\right)\right]^2}, \tag{4.2}$$

where $\hat{F}(v) = \int_c^v \hat{f}(z)\,dz$. Here and below, c is the lower bound of bidders' private value. We choose $c = \min_{m=1,2,\dots M}\left(\log(V_{m|3})\right)$, since no information about $F(v)$ for $v < c$ can be observed. The reader should note that with our objective function this value does not affect our estimates. In order to estimate the unknown distribution of v we employ the method proposed by Coppejans and Gallant (2002) and use the hermite series to approximate the unknown distribution. Gallant and Nychka (1987), Fenton and Gallant (1996) and Coppejans and Gallant (2002) provide details on how to use this method to approximate the unknown distribution of private values. The optimal series length varies according to the data set under consideration. Coppejans and Gallant (2002) proposed a cross-validation strategy by employing the Integrated Squared Error (ISE) criterion to choose the optimal series length k^*. The ISE in their paper is defined as:

$$\begin{aligned} ISE\left(\hat{f}\right) &= \int \hat{f}^2(y)\,dy - 2\int \hat{f}(y)\,f(y)\,dy + \int f^2(y)\,dy \\ &= M_{(1)} - 2M_{(2)} + M_{(3)} \end{aligned} \tag{4.3}$$

Here, $\hat{f}(y)$ is an estimator of true density $f(y)$ of interest.

Here what we are interested is a conditional density. Along the line of Coppejans and Gallant (2002), we propose Weighted Integrated Squared Error (WISE) which serves as our criteria in selecting the optimal series length. WISE is defined as follows:

$$\begin{aligned} WISE(\hat{f}) &= \int\int (\hat{f}(y|x) - f(y|x))^2 f(x)dydx \\ &= \int\int \hat{f}(y|x)^2 dy f(x)dx - 2\int\int \hat{f}(y|x)f(y|x)f(x)dydx \\ &\quad + \int\int f(y|x)^2 dy f(x)dx \\ &= Q_1 - 2Q_2 + Q_3, \end{aligned} \tag{4.4}$$

where $\hat{f}(y|x)$ is an estimator of true conditional density $f(y|x)$. In implementing the cross-validation strategy, first, we randomly partition the data set under consideration into 5 groups, denoted by χ_j, $j = 1,\dots,5$, making the sizes of these groups as close to equal as possible. Let $\hat{f}_{j,k}(\cdot)$ denote the semi-nonparametric estimate obtained from the sub-sample that remains after deletion of the j'th group when k is used as a series length. The cumulative distribution associated with $\hat{f}_{j,k}(\cdot)$ is denoted by $\hat{F}_{j,k}(\cdot)$. Since the third term only involves true densities, we only need to look at the first two terms. The estimates of the two terms are defined as below:

$$\hat{Q}_1(k) = 1/M \sum_{j=1}^{5} \sum_{(x_m, y_m) \in \chi_j} \int [\hat{f}_{j,k}(y|x_m)]^2 dy \tag{4.5}$$

$$\hat{Q}_2(k) = 1/M \sum_{j=1}^{5} \sum_{(x_m, y_m) \in \chi_j} \hat{f}_{j,k}(y_m|x_m). \tag{4.6}$$

We also define

$$CVH\,(k) = \hat{Q}_1\,(k) - 2\hat{Q}_2\,(k)\,. \tag{4.7}$$

It is worth mentioning that our criteria is WISE, and hence $\hat{Q}_1(k)$ and $\hat{Q}_2(k)$ are not the same as what were defined in Song (2004). According to Coppejans and Gallant (2002), a typical graph of $CVH\,(k)$ versus k is that $CVH\,(k)$ falls as k increases when k is small, periodically drops abruptly, and flattens right after the final abrupt drop. They recommend a choice of k which brings the last abrupt drop of $CVH\,(k)$. Our result is listed in Table 4.9 and shows that the abrupt drop of $CVH\,(k)$ occurs when k changes from 1 to 2. The small increase in $CVH(k)$when k changes from 3 to 4 is likely due to overfitting. The CVH approach proposed in Coppejans and Gallant (2002) is Hold-out-sample Cross-validation. As k increases, over-fitting the estimation sample can generate a poor estimate of the underlying distribution and may lead to a higher CVH value.

The density function of v_m follows immediately as:

$$f\,(v_m) = \frac{\left[1 + a_1\left(\frac{v_m - u}{\sigma}\right) + a_2\left(\frac{v_m - u}{\sigma}\right)^2\right]^2 \phi\,(v_m; u, \sigma, c)}{\int_c^{\infty}\left[1 + a_1\left(\frac{z-u}{\sigma}\right) + a_2\left(\frac{z-u}{\sigma}\right)^2\right]^2 \phi\,(z; u, \sigma, c)\, dz}. \tag{4.8}$$

The nonparametric maximum likelihood estimator is then defined as:

$$\begin{aligned}\left(\hat{\beta}, \hat{a}, \hat{u}, \hat{\sigma}\right) &= \arg \max_{(\beta, a_1, a_2, u) \in \mathbb{R}^{10}, \sigma \in \mathbb{R}_{++}} L_M\left(\hat{f}\right) \\ &= \arg \max_{(\beta, a_1, a_2, u) \in \mathbb{R}^{10}, \sigma \in \mathbb{R}_{++}} \frac{1}{M} \sum_{m=1}^{M} \ln \frac{2\left[1 - \hat{F}\left(v_{m|2}\right)\right] \hat{f}\left(v_{m|2}\right)}{\left[1 - \hat{F}\left(v_{m|3}\right)\right]^2}.\end{aligned} \tag{4.9}$$

One criticism of this method is that the third highest bids may not reflect the bidders' private values since they utilize the second and third highest bids as estimates of the second and the third highest bidders' private values. We follow Song (2004) by using data in which the first or second highest bidder submitted a cutoff price greater than the third highest bid late in the auction. To determine how late is sufficient, Song (2004) provides a method based on the CVH using a modified formula for $\hat{Q}_1$ and $\hat{Q}_2$. Following her method, we consider a sequence of 6 sub data sets, $A_{w1}, \cdots, A_{w6}$, with different window sizes, arbitrarily chosen so that the size difference between two adjacent subsets is similar. We choose window sizes as $w1 = 5\,\text{min}$, $w2 = 15\,\text{min}$, $w3 = 40\,\text{min}$, $w4 = 2\,\text{h}$, $w5 = 3.5\,\text{h}$ and $w6$ is all. A_{w1} represents the auction set in which the first or second highest bidder submits a bid greater than the third highest bid no earlier than 5 min before the auction ends. Other sub data sets are defined in the similar way. Obviously, we have $A_{w1} \subset A_{w2} \subset \cdots \subset A_{w6}$. It is intuitive that the third highest bids are more likely to reflect the third highest valuations for auctions in set A_{w1} than auctions in other sub sets. However, A_{w1} has the least number of observations and thus a potentially larger sample variance. Song's approach considers this trade-off by applying the same cross-validation strategy that is used for choosing the optimal series length and suggests choosing the window size which has the smallest CVH_{wi}. For each auction set A_{wi}, we calculate CVH_{wi}. Corresponding to Eq. (4.7), CVH_{wi} is defined as

$$CVH_{wi}(k^*) = \hat{Q}_{1_{wi}}(k^*) - 2\hat{Q}_{2_{wi}}(k^*),$$

where

$$\hat{Q}_{1_{wi}}(k^*) = 1/M_{wi} \sum_{j=1}^{5} \sum_{(x_m, y_m) \in \chi_j \cap A_{wi}} \int [\hat{f}_{j,k^*}(y|x_m)]^2 dy$$

$$\hat{Q}_{2_{wi}}(k^*) = 1/M_{wi} \sum_{j=1}^{5} \sum_{(x_m, y_m) \in \chi_j \cap A_{wi}} \hat{f}_{j,k^*}(y_m|x_m),$$

where M_{wi} is the sample size of subset A_{wi}. We present the results in Table 4.10. It is clear that CVH_{wi} decreases when window size increases from $w1$ to $w4$. The values of CVH_{w4} and CVH_{w5} are almost identical to each other. The change of window size from $w5$ to $w6$ causes a dramatic increase in CVH_{wi}. Since our analysis is based on semi-nonparametric and nonparametric methods, we want to keep as much data as possible. We choose $w5 = 3.5\,\text{h}$ instead of $w4 = 2\,\text{h}$ as our optimal window size since the difference between CVH_{w4} and CVH_{w5} is rather small.

4.3 The Data Set and Our Collection Techniques

At the time our data set was collected, eBay saved all information about closed auctions on their website for a month after the auction closed. This allowed people who participated in the auction to verify the outcome and provides the source for our data set. Our data was collected using a "spider" program which periodically searches eBay for recently closed computer monitor auctions and downloads the pages giving the item description and the bid history. Software development was done in Python—a multi-platform, multi-OS, object-oriented programming language. It is divided into three parts. It first goes to eBay's site and collects the item description page and the bidding history page. It next parses the web pages and makes a database entry for each closed auction. The final part iterates through the stored database entries and creates a tab-delimited ASCII file.

The original data processing program did not process all of the data. It provided us with the core of the data which was augmented with further processing of the raw html files. Using string searches we have managed to collect extensive descriptive information for the entire data set. With further data processing we have managed to collect all of the bidding histories.

Running this program from February 23, 2000 to June 11, 2000 we were able to capture information on approximately 9,000 English auctions of computer monitors, effectively all monitors auctioned during that time period. We excluded any non-working, touch screen, LCD monitors, Apple monitors, or other types of monitors that are bought for different purposes than the monitors in our sample. Also, if there were any bid retractions or cancellations (this happened in 7.4 % of the auctions) we dropped the observation because the retractions might indicate collusion. We also deleted several auctions in which the auctioneer cancelled the auction early (usually within 10–15 min of the beginning of the auction.)

Descriptive variables except for monitor size were constructed using string searches. In Gonzalez et al. (2009) the strings that were used for each variable are detailed. This allowed us to collect data on whether there was a secret reservation price, whether it was met, monitor resolutions, dot pitch, whether a warranty was offered, several different brand names, whether the monitor was new, like-new, or refurbished, and whether it was a flat screened monitor. "Brand name" is used for monitors that are from one of the ten largest firms represented in our data set. These firms are Sony, Compaq, NEC, IBM, Hewlett Packard, Dell, Gateway, Viewsonic, Sun, and Hitachi in order of size. Sony has close to a 10 % market share while the smallest have close to a 3 % market share. These ten firms represent 59 % of the market. Dot pitch and resolution are not reported in all of the auctions. Dot Pitch is reported in 42 % of the auctions, resolution in 64 %.

Since selecting a relatively homogeneous data set is important in conducting and interpreting results from nonparametric analysis we dropped all auctions that were not clearly for 17″ color PC monitors. Monitor size has the most pronounced and significant effect on bidders' private values. Since we need information for both the second and third highest bids in order to estimate the models, we dropped the auctions that had less than three bidders. As this sample is relatively more competitive than the original sample, owing to a higher number of bidders, we refer to this sample as the "competitive" sample. This gives us 476 observations. To makc the data set even more homogeneous, we also drop 12 auctions in which warranties were offered on the auctioned monitors. Our final data set has 464 observations.

In estimating the distribution of bidders' private values with the semi-nonparametric approach, we used the following seven control variables: monitor dot pitch (0 is used when no dot pitch is reported), dummy for the cases when no dot pitch is reported, monitor resolution (0 is used when no resolution is reported), dummy for the cases when no resolution is reported, condition of auctioned items (2 for new, 1 for like new or refurbished, 0 for no condition report), dummy for flat screen and dummy for brand name. We use 1 for both "like new" and "refurbished" because we did not see significant sample mean difference for these two categories and there are only 17 observations with condition specified as "like new" in our sample. Descriptive statistics of the variables for the sample are presented in Table 4.8.

Notice that we do not use auctioneer's feedback rating—a reputation system on eBay—in our estimates. While this variable may affect entry under the private value assumption it cannot affect bids conditional on entry.

4.4 Estimates

For the results that follow we choose the optimal hermite series number as $k^* = 2$ and the optimal window size as $w5 = 3.5$ h, i.e., we choose the auctions where the first or second highest bidder submitted a bid greater than the third highest bid no earlier than 3.5 h before the auction ended. This yields a sample of 376 observations on which to base our semi-nonparametric estimates of consumer surplus. The estimated parameters are in Table 4.1.

Table 4.1 Semi-nonparametric estimates

Dot pitch	−7.9842[a]
.	(0.1310)
Dummy, no dot pitch	−1.9606[a]
.	(0.0347)
Resolution	0.0486[a]
.	(0.0051)
Dummy, no resolution	−0.1024[a]
.	(0.0060)
Dummy, brand name	−0.0465[a]
.	(0.0005)
Dummy, flat screen	−0.0769[a]
.	(0.0004)
Status	0.0568[a]
.	(0.0001)
Number of auctions	376

[a]Significant at the 1 % confidence level

Table 4.2 Statistics of estimated distribution

	Mean	Standard deviation
SNP	\$30.18	\$26.77
NP	\$28.26	\$26.63

The coefficients except for the ones on "Brand Name" and "Flat Screen" dummies have the expected sign and are highly significant. A smaller dot pitch is better so we expect the coefficient on the log of dot pitch to be negative, likewise a larger resolution and better condition are both good so those coefficients should be positive. When no dot pitch or resolution are reported the bidders expect a worse than average value for these variables. "Brand Name" means popular brand, which includes ten brands in our data set. There is no consensus on what the sign should be for the variable "Brand Name". Both positive and negative results have been seen in literature. In our study, we find a negative effect of "Brand Name" on bidders' private value. The coefficient on "Flat Screen" is negative and significant which does not suit our intuition. However, since the magnitude of the estimate is tiny, we have a reason to believe that the "Flat dummy" does not play an important role in determining the bidder's private. Of course, another possible reason for the incorrect sign on "Flat dummy" might be because we use semi-nonparametric estimation method.

Our consumer surplus estimates are based on these coefficients. Because the data we use for the analysis is relatively homogeneous, we also present nonparametric results as comparison. In the nonparametric estimation, we use Song's method without considering the control variables. The estimated expectation and standard deviation of bidders' private valuation are in Table 4.2. SNP and NP denote semi-nonparametric and nonparametric methods respectively.

In the semi-nonparametric analysis, the mean, standard deviation are computed with the median values of $x_1, x_2, \cdots$, and x_7.

4.5 Structural Consumer Surplus and Consumer Share of Surplus

In order to investigate the welfare impact of eBay, we calculate the consumer surplus and consumer share of surplus. Consumer surplus in auction m is calculated as:

$$CS_m = V_{m|1} - p_m, \tag{4.10}$$

where p_m denotes the price the winner paid, which equals to the second highest bid in eBay auctions. $V_{m|1}$ denotes the valuation of the winner. Since we do not observe $V_{m|1}$, we estimate the expected consumer surplus as:

$$E\left(CS_m|\hat{V}_{m|2}\right) = e^{x_m'\hat{\beta}} \int_{\hat{v}_{m|2}}^{\infty} \frac{f(v)}{1 - F\left(\hat{v}_{m|2}\right)} e^{v} dv - p_m \tag{4.11}$$

Table 4.3 Structural consumer surplus

	Mean	Median	Std. dev.	Min	Max
SNP	\$28.32	\$28.31	\$3.85	\$16.94	\$51.06
NP	\$28.57	\$28.31	\$1.57	\$19.28	\$39.28
PL	\$52.54	\$39.69	\$38.23	\$13.51	\$210.09

Again, $\hat{v}_{m|2}$ is the estimator of $v_{m|2}$ calculated based on model (4.1) with estimated coefficient $\hat{\beta}$ and x_m, which is the vector of the values of control variables in auction m; and p_m is the price. For comparison we include the parametric estimates(PL) wherein private values are distributed as half-logistic. These preferred estimates are based on a battery of nonparametric good-of-fit tests of a number of parametric distributions for private values. The descriptive statistics of expected consumer surplus from our SNP, NP methods, and PL approaches are presented in Table 4.3.

Notice that the distribution of consumer surplus based on the parametric method is highly skewed. For this reason here and below we focus on the median values, not the averages, for comparison among the three methodologies, since for the SNP and NP estimates the median and mean are quite similar. There could be at least two reasons for the significant divergence of parametric and semi-nonparametric and nonparametric estimates. Of course one reason could be the more flexible distribution of private values in the semi-nonparametric and nonparametric methodologies. However, it could be because the auctions used for the semi-nonparametric and nonparametric auctions are more competitive. Since in order to estimate the semi-nonparametric and nonparametric models, all auctions with less than three bidders were dropped and thus the average number of bidders in the semi-nonparametric and nonparametric data subset is 8.1, versus 6.8 for the parametric data set. Since we use the parametric estimates of the coefficients to estimate the consumer surplus, the results are still distribution dependent.

While the amount of consumer surplus in an auction is a significant statistic it reveals only one dimension of the surplus being generated. If the value of the average monitor is high relative to the surplus even if the size of the surplus is substantial the fraction of the surplus captured by consumers might be small. A low share of surplus indicates that auctions under consideration were highly competitive, and that auctioneers were earning large profits on eBay. Hence, the consumer share of surplus is another important measure to understand the eBay auction market. This measure is the fraction of total surplus that is captured by the consumers and is defined as:

$$CSS_m = \frac{CS_m}{V_{m|1} - V_{m|a}} = \frac{V_{m|1} - p_m}{V_{m|1} - V_{m|a}}. \tag{4.12}$$

where $V_{m|1}$ is the winning bidder's private valuation in auction m, p_m is the price, and $V_{m|a}$ is the value the auctioneer places on the item auctioned. Although we do not have a direct measure of $V_{m|a}$ we do know that its lower bound is 0. One could use the auctioneer's reservation price to produce a tighter bound. Theoretically this

Table 4.4 Structural lower bound of consumer share of surplus

	Mean (%)	Median (%)	Min (%)	Max (%)
SNP	20.63	19.03	9.52	62.84
NP	20.83	18.98	9.96	64.91
PL	33.90	30.30	8.70	99.90

Table 4.5 Medians lower bound of consumer share of surplus

	SNP	NP	PL
MCSS (%)	18.93	18.98	28.41

should be equal to the auctioneer's reservation value, but when one looks at the data one realizes that if that were true almost all auctioneers do not value their good. Thus using this information would not change much and we obviously do not have a correct theory for the relationship between reservation prices and reservation values. Thus it is better to ignore this value, and we can estimate a lower bound for the consumer share of surplus as:

$$CSS_m = \frac{V_{m|1} - p_m}{V_{m|1}} = 1 - \frac{p_m}{V_{m|1}} \in [0, 1] . \tag{4.13}$$

We also note that CSS_m is less sensitive to outliers than CS_m. Although we do not directly observe CSS_m we can derive the expected consumer share of surplus in auction m:

$$E\left(CSS_m|\hat{V}_{m|2}\right) = 1 - p_m e^{-x_m'\hat{\beta}} \int_{\hat{v}_{m|2}}^{\infty} \frac{f(v)}{1 - F\left(\hat{v}_{m|2}\right)} e^{-v} dv. \tag{4.14}$$

Estimates of this expectation are in Table 4.4.

In Table 4.4, PL again represents the parametric method with the assumption of half-logistic distributed private valuations. The results from SNP and NP are comparable, however, obviously lower than those from PL except for the minimum. Again this could be due to differences in methodology or the fact that there were more bidders on average in the semi-nonparametric and nonparametric data set.

For comparison with other analyses it is useful to substitute and examine the median values of the lower bounds of the consumer share of surplus. In this analysis we use the median price and median consumer's value. In general this is easily computed from the reported coefficients and descriptive statistics. To construct the median consumer's value (if it is not immediately given) one uses the sales price and the coefficients of the regression. If the median price is p_m and x_m the median values of the right hand side variables then with a log linear specification this is $p_m e^{-x_m'\beta}$. These results are shown in Table 4.5. The median winning price p_m is \$120 for the data used in semi-nonparametric and nonparametric methods and \$100 for the data used in parametric estimation.

We can see that the results are very close, although the consumer share of surplus from SNP and NP are smaller than that from PL. In Song (2004), the consumer share of surplus for yearbook auctions is 53 % if calculated using the same methodology. Song's result is significantly higher than all of the results above. The difference can be explained with competition levels involved. The average number of bidders is 3.6 in Song (2004), which is significantly lower than either subset of monitor auctions. More competition on the bidders' side would appear to result in lower consumer share of surplus.

4.6 Distribution Free Consumer Surplus and Consumer Share of Surplus

A problem with both parametric and semi-nonparametric and nonparametric estimation is upper tail sensitivity. The parameters determining the weight on the upper tail are determined by observations at the center of the distribution, thus the upper tail can be easily too thick or too thin. For extreme value statistics like consumer surplus this can cause significant problems. It would be desirable to find an alternative method that is not as sensitive to the underlying distribution.

A secondary problem is that there is no simple method to estimate consumer surplus if one does not use structural estimation. Thus this important statistic is often overlooked in empirical analysis. It is possible to estimate consumer surplus without performing structural estimation but it requires additional assumptions. One that we pursue in this section is that the set of potential bidders is constant for all auctions, which is not equivalent to assuming a constant set of active bidders. Randomizing the entry order over the set of potential bidders would produce a large variation in the number of active bidders. However, we do require this number to be nonstochastic and that it does not vary from auction to auction, which is often implicit in interpreting results from many distribution free auction studies.

In structural estimations the following methodology produces an alternative way to measure consumer surplus and provides a potentially more robust picture of the size of the consumer surplus. Let N be the number of potential bidders. Then it is clear that the distribution of the first order statistic—$H^{(1)}(V|N)$—first order stochastically dominates the distribution of the second order statistic—$H^{(2)}(V|N)$. Utilizing the fact that it is a lower bound for $H^{(1)}(V|N)$ one can produce a lower bound for consumer surplus. Under reasonable assumptions on $H^{(2)}(V|N)$ we know that:

$$H^{(2)}(V|N) = \lim_{M\to\infty} \frac{\#\left(m' \in M \,|\, p_{m'}e^{-x'_{m'}\hat{\beta}} \le V\right)}{M}. \tag{4.15}$$

For finite M of course the right hand side is only an alternative estimator for $H^{(2)}(V|N)$. If the potential number of bidders is stochastic or due to simple bad

Table 4.6 Distribution free consumer surplus

	Mean	Median	Std. dev.	Min	Max
SNP	\$44.47	\$39.64	\$17.36	\$0	\$119.89
NP	\$41.48	\$37.02	\$16.06	\$0	\$112.50
PL, all data	\$65.47	\$45.69	\$53.25	\$0	\$1,185.82
PL, SNP data	\$40.88	\$36.65	\$16.60	\$0	\$130.63

draws we can have $H^{(2)}(V|N) < \frac{\#\left(m' \in M | p_{m'} e^{-x'_{m'}\hat{\beta}} \leq V\right)}{M}$ for some V. As we will show with our data, it is possible that this estimator has a fatter upper tail than the structural estimates. We essentially construct the estimator by setting up a counter factual wherein the price setter in auction m' wins auction m instead. Averaging this over the m' that could have won auction m we derive an estimate of the consumer surplus in auction m. This statistic can easily be calculated using only the estimated coefficients and the data. Let 1_x be the indicator function which is 1 if x is true, 0 otherwise. Based on Model (4.1) and this estimating approach, consumer surplus can be derived as:

$$\widehat{CS}_m = e^{x'_m \hat{\beta}} \frac{\sum_{m'=1}^{T} p_{m'} e^{-x'_{m'}\hat{\beta}} 1_{p_{m'} e^{-x'_{m'}\hat{\beta}} \geq p_m e^{-x'_m \hat{\beta}}}}{\#\left(m' \in T | p_{m'} e^{-x'_{m'}\hat{\beta}} \geq p_m e^{-x'_m \hat{\beta}}\right)} - p_m. \tag{4.16}$$

We refer to this as the **distribution free consumer surplus** because it does not require nor make use of any estimates of the distribution of the error term. The descriptive statistics for this estimate of consumer surplus are in Table 4.6.

The minimum consumer surplus is zero by construction. Interestingly, median estimates of this measure of consumer surplus are higher than those based on the structural estimates we presented earlier, due to the presence of outliers. These outliers could either be due to bad draws from the underlying distribution or due to the number of potential bidders being stochastic. Either problem could cause a given auction to be quite competitive and result in a relatively high value for the price setting bidder resulting in larger distribution free estimates of consumer surplus in every auction. To take account of the outliers we trim both the top and bottom varying percentages to see how much trimming is necessary to stabilize the estimated consumer surplus. For the parametric and nonparametric methodologies we estimates stabilize with 2 % total trimming. For the semi-nonparametric methodology 8 % total trimming was necessary. The statistics generated without any trimming are significantly larger with the difference in medians about \$10 for the semi-nonparametric and nonparametric and \$6 for the parametric estimates.

Recall our findings above wherein the parametric structural estimates of consumer surplus where larger than those based on the semi-nonparametric and nonparametric estimates. These differences have at least two causes. One is that the parametric methodology is less flexible. Another is that we utilize a more

Table 4.7 Distribution free, lower bound of consumer share of surplus

	Mean (%)	Median (%)	Min (%)	Max(%)
SNP	28.34	25.16	0	91.05
NP	27.20	23.58	0	91.43
PL, all data	32.42	26.35	0	99.90
PL, SNP data	23.62	19.83	0	90.44

competitive data set for the semi- and nonparametric estimations. The last row in Table 4.7 above points to the latter rationale. When we estimate the distribution free consumer surplus using the data set where matching allowed us to utilize the semi- and nonparametric methods we find that the estimates are a bit lower than the semi- and nonparametric estimates, but comparable. Indeed, when one compares these estimates of consumer surplus with those in the row above it is clear that a major explanation for differences in estimates of consumer surplus are due to selecting a more competitive data set for the semi- and nonparametric estimates.

The new measure of consumer share of surplus also will be less sensitive to these outliers and would provide a potentially more robust picture of how much surplus is being generated. In the consumer share of surplus the value of the counter factual is always between zero and one and this normalization also makes the statistic less sensitive to outliers. The statistic is:

$$\widehat{CSS}_m = 1 - p_m e^{-x_m'\hat{\beta}} \frac{\sum_{m'=1}^{M} \frac{1}{p_{m'} e^{-x_{m'}'\hat{\beta}}} 1_{p_{m'} e^{-x_{m'}'\hat{\beta}} \geq p_m e^{-x_m'\hat{\beta}}}}{\# \left(m' \in M \,|\, p_{m'} e^{-x_{m'}'\hat{\beta}} \geq p_m e^{-x_m'\hat{\beta}} \right)}, \tag{4.17}$$

Estimates of this new measure of the share of consumer surplus are given in Table 4.7.

These results are consistent with those in Table 4.6 and indicate that the median distribution-free semi-nonparametric and nonparametric estimates are somewhat higher than their structural counterparts, with a difference of about 6 % for SNP and 5 % for NP. The corresponding consumer share measure based on the parametric estimates is lower than that its structural counterpart by about 4 %. When we use the parametric model to estimate consumer surplus using the data set based on the matching needed to employ our semi-nonparametric estimators it is now the lowest estimate of all, as in Table 4.6, which we would expect as estimated average values are lower for both consumer surplus and consumer's share of surplus. This would suggest that estimates of consumer surplus fall significantly when these statistics are high and have little impact on them when they are low. Thus if we estimated the parametric model on the restricted data set it is likely that the consumer's surplus and consumer's share of surplus will be higher.

The advantages of this particular distribution free methodology are twofold. First it is easy and immediate to calculate after any estimation. Second it appears to be relatively robust. Its disadvantage is the assumption that the pool of potential bidders is the same for each auction.

4.7 Conclusion

In this paper we estimate consumer surplus for eBay computer monitor auctions with semi-nonparametric and nonparametric methods. We compare our results with estimates based on parametric assumptions on the distributions of private values. We also develop a new technique, a distribution free technique, to estimate these important statistics. This new technique provides robustness checks for our estimates. We also develop a new method that places a lower bound on the consumers' benefit from these auctions, the consumer share of surplus. This provides more insight into the degree of competition in these auctions.

The general conclusions from our empirical study is that the market for computer monitors on eBay was competitive, but not at the extreme, from February 23, 2000 to June 11, 2000. It seems that the median consumer was capturing around $28 in consumer surplus or 19 % of the total surplus available. This suggests that the auctioneers were capturing at most 81 % of the total surplus. While this is a hefty share this does not take into account the unknown value that auctioneers place on their computer monitors. It would be interesting to know what share of the surplus consumers are capturing in a similar market today. Since eBay is an auction marketplace, high profits will draw more auctioneers to the market and high consumer surplus will draw more bidders. However, it is much more costly to become an auctioneer and thus the number of auctioneers per bidder is likely to have increased over time.

We would like to encourage more analysts to estimate the consumer surplus and consumer share of surplus generated in online auctions. It would be worthwhile to develop a more general picture of how much eBay is benefitting our economy. In this vein we point out that our distribution form methodology does not require the standard structural assumptions necessary to estimate consumer surplus and seems to produce estimates that are close to structural estimates, especially if the data is trimmed by reasonable trimming factors.

Acknowledgements We would like to thank Sandra Campo and participants at the Conference on Auctions and Games, Virginia Polytechnic Institute and State University, Blacksburg, VA, October 12–14, 2007 as well as Ravi Bapna and participants of the *FTC Roundtable: Economics of Internet Auctions*, October 27th, 2005, Washington, DC for insightful and needed criticism on earlier drafts of this paper. The usual caveat applies.

Appendix 1

Tables and Descriptive Statistics

Table 4.8 Descriptive statistics of key variables

	Average	Median	Std. dev.	Skewness	Maximum	Minimum
Sales price	124.27	120	2.12	0.82	355	10.5
Number of bidders	7.82	7	0.15	0.57	20	3
The length of the auction	5.30	5	0.10	0.40	10	3
Size	17	17	1	2.73	17	17
Dot pitch[a]	0.57	1	1.03	0.72	1	0.2
Dummy, dot pitch not reported	0.58	1	0.02	−0.32	1	0
Resolution[a]	86.74	800	1.17	0.57	1,600	1
Dummy, resolution not reported	0.36	0	0.02	0.58	1	0
Dummy, new monitor	0.08	0	0.010	3.23	1	0
Dummy, like-new monitor	0.04	0	0.01	4.79	1	0
Dummy, refurbished monitor	0.13	0	0.02	2.19	1	0
Dummy, warranty on monitor	0	0	0	0	0	0
Dummy, brand name monitor	0.59	1	0.02	−0.38	1	0
Dummy, flat screen monitor	0.28	0	0.02	1.01	1	0
Seller's feedback	42.87	57	1.09	0.76	4,344	1

[a]Statistics for these variables are only for items where a value was reported

Appendix 2

Tables of Semi-nonparametric Estimation

Table 4.9 Relations between CVH and k

	k = 0	k = 1	k = 2	k = 3	k = 4
CVH	−3.83	−3.83	−3.89	−3.89	−3.88

Table 4.10 Relations between CVH and window size, k* = 2

	w1 ≤ 5 min	w2 ≤ 15 min	w3 ≤ 40 min	w4 ≤ 2 h	w5 ≤ 3.5 h	w5 = all
CVH	−4.65	−4.69	−4.71	−4.72	−4.72	−4.62

References

Adams CP (2007) Estimating demand from eBay prices. Int J Ind Organ 25:1213–1232

Athey S, Haile PA (2002) Identification of standard auction models. Econometrica 65:1097–1128

Athey S, Haile PA (2005) Nonparametric approaches to auctions. In: Heckman JJ, Leamer E (eds) Handbook of econometrics, vol 6. Elsevier, Amsterdam

Bajari P, Hortaçsu A (2003) Winner's curse, reserve prices and endogenous entry: empirical insights from eBay auctions. RAND J Econ 34:329–355

Bapna R, Goes P, Gupta A (2003a) Analysis and design of business-to-consumer online auctions. Manag Sci 49:85–101

Bapna R, Goes P, Gupta A (2003b) Replicating online yankee auctions to analyze auctioneers' and bidders' strategies. Inf Syst Res 14:244–268

Bapna R, Goes P, Gupta A, Jin Y (2004) User heterogeneity and its impact on electronic auction market design: an empirical exploration. MIS Q 28:21–43

Bapna R, Jank W, Shmueli G (2008) Consumer surplus in online auctions. Inf Syst Res 19:400–416

Bulbul Toklu S (2010) Methodology: structural parametric and nonparametric methods for online auctions. Mimeo. Available at http://www.owlnet.rice.edu/\char126\relaxseda.bulbul/

Carare O (2001) Need for speed: demand estimation using auction data. Economics Working Paper, Rutgers University. Available at http://econweb.rutgers.edu/carare/ns.pdf

Coppejans M, Gallant AR (2002) Cross-validated snp density estimates. J Econ 110:27–65

Ely JC, Hossain T (2009) Sniping and squatting in auction markets. Am Econ J Microecon 1:68–94

Fenton V, Gallant AR (1996) Qualitative and asymptotic performance of SNP density estimators. Journal of Econometrics, 74:77–118

Gallant AR, Nychka DW (1987) Semi-nonparametric maximum likelihood estimation. Econometrica 55:363–390

Gonzalez R (2002) Essays in structural parametric and semi-parametric estimation of auction and agency models. Unpublished dissertation, Rice University

Gonzalez R, Hasker K, Sickles RC (2009) An analysis of strategic behavior in eBay auctions. Singap Econ Rev 54:441–472

Haile PA, Tamer ET (2003) Inference with an incomplete model of English auctions. J Political Econ 111:1–51

Hasker K, Sickles RC (2010) eBay in the economic literature: analysis of an auction marketplace. Rev Ind Organ 37:3–42

Laffont JJ, Ossard H, Vuong Q (1995) Econometrics of first-price auctions. Econometrica 63:953–980
Lucking-Reiley D, Bryan D, Prasad N, Reeves D (2007) Pennies from eBay: the determinants of price in online auctions. J Ind Econ 55:223–233
Nekipelov D (2007) Entry deterrence and learning prevention on eBay. Working paper. University of California, Berkeley, webpage https://www.econ.berkeley.edu/faculty/837
Roth AE, Ockenfels A (2002) Last-minute bidding and the rules for ending second-price auctions: evidence from eBay and Amazon auctions on the internet. Am Econ Rev 92:1093–1103
Sailer K (2006) Searching the eBay marketplace. University of Munich, Department of Economics Discussion Papers, Number 1234
Song U (2004) Nonparametric estimation of an eBay auction model with an unknown number of bidders. Mimeo. Available at http://faculty.arts.ubc.ca/usong/eBay.pdf

Chapter 5
Inference in Two-Step Panel Data Models with Time-Invariant Regressors: Bootstrap Versus Analytic Estimators

Scott E. Atkinson and Christopher Cornwell

5.1 Introduction

Panel data are useful because of the opportunity they afford the researcher to control for unobserved heterogeneity or effects that do not vary over time. Typically, exploiting this opportunity means employing the fixed-effects (FE) estimator, because it produces consistent estimates of the coefficients of time-varying variables under weak assumptions about their relationship with the effects. As is well-understood, the FE estimator achieves this through a data transformation that eliminates the effects. The downside to FE estimation, however, is that this data transformation also eliminates any time-invariant variables. Consequently, the FE estimator is sometimes abandoned entirely for a random-effects (RE) approach, whose requirements for consistency frequently are not satisfied, since unobserved heterogeneity is often correlated with the regressors.

While the partial effects of time-invariant variables can be recovered in a second-step regression, this fact is generally omitted in most textbook treatments of panel-data methods (Wooldridge 2010 is an exception). The practical necessity of recovering the partial effects of time-invariant variables shows up in many different empirical contexts. In the familiar exercise of estimating wage regressions, human-capital variables such as experience and tenure are taken to be correlated with the unobserved effect, which is commonly interpreted as "ability". While FE estimation eliminates such time-invariant unobservables, it also eliminates race, gender and education (when schooling is completed before the sample period), the effects of which are of great interest. Similarly, when estimating production relationships, inputs may be correlated with fixed "environmental" factors, which again would

---

S.E. Atkinson (✉) • C. Cornwell
Department of Economics, Terry College of Business, University of Georgia,
503 Brooks Hall, 310 Herty Drive, Athens, GA 30602, USA
e-mail: atknsn@uga.edu; cowrnl@uga.edu

R.C. Sickles and W.C. Horrace (eds.), *Festschrift in Honor of Peter Schmidt: Econometric Methods and Applications*, DOI 10.1007/978-1-4899-8008-3_5,

swept away by the FE estimator. However, policy-relevant firm characteristics, such as public or private ownership in the case of electric utilities, would be swept away as well.

Interest in recovering the partial effects of time-invariant variables may be even more common in panels of state and country-level aggregates, as with empirical growth and comparative political-economy studies, where policy-relevant fixed institutional variables are differenced out of a FE regression. The recovery of these partial effects motivated the work of Plümper and Troeger (2007), who proposed a three-step method for estimating the effects of time-invariant variables in linear panel-data models. Plümper's and Troeger's so-called "fixed-effects vector decomposition" (FEVD) became widely utilized through their Stata program (xtfevd) that computes the estimator and corresponding standard errors. However, as shown in the critiques of Breusch et al. (2011) and Greene (2011), the main substantive claims about the FEVD estimator are false. Importantly, from our perspective, the standard errors produced by the FEVD estimator are incorrect, because their method does not estimate the correct asymptotic covariance matrix, which should incorporate the first-step estimated covariance matrix.

In this paper, we focus on the two-step estimation procedure and compare conventional inference based on the asymptotic formula to bootstrap alternatives. Bootstrapping has a natural appeal, because of the complications associated with estimating the asymptotic covariance matrix and the inherent finite-sample bias of the resulting standard errors. Our paper contributes to the panel data and bootstrapping literature in four ways. First, we derive the correct asymptotic covariance matrix for the second-step coefficient estimators, allowing for heteroskedasticity and autocorrelation of unknown form. Second, we develop the steps required to perform bootstrap estimation of the covariance matrix of the second-step estimated coefficients. Third, we prove that the pairs and wild bootstrap coefficient estimators are unbiased. This stands in contrast to Flachaire (2005) who asserts that the pairs is a biased estimator. Unbiasedness implies that the error in rejection probability (ERP) of corresponding t-tests, measured as the difference between their actual and nominal size, should be small.

Finally, using Monte Carlo methods, we compare the size and power of the naive asymptotic estimator, which ignores the first-step estimation error, the correct asymptotic covariance matrix estimator, which does not, and the bootstrap alternatives. We consider a variety of panel sizes (N) and lengths (T) relevant to the common large-N, small-T setting. We find that the bootstrap methods consistently provide more accurate inference than the asymptotic formulae. The performance gain is largest for N less than 250 and shrinks as N grows. Although a small ERP remains for the correct asymptotic covariance matrix estimator when $N = 1{,}000$, as N grows to 250 and beyond, both bootstrap estimators generally produce the correct size. Comparing the two bootstrap methods, the pairs tends to moderately over-reject and the wild to moderately under-reject for smaller values of N, with the pairs having a slightly smaller ERP. While we find a slight advantage of the pairs method over the others in terms of power with $N = 250$ and $T = 5$, few differences are observed with larger values of N.

The remainder of this paper is organized as follows. Section 5.2 introduces the model and two-step estimator. Section 5.3 presents the correct asymptotic covariance matrix for the second-step estimator and outlines the bootstrap alternatives for second-step standard-error estimation. In Sect. 5.4, we review previous studies of the wild and pairs procedures and prove that they are both unbiased for the problems we address. Section 5.5 explains our Monte Carlo experiments and reports our findings on the size and power of t-tests produced by conventional and bootstrap procedures. Conclusions follow in Sect. 5.6.

5.2 The Two-Step Model and Parameter Estimation

We consider estimation of linear panel-data models of the form

$$y_{it} = \mathbf{x}_{it}\beta + \mathbf{z}_i\gamma + \xi_{it} \quad i = 1, \ldots, N; t = 1, \ldots, T, \tag{5.1}$$

where $\xi_{it} = c_i + e_{it}$, y_{it} is the dependent variable, $\mathbf{x}_{it}$ is a $(1 \times K)$ vector of time-varying regressors, $\mathbf{z}_i$ is a $(1 \times G)$ vector of time-invariant regressors, c_i is an unobserved effect that is fixed for the cross-section unit, and e_{it} is an error term.[1] The e_{it} may be heteroscedastic and serially correlated. The coefficient vectors, β and γ, are $(K \times 1)$ and $(G \times 1)$, respectively. For most of the discussion that follows we work with the form of the model that combines all T observations for each cross-section unit:

$$\mathbf{y}_i = \mathbf{X}_i\beta + (\mathbf{j}_T \otimes \mathbf{z}_i)\gamma + +\mathbf{j}_T c_i + \mathbf{e}_i, \tag{5.2}$$

where $\mathbf{X}_i$ is $(T \times K)$, $\mathbf{j}_T$ is a T-vector of ones, and $\mathbf{y}_i$ and $\mathbf{e}_i$ are $(T \times 1)$ vectors.

Our interest is in estimating γ, allowing for the possibility that some or all of the variables in $\mathbf{X}_i$ are correlated with the unobserved effect. Formally, we adopt the standard FE assumption that

$$E(e_{it} \,|\, \mathbf{X}_i, \mathbf{z}_i, c_i) = 0, \quad t = 1, \ldots, T. \tag{5.3}$$

Additionally, we assume

$$E(c_i \,|\, \mathbf{z}_i) = 0, \tag{5.4}$$

which treats the time-invariant variables as uncorrelated with the unobserved effects. We invoke (5.4) to focus attention on the transmission of the first-step estimation

[1] Although the model setup assumes a balanced panel, this is not necessary. The asymptotic covariance matrix and bootstrap procedures can readily accommodate settings in which the number of time-series observations varies with the cross-section unit.

error to the second step, without the confounding influence of endogeneity in $\mathbf{z}_i$. While this is a strong assumption, it is reasonable in some of the empirical contexts referenced above. For example, in the production relationships category, Agee et al. (2009, 2012) use directional distance functions to estimate the efficiency of a household's production of health and human capital in children. In both cases, all time-invariant child and household characteristics are treated as exogenous on the grounds that the characteristics are either fixed by nature (e.g., race and gender) or by circumstances of the household or the parents. County, state, and country-level panels provide other examples, many of which come from social science papers outside of economics (as described in Plümper and Troeger (2007)). A common practice has been either to include time-invariant variables in a pooled ordinary least-squares (POLS) or RE regression, or use FE estimation and ignore them. Knack (1993), which is concerned with the relationship between the prospect of jury service and voter registration, does both. Over Knack's two-year panel, certain state characteristics, like whether there is a senate contest, are time-invariant. Because the timing of senate contests are fixed by law, this indicator is exogenous. Knack estimates OLS regressions on each year separately, including the fixed characteristics, and FE regressions using both years of the panel, dropping these characteristics.[2]

In the two-step approach to estimating γ, we begin by applying FE to (5.1), which produces

$$\hat{\beta}_{FE} = \left(\sum_i \mathbf{X}_i'\mathbf{Q}_T\mathbf{X}_i\right)^{-1} \sum_i \mathbf{X}_i'\mathbf{Q}_T\mathbf{y}_i, \tag{5.5}$$

where $\mathbf{Q}_T = \mathbf{I}_T - \mathbf{j}_T(\mathbf{j}_T'\mathbf{j}_T)^{-1}\mathbf{j}_T'$ is the idempotent projection that time de-means the data. The FE estimator is unbiased and consistent under (5.3).

Next, we take $\hat{\beta}_{FE}$ and compute individual or group-level residuals,

$$\hat{\delta}_i = \bar{y}_i - \bar{\mathbf{x}}_i\hat{\beta}_{FE}, \tag{5.6}$$

and formulate the second-step regression model

$$\hat{\delta}_i = \mathbf{z}_i\gamma + u_i, \tag{5.7}$$

where

$$u_i = \bar{\xi}_i - \bar{\mathbf{x}}_i(\hat{\beta}_{FE} - \beta), \tag{5.8}$$

[2]Atkinson and Cornwell (2013) extend the analysis here to allow some of the elements of $\mathbf{z}_i$ to be correlated with the unobserved effect.

$\bar{\xi}_i = c_i + \bar{e}_i$, the over-bar indicates the sample-period mean for unit i (e.g., $\bar{\mathbf{x}}_i = \frac{1}{T}\sum_t \mathbf{x}_{it}$), and the first element of $\mathbf{z}_i$ is 1. Equation (5.8) is obtained by combining (5.7), (5.6), and the sample-period mean for unit i of (5.2). We then estimate γ by applying OLS to (5.7).[3] The resulting estimator, which we label $\hat{\gamma}_{FE}$ because it is derived from $\hat{\beta}_{FE}$, can be written as

$$\hat{\gamma}_{FE} = \left(\sum_i \mathbf{z}_i'\mathbf{z}_i\right)^{-1}\left(\sum_i \mathbf{z}_i'\hat{\delta}_i\right). \tag{5.9}$$

5.3 Second-Step Standard-Error Estimation

In this section, we first derive the asymptotic covariance matrix of $\hat{\gamma}_{FE}$ and explain how to estimate it consistently. Then we outline the procedures for computing the wild and pairs bootstrap alternatives.

5.3.1 *Asymptotic Covariance Matrix*

As Wooldridge (2010) points out, the asymptotic covariance matrix for $\hat{\gamma}_{FE}$ can be obtained by applying standard arguments for two-step estimators (see, for example, Murphy and Topel 1985). We begin by writing the sampling error of $\hat{\gamma}_{FE}$ as

$$\hat{\gamma}_{FE} - \gamma = \left(\sum_i \mathbf{z}_i'\mathbf{z}_i\right)^{-1}\left(\sum_i \mathbf{z}_i' u_i\right). \tag{5.10}$$

Then we can show that $\sqrt{N}(\hat{\gamma}_{FE} - \gamma)$ is asymptotically normal with a limiting covariance matrix that can be expressed as

$$(\mathbf{B}_{zz})^{-1}\,\mathbf{A}\,(\mathbf{B}_{zz})^{-1}, \tag{5.11}$$

where, $\mathbf{B}_{zz} = \text{plim}\frac{1}{N}\sum_i \mathbf{z}_i'\mathbf{z}_i$. As implied by (5.8)

$$\mathbf{A} = \text{plim}\frac{1}{N}\sum_i \bar{\xi}_i^2\mathbf{z}_i'\mathbf{z}_i + \text{plim}\frac{1}{N}\sum_i \mathbf{z}_i'\bar{\mathbf{x}}_i\,\mathbf{V}_{\hat{\beta}_{FE}}\,\bar{\mathbf{x}}_i'\mathbf{z}_i, \tag{5.12}$$

where $\mathbf{V}_{\hat{\beta}_{FE}}$ is the limiting covariance matrix of $\sqrt{N}(\hat{\beta}_{FE} - \beta)$.

---

[3]As discussed in Atkinson and Cornwell (2013), allowing some of the elements of $\mathbf{z}_i$ to be correlated with the unobserved effect leads to the two-step "simple, consistent" instrumental variables estimator of Hausman and Taylor (1981). From this perspective, you can view our two-step estimator as an instrumental variables estimator using $[\mathbf{Q}_T\mathbf{X}_i, (j_T \otimes \mathbf{z}_i)]$ as instruments.

A consistent estimator of the asymptotic covariance matrix of $\hat{\gamma}_{FE}$ hinges on the consistent estimation of $\mathbf{A}$. The latter is accomplished by utilizing the robust covariance matrix estimator of $\mathbf{V}_{\hat{\beta}_{FE}}$,

$$\hat{\mathbf{V}}_{\hat{\beta}_{FE}} = \left(\sum_i \mathbf{X}_i'\mathbf{Q}_T\mathbf{X}_i\right)^{-1} \sum_i \mathbf{X}_i'\mathbf{Q}_T\hat{\mathbf{e}}_i\hat{\mathbf{e}}_i'\mathbf{Q}_T\mathbf{X}_i \left(\sum_i \mathbf{X}_i'\mathbf{Q}_T\mathbf{X}_i\right)^{-1} \tag{5.13}$$

(see Arellano 1987), and extracting an estimator of ξ_i from the group-level version of (5.1) evaluated at $(\hat{\beta}_{FE}, \hat{\gamma}_{FE})$.

5.3.2 *Bootstrap Methods*

There are two important reasons to prefer bootstrap estimators of standard errors to estimators based on asymptotic formulae. First, bootstrapping standard errors is often easier than estimating the asymptotic covariance matrix. Second, bootstrapping often produces better small-sample performance in terms of ERP.

We consider the wild and pairs bootstrap procedures because they produce estimated standard errors that are robust to heteroskedasticity. Davidson and Flachaire (2008) have shown that the wild bootstrap yields a heteroskedasticity-consistent covariance matrix estimator when the residuals are divided by h_i, the diagonal element of the projection matrix corresponding to the right-hand-side variables of the original equation estimated. T. Lancaster (2003, A note on bootstraps and robustness, unpublished manuscript. Department of Economics, Brown University) has proven that the pairs bootstrap yields a similar covariance estimator. Below we outline how each can be adapted to our two-step estimation problem.

Following Cameron and Trivedi (2005), for fixed-T panels, consistent (as $N \to \infty$) standard errors can be obtained by using cross-sectional resampling. Hence, we employ this method for both the pairs and wild bootstrap, assuming no cross-sectional or temporal dependence.[4]

5.3.2.1 Wild Bootstrap Estimator

The wild bootstrap procedure can the applied to the estimation of the standard errors of $\hat{\gamma}_{FE}$ by executing the following steps.

[4]Also, see Kapetanios (2008), who shows that if the data do not exhibit cross-sectional dependence but exhibit temporal dependence, then cross-sectional resampling is superior to block bootstrap resampling. Further, he shows that cross-sectional resampling provides asymptotic refinements. Monte Carlo results using these assumptions indicate the superiority of the cross-sectional method.

1. Compute $\hat{\beta}_{FE}$ in (5.5).
2. Using $\hat{\beta}_{FE}$, compute $\hat{\delta}_i$ in (5.6).
3. Compute $\hat{\gamma}_{FE}$ in (5.9).
4. Since $\xi_{it} = c_i + e_{it}$ in (5.1), compute

$$\hat{\xi}_{it} = y_{it} - \mathbf{x}_{it}\hat{\beta}_{FE} - \mathbf{z}_i\hat{\gamma}_{FE}, \tag{5.14}$$

   Then define $f(\hat{\xi}_{it})$ as:

$$f(\hat{\xi}_{it}) = \frac{\hat{\xi}_{it}}{(1-h_{it})^{1/2}},$$

   where h_{it} is the diagonal element of the projection matrix corresponding to the right-hand-side variables of (5.2). Thus, the transformed residual is homoskedastic by definition so long as the error term, ξ_{it}, is homoskedastic.[5]
5. We follow Davidson and Flachaire (2008) and MacKinnon (2002) and define ϵ_i as the two-point Rademacher distribution:

$$\epsilon_i = \begin{cases} -1 \text{ with probability } \frac{1}{2} \\ \;\;\,1 \text{ with probability } \frac{1}{2} \end{cases}. \tag{5.15}$$

   This assigns the same value to all T observations for each i. Then, we generate

$$y_{it}^w = \mathbf{x}_{it}\hat{\beta}_{FE} + \mathbf{z}_i\hat{\gamma}_{FE} + \xi_{it}^w, \tag{5.16}$$

   where

$$\xi_{it}^w = f(\hat{\xi}_{it})\epsilon_i. \tag{5.17}$$

   Davidson and Flachaire (2008) provide evidence that this version of the wild bootstrap is superior to other wild methods. This is due to the fact that $E(\epsilon_i) = 0$, $E(\epsilon_i^2) = 1$, $E(\epsilon_i^3) = 0$, and $E(\epsilon_i^4) = 1$. Since $\hat{\xi}_{it}$ and ϵ_i are independent, $E(\xi_{it}^w) = E(\hat{\xi}_{it})\epsilon_i\vartheta = 0$, its variance is that of $\hat{\xi}_{it}\vartheta$, its third moment is zero (which implies zero skewness in $\hat{\xi}_{it}$), but its fourth moment is again that of $\hat{\xi}_{it}\vartheta$. Thus, the first, second, and fourth moments of $\hat{\xi}_{it}\vartheta$ are reproduced exactly in the wild bootstrap data using (5.15).
6. Compute the FE estimator of $\hat{\beta}$ using the wild bootstrap data:

$$\hat{\beta}_{FE}^w = \left(\sum_i \mathbf{X}_i'\mathbf{Q}_T\mathbf{X}_i\right)^{-1}\sum_i \mathbf{X}_i'\mathbf{Q}_T\mathbf{y}_i^w. \tag{5.18}$$

[5]Further, this transformation is needed to obtain a heteroskedastic-consistent covariance matrix as explained above.

7. Compute the group-mean residuals as

$$\delta_i^w = \bar{y}_i^w - \bar{\mathbf{x}}_i \hat{\beta}_{FE}^w. \tag{5.19}$$

Note that in step (5) it was necessary to generate y_{it}^w rather than time-demeaned y_{it}, because in the current step one must compute group means to generate the residuals. Group means cannot be recovered from the time-demeaned data.

8. Formulate the true bootstrap model

$$\delta_i^w = \mathbf{z}_i \hat{\gamma}_{FE} + u_i^w, \tag{5.20}$$

where u_i^w is a bootstrap error, and compute the second-step estimator of $\hat{\gamma}_{FE}$ using the bootstrap data:

$$\hat{\gamma}_{FE}^w = \left(\sum_i \mathbf{z}_i' \mathbf{z}_i \right)^{-1} \sum_i \mathbf{z}_i' \delta_i^w. \tag{5.21}$$

9. Iterate steps 5–8 and compute the sample standard deviation of $\hat{\gamma}_{FE}^w$, $s_{\hat{\gamma},w}$, as an estimator of the standard error of $\hat{\gamma}_{FE}$, where w denotes the wild procedure.

5.3.2.2 Pairs Bootstrap Estimator

The pairs bootstrap procedure discussed in T. Lancaster (2003, A note on bootstraps and robustness, unpublished manuscript. Department of Economics, Brown University) can be extended to our problem as follows:

1. Compute $\hat{\beta}_{FE}$ in (5.5).
2. Using $\hat{\beta}_{FE}$, compute $\hat{\delta}_i$ in (5.6).
3. Compute $\hat{\gamma}_{FE}$ in (5.9).
4. Draw randomly with replacement among $i = 1, \ldots, N$ blocks, using all T observations in the chosen block, with probability $1/T$ from $\{y_{it}, \mathbf{x}_{it}, \mathbf{z}_{it}\}$ to obtain $\{y_{it}^p, \mathbf{x}_{it}^p, \mathbf{z}_{it}^p\}$, where the superscript denotes the pairs estimator. Resampling all variables in this manner preserves the correlation of the corresponding time-invariant and group-mean variables in the second-step regression with the first-step variables.
5. For the pairs bootstrap, define $\boldsymbol{\xi}_i^p$ as a $(T \times 1)$ vector made up of $\{\xi_{i1}^p, \ldots, \xi_{iT}^p\}$ for observation i. Write the first-step regression model with unknown error term, $\boldsymbol{\xi}_i^p$, as

$$\mathbf{y}_i^p = \mathbf{X}_i^p \hat{\beta}_{FE} + (\mathbf{j}_T \otimes \mathbf{z}_i^p) \hat{\gamma}_{FE} + \boldsymbol{\xi}_i^p. \tag{5.22}$$

Compute the FE estimator of $\hat{\beta}$ using the pairs bootstrap data $(\mathbf{y}_i^p, \mathbf{X}_i^p)$

$$\hat{\beta}_{FE}^{p} = \left(\sum_{i} \mathbf{X}_i^{p'} \mathbf{Q}_T \mathbf{X}_i^{p}\right)^{-1} \sum_{i} \mathbf{X}_i^{p'} \mathbf{Q}_T \mathbf{y}_i^{p}. \tag{5.23}$$

6. Using $\hat{\beta}_{FE}^{p}$ compute the residuals

$$\delta_i^p = \bar{y}_i^p - \bar{\mathbf{x}}_i^p \hat{\beta}_{FE}^{p}. \tag{5.24}$$

7. Formulate the second-step pairs bootstrap model as

$$\delta_i^p = \mathbf{z}_i^p \hat{\gamma}_{FE} + u_i^p, \tag{5.25}$$

where u_i^p is the pairs second-step error, then compute the second-step estimator of $\hat{\gamma}_{FE}$ using the bootstrap data:

$$\hat{\gamma}_{FE}^{p} = \left(\sum_{i} \mathbf{z}_i^{p'} \mathbf{z}_i^{p}\right)^{-1} \sum_{i} \mathbf{z}_i^{p'} \delta_i^{p}. \tag{5.26}$$

8. Iterate steps 4–7 and compute the sample standard deviation of $\hat{\gamma}_{FE}^{p}$, $s_{\hat{\gamma},p}$, as an estimator of the standard error of $\hat{\gamma}_{FE}$.

5.4 The Size and Power of Bootstrap Estimators

5.4.1 Previous Studies of the Size and Power of Bootstrap Estimators

We are unaware of any Monte Carlo study that examines the ERP and size of estimator t-values for two-step panel-data models of the type we consider. However, there is a substantial literature on bootstrap performance in cross-section regressions. Horowitz (2001) compares the actual size of the pairs and wild bootstrap to the size associated with the asymptotic formula for White's information matrix test, the t-test in a heteroskedastic regression model, and the t-test in a Box-Cox regression model. For relatively small sample sizes, he finds that the wild and pairs dramatically reduce the ERP of the asymptotic formulas, and in many cases the wild essentially eliminates this error. The wild method outperforms the pairs and both outperform the jackknife method. Davidson and Flachaire (2008) obtain similar results when they compare the wild and pairs estimators to those obtained using the asymptotic formula. Using an Edgeworth expansion, they trace the wild's advantage to the fact that the ERPs of the pairs depend on more higher-order raw moments of the original errors and the bootstrap residuals, which are greater under heteroskedasticity. With homoskedastic errors, there is little difference between the wild and pairs estimators and their ERP is very small. The results we present below are consistent with this finding. Inference based on the asymptotic formula also improves, but exhibits a substantially larger ERP.

In summary, for single-equation models with heteroskedastic errors, Monte Carlo results generally show that the wild bootstrap outperforms the pairs and that both improve on inference based on the estimator of the asymptotic formula. However, we are not aware of bootstrap performance comparisons that address the empirical context of a two-step panel data model, where estimation error from the first step is the primary complicating factor. Next, we analytically examine the wild and pairs procedures for the two-step estimation problem, identifying the conditions required for both to be unbiased.

5.4.2 *The Unbiasedness of Our Two-Step Bootstrap Estimators*

The unbiasedness of the first and second-step wild estimators follows directly from the fact that the ϵ_i are zero-mean random variables generated independently of ξ_{it}. See Theorems 1 and 2 in the Appendix. Flachaire (2005) compares the conditional expectation of the bootstrap error given the explanatory variables for the wild versus pairs methods in a simple linear model. In terms of our setup, he asserts that the wild bootstrap satisfies $E(u_i^w|\mathbf{z}_i) = 0$, and hence is unbiased.

He also asserts that the pairs does not satisfy $E(u_i^p|\mathbf{z}_i^p) \neq 0$, and therefore is biased (because u_i^p depends on $\mathbf{z}_i^p$). Thus, he argues that the wild should produce a smaller ERP than the pairs estimator. In the Appendix, however, we prove that both estimators are unbiased given the exogeneity conditions (5.3) and (5.4).

To show that the pairs estimator is unbiased, we need to reformulate it in terms of the residual of the original model. Since by definition $\mathbf{y}_i$ equals the fitted model plus the residual for observation i,

$$\sqrt{v_i}\mathbf{y}_i = \sqrt{v_i}\mathbf{X}_i\hat{\beta}_{FE} + \sqrt{v_i}(\mathbf{j}_T \otimes \mathbf{z}_i)\hat{\gamma}_{FE} + \sqrt{v_i}\hat{\boldsymbol{\xi}}_i, \tag{5.27}$$

where v_i specifies number of times (from 0 to N) that each $(\mathbf{y}_i, \mathbf{X}_i)$ pair for observation i is reused in the pairs bootstrap sample. Using $(\sqrt{v_i}\mathbf{y}_i, \sqrt{v_i}\mathbf{X}_i)$ we obtain an alternative formulation of the pairs first-step estimator as

$$\hat{\beta}_{FE}^p = \left(\sum_i v_i\mathbf{X}_i'\mathbf{Q}_T\mathbf{X}_i\right)^{-1}\sum_i v_i\mathbf{X}_i'\mathbf{Q}_T\mathbf{y}_i. \tag{5.28}$$

Hence, (5.28) becomes a weighted regression version of (5.23), where $\mathbf{y}_i^p$ is replaced by $\sqrt{v_i}\mathbf{y}_i$, $\mathbf{X}_i^p$ is replaced by $\sqrt{v_i}\mathbf{X}_i$, and $(\mathbf{j}_T \otimes \mathbf{z}_i^p)$ is replaced by $\sqrt{v_i}(\mathbf{j}_T \otimes \mathbf{z}_i)$. Again by definition, reformulate (5.25) as

$$\sqrt{v_i}\delta_i = \sqrt{v_i}\mathbf{z}_i\hat{\gamma}_{FE} + \sqrt{v_i}\hat{u}_i. \tag{5.29}$$

where $\hat{u}_i$ is the residual computed from (5.7) and obtain a more useful formulation of the second-step pairs estimator as

$$\hat{\gamma}_{FE}^{p} = \left(\sum_i v_i \mathbf{z}_i' \mathbf{z}_i\right)^{-1} \sum_i v_i \mathbf{z}_i' \delta_i. \tag{5.30}$$

Theorem 3 says that the pairs estimator is unbiased in the first step if $E(\mathbf{Q}_T \hat{\boldsymbol{\xi}}_i | v_i, \mathbf{X}_i) = 0$. This result also applies to any linear, single-equation model estimated by the pairs estimator. Finally, using (5.30), and assuming that (5.3), (5.4), and Theorem 3 hold, Theorem 4 shows that in the second step, the pairs estimator is unbiased for $\hat{\gamma}_{FE}$.

Davidson and MacKinnon (1999) demonstrate that the ERP depends on estimator bias. Thus, a biased bootstrap estimator should have a larger ERP than an unbiased estimator assuming that the errors, ξ_i, are i.i.d.[6] The size of t-values for both the second-step wild and pairs estimators should be highly accurate since their biases are zero, given that the assumptions in (5.3) and (5.4) hold.

5.5 Monte Carlo Estimation

5.5.1 Data Generation

We create the data for the Monte Carlo experiments in the following steps.

1. Generate the x_{itk} and z_{itg} ($k = 1, \ldots, 10$; $g = 1, \ldots, 3$) as multivariate normal with zero means and unit variances. We set $cov(z_g, z_{g'}) = 0.2,\ g \neq g'$ (implying simple correlations of 0.2), $cov(x_k, x_{k'}) = 0.3,\ k \neq k'$. We also set $cov(x_k, z_g) = 0.3$ and draw x_{itk} and z_{itg}. For each g, we then create the group mean of z_{itg} and use this for z_{ig} (which is time invariant) so that the group means of x_k and z_g have correlation of 0.3.
2. Generate c_i and e_{it} as i.i.d. normal random variables with mean zero and variance of 10 and 100, respectively. The large variance for e_{it} guarantees a relatively low R^2 for the first-step regression. This in turn implies a greater difference between the estimated "naive" and correct asymptotic covariance matrices for the second-step coefficients.
3. Using the data from steps 1–2, generate y_{it} in Eq. (5.1).

The bootstrap estimators do not require the i.i.d. assumption. As described in Sect. 5.3.2, they have heteroskedastic-consistent covariance matrices. Using cross-sectional resampling as defined above, these bootstrap methods will deal with dependent data by generating correlated errors that exhibit approximately the

[6] As indicated above, Davidson and Flachaire (2008) find that many other factors in addition to bias, especially heteroskedasticity, can increase the ERP of bootstrap and asymptotic estimators.

same pattern of autocorrelation as ξ_{it}. However, in this paper we focus on the i.i.d. case (as defined in step two), because our primary interest here is how the bootstrap estimators handle the transmission of the first-step estimation error to the second step relative to the analytical alternative in the simplest of contexts. In Atkinson and Cornwell (2013), we explore the effects, in some cases substantial, of heteroskedasticity and serial correlation in the ξ_{it} on the second-step inference problem.

5.5.2 Monte Carlo Results

We perform a number of Monte Carlo experiments to compare the actual size and power of the t-statistics derived from four estimators of the covariance matrix of $\hat{\gamma}$– a "naive" method which is the asymptotic formula without adjusting for the first-step parameter estimators, the correct asymptotic formula which makes this adjustment, the pairs bootstrap, and the wild bootstrap. For our size calculations, we assume that $\beta = \gamma = 1$ during data generation and test the null that $\gamma = 1$ using a two-sided equal-tailed 95 % confidence interval, so that the total type-I error is $\alpha = 0.05$.

We set the number of bootstrap draws, B, to 399 following MacKinnon (2002) who states that while this number may be smaller than should be used in practice, any randomness due to B of this size averages out across the replications. We find this to be true for our experiments where larger values of B did not change our results on ERP up to three significant digits beyond the decimal point. Within each of $M(m = 1, \ldots, M)$ Monte Carlo trials, for each bootstrap method, we estimate the unrestricted model and obtain $\hat{\gamma}^*_{m,b,g}$, the bootstrap estimator of $\hat{\gamma}_{m,g}$, $b = 1, \ldots, B$. For each m, we calculate the actual size of the test-statistic,

$$t^*_{m,g} = (\hat{\gamma}_{m,g} - \gamma_g)/s^*_{m,g}, \quad g = 1, \ldots, G, \tag{5.31}$$

where $s^*_{m,g}$ is the bootstrap estimator of the standard error of $\hat{\gamma}_{m,g}$, computed as the standard deviation of $\hat{\gamma}^*_{m,b,g}$ over all bootstrap replications. Note that the $t^*_{m,g}$ statistic is not asymptotically pivotal and no asymptotic refinements obtain; however, we employ it since applied researchers may have difficulty computing the asymptotic formula. See MacKinnon (2002) for details.

For each Monte Carlo trial, m, we calculate the size for each bootstrap estimator as the percentage of $t^*_{m,g}$ values greater than the nominal level of $t^*_{\alpha/2} = 1.96$ or less than the nominal level of $t^*_{1-\alpha/2} = -1.96$, with $\alpha = 0.05$. We choose $M = 1{,}999$, so that $\frac{1}{2}\alpha(M + 1)$ is an integer.

For each Monte Carlo trial, we compute the size for the naive and asymptotic formula methods using

$$t_{m,g} = (\hat{\gamma}_{m,g} - \gamma_g)/s_{\hat{\gamma}_{m,g}}, \tag{5.32}$$

Table 5.1 Monte Carlo actual size calculations

	$T = 5$			$T = 10$			$T = 20$		
	γ_1	γ_2	γ_3	γ_1	γ_2	γ_3	γ_1	γ_2	γ_3
$N = 50$									
Naive	0.080	0.077	0.088	0.073	0.085	0.085	0.070	0.085	0.084
Asy.	0.069	0.069	0.080	0.070	0.081	0.083	0.070	0.084	0.083
Pairs	0.051	0.051	0.051	0.051	0.051	0.051	0.051	0.051	0.051
Wild	0.046	0.047	0.046	0.046	0.046	0.046	0.047	0.046	0.046
Avg.	0.062	0.061	0.066	0.060	0.066	0.066	0.059	0.066	0.066
$N = 100$									
Naive	0.067	0.073	0.058	0.057	0.070	0.067	0.067	0.073	0.070
Asy.	0.060	0.069	0.055	0.055	0.069	0.065	0.066	0.072	0.069
Pairs	0.050	0.051	0.050	0.050	0.051	0.051	0.050	0.050	0.050
Wild	0.048	0.048	0.048	0.048	0.048	0.048	0.048	0.048	0.048
Avg.	0.056	0.060	0.053	0.052	0.059	0.058	0.058	0.061	0.059
$N = 250$									
Naive	0.055	0.064	0.055	0.051	0.061	0.064	0.061	0.053	0.055
Asy.	0.053	0.062	0.051	0.051	0.060	0.062	0.061	0.052	0.054
Pairs	0.050	0.049	0.050	0.050	0.050	0.050	0.050	0.050	0.050
Wild	0.050	0.049	0.049	0.049	0.049	0.049	0.049	0.049	0.049
Avg.	0.052	0.056	0.051	0.050	0.055	0.056	0.055	0.051	0.052
$N = 500$									
Naive	0.057	0.050	0.065	0.057	0.060	0.051	0.043	0.056	0.055
Asy.	0.052	0.048	0.062	0.057	0.059	0.050	0.042	0.055	0.053
Pairs	0.050	0.050	0.050	0.050	0.050	0.050	0.050	0.050	0.050
Wild	0.050	0.050	0.049	0.050	0.050	0.049	0.049	0.050	0.050
Avg.	0.052	0.049	0.056	0.053	0.054	0.050	0.046	0.053	0.052
$N = 1{,}000$									
Naive	0.051	0.054	0.053	0.048	0.045	0.048	0.053	0.047	0.052
Asy.	0.049	0.050	0.050	0.048	0.044	0.048	0.053	0.047	0.051
Pairs	0.050	0.050	0.050	0.050	0.050	0.050	0.050	0.050	0.050
Wild	0.050	0.050	0.050	0.050	0.050	0.050	0.050	0.050	0.050
Avg.	0.050	0.051	0.050	0.049	0.047	0.049	0.051	0.048	0.051

where $s_{\hat{\gamma}_{m,g}}$ for the naive method is the standard error estimator ignoring the existence of first-step random variables and for the asymptotic method is the square root of the gth diagonal element of (5.13). Then, we estimate size over all M observations as the percentage of times that $t_{m,g}$ exceeds the nominal level of $t^*_{\alpha/2} = 1.96$ or is less than the nominal level of $t^*_{1-\alpha/2} = -1.96$ for $\alpha = 0.05$.

Because we are interested in performance under large-N asymptotics, we consider the following cases: $N = 50, 100, 250, 500$ and $1{,}000$ crossed with $T = 5, 10$ and 20. We compute the actual size, also termed type-I error or rejection probability (RP), and the absolute value of the ERP. Table 5.1 reports actual RPs, while Table 5.2 reports the sum over all parameters of the absolute ERPs.

Table 5.2 Total Monte Carlo ERP

	$T = 5$	$T = 10$	$T = 20$
$N = 50$			
Naive	0.095	0.093	0.088
Asy.	0.067	0.083	0.086
Pairs	0.004	0.004	0.003
Wild	0.011	0.012	0.011
Avg.	0.044	0.048	0.047
$N = 100$			
Naive	0.047	0.043	0.059
Asy.	0.034	0.039	0.056
Pairs	0.001	0.001	0.001
Wild	0.005	0.005	0.005
Avg.	0.022	0.022	0.030
$N = 250$			
Naive	0.023	0.025	0.018
Asy.	0.015	0.022	0.017
Pairs	0.001	0.000	0.000
Wild	0.002	0.002	0.003
Avg.	0.010	0.012	0.009
$N = 500$			
Naive	0.022	0.017	0.017
Asy.	0.016	0.016	0.016
Pairs	0.000	0.000	0.000
Wild	0.001	0.001	0.001
Avg.	0.010	0.009	0.009
$N = 1{,}000$			
Naive	0.007	0.009	0.008
Asy.	0.002	0.010	0.007
Pairs	0.001	0.000	0.000
Wild	0.001	0.001	0.001
Avg.	0.002	0.005	0.004

Table 5.1 shows that the naive and asymptotic methods seriously over-reject for small values of N, the pairs bootstrap slightly over-rejects, and the wild bootstrap under-rejects. Both bootstrap methods are considerably more accurate than the non-bootstrap methods, with the advantage going to the pairs. For $N = 50$, actual sizes are 0.051 for the pairs and between 0.046 and 0.047 for the wild, but range from 0.069 to 0.088 for the non-bootstrap methods. Thus, the upward bias of the pairs is extremely small (2 %); the downward bias of the wild is larger (6–8 %), but still far smaller than the bias of the conventional methods (at least 40 %).

Increasing N generally improves the accuracy of all methods, but the performance rankings do not change. By N of 250, the bootstrap methods produces the correct, or very close to the correct, size in every case, while the conventional methods still overstate the significance of t-values by at least 10 % in more than half of the cases. Increasing N to 500 and then 1,000 brings actual and nominal size into alignment in every bootstrap case. However, even when $N = 1{,}000$, the conventional approaches get the size right in only two cases and are off by as much as 12 % in the others.

The sums of absolute ERPs in Table 5.2 concisely summarize the advantage of the bootstrap methods. For $N > 50$, the pairs bootstrap absolute ERP sum never exceeds 0.001. The wild bootstrap is not as impressive for smaller values of N, but competes with the pairs when N is at least 250. In contrast, the absolute ERP sums of conventional methods are often an order of magnitude larger, even for N as large as 500.

To quantify the roles of N and T in reducing size distortions we regress the ln(actual size) for each estimated coefficient on the logs of N and T by method, where the observations are the 15 combinations of N and T considered in Table 5.3. Asymptotic t-values are reported in parentheses. The results show that increasing N by a given percentage affects size to a considerably greater degree than increasing T by the same percentage. The cross-section dimension effect is also always highly significant, whereas the panel length is never significant at even the 10- % level. This makes sense, because T affects second-step estimation only through its effect on $\hat{\beta}_{FE}$ and its estimated covariance matrix.

Finally we examine the power of the conventional and bootstrap tests, computed using level-adjusted sizes. Since both bootstrap methods always reject less frequently than the conventional methods, the former will appear to have less power. Therefore, we compute power based on level-adjusted $t^*_{m,g}$ values, so that critical values are used for which the actual RP is exactly equal to the nominal RP.[7] These levels, $t^*_{\alpha/2,g}$ and $t^*_{1-\alpha/2,g}$, are the $\alpha/2$ and $1-\alpha/2$ quantiles of the sorted $t^*_{m,g}$. For each Monte Carlo replication, they are found by first sorting the $t^*_{m,g}$ values from large to small and then taking the $(\alpha/2)(B+1)$ and $(1-\alpha/2)(B+1)$ values for each g. We compute the power curves for γ_3 for each method as the alternative value of γ_3 (denoted as ALT in the figures) is increased from -1 to 1 in increments of .1 by calculating the percentage of the B bootstrap estimates that fall outside the critical region. For the conventional methods, we use the same range of alternative parameter values to compute power as the percentage of M Monte Carlo estimates that falls outside the interval defined by their level-adjusted t-values, computed using the same sorting method just described.

Figures 5.1–5.3 present the power curves for $N = 250, 500$, and 1000, where $T = 5$ throughout. With $N = 250$, the pairs method holds a slight advantage in terms of power. However, with larger values of N, all methods are highly similar. With $N = 250$ the power of all methods is quite low relative to $N = 1000$, where power has risen to approximately .7 for alternatives of -1 and 1.

[7] See Davidson and MacKinnon (2006a,b) for further discussion.

Table 5.3 Regressions explaining ln (actual size) (number of observations = 15)

	Intercept	ln(N)	ln(T)	R^2
Naive				
γ_1	2.5426	−0.1277	−0.0369	0.7180
	(15.4134)**	(−5.4644)**	(−0.8293)	
γ_2	2.8238	−0.1766	−0.0173	0.8894
	(22.2146)**	(−9.8096)**	(−0.5066)	
γ_3	2.6794	−0.1550	−0.0073	0.7569
	(14.9573)**	(−6.1099)**	(−0.1514)	
Avg.	2.6819	−0.1531	−0.0205	0.7881
Asy.				
γ_1	2.3006	−0.1128	0.0169	0.6857
	(14.7321)**	(−5.1009)**	(0.4023)	
γ_2	2.6490	−0.1663	0.0211	0.8702
	(20.1923)**	(−8.9502)**	(0.5962)	
γ_3	2.5232	−0.1474	0.0282	0.7411
	(14.1429)**	(−5.8312)**	(0.5873)	
Avg.	2.4910	−0.1422	0.0221	0.7657
Pairs				
γ_1	1.6651	−0.0088	−0.0008	0.8064
	(188.2853)**	(−7.0626)**	(−0.3330)	
γ_2	1.6575	−0.0083	0.0013	0.6901
	(146.0756)**	(−5.1508)**	(0.4405)	
γ_3	1.6622	−0.0088	0.0000	0.8025
	(187.1058)**	(−6.9817)**	(0.0179)	
Avg.	1.6616	−0.0086	0.0002	0.7663
Wild				
γ_1	1.4655	0.0220	−0.0014	0.7810
	(61.5810)**	(6.5375)**	(−0.2115)	
γ_2	1.4651	0.0229	−0.0035	0.8314
	(69.5469)**	(7.6683)**	(−0.6200)	
γ_3	1.4590	0.0228	−0.0009	0.8420
	(72.5098)**	(7.9953)**	(−0.1599)	
Avg.	1.4632	0.0226	−0.0019	0.8181

** indicates significance of the t-values at the .05 level using a two-tailed asymptotic-t test.

5.6 Conclusions

The primary advantage of panel data is the ability they provide to control for unobserved heterogeneity or effects that are time-invariant. The fixed-effects (FE) estimator is by far the most popular technique for exploiting this advantage, because it makes no assumption about the relationship between the explanatory variables in the model and the effects. However, a well-known problem with the FE estimator is that any time-invariant regressor in the model is swept away by the data transformation that eliminates the effects. The partial effects of time-invariant

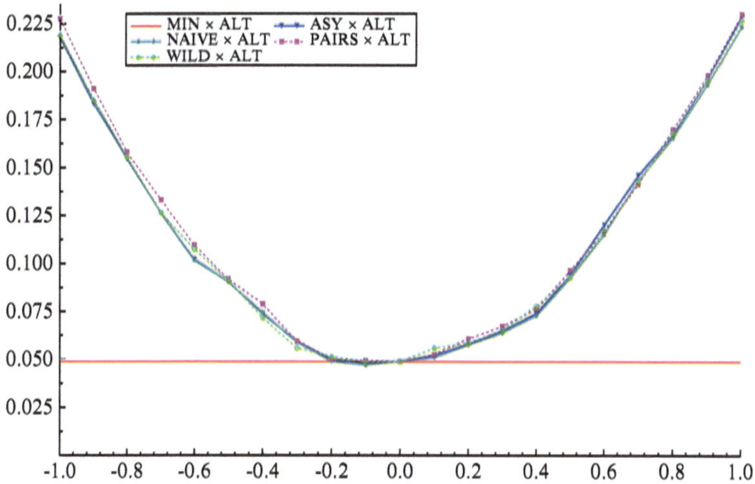

Fig. 5.1 Power vs. H_A for $N = 250$, $t = 5$ for γ_3

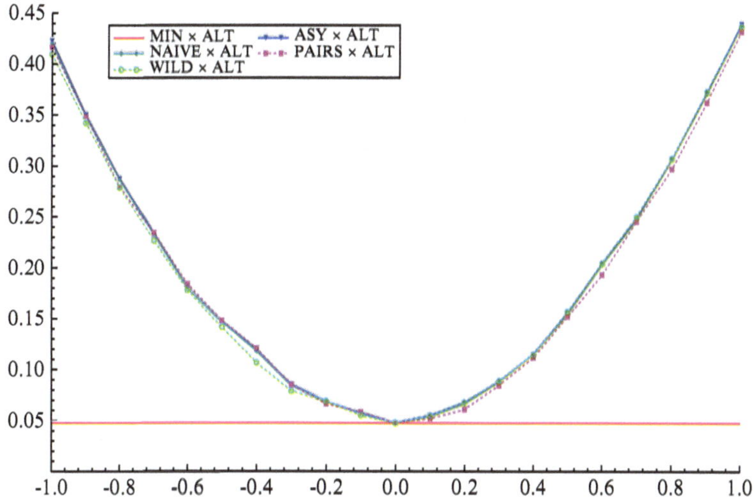

Fig. 5.2 Power vs. H_A for $N = 500$, $t = 5$ for γ_3

variables can be estimated in a second-step regression, but this fact is generally overlooked in textbook discussions of panel-data methods.

In this paper, we have shown how to conduct inference on the coefficients of time-invariant variables in linear panel-data models, estimated in a two-step framework. Our estimation framework is rooted in Hausman and Taylor's (1981) "consistent, but inefficient" estimator, albeit under weaker FE assumptions. We derive the asymptotic covariance matrix of the two-step estimator and compare inference based on the asymptotic standard errors with bootstrap alternatives. Bootstrapping

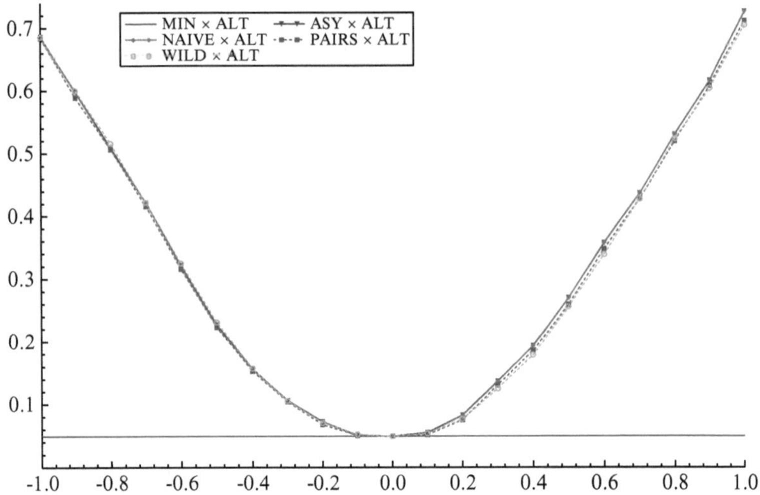

Fig. 5.3 Power vs. H_A for $N = 1000$, $t = 5$ for γ_3

has a natural appeal, because of the complications associated with estimating the asymptotic covariance matrix and the inherent finite-sample bias of the resulting standard errors. We adapt the pairs and wild bootstrap to this two-step problem. Then we prove that both bootstrap coefficient estimators are unbiased, a result that is important since bootstrap ERPs are a function of bias. Using Monte Carlo methods, we compare the size and power of the naive asymptotic estimator, which ignores the first-step estimation error, the correct asymptotic covariance matrix estimator, which does not, and the bootstrap alternatives.

In terms of size, bootstrap methods are the clear winners. For values of N less than 250, the pairs somewhat over-rejects and the wild somewhat under-rejects, with the pairs having a small advantage. The positive ERP of the pairs is 2 %, while the negative ERP of the wild is 6–8 %. In contrast, both are considerably more accurate than the methods based on asymptotic formulae, which are typically biased by more than 40 %. For values of N equal to 250 and larger, the bootstrap methods converge to the correct size and the advantage of the pairs becomes negligible. The correct asymptotic covariance matrix estimator remains somewhat biased even for $N = 1{,}000$. The pairs bootstrap method slightly out-performs the other methods in terms of power with $N = 250$, although power curves are highly similar with larger values of N.

The Monte Carlo findings are consistent with the results of our analytical examination of the pairs and wild bootstrap procedures. The implication of these results is that both bootstrap ERPs should be very close to zero. The bottom line of both our Monte Carlo exercise and analytical results is that researchers interested in estimating the effects of time-invariant variables in a two-step framework should rely on bootstrapped standard errors. This conclusion holds particularly strongly in small-N panels like those encountered in cross-state and cross-country studies.

What remains is to consider the advantages to bootstrapping when some of the second-step regression variables may be correlated with the unobserved effects and when the true model errors are heteroskedastic and autocorrelated. Atkinson and Cornwell (2013) extend the work of this paper to that case.

Appendix

Unbiasedness of the Wild First-Step Estimator, $\hat{\beta}^w_{FE}$

Lemma 1: *Since ϵ_i is drawn independently and $E(\epsilon_i = 0)$, $E(\boldsymbol{\xi}^w_i|\mathbf{X}_i) = 0$.*

Proof of Lemma 1: From (5.17), $\boldsymbol{\xi}^w_i = \hat{\boldsymbol{\xi}}_i\epsilon_i\vartheta$. Thus, $E(\boldsymbol{\xi}^w_i|\mathbf{X}_i) = E(\hat{\boldsymbol{\xi}}_i\epsilon_i\vartheta|\mathbf{X}_i) = E(\hat{\boldsymbol{\xi}}_i|\mathbf{X}_i)\vartheta E(\epsilon_i|\mathbf{X}_i) = E(\hat{\boldsymbol{\xi}}_i|\mathbf{X}_i)\vartheta E(\epsilon_i) = 0$, since ϵ_i is independent of $\hat{\boldsymbol{\xi}}_i$ and $\mathbf{X}_i$ and in addition $E(\epsilon_i) = 0$ by definition in (5.15). ■

Theorem 1: *Given the FE conditional-mean assumption in (5.3) and Lemma 1, the wild bootstrap first-step estimator $\hat{\beta}^w_{FE}$ is unbiased for $\hat{\beta}_{FE}$.*

Proof of Theorem 1: Writing the vector form of (5.16) as $\mathbf{y}^w_i = \mathbf{X}_i\hat{\beta}_{FE} + \mathbf{z}_i\hat{\gamma}_{FE} + \boldsymbol{\xi}^w_i$ and substituting into (5.18), the first-step wild estimator can be written as

$$\hat{\beta}^w_{FE} = \hat{\beta}_{FE} + \left(\sum_i \mathbf{X}_i'\mathbf{Q}_T\mathbf{X}_i\right)^{-1}\sum_i \mathbf{X}_i'\mathbf{Q}_T\boldsymbol{\xi}^w_i, \tag{5.33}$$

where $\boldsymbol{\xi}^w_i$ is a $(T \times 1)$ vector. Then

$$E(\hat{\beta}^w_{FE}|\mathbf{X}_i) = \hat{\beta}_{FE} + \left(\sum_i \mathbf{X}_i'\mathbf{Q}_T\mathbf{X}_i\right)^{-1}\sum_i \mathbf{X}_i'\mathbf{Q}_T E(\boldsymbol{\xi}^w_i|\mathbf{X}_i) = \hat{\beta}_{FE}, \tag{5.34}$$

using Lemma 1. Further, $E[E(\hat{\beta}^w_{FE}|\mathbf{X}_i)] = E(\hat{\beta}^w_{FE}) = \hat{\beta}_{FE}$. ■

Unbiasedness of the Wild Second-Step Estimator, $\hat{\gamma}^w_{FE}$

To show that the second-step wild estimator is unbiased, we substitute (5.19) into (5.20) to obtain

$$u^w_i = \bar{y}^w_i - \bar{\mathbf{x}}_i\hat{\beta}^w_{FE} - \mathbf{z}_i\hat{\gamma}_{FE}. \tag{5.35}$$

Now average (5.16) over t to obtain

$$\bar{y}_i^w = \bar{\mathbf{x}}_i \hat{\beta}_{FE} + \mathbf{z}_i \hat{\gamma}_{FE} + \bar{\xi}_i^w \tag{5.36}$$

and substitute (5.36) into (5.35) to yield

$$u_i^w = \bar{\mathbf{x}}_i (\hat{\beta}_{FE} - \hat{\beta}_{FE}^w) + \bar{\xi}_i^w. \tag{5.37}$$

Lemma 2: *Since ϵ_i is drawn independently and $E(\epsilon_i = 0)$, $E(\bar{\xi}_{it}^w | \mathbf{z}_i, \bar{\mathbf{x}}_i) = 0$.*

Proof of Lemma 2: Use the definition of ξ_{it}^w in (5.17) and condition on $\mathbf{z}_i, \bar{\mathbf{x}}_i$. Then use the independence of ϵ_i from $\mathbf{z}_i, \bar{\mathbf{x}}_i$. ■

Theorem 2: *Given Theorem 1 and Lemma 2, the wild second-step estimator, $\hat{\gamma}_{FE}^w$, is unbiased for $\hat{\gamma}_{FE}$.*

Proof of Theorem 2:

$$\begin{aligned} E(\hat{\gamma}_{FE}^w | \mathbf{z}_i, \bar{\mathbf{x}}_i) &= \hat{\gamma}_{FE} + \left(\sum_i \mathbf{z}_i' \mathbf{z}_i \right)^{-1} \left(\sum_i \mathbf{z}_i' E(u_i^w | \mathbf{z}_i, \bar{\mathbf{x}}_i) \right) \\ &= \hat{\gamma}_{FE} + \left(\sum_i \mathbf{z}_i' \mathbf{z}_i \right)^{-1} \left(\sum_i \mathbf{z}_i' E\{[\bar{\mathbf{x}}_i (\hat{\beta}_{FE} - \hat{\beta}_{FE}^w) + \bar{\xi}_i^w] | \mathbf{z}_i, \bar{\mathbf{x}}_i\} \right) \\ &= \hat{\gamma}_{FE}, \end{aligned} \tag{5.38}$$

after substituting from (5.37) for u_i^w and then applying Theorem 1 and Lemma 2. Finally, $E[E(\hat{\gamma}_{FE}^w | \mathbf{z}_i, \bar{\mathbf{x}}_i)] = E(\hat{\gamma}_{FE}^w) = \hat{\gamma}_{FE}$. ■

Unbiasedness of the Pairs First-Step Estimator, $\hat{\boldsymbol{\beta}}_{FE}^p$

To show the unbiasedness of the pairs first-step estimator, we need (5.3).

Lemma 3: *Given (5.3), $E(\mathbf{Q}_T \hat{\boldsymbol{\xi}}_i | v_i, \mathbf{X}_i) = 0$.*

Proof of Lemma 3: First,

$$\begin{aligned} E(\mathbf{Q}_T \hat{\boldsymbol{\xi}}_i | v_i, \mathbf{X}_i) &= E(\mathbf{M}_i \mathbf{Q}_T \boldsymbol{\xi}_i | v_i, \mathbf{X}_i) \\ &= E(\mathbf{Q}_T \boldsymbol{\xi}_i | v_i, \mathbf{X}_i) - \mathbf{Q}_T \mathbf{X}_i \left(\sum_i \mathbf{X}_i' \mathbf{Q}_T \mathbf{X}_i \right)^{-1} \mathbf{X}_i' \mathbf{Q}_T E(\mathbf{Q}_T \boldsymbol{\xi}_i | v_i, \mathbf{X}_i) \\ &= 7E\{\mathbf{Q}_T [(\mathbf{j}_T \otimes c_i) + \mathbf{e}_i] | v_i, \mathbf{X}_i\} \\ &\quad - \mathbf{Q}_T \mathbf{X}_i \left(\sum_i \mathbf{X}_i' \mathbf{Q}_T \mathbf{X}_i \right)^{-1} \mathbf{X}_i' \mathbf{Q}_T E\{\mathbf{Q}_T [(\mathbf{j}_T \otimes c_i) + \mathbf{e}_i] \\ &\quad \times | v_i, \mathbf{X}_i\}, \end{aligned} \tag{5.39}$$

using $\mathbf{M}_i = \mathbf{I}_T - \mathbf{Q}_T\mathbf{X}_i\left(\sum_i \mathbf{X}_i'\mathbf{Q}_T\mathbf{X}_i\right)^{-1}\mathbf{X}_i'\mathbf{Q}_T$ and $\boldsymbol{\xi}_i = (\mathbf{j}_T \otimes c_i) + \mathbf{e}_i$. Then, using (5.3) and the fact that $\mathbf{Q}_T$ eliminates c_i completes the proof. ■

Theorem 3: *Given Lemma 3, the bootstrap pairs first-step estimator, $\hat{\beta}^p_{FE}$, is unbiased for $\hat{\beta}_{FE}$.*

Proof of Theorem 3: Substitute $\mathbf{Q}_T\mathbf{y}_i$ in (5.28) and take expectations. Then

$$\begin{aligned} E(\hat{\beta}^p_{FE}|v_i, \mathbf{X}_i) &= \hat{\beta}_{FE} + \left(\sum_i v_i \mathbf{X}_i'\mathbf{Q}_T\mathbf{X}_i\right)^{-1} \sum_i v_i \mathbf{X}_i'\mathbf{Q}_T E(\mathbf{Q}_T\hat{\boldsymbol{\xi}}_i|v_i, \mathbf{X}_i) \\ &= \hat{\beta}_{FE}, \end{aligned} \tag{5.40}$$

using Lemma 3. ■

Unbiasedness of the Pairs Second-Step Estimator, $\hat{\gamma}^p_{FE}$

Theorem 4: *Given (5.3), (5.4), and Theorem 3, the pairs second-step estimator, $\hat{\gamma}^p_{FE}$, is unbiased for $\hat{\gamma}_{FE}$.*

Proof of Theorem 4: Substituting (5.29) into (5.30) we obtain

$$\hat{\gamma}^p_{FE} = \hat{\gamma}_{FE} + \left(\sum_i v_i \mathbf{z}_i'\mathbf{z}_i\right)^{-1}\left(\sum_i v_i \mathbf{z}_i'\hat{u}_i\right). \tag{5.41}$$

We can relate $\hat{u}_i$ to u_i as follows:

$$\hat{u}_i = u_i - \mathbf{z}_i\left(\sum_i \mathbf{z}_i'\mathbf{z}_i\right)^{-1}\sum_i \mathbf{z}_i'u_i. \tag{5.42}$$

Then substitute (5.42) into (5.41) to obtain

$$\hat{\gamma}^p_{FE} = \hat{\gamma}_{FE} + \left(\sum_i v_i \mathbf{z}_i'\mathbf{z}_i\right)^{-1}\sum_i v_i \mathbf{z}_i'u_i - \left(\sum_i \mathbf{z}_i'\mathbf{z}_i\right)^{-1}\sum_i \mathbf{z}_i'u_i \tag{5.43}$$

Conditioning on $(\mathbf{z}_i, \bar{\mathbf{x}}_i, v_i)$, we use (5.8) and take the expectation of both sides to obtain

$$E(u_i|\mathbf{z}_i, \bar{\mathbf{x}}_i, v_i) = E(\bar{\xi}_i|\mathbf{z}_i, v_i) + \bar{\mathbf{x}}_i E[(\hat{\beta}_{FE} - \beta)|\mathbf{z}_i, \bar{\mathbf{x}}_i, v_i]. \tag{5.44}$$

The first term on the right-hand-side of (5.44) is zero due to (5.3) and (5.4), while $\hat{\beta}_{FE}$ is unbiased for β from Theorem 3. ■

References

Agee MD, Atkinson SE, Crocker TD (2009) Multi-input and multi-output estimation of the efficiency of child health production: a two-step panel data approach. South Econ J 75:909–927

Agee MD, Atkinson SE, Crocker TD (2012) Child maturation, time-invariant, and time-varying inputs: their interaction in the production of human capital. J Product Anal 35:29–44

Arellano M (1987) Computing robust standard errors for within-groups estimators, Oxf Bull Econ Stat 49:431–34

Atkinson SE, Cornwell C (2013) Inference in two-step panel data models with weak instruments and time-invariant regressors: bootstrap versus analytic estimators. Working paper, University of Georgia

Breusch T, Ward MB, Nguyen HTM, Kompas T (2011) On the fixed-effects vector decomposition. Polit Anal 19:123–134

Cameron AC, Trivedi, PK (2005) Microeconometrics: methods and applications. Cambridge University Press, New York

Davidson R, Flachaire, E (2008) The wild bootstrap, tamed at last. J Econom 146:162–169

Davidson R, MacKinnon, JG (1999) Size distortion of bootstrap tests. Econom Theory 15:361–376

Davidson R, MacKinnon, JG (2006) The power of bootstrap and asymptotic tests. J Econom 133:421–441

Davidson R, MacKinnon, JG (2006) Bootstrap methods in econometrics. Chapter 23 In: Mills TC, Patterson KD (ed) Palgrave handbooks of econometrics: Volume I Econometric Theory. Palgrave Macmillan, Basingstoke, pp 812–838

Flachaire E (2005) Bootstrapping Heteroskedastic regression models: wild bootsrap vs. pairs bootstrap. Comput Stat Data Anal 2005:361–376

Greene WH (2011) Fixed effects vector decomposition: A magical solution to the problem of time-invariant variables in fixed effects models? Polit Anal 19:135–146

Hausman JA, Taylor W (1981) Panel data and unobservable individual effects. Econometrica 49:1377–1399

Horowitz J (2001) The bootstrap. In: Heckman JJ, Leamer E (ed) Handbook of econometrics, vol 5, ch. 52. North-Holland, New York

Kapetanios G (2008) A bootstrap procedure for panel data sets with many cross-sectional units. Econom J 11:377–395

Knack S (1993) The voter participation effects of selecting jurors from registration. J Law Econ 36:99–114

MacKinnon JG (2002) Bootstrap inference in econometrics. Can J Econ 35:615–645

Murphy KM, Topel RH, (1985) Estimation and inference in two-step econometric models. J Bus Econ Stat 3:88–97

Plümper T, Troeger VE (2007) Efficient estimation of time-invariant and rarely changing variables in finite sample panel analysis with unit fixed effects. Polit Anal 15:124–139

Wooldridge JM (2010) Econometric analysis of cross section and panel data, 2nd edn. MIT: Cambridge

Chapter 6
International Evidence on Cross-Price Effects of Food and Other Goods

James L. Seale, Jr., Cody P. Dahl, Charles B. Moss, and Anita Regmi

6.1 Introduction

A change in the price of a good affects the demand for that good and for other goods as well. Understanding and measuring the interaction between the price and consumption of goods among countries with diverse income levels improve the ability of researchers and policy makers to project changing consumption patterns and their effects on rich and poor countries. Price and income elasticities are critical tools for these analyses, but estimation of these are sometimes hampered by the lack of data consistent over countries and geographic regions. The International Comparison Project (ICP) provides such data, making important advancements in cross-country-demand analyses possible.[1] Although cross-country-demand studies

[1]Kravis et al. (1975) conduct phase I, Kravis et al. (1978, 1982) conduct phases II and III, the United Nations Statistical Office conducts Phases IV and V, and a consortium coordinated by the World Bank conducts the 1996 ICP. See Seale and Regmi (2006) for a more thorough discussion of the data and issues involved in using them to estimate and model cross-country demand systems.

J.L. Seale, Jr. (✉) • C.B. Moss
University of Florida, Food and Resource Economics, P.O. Box 110240, Gainesville, FL 32611-0240, USA
e-mail: jseale@ufl.edu; cbmoss@ufl.edu

C.P. Dahl
Hancock Agricultural Investment Group, 99 High Street, 26th Floor, Boston, MA 02110-2320
e-mail: CDahl@hnrg.com

A. Regmi
CGIAR Consortium Office c/o AGROPOLIS INTERNATIONAL, Avenue Agropolis, F-34394 Montpellier Cedex 5, France
e-mail: anita.regmi@cgiar.org

R.C. Sickles and W.C. Horrace (eds.), *Festschrift in Honor of Peter Schmidt: Econometric Methods and Applications*, DOI 10.1007/978-1-4899-8008-3_6,

that do not use ICP data are mentioned, this paper emphasizes those that do. In particular, the focus of the paper is not on income or own-price elasticities of demand, but on cross-price elasticities of demand for a large and income diverse set of countries.

Many cross-country-demand studies calculate and report expenditure or own-price elasticities of demand. Early international comparison studies fit demand models to time-series data on a country-by-country basis and report expenditure or own-price elasticities (e.g., Houthakker 1957; Gamaletsos 1973; Parks and Barten 1973; Selvanathan and Selvanathan 1993; and Chen 1999b). Following Houthakker (1965), other authors fit demand systems to pooled time-series data and report either expenditure or own-price elasticities (e.g., Pollack and Wales 1987; Clements and Selvanathan 1994; Chen 1999a, c; Yu et al. 2003; Reimer 2003; and Clements et al. 2006).

Studies that use ICP data and report own-price elasticities of demand are Finke et al. (1984), Chen (1994), Clements and Chen (1996), Regmi et al. (2001), Seale et al. (2003), and Seale and Regmi (2006, 2009). Other studies that use ICP data to estimate cross-country-demand systems report expenditure or Engel elasticities of demand but no price elasticities (e.g., Clements et al. 1979; Finke et al. 1983; Theil et al. 1980; Seale and Theil 1991a; Wang et al. 1997; Cole et al. 1998; Cranfield et al. 1998a, 2000; Reimer and Hertel 2003; Cranfield et al. 2005, 2007) while others report no elasticities at all (e.g., Cranfield et al. 1998b, 2003; and Reimer and Hertel 2004; Clements and Chen 2010).

Few studies that fit demand systems to cross-country data calculate and report cross-price elasticities of demand. Goldberger and Gamaletsos (1970) report and compare cross-price elasticities of demand for five goods in 11 OECD countries, but they estimate the sample mean elasticities of each country separately with time-series data and not as a cross-country-demand system. Lluch and Powell (1975) fit the linear expenditure system to time-series data of 19 countries for eight goods and report the cross-price elasticities of seven goods with respect to food price at sample means. Three studies (i.e., Theil and Finke 1985 (also reported in Theil 1987); Theil et al. 1989; and Seale and Theil 1991b) calculate and report cross-price elasticities for two goods, food and nonfood, by fitting a demand system to ICP data. Additionally, Theil and Finke (1985) (also in Theil 1987, Table 2.10, p. 67) calculate cross-price elasticities of demand for food and nonfood for 13 real (1975) per-capita income levels expressed as a percentage of the United States (U.S.) level, basing their calculations on parameter estimates of Finke et al. (1983). TCS fit a 10-good-demand system to pooled ICP data of 1970, 1975 and 1980 and use their resulting parameter estimates to calculate and report cross-price elasticities of food and nonfood for 60 countries in 1980. Seale and Theil (1991b) calculate their reported cross-price elasticities of food and nonfood for 60 countries in 1980 using parameter estimates of Fiebig et al. (1988) who fit a 10-good-demand system to the pooled ICP data of the 60 countries for the years 1970, 1975 and 1980.

More recently, Seale et al. (SRB 2003) and Seale and Regmi (SR 2006) fit a two-stage-demand system to data from the 1996 ICP. Seale and Regmi (SR 2009) use maximum likelihood (ML) to estimate the parameters of the Florida model and correct for group heteroskedasticity.[2] SRB and SR (2006) also use the parameter estimates from the first stage of the two-stage-demand system to calculate the income elasticities and three own-price elasticities of demand for nine goods. No one to date, however, calculates the cross-price elasticities of demand using more than a two-good, cross-country-demand system.

This paper develops a methodology to calculate theoretically consistent cross-price elasticities of demand by using the parameter estimates of the Florida model and real income per-capita statistics from a large and diverse set of 114 countries. The next section presents a review of the literature, followed by a brief discussion of the ICP data and the methodology for obtaining cross-price elasticities. The details of the Florida model are presented in Appendix A while the formulae of the cross-price elasticities are developed in Appendix B. The empirical section reports the cross-price elasticities of a two-good demand system – food and nonfood – from the 114-country sample, and compares these elasticities with those of TCS (pp. 116–117) for the 41 countries in both studies. This is followed by the presentation and discussion of the cross-price elasticities of the nine goods which are reported and discussed for three income groupings of the 114 countries and for each of the 114 countries. In the conclusions, comments are made and implications drawn.

6.2 Review of Literature

Cross-country demand analysis for goods and services has come a long way since the pioneering work of Hendrik Houthakker (1957). Clements and Theil (1979) and Suhm (1979) are first to apply a cross-country-demand system to ICP data by fitting Working's (1943) model to 1975 ICP data of 15 countries on four and eight groups of consumer goods ("goods" hereafter), respectively.[3]

Working fit his model to U.S. household data by assuming that all households face the same prices. Accordingly, Working's model accounts for variation in income but not in prices. Working's model is appropriate to use in cross-country-demand analysis if it is reasonable to assume that the price of goods are the same in each country. Since consumers in different countries often pay different prices for the same-type goods, the equal-price assumption is generally too restrictive and prevents analysis of how, in different countries, the demand for goods changes in response to a change in the own price or in the price of other goods.

---

[2]TCS who developed the model originally referred to it as the Working-PI (preference independence) model (TCS, p. 41). Seale et al. (1991) are first to refer to it as the Florida model in the tradition of naming a demand-system model for its place of origin (e.g., Rotterdam model (Theil 1965), the CBS model (Keller and van Driel 1985), and the NBR model (Neves 1987)). Theil in later writings also refers to it as the Florida model (Theil 1996. p. 3, 60; 1997). The model is described in detail in Appendix A.

[3]Working's model is an Engel curve model that describes the budget shares of goods as linear functions of the log of total consumption expenditure (income).

Theil et al. (TSM 1980) apply the differential approach to consumption theory to the cross-country Working's model and add a price term to account for the substitution effects among goods that result from a price change. TSM fit their model to data compiled by Suhm (1979) and, adding the constraint of preference independence among goods (additive utility), estimate the parameters of the model with ML.

Others successfully apply the TSM model to data from the ICP. Finke et al. (1983) fit the TSM model to data from 30 countries using the 1975 ICP statistics on 10 goods.[4] Fiebig et al. (1987) disaggregate the 1975 ICP data further into an 11-good demand system that includes energy. Fiebig et al. (FST 1988) individually apply the TSM model (with 10 goods) to 15 countries from the 1970 ICP, 30 countries from the 1975 ICP, and 24 (of 30) countries that participate in both Phases III (1975 ICP) and IV (1980 ICP). FST also pool the data from the 30 countries (in the 1975 ICP) by linking country data in 1975 to 1970 and 1980 to 1975. Since the resulting data are stochastically dependent across time, FST extend the TSM model to incorporate an autoregressive process (AR (1)) that corrects for serial correlation.[5]

Seale and Theil (1987) extend the analysis of FST in three ways: they increase the FST sample size from 30 countries to 58 countries by adding the Phase IV (1980) data of 28 additional countries that did not participate in the ICP prior to Phase IV; they note that the size of the error covariance matrices, when applying the TSM model to the data containing the new 28 countries, is about twice the size of the error covariance matrices of the FST groupings; and, in estimating the pooled-data parameters, they multiply by two the error covariance matrix with the new 28 countries in the computations of the ML estimator to correct for group heteroskedasticity.

TCS modify the TSM model by using a different parameterization of the model. The resulting model, the Florida model, describes the budget share of a good as a function of, in addition to an income term and a substitution term, a pure price term. TCS, using a 10-good classification, fit the new model to the ICP data of Phases II, III, and IV, individually, and, after a series of tests, fit the new model to the data pooled across time. TCS estimate all parameters of the Florida model with ML, including an autoregressive and heteroskedasticity parameters, by an iterative grid search. In a subsequent paper, Seale et al. (SWK 1991) fit the Florida model to the TCS data disaggregated into an 11-good system, including energy, and estimate all parameters with the ML scoring method (Harvey 1990, p. 320). Seale, Regmi and Bernstein (SRB) and Seale and Regmi (SR 2006, 2009) fit the model to the 1996 ICP

[4]Kravis et al. (1982) fit the linear expenditure system (LES) to four broad categories of goods, but a careful reading of their footnote 47, p. 386, makes it clear that their LES analysis is independent of the ICP multilateral data. They do, however, fit a double-log model to ICP Phase III data for 25 summary categories of goods and for 103 detailed categories of goods in 30 countries.

[5]If the error term, say, of the food budget share is positive and large for country c in 1970 (Phase II), it is likely that this country will also have a positive error term for food in 1975 (Phase III). The AR(1) process is a simple method to account for stable but different preference structures across countries.

data of 114 countries for nine goods in the first stage of a two-stage-demand system and estimate the parameters with a heteroskedastic-corrected-maximum-likelihood estimator.[6] More recently, Clements and Chen (2010) fit the Florida model to ICP data for the purpose of measuring the affluence of nations based on food budget shares that allow for difference in food prices, and Seale and Solano (2012) estimate the cross-country demand for energy with the Florida model.

6.3 Data

When available, cross-country consumption data that include rich and poor countries are attractive for demand analysis. The variability of consumption, income, and prices is generally greater than time-series data of a single country or household data (Selvanathan and Selvanathan 1993). However, using consumption data for a large number of countries, goods, and services can be challenging. Firstly, international data are generally reported in national currency units and conversion to a single currency denomination is required. One possible way is to convert national currency units into base-country units with official exchange rates. However, doing so is fraught with problems. One is that conversion by official exchange rates leads to converted expenditure data that overstate the poverty of low-income countries (Kravis et al. 1982). Also, expenditure data converted by official exchange rates can lead to spurious results because of wide fluctuations in official exchange rates over time that are independent of personal expenditures (Theil et al. 1989). Further, official exchange rates are not connected to changes in demand for non-traded goods and services.

The ICP, originally established by Kravis and his colleagues at University of Pennsylvania, uses a currency-exchange methodology based on purchasing-power parity (PPP) and provides comparable gross-domestic product and consumption data based on PPP conversions for a large number of consumption items across countries (Kravis et al. 1975). PPP is the number of local currency units required to buy equivalent goods with a unit of base-country currency. The measure converts different national currencies to a single-base currency based upon the number of units it takes to purchase the same bundle of goods in the base country. As such, it more closely relates consumption expenditures across countries than conversion by official exchange rates. Further, this method is not susceptible to the vagaries of exchange rate fluctuations, and, unlike official exchange rates, it accounts for both traded and non-traded goods and services (Reimer and Hertel 2004).

The paper analyzes the 1996 ICP data collected between 1993 and 1996 by six agencies contracted by the United Nations for countries in Asia, Africa, the Middle

---

[6] To differentiate the preference structure in the two stages, these authors refer to the first-stage (second-stage) model as the Florida-PI (Slutsky) model. In this paper, we forego this differentiation and simply refer to the preference independent form as the Florida model.

East, the Caribbean, Latin America, Organization for Economic Co-Operation and Development (OECD), and the Commonwealth of Independent States (CIS).[7] Price and expenditure data at disaggregate levels are collected in each region. Real volumes (quantities) are obtained with the Geary-Khamis method and are expressed in terms of the base-country currency (in most cases the 1996 United States (U.S.) dollar) that are comparable across countries.[8] A major advantage of the Geary-Khamis method is that the resulting volumes (quantities) are additive in that subcategory volumes sum to the calculated category volume (United Nations, 1986–1987; World Bank 1993).

Two of the regions, Asia and Latin America, did not express the data relative to that of the U.S. dollar but relative to currencies of Hong Kong and Mexico, respectively. To make the data comparable across all countries, SRB (2003) transform the data in two ways. Because Mexico is included in the OECD-country data, conversion of the Latin America data to be comparable to the U.S. is straight forward. Making the Asian data comparable to the other countries is more challenging. In the first step, SBR re-express the Asian data relative to that of Japan that are included in the OECD-country data. The resulting transformed Asian data still have scaling problems. Next, SRB compare the PPP-based per capita real consumption from the 1996 ICP data to those from the World Bank's World Development Indicators (WDI 2001), and they notice a close match for all countries except those in Asia. Accordingly, they use the WDI rankings as a new scale for the Asian data. For example, Hong Kong's PPP real per capita personal consumption in 1996 (according to the WDI 2001) is 79.8% that of the U.S. level, and SR multiply the real per capita volumes (in 1996 international dollars) of the broad consumption categories of Asian countries by 79.8 to get real volumes relative to those of the U.S. This process adequately corrects the scaling problem encountered within the Asian-country data.

While 115 countries are included in the 1996 ICP, one country, Herzegovina, does not have associated population data. As all expenditures and real volumes are converted for analysis on a per capita basis, Herzegovina is omitted from the sample. The resulting 114 countries are presented in Table 6.1.

The analysis is confined to the consumption component of gross domestic product and, in particular, to nine consumption categories: food, beverages and tobacco; clothing and footwear; gross rent, fuel and power; house furnishings and operations; medical care; transport and communications; recreation; education; and other items. The food, beverages and tobacco group includes food prepared and consumed at home plus beverages and tobacco, but it does not include food

[7]Over the years, the number of countries included in the ICP has increased: 10 countries in the 1970 Phase I (Kravis et al. 1975); 16 countries in the 1970 Phase II (Kravis et al. 1978); 34 countries in the 1975 Phase III (Kravis et al. 1982); 60 countries in the 1980 Phase IV (United Nations 1986–1987); and 115 countries in 1996.

[8]See TCS, Appendix A, for a discussion of the Geary-Khamis methodology and how to estimate PPPs based upon it.

Table 6.1 Normalized per capita real income and food budget shares (from 1996 ICP)

Country	Per capita real income US = 100	Food share of total expenditure	Country	Per capita real income US = 100	Food share of total expenditure	Country	Per capita real income US = 100	Food share of total expenditure
Low-income countries	*Percent*		***Middle-income countries***	*Percent*		***High-income countries***	*Percent*	
Tanzania	2.04	73.24	Ukraine	15.28	45.03	Czech Republic	45.08	25.00
Nigeria	2.88	72.97	Philippines	16.32	48.35	Greece	48.48	21.17
Tajikistan	3.37	68.94	Peru	16.76	30.31	Korea	49.45	31.64
Zambia	3.46	60.81	Botswana	16.81	32.80	Portugal	50.54	23.23
Yemen	3.47	61.13	Thailand	17.03	28.56	Spain	50.84	17.52
Malawi	3.81	53.35	Morocco	17.56	45.61	Ireland	52.19	16.59
Madagascar	3.81	65.88	Venezuela	17.71	29.47	Singapore	53.64	13.04
Mali	3.91	53.27	Macedonia	18.51	34.73	Mauritius	55.77	28.12
Mongolia	3.94	58.74	Belize	18.55	31.17	Israel	57.73	17.70
Benin	4.88	55.40	Egypt	18.58	48.08	New Zealand	58.54	15.19
Kenya	5.35	45.82	St Vincent and Grenadines	18.70	35.87	Finland	58.72	14.67
Sierra Leone	5.80	62.09	Swaziland	19.67	27.48	Bahamas	59.35	35.73
Nepal	5.81	57.88	Lebanon	20.07	39.33	Sweden	63.82	13.26
Turkmenistan	6.04	50.82	Belarus	20.25	50.45	Netherlands	64.58	13.29
Congo	6.51	46.92	Kazakhstan	20.33	51.82	France	68.20	15.34
Senegal	6.94	53.35	Dominica	20.33	38.27	United Kingdom	68.55	16.37
Vietnam	7.10	64.75	Latvia	21.43	41.76	Belgium	69.32	14.36
Bangladesh	7.16	56.05	St Lucia	21.55	46.62	Norway	69.51	15.98
Pakistan	8.23	46.99	Brazil	21.68	22.71	Italy	70.07	16.59
Azerbaijan	8.76	73.51	Bulgaria	21.80	30.70	Austria	71.51	13.53
Cote d'Ivoire	8.99	44.32	Russia	22.47	34.35	Germany	71.79	13.09
Paraguay	9.14	27.27	Fiji	23.25	36.28	Australia	73.17	15.07

(continued)

Table 6.1 (continued)

Country	Per capita real income US = 100	Food share of total expenditure	Country	Per capita real income US = 100	Food share of total expenditure	Country	Per capita real income US = 100	Food share of total expenditure
Uzbekistan	9.54	48.33	Grenada	23.26	40.99	Japan	74.12	14.88
Kyrgyzstan	9.57	47.15	Turkey	23.65	32.60	Canada	75.41	11.68
Cameroon	9.64	43.80	Lithuania	24.31	40.42	Bermuda	78.21	14.23
Moldova	9.65	43.45	Romania	24.80	45.26	Switzerland	79.36	14.57
Bolivia	10.10	42.52	Iran	25.80	32.55	Barbados	79.55	11.10
Ecuador	10.27	29.09	Mexico	26.31	26.63	Hong Kong	79.86	10.28
Armenia	10.74	69.66	Bahrain	26.91	28.55	Iceland	80.11	18.90
Sri Lanka	10.79	63.55	Chile	27.34	22.96	Denmark	80.85	14.02
Jordan	11.37	37.67	Antigua and Barbuda	27.34	36.12	Luxemburg	97.17	17.08
Albania	12.25	69.26	Poland	28.27	30.65	United States	100.00	9.73
Indonesia	12.56	50.62	Trinidad and Tobago	29.06	22.06			
Jamaica	12.63	34.78	Estonia	29.87	33.45			
Zimbabwe	12.71	25.58	Gabon	30.07	47.94			
Guinea	13.03	43.69	Tunisia	30.72	35.95			
Syria	13.79	47.92	St Kitts and Nevis	31.11	36.33			
Georgia	13.92	47.39	Uruguay	31.38	25.25			
			Slovakia	31.87	32.06			
			Hungary	34.57	22.54			
			Argentina	38.49	32.79			
			Oman	40.26	24.14			
			Qatar	42.57	26.22			
			Slovenia	43.67	21.34			
Low-income average	8.00	52.58	*Middle-income average*	24.91	34.69	*High-income average*	67.36	16.97

Source: Seale and Regmi (2009), Table 12.2, pp. 158–59

consumed away from home that is included in recreation. The nine consumption categories in this analysis are the same aggregate categories of SRB and SR (2009).

The 114 countries are divided into low-, middle-, and high-income countries based on real income per capita relative to that of the U.S.[9] Low-income countries represent countries with real income per capita less than 15% of the real income per capita in the U.S. Middle-income countries represent countries with real income per capita equal to or greater than 15% but less that 45% of the real income per capita in the U.S., and high-income countries represent those with real income per capita equal to or greater than 45% of the real income per capita in the U.S. (Table 6.1). The majority of Sub-Saharan African countries, poor transition economies such as Mongolia and Turkmenistan, and low-income Middle Eastern and Asian countries such as Yemen and Nepal fall within the low-income group. High-income countries include most Western European countries, Australia, New Zealand, Canada, and the U.S. Middle-income countries include many Latin American countries, North African countries, and better-off transition economies such as Estonia, Hungary, and Slovenia.

6.4 Methodology

The purpose of demand analysis is to discover empirical regularities in consumption patterns. Although single-equation methods have been used in past demand analysis, it is now generally agreed that a systems approach to demand is more appropriate. One main reason is that the demands for different goods are related through the consumer's budget constraint. If a consumer purchases more of one good, she must consume less of at least one other good.

The goal of this study is to estimate the effect of a price change of a good on the quantity demanded of the other remaining goods by calculating cross-price elasticities of demand. A cross-price elasticity measures the percent change in the quantity demanded of good i from a 1% change in the price of good j, i not equal to j. When i is equal to j, the price elasticity is referred to as an own-price elasticity of demand.

Three prominent types of price elasticities are the Frisch, Slutsky, and Cournot price elasticities. The three elasticities differ depending upon assumptions concerning income after a price change. After a price change, the Frisch price elasticity results from compensating the consumer with the amount of income that keeps the marginal utility of income constant. The Slutsky price elasticity results from compensating the consumer with the amount of income that keeps real income constant and is the price elasticity most often used in the measurement of welfare

[9]Note that this classification is merely done to facilitate analysis and is not based on any generally accepted criteria for classification. Since the classification is based on the ICP data used in this analysis, some countries may be in a group with which they normally would not be associated.

from changes in price. The Cournot price elasticity results from constraining the nominal income of the consumer to remain unchanged after a change in price.[10] Because it is composed of both the substitution effect and the income effect of a price change, it more closely measures the market response of quantity demanded when price changes. Cournot elasticities are often used in econometric and simulation models.

The first step to estimating cross-price elasticities is to fit a demand system to the data for, in our case, nine aggregate goods for 114 countries. Then, based on estimated parameters, cross-price elasticities may be calculated. We choose the Florida model for analysis and estimate its parameters with maximum likelihood (ML).[11] The Florida model is developed by TCS (1989) for the specific purpose of fitting their cross-country-demand system to ICP data. It possesses several characteristics that are important in model choice for cross-country demand analysis. One is that the model's marginal shares vary with income levels such that they increase (decrease) as income levels increase for luxury (necessity) goods. This allows the calculation of income and price elasticities for individual countries that follow the predictions of economic theory as opposed to those with constant marginal shares that would result in elasticities that go against such economic predictions. For example, Engel's law predicts that budget shares for necessities such as food decrease as income levels increase. Accordingly, the budget share for food is expected to be larger for a poor country such as Tanzania than that of the U.S. Economic theory also suggests that income and price elasticities of demand for food are larger for a poor country than for a rich one (Timmer 1981). If a model's marginal shares are constant as they are for the linear expenditure system (LES), income and price elasticities of demand would be smaller for poor countries than for rich ones.

Another reason for choosing the Florida model for analysis is that its price terms are relative prices instead of absolute prices. While the real volume (quantity) data of the ICP are measured in international dollars and thus comparable across countries, price and nominal expenditure data are measured in national currencies. By proper deflation of absolute prices, the price terms of the Florida model are relative prices and thus nondenominational. Other popular demand systems such as the almost ideal demand system (Deaton and Muellbauer 1980) and the quadratic almost ideal demand system (Banks et al. 1997) have prices expressed in absolute terms so that they are not suitable for fitting the ICP data. The use of the Florida model for estimation also facilitates the calculation of three-types of

[10]The Slutsky and Hicksian price elasticities are sometimes referred to as the compensated price elasticities. However, the Slutsky and Hicks compensation methods differ. The Slutsky (Hicks) compensation keeps real income constant after a price change by the amount necessary that would allow the consumer to continue consuming the same bundle of goods (remain on the same indifference curve) that existed prior to the price change (Friedman 1976, pp. 50–54). The Cournot price elasticity is sometimes referred to as the uncompensated or ordinary price elasticity that is derived from the ordinary or Marshallian demand curve.

[11]Clements and Chen (2010) point out that the Florida model "is probably the most extensively applied and assessed in a cross-country context."

price elasticities. The details of the Florida model and its derivation are discussed in Appendix A. Formulae for calculating cross-price elasticities are derived and presented in Appendix B.

6.5 Empirical Results

SR (2009) calculate and report income and three types of own-price elasticities of demand for nine goods in 114 countries participating in the 1996 ICP. They do not report the marginal shares of the 114 countries or the cross-price elasticities of demand for the nine goods. In this section, we extend the analyses to calculate and report the marginal shares in the 114 countries for the nine goods. Next, we examine a two-good-demand system for food (including beverages and tobacco) and nonfood, calculate the cross-price elasticities using the parameter estimates of SR (2009), and compare our results with the cross-price elasticities of TCS. Finally, we calculate and report the Slutsky and Cournot cross-price elasticities of demand for the nine-good system across 114 countries using Eqs. (6.19a), (6.19b), (6.20a), and (6.20b). The minimal requirements to calculate the Slutsky and Cournot cross-price elasticities of demand are parameter estimates of the Florida model and the natural log of the real income per capita of the 114 countries.

6.5.1 Marginal Shares

Marginal shares sum to one over all goods and measure how consumers allocate an additional unit of income among, in our case, nine broad categories of goods. Marginal shares are also used to calculate income and price elasticities. The marginal shares of all 114 countries are calculated using Eq. (6.16) and are reported along with the averages of the three-country groupings by income levels in the Table 6.6. A striking pattern emerges with low-income countries allocating an additional unit of income at a higher (lower) relative share than do high- and middle-income countries for necessities (luxuries). For example, if incomes go up by $1 across all countries, the expenditures on food would increase by 54 cents in Tanzania and by 2 cents in the U.S., a difference in magnitude of 27 times!

An additional dollar of income in Tanzania would increase expenditures on other, recreation, and medical care by 5 cents, 3 cents, and 4 cents, respectively. In contrast, an additional dollar in the U.S. would increase expenditure on these three goods by 18 cents, 9 cents, and 13 cents, respectively, for a difference in magnitudes of between 3 and 4 times. The difference in the magnitude of spending between consumers in the two countries is about double for clothing and footwear, gross rent, fuel and power, housing furnishings and operations, and transportation and communications while it is only about 1.3 times for education.

Table 6.2 Parameters from maximum likelihood estimations

Good or parameter (1)	Pooled data, 1980 normalization[a] (2)	1996 data, 114 countries[b] (3)
	Coefficient ϕ	
Income flexibility	−.723 (.025)	−.809 (.021)
	Coefficient β_i	
Food, beverage, tobacco	−.134 (.009)	−.135 (.006)
Clothing, footwear	−.004 (.003)	−.006 (.002)
Gross rent, fuel and power	.018 (.004)	.027 (.004)
House furnishings, operations	.014 (.003)	.012 (.001)
Medical care	.022 (.003)	.024 (.003)
Transport and communications	.030 (.004)	.021 (.003)
Recreation	.018 (.002)	.020 (.002)
Education	.005 (.004)	.005 (.002)
Other	.030 (.003)	.032 (.003)
	Coefficient α_i	
Food, beverage, tobacco	.214 (.015)	.151 (.011)
Clothing and footwear	.078 (.004)	.059 (.004)
Gross rent, fuel and power	.146 (.006)	.179 (.008)
House furnishings, operations	.087 (.004)	.077 (.004)
Medical care	.089 (.004)	.106 (.005)
Transport and communications	.126 (.006)	.133 (.006)
Recreation	.069 (.003)	.074 (.004)
Education	.066 (.005)	.074 (.004)
Other	.124 (.005)	.147 (.006)
	Coefficient K_g	
K_1	1.606	1.089 (.114)
K_2		1.294 (.080)

[a]Column (2) figures are from Table 5.4, column 3, page 105, TCS (1989). The estimate of−.134 for food, beverages, tobacco is simply obtained by summing TCS's parameter estimates of food,−.135, and beverages and tobacco, .001
[b]Column (3) figures are from Table 12.5, column (4), Seale and Regmi (2009)

6.5.2 *Cross-Price Elasticities in a Two-Good-Demand System*

In a two-good-demand system, the Slutsky cross-price terms are equal to the negative of the corresponding Slutsky own-price terms. Cournot cross-price elasticities, however, are not equal to the negative of the corresponding Cournot own-price elasticities. Their calculations are based on Eq. (6.20b) or Eq. (6.21b), on the alpha and beta of food, beverages and tobacco (referred to as food hereafter) and on phi from column (3), Table 6.2. The alpha and beta for nonfood equal one minus the alpha of food and the negative of the beta of food, respectively, a result of the adding-up conditions of Eq. (6.2). The standard deviations for the elasticities are computed by bootstrapping. Specifically, we draw 10,000 sets of parameters from the distribution that maximized the likelihood function given the sample. Using each draw, we then compute the elasticities (both Slutsky and Cournot). Finally, we compute the standard deviation for this sample of elasticities.

The calculated cross-price elasticities of the 114 countries in the food and nonfood demand system (Table 6.3) indicate that the Slutsky cross-price elasticity of demand for food with respect to a change in nonfood price is higher in the middle-income countries than in the low- and high-income countries. This result is consistent with the thinking that middle-income countries lie at the threshold where consumers are likely to upgrade their consumption patterns. As a Slutsky price elasticity measures the expenditure response to a price change without any change in real income, middle-income consumers are free to switch to goods which may have become relatively cheaper with a change in the price of a given good. However, low-income consumers with less disposable income may be constrained by the need to meet their subsistence consumption baskets and are less able to take advantage of a price change.

The Slutsky cross-price elasticities of demand for food with respect to a change in nonfood price (food-nonfood elasticities) and for nonfood with respect to a change in food price (nonfood-food elasticities) are all positive and, except for those of Luxembourg and U.S., are statistically different from zero ($\alpha = .05$). When compared to the point estimates of the U.S., the Slutsky food-nonfood elasticities are all statistically different except for that of Luxembourg ($\alpha = .05$), and the Slutsky nonfood-food elasticities are all statistically different when income is less than that of Switzerland's ($\alpha = .05$). The Slutsky nonfood-food elasticities are larger than the corresponding ones for food-nonfood elasticities in countries with real income per capita less than that of Pakistan. Starting with Pakistan and countries thereafter, the Slutsky food-nonfood elasticity is greater than the nonfood-food elasticity. Further, quantities demanded for food and nonfood are more sensitive in low- and middle-income countries to compensated cross-price changes than in high-income countries. The average food-nonfood elasticities of the group of low- and middle-income countries equal approximately one and a half times that of the average of the high-income group of countries. The average nonfood-food elasticities of the low-income and middle-income countries are six and three times larger, respectively, than that of the high-income group. The demand for food with respect to a change in the price of nonfood in Tanzania is about four times more sensitive than that in the U.S. Most striking is that the demand for nonfood with respect to a change in the price of food is 42 times more sensitive in Tanzania than in the U.S.

The Cournot cross-price elasticity equals the corresponding Slutsky elasticity minus a positive income term Eq. (6.21b), and it is markedly different from the corresponding Slutsky elasticity. For low-income countries with real income per capita of about 13% or less than that of the U.S., the Cournot food-nonfood elasticity is positive, indicating that the income effect is smaller than the substitution effect and that, in these countries, if nonfood price rises, expenditures on food will increase. However, except for the lowest income countries starting below Senegal, these positive elasticities are not significantly different from zero ($\alpha = .05$). For the other countries, the income effects are larger than the substitution effects, and the elasticities are negative. Most however are statistically the same as zero until reaching countries with income greater than Slovakia except for that of Luxembourg and U.S. which are statistically the same as zero ($\alpha = .05$). In comparison with

Table 6.3 Cross-price elasticities in a two-good-demand system across 114 countries from 1996 ICP

	Food		Non food			Food		Non food			Food		Non food	
Country	Slutsky	Cournot	Slutsky	Cournot	Country	Slutsky	Cournot	Slutsky	Cournot	Country	Slutsky	Cournot	Slutsky	Cournot
Tanzania	0.296[a,b]	0.038[a,b]	0.623[a,b]	−0.340[a,b]	Ukraine	0.393[a,b]	−0.003	0.268[a,b]	−0.230[a,b]	Czech Republic	0.338[a,b]	−0.015[a]	0.118[a,b]	−0.188[a,b]
Nigeria	0.320[a,b]	0.031[a,b]	0.548[a,b]	−0.315[a,b]	Philippines	0.393[a,b]	−0.004	0.258[a,b]	−0.227[a,b]	Greece	0.327[a,b]	−0.016[a]	0.108[a,b]	−0.185[a,b]
Tajikistan	0.330[a,b]	0.027[a,b]	0.517[a,b]	−0.305[a,b]	Peru	0.394[a,b]	−0.004	0.255[a,b]	−0.226[a,b]	Korea	0.324[a,b]	−0.016[a]	0.106[a,b]	−0.185[a,b]
Zambia	0.332[a,b]	0.027[a,b]	0.512[a,b]	−0.303[a,b]	Botswana	0.394[a,b]	−0.004	0.254[a,b]	−0.226[a,b]	Portugal	0.320[a,b]	−0.016[a]	0.103[a,b]	−0.184[a,b]
Yemen	0.332[a,b]	0.027[a,b]	0.512[a,b]	−0.303[a,b]	Thailand	0.394[a,b]	−0.005	0.252[a,b]	−0.225[a,b]	Spain	0.319[a,b]	−0.016[a]	0.102[a,b]	−0.184[a,b]
Malawi	0.338[a,b]	0.025[a,b]	0.494[a,b]	−0.297[a,b]	Morocco	0.393[a,b]	−0.005	0.248[a,b]	−0.224[a,b]	Ireland	0.314[a,b]	−0.016[a]	0.099[a,b]	−0.183[a,b]
Madagascar	0.338[a,b]	0.024[a,b]	0.494[a,b]	−0.297[a,b]	Venezuela	0.393[a,b]	−0.005	0.247[a,b]	−0.224[a,b]	Singapore	0.309[a,b]	−0.016[a]	0.095[a,b]	−0.182[a,b]
Mali	0.340[a,b]	0.024[a,b]	0.489[a,b]	−0.296[a,b]	Macedonia	0.393[a,b]	−0.006	0.240[a,b]	−0.222[a,b]	Mauritius	0.301[a,b]	−0.016[a]	0.090[a,b]	−0.180[a,b]
Mongolia	0.340[a,b]	0.024[a,b]	0.488[a,b]	−0.295[a,b]	Belize	0.393[a,b]	−0.006	0.240[a,b]	−0.222[a,b]	Israel	0.294[a,b]	−0.015[a]	0.085[a,b]	−0.179[a,b]
Benin	0.353[a,b]	0.019[a,b]	0.449[a,b]	−0.283[a,b]	Egypt	0.393[a,b]	−0.006	0.240[a,b]	−0.222[a,b]	New Zealand	0.291[a,b]	−0.015[a]	0.084[a,b]	−0.179[a,b]
Kenya	0.358[a,b]	0.017[a,b]	0.433[a,b]	−0.278[a,b]	St. Vincent and Grenadines	0.393[a,b]	−0.006	0.239[a,b]	−0.221[a,b]	Finland	0.290[a,b]	−0.015[a]	0.083[a,b]	−0.179[a,b]
Sierra Leone	0.362[a,b]	0.016[a,b]	0.419[a,b]	−0.274[a,b]	Swaziland	0.393[a,b]	−0.007	0.232[a,b]	−0.219[a,b]	Bahamas	0.288[a,b]	−0.015[a]	0.082[a,b]	−0.178[a,b]
Nepal	0.362[a,b]	0.016[a,b]	0.419[a,b]	−0.274[a,b]	Lebanon	0.392[a,b]	−0.007	0.229[a,b]	−0.219[a,b]	Sweden	0.269[a,b]	−0.015[a]	0.072[a,b]	−0.176[a,b]
Turkmenistan	0.364[a,b]	0.015[a,b]	0.412[a,b]	−0.272[a,b]	Belarus	0.392[a,b]	−0.007	0.228[a,b]	−0.218[a,b]	Netherlands	0.266[a,b]	−0.015[a]	0.071[a,b]	−0.175[a,b]
Congo	0.368[a,b]	0.013[a,b]	0.400[a,b]	−0.268[a,b]	Kazakhstan	0.392[a,b]	−0.007	0.227[a,b]	−0.218[a,b]	France	0.251[a,b]	−0.014[a]	0.064[a,b]	−0.173[a]
Senegal	0.371[a,b]	0.012[b]	0.389[a,b]	−0.265[a,b]	Dominica	0.392[a,b]	−0.007	0.227[a,b]	−0.218[a,b]	United Kingdom	0.249[a,b]	−0.014[a]	0.063[a,b]	−0.173[a]
Vietnam	0.372[a,b]	0.011[b]	0.386[a,b]	−0.264[a,b]	Latvia	0.391[a,b]	−0.008	0.220[a,b]	−0.216[a,b]	Belgium	0.246[a,b]	−0.014[a]	0.062[a,b]	−0.173[a]
Bangladesh	0.372[a,b]	0.011[b]	0.384[a,b]	−0.264[a,b]	St. Lucia	0.391[a,b]	−0.008	0.219[a,b]	−0.216[a,b]	Norway	0.245[a,b]	−0.014[a]	0.061[a,b]	−0.173[a]
Pakistan	0.378[a,b]	0.009[b]	0.362[a,b]	−0.257[a,b]	Brazil	0.391[a,b]	−0.008	0.218[a,b]	−0.216[a,b]	Italy	0.242[a,b]	−0.014[a]	0.060[a,b]	−0.173[a]
Azerbaijan	0.380[a,b]	0.007	0.352[a,b]	−0.254[a,b]	Bulgaria	0.391[a,b]	−0.008	0.217[a,b]	−0.215[a,b]	Austria	0.236[a,b]	−0.014[a]	0.058[a,b]	−0.172[a]
Cote d'Ivoire	0.381[a,b]	0.007	0.348[a,b]	−0.253[a,b]	Russia	0.390[a,b]	−0.009	0.213[a,b]	−0.214[a,b]	Germany	0.235[a,b]	−0.014[a]	0.057[a,b]	−0.172[a]
Paraguay	0.382[a,b]	0.006	0.345[a,b]	−0.252[a,b]	Fiji	0.389[a,b]	−0.009	0.208[a,b]	−0.213[a,b]	Australia	0.228[a,b]	−0.013[a]	0.055[a,b]	−0.171[a]

Uzbekistan	0.383[a,b]	0.006	0.339[a,b]	−0.250[a,b]	Grenada	0.389[a,b]	−0.009	0.208[a,b]	−0.213[a,b]	Japan	0.224[a,b]	−0.013[a]	0.053[a,b]	−0.171[a]
Kyrgyzstan	0.383[a,b]	0.006	0.338[a,b]	−0.250[a,b]	Turkey	0.389[a,b]	−0.009	0.206[a,b]	−0.212[a,b]	Canada	0.218[a,b]	−0.013[a]	0.051[a,b]	−0.170[a]
Cameroon	0.384[a,b]	0.005	0.337[a,b]	−0.250[a,b]	Lithuania	0.388[a,b]	−0.010	0.202[a,b]	−0.211[a,b]	Bermuda	0.204[a,b]	−0.012[a]	0.046[a,b]	−0.169[a]
Moldova	0.384[a,b]	0.005	0.337[a,b]	−0.250[a,b]	Romania	0.387[a,b]	−0.010	0.199[a,b]	−0.210[a,b]	Switzerland	0.198[a,b]	−0.012[a]	0.044[a]	−0.168[a]
Bolivia	0.385[a,b]	0.005	0.330[a,b]	−0.247[a,b]	Iran	0.385[a,b]	−0.011	0.194[a,b]	−0.209[a,b]	Barbados	0.197[a,b]	−0.012[a]	0.044[a]	−0.168[a]
Ecuador	0.386[a,b]	0.004	0.327[a,b]	−0.247[a,b]	Mexico	0.385[a,b]	−0.011	0.191[a,b]	−0.208[a,b]	Hong Kong	0.196[a,b]	−0.012[a]	0.043[a]	−0.168[a]
Armenia	0.387[a,b]	0.003	0.320[a,b]	−0.245[a,b]	Bahrain	0.384[a,b]	−0.011	0.188[a,b]	−0.207[a,b]	Iceland	0.194[a,b]	−0.012[a]	0.043[a]	−0.168[a]
Sri Lanka	0.387[a,b]	0.003	0.320[a,b]	−0.245[a,b]	Chile	0.383[a,b]	−0.011	0.186[a,b]	−0.207[a,b]	Denmark	0.191[a]	−0.012[a]	0.042[a]	−0.168[a]
Jordan	0.388[a,b]	0.002	0.312[a,b]	−0.242[a,b]	Antigua and Barbuda	0.383[a,b]	−0.011	0.186[a,b]	−0.207[a,b]	Luxembourg	0.100	−0.007	0.018	−0.161[a]
Albania	0.390[a,b]	0.001	0.301[a,b]	−0.239[a,b]	Poland	0.381[a,b]	−0.012	0.181[a,b]	−0.205[a,b]	United States	0.082	−0.005	0.015	−0.160[a]
Indonesia	0.391[a,b]	0.001	0.297[a,b]	−0.238[a,b]	Trinidad and Tobago	0.380[a,b]	−0.012	0.177[a,b]	−0.204[a,b]					
Jamaica	0.391[a,b]	0.000	0.296[a,b]	−0.238[a,b]	Estonia	0.378[a,b]	−0.012	0.174[a,b]	−0.203[a,b]					
Zimbabwe	0.391[a,b]	0.000	0.295[a,b]	−0.237[a,b]	Gabon	0.378[a,b]	−0.012	0.173[a,b]	−0.203[a,b]					
Guinea	0.391[a,b]	0.000	0.291[a,b]	−0.236[a,b]	Tunisia	0.376[a,b]	−0.013	0.170[a,b]	−0.202[a,b]					
Syria	0.392[a,b]	−0.001	0.283[a,b]	−0.234[a,b]	St. Kitts and Nevis	0.376[a,b]	−0.013	0.168[a,b]	−0.202[a,b]					
Georgia	0.392[a,b]	−0.001	0.282[a,b]	−0.234[a,b]	Uruguay	0.375[a,b]	−0.013	0.167[a,b]	−0.201[a,b]					
					Slovakia	0.374[a,b]	−0.013	0.165[a,b]	−0.201[a,b]					
					Hungary	0.368[a,b]	−0.014[a]	0.154[a,b]	−0.198[a,b]					
					Argentina	0.357[a,b]	−0.015[a]	0.139[a,b]	−0.194[a,b]					
					Oman	0.353[a,b]	−0.015[a]	0.133[a,b]	−0.192[a,b]					
					Qatar	0.346[a,b]	−0.015[a]	0.126[a,b]	−0.190[a,b]					
					Slovenia	0.342[a,b]	−0.015[a]	0.122[a,b]	−0.189[a,b]					

[a]Statistically different from zero at 0.05 significance level
[b]Statistically different from point estimate of U.S. at 0.05 significance level

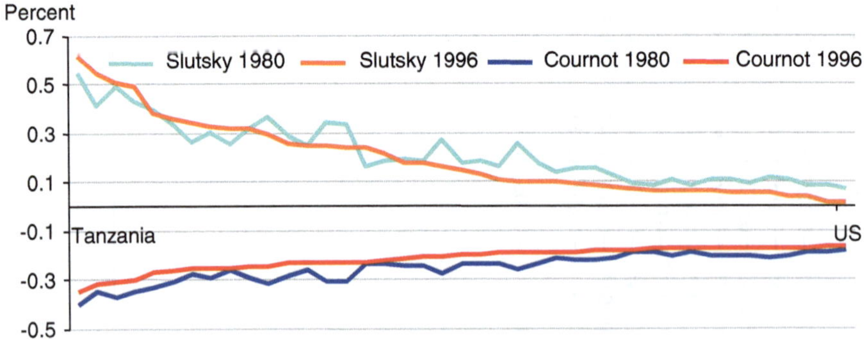

Fig. 6.1 Nonfood cross-price elasticity with food price change (Source: 1980 from Theil et al. 1989. Forty one countries are listed in order of increasing affluence)

the elasticity estimate of the U.S., countries with income less than Azerbaijan have Cournot food-nonfood elasticities that are statistically different ($\alpha = .05$). All estimated Cournot elasticities are small in magnitude. Considering that food is a necessity, the relatively inelastic Cournot cross-price elasticity estimates are consistent with our expectations.

The pattern is markedly different for the nonfood consumption category, since taken together nonfood is a luxury good. All Cournot nonfood-food elasticities are negative and statistically different from zero ($\alpha = .05$). Starting with the poorest country, Tanzania, and traveling towards richer ones, the Cournot nonfood-food elasticity gradually declines in absolute value from −.43 in Tanzania to −.16 in the U.S. This has significant implication on economies rich and poor. When food price increases, the nonfood sector of an economy will shrink, particularly in poor countries but also in rich ones. When compared to the point estimate of the U.S., countries with income less than France have Cournot nonfood-food elasticities statistically different ($\alpha = .05$).

Forty-one countries in this study are also in the study of TCS making a comparison of cross-price elasticities of food and nonfood possible across time, 1980–1996. Our cross-price elasticities for the 41 countries and those of TCS (columns (11) and (12) of Table 5.8, pp. 116–117 (TCS)) are plotted in Figs. 6.1 and 6.2. First, it is important to note that real income per capita relative to the U.S. decreases from 1980 to 1996 for the poorest countries while it increases for the other more affluent ones. Both studies find that the nonfood-food elasticity decreases with affluence while the food-nonfood elasticity first increases with affluence before decreasing. When comparing the Slutsky elasticities over time, they are smaller in 1996 for the countries that increase real income per capita between 1980 and 1996 relative to the U.S., but larger for the others. The finding is reasonable as one expects price elasticities to become less elastic as income increases (Timmer 1981).

The Cournot nonfood-food elasticities in both studies decrease absolutely with affluence and all in 1980 are absolutely larger than corresponding ones in 1996.

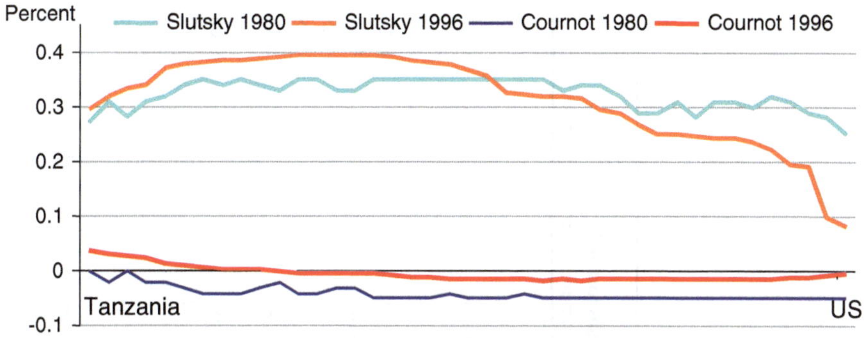

Fig. 6.2 Food cross-price elasticity with nonfood price change (Source: 1980 from Theil et al. 1989. Forty one countries are listed in order of increasing affluence)

All Cournot food-nonfood elasticities are negative in 1980 while most are negative in 1996 except for the poorest countries. Comparisons over time indicate that the 1996 values are generally smaller than the 1980 ones in absolute values. The exception is again for some of the lowest income countries where the 1996 elasticities are positive and larger than the negative values of 1980. Despite the differences we note between the 1996 and 1980 elasticities, the cross-price elasticities for a two-good-demand system using estimates from 1996 ICP data appear reasonable and offer sufficient support for estimating cross-price elasticities for the nine-good-demand system.

6.5.3 Cross-Price Elasticities in a Nine-Good-Demand System Across Three Income Groupings

While cross-price elasticities are calculated and reported in Tables 6.7, 6.8, 6.9, 6.10, 6.11, 6.12, 6.13, 6.14, and 6.15 on a country-by-country basis for the nine goods, it is convenient to summarize the results by calculating and reporting averages of three groupings: low-; middle-; and high-income countries (Tables 6.4 and 6.5). Within a country grouping, the Slutsky cross-price elasticities of the nine-good-demand system are bigger in magnitude for more luxurious consumption items such as recreation than for the two necessity items, food, and clothing and footwear (Table 6.4). When a price changes with respect to one of the two necessities, the Slutsky cross-price elasticities of the other eight goods are the greatest among low-income countries and decrease in magnitude as countries become wealthier. The opposite is generally the case when price changes with respect to one of the seven more luxurious goods.

The substitution effects of the eight goods in the low- and middle-income countries, on average, for a change in the price of food are substantial. For example,

Table 6.4 Slutsky (compensated) own- and cross-price elasticities for a nine-good demand system

	Food, beverage and tobacco	Clothing and footwear	Gross rent, fuel and power	House furnishings and operations	Medical care	Education	Transport and communication	Recreation	Other
1% change in price of	*Percent change in quantity demanded*								
Low-income countries									
Food, beverage and tobacco	*−0.37*	0.28	0.38	0.38	0.51	0.33	0.39	0.63	0.49
Clothing and footwear	0.04	*−0.69*	0.07	0.07	0.09	0.06	0.07	0.11	0.09
Gross rent, fuel and power	0.08	0.10	*−0.88*	0.14	0.18	0.12	0.14	0.22	0.17
House operations	0.03	0.04	0.06	*−0.95*	0.08	0.05	0.06	0.09	0.07
Medical care	0.04	0.05	0.07	0.07	*−1.24*	0.06	0.07	0.11	0.08
Education	0.04	0.05	0.07	0.07	0.09	*−0.82*	0.07	0.11	0.08
Transport and communication	0.06	0.07	0.10	0.10	0.13	0.13	*−0.93*	0.16	0.13
Recreation	0.02	0.03	0.04	0.04	0.05	0.04	0.04	*−1.59*	0.05
Other	0.05	0.07	0.09	0.09	0.12	0.08	0.10	0.15	*−1.17*
Middle-income countries									
Food, beverage and tobacco	*−0.38*	0.15	0.20	0.20	0.23	0.18	0.20	0.24	0.22
Clothing and footwear	0.03	*−0.69*	0.06	0.06	0.07	0.05	0.06	0.07	0.07
Gross rent, fuel and power	0.08	0.12	*−0.80*	0.16	0.18	0.15	0.16	0.19	0.18
House operations	0.04	0.05	0.07	*−0.89*	0.08	0.06	0.07	0.08	0.08

Medical care	0.05	0.07	0.09	0.09	*−0.98*	0.08	0.09	0.11	0.10
Education	0.03	0.05	0.07	0.07	0.08	*−0.81*	0.07	0.08	0.08
Transport and communication	0.06	0.09	0.12	0.12	0.13	0.13	*−0.85*	0.14	0.13
Recreation	0.03	0.05	0.06	0.06	0.07	0.06	0.06	*−1.09*	0.07
Other	0.06	0.10	0.13	0.13	0.14	0.12	0.13	0.15	*−0.93*
High-income countries									
Food, beverage and tobacco	*−0.25*	0.05	0.07	0.07	0.07	0.06	0.07	0.08	0.07
Clothing and footwear	0.02	*−0.69*	0.05	0.05	0.06	0.05	0.05	0.06	0.06
Gross rent, fuel and power	0.05	0.14	*−0.76*	0.18	0.20	0.17	0.18	0.21	0.20
House operations	0.02	0.06	0.08	*−0.86*	0.08	0.07	0.08	0.09	0.08
Medical care	0.03	0.09	0.11	0.11	*−0.89*	0.10	0.11	0.13	0.12
Education	0.02	0.06	0.07	0.07	0.08	*−0.80*	0.07	0.08	0.08
Transport and communication	0.04	0.11	0.14	0.14	0.15	0.15	*−0.81*	0.15	0.15
Recreation	0.02	0.06	0.08	0.08	0.09	0.07	0.08	*−0.96*	0.09
Other	0.04	0.12	0.16	0.16	0.17	0.14	0.16	0.17	*−0.84*

Note: Own-price (cross-price) elasticities are reported on diagonals (off-diagonals). Own-price elasticities are from Seale and Regmi (2009), Table 12.9, p. 291

Table 6.5 Cournot (uncompensated) own-and cross-price elasticities for a nine-good demand system

	Food, beverage and tobacco	Clothing and footwear	Gross rent, fuel and power	House furnishings and operations	Medical care	Education	Transport and communication	Recreation	Other
Percent price change in	*Percent change in demanded*								
Low-income countries									
Food, beverage and tobacco	*−0.74*	−0.19	−0.26	−0.26	−0.34	−0.22	−0.27	−0.43	−0.33
Clothing and footwear	−0.01	*−0.76*	−0.02	−0.02	−0.03	−0.02	−0.02	−0.04	−0.03
Gross rent, fuel and power	0.00	0.00	*−1.01*	0.00	0.00	0.00	0.00	0.00	0.00
House operations	0.00	0.00	0.00	*−1.01*	0.00	0.00	0.00	0.00	0.00
Medical care	0.01	0.01	0.01	0.01	*−0.31*	0.01	0.01	0.02	0.02
Education	−0.01	−0.01	−0.01	−0.01	−0.01	*−0.88*	−0.01	−0.02	−0.01
Transport and communication	0.00	0.00	0.00	0.00	0.00	0.00	*−1.03*	0.01	0.00
Recreation	0.01	0.01	0.02	0.02	0.02	0.01	0.02	*−1.63*	0.02
Other	0.01	0.01	0.02	0.02	0.02	0.02	0.03	0.02	*−1.26*
Middle-income countries									
Food, beverage and tobacco	*−0.59*	−0.16	−0.21	−0.21	−0.23	−0.19	−0.21	−0.25	−0.23
Clothing and footwear	−0.01	*−0.76*	−0.02	−0.02	−0.02	−0.02	−0.02	−0.03	−0.02
Gross rent, fuel and power	0.00	0.00	*−0.97*	−0.01	−0.01	−0.01	−0.01	−0.01	−0.01

House operations	0.00	0.00	0.00	*−0.97*	0.00	0.00	0.00	0.00	0.00
Medical care	0.00	0.01	0.01	0.01	*−1.07*	0.01	0.01	0.01	0.01
Education	−0.01	−0.01	−0.01	−0.01	−0.01	*−0.88*	−0.01	−0.01	−0.01
Transport and communication	0.00	0.00	0.00	0.00	0.00	0.00	*−0.98*	0.00	0.00
Recreation	0.00	0.01	0.01	0.01	0.01	0.01	0.01	*−1.15*	0.01
Other	0.00	0.01	0.01	0.01	0.01	0.01	0.01	0.01	*−1.06*
High-income countries									
Food, beverage and tobacco	*−0.32*	−0.14	−0.17	−0.17	−0.19	−0.16	−0.17	−0.19	−0.19
Clothing and footwear	−0.01	*−0.75*	−0.02	−0.02	−0.02	−0.02	−0.02	−0.02	−0.02
Gross rent, fuel and power	0.00	−0.01	*−0.95*	−0.01	−0.01	−0.01	−0.01	−0.01	−0.01
House operations	0.00	0.00	−0.01	*−0.94*	−0.01	0.00	−0.01	−0.01	−0.01
Medical care	0.00	0.0	0.00	0.00	−1.01	0.00	0.00	0.00	0.00
Education	0.00	−0.01	−0.01	−0.01	−0.01	*−0.88*	−0.01	−0.01	−0.01
Transport and communication	0.00	−0.01	−0.01	−0.01	−0.01	−0.01	*−0.95*	−0.01	−0.01
Recreation	0.00	0.00	0.00	0.00	0.00	0.00	0.00	*−1.05*	0.00
Other	0.00	0.00	0.00	0.00	0.00	0.00	0.00	0.00	*−1.01*

Note: Own-price (cross-price) elasticities are on diagonals (off-diagonals). Own-price elasticities are from Seale and Regmi (2009), Table 12.10, p. 297

a 1% increase in the price of food, if real income is unchanged (compensated), will increase, on average, the demand for the other eight goods between .63% (.24%) for recreation and .28% (.15%) for clothing and footwear in low- (middle-) income countries. The substitution effects in the high-income countries are substantially less. A 1% increase in the price of food, when real income remains constant, will increase the quantity demanded for clothing and footwear, on average, by .05%, for recreation by .08%, and for the other six goods by .07% each.

If the price of one of the eight nonfood goods in low-, middle-, and high-income countries increases, *ceteris paribus*, by 1%, the average demand for the other eight goods will increase by .20% or less. The exceptions in low- and high-income countries are for recreation (.22% and .21%, respectively) when the price of gross rent, fuel and power changes by 1%.

A comparison of Tables 6.4 and 6.5 indicates that the income effect of a price change may be large. When price changes for either food or clothing and footwear, the two necessity goods, all Cournot cross-price elasticities are negative. Negative Cournot cross-price elasticities also result from a change in the price of education for all goods in all groups except for food in high-income countries where the elasticity is zero. In the cases of gross rent, fuel and power, house furnishings and operations, and transportation and communications, the substitution effect outweighs the income effect in the low-income group, on average, but, for the other two income groupings, the opposite is true. For medical care and other, the substitution effects are larger than the income effects, so that, on average across the three groupings, the cross-price elasticities are all positive.[12] For recreation, all cross-price elasticities are positive across all groups. The values of these elasticities for all goods generally tend to be the largest for the poorest countries and decrease in magnitude as countries become wealthier.

It is of particular interest, given the recent attention to the poverty impacts of increases in food prices, to look more closely at the Cournot cross-price elasticities when the price of food changes. An increase in the price of food will have a depressing impact on the economies of all three income groupings in that it decreases the demand for all the other eight goods due to the income effects of the price change being larger than the substitution effects. These cross-price elasticities are largest, on average, for low-income countries, followed by middle-income countries, and smallest for high-income countries. The range in elasticities among the eight other goods is between −.43% (−.25%) for recreation and −.19% (−.16%) for clothing and footwear in the low- (middle-) income group. In high-income countries, though smaller, the effects of a food-price change on the other eight goods is substantial ranging from .19% for recreation to .14% for clothing and footwear.

[12]The cross-price elasticities with respect to changes in the price of medical care and other are positive for all counties except for the two or three wealthiest counties, respectively (Table 6.11 and Table 6.15).

The combined substitution and income effects with respect to a price change of one of the eight nonfood goods in all groups are relatively small, and all respective Cournot cross-price elasticities are close to zero. The largest negative cross-price elasticity is for recreation when the price of clothing and footwear changes, and its value is only −.04. Even in the cases where the substitution effect is larger than the income effect (e.g., the cross-price elasticities are positive), the values are still close to zero.

6.5.4 Cross-Price Elasticities in a Nine-Good-Demand System Across Individual Countries

Cross-price elasticities are calculated on a country-by-country basis, and the standard deviations for the elasticities are computed by bootstrapping. Specifically, we draw 10,000 sets of parameters from the distribution that maximized the likelihood function given the sample. Using each draw, we then compute the elasticities (both Slutsky and Cournot). Finally, we compute the standard deviation for this sample of elasticities. Tables 6.7, 6.8, 6.9, 6.10, 6.11, 6.12, 6.13, 6.14, and 6.15 contain the Slutsky and Cournot cross-price elasticities of demand for each of the eight of nine aggregate goods with respect to a change in the price of the ninth good for all 114 countries. Examination of these tables clearly establishes that the cross-price elasticities with respect to a change in the price of food are largest for all countries, both in terms of the Slutsky and Cournot cross-price elasticities.

6.5.4.1 Slutsky Cross-Price Elasticities

All Slutsky cross-price elasticities are positive (Tables 6.7, 6.8, 6.9, 6.10, 6.11, 6.12, 6.13, 6.14, and 6.15). The largest among the eight goods are for a change in the price of food, and almost all of these with respect to a food price change are statistically different from zero ($\alpha = .05$). The exceptions are for medical care, transport and communication, and other among the poorest countries and for transport and communications and other for the two richest countries, Luxembourg and the U.S. Additionally, most of the Slutsky cross-price elasticities with respect to a change in food price are statistically different from the point estimate of the U.S. The exceptions again are the same commodities and poor countries with elasticities not significantly different from zero plus some of the richest countries for all eight commodities. In terms of magnitude, the Slutsky cross-price elasticity for the other necessity, clothing and footwear, is the smallest among the eight goods in response to a change in food price (Table 6.7). In Tanzania, the poorest country in the sample, a 1% increase in the price of food will increase the compensated demand for clothing and footwear by .41% while it increases the quantities demanded of medical care and of other items by over 1.0%. For Nigeria, the second poorest country, it increases the demand for recreation by 2.6%. As one travels from the poorest countries to richer ones, the Slutsky cross-price elasticities with respect to a change in food price decrease. When reaching the U.S., all these elasticities are small in the order of .02% for gross rent, fuel and power, medical care, transportation and communications, recreation, and other and .01% for three remaining goods. Still, except for transportation and communication and other, these elasticities are statistically different from zero ($\alpha = .05$). The Slutsky cross-price elasticities of recreation, the most luxurious good, are largest among the eight goods with respect to a food price change and range from 2.62 for Nigeria (statistically different from zero and elasticity estimate of U.S.) to .02 for the U.S. (also statistically different from zero).

Although smaller, all Slutsky cross-price elasticities with respect to a 1% change in the price of clothing and footwear, the other necessity, decrease in value as one travels from the poorest to the richest country (Table 6.8). As with respect to a change in food price, all these are statistically different from zero except in the case of medical care, transport and communications, and other for the poorest countries and for food for Luxembourg and U.S. Also for food with respect to a change in clothing and footwear, all elasticities are statistically different from that of the U.S. except for the five next richest countries. The largest elasticities are recreation's and while all are statistically different from zero ($\alpha = .05$), many are statistically the same as that of the U.S. with the exceptions being the poorest countries with income less than that of Peru. For Nigeria, the second poorest country, its cross-price elasticities range from .39% for recreation to .05% for food. Once reaching the affluence of the U.S., the elasticities range from .06% for recreation to .00% for food.

The pattern is different for a change in the price of a luxury good when real income is compensated. In some cases, the values increase initially when traveling from poor to rich countries before decreasing thereafter, in others the values steadily increase throughout while in still others they initially decrease before increasing in value. For example, when the price of gross rent, fuel and power increases by 1%, the quantity demanded of food will increase in value until reaching Russia where it decreases in value thereafter until reaching the U.S. Its effect on medical care, recreation and other items is opposite as the elasticities decrease initially before reaching a minimum and then increase in value thereafter. The quantity demanded of recreation is most sensitive to a cross-price change in poor as well as rich countries. The second most affected good is medical care.

Statistical significance of the Slutsky cross-price elasticities are similar with respect to a price change of the different luxury goods. Generally, the poorest countries have elasticity estimates that are not significantly different from zero ($\alpha = .05$) for medical care, transport and communications and other, and generally the food cross-price elasticities are insignificant for Luxembourg and U.S. Statistical difference in the elasticity estimates from those of the U.S. vary depending on which luxury good price changes. For example, except for the food cross-price elasticity with respect to a change in recreation price, those for the seven other goods are not statistically different from those of the U.S. The cross-price elasticities with respect to a change in medical care price are most different from those with respect to a recreation price change. Most are statistically different from those of the U.S. for the low- and middle-income countries. Upon reaching the rich countries, all elasticities except for that of food are statistically the same as those of the U.S. It is noteworthy that the food cross-price elasticities are most often statistically different from zero and most often statistically different from the elasticity estimates of the U.S. for both luxury and necessity goods.

6.5.4.2 Cournot Cross-Price Elasticities

Cournot cross-price elasticities of demand for the other seven goods with respect to a change in the two necessity goods (i.e., food and clothing and footwear) are all negative for all countries (Tables 6.7 and 6.8). This occurs when the income effect of a price change outweighs the substitution effect. Further, most of these elasticities are statistically different from zero ($\alpha = .05$), and for food most are statistically different from those of the U.S. The resulting elasticity estimates show that increases in the price of these two necessities have depressing effects on the economies of low-, middle-, and high-income countries. This is particularly true for an increase in food price as the elasticities with respect to a food price change are absolutely greater than those with respect to a change in the price of clothing and footwear. A 1% increase in the price of food holding nominal income constant will decrease the demand for clothing and footwear by .22% in Tanzania and by .13% in the U.S. Its effects on the luxury goods in all countries are even more depressing with recreation being the most sensitive. The recreation-food elasticity in Nigeria is −1.51 while it is −.18 in the U.S. Changes in the quantity demanded for the other six luxury goods in response to a change in food price are also substantial even for a wealthy country like the U.S. In particular, medical care expenditures are reduced by .71% in Tanzania and .17% in the U.S. These results indicate that a food price increase affects health in all countries beyond the nutritional aspects. Given such large negative effects that a food price increase has on the entire economy, it is not surprising that high food prices in recent years contribute to food riots in many parts of the world (Faiola 2008).

Similarly but in smaller magnitude, a price increase for clothing and footwear will have a depressing effect on a country's economy. For example, a 1% increase in the price of clothing and footwear when nominal income is uncompensated will decrease the demand for the seven luxury goods by .13% (recreation) or less in Nigeria and by .02% in the U.S. It has the smallest effect on food with an elasticity of only −.02% in Tanzania and −.00 in the U.S.

Table 6.6 Distribution of additional one unit of income across expenditure categories, 114 countries in 1996[a]

	Food, beverage and tobacco	Clothing and footwear	Gross rent, fuel and power	House furnishing and operations	Medical care	Education	Transport and communication	Recreation	Other
Low-income country									
Tanzania	0.54	0.08	0.10	0.04	0.04	0.06	0.07	0.03	0.05
Nigeria	0.50	0.07	0.11	0.05	0.04	0.06	0.08	0.02	0.06
Tajikistan	0.47	0.07	0.11	0.05	0.05	0.06	0.08	0.03	0.07
Zambia	0.47	0.07	0.11	0.05	0.05	0.06	0.08	0.03	0.07
Yemen	0.47	0.07	0.11	0.05	0.05	0.06	0.08	0.03	0.07
Malawi	0.46	0.07	0.12	0.05	0.05	0.06	0.09	0.03	0.07
Madagascar	0.46	0.07	0.12	0.05	0.05	0.06	0.09	0.03	0.07
Mali	0.45	0.07	0.12	0.05	0.05	0.06	0.09	0.03	0.07
Mongolia	0.45	0.07	0.12	0.05	0.05	0.06	0.09	0.03	0.07
Benin	0.42	0.07	0.12	0.05	0.06	0.06	0.09	0.03	0.08
Kenya	0.41	0.07	0.13	0.05	0.06	0.06	0.09	0.04	0.08
Sierra Leone	0.40	0.07	0.13	0.06	0.06	0.06	0.09	0.04	0.09
Nepal	0.40	0.07	0.13	0.06	0.06	0.06	0.09	0.04	0.09
Turkmenistan	0.40	0.07	0.13	0.06	0.06	0.06	0.09	0.04	0.09
Congo	0.39	0.07	0.13	0.06	0.06	0.07	0.10	0.04	0.09
Senegal	0.38	0.07	0.13	0.06	0.07	0.07	0.10	0.04	0.09
Vietnam	0.37	0.07	0.13	0.06	0.07	0.07	0.10	0.04	0.09
Bangladesh	0.37	0.07	0.13	0.06	0.07	0.07	0.10	0.04	0.09
Pakistan	0.35	0.07	0.14	0.06	0.07	0.07	0.10	0.04	0.10
Azerbaijan	0.35	0.07	0.14	0.06	0.07	0.07	0.10	0.05	0.10
Cote d'Ivoire	0.34	0.07	0.14	0.06	0.07	0.07	0.10	0.05	0.10
Paraguay	0.34	0.07	0.14	0.06	0.07	0.07	0.10	0.05	0.10

Uzbekistan	0.33	0.07	0.14	0.06	0.07	0.07	0.10	0.05	0.10
Kyrgyzstan	0.33	0.07	0.14	0.06	0.07	0.07	0.10	0.05	0.10
Cameroon	0.33	0.07	0.14	0.06	0.07	0.07	0.10	0.05	0.10
Moldova	0.33	0.07	0.14	0.06	0.07	0.07	0.10	0.05	0.10
Bolivia	0.33	0.07	0.14	0.06	0.07	0.07	0.11	0.05	0.10
Ecuador	0.32	0.07	0.14	0.06	0.08	0.07	0.11	0.05	0.11
Armenia	0.32	0.07	0.15	0.06	0.08	0.07	0.11	0.05	0.11
Sri Lanka	0.32	0.07	0.15	0.06	0.08	0.07	0.11	0.05	0.11
Jordan	0.31	0.07	0.15	0.06	0.08	0.07	0.11	0.05	0.11
Albania	0.30	0.07	0.15	0.06	0.08	0.07	0.11	0.05	0.11
Indonesia	0.30	0.07	0.15	0.06	0.08	0.07	0.11	0.05	0.11
Jamaica	0.30	0.07	0.15	0.06	0.08	0.07	0.11	0.05	0.11
Zimbabwe	0.29	0.07	0.15	0.06	0.08	0.07	0.11	0.05	0.11
Guinea	0.29	0.07	0.15	0.07	0.08	0.07	0.11	0.05	0.11
Syria	0.28	0.07	0.15	0.07	0.08	0.07	0.11	0.05	0.11
Georgia	0.28	0.06	0.15	0.07	0.08	0.07	0.11	0.05	0.11
Middle-income country									
Ukraine	0.27	0.06	0.16	0.07	0.08	0.07	0.11	0.06	0.12
Philippines	0.26	0.06	0.16	0.07	0.09	0.07	0.12	0.06	0.12
Peru	0.26	0.06	0.16	0.07	0.09	0.07	0.12	0.06	0.12
Botswana	0.26	0.06	0.16	0.07	0.09	0.07	0.12	0.06	0.12
Thailand	0.26	0.06	0.16	0.07	0.09	0.07	0.12	0.06	0.12
Morocco	0.25	0.06	0.16	0.07	0.09	0.07	0.12	0.06	0.12
Venezuela	0.25	0.06	0.16	0.07	0.09	0.07	0.12	0.06	0.12
Macedonia	0.24	0.06	0.16	0.07	0.09	0.07	0.12	0.06	0.12
Belize	0.24	0.06	0.16	0.07	0.09	0.07	0.12	0.06	0.12
Egypt	0.24	0.06	0.16	0.07	0.09	0.07	0.12	0.06	0.12

(continued)

Table 6.6 (continued)

	Food, beverage and tobacco	Clothing and footwear	Gross rent, fuel and power	House furnishing and operations	Medical care	Education	Transport and communication	Recreation	Other
St. Vincent and Grenadines	0.24	0.06	0.16	0.07	0.09	0.07	0.12	0.06	0.12
Swaziland	0.24	0.06	0.16	0.07	0.09	0.07	0.12	0.06	0.13
Lebanon	0.23	0.06	0.16	0.07	0.09	0.07	0.12	0.06	0.13
Belarus	0.23	0.06	0.16	0.07	0.09	0.07	0.12	0.06	0.13
Kazakhstan	0.23	0.06	0.16	0.07	0.09	0.07	0.12	0.06	0.13
Dominica	0.23	0.06	0.16	0.07	0.09	0.07	0.12	0.06	0.13
Latvia	0.22	0.06	0.16	0.07	0.09	0.07	0.12	0.06	0.13
St. Lucia	0.22	0.06	0.16	0.07	0.09	0.07	0.12	0.06	0.13
Brazil	0.22	0.06	0.16	0.07	0.09	0.07	0.12	0.06	0.13
Bulgaria	0.22	0.06	0.16	0.07	0.09	0.07	0.12	0.06	0.13
Russia	0.22	0.06	0.17	0.07	0.09	0.07	0.12	0.06	0.13
Fiji	0.21	0.06	0.17	0.07	0.09	0.07	0.12	0.07	0.13
Grenada	0.21	0.06	0.17	0.07	0.09	0.07	0.12	0.07	0.13
Turkey	0.21	0.06	0.17	0.07	0.10	0.07	0.12	0.07	0.13
Lithuania	0.21	0.06	0.17	0.07	0.10	0.07	0.12	0.07	0.13
Romania	0.20	0.06	0.17	0.07	0.10	0.07	0.12	0.07	0.13
Iran	0.20	0.06	0.17	0.07	0.10	0.07	0.13	0.07	0.13
Mexico	0.20	0.06	0.17	0.07	0.10	0.07	0.13	0.07	0.14
Bahrain	0.19	0.06	0.17	0.07	0.10	0.07	0.13	0.07	0.14
Chile	0.19	0.06	0.17	0.07	0.10	0.07	0.13	0.07	0.14
Antigua and Barbuda	0.19	0.06	0.17	0.07	0.10	0.07	0.13	0.07	0.14
Poland	0.19	0.06	0.17	0.07	0.10	0.07	0.13	0.07	0.14

Trinidad and Tobago	0.18	0.06	0.17	0.07	0.10	0.07	0.13	0.07	0.14
Estonia	0.18	0.06	0.17	0.07	0.10	0.07	0.13	0.07	0.14
Gabon	0.18	0.06	0.17	0.07	0.10	0.07	0.13	0.07	0.14
Tunisia	0.18	0.06	0.17	0.08	0.10	0.07	0.13	0.07	0.14
St. Kitts and Nevis	0.17	0.06	0.17	0.08	0.10	0.07	0.13	0.07	0.14
Uruguay	0.17	0.06	0.17	0.08	0.10	0.07	0.13	0.07	0.14
Slovakia	0.17	0.06	0.17	0.08	0.10	0.07	0.13	0.07	0.14
Hungary	0.16	0.06	0.18	0.08	0.10	0.07	0.13	0.07	0.14
Argentina	0.14	0.06	0.18	0.08	0.11	0.07	0.13	0.08	0.15
Oman	0.14	0.06	0.18	0.08	0.11	0.07	0.14	0.08	0.15
Qatar	0.13	0.06	0.18	0.08	0.11	0.07	0.14	0.08	0.15
Slovenia	0.13	0.06	0.18	0.08	0.11	0.07	0.14	0.08	0.15
High-income country									
Czech Republic	0.12	0.06	0.18	0.08	0.11	0.07	0.14	0.08	0.15
Greece	0.11	0.06	0.19	0.08	0.11	0.08	0.14	0.08	0.16
Korea	0.11	0.06	0.19	0.08	0.11	0.08	0.14	0.08	0.16
Portugal	0.11	0.06	0.19	0.08	0.11	0.08	0.14	0.08	0.16
Spain	0.11	0.06	0.19	0.08	0.11	0.08	0.14	0.08	0.16
Ireland	0.10	0.06	0.19	0.08	0.11	0.08	0.14	0.08	0.16
Singapore	0.10	0.06	0.19	0.08	0.12	0.08	0.14	0.08	0.16
Mauritius	0.09	0.06	0.19	0.08	0.12	0.08	0.14	0.08	0.16
Israel	0.09	0.06	0.19	0.08	0.12	0.08	0.14	0.08	0.16
New Zealand	0.09	0.06	0.19	0.08	0.12	0.08	0.14	0.08	0.16
Finland	0.09	0.06	0.19	0.08	0.12	0.08	0.14	0.08	0.16
Bahamas	0.09	0.06	0.19	0.08	0.12	0.08	0.14	0.08	0.16
Sweden	0.08	0.06	0.19	0.08	0.12	0.08	0.14	0.09	0.16
Netherlands	0.07	0.06	0.19	0.08	0.12	0.08	0.15	0.09	0.16
France	0.07	0.06	0.20	0.08	0.12	0.08	0.15	0.09	0.17

(continued)

Table 6.6 (continued)

	Food, beverage and tobacco	Clothing and footwear	Gross rent, fuel and power	House furnishing and operations	Medical care	Education	Transport and communication	Recreation	Other
United Kingdom	0.07	0.06	0.20	0.08	0.12	0.08	0.15	0.09	0.17
Belgium	0.07	0.06	0.20	0.08	0.12	0.08	0.15	0.09	0.17
Norway	0.06	0.06	0.20	0.08	0.12	0.08	0.15	0.09	0.17
Italy	0.06	0.06	0.20	0.08	0.12	0.08	0.15	0.09	0.17
Austria	0.06	0.06	0.20	0.08	0.12	0.08	0.15	0.09	0.17
Germany	0.06	0.06	0.20	0.08	0.12	0.08	0.15	0.09	0.17
Australia	0.06	0.06	0.20	0.09	0.12	0.08	0.15	0.09	0.17
Japan	0.06	0.06	0.20	0.09	0.12	0.08	0.15	0.09	0.17
Canada	0.05	0.06	0.20	0.09	0.12	0.08	0.15	0.09	0.17
Bermuda	0.05	0.05	0.20	0.09	0.12	0.08	0.15	0.09	0.17
Switzerland	0.05	0.05	0.20	0.09	0.12	0.08	0.15	0.09	0.17
Barbados	0.05	0.05	0.20	0.09	0.12	0.08	0.15	0.09	0.17
Hong Kong	0.05	0.05	0.20	0.09	0.12	0.08	0.15	0.09	0.17
Iceland	0.05	0.05	0.20	0.09	0.12	0.08	0.15	0.09	0.17
Denmark	0.04	0.05	0.20	0.09	0.12	0.08	0.15	0.09	0.17
Luxembourg	0.02	0.05	0.21	0.09	0.13	0.08	0.15	0.09	0.18
United States	0.02	0.05	0.21	0.09	0.13	0.08	0.15	0.09	0.18
Low-income average	0.373	0.069	0.134	0.058	0.067	0.066	0.098	0.042	0.093
Middle-income average	0.209	0.062	0.167	0.072	0.096	0.072	0.124	0.066	0.133
High-income average	0.072	0.056	0.195	0.084	0.120	0.077	0.146	0.086	0.166

[a]Countries are reported based on ascending per capita real income levels

These calculations are based on the marginal shares expressed in Eq. (6.12)

Table 6.7 Slutsky and Cournot cross-price elasticities with change in food, beverages and tobacco price, 114 countries in 1996[a]

	Clothing and footwear		Gross rent, fuel and power		House furnishing and operations		Medical care		Education		Transport and communication		Recreation[b]		Other	
	Slutsky	Cournot	Slutsky	Cournot	Slutsky	Cournot	Slutsky	Cournot	Slutsky	Cournot	Slutsky	Cournot	Slutsky	Cournot	Slutsky	Cournot
Low-income country																
Tanzania	0.408	−0.222	0.601	−0.328	0.596	−0.325	1.294[c,d]	−0.706[c,d]	0.479	−0.261	0.621[c,d]	−0.339[c,d]			1.149[c,d]	−0.626[c,d]
Nigeria	0.372	−0.214	0.533	−0.306	0.529	−0.304	0.869	−0.499[d]	0.437	−0.251	0.547[c,d]	−0.314[c,d]	2.622	−1.506	0.818[c,d]	−0.469[c,d]
Tajikistan	0.356	−0.210	0.504	−0.297	0.501	−0.295	0.763	−0.449	0.417	−0.246	0.516[c,d]	−0.304[c,d]	1.524	−0.898	0.727[c,d]	−0.428[c,d]
Zambia	0.353	−0.209	0.499	−0.295	0.496	−0.293	0.747	−0.442	0.414	−0.245	0.511[c,d]	−0.302[c,d]	1.427	−0.845	0.713[c,d]	−0.422[c,d]
Yemen	0.353	−0.209	0.498	−0.295	0.495	−0.293	0.746	−0.442	0.414	−0.245	0.510[c,d]	−0.302[c,d]	1.421	−0.841	0.712[c,d]	−0.422[c,d]
Malawi	0.343	−0.207	0.482	−0.290	0.479	−0.288	0.696	−0.419	0.402	−0.242	0.493[c,d]	−0.297[c,d]	1.176	−0.708	0.669[c,d]	−0.403[c,d]
Madagascar	0.343	−0.206	0.481	−0.290	0.479	−0.288	0.695	−0.419	0.402	−0.242	0.492[c,d]	−0.296[c,d]	1.172	−0.706	0.668[c,d]	−0.402[c,d]
Mali	0.340	−0.206	0.477	−0.289	0.474	−0.287	0.683	−0.413	0.399	−0.241	0.488[c,d]	−0.295[c,d]	1.121	−0.678	0.657[c,d]	−0.397[c,d]
Mongolia	0.340	−0.206	0.476	−0.288	0.473	−0.287	0.680	−0.412	0.398	−0.241	0.486[c,d]	−0.295[c,d]	1.109	−0.672	0.654[c,d]	−0.396[c,d]
Benin	0.317	−0.200	0.439	−0.277	0.437	−0.276	0.591	−0.373	0.372	−0.235	0.448	−0.283	0.828	−0.522	0.574[c,d]	−0.362[c,d]
Kenya	0.308	−0.198	0.424	−0.273	0.422	−0.271	0.559	−0.359	0.361	−0.232	0.432	−0.278	0.750	−0.482	0.544[c,d]	−0.350[c,d]
Sierra Leone	0.299	−0.196	0.411	−0.269	0.409	−0.267	0.532	−0.348	0.351	−0.230	0.418	−0.274	0.692	−0.453	0.519	−0.340[d]
Nepal	0.299	−0.196	0.410	−0.269	0.408	−0.267	0.532	−0.348	0.351	−0.230	0.418	−0.273	0.691	−0.452	0.519	−0.339[d]
Turkmenistan	0.295	−0.195	0.404	−0.267	0.402	−0.265	0.520	−0.343	0.346	−0.229	0.411	−0.271	0.667	−0.440	0.508[c,d]	−0.335[c,d]
Congo	0.288	−0.193	0.392	−0.263	0.391	−0.262	0.498	−0.334	0.337	−0.226	0.399	−0.268	0.624	−0.419	0.487[c,d]	−0.327[c,d]
Senegal	0.281	−0.191	0.382	−0.260	0.381	−0.259	0.480	−0.327	0.330	−0.224	0.389	−0.265	0.592	−0.403	0.470	−0.320
Vietnam	0.279	−0.191	0.379	−0.259	0.377	−0.258	0.474	−0.324	0.327	−0.224	0.385	−0.263	0.581	−0.398	0.464	−0.318
Bangladesh	0.278	−0.191	0.377	−0.259	0.376	−0.258	0.472	−0.323	0.326	−0.224	0.383	−0.263	0.577	−0.396	0.462	−0.317
Pakistan	0.264	−0.187	0.356	−0.253	0.354	−0.252	0.436	−0.309	0.309	−0.219	0.361	−0.256	0.519	−0.368	0.428	−0.304

(continued)

Table 6.7 (continued)

	Clothing and footwear		Gross rent, fuel and power		House furnishing and operations		Medical care		Education		Transport and communication		Recreation[b]		Other	
	Slutsky	Cournot	Slutsky	Cournot	Slutsky	Cournot	Slutsky	Cournot	Slutsky	Cournot	Slutsky	Cournot	Slutsky	Cournot	Slutsky	Cournot
Azerbaijan	0.257	−0.186	0.346	−0.250	0.345	−0.249	0.421	−0.304	0.302	−0.218	0.351	−0.254	0.495	−0.357	0.414	−0.298
Cote d'Ivoire	0.255	−0.185	0.342	−0.249	0.341	−0.248	0.415	−0.301	0.299	−0.217	0.347	−0.252	0.486	−0.353	0.408	−0.296
Paraguay	0.253	−0.184	0.340	−0.248	0.339	−0.247	0.411	−0.300	0.297	−0.216	0.345	−0.252	0.480	−0.350	0.404	−0.295
Uzbekistan	0.248	−0.183	0.333	−0.246	0.332	−0.245	0.401	−0.296	0.291	−0.215	0.338	−0.250	0.466	−0.344	0.395	−0.291
Kyrgyzstan	0.248	−0.183	0.333	−0.246	0.332	−0.245	0.401	−0.296	0.291	−0.215	0.338	−0.250	0.465	−0.343	0.394	−0.291
Cameroon	0.247	−0.183	0.332	−0.246	0.331	−0.245	0.399	−0.295	0.290	−0.215	0.337	−0.249	0.462	−0.342	0.392	−0.291
Moldova	0.247	−0.183	0.332	−0.246	0.330	−0.245	0.399	−0.295	0.290	−0.215	0.336	−0.249	0.462	−0.342	0.392	−0.291
Bolivia	0.243	−0.182	0.325	−0.244	0.324	−0.243	0.388	−0.291	0.285	−0.214	0.329	−0.247	0.447	−0.336	0.383	−0.287
Ecuador	0.241	−0.182	0.322	−0.243	0.321	−0.242	0.385	−0.290	0.283	−0.213	0.327	−0.246	0.442	−0.333	0.379	−0.286
Armenia	0.236	−0.180	0.316	−0.241	0.315	−0.240	0.375	−0.286	0.277	−0.212	0.320	−0.244	0.428	−0.327	0.370	−0.282
Sri Lanka	0.236	−0.180	0.315	−0.241	0.314	−0.240	0.374	−0.286	0.277	−0.212	0.319	−0.244	0.427	−0.327	0.369	−0.282
Jordan	0.230	−0.179	0.307	−0.239	0.306	−0.238	0.363	−0.282	0.270	−0.210	0.311	−0.242	0.412	−0.320	0.358	−0.278
Albania	0.223	−0.177	0.296	−0.236	0.295	−0.235	0.348	−0.276	0.261	−0.208	0.300	−0.239	0.391	−0.311	0.343	−0.273
Indonesia	0.220	−0.176	0.293	−0.235	0.292	−0.234	0.343	−0.275	0.259	−0.207	0.296	−0.238	0.385	−0.308	0.338	−0.271
Jamaica	0.220	−0.176	0.292	−0.234	0.291	−0.234	0.341	−0.274	0.258	−0.207	0.296	−0.237	0.383	−0.308	0.337	−0.271
Zimbabwe	0.219	−0.176	0.291	−0.234	0.290	−0.233	0.340	−0.274	0.257	−0.207	0.295	−0.237	0.382	−0.307	0.336	−0.270
Guinea	0.217	−0.176	0.287	−0.233	0.286	−0.232	0.335	−0.272	0.254	−0.206	0.291	−0.236	0.375	−0.304	0.331	−0.268
Syria	0.211	−0.174	0.279	−0.231	0.278	−0.230	0.324	−0.268	0.247	−0.204	0.283	−0.234	0.361	−0.298	0.320	−0.265
Georgia	0.210	−0.174	0.278	−0.230	0.277	−0.230	0.322	−0.267	0.246	−0.204	0.281	−0.233	0.359	−0.297	0.319	−0.264
Middle-income country																
Ukraine	0.200	−0.172	0.265	−0.227	0.264	−0.226	0.305	−0.261	0.235	−0.201	0.268	−0.229	0.336	−0.288	0.301	−0.258
Philippines	0.194	−0.170	0.255	−0.224	0.254	−0.223	0.293	−0.257	0.227	−0.200	0.258	−0.227	0.321	−0.282	0.289	−0.254

Peru	0.191	−0.169	0.251	−0.223	0.251	−0.222	0.288	−0.255	0.224	−0.199	0.254	−0.226	0.315	−0.280	0.285	−0.252
Botswana	0.191	−0.169	0.251	−0.223	0.250	−0.222	0.287	−0.255	0.224	−0.199	0.254	−0.225	0.315	−0.279	0.284	−0.252
Thailand	0.189	−0.169	0.249	−0.222	0.248	−0.222	0.285	−0.254	0.222	−0.198	0.252	−0.225	0.312	−0.278	0.282	−0.251
Morocco	0.186	−0.168	0.245	−0.221	0.244	−0.221	0.279	−0.252	0.219	−0.197	0.248	−0.224	0.305	−0.276	0.276	−0.250
Venezuela	0.185	−0.168	0.244	−0.221	0.243	−0.220	0.278	−0.252	0.218	−0.197	0.246	−0.223	0.303	−0.275	0.275	−0.249
Macedonia	0.181	−0.167	0.237	−0.219	0.237	−0.218	0.270	−0.249	0.212	−0.196	0.240	−0.222	0.294	−0.271	0.267	−0.247
Belize	0.181	−0.167	0.237	−0.219	0.236	−0.218	0.270	−0.249	0.212	−0.196	0.240	−0.221	0.294	−0.271	0.267	−0.246
Egypt	0.180	−0.167	0.237	−0.219	0.236	−0.218	0.269	−0.249	0.212	−0.196	0.240	−0.221	0.293	−0.271	0.267	−0.246
St. Vincent and Grenadines	0.180	−0.167	0.236	−0.219	0.235	−0.218	0.268	−0.248	0.211	−0.196	0.239	−0.221	0.292	−0.270	0.265	−0.246
Swaziland	0.175	−0.165	0.229	−0.217	0.228	−0.216	0.259	−0.245	0.205	−0.194	0.231	−0.219	0.281	−0.266	0.257	−0.243
Lebanon	0.173	−0.165	0.226	−0.216	0.226	−0.215	0.256	−0.244	0.203	−0.194	0.229	−0.218	0.277	−0.265	0.253	−0.242
Belarus	0.172	−0.165	0.225	−0.216	0.224	−0.215	0.254	−0.244	0.202	−0.193	0.227	−0.218	0.275	−0.264	0.252	−0.241
Kazakhstan	0.171	−0.164	0.224	−0.216	0.224	−0.215	0.254	−0.244	0.201	−0.193	0.227	−0.218	0.275	−0.264	0.251	−0.241
Dominica	0.171	−0.164	0.224	−0.216	0.224	−0.215	0.254	−0.244	0.201	−0.193	0.227	−0.218	0.275	−0.264	0.251	−0.241
Latvia	0.166	−0.163	0.217	−0.214	0.217	−0.213	0.245	−0.240	0.195	−0.192	0.219	−0.216	0.264	−0.260	0.242	−0.238
St. Lucia	0.165	−0.163	0.216	−0.213	0.216	−0.213	0.244	−0.240	0.194	−0.191	0.219	−0.216	0.263	−0.259	0.241	−0.238
Brazil	0.165	−0.163	0.215	−0.213	0.215	−0.212	0.243	−0.240	0.193	−0.191	0.218	−0.215	0.262	−0.259	0.240	−0.238
Bulgaria	0.164	−0.163	0.215	−0.213	0.214	−0.212	0.242	−0.240	0.193	−0.191	0.217	−0.215	0.261	−0.258	0.239	−0.237
Russia	0.161	−0.162	0.211	−0.212	0.210	−0.211	0.237	−0.238	0.189	−0.190	0.213	−0.214	0.255	−0.256	0.234	−0.236
Fiji	0.158	−0.161	0.206	−0.210	0.205	−0.210	0.231	−0.236	0.185	−0.189	0.208	−0.213	0.248	−0.254	0.229	−0.234
Grenada	0.158	−0.161	0.206	−0.210	0.205	−0.210	0.231	−0.236	0.185	−0.189	0.208	−0.213	0.248	−0.254	0.229	−0.234

(continued)

Table 6.7 (continued)

	Clothing and footwear		Gross rent, fuel and power		House furnishing and operations		Medical care		Education		Transport and communication		Recreation[b]		Other	
	Slutsky	Cournot	Slutsky	Cournot	Slutsky	Cournot	Slutsky	Cournot	Slutsky	Cournot	Slutsky	Cournot	Slutsky	Cournot	Slutsky	Cournot
Turkey	0.156	−0.161	0.204	−0.210	0.203	−0.209	0.228	−0.235	0.183	−0.189	0.206	−0.212	0.245	−0.253	0.226	−0.233
Lithuania	0.153	−0.160	0.200	−0.209	0.199	−0.208	0.223	−0.234	0.180	−0.188	0.202	−0.211	0.240	−0.251	0.222	−0.232
Romania	0.151	−0.159	0.197	−0.208	0.197	−0.207	0.220	−0.232	0.178	−0.187	0.199	−0.210	0.236	−0.249	0.218	−0.230
Iran	0.147	−0.158	0.192	−0.207	0.191	−0.206	0.214	−0.230	0.173	−0.186	0.193	−0.209	0.229	−0.247	0.212	−0.228
Mexico	0.145	−0.158	0.189	−0.206	0.188	−0.205	0.210	−0.229	0.171	−0.186	0.191	−0.208	0.225	−0.245	0.209	−0.227
Bahrain	0.143	−0.157	0.186	−0.205	0.185	−0.204	0.207	−0.228	0.168	−0.185	0.188	−0.207	0.221	−0.244	0.205	−0.226
Chile	0.142	−0.157	0.184	−0.205	0.184	−0.204	0.205	−0.227	0.166	−0.185	0.186	−0.206	0.219	−0.243	0.203	−0.226
Antigua and Barbuda	0.141	−0.157	0.184	−0.204	0.183	−0.204	0.204	−0.227	0.166	−0.185	0.185	−0.206	0.218	−0.243	0.203	−0.225
Poland	0.138	−0.156	0.179	−0.203	0.179	−0.203	0.199	−0.226	0.162	−0.184	0.181	−0.205	0.212	−0.240	0.197	−0.224
Trinidad and Tobago	0.135	−0.156	0.176	−0.202	0.175	−0.202	0.195	−0.224	0.159	−0.183	0.177	−0.204	0.207	−0.239	0.193	−0.222
Estonia	0.132	−0.155	0.172	−0.201	0.171	−0.201	0.190	−0.223	0.156	−0.182	0.173	−0.203	0.202	−0.237	0.189	−0.221
Gabon	0.132	−0.155	0.171	−0.201	0.170	−0.200	0.189	−0.222	0.155	−0.182	0.172	−0.203	0.201	−0.237	0.188	−0.221
Tunisia	0.129	−0.154	0.168	−0.200	0.168	−0.200	0.186	−0.221	0.152	−0.181	0.170	−0.202	0.198	−0.235	0.184	−0.220
St. Kitts and Nevis	0.128	−0.154	0.166	−0.200	0.166	−0.199	0.184	−0.221	0.151	−0.181	0.168	−0.201	0.195	−0.234	0.182	−0.219
Uruguay	0.127	−0.154	0.165	−0.199	0.165	−0.199	0.182	−0.220	0.150	−0.181	0.167	−0.201	0.194	−0.234	0.181	−0.219
Slovakia	0.126	−0.153	0.163	−0.199	0.163	−0.198	0.180	−0.219	0.148	−0.180	0.165	−0.201	0.191	−0.233[d]	0.179	−0.218
Hungary	0.118	−0.151	0.152	−0.196	0.152	−0.195	0.167	−0.216	0.138	−0.178	0.154	−0.198	0.177	−0.228[d]	0.166	−0.214
Argentina	0.107	−0.149	0.138	−0.192	0.138	−0.192	0.151	−0.210	0.126	−0.175	0.139	−0.194	0.159	−0.222[d]	0.150	−0.209
Oman	0.102	−0.147	0.132	−0.190	0.132	−0.190	0.144	−0.208	0.120	−0.174	0.133	−0.192	0.152	−0.219[d]	0.143	−0.207
Qatar	0.097	−0.146	0.125	−0.188	0.124	−0.188	0.136	−0.206	0.114	−0.172	0.126	−0.190	0.143	−0.216[d]	0.135	−0.204
Slovenia	0.094	−0.145	0.121	−0.188	0.121	−0.187	0.132	−0.205	0.111	−0.171	0.122	−0.189	0.139	−0.215[d]	0.131	−0.203

High-income country																
Czech Republic	0.091	−0.145	0.117	−0.186	0.117	−0.186	0.128	−0.203	0.107	−0.170	0.118	−0.188	0.134	−0.213[d]	0.127	−0.202
Greece	0.083	−0.143	0.108	−0.184	0.107	−0.183	0.117	−0.200	0.098	−0.168	0.108	−0.185	0.122	−0.209[d]	0.116	−0.199
Korea	0.082	−0.142	0.105	−0.183	0.105	−0.183	0.114	−0.199	0.096	−0.168	0.106	−0.185	0.119	−0.208[d]	0.113	−0.198
Portugal	0.079	−0.142	0.102	−0.182	0.102	−0.182	0.111	−0.198	0.093	−0.167	0.103	−0.184	0.116	−0.207[d]	0.110	−0.197
Spain	0.079	−0.142	0.101	−0.182	0.101	−0.182	0.110	−0.198	0.093	−0.167	0.102	−0.184	0.115	−0.207[d]	0.109	−0.197
Ireland	0.076	−0.141	0.098	−0.181	0.098	−0.181	0.106	−0.197	0.090	−0.166	0.099	−0.183	0.111	−0.206[d]	0.106	−0.195
Singapore	0.073	−0.140	0.094	−0.180	0.094	−0.180[d]	0.102	−0.195	0.086	−0.165	0.095	−0.182	0.107	−0.204[d]	0.102	−0.194
Mauritius	0.069	−0.139	0.089	−0.179	0.089	−0.179[d]	0.097	−0.194	0.082	−0.164	0.090	−0.180	0.101	−0.202[d]	0.096	−0.193
Israel	0.066	−0.138	0.085	−0.178	0.085	−0.177[d]	0.092	−0.192	0.078	−0.163	0.085	−0.179	0.096	−0.201[d]	0.091	−0.191
New Zealand	0.065	−0.138	0.083	−0.177	0.083	−0.177[d]	0.090	−0.192	0.076	−0.163[d]	0.084	−0.179	0.094	−0.200[d]	0.089	−0.191[d]
Finland	0.064	−0.138	0.083	−0.177	0.082	−0.177[d]	0.089	−0.191	0.076	−0.163[d]	0.083	−0.179	0.093	−0.200[d]	0.089	−0.190[d]
Bahamas	0.063	−0.138	0.081	−0.177	0.081	−0.177[d]	0.088	−0.191	0.075	−0.162[d]	0.082	−0.178	0.091	−0.199[d]	0.087	−0.190[d]
Sweden	0.056	−0.136	0.072	−0.174	0.072	−0.174[d]	0.077	−0.188	0.066	−0.160[d]	0.072	−0.176	0.081	−0.196[d]	0.077	−0.187[d]
Netherlands	0.055	−0.136[d]	0.070	−0.174	0.070	−0.174[d]	0.076	−0.187	0.065	−0.160[d]	0.071	−0.175	0.079	−0.195[d]	0.075	−0.186[d]
France	0.049	−0.134[d]	0.063	−0.172	0.063	−0.172[d]	0.068	−0.185	0.058	−0.159[d]	0.064	−0.173	0.071	−0.193[d]	0.068	−0.184[d]
United Kingdom	0.049	−0.134[d]	0.063	−0.172	0.063	−0.172[d]	0.067	−0.185	0.058	−0.158[d]	0.063	−0.173	0.070	−0.192[d]	0.067	−0.184[d]
Belgium	0.048	−0.134[d]	0.061	−0.172	0.061	−0.171[d]	0.066	−0.184	0.056	−0.158[d]	0.062	−0.173	0.068	−0.192[d]	0.065	−0.184[d]
Norway	0.047	−0.134[d]	0.061	−0.172	0.061	−0.171[d]	0.065	−0.184	0.056	−0.158[d]	0.061	−0.173	0.068	−0.192[d]	0.065	−0.183[d]
Italy	0.047	−0.134[d]	0.060	−0.171[d]	0.060	−0.171[d]	0.064	−0.184	0.055	−0.158[d]	0.060	−0.172	0.067	−0.191[d]	0.064	−0.183[d]
Austria	0.045	−0.133[d]	0.057	−0.171[d]	0.057	−0.170[d]	0.061	−0.183	0.053	−0.157[d]	0.058	−0.172	0.064	−0.190[d]	0.061	−0.182[d]

(continued)

Table 6.7 (continued)

	Clothing and footwear		Gross rent, fuel and power		House furnishing and operations		Medical care		Education		Transport and communication		Recreation[b]		Other	
	Slutsky	Cournot	Slutsky	Cournot	Slutsky	Cournot	Slutsky	Cournot	Slutsky	Cournot	Slutsky	Cournot	Slutsky	Cournot	Slutsky	Cournot
Germany	0.044	−0.133[d]	0.057	−0.170[d]	0.057	−0.170[d]	0.061	−0.183	0.052	−0.157[d]	0.057	−0.172	0.063	−0.190[d]	0.061	−0.182[d]
Australia	0.042	−0.133[d]	0.054	−0.170[d]	0.054	−0.169[d]	0.058	−0.182[d]	0.050	−0.157[d]	0.055	−0.171	0.061	−0.189[d]	0.058	−0.181[d]
Japan	0.041	−0.132[d]	0.053	−0.169[d]	0.053	−0.169[d]	0.056	−0.182[d]	0.049	−0.156[d]	0.053	−0.170	0.059	−0.189[d]	0.056	−0.181[d]
Canada	0.039	−0.132[d]	0.050	−0.169[d]	0.050	−0.168[d]	0.054	−0.181[d]	0.046	−0.156[d]	0.051	−0.170[d]	0.056	−0.188[d]	0.054	−0.180[d]
Bermuda	0.036	−0.131[d]	0.046	−0.168[d]	0.046	−0.167[d]	0.049	−0.180[d]	0.042	−0.155[d]	0.046	−0.169[d]	0.051	−0.186[d]	0.049	−0.179[d]
Switzerland	0.034[d]	−0.131[d]	0.044[d]	−0.167[d]	0.044	−0.167[d]	0.047[d]	−0.179[d]	0.041	−0.154[d]	0.044[d]	−0.168[d]	0.049	−0.186[d]	0.047[d]	−0.178[d]
Barbados	0.034[d]	−0.131[d]	0.044[d]	−0.167[d]	0.043[d]	−0.167[d]	0.047[d]	−0.179[d]	0.040[d]	−0.154[d]	0.044[d]	−0.168[d]	0.048	−0.186[d]	0.046[d]	−0.178[d]
Hong Kong	0.034[d]	−0.130[d]	0.043[d]	−0.167[d]	0.043[d]	−0.167[d]	0.046[d]	−0.179[d]	0.040[d]	−0.154[d]	0.043[d]	−0.168[d]	0.048	−0.185[d]	0.046[d]	−0.178[d]
Iceland	0.033[d]	−0.130[d]	0.043[d]	−0.167[d]	0.043[d]	−0.166[d]	0.046[d]	−0.179[d]	0.039[d]	−0.154[d]	0.043[d]	−0.168[d]	0.047[d]	−0.185[d]	0.045[d]	−0.178[d]
Denmark	0.032[d]	−0.130[d]	0.042[d]	−0.166[d]	0.041[d]	−0.166[d]	0.044[d]	−0.178[d]	0.038[d]	−0.154[d]	0.042[d]	−0.168[d]	0.046[d]	−0.185[d]	0.044[d]	−0.177[d]
Luxembourg	0.014[d]	−0.126[d]	0.018[d]	−0.160[d]	0.018[d]	−0.160[d]	0.019[d]	−0.171[d]	0.017[d]	−0.149[d]	0.018[c,d]	−0.161[d]	0.020[d]	−0.177[d]	0.019[c,d]	−0.170[d]
United States	0.011	−0.125	0.015	−0.159	0.014	−0.159	0.015	−0.170	0.013	−0.148	0.015[c]	−0.160	0.016	−0.175	0.015[c]	−0.169
Low-income average	0.278	−0.191	0.381	−0.260	0.379	−0.259	0.509	−0.343	0.327	−0.224	0.388	−0.265	0.708	−0.470	0.493	−0.332
Middle-income average	0.154	−0.160	0.202	−0.209	0.201	−0.209	0.227	−0.235	0.182	−0.188	0.204	−0.212	0.245	−0.253	0.225	−0.233
High-income average	0.053	−0.135	0.068	−0.173	0.067	−0.173	0.073	−0.187	0.062	−0.159	0.068	−0.175	0.076	−0.194	0.072	−0.186

[a]Countries are reported based on ascending per capita real income levels
[b]As the estimated budget share was negative for Tanzania we do not report the elasticity for this country
[c]Elasticity estimate is not significantly different from zero at 0.05 level
[d]Elasticity estimate is not significantly different from the point estimate of the United States at 0.05 level

Table 6.8 Slutsky and Cournot cross-price elasticities with change in clothing and footwear price, 114 countries in 1996[a]

	Food, beverage and tobacco		Gross rent, fuel and power		House operations		Medical care		Education		Transport and communication		Recreation[b]		Other	
	Slutsky	Cournot	Slutsky	Cournot	Slutsky	Cournot	Slutsky	Cournot	Slutsky	Cournot	Slutsky	Cournot	Slutsky	Cournot	Slutsky	Cournot
Low-income country																
Tanzania	0.049	−0.016	0.084	−0.028	0.084	−0.028[d]	0.182[c,d]	−0.060[c,d]	0.067	−0.022[d]	0.087[c,d]	−0.029[c,d]			0.161[c,d]	−0.053[c,d]
Nigeria	0.047	−0.016	8.00	−0.027[d]	0.079	−0.026[d]	0.130[d]	−0.043[d]	0.065	−0.022[d]	0.082[c,d]	−0.027[c,d]	0.392	−0.131[d]	0.122[c,d]	−0.041[c,d]
Tajikistan	0.046	−0.015	0.078	−0.026[d]	0.077	−0.026[d]	0.118	−0.039	0.064	−0.022[d]	0.080[c,d]	−0.027[c,d]	0.235	−0.079[d]	0.112[c,d]	−0.037[c,d]
Zambia	0.046	−0.015	0.077	−0.026[d]	0.077	−0.026[d]	0.116	−0.039	0.064	−0.021[d]	0.079[c,d]	−0.027[c,d]	0.221	−0.074[d]	0.111[c,d]	−0.037[c,d]
Yemen	0.046	−0.015	0.077	−0.026[d]	0.077	−0.026[d]	0.116	−0.039	0.064	−0.021[d]	0.079[c,d]	−0.026[c,d]	0.220	−0.074[d]	0.110[c,d]	−0.037[c,d]
Malawi	0.045	−0.015	0.076	−0.026[d]	0.076	−0.025[d]	0.110	−0.037	0.064	−0.021[d]	0.078[c,d]	−0.026[c,d]	0.186	−0.062[d]	0.106[c,d]	−0.035[c,d]
Madagascar	0.045	−0.015	0.076	−0.026[d]	0.076	−0.025[d]	0.110	−0.037	0.064	−0.021[d]	0.078[c,d]	−0.026[c,d]	0.186	−0.062[d]	0.106[c,d]	−0.035[c,d]
Mali	0.045	−0.015	0.076	−0.025[d]	0.075	−0.025[d]	0.109	−0.036	0.064	−0.021[d]	0.078[c,d]	−0.026[c,d]	0.178	−0.060[d]	0.105[c,d]	−0.035[c,d]
Mongolia	0.045	−0.015	0.076	−0.025[d]	0.075	−0.025[d]	0.108	−0.036	0.063	−0.021[d]	0.078[c,d]	−0.026[c,d]	0.177	−0.059[d]	0.104[c,d]	−0.035[c,d]
Benin	0.044	−0.015	0.074	−0.025[d]	0.073	−0.025[d]	0.099	−0.033	0.062	−0.021[d]	0.075[c,d]	−0.025[d]	0.139	−0.047[d]	0.096[c,d]	−0.032[c,d]
Kenya	0.043	−0.015	0.073	−0.025[d]	0.072	−0.024[d]	0.096	−0.032	0.062	−0.021[d]	0.074[c]	−0.025	0.128	−0.043[d]	0.093[c,d]	−0.031[c,d]
Sierra Leone	0.042	−0.014	0.072	−0.024[d]	0.071	−0.024[d]	0.093	−0.032	0.061	−0.021[d]	0.073	−0.025	0.121	−0.041[d]	0.091[d]	−0.031[d]
Nepal	0.042	−0.014	0.072	−0.024[d]	0.071	−0.024[d]	0.093	−0.031	0.061	−0.021[d]	0.073	−0.025	0.121	−0.041[d]	0.091[d]	−0.031[d]
Turkmenistan	0.042	−0.014	0.071	−0.024[d]	0.071	−0.024[d]	0.092	−0.031	0.061	−0.021[d]	0.073[c]	−0.025	0.118	−0.040[d]	0.090[c,d]	−0.030[c,d]
Congo	0.042	−0.014	0.071	−0.024[d]	0.070	−0.024[d]	0.090	−0.030	0.061	−0.021[d]	0.072[c]	−0.024	0.112	−0.038[d]	0.088[c,d]	−0.030[c,d]
Senegal	0.041	−0.014	0.070	−0.024[d]	0.070	−0.024[d]	0.088	−0.030	0.060	−0.021[d]	0.071	−0.024	0.108	−0.037[d]	0.086[d]	−0.029[d]
Vietnam	0.041	−0.014	0.070	−0.024[d]	0.069	−0.024[d]	0.087	−0.030	0.060	−0.021[d]	0.071	−0.024	0.107	−0.036[d]	0.086	−0.029[d]
Bangladesh	0.041	−0.014	0.070	−0.024[d]	0.069	−0.024[d]	0.087	−0.030	0.060	−0.021[d]	0.071	−0.024	0.107	−0.036[d]	0.085	−0.029[d]
Pakistan	0.040	−0.014	0.068	−0.023[d]	0.068	−0.023[d]	0.084	−0.029	0.059	−0.020[d]	0.069	−0.024	0.100	−0.034[d]	0.082	−0.028[d]
Azerbaijan	0.039	−0.013	0.068	−0.023[d]	0.068	−0.023[d]	0.082	−0.028	0.059	−0.020[d]	0.069	−0.024	0.097	−0.033[d]	0.081	−0.028[d]
Cote d'Ivoire	0.039	−0.013	0.068	−0.023[d]	0.067	−0.023[d]	0.082	−0.028	0.059	−0.020[d]	0.069	−0.024	0.096	−0.033[d]	0.081	−0.028[d]
Paraguay	0.039	−0.013	0.067	−0.023[d]	0.067	−0.023[d]	0.082	−0.028[d]	0.059	−0.020[d]	0.068	−0.023	0.095	−0.033[d]	0.080	−0.028[d]
Uzbekistan	0.039	−0.013	0.067	−0.023[d]	0.067	−0.023[d]	0.081	−0.028[d]	0.059	−0.020[d]	0.068	−0.023	0.094	−0.032[d]	0.079	−0.027[d]
Kyrgyzstan	0.039	−0.013	0.067	−0.023[d]	0.067	−0.023[d]	0.081	−0.028[d]	0.059	−0.020[d]	0.068	−0.023	0.094	−0.032[d]	0.079	−0.027[d]

(continued)

Table 6.8 (continued)

	Food, beverage and tobacco		Gross rent, fuel and power		House operations		Medical care		Education		Transport and communication		Recreation[b]		Other	
	Slutsky	Cournot	Slutsky	Cournot	Slutsky	Cournot	Slutsky	Cournot	Slutsky	Cournot	Slutsky	Cournot	Slutsky	Cournot	Slutsky	Cournot
Cameroon	0.039	−0.013	0.067	−0.023[d]	0.067	−0.023[d]	0.081	−0.028[d]	0.059	−0.020[d]	0.068	−0.023	0.093	−0.032[d]	0.079	−0.027[d]
Moldova	0.039	−0.013	0.067	−0.023[d]	0.067	−0.023[d]	0.080	−0.028[d]	0.059	−0.020[d]	0.068	−0.023	0.093	−0.032[d]	0.079	−0.027[d]
Bolivia	0.038	−0.013	0.067	−0.023[d]	0.066	−0.023[d]	0.080	−0.027[d]	0.058	−0.020[d]	0.068	−0.023	0.092	−0.032[d]	0.078	−0.027[d]
Ecuador	0.038	−0.013	0.066	−0.023[d]	0.066	−0.023[d]	0.079	−0.027[d]	0.058	−0.020[d]	0.067	−0.023	0.091	−0.031[d]	0.078	−0.027[d]
Armenia	0.038	−0.013	0.066	−0.023[d]	0.066	−0.023[d]	0.078	−0.027[d]	0.058	−0.020[d]	0.067	−0.023	0.090	−0.031[d]	0.077	−0.027[d]
Sri Lanka	0.038	−0.013	0.066	−0.023[d]	0.066	−0.023[d]	0.078	−0.027[d]	0.058	−0.020[d]	0.067	−0.023	0.089	−0.031[d]	0.077	−0.027[d]
Jordan	0.037	−0.013	0.066	−0.023[d]	0.065	−0.023[d]	0.077	−0.027[d]	0.058	−0.020[d]	0.066	−0.023	0.088	−0.030[d]	0.076	−0.026[d]
Albania	0.037	−0.013	0.065	−0.022[d]	0.065	−0.022[d]	0.076	−0.026[d]	0.057	−0.020[d]	0.066	−0.023	0.086	−0.030[d]	0.075	−0.026[d]
Indonesia	0.036	−0.013	0.065	−0.022[d]	0.065	−0.022[d]	0.076	−0.026[d]	0.057	−0.020[d]	0.066	−0.023	0.085	−0.029[d]	0.075	−0.026[d]
Jamaica	0.036	−0.013	0.065	−0.022[d]	0.064	−0.022[d]	0.076	−0.026[d]	0.057	−0.020[d]	0.066	−0.023	0.085	−0.029[d]	0.075	−0.026[d]
Zimbabwe	0.036	−0.013	0.065	−0.022[d]	0.064	−0.022[d]	0.076	−0.026[d]	0.057	−0.020[d]	0.065	−0.023	0.085	−0.029[d]	0.075	−0.026[d]
Guinea	0.036	−0.012	0.064	−0.022[d]	0.064	−0.022[d]	0.075	−0.026[d]	0.057	−0.020[d]	0.065	−0.023	0.084	−0.029[d]	0.074	−0.026[d]
Syria	0.036	−0.012	0.064	−0.022[d]	0.064	−0.022[d]	0.074	−0.026[d]	0.057	−0.020[d]	0.065	−0.022	0.083	−0.029[d]	0.073	−0.025[d]
Georgia	0.036	−0.012	0.064	−0.022[d]	0.064	−0.022[d]	0.074	−0.026[d]	0.057	−0.020	0.065	−0.022	0.082	−0.029[d]	0.073	−0.025[d]
Middle-income country																
Ukraine	0.035	−0.012	0.063	−0.022[d]	0.063	−0.022[d]	0.073	−0.025[d]	0.056	−0.020[d]	0.064	−0.022	0.080	−0.028[d]	0.072	−0.025[d]
Philippines	0.034	−0.012	0.063	−0.022[d]	0.062	−0.022[d]	0.072	−0.025[d]	0.056	−0.019[d]	0.063	−0.022[d]	0.079	−0.027[d]	0.071	−0.025[d]
Peru	0.034	−0.012	0.062	−0.022[d]	0.062	−0.022[d]	0.071	−0.025[d]	0.056	−0.019[d]	0.063	−0.022[d]	0.078[d]	−0.027[d]	0.071	−0.025[d]
Botswana	0.034	−0.012	0.062	−0.022[d]	0.062	−0.022[d]	0.071	−0.025[d]	0.056	−0.019[d]	0.063	−0.022[d]	0.078[d]	−0.027[d]	0.071	−0.025[d]
Thailand	0.034	−0.012	0.062	−0.022[d]	0.062	−0.022[d]	0.071	−0.025[d]	0.056	−0.019[d]	0.063	−0.022[d]	0.078[d]	−0.027[d]	0.070	−0.025[d]
Morocco	0.033	−0.012	0.062	−0.022[d]	0.062	−0.022[d]	0.071	−0.025[d]	0.055	−0.019[d]	0.063	−0.022[d]	0.077[d]	−0.027[d]	0.070	−0.024[d]
Venezuela	0.033	−0.012	0.062	−0.022[d]	0.062	−0.022[d]	0.071	−0.025[d]	0.055	−0.019[d]	0.063	−0.022[d]	0.077[d]	−0.027[d]	0.070	−0.024[d]
Macedonia	0.033	−0.012	0.062	−0.022[d]	0.061	−0.021[d]	0.070	−0.024[d]	0.055	−0.019[d]	0.062	−0.022[d]	0.076[d]	−0.027[d]	0.069	−0.024[d]
Belize	0.033	−0.012	0.062	−0.022[d]	0.061	−0.021[d]	0.070	−0.024[d]	0.055	−0.019[d]	0.062	−0.022[d]	0.076[d]	−0.027[d]	0.069	−0.024[d]
Egypt	0.033	−0.012	0.062	−0.022[d]	0.061	−0.021[d]	0.070	−0.024[d]	0.055	−0.019[d]	0.062	−0.022[d]	0.076[d]	−0.027[d]	0.069	−0.024[d]

St. Vincent and Grenadines	0.033	−0.011	0.062	−0.022[d]	0.061	−0.021[d]	0.070	−0.024[d]	0.055	−0.019[d]	0.062	−0.022[d]	0.076[d]	−0.027[d]	0.069	−0.024[d]
Swaziland	0.032	−0.011	0.061	−0.021[d]	0.061	−0.021[d]	0.069	−0.024[d]	0.055	−0.019[d]	0.062	−0.022[d]	0.075[d]	−0.026[d]	0.069	−0.024[d]
Lebanon	0.032	−0.011	0.061	−0.021[d]	0.061	−0.021[d]	0.069	−0.024[d]	0.055	−0.019[d]	0.062	−0.022[d]	0.075[d]	−0.026[d]	0.068	−0.024[d]
Belarus	0.032	−0.011	0.061	−0.021[d]	0.061	−0.021[d]	0.069	−0.024[d]	0.055	−0.019[d]	0.062	−0.022[d]	0.075[d]	−0.026[d]	0.068	−0.024[d]
Kazakhstan	0.032	−0.011	0.061	−0.021[d]	0.061	−0.021[d]	0.069	−0.024[d]	0.055	−0.019[d]	0.062	−0.022[d]	0.075[d]	−0.026[d]	0.068	−0.024[d]
Dominica	0.032	−0.011	0.061	−0.021[d]	0.061	−0.021[d]	0.069	−0.024[d]	0.055	−0.019[d]	0.062	−0.022[d]	0.075[d]	−0.026[d]	0.068	−0.024[d]
Latvia	0.031	−0.011	0.060	−0.021[d]	0.060	−0.021[d]	0.068	−0.024[d]	0.054	−0.019[d]	0.061	−0.021[d]	0.074[d]	−0.026[d]	0.068	−0.024[d]
St. Lucia	0.031	−0.011	0.060	−0.021[d]	0.060	−0.021[d]	0.068	−0.024[d]	0.054	−0.019[d]	0.061	−0.021[d]	0.073[d]	−0.026[d]	0.067	−0.024[d]
Brazil	0.031	−0.011	0.060	−0.021[d]	0.060	−0.021[d]	0.068	−0.024[d]	0.054	−0.019[d]	0.061	−0.021[d]	0.073[d]	−0.026[d]	0.067	−0.024[d]
Bulgaria	0.031	−0.011	0.060	−0.021[d]	0.060	−0.021[d]	0.068	−0.024[d]	0.054	−0.019[d]	0.061	−0.021[d]	0.073[d]	−0.026[d]	0.067	−0.024[d]
Russia	0.031	−0.011	0.060	−0.021[d]	0.060	−0.021[d]	0.068	−0.024[d]	0.054	−0.019[d]	0.061	−0.021[d]	0.073[d]	−0.026[d]	0.067	−0.024[d]
Fiji	0.031	−0.011	0.060	−0.021[d]	0.060	−0.021[d]	0.067	−0.024[d]	0.054	−0.019[d]	0.060	−0.021[d]	0.072[d]	−0.025[d]	0.067	−0.023[d]
Grenada	0.031	−0.011	0.060	−0.021[d]	0.060	−0.021[d]	0.067	−0.024[d]	0.054	−0.019[d]	0.060	−0.021[d]	0.072[d]	−0.025[d]	0.067	−0.023[d]
Turkey	0.030	−0.011	0.060	−0.021[d]	0.060	−0.021[d]	0.067	−0.024[d]	0.054	−0.019[d]	0.060	−0.021[d]	0.072[d]	−0.025[d]	0.066	−0.023[d]
Lithuania	0.030	−0.011	0.060[d]	−0.021[d]	0.059	−0.021[d]	0.067	−0.023[d]	0.054	−0.019[d]	0.060	−0.021[d]	0.071[d]	−0.025[d]	0.066	−0.023[d]
Romania	0.030	−0.011	0.059[d]	−0.021[d]	0.059	−0.021[d]	0.066	−0.023[d]	0.054	−0.019[d]	0.060	−0.021[d]	0.071[d]	−0.025[d]	0.066	−0.023[d]
Iran	0.030	−0.010	0.059[d]	−0.021[d]	0.059[d]	−0.021[d]	0.066	−0.023[d]	0.053	−0.019[d]	0.060	−0.021[d]	0.071[d]	−0.025[d]	0.065	−0.023[d]
Mexico	0.029	−0.010	0.059[d]	−0.021[d]	0.059[d]	−0.021[d]	0.066	−0.023[d]	0.053	−0.019[d]	0.060	−0.021[d]	0.070[d]	−0.025[d]	0.065[d]	−0.023[d]
Bahrain	0.029	−0.010	0.059[d]	−0.021[d]	0.059[d]	−0.021[d]	0.065	−0.023[d]	0.053[d]	−0.019[d]	0.059	−0.021[d]	0.070[d]	−0.025[d]	0.065[d]	−0.023[d]
Chile	0.029	−0.010	0.059[d]	−0.021[d]	0.059[d]	−0.021[d]	0.065	−0.023[d]	0.053[d]	−0.019[d]	0.059	−0.021[d]	0.070[d]	−0.025[d]	0.065[d]	−0.023[d]
Antigua and Barbuda	0.029	−0.010	0.059[d]	−0.021[d]	0.059[d]	−0.021[d]	0.065	−0.023[d]	0.053[d]	−0.019[d]	0.059	−0.021[d]	0.070[d]	−0.025[d]	0.065[d]	−0.023[d]
Poland	0.029	−0.010	0.058[d]	−0.021[d]	0.058[d]	−0.021[d]	0.065	−0.023[d]	0.053[d]	−0.019[d]	0.059	−0.021[d]	0.069[d]	−0.025[d]	0.064[d]	−0.023[d]
Trinidad and Tobago	0.028	−0.010	0.058[d]	−0.021[d]	0.058[d]	−0.021[d]	0.065	−0.023[d]	0.053[d]	−0.019[d]	0.059	−0.021[d]	0.069[d]	−0.024[d]	0.064[d]	−0.023[d]
Estonia	0.028	−0.010	0.058[d]	−0.021[d]	0.058[d]	−0.021[d]	0.064	−0.023[d]	0.053[d]	−0.019[d]	0.059	−0.021[d]	0.068[d]	−0.024[d]	0.064[d]	−0.023[d]
Gabon	0.028	−0.010	0.058[d]	−0.021[d]	0.058[d]	−0.021[d]	0.064	−0.023[d]	0.053[d]	−0.019[d]	0.059	−0.021[d]	0.068[d]	−0.024[d]	0.064[d]	−0.023[d]
Tunisia	0.028	−0.010	0.058[d]	−0.021[d]	0.058[d]	−0.020[d]	0.064[d]	−0.023[d]	0.052[d]	−0.019[d]	0.058	−0.021[d]	0.068[d]	−0.024[d]	0.063[d]	−0.023[d]

(continued)

Table 6.8 (continued)

	Food, beverage and tobacco		Gross rent, fuel and power		House operations		Medical care		Education		Transport and communication		Recreation[b]		Other	
	Slutsky	Cournot	Slutsky	Cournot	Slutsky	Cournot	Slutsky	Cournot	Slutsky	Cournot	Slutsky	Cournot	Slutsky	Cournot	Slutsky	Cournot
St. Kitts and Nevis	0.027	−0.010	0.058[d]	−0.021[d]	0.058[d]	−0.020[d]	0.064[d]	−0.023[d]	0.052[d]	−0.019[d]	0.058	−0.021[d]	0.068[d]	−0.024[d]	0.063[d]	−0.023[d]
Uruguay	0.027	−0.010	0.058[d]	−0.021[d]	0.058[d]	−0.020[d]	0.064[d]	−0.023[d]	0.052[d]	−0.019[d]	0.058	−0.021[d]	0.068[d]	−0.024[d]	0.063[d]	−0.022[d]
Slovakia	0.027	−0.010	0.058[d]	−0.020[d]	0.057[d]	−0.020[d]	0.064[d]	−0.023[d]	0.052[d]	−0.019[d]	0.058	−0.021[d]	0.067[d]	−0.024[d]	0.063[d]	−0.022[d]
Hungary	0.026	−0.009	0.057[d]	−0.020[d]	0.057[d]	−0.020[d]	0.063[d]	−0.022[d]	0.052[d]	−0.018[d]	0.057[d]	−0.021[d]	0.066[d]	−0.024[d]	0.062[d]	−0.022[d]
Argentina	0.025	−0.009	0.056[d]	−0.020[d]	0.056[d]	−0.020[d]	0.062[d]	−0.022[d]	0.051[d]	−0.018[d]	0.057[d]	−0.020[d]	0.065[d]	−0.023[d]	0.061[d]	−0.022[d]
Oman	0.024	−0.009	0.056[d]	−0.020[d]	0.056[d]	−0.020[d]	0.061[d]	−0.022[d]	0.051[d]	−0.018[d]	0.056[d]	−0.020[d]	0.064[d]	−0.023[d]	0.061[d]	−0.022[d]
Qatar	0.023	−0.008	0.056[d]	−0.020[d]	0.055[d]	−0.020[d]	0.061[d]	−0.022[d]	0.051[d]	−0.018[d]	0.056[d]	−0.020[d]	0.064[d]	−0.023[d]	0.060[d]	−0.022[d]
Slovenia	0.023	−0.008	0.055[d]	−0.020[d]	0.055[d]	−0.020[d]	0.060[d]	−0.022[d]	0.051[d]	−0.018	0.056[d]	−0.020[d]	0.063[d]	−0.023[d]	0.060[d]	−0.022[d]
High-income country																
Czech Republic	0.022	−0.008	0.055[d]	−0.020[d]	0.055[d]	−0.020[d]	0.060[d]	−0.022[d]	0.050[d]	−0.018[d]	0.056[d]	−0.020[d]	0.063[d]	−0.023[d]	0.060[d]	−0.021[d]
Greece	0.021	−0.008	0.055[d]	−0.020[d]	0.055[d]	−0.020[d]	0.059[d]	−0.021[d]	0.050[d]	−0.018[d]	0.055[d]	−0.020[d]	0.062[d]	−0.022[d]	0.059[d]	−0.021[d]
Korea	0.021	−0.008	0.054[d]	−0.020[d]	0.054[d]	−0.020[d]	0.059[d]	−0.021[d]	0.050[d]	−0.018[d]	0.055[d]	−0.020[d]	0.062[d]	−0.022[d]	0.059[d]	−0.021[d]
Portugal	0.021	−0.007	0.054[d]	−0.020[d]	0.054[d]	−0.020[d]	0.059[d]	−0.021[d]	0.050[d]	−0.018[d]	0.055[d]	−0.020[d]	0.062[d]	−0.022[d]	0.059[d]	−0.021[d]
Spain	0.021	−0.007	0.054[d]	−0.020[d]	0.054[d]	−0.020[d]	0.059[d]	−0.021[d]	0.050[d]	−0.018[d]	0.055[d]	−0.020[d]	0.062[d]	−0.022[d]	0.059[d]	−0.021[d]
Ireland	0.020	−0.007	0.054[d]	−0.020[d]	0.054[d]	−0.020[d]	0.059[d]	−0.021[d]	0.050[d]	−0.018[d]	0.055[d]	−0.020[d]	0.061[d]	−0.022[d]	0.058[d]	−0.021[d]
Singapore	0.020	−0.007	0.054[d]	−0.020[d]	0.054[d]	−0.019[d]	0.058[d]	−0.021[d]	0.049[d]	−0.018[d]	0.054[d]	−0.020[d]	0.061[d]	−0.022[d]	0.058[d]	−0.021[d]
Mauritius	0.019	−0.007	0.054[d]	−0.019[d]	0.054[d]	−0.019[d]	0.058[d]	−0.021[d]	0.049[d]	−0.018[d]	0.054[d]	−0.020[d]	0.061[d]	−0.022[d]	0.058[d]	−0.021[d]
Israel	0.018	−0.007	0.053[d]	−0.019[d]	0.053[d]	−0.019[d]	0.058[d]	−0.021[d]	0.049[d]	−0.018[d]	0.054[d]	−0.020[d]	0.060[d]	−0.022[d]	0.057[d]	−0.021[d]
New Zealand	0.018	−0.007	0.053[d]	−0.019[d]	0.053[d]	−0.019[d]	0.058[d]	−0.021[d]	0.049[d]	−0.018[d]	0.054[d]	−0.020[d]	0.060[d]	−0.022[d]	0.057[d]	−0.021[d]
Finland	0.018	−0.007	0.053[d]	−0.019[d]	0.053[d]	−0.019[d]	0.058[d]	−0.021[d]	0.049[d]	−0.018[d]	0.054[d]	−0.020[d]	0.060[d]	−0.022[d]	0.057[d]	−0.021[d]
Bahamas	0.018	−0.006	0.053[d]	−0.019[d]	0.053[d]	−0.019[d]	0.058[d]	−0.021[d]	0.049[d]	−0.018[d]	0.054[d]	−0.019[d]	0.060[d]	−0.022[d]	0.057[d]	−0.021[d]
Sweden	0.016	−0.006	0.053[d]	−0.019[d]	0.053[d]	−0.019[d]	0.057[d]	−0.021[d]	0.049[d]	−0.018[d]	0.053[d]	−0.019[d]	0.059[d]	−0.022[d]	0.057[d]	−0.021[d]

Netherlands	0.016	−0.006	0.053[d]	−0.019[d]	0.053[d]	−0.019[d]	0.057[d]	−0.021[d]	0.048[d]	−0.018[d]	0.053[d]	−0.019[d]	0.059[d]	−0.022[d]	0.056[d]	−0.021[d]
France	0.015	−0.005	0.052[d]	−0.019[d]	0.052[d]	−0.019[d]	0.056[d]	−0.021[d]	0.048[d]	−0.018[d]	0.053[d]	−0.019[d]	0.059[d]	−0.021[d]	0.056[d]	−0.020[d]
United Kingdom	0.015	−0.005	0.052[d]	−0.019[d]	0.052[d]	−0.019[d]	0.056[d]	−0.021[d]	0.048[d]	−0.018[d]	0.053[d]	−0.019[d]	0.059[d]	−0.021[d]	0.056[d]	−0.020[d]
Belgium	0.015	−0.005	0.052[d]	−0.019[d]	0.052[d]	−0.019[d]	0.056[d]	−0.021[d]	0.048[d]	−0.018[d]	0.053[d]	−0.019[d]	0.058[d]	−0.021[d]	0.056[d]	−0.020[d]
Norway	0.015	−0.005	0.052[d]	−0.019[d]	0.052[d]	−0.019[d]	0.056[d]	−0.021[d]	0.048[d]	−0.018[d]	0.053[d]	−0.019[d]	0.058[d]	−0.021[d]	0.056[d]	−0.020[d]
Italy	0.014	−0.005	0.052[d]	−0.019[d]	0.052[d]	−0.019[d]	0.056[d]	−0.020[d]	0.048[d]	−0.018[d]	0.053[d]	−0.019[d]	0.058[d]	−0.021[d]	0.056[d]	−0.020[d]
Austria	0.014	−0.005	0.052[d]	−0.019[d]	0.052[d]	−0.019[d]	0.056[d]	−0.020[d]	0.048[d]	−0.018[d]	0.052[d]	−0.019[d]	0.058[d]	−0.021[d]	0.056[d]	−0.020[d]
Germany	0.014	−0.005	0.052[d]	−0.019[d]	0.052[d]	−0.019[d]	0.056[d]	−0.020[d]	0.048[d]	−0.018[d]	0.052[d]	−0.019[d]	0.058[d]	−0.021[d]	0.056[d]	−0.020[d]
Australia	0.013	−0.005	0.052[d]	−0.019[d]	0.052[d]	−0.019[d]	0.056[d]	−0.020[d]	0.048[d]	−0.018[d]	0.052[d]	−0.019[d]	0.058[d]	−0.021[d]	0.055[d]	−0.020[d]
Japan	0.013	−0.005	0.052[d]	−0.019[d]	0.052[d]	−0.019[d]	0.056[d]	−0.020[d]	0.048[d]	−0.017[d]	0.052[d]	−0.019[d]	0.058[d]	−0.021[d]	0.055[d]	−0.020[d]
Canada	0.013	−0.005	0.052[d]	−0.019[d]	0.052[d]	−0.019[d]	0.055[d]	−0.020[d]	0.048[d]	−0.017[d]	0.052[d]	−0.019[d]	0.058[d]	−0.021[d]	0.055[d]	−0.020[d]
Bermuda	0.012	−0.004	0.051[d]	−0.019[d]	0.051[d]	−0.019[d]	0.055[d]	−0.020[d]	0.047[d]	−0.017[d]	0.052[d]	−0.019[d]	0.057[d]	−0.021[d]	0.055[d]	−0.020[d]
Switzerland	0.011	−0.004	0.051[d]	−0.019[d]	0.051[d]	−0.019[d]	0.055[d]	−0.020[d]	0.047[d]	−0.017[d]	0.052[d]	−0.019[d]	0.057[d]	−0.021[d]	0.055[d]	−0.020[d]
Barbados	0.011[d]	−0.004	0.051[d]	−0.019[d]	0.051[d]	−0.019[d]	0.055[d]	−0.020[d]	0.047[d]	−0.017[d]	0.052[d]	−0.019[d]	0.057[d]	−0.021[d]	0.055[d]	−0.020[d]
Hong Kong	0.011[d]	−0.004	0.051[d]	−0.019[d]	0.051[d]	−0.019[d]	0.055[d]	−0.020[d]	0.047[d]	−0.017[d]	0.052[d]	−0.019[d]	0.057[d]	−0.021[d]	0.055[d]	−0.020[d]
Iceland	0.011[d]	−0.004	0.051[d]	−0.019[d]	0.051[d]	−0.019[d]	0.055[d]	−0.020[d]	0.047[d]	−0.017[d]	0.052[d]	−0.019[d]	0.057[d]	−0.021[d]	0.055[d]	−0.020[d]
Denmark	0.011[d]	−0.004	0.051[d]	−0.019[d]	0.051[d]	−0.019[d]	0.055[d]	−0.020[d]	0.047[d]	−0.017[d]	0.052[d]	−0.019[d]	0.057[d]	−0.021[d]	0.055[d]	−0.020[d]
Luxembourg	0.005[c,d]	−0.002[c,d]	0.050[d]	−0.019[d]	0.050[d]	−0.018[d]	0.053[d]	−0.020[d]	0.046[d]	−0.017[d]	0.050[d]	−0.019[d]	0.055[d]	−0.020[d]	0.053[d]	−0.020[d]
United States	0.004[c,d]	−0.002[c]	0.050	−0.018	0.050	−0.018	0.053	−0.020	0.046	−0.017	0.050	−0.019	0.055	−0.020	0.053	−0.020
Low-income average	0.041	−0.014	0.070	−0.024	0.070	−0.024	0.092	−0.031	0.060	−0.021	0.071	−0.024	0.126	−0.043	0.089	−0.030
Middle-income average	0.030	−0.011	0.060	−0.021	0.060	−0.021	0.067	−0.024	0.054	−0.019	0.060	−0.021	0.072	−0.025	0.066	−0.023
High-income average	0.015	−0.006	0.053	−0.019	0.052	−0.019	0.057	−0.021	0.048	−0.018	0.053	−0.019	0.059	−0.021	0.056	−0.021

[a]Countries are reported based on ascending per capita real income levels
[b]As the estimated budget share was negative for Tanzania we do not report the elasticity for this country
[c]Elasticity estimate is not significantly different from zero at 0.05 level
[d]Elasticity estimate is not significantly different from the point estimate of the United States at 0.05 level

Table 6.9 Slutsky and Cournot cross-price elasticities with change in gross rent/fuel/power price, 114 countries in 1996[a]

	Food, beverage and tobacco		Clothing and footwear		House operations		Medical care		Education		Transport and communication		Recreation[b]		Other	
	Slutsky	Cournot	Slutsky	Cournot	Slutsky	Cournot	Slutsky	Cournot	Slutsky	Cournot	Slutsky	Cournot	Slutsky	Cournot	Slutsky	Cournot
Low-income country																
Tanzania	0.065	0.006[c,d]	0.075	0.007[c]	0.110	0.011[c]	0.240[c,d]	0.023[c]	0.089	0.009[c]	0.115[c,d]	0.011[c,d]			0.213[c,d]	0.021[c]
Nigeria	0.070	0.005[c,d]	0.082	0.006[c]	0.117	0.008[c]	0.192[d]	0.013[c]	0.097	0.007[c]	0.121[c,d]	0.008[c,d]	0.580	0.040[c]	0.181[c,d]	0.012[c]
Tajikistan	0.072	0.004[c,d]	0.085	0.005[c]	0.120	0.007[c]	0.183[d]	0.011[c]	0.100	0.006[c]	0.124[c,d]	0.007[c,d]	0.366	0.021[c]	0.175[c,d]	0.010[c]
Zambia	0.072	0.004[c,d]	0.086	0.005[c]	0.121	0.007[c]	0.182[d]	0.010[c]	0.101	0.006[c]	0.124[c,d]	0.007[c,d]	0.348	0.019[c]	0.174[c,d]	0.010[c]
Yemen	0.072	0.004[c,d]	0.086	0.005[c]	0.121	0.007[c]	0.182[d]	0.010[c]	0.101	0.006[c]	0.124[c,d]	0.007[c,d]	0.346	0.019[c]	0.174[c,d]	0.010[c]
Malawi	0.073	0.004[c,d]	0.088	0.004[c]	0.123	0.006[c]	0.178[d]	0.009[c]	0.103	0.005[c]	0.126[c,d]	0.006[c,d]	0.301	0.015[c]	0.171[c,d]	0.008[c]
Madagascar	0.073	0.004[c,d]	0.088	0.004[c]	0.123	0.006[c]	0.178[d]	0.009[c]	0.103	0.005[c]	0.126[c,d]	0.006[c,d]	0.301	0.015[c]	0.171[c,d]	0.008[c]
Mali	0.074	0.003[c,d]	0.088	0.004[c]	0.123	0.006[c]	0.178[d]	0.008[c]	0.104	0.005[c]	0.127[c,d]	0.006[c,d]	0.291	0.014[c]	0.171[c,d]	0.008[c]
Mongolia	0.074	0.003[c,d]	0.089	0.004[c]	0.123	0.006[c]	0.177[d]	0.008[c]	0.104	0.005[c]	0.127[c,d]	0.006[c,d]	0.289	0.014[c]	0.171[c,d]	0.008[c]
Benin	0.076	0.003[c,d]	0.093	0.003[c]	0.128	0.004[c]	0.173[d]	0.006[c]	0.109	0.004[c]	0.131[d]	0.004[c,d]	0.242	0.008[c]	0.168[c,d]	0.006[c]
Kenya	0.077	0.002[c,d]	0.095	0.003[c]	0.130	0.004[c]	0.172[d]	0.005[c]	0.111	0.003[c]	0.133[d]	0.004[c,d]	0.230	0.007[c]	0.167[c,d]	0.005[c]
Sierra Leone	0.078	0.002[c,d]	0.096	0.002[c]	0.131	0.003[c]	0.171	0.004[c]	0.113	0.003[c]	0.134[d]	0.003[c,d]	0.222	0.005[c]	0.167[d]	0.004[c]
Nepal	0.078	0.002[c,d]	0.096	0.002[c]	0.131	0.003[c]	0.171	0.004[c]	0.113	0.003[c]	0.134[d]	0.003[c,d]	0.222	0.005[c]	0.167[d]	0.004[c]
Turkmenistan	0.078	0.002[c,d]	0.097	0.002[c]	0.132	0.003[c]	0.171	0.004[c]	0.114	0.002[c]	0.135[d]	0.003[c,d]	0.219	0.005[c]	0.167[c,d]	0.004[c]
Congo	0.079	0.001[c,d]	0.098	0.002[c]	0.134	0.002[c]	0.170	0.003[c]	0.115	0.002[c]	0.137[d]	0.002[c,d]	0.214	0.004[c]	0.167[c,d]	0.003[c]
Senegal	0.080	0.001[c,d]	0.100	0.001[c]	0.135	0.002[c]	0.170	0.002[c]	0.117	0.002[c]	0.138[d]	0.002[c,d]	0.210	0.003[c]	0.167[d]	0.002[c]
Vietnam	0.080	0.001[c,d]	0.100	0.001[c]	0.135	0.002[c]	0.170	0.002[c]	0.117	0.002[c]	0.138[d]	0.002[c,d]	0.209	0.003[c]	0.167[d]	0.002[c]
Bangladesh	0.080	0.001[c,d]	0.100	0.001[c]	0.136	0.002[c]	0.170	0.002[c]	0.118	0.001[c]	0.138[d]	0.002[c,d]	0.208	0.003[c]	0.167[d]	0.002[c]
Pakistan	0.081	0.000[c,d]	0.103	0.001[c]	0.139	0.001[c]	0.170	0.001[c]	0.121	0.001[c]	0.141[d]	0.001[c,d]	0.203	0.001[c]	0.167[d]	0.001[c]
Azerbaijan	0.081	0.000[c,d]	0.104	0.000[c]	0.140	0.000[c]	0.171	0.001[c]	0.122	0.000[c]	0.142[d]	0.000[c,d]	0.201	0.001[c]	0.168[d]	0.000[c]

Cote d'Ivoire	0.081	0.000[c,d]	0.105	0.000[c]	0.140	0.000[c]	0.171	0.000[c]	0.123	0.000[c]	0.143[d]	0.000[c,d]	0.200	0.000[c]	0.168[d]	0.000[c]
Paraguay	0.082	0.000[c,d]	0.105	0.000[c]	0.141	0.000[c]	0.171	0.000[c]	0.123	0.000[c]	0.143[d]	0.000[c,d]	0.200	0.000[c]	0.168[d]	0.000[c]
Uzbekistan	0.082	0.000[c,d]	0.106	0.000[c]	0.142	0.000[c]	0.171	0.000[c]	0.124	0.000[c]	0.144[d]	0.000[c,d]	0.199	0.000[c]	0.168[d]	0.000[c]
Kyrgyzstan	0.082	0.000[c,d]	0.106	0.000[c]	0.142	0.000[c]	0.171	0.000[c]	0.124	0.000[c]	0.144[d]	0.000[c,d]	0.198	0.000[c]	0.168[d]	0.000[c]
Cameroon	0.082	0.000[c,d]	0.106	0.000[c]	0.142	0.000[c]	0.171	0.000[c]	0.124	0.000[c]	0.144[d]	0.000[c,d]	0.198	0.000[c]	0.168[d]	0.000[c]
Moldova	0.082	0.000[c,d]	0.106	0.000[c]	0.142	0.000[c]	0.171	0.000[c]	0.125	0.000[c]	0.144[d]	0.000[c,d]	0.198	0.000[c]	0.168[d]	0.000[c]
Bolivia	0.082	0.000[c,d]	0.107	0.000[c]	0.143	0.000[c]	0.171	−0.001[c]	0.126	0.000[c]	0.145[d]	0.000[c,d]	0.197	−0.001[c]	0.169[d]	−0.001[c]
Ecuador	0.082	0.000[c,d]	0.107	0.000[c]	0.143	−0.001[c]	0.171	−0.001[c]	0.126	−0.001[c]	0.146[d]	−0.001[c,d]	0.197	−0.001[c]	0.169[d]	−0.001[c]
Armenia	0.082	−0.001[c,d]	0.108	−0.001[c]	0.144	−0.001[c]	0.172	−0.001[c,d]	0.127	−0.001[c]	0.147[d]	−0.001[c,d]	0.196	−0.001[c]	0.169[d]	−0.001[c,d]
Sri Lanka	0.083	−0.001[c,d]	0.108	−0.001[c]	0.144	−0.001[c]	0.172	−0.001[c,d]	0.127	−0.001[c]	0.147[d]	−0.001[c,d]	0.196	−0.001[c]	0.169[d]	−0.001[c,d]
Jordan	0.083	−0.001[c,d]	0.109	−0.001[c]	0.145	−0.001[c]	0.172	−0.001[c,d]	0.128	−0.001[c]	0.148[d]	−0.001[c,d]	0.195	−0.002[c]	0.170[d]	−0.001[c,d]
Albania	0.083	−0.001[c,d]	0.111	−0.001[c]	0.147	−0.002[c]	0.173	−0.002[c,d]	0.130	−0.002[c]	0.149[d]	−0.002[c,d]	0.195	−0.002[c]	0.171[d]	−0.002[c,d]
Indonesia	0.083	−0.001[c,d]	0.111	−0.001[c]	0.147	−0.002[c]	0.173	−0.002[c,d]	0.131	−0.002[c]	0.150[d]	−0.002[c,d]	0.194	−0.002[c]	0.171[d]	−0.002[c,d]
Jamaica	0.083	−0.001[c,d]	0.111	−0.001[c]	0.147	−0.002[c]	0.173	−0.002[c,d]	0.131	−0.002[c]	0.150[d]	−0.002[c,d]	0.194	−0.003[c]	0.171[d]	−0.002[c,d]
Zimbabwe	0.083	−0.001[c,d]	0.111	−0.001[c]	0.148	−0.002[c]	0.173	−0.002[c,d]	0.131	−0.002[c]	0.150[d]	−0.002[c,d]	0.194	−0.003[c]	0.171[d]	−0.002[c,d]
Guinea	0.083	−0.001[c,d]	0.112	−0.002[c]	0.148	−0.002[c]	0.173	−0.002[c,d]	0.131	−0.002[c]	0.150[d]	−0.002[c,d]	0.194	−0.003[c]	0.171[d]	−0.002[c,d]
Syria	0.083	−0.001[c,d]	0.113	−0.002[c]	0.149	−0.002[c,d]	0.174	−0.003[c,d]	0.133	−0.002[c,d]	0.152[d]	−0.002[c,d]	0.194	−0.003[c]	0.172[d]	−0.003[c,d]
Georgia	0.083	−0.001[c,d]	0.113	−0.002[c]	0.150	−0.003[c,d]	0.174	−0.003[d]	0.133	−0.002[c,d]	0.152[d]	−0.003[c,d]	0.194	−0.003[c]	0.172[d]	−0.003[c,d]
Middle-income country																
Ukraine	0.084	−0.002[c,d]	0.115	−0.002[c,d]	0.151	−0.003[c,d]	0.175	−0.004[c,d]	0.135	−0.003[c,d]	0.154[d]	−0.003[c,d]	0.193	−0.004[c,d]	0.173[d]	−0.004[c,d]
Philippines	0.084	−0.002[c,d]	0.116	−0.003[c,d]	0.153	−0.003[c,d]	0.176	−0.004[c,d]	0.137	−0.003[c,d]	0.155[d]	−0.004[c,d]	0.193	−0.004[c,d]	0.174[d]	−0.004[c,d]
Peru	0.083	−0.002[c,d]	0.117	−0.003[c,d]	0.153	−0.004[c,d]	0.176	−0.004[c,d]	0.137	−0.003[c,d]	0.156[d]	−0.004[c,d]	0.193	−0.005[c,d]	0.174[d]	−0.004[c,d]
Botswana	0.083	−0.002[c,d]	0.117	−0.003[c,d]	0.153	−0.004[c,d]	0.176	−0.004[c,d]	0.137	−0.003[c,d]	0.156[d]	−0.004[c,d]	0.193	−0.005[c,d]	0.174[d]	−0.004[c,d]
Thailand	0.083	−0.002[c,d]	0.117	−0.003[c,d]	0.154	−0.004[c,d]	0.176	−0.004[c,d]	0.138	−0.003[c,d]	0.156[d]	−0.004[c,d]	0.193	−0.005[c,d]	0.174[d]	−0.004[c,d]
Morocco	0.083	−0.002[c,d]	0.118	−0.003[c,d]	0.154	−0.004[c,d]	0.177	−0.004[c,d]	0.138	−0.004[c,d]	0.157[d]	−0.004[c,d]	0.193	−0.005[c,d]	0.175[d]	−0.004[c,d]

(continued)

Table 6.9 (continued)

	Food, beverage and tobacco		Clothing and footwear		House operations		Medical care		Education		Transport and communication		Recreation^{b}		Other	
	Slutsky	Cournot	Slutsky	Cournot	Slutsky	Cournot	Slutsky	Cournot	Slutsky	Cournot	Slutsky	Cournot	Slutsky	Cournot	Slutsky	Cournot
Venezuela	0.083	−0.002^{c,d}	0.118	−0.003^{c,d}	0.155	−0.004^{c,d}	0.177	−0.005^{c,d}	0.138	−0.004^{c,d}	0.157^{d}	−0.004^{c,d}	0.193	−0.005^{c,d}	0.175^{d}	−0.005^{c,d}
Macedonia	0.083	−0.002^{c,d}	0.119	−0.003^{c,d}	0.156	−0.004^{c,d}	0.177	−0.005^{c,d}	0.139	−0.004^{c,d}	0.158^{d}	−0.004^{c,d}	0.193	−0.005^{c,d}	0.175^{d}	−0.005^{c,d}
Belize	0.083	−0.002^{c,d}	0.119	−0.003^{c,d}	0.156	−0.004^{c,d}	0.177	−0.005^{c,d}	0.139	−0.004^{c,d}	0.158^{d}	−0.004^{c,d}	0.193	−0.005^{c,d}	0.176^{d}	−0.005^{c,d}
Egypt	0.083	−0.002^{c,d}	0.119	−0.003^{c,d}	0.156	−0.004^{c,d}	0.177	−0.005^{c,d}	0.140	−0.004^{c,d}	0.158^{d}	−0.004^{c,d}	0.193	−0.005^{c,d}	0.176^{d}	−0.005^{c,d}
St. Vincent and Grenadines	0.083	−0.002^{c,d}	0.119	−0.003^{c,d}	0.156	−0.004^{c,d}	0.177	−0.005^{c,d}	0.140	−0.004^{c,d}	0.158^{d}	−0.004^{c,d}	0.193	−0.005^{c,d}	0.176^{d}	−0.005^{c,d}
Swaziland	0.083	−0.002^{c,d}	0.120	−0.004^{c,d}	0.157	−0.005^{c,d}	0.178	−0.005^{c,d}	0.141	−0.004^{c,d}	0.159^{d}	−0.005^{c,d}	0.193	−0.006^{c,d}	0.176^{d}	−0.005^{c,d}
Lebanon	0.083	−0.003^{c,d}	0.120	−0.004^{c,d}	0.157	−0.005^{c,d}	0.178	−0.005^{c,d}	0.141	−0.004^{c,d}	0.159^{d}	−0.005^{c,d}	0.193	−0.006^{c,d}	0.177^{d}	−0.005^{c,d}
Belarus	0.083	−0.003^{c,d}	0.120	−0.004^{c,d}	0.157	−0.005^{c,d}	0.178	−0.005^{c,d}	0.141	−0.004^{c,d}	0.160^{d}	−0.005^{c,d}	0.193	−0.006^{c,d}	0.177^{d}	−0.005^{c,d}
Kazakhstan	0.083	−0.003^{c,d}	0.121	−0.004^{c,d}	0.157	−0.005^{c,d}	0.178	−0.005^{c,d}	0.142	−0.004^{c,d}	0.160^{d}	−0.005^{c,d}	0.193	−0.006^{c,d}	0.177^{d}	−0.005^{c,d}
Dominica	0.083	−0.003^{c,d}	0.121	−0.004^{c,d}	0.158	−0.005^{c,d}	0.178	−0.005^{c,d}	0.142	−0.004^{c,d}	0.160^{d}	−0.005^{c,d}	0.193	−0.006^{c,d}	0.177^{d}	−0.005^{c,d}
Latvia	0.083	−0.003^{c,d}	0.122	−0.004^{c,d}	0.159	−0.005^{c,d}	0.179	−0.006^{c,d}	0.143	−0.005^{c,d}	0.161^{d}	−0.005^{c,d}	0.193	−0.006^{c,d}	0.178^{d}	−0.006^{c,d}
St. Lucia	0.083	−0.003^{c,d}	0.122	−0.004^{c,d}	0.159	−0.005^{c,d}	0.179	−0.006^{c,d}	0.143	−0.005^{c,d}	0.161^{d}	−0.005^{c,d}	0.194	−0.006^{c,d}	0.178^{d}	−0.006^{c,d}
Brazil	0.083	−0.003^{c,d}	0.122	−0.004^{c,d}	0.159	−0.005^{c,d}	0.179	−0.006^{c,d}	0.143	−0.005^{c,d}	0.161^{d}	−0.005^{c,d}	0.194	−0.006^{c,d}	0.178^{d}	−0.006^{c,d}
Bulgaria	0.083	−0.003^{c,d}	0.122	−0.004^{c,d}	0.159	−0.005^{c,d}	0.179	−0.006^{c,d}	0.143	−0.005^{c,d}	0.161^{d}	−0.005^{c,d}	0.194	−0.006^{c,d}	0.178^{d}	−0.006^{c,d}
Russia	0.083	−0.003^{c,d}	0.122	−0.004^{c,d}	0.160	−0.005^{c,d}	0.180	−0.006^{c,d}	0.144	−0.005^{c,d}	0.162^{d}	−0.005^{c,d}	0.194	−0.007^{c,d}	0.178^{d}	−0.006^{c,d}
Fiji	0.082	−0.003^{c,d}	0.123	−0.004^{c,d}	0.160	−0.006^{c,d}	0.180	−0.006^{c,d}	0.145	−0.005^{c,d}	0.162^{d}	−0.006^{c,d}	0.194	−0.007^{c,d}	0.179^{d}	−0.006^{c,d}
Grenada	0.082	−0.003^{c,d}	0.123	−0.004^{c,d}	0.160	−0.006^{c,d}	0.180	−0.006^{c,d}	0.145	−0.005^{c,d}	0.162^{d}	−0.006^{c,d}	0.194	−0.007^{c,d}	0.179^{d}	−0.006^{c,d}
Turkey	0.082	−0.003^{c,d}	0.123	−0.004^{c,d}	0.161	−0.006^{c,d}	0.180	−0.006^{c,d}	0.145	−0.005^{c,d}	0.163^{d}	−0.006^{c,d}	0.194	−0.007^{c,d}	0.179^{d}	−0.006^{c,d}
Lithuania	0.082	−0.003^{c,d}	0.124	−0.005^{c,d}	0.161	−0.006^{c,d}	0.181	−0.007^{c,d}	0.146	−0.005^{c,d}	0.163^{d}	−0.006^{c,d}	0.194	−0.007^{c,d}	0.179^{d}	−0.007^{c,d}
Romania	0.082	−0.003^{c,d}	0.124	−0.005^{c,d}	0.162	−0.006^{c,d}	0.181	−0.007^{c,d}	0.146	−0.005^{c,d}	0.164^{d}	−0.006^{c,d}	0.194	−0.007^{c,d}	0.180^{d}	−0.007^{c,d}
Iran	0.081	−0.003^{c,d}	0.125	−0.005^{c,d}	0.163	−0.006^{c,d}	0.182^{d}	−0.007^{c,d}	0.147	−0.006^{c,d}	0.165^{d}	−0.006^{c,d}	0.195	−0.007^{c,d}	0.180^{d}	−0.007^{c,d}

Mexico	0.081	−0.003[c,d]	0.125	−0.005[c,d]	0.163	−0.006[c,d]	0.182[d]	−0.007[c,d]	0.147	−0.006[c,d]	0.165[d]	−0.006[c,d]	0.195	−0.008[c,d]	0.181[d]	−0.007[c,d]
Bahrain	0.081	−0.003[c,d]	0.126	−0.005[c,d]	0.163	−0.007[c,d]	0.182[d]	−0.007[c,d]	0.148	−0.006[c,d]	0.165[d]	−0.007[c,d]	0.195	−0.008[c,d]	0.181[d]	−0.007[c,d]
Chile	0.081	−0.003[c,d]	0.126	−0.005[c,d]	0.164	−0.007[c,d]	0.183[d]	−0.007[c,d]	0.148	−0.006[c,d]	0.166[d]	−0.007[c,d]	0.195	−0.008[c,d]	0.181[d]	−0.007[c,d]
Antigua and Barbuda	0.081	−0.003[c,d]	0.126	−0.005[c,d]	0.164	−0.007[c,d]	0.183[d]	−0.007[c,d]	0.148	−0.006[c,d]	0.166[d]	−0.007[c,d]	0.195	−0.008[c,d]	0.181[d]	−0.007[c,d]
Poland	0.080	−0.003[c,d]	0.127	−0.005[c,d]	0.164	−0.007[c,d]	0.183[d]	−0.008[c,d]	0.149	−0.006[c,d]	0.166[d]	−0.007[c,d]	0.195	−0.008[c,d]	0.182[d]	−0.008[c,d]
Trinidad and Tobago	0.080	−0.003[c,d]	0.127	−0.005[c,d]	0.165	−0.007[c,d]	0.183[d]	−0.008[c,d]	0.150	−0.006[c,d]	0.167[d]	−0.007[c,d]	0.195	−0.008[c,d]	0.182[d]	−0.008[c,d]
Estonia	0.080	−0.003[c,d]	0.128	−0.005[c,d]	0.166	−0.007[c,d]	0.184[d]	−0.008[c,d]	0.150	−0.006[c,d]	0.168[d]	−0.007[c,d]	0.196	−0.008[c,d]	0.182[d]	−0.008[c,d]
Gabon	0.080	−0.003[c,d]	0.128	−0.006[c,d]	0.166	−0.007[c,d]	0.184[d]	−0.008[c,d]	0.151	−0.007[c,d]	0.168[d]	−0.007[c,d]	0.196	−0.008[c,d]	0.183[d]	−0.008[c,d]
Tunisia	0.079	−0.003[c,d]	0.128	−0.006[c,d]	0.166	−0.007[c,d]	0.184[d]	−0.008[c,d]	0.151	−0.007[c,d]	0.168[d]	−0.007[c,d]	0.196	−0.009[c,d]	0.183[d]	−0.008[c,d]
St. Kitts and Nevis	0.079	−0.004[c,d]	0.129	−0.006[c,d]	0.167	−0.007[c,d]	0.185[d]	−0.008[c,d]	0.151	−0.007[c,d]	0.168[d]	−0.007[c,d]	0.196	−0.009[c,d]	0.183[d]	−0.008[c,d]
Uruguay	0.079	−0.004[c,d]	0.129	−0.006[c,d]	0.167	−0.007[c,d]	0.185[d]	−0.008[c,d]	0.151	−0.007[c,d]	0.169[d]	−0.008[c,d]	0.196	−0.009[c,d]	0.183[d]	−0.008[c,d]
Slovakia	0.079	−0.004[c,d]	0.129	−0.006[c,d]	0.167	−0.008[c,d]	0.185[d]	−0.008[c,d]	0.152	−0.007[c,d]	0.169[d]	−0.008[c,d]	0.196	−0.009[c,d]	0.184[d]	−0.008[c,d]
Hungary	0.077	−0.004[c,d]	0.131	−0.006[c,d]	0.169	−0.008[c,d]	0.186[d]	−0.009[c,d]	0.154	−0.007[c,d]	0.171[d]	−0.008[c,d]	0.197	−0.009[c,d]	0.185[d]	−0.009[c,d]
Argentina	0.075	−0.004[c,d]	0.133[d]	−0.007[c,d]	0.171	−0.009[c,d]	0.188[d]	−0.009[c,d]	0.156	−0.008[c,d]	0.173[d]	−0.009[c,d]	0.198	−0.010[c,d]	0.187[d]	−0.009[c,d]
Oman	0.074	−0.004[c,d]	0.133[d]	−0.007[c,d]	0.172	−0.009[c,d]	0.189[d]	−0.010[c,d]	0.157	−0.008[c,d]	0.174[d]	−0.009[c,d]	0.199	−0.010[c,d]	0.187[d]	−0.010[c,d]
Qatar	0.073	−0.004[c,d]	0.135[d]	−0.007[c,d]	0.173	−0.009[c,d]	0.189[d]	−0.010[c,d]	0.158[d]	−0.008[c,d]	0.175[d]	−0.009[c,d]	0.199	−0.011[c,d]	0.188[d]	−0.010[c,d]
Slovenia	0.072	−0.004[c,d]	0.135[d]	−0.007[c,d]	0.174[d]	−0.009[c,d]	0.190[d]	−0.010[c,d]	0.159[d]	−0.009[c,d]	0.176[d]	−0.009[c,d]	0.200	−0.011[c,d]	0.189[d]	−0.010[c,d]
High-income country																
Czech Republic	0.071	−0.004[c,d]	0.136[d]	−0.007[c,d]	0.174[d]	−0.010[c,d]	0.190[d]	−0.010[c,d]	0.160[d]	−0.009[c,d]	0.176[d]	−0.010[c,d]	0.200	−0.011[c,d]	0.189[d]	−0.010[c,d]
Greece	0.069	−0.004[c,d]	0.137[d]	−0.008[c,d]	0.176[d]	−0.010[c,d]	0.192[d]	−0.011[c,d]	0.161[d]	−0.009[c,d]	0.178[d]	−0.010[c,d]	0.201	−0.011[c,d]	0.190[d]	−0.011[c,d]
Korea	0.068	−0.004[c,d]	0.137[d]	−0.008[c,d]	0.176[d]	−0.010[c,d]	0.192[d]	−0.011[c,d]	0.162[d]	−0.009[c,d]	0.178[d]	−0.010[c,d]	0.201	−0.011[c,d]	0.191[d]	−0.011[c,d]
Portugal	0.067	−0.004[c,d]	0.138[d]	−0.008[c,d]	0.177[d]	−0.010[c,d]	0.192[d]	−0.011[c d]	0.162[d]	−0.009[c d]	0.179[d]	−0.010[c,d]	0.201[d]	−0.012[c,d]	0.191[d]	−0.011[c,d]
Spain	0.067	−0.004[c,d]	0.138[d]	−0.008[c,d]	0.177[d]	−0.010[c,d]	0.192[d]	−0.011[c,d]	0.162[d]	−0.009[c,d]	0.179[d]	−0.010[c,d]	0.201[d]	−0.012[c,d]	0.191[d]	−0.011[c,d]

(continued)

Table 6.9 (continued)

	Food, beverage and tobacco		Clothing and footwear		House operations		Medical care		Education		Transport and communication		Recreation[b]		Other	
	Slutsky	Cournot	Slutsky	Cournot	Slutsky	Cournot	Slutsky	Cournot	Slutsky	Cournot	Slutsky	Cournot	Slutsky	Cournot	Slutsky	Cournot
Ireland	0.066	−0.004[c,d]	0.138[d]	−0.008[c,d]	0.178[d]	−0.010[c,d]	0.193[d]	−0.011[c,d]	0.163[d]	−0.010[c,d]	0.179[d]	−0.010[c,d]	0.202[d]	−0.012[c,d]	0.192[d]	−0.011[c,d]
Singapore	0.065	−0.004[c,d]	0.139[d]	−0.008[c,d]	0.178[d]	−0.011[c,d]	0.193[d]	−0.011[c,d]	0.164[d]	−0.010[c,d]	0.180[d]	−0.011[c,d]	0.202[d]	−0.012[c,d]	0.192[d]	−0.011[c,d]
Mauritius	0.063	−0.004[d]	0.140[d]	−0.008[c,d]	0.179[d]	−0.011[c,d]	0.194[d]	−0.012[c,d]	0.165[d]	−0.010[c,d]	0.181[d]	−0.011[c,d]	0.203[d]	−0.012[c,d]	0.193[d]	−0.012[c,d]
Israel	0.062	−0.004[d]	0.140[d]	−0.009[c,d]	0.180[d]	−0.011[c,d]	0.195[d]	−0.012[c,d]	0.165[d]	−0.010[c,d]	0.181[d]	−0.011[c,d]	0.203[d]	−0.012[c,d]	0.194[d]	−0.012[c,d]
New Zealand	0.061	−0.004[d]	0.140[d]	−0.009[c,d]	0.180[d]	−0.011[c,d]	0.195[d]	−0.012[c,d]	0.166[d]	−0.010[c,d]	0.182[d]	−0.011[c,d]	0.203[d]	−0.012[c,d]	0.194[d]	−0.012[c,d]
Finland	0.061	−0.004[d]	0.141[d]	−0.009[c,d]	0.180[d]	−0.011[c,d]	0.195[d]	−0.012[c,d]	0.166[d]	−0.010[c,d]	0.182[d]	−0.011[c,d]	0.203[d]	−0.013[c,d]	0.194[d]	−0.012[c,d]
Bahamas	0.060	−0.004[d]	0.141[d]	−0.009[d]	0.180[d]	−0.011[c,d]	0.195[d]	−0.012[c,d]	0.166[d]	−0.010[c,d]	0.182[d]	−0.011[c,d]	0.204[d]	−0.013[c,d]	0.194[d]	−0.012[c,d]
Sweden	0.057	−0.004[d]	0.142[d]	−0.009[d]	0.182[d]	−0.012[c,d]	0.196[d]	−0.012[d]	0.168[d]	−0.011[c,d]	0.184[d]	−0.012[d]	0.205[d]	−0.013[c,d]	0.195[d]	−0.012[d]
Netherlands	0.056	−0.004[d]	0.142[d]	−0.009[d]	0.182[d]	−0.012[c,d]	0.197[d]	−0.013[d]	0.168[d]	−0.011[d]	0.184[d]	−0.012[d]	0.205[d]	−0.013[c,d]	0.196[d]	−0.012[d]
France	0.053	−0.003[d]	0.143[d]	−0.009[d]	0.183[d]	−0.012[d]	0.198[d]	−0.013[d]	0.169[d]	−0.011[d]	0.185[d]	−0.012[d]	0.205[d]	−0.013[c,d]	0.197[d]	−0.013[d]
United Kingdom	0.052	−0.003[d]	0.143[d]	−0.009[d]	0.183[d]	−0.012[d]	0.198[d]	−0.013[d]	0.169[d]	−0.011[d]	0.185[d]	−0.012[d]	0.206[d]	−0.013[c,d]	0.197[d]	−0.013[d]
Belgium	0.052	−0.003[d]	0.144[d]	−0.009[d]	0.184[d]	−0.012[d]	0.198[d]	−0.013[d]	0.169[d]	−0.011[d]	0.185[d]	−0.012[d]	0.206[d]	−0.013[c,d]	0.197[d]	−0.013[d]
Norway	0.051	−0.003[d]	0.144[d]	−0.009[d]	0.184[d]	−0.012[d]	0.198[d]	−0.013[d]	0.170[d]	−0.011[d]	0.185[d]	−0.012[d]	0.206[d]	−0.013[c,d]	0.197[d]	−0.013[d]
Italy	0.051	−0.003[d]	0.144[d]	−0.009[d]	0.184[d]	−0.012[d]	0.198[d]	−0.013[d]	0.170[d]	−0.011[d]	0.185[d]	−0.012[d]	0.206[d]	−0.014[c,d]	0.197[d]	−0.013[d]
Austria	0.049	−0.003[d]	0.144[d]	−0.010[d]	0.184[d]	−0.012[d]	0.198[d]	−0.013[d]	0.170[d]	−0.011[d]	0.186[d]	−0.012[d]	0.206[d]	−0.014[d]	0.197[d]	−0.013[d]
Germany	0.049	−0.003[d]	0.144[d]	−0.010[d]	0.184[d]	−0.012[d]	0.198[d]	−0.013[d]	0.170[d]	−0.011[d]	0.186[d]	−0.012[d]	0.206[d]	−0.014[d]	0.197[d]	−0.013[d]

Australia	0.048	−0.003[d]	0.145[d]	−0.010[d]	0.185[d]	−0.012[d]	0.199[d]	−0.013[d]	0.171[d]	−0.011[d]	0.186[d]	−0.012[d]	0.206[d]	−0.014[d]	0.198[d]	−0.013[d]
Japan	0.047	−0.003[d]	0.145[d]	−0.010[d]	0.185[d]	−0.012[d]	0.199[d]	−0.013[d]	0.171[d]	−0.011[d]	0.187[d]	−0.013[d]	0.207[d]	−0.014[d]	0.198[d]	−0.013[d]
Canada	0.046	−0.003[d]	0.145[d]	−0.010[d]	0.185[d]	−0.013[d]	0.199[d]	−0.013[d]	0.171[d]	−0.012[d]	0.187[d]	−0.013[d]	0.207[d]	−0.014[d]	0.198[d]	−0.013[d]
Bermuda	0.043	−0.003[d]	0.146[d]	−0.010[d]	0.186[d]	−0.013[d]	0.200[d]	−0.014[d]	0.172[d]	−0.012[d]	0.188[d]	−0.013[d]	0.207[d]	−0.014[d]	0.199[d]	−0.014[d]
Switzerland	0.042	−0.003[d]	0.146[d]	−0.010[d]	0.187[d]	−0.013[d]	0.200[d]	−0.014[d]	0.173[d]	−0.012[d]	0.188[d]	−0.013[d]	0.208[d]	−0.014[d]	0.199[d]	−0.014[d]
Barbados	0.041	−0.003[d]	0.146[d]	−0.010[d]	0.187[d]	−0.013[d]	0.200[d]	−0.014[d]	0.173[d]	−0.012[d]	0.188[d]	−0.013[d]	0.208[d]	−0.014[d]	0.199[d]	−0.014[d]
Hong Kong	0.041[d]	−0.003[d]	0.146[d]	−0.010[d]	0.187[d]	−0.013[d]	0.200[d]	−0.014[d]	0.173[d]	−0.012[d]	0.188[d]	−0.013[d]	0.208[d]	−0.014[d]	0.199[d]	−0.014[d]
Iceland	0.041[d]	−0.003[d]	0.146[d]	−0.010[d]	0.187[d]	−0.013[d]	0.200[d]	−0.014[d]	0.173[d]	−0.012[d]	0.188[d]	−0.013[d]	0.208[d]	−0.014[d]	0.199[d]	−0.014[d]
Denmark	0.040[d]	−0.003[d]	0.146[d]	−0.010[d]	0.187[d]	−0.013[d]	0.201[d]	−0.014[d]	0.173[d]	−0.012[d]	0.189[d]	−0.013[d]	0.208[d]	−0.014[d]	0.200[d]	−0.014[d]
Luxembourg	0.021[c,d]	−0.002[c,d]	0.150[d]	−0.011[d]	0.191[d]	−0.014[d]	0.204[d]	−0.015[d]	0.177[d]	−0.013[d]	0.192[d]	−0.014[d]	0.211[d]	−0.015[d]	0.203[d]	−0.015[d]
United States	0.017[c]	−0.001[c]	0.150	−0.011	0.191	−0.014	0.204	−0.015	0.178	−0.013	0.193	−0.014	0.211	−0.016	0.204	−0.015
Low-income average	0.079	0.001	0.100	0.001	0.136	0.002	0.175	0.003	0.118	0.002	0.139	0.002	0.236	0.005	0.171	0.003
Middle-income average	0.081	−0.003	0.124	−0.004	0.161	−0.006	0.181	−0.007	0.145	−0.005	0.163	−0.006	0.195	−0.007	0.179	−0.006
High-income average	0.052	−0.003	0.143	−0.009	0.183	−0.012	0.197	−0.013	0.168	−0.011	0.184	−0.012	0.205	−0.013	0.196	−0.013

[a]Countries are reported based on ascending per capita real income levels

[b]As the estimated budget share was negative for Tanzania we do not report the elasticity for this country

[c]Elasticity estimate is not significantly different from zero at 0.05 level

[d]Elasticity estimate is not significantly different from the point estimate of the United States at 0.05 level

Table 6.10 Slutsky and Cournot cross-price elasticities with change in house furnishings and operations price, 114 countries in 1996[a]

	Food, beverage and tobacco		Clothing and footwear		Gross rent, fuel and power		Medical care		Education		Transport and communication		Recreation[b]		Other	
	Slutsky	Cournot	Slutsky	Cournot	Slutsky	Cournot	Slutsky	Cournot	Slutsky	Cournot	Slutsky	Cournot	Slutsky	Cournot	Slutsky	Cournot
Low-income country																
Tanzania	0.028	0.003[c,d]	0.033	0.003[c]	0.048	0.004[c]	0.104[c,d]	0.009[c,d]	0.039	0.003[c]	0.050[c,d]	0.004[c,d]			0.093[c,d]	0.008[c,d]
Nigeria	0.030	0.002[c,d]	0.036	0.002[c]	0.051	0.003[c]	0.084[c,d]	0.005[c]	0.042	0.003[c]	0.053[c,d]	0.003[c,d]	0.252	0.016[c]	0.079[c,d]	0.005[c,d]
Tajikistan	0.031	0.002[c,d]	0.037	0.002[c]	0.053	0.003[c]	0.080[d]	0.004[c]	0.044	0.002[c]	0.054[c,d]	0.003[c,d]	0.159	0.008[c]	0.076[c,d]	0.004[c,d]
Zambia	0.031	0.002[c,d]	0.037	0.002[c]	0.053	0.003[c]	0.079[d]	0.004[c]	0.044	0.002[c]	0.054[c,d]	0.003[c,d]	0.151	0.008[c]	0.076[c,d]	0.004[c,d]
Yemen	0.031	0.002[c,d]	0.037	0.002[c]	0.053	0.003[c]	0.079[d]	0.004[c]	0.044	0.002[c]	0.054[c,d]	0.003[c,d]	0.151	0.007[c]	0.075[c,d]	0.004[c,d]
Malawi	0.032	0.001[c,d]	0.038	0.002[c]	0.054	0.002[c]	0.077[d]	0.003[c]	0.045	0.002[c]	0.055[c,d]	0.002[c,d]	0.131	0.006[c]	0.074[c,d]	0.003[c,d]
Madagascar	0.032	0.001[c,d]	0.038	0.002[c]	0.054	0.002[c]	0.077[d]	0.003[c]	0.045	0.002[c]	0.055[c,d]	0.002[c,d]	0.131	0.006[c]	0.074[c,d]	0.003[c,d]
Mali	0.032	0.001[c,d]	0.038	0.002[c]	0.054	0.002[c]	0.077[d]	0.003[c]	0.045	0.002[c]	0.055[c,d]	0.002[c,d]	0.127	0.005[c]	0.074[c,d]	0.003[c,d]
Mongolia	0.032	0.001[c,d]	0.038	0.002[c]	0.054	0.002[c]	0.077[d]	0.003[c]	0.045	0.002[c]	0.055[c,d]	0.002[c,d]	0.126	0.005[c]	0.074[c,d]	0.003[c,d]
Benin	0.033	0.001[c,d]	0.040	0.001[c]	0.056	0.002[c]	0.075[d]	0.002[c]	0.047	0.001[c]	0.057[d]	0.002[c,d]	0.105	0.003[c]	0.073[c,d]	0.002[c,d]
Kenya	0.033	0.001[c,d]	0.041	0.001[c]	0.057	0.001[c]	0.074[d]	0.002[c]	0.048	0.001[c]	0.058[d]	0.001[c]	0.100	0.002[c]	0.072[c,d]	0.002[c,d]
Sierra Leone	0.034	0.001[c,d]	0.042	0.001[c]	0.057	0.001[c]	0.074[d]	0.001[c]	0.049	0.001[c]	0.058[d]	0.001[c]	0.096	0.002[c]	0.072[d]	0.001[c]
Nepal	0.034	0.001[c,d]	0.042	0.001[c]	0.057	0.001[c]	0.074[d]	0.001[c]	0.049	0.001[c]	0.058[d]	0.001[c]	0.096	0.002[c]	0.072[d]	0.001[c]
Turkmenistan	0.034	0.001[c,d]	0.042	0.001[c]	0.058	0.001[c]	0.074[d]	0.001[c]	0.049	0.001[c]	0.059[d]	0.001[c]	0.095	0.002[c]	0.072[c,d]	0.001[c]
Congo	0.034	0.000[c,d]	0.043	0.001[c]	0.058	0.001[c]	0.074[d]	0.001[c]	0.050	0.001[c]	0.059[d]	0.001[c]	0.093	0.001[c]	0.072[c,d]	0.001[c,d]
Senegal	0.034	0.000[c,d]	0.043	0.000[c]	0.059	0.001[c]	0.074[d]	0.001[c]	0.051	0.001[c]	0.060[d]	0.001[c]	0.091	0.001[c]	0.072[d]	0.001[c]
Vietnam	0.035	0.000[c,d]	0.043	0.000[c]	0.059	0.001[c]	0.074[d]	0.001[c]	0.051	0.000[c]	0.060[d]	0.001[c]	0.090	0.001[c]	0.072[d]	0.001[c]
Bangladesh	0.035	0.000[c,d]	0.043	0.000[c]	0.059	0.000[c]	0.074[d]	0.001[c]	0.051	0.000[c]	0.060[d]	0.001[c]	0.090	0.001[c]	0.072[d]	0.001[c]
Pakistan	0.035	0.000[c,d]	0.045	0.000[c]	0.060	0.000[c]	0.074[d]	0.000[c]	0.052	0.000[c]	0.061[d]	0.000[c]	0.088	0.000[c]	0.072[d]	0.000[c]
Azerbaijan	0.035	0.000[c,d]	0.045	0.000[c]	0.061	0.000[c]	0.074[d]	0.000[c]	0.053	0.000[c]	0.062[d]	0.000[c]	0.087	0.000[c]	0.073[d]	0.000[c]

Cote d'Ivoire	0.035	0.000[c,d]	0.045	0.000[c]	0.061	0.000[c]	0.074[d]	0.000[c]	0.053	0.000[c]	0.062[d]	0.000[c]	0.087	0.000[c]	0.073[d]	0.000[c]
Paraguay	0.035	0.000[c,d]	0.045	0.000[c]	0.061	0.000[c]	0.074[d]	0.000[c]	0.053	0.000[c]	0.062[d]	0.000[c]	0.086	0.000[c]	0.073[d]	0.000[c]
Uzbekistan	0.035	0.000[c,d]	0.046	0.000[c]	0.062	0.000[c]	0.074	0.000[c]	0.054	0.000[c]	0.062[d]	0.000[c]	0.086	0.000[c]	0.073[d]	0.000[c]
Kyrgyzstan	0.035	0.000[c,d]	0.046	0.000[c]	0.062	0.000[c]	0.074	0.000[c]	0.054	0.000[c]	0.062[d]	0.000[c]	0.086	0.000[c]	0.073[d]	0.000[c]
Cameroon	0.035	0.000[c,d]	0.046	0.000[c]	0.062	0.000[c]	0.074	0.000[c]	0.054	0.000[c]	0.063[d]	0.000[c]	0.086	0.000[c]	0.073[d]	0.000[c]
Moldova	0.035	0.000[c,d]	0.046	0.000[c]	0.062	0.000[c]	0.074	0.000[c]	0.054	0.000[c]	0.063[d]	0.000[c]	0.086	0.000[c]	0.073[d]	0.000[c]
Bolivia	0.036	0.000[c,d]	0.046	0.000[c]	0.062	0.000[c]	0.074	−0.001[c]	0.054	0.000[c]	0.063[d]	0.000[c]	0.085	−0.001[c]	0.073[d]	−0.001[c]
Ecuador	0.036	0.000[c,d]	0.046	0.000[c]	0.062	0.000[c]	0.074	−0.001[c]	0.055	0.000[c]	0.063[d]	−0.001[c]	0.085	−0.001[c]	0.073[d]	−0.001[c]
Armenia	0.036	0.000[c,d]	0.047	0.000[c]	0.063	−0.001[c]	0.074	−0.001[c]	0.055	−0.001[c]	0.063[d]	−0.001[c]	0.085	−0.001[c]	0.073[d]	−0.001[c]
Sri Lanka	0.036	0.000[c,d]	0.047	0.000[c]	0.063	−0.001[c]	0.074	−0.001[c]	0.055	−0.001[c]	0.063[d]	−0.001[c]	0.085	−0.001[c]	0.073[d]	−0.001[c]
Jordan	0.036	0.000[c,d]	0.047	−0.001[c]	0.063	−0.001[c]	0.074	−0.001[c]	0.056	−0.001[c]	0.064[d]	−0.001[c]	0.085	−0.001[c]	0.073[d]	−0.001[c]
Albania	0.036	−0.001[c,d]	0.048	−0.001[c]	0.064	−0.001[c]	0.075	−0.001[c]	0.056	−0.001[c]	0.065[d]	−0.001[c]	0.084	−0.001[c]	0.074[d]	−0.001[c]
Indonesia	0.036	−0.001[c,d]	0.048	−0.001[c]	0.064	−0.001[c]	0.075	−0.001[c]	0.056	−0.001[c]	0.065[d]	−0.001[c]	0.084	−0.001[c]	0.074[d]	−0.001[c]
Jamaica	0.036	−0.001[c,d]	0.048	−0.001[c]	0.064	−0.001[c]	0.075	−0.001[c]	0.057	−0.001[c]	0.065[d]	−0.001[c]	0.084	−0.001[c]	0.074[d]	−0.001[c]
Zimbabwe	0.036	−0.001[c,d]	0.048	−0.001[c]	0.064	−0.001[c]	0.075	−0.001[c]	0.057	−0.001[c]	0.065[d]	−0.001[c]	0.084	−0.001[c]	0.074[d]	−0.001[c]
Guinea	0.036	−0.001[c,d]	0.048	−0.001[c]	0.064	−0.001[c]	0.075	−0.001[c]	0.057	−0.001[c]	0.065[d]	−0.001[c]	0.084	−0.001[c]	0.074[d]	−0.001[c]
Syria	0.036	−0.001[c,d]	0.049	−0.001[c]	0.065	−0.001[c]	0.075	−0.001[c]	0.057	−0.001[c]	0.066[d]	−0.001[c]	0.084	−0.002[c]	0.074[d]	−0.001[c]
Georgia	0.036	−0.001[c,d]	0.049	−0.001[c]	0.065	−0.001[c]	0.075	−0.002[c]	0.057	−0.001[c]	0.066[d]	−0.001[c]	0.084	−0.002[c]	0.074[d]	−0.001[c]

(continued)

Table 6.10 (continued)

	Food, beverage and tobacco		Clothing and footwear		Gross rent, fuel and power		Medical care		Education		Transport and communication		Recreation[b]		Other	
	Slutsky	Cournot	Slutsky	Cournot	Slutsky	Cournot	Slutsky	Cournot	Slutsky	Cournot	Slutsky	Cournot	Slutsky	Cournot	Slutsky	Cournot
Middle-income country																
Ukraine	0.036	−0.001[c,d]	0.050	−0.001[c]	0.066	−0.002[c]	0.076	−0.002[c]	0.058	−0.001[c]	0.066[d]	−0.002[c]	0.084	−0.002[c]	0.075[d]	−0.002[c]
Philippines	0.036	−0.001[c,d]	0.050	−0.001[c]	0.066	−0.002[c]	0.076	−0.002[c]	0.059	−0.002[c]	0.067[d]	−0.002[c]	0.083	−0.002[c]	0.075[d]	−0.002[c]
Peru	0.036	−0.001[c,d]	0.050	−0.001[c]	0.067	−0.002[c]	0.076	−0.002[c]	0.059	−0.002[c]	0.067[d]	−0.002[c]	0.083	−0.002[c]	0.075[d]	−0.002[c]
Botswana	0.036	−0.001[c,d]	0.051	−0.001[c]	0.067	−0.002[c]	0.076	−0.002[c]	0.059	−0.002[c]	0.067[d]	−0.002[c]	0.083	−0.002[c]	0.075[d]	−0.002[c]
Thailand	0.036	−0.001[c,d]	0.051	−0.001[c]	0.067	−0.002[c]	0.076	−0.002[c]	0.059	−0.002[c]	0.067[d]	−0.002[c]	0.083	−0.002[c]	0.075[d]	−0.002[c]
Morocco	0.036	−0.001[c,d]	0.051	−0.001[c]	0.067	−0.002[c]	0.076	−0.002[c]	0.060	−0.002[c]	0.068[d]	−0.002[c]	0.083	−0.002[c]	0.076[d]	−0.002[c]
Venezuela	0.036	−0.001[c,d]	0.051	−0.001[c]	0.067	−0.002[c]	0.076	−0.002[c]	0.060	−0.002[c]	0.068[d]	−0.002[c]	0.083	−0.002[c]	0.076[d]	−0.002[c]
Macedonia	0.036	−0.001[c,d]	0.051	−0.002[c]	0.067	−0.002[c]	0.077	−0.002[c]	0.060	−0.002[c]	0.068[d]	−0.002[c]	0.083	−0.003[c]	0.076[d]	−0.002[c]
Belize	0.036	−0.001[c,d]	0.051	−0.002[c]	0.067	−0.002[c]	0.077	−0.002[c]	0.060	−0.002[c]	0.068[d]	−0.002[c]	0.083	−0.003[c]	0.076[d]	−0.002[c]
Egypt	0.036	−0.001[c,d]	0.051	−0.002[c]	0.067	−0.002[c]	0.077	−0.002[c]	0.060	−0.002[c]	0.068[d]	−0.002[c]	0.083	−0.003[c]	0.076[d]	−0.002[c]
St. Vincent and Grenadines	0.036	−0.001[c,d]	0.051	−0.002[c]	0.067	−0.002[c]	0.077	−0.002[c]	0.060	−0.002[c]	0.068[d]	−0.002[c]	0.083	−0.003[c]	0.076[d]	−0.002[c]
Swaziland	0.036	−0.001[c,d]	0.052	−0.002[c]	0.068	−0.002[c]	0.077	−0.002[c]	0.061	−0.002[c]	0.069[d]	−0.002[cd]	0.083	−0.003[c]	0.076[d]	−0.002[c]
Lebanon	0.036	−0.001[c,d]	0.052	−0.002[c]	0.068	−0.002[c]	0.077	−0.003[c]	0.061	−0.002[c]	0.069[d]	−0.002[c,d]	0.083	−0.003[c]	0.076[d]	−0.003[c]
Belarus	0.036	−0.001[c,d]	0.052	−0.002[c]	0.068	−0.002[c]	0.077	−0.003[c]	0.061	−0.002[c]	0.069[d]	−0.002[c,d]	0.083	−0.003[c]	0.076[d]	−0.003[c]
Kazakhstan	0.036	−0.001[c,d]	0.052	−0.002[c]	0.068	−0.002[c]	0.077	−0.003[c]	0.061	−0.002[c]	0.069[d]	−0.002[c,d]	0.083	−0.003[c]	0.076[d]	−0.003[c]
Dominica	0.036	−0.001[c,d]	0.052	−0.002[c]	0.068	−0.002[c]	0.077	−0.003[c]	0.061	−0.002[c]	0.069[d]	−0.002[c,d]	0.083	−0.003[c]	0.076[d]	−0.003[c]
Latvia	0.036	−0.001[c,d]	0.052	−0.002[c]	0.069	−0.002[c]	0.077[d]	−0.003[c]	0.062	−0.002[c]	0.069[d]	−0.002[c,d]	0.084	−0.003[c]	0.077[d]	−0.003[c]
St. Lucia	0.036	−0.001[c,d]	0.053	−0.002[c]	0.069	−0.002[c]	0.077[d]	−0.003[c]	0.062	−0.002[c]	0.069[d]	−0.002[c,d]	0.084	−0.003[c]	0.077[d]	−0.003[c]
Brazil	0.036	−0.001[c,d]	0.053	−0.002[c]	0.069	−0.002[c]	0.077[d]	−0.003[c]	0.062	−0.002[c]	0.070[d]	−0.002[c,d]	0.084	−0.003[c]	0.077[d]	−0.003[c]
Bulgaria	0.036	−0.001[c,d]	0.053	−0.002[c]	0.069	−0.002[c]	0.077[d]	−0.003[c]	0.062	−0.002[c]	0.070[d]	−0.002[c,d]	0.084	−0.003[c]	0.077[d]	−0.003[c]
Russia	0.036	−0.001[c,d]	0.053	−0.002[c]	0.069	−0.003[c]	0.078[d]	−0.003[c]	0.062	−0.002[c]	0.070[d]	−0.003[c,d]	0.084	−0.003[c]	0.077[d]	−0.003[c]

Fiji	0.036	−0.001[c,d]	0.053	−0.002[c]	0.069	−0.003[c]	0.078[d]	−0.003[c]	0.062	−0.002[c]	0.070[d]	−0.003[c,d]	0.084	−0.003[c]	0.077[d]	−0.003[c,d]
Grenada	0.036	−0.001[c,d]	0.053	−0.002[c]	0.069	−0.003[c]	0.078[d]	−0.003[c]	0.062	−0.002[c]	0.070[d]	−0.003[c,d]	0.084	−0.003[c]	0.077[d]	−0.003[c,d]
Turkey	0.035	−0.001[c,d]	0.053	−0.002[c]	0.070	−0.003[c]	0.078[d]	−0.003[c,d]	0.063	−0.002[c]	0.070[d]	−0.003[c,d]	0.084	−0.003[c]	0.077[d]	−0.003[c,d]
Lithuania	0.035	−0.001[c,d]	0.054	−0.002[c]	0.070	−0.003[c]	0.078[d]	−0.003[c,d]	0.063	−0.002[c]	0.071[d]	−0.003[c,d]	0.084	−0.003[c]	0.077[d]	−0.003[c,d]
Romania	0.035	−0.001[c,d]	0.054	−0.002[c]	0.070	−0.003[c]	0.078[d]	−0.003[c,d]	0.063	−0.003[c]	0.071[d]	−0.003[c,d]	0.084	−0.003[c]	0.078[d]	−0.003[c,d]
Iran	0.035	−0.001[c,d]	0.054	−0.002[c]	0.070	−0.003[c]	0.078[d]	−0.003[c,d]	0.063	−0.003[c]	0.071[d]	−0.003[c,d]	0.084	−0.003[c]	0.078[d]	−0.003[c,d]
Mexico	0.035	−0.001[c,d]	0.054	−0.002[c]	0.071	−0.003[c]	0.079[d]	−0.003[c,d]	0.064	−0.003[c]	0.071[d]	−0.003[c,d]	0.084	−0.004[c]	0.078[d]	−0.003[c,d]
Bahrain	0.035	−0.001[c,d]	0.054	−0.002[c]	0.071	−0.003[c]	0.079[d]	−0.003[c,d]	0.064	−0.003[c]	0.071[d]	−0.003[c,d]	0.084	−0.004[c]	0.078[d]	−0.003[c,d]
Chile	0.035	−0.001[c,d]	0.054	−0.002[c]	0.071	−0.003[c]	0.079[d]	−0.003[c,d]	0.064	−0.003[c]	0.072[d]	−0.003[c,d]	0.084	−0.004[c]	0.078[d]	−0.003[c,d]
Antigua and Barbuda	0.035	−0.002[c,d]	0.054	−0.002[c]	0.071	−0.003[c]	0.079[d]	−0.003[c,d]	0.064	−0.003[c]	0.072[d]	−0.003[c,d]	0.084	−0.004[c]	0.078[d]	−0.003[c,d]
Poland	0.035	−0.002[d]	0.055	−0.002	0.071	−0.003	0.079[d]	−0.003[c,d]	0.064	−0.003[d]	0.072[d]	−0.003[c,d]	0.084	−0.004	0.078[d]	−0.003[c,d]
Trinidad and Tobago	0.035	−0.002[d]	0.055	−0.002	0.071	−0.003[d]	0.079[d]	−0.004[d]	0.065	−0.003[d]	0.072[d]	−0.003[d]	0.084	−0.004	0.079[d]	−0.004[c,d]
Estonia	0.034	−0.002[d]	0.055	−0.003	0.072	−0.003[d]	0.079[d]	−0.004[d]	0.065	−0.003[d]	0.072[d]	−0.003[d]	0.084	−0.004	0.079[d]	−0.004[d]
Gabon	0.034	−0.002[d]	0.055	−0.003	0.072	−0.003[d]	0.079[d]	−0.004[d]	0.065	−0.003[d]	0.072[d]	−0.003[d]	0.084	−0.004	0.079[d]	−0.004[d]
Tunisia	0.034	−0.002[d]	0.055	−0.003[d]	0.072	−0.003[d]	0.080[d]	−0.004[d]	0.065	−0.003[d]	0.073[d]	−0.003[d]	0.085	−0.004[d]	0.079[d]	−0.004[d]
St. Kitts and Nevis	0.034	−0.002[d]	0.056	−0.003[d]	0.072	−0.003[d]	0.080[d]	−0.004[d]	0.065	−0.003[d]	0.073[d]	−0.003[d]	0.085	−0.004[d]	0.079[d]	−0.004[d]
Uruguay	0.034	−0.002[d]	0.056	−0.003[d]	0.072	−0.003[d]	0.080[d]	−0.004[d]	0.065	−0.003[d]	0.073[d]	−0.003[d]	0.085	−0.004[d]	0.079[d]	−0.004[d]
Slovakia	0.034	−0.002[d]	0.056	−0.003[d]	0.072	−0.003[d]	0.080[d]	−0.004[d]	0.066	−0.003[d]	0.073[d]	−0.003[d]	0.085	−0.004[d]	0.079[d]	−0.004[d]
Hungary	0.033	−0.002[d]	0.056	−0.003[d]	0.073	−0.004[d]	0.080[d]	−0.004[d]	0.066	−0.003[d]	0.074[d]	−0.004[d]	0.085	−0.004[d]	0.080[d]	−0.004[d]
Argentina	0.032	−0.002[d]	0.057[d]	−0.003[d]	0.074[d]	−0.004[d]	0.081[d]	−0.004[d]	0.067[d]	−0.004[d]	0.075[d]	−0.004[d]	0.085[d]	−0.005[d]	0.080[d]	−0.004[d]
Oman	0.032	−0.002[d]	0.058[d]	−0.003[d]	0.074[d]	−0.004[d]	0.081[d]	−0.004[d]	0.068[d]	−0.004[d]	0.075[d]	−0.004[d]	0.086[d]	−0.005[d]	0.081[d]	−0.004[d]
Qatar	0.031	−0.002[d]	0.058[d]	−0.003[d]	0.075[d]	−0.004[d]	0.082[d]	−0.005[d]	0.068[d]	−0.004[d]	0.075[d]	−0.004[d]	0.086[d]	−0.005[d]	0.081[d]	−0.005[d]
Slovenia	0.031	−0.002[d]	0.058[d]	−0.003[d]	0.075[d]	−0.004[d]	0.082[d]	−0.005[d]	0.069[d]	−0.004[d]	0.076[d]	−0.004[d]	0.086[d]	−0.005[d]	0.081[d]	−0.005[d]

(continued)

Table 6.10 (continued)

	Food, beverage and tobacco		Clothing and footwear		Gross rent, fuel and power		Medical care		Education		Transport and communication		Recreation[b]		Other	
	Slutsky	Cournot	Slutsky	Cournot	Slutsky	Cournot	Slutsky	Cournot	Slutsky	Cournot	Slutsky	Cournot	Slutsky	Cournot	Slutsky	Cournot
High-income country																
Czech Republic	0.031	−0.002	0.058[d]	−0.003[d]	0.075[d]	−0.004[d]	0.082[d]	−0.005[d]	0.069[d]	−0.004[d]	0.076[d]	−0.004[d]	0.086[d]	−0.005[d]	0.082[d]	−0.005[d]
Greece	0.030	−0.002	0.059[d]	−0.003[d]	0.076[d]	−0.004[d]	0.083[d]	−0.005[d]	0.070[d]	−0.004[d]	0.077[d]	−0.005[d]	0.087[d]	−0.005[d]	0.082[d]	−0.005[d]
Korea	0.029	−0.002	0.059[d]	−0.004[d]	0.076[d]	−0.005[d]	0.083[d]	−0.005[d]	0.070[d]	−0.004[d]	0.077[d]	−0.005[d]	0.087[d]	−0.005[d]	0.082[d]	−0.005[d]
Portugal	0.029	−0.002	0.059[d]	−0.004[d]	0.076[d]	−0.005[d]	0.083[d]	−0.005[d]	0.070[d]	−0.004[d]	0.077[d]	−0.005[d]	0.087[d]	−0.005[d]	0.082[d]	−0.005[d]
Spain	0.029	−0.002	0.059[d]	−0.004[d]	0.076[d]	−0.005[d]	0.083[d]	−0.005[d]	0.070[d]	−0.004[d]	0.077[d]	−0.005[d]	0.087[d]	−0.005[d]	0.082[d]	−0.005[d]
Ireland	0.028	−0.002	0.060[d]	−0.004[d]	0.077[d]	−0.005[d]	0.083[d]	−0.005[d]	0.070[d]	−0.004[d]	0.077[d]	−0.005[d]	0.087[d]	−0.005[d]	0.083[d]	−0.005[d]
Singapore	0.028	−0.002	0.060[d]	−0.004[d]	0.077[d]	−0.005[d]	0.083[d]	−0.005[d]	0.071[d]	−0.004[d]	0.078[d]	−0.005[d]	0.087[d]	−0.005[d]	0.083[d]	−0.005[d]
Mauritius	0.027	−0.002	0.060[d]	−0.004[d]	0.077[d]	−0.005[d]	0.084[d]	−0.005[d]	0.071[d]	−0.004[d]	0.078[d]	−0.005[d]	0.087[d]	−0.005[d]	0.083[d]	−0.005[d]
Israel	0.027	−0.002	0.060[d]	−0.004[d]	0.078[d]	−0.005[d]	0.084[d]	−0.005[d]	0.071[d]	−0.005[d]	0.078[d]	−0.005[d]	0.088[d]	−0.006[d]	0.083[d]	−0.005[d]
New Zealand	0.026	−0.002	0.061[d]	−0.004[d]	0.078[d]	−0.005[d]	0.084[d]	−0.005[d]	0.071[d]	−0.005[d]	0.078[d]	−0.005[d]	0.088[d]	−0.006[d]	0.084[d]	−0.005[d]
Finland	0.026	−0.002	0.061[d]	−0.004[d]	0.078[d]	−0.005[d]	0.084[d]	−0.005[d]	0.071[d]	−0.005[d]	0.078[d]	−0.005[d]	0.088[d]	−0.006[d]	0.084[d]	−0.005[d]
Bahamas	0.026	−0.002	0.061[d]	−0.004[d]	0.078[d]	−0.005[d]	0.084[d]	−0.005[d]	0.072[d]	−0.005[d]	0.078[d]	−0.005[d]	0.088[d]	−0.006[d]	0.084[d]	−0.005[d]
Sweden	0.024	−0.002	0.061[d]	−0.004[d]	0.079[d]	−0.005[d]	0.085[d]	−0.006[d]	0.072[d]	−0.005[d]	0.079[d]	−0.005[d]	0.088[d]	−0.006[d]	0.084[d]	−0.006[d]
Netherlands	0.024	−0.002	0.061[d]	−0.004[d]	0.079[d]	−0.005[d]	0.085[d]	−0.006[d]	0.072[d]	−0.005[d]	0.079[d]	−0.005[d]	0.088[d]	−0.006[d]	0.084[d]	−0.006[d]
France	0.023	−0.002	0.062[d]	−0.004[d]	0.079[d]	−0.005[d]	0.085[d]	−0.006[d]	0.073[d]	−0.005[d]	0.080[d]	−0.005[d]	0.089[d]	−0.006[d]	0.085[d]	−0.006[d]
United Kingdom	0.023	−0.002	0.062[d]	−0.004[d]	0.079[d]	−0.005[d]	0.085[d]	−0.006[d]	0.073[d]	−0.005[d]	0.080[d]	−0.005[d]	0.089[d]	−0.006[d]	0.085[d]	−0.006[d]
Belgium	0.022	−0.002	0.062[d]	−0.004[d]	0.079[d]	−0.005[d]	0.085[d]	−0.006[d]	0.073[d]	−0.005[d]	0.080[d]	−0.005[d]	0.089[d]	−0.006[d]	0.085[d]	−0.006[d]
Norway	0.022	−0.001	0.062[d]	−0.004[d]	0.079[d]	−0.005[d]	0.085[d]	−0.006[d]	0.073[d]	−0.005[d]	0.080[d]	−0.005[d]	0.089[d]	−0.006[d]	0.085[d]	−0.006[d]

Italy	0.022	−0.001	0.062[d]	−0.004[d]	0.079[d]	−0.005[d]	0.085[d]	−0.006[d]	0.073[d]	−0.005[d]	0.080[d]	−0.005[d]	0.089[d]	−0.006[d]	0.085[d]	−0.006[d]
Austria	0.021	−0.001	0.062[d]	−0.004[d]	0.080[d]	−0.005[d]	0.085[d]	−0.006[d]	0.073[d]	−0.005[d]	0.080[d]	−0.005[d]	0.089[d]	−0.006[d]	0.085[d]	−0.006[d]
Germany	0.021	−0.001	0.062[d]	−0.004[d]	0.080[d]	−0.005[d]	0.085[d]	−0.006[d]	0.073[d]	−0.005[d]	0.080[d]	−0.005[d]	0.089[d]	−0.006[d]	0.085[d]	−0.006[d]
Australia	0.021	−0.001[d]	0.062[d]	−0.004[d]	0.080[d]	−0.005[d]	0.086[d]	−0.006[d]	0.074[d]	−0.005[d]	0.080[d]	−0.006[d]	0.089[d]	−0.006[d]	0.085[d]	−0.006[d]
Japan	0.020	−0.001[d]	0.062[d]	−0.004[d]	0.080[d]	−0.006[d]	0.086[d]	−0.006[d]	0.074[d]	−0.005[d]	0.080[d]	−0.006[d]	0.089[d]	−0.006[d]	0.085[d]	−0.006[d]
Canada	0.020	−0.001[d]	0.063[d]	−0.004[d]	0.080[d]	−0.006[d]	0.086[d]	−0.006[d]	0.074[d]	−0.005[d]	0.081[d]	−0.006[d]	0.089[d]	−0.006[d]	0.085[d]	−0.006[d]
Bermuda	0.018	−0.001[d]	0.063[d]	−0.004[d]	0.080[d]	−0.006[d]	0.086[d]	−0.006[d]	0.074[d]	−0.005[d]	0.081[d]	−0.006[d]	0.089[d]	−0.006[d]	0.086[d]	−0.006[d]
Switzerland	0.018	−0.001[d]	0.063[d]	−0.004[d]	0.081[d]	−0.006[d]	0.086[d]	−0.006[d]	0.074[d]	−0.005[d]	0.081[d]	−0.006[d]	0.089[d]	−0.006[d]	0.086[d]	−0.006[d]
Barbados	0.018	−0.001[d]	0.063[d]	−0.004[d]	0.081[d]	−0.006[d]	0.086[d]	−0.006[d]	0.074[d]	−0.005[d]	0.081[d]	−0.006[d]	0.089[d]	−0.006[d]	0.086[d]	−0.006[d]
Hong Kong	0.018	−0.001[d]	0.063[d]	−0.004[d]	0.081[d]	−0.006[d]	0.086[d]	−0.006[d]	0.074[d]	−0.005[d]	0.081[d]	−0.006[d]	0.090[d]	−0.006[d]	0.086[d]	−0.006[d]
Iceland	0.018	−0.001[d]	0.063[d]	−0.004[d]	0.081[d]	−0.006[d]	0.086[d]	−0.006[d]	0.074[d]	−0.005[d]	0.081[d]	−0.006[d]	0.090[d]	−0.006[d]	0.086[d]	−0.006[d]
Denmark	0.017[d]	−0.001[d]	0.063[d]	−0.004[d]	0.081[d]	−0.006[d]	0.086[d]	−0.006[d]	0.075[d]	−0.005[d]	0.081[d]	−0.006[d]	0.090[d]	−0.006[d]	0.086[d]	−0.006[d]
Luxembourg	0.009[cd]	−0.001[d]	0.065[d]	−0.005[d]	0.082[d]	−0.006[d]	0.088[d]	−0.007[d]	0.076[d]	−0.006[d]	0.083[d]	−0.006[d]	0.091[d]	−0.007[d]	0.087[d]	−0.007[d]
United States	0.007[c]	−0.001	0.065	−0.005	0.083	−0.006	0.088	−0.007	0.077	−0.006	0.083	−0.006	0.091	−0.007	0.088	−0.007
Low-income average	0.034	0.000	0.043	0.000	0.059	0.001	0.076	0.001	0.051	0.000	0.060	0.001	0.102	0.002	0.074	0.001
Middle-income average	0.035	−0.001	0.053	−0.002	0.070	−0.003	0.078	−0.003	0.063	−0.002	0.070	−0.003	0.084	−0.003	0.077	−0.003
High-income average	0.023	−0.001	0.061	−0.004	0.079	−0.005	0.085	−0.006	0.073	−0.005	0.079	−0.005	0.088	−0.006	0.084	−0.006

[a]Countries are reported based on ascending per capita real income levels

[b]As the estimated budget share was negative for Tanzania we do not report the elasticity for this country

[c]Elasticity estimate is not significantly different from zero at 0.05 level

[d]Elasticity estimate is not significantly different from the point estimate of the United States at 0.05 level

Table 6.11 Slutsky and Cournot cross-price elasticities with change in medical care price, 114 countries in 1996[a]

	Food, beverage and tobacco		Clothing and footwear		Gross rent, fuel and power		House furnishing and operations		Education		Transport and communication		Recreation[b]		Other	
	Slutsky	Cournot	Slutsky	Cournot	Slutsky	Cournot	Slutsky	Cournot	Slutsky	Cournot	Slutsky	Cournot	Slutsky	Cournot	Slutsky	Cournot
Low-income country																
Tanzania	0.024	0.014	0.027	0.016	0.040	0.023	0.040	0.023	0.032	0.019	0.042[c,d]	0.024[c,d]			0.077[c]	0.045[c,d]
Nigeria	0.028	0.012	0.034	0.014	0.048	0.021	0.048	0.020	0.039	0.017	0.049[c,d]	0.021[c,d]	0.236	0.101	0.074[c]	0.032[c,d]
Tajikistan	0.030	0.012	0.036	0.014	0.051	0.019	0.051	0.019	0.043	0.016	0.053[c,d]	0.020[c,d]	0.156	0.059	0.074[c]	0.028[c,d]
Zambia	0.031	0.011	0.037	0.014	0.052	0.019	0.052	0.019	0.043	0.016	0.053[c,d]	0.020[c,d]	0.149	0.055	0.074[c]	0.027[c,d]
Yemen	0.031	0.011	0.037	0.014	0.052	0.019	0.052	0.019	0.043	0.016	0.053[c,d]	0.020[c,d]	0.148	0.055	0.074[c]	0.027[c,d]
Malawi	0.032	0.011	0.038	0.013	0.054	0.018	0.054	0.018	0.045	0.015	0.055[c,d]	0.019[c,d]	0.132	0.045	0.075[c]	0.026[c,d]
Madagascar	0.032	0.011	0.039	0.013	0.054	0.018	0.054	0.018	0.045	0.015	0.055[c,d]	0.019[c,d]	0.132	0.045	0.075[c]	0.026[c,d]
Mali	0.032	0.011	0.039	0.013	0.055	0.018	0.054	0.018	0.046	0.015	0.056[c,d]	0.019[c,d]	0.129	0.043	0.075[c]	0.025[c,d]
Mongolia	0.033	0.011	0.039	0.013	0.055	0.018	0.054	0.018	0.046	0.015	0.056[c,d]	0.019[c,d]	0.128	0.043	0.075[c]	0.025[c,d]
Benin	0.035	0.010	0.043	0.012	0.059	0.017	0.059	0.017	0.050	0.014	0.061[d]	0.017	0.112	0.032	0.078[c]	0.022[c,d]
Kenya	0.036	0.010	0.045	0.012	0.061	0.016	0.061	0.016	0.052	0.014	0.062[d]	0.016	0.108	0.028	0.079	0.021[c,d]
Sierra Leone	0.037	0.009	0.046	0.011	0.063	0.016	0.063	0.015	0.054	0.013	0.064[d]	0.016	0.106	0.026	0.080	0.020
Nepal	0.037	0.009	0.046	0.011	0.063	0.016	0.063	0.015	0.054	0.013	0.064[d]	0.016	0.106	0.026	0.080	0.020
Turkmenistan	0.038	0.009	0.047	0.011	0.064	0.015	0.064	0.015	0.055	0.013	0.065[d]	0.016	0.105	0.025	0.080[c]	0.019[c,d]
Congo	0.039	0.009	0.048	0.011	0.065	0.015	0.065	0.015	0.056	0.013	0.067[d]	0.015	0.104	0.024	0.081[c]	0.018[c,d]
Senegal	0.039	0.008	0.049	0.011	0.067	0.014	0.067	0.014	0.058	0.012	0.068[d]	0.015	0.103	0.022	0.082	0.018
Vietnam	0.039	0.008	0.050	0.010	0.067	0.014	0.067	0.014	0.058	0.012	0.068[d]	0.014	0.103	0.022	0.082	0.017

Bangladesh	0.040	0.008	0.050	0.010	0.067	0.014	0.067	0.014	0.058	0.012	0.069[d]	0.014	0.103	0.022	0.083	0.017
Pakistan	0.041	0.008	0.052	0.010	0.070	0.013	0.070	0.013	0.061	0.012	0.071	0.013	0.103	0.019	0.085	0.016
Azerbaijan	0.042	0.007	0.053	0.010	0.072	0.013	0.071	0.013	0.062	0.011	0.073	0.013	0.102	0.018	0.086	0.015
Cote d'Ivoire	0.042	0.007	0.054	0.009	0.072	0.013	0.072	0.013	0.063	0.011	0.073	0.013	0.102	0.018	0.086	0.015
Paraguay	0.042	0.007	0.054	0.009	0.073	0.013	0.072	0.013	0.063	0.011	0.074	0.013	0.103	0.018	0.086	0.015
Uzbekistan	0.042	0.007	0.055	0.009	0.073	0.012	0.073	0.012	0.064	0.011	0.075	0.013	0.103	0.017	0.087	0.015
Kyrgyzstan	0.042	0.007	0.055	0.009	0.074	0.012	0.073	0.012	0.064	0.011	0.075	0.013	0.103	0.017	0.087	0.015
Cameroon	0.042	0.007	0.055	0.009	0.074	0.012	0.073	0.012	0.064	0.011	0.075	0.012	0.103	0.017	0.087	0.015
Moldova	0.042	0.007	0.055	0.009	0.074	0.012	0.073	0.012	0.064	0.011	0.075	0.012	0.103	0.017	0.087	0.015
Bolivia	0.043	0.007	0.056	0.009	0.075	0.012	0.074	0.012	0.065	0.011	0.076	0.012	0.103	0.017	0.088	0.014
Ecuador	0.043	0.007	0.056	0.009	0.075	0.012	0.075	0.012	0.066	0.010	0.076	0.012	0.103	0.016	0.088	0.014
Armenia	0.043	0.007	0.057	0.009	0.076	0.012	0.076	0.012	0.067	0.010	0.077	0.012	0.103	0.016	0.089	0.014
Sri Lanka	0.043	0.007	0.057	0.009	0.076	0.012	0.076	0.012	0.067	0.010	0.077	0.012	0.103	0.016	0.089	0.014
Jordan	0.044	0.006	0.058	0.008	0.077	0.011	0.077	0.011	0.068	0.010	0.078	0.011	0.103	0.015	0.090	0.013
Albania	0.044	0.006	0.059	0.008	0.079	0.011	0.078	0.011	0.069	0.010	0.080	0.011	0.104	0.014	0.091	0.013
Indonesia	0.044	0.006	0.060	0.008	0.079	0.011	0.079	0.011	0.070	0.009	0.080	0.011	0.104	0.014	0.091	0.012
Jamaica	0.045	0.006	0.060	0.008	0.079	0.011	0.079	0.011	0.070	0.009	0.080	0.011	0.104	0.014	0.092	0.012
Zimbabwe	0.045	0.006	0.060	0.008	0.079	0.011	0.079	0.011	0.070	0.009	0.080	0.011	0.104	0.014	0.092	0.012
Guinea	0.045	0.006	0.060	0.008	0.080	0.010	0.080	0.010	0.071	0.009	0.081	0.011	0.104	0.014	0.092	0.012
Syria	0.045	0.006	0.061	0.008	0.081	0.010	0.081	0.010	0.072	0.009	0.082	0.010	0.105	0.013	0.093	0.012
Georgia	0.045	0.006	0.061	0.008	0.081	0.010	0.081	0.010	0.072	0.009	0.082	0.010	0.105	0.013	0.093	0.012

(continued)

Table 6.11 (continued)

	Food, beverage and tobacco		Clothing and footwear		Gross rent, fuel and power		House furnishing and operations		Education		Transport and communication		Recreation[b]		Other	
	Slutsky	Cournot	Slutsky	Cournot	Slutsky	Cournot	Slutsky	Cournot	Slutsky	Cournot	Slutsky	Cournot	Slutsky	Cournot	Slutsky	Cournot
Middle-income country																
Ukraine	0.046	0.005	0.063	0.007	0.083	0.009	0.083	0.009	0.074	0.008	0.084	0.010	0.106	0.012	0.095	0.011
Philippines	0.046	0.005	0.064	0.007	0.085	0.009	0.084	0.009	0.075	0.008	0.085	0.009	0.106	0.011	0.096	0.010
Peru	0.046	0.005	0.065	0.007	0.085	0.009	0.085	0.009	0.076	0.008	0.086	0.009	0.107	0.011	0.096	0.010
Botswana	0.046	0.005	0.065	0.007	0.085	0.009	0.085	0.009	0.076	0.008	0.086	0.009	0.107	0.011	0.096	0.010
Thailand	0.046	0.005	0.065	0.007	0.085	0.009	0.085	0.009	0.076	0.008	0.086	0.009	0.107	0.011	0.097	0.010
Morocco	0.046	0.005	0.065	0.007	0.086	0.009	0.086	0.009	0.077	0.008	0.087	0.009	0.107	0.011	0.097	0.010
Venezuela	0.046	0.005	0.066	0.007	0.086	0.009	0.086	0.009	0.077	0.008	0.087	0.009	0.107	0.011	0.097	0.010
Macedonia	0.047	0.004	0.066	0.006	0.087	0.008	0.087	0.008	0.078	0.007	0.088	0.008	0.108	0.010	0.098	0.009
Belize	0.047	0.004	0.066	0.006	0.087	0.008	0.087	0.008	0.078	0.007	0.088	0.008	0.108	0.010	0.098	0.009
Egypt	0.047	0.004	0.066	0.006	0.087	0.008	0.087	0.008	0.078	0.007	0.088	0.008	0.108	0.010	0.098	0.009
St. Vincent and Grenadines	0.047	0.004	0.066	0.006	0.087	0.008	0.087	0.008	0.078	0.007	0.088	0.008	0.108	0.010	0.098	0.009
Swaziland	0.047	0.004	0.067	0.006	0.088	0.008	0.088	0.008	0.079	0.007	0.089	0.008	0.109	0.010	0.099	0.009
Lebanon	0.047	0.004	0.068	0.006	0.089	0.008	0.088	0.008	0.080	0.007	0.090	0.008	0.109	0.010	0.099	0.009
Belarus	0.047	0.004	0.068	0.006	0.089	0.008	0.089	0.008	0.080	0.007	0.090	0.008	0.109	0.010	0.100	0.009
Kazakhstan	0.047	0.004	0.068	0.006	0.089	0.008	0.089	0.008	0.080	0.007	0.090	0.008	0.109	0.010	0.100	0.009
Dominica	0.047	0.004	0.068	0.006	0.089	0.008	0.089	0.008	0.080	0.007	0.090	0.008	0.109	0.010	0.100	0.009
Latvia	0.047	0.004	0.069	0.006	0.090	0.008	0.090	0.007	0.081	0.007	0.091	0.008	0.110	0.009	0.101	0.008
St. Lucia	0.047	0.004	0.069	0.006	0.090	0.007	0.090	0.007	0.081	0.007	0.091	0.008	0.110	0.009	0.101	0.008
Brazil	0.047	0.004	0.069	0.006	0.090	0.007	0.090	0.007	0.081	0.007	0.091	0.008	0.110	0.009	0.101	0.008
Bulgaria	0.047	0.004	0.069	0.006	0.090	0.007	0.090	0.007	0.081	0.007	0.091	0.007	0.110	0.009	0.101	0.008

Russia	0.047	0.004	0.070	0.006	0.091	0.007	0.091	0.007	0.082	0.007	0.092	0.007	0.110	0.009	0.101	0.008
Fiji	0.047	0.004	0.070	0.005	0.092	0.007	0.091	0.007	0.083	0.006	0.093	0.007	0.111	0.008	0.102	0.008
Grenada	0.047	0.004	0.070	0.005	0.092	0.007	0.091	0.007	0.083	0.006	0.093	0.007	0.111	0.008	0.102	0.008
Turkey	0.047	0.004	0.071	0.005	0.092	0.007	0.092	0.007	0.083	0.006	0.093	0.007	0.111	0.008	0.102	0.008
Lithuania	0.047	0.003	0.071	0.005	0.093	0.007	0.092	0.007	0.083	0.006	0.094	0.007	0.111	0.008	0.103	0.008
Romania	0.047	0.003	0.071	0.005	0.093	0.007	0.093	0.007	0.084	0.006	0.094	0.007	0.111	0.008	0.103	0.007
Iran	0.047	0.003[c]	0.072	0.005	0.094	0.006	0.094	0.006	0.085	0.006	0.095	0.007	0.112	0.008	0.104	0.007
Mexico	0.047	0.003[c]	0.072	0.005[c]	0.094	0.006[c]	0.094	0.006	0.085	0.006	0.095	0.006[c]	0.112	0.008	0.104	0.007[c]
Bahrain	0.047	0.003[c,d]	0.073	0.005[c]	0.095	0.006[c]	0.094	0.006	0.086	0.006	0.096	0.006[c]	0.113	0.007	0.105	0.007[c]
Chile	0.047	0.003[c,d]	0.073	0.005[c]	0.095	0.006[c]	0.095	0.006	0.086	0.006	0.096	0.006[c]	0.113	0.007	0.105	0.007[c]
Antigua and Barbuda	0.047	0.003[c,d]	0.073	0.005[c]	0.095	0.006[c]	0.095	0.006	0.086	0.006	0.096	0.006[c]	0.113	0.007	0.105	0.007[c]
Poland	0.047	0.003[c,d]	0.074	0.005[c]	0.096	0.006[c]	0.095	0.006[c]	0.087	0.005[c]	0.097	0.006[c]	0.113	0.007	0.105	0.007[c]
Trinidad and Tobago	0.047	0.003[c,d]	0.074	0.004[c]	0.096	0.006[c]	0.096	0.006[c]	0.087	0.005[c]	0.097	0.006[c]	0.114	0.007[c]	0.106	0.006[c]
Estonia	0.047	0.003[c,d]	0.075	0.004[c]	0.097	0.006[c]	0.097	0.006[c]	0.088	0.005[c]	0.098	0.006[c]	0.114	0.007[c]	0.106	0.006[c]
Gabon	0.046	0.003[c,d]	0.075	0.004[c]	0.097	0.006[c]	0.097	0.006[c]	0.088	0.005[c]	0.098	0.006[c]	0.114	0.007[c]	0.107	0.006[c]
Tunisia	0.046	0.003[c,d]	0.075	0.004[c]	0.097	0.005[c]	0.097	0.005[c]	0.088	0.005[c]	0.098[d]	0.006[c,d]	0.114	0.006[c]	0.107	0.006[c]
St. Kitts and Nevis	0.046	0.003[c,d]	0.075	0.004[c,d]	0.098	0.005[c,d]	0.097	0.005[c]	0.088	0.005[c]	0.099[d]	0.005[c,d]	0.115	0.006[c]	0.107	0.006[c,d]
Uruguay	0.046	0.003[c,d]	0.075	0.004[c,d]	0.098	0.005[c,d]	0.098	0.005[c]	0.089	0.005[c]	0.099[d]	0.005[c,d]	0.115	0.006[c]	0.107	0.006[c,d]
Slovakia	0.046	0.002[c,d]	0.076	0.004[c,d]	0.098	0.005[c,d]	0.098	0.005[c]	0.089	0.005[c]	0.099[d]	0.005[c,d]	0.115	0.006[c]	0.108	0.006[c,d]
Hungary	0.046	0.002[c,d]	0.077	0.004[c,d]	0.100	0.005[c,d]	0.100	0.005[c,d]	0.091	0.004[c,d]	0.101[d]	0.005[c,d]	0.116	0.006[c,d]	0.109	0.005[c,d]
Argentina	0.045	0.002[c,d]	0.079	0.003[c,d]	0.102	0.004[c,d]	0.102	0.004[c,d]	0.093	0.004[c,d]	0.103[d]	0.004[c,d]	0.118	0.005[c,d]	0.111[d]	0.005[c,d]
Oman	0.044	0.002[c,d]	0.080	0.003[c,d]	0.103	0.004[c,d]	0.103	0.004[c,d]	0.094	0.004[c,d]	0.104[d]	0.004[c,d]	0.118	0.005[c,d]	0.112[d]	0.004[c,d]
Qatar	0.044	0.002[c,d]	0.081	0.003[c,d]	0.104	0.004[c,d]	0.104	0.004[c,d]	0.095	0.003[c,d]	0.105[d]	0.004[c,d]	0.119	0.004[c,d]	0.113[d]	0.004[c,d]
Slovenia	0.043	0.001[c,d]	0.081	0.003[c,d]	0.104	0.004[c,d]	0.104	0.004[c,d]	0.095	0.003[c,d]	0.105[d]	0.004[c,d]	0.120	0.004[c,d]	0.113[d]	0.004[c,d]

(continued)

Table 6.11 (continued)

	Food, beverage and tobacco		Clothing and footwear		Gross rent, fuel and power		House furnishing and operations		Education		Transport and communication		Recreation[b]		Other	
	Slutsky	Cournot	Slutsky	Cournot	Slutsky	Cournot	Slutsky	Cournot	Slutsky	Cournot	Slutsky	Cournot	Slutsky	Cournot	Slutsky	Cournot
High-income country																
Czech Republic	0.043	0.001[c,d]	0.082[d]	0.003[c,d]	0.105	0.003[c,d]	0.105	0.003[c,d]	0.096	0.003[c,d]	0.106[d]	0.003[c,d]	0.120	0.004[c,d]	0.114[d]	0.004[c,d]
Greece	0.042	0.001[c,d]	0.083[d]	0.002[c,d]	0.107	0.003[c,d]	0.106	0.003[c,d]	0.098	0.003[c,d]	0.107[d]	0.003[c,d]	0.121	0.003[c,d]	0.115[d]	0.003[c,d]
Korea	0.041	0.001[c,d]	0.083[d]	0.002[c,d]	0.107[d]	0.003[c,d]	0.107	0.003[c,d]	0.098	0.003[c,d]	0.108[d]	0.003[c,d]	0.122	0.003[c,d]	0.115[d]	0.003[c,d]
Portugal	0.041	0.001[c,d]	0.083[d]	0.002[c,d]	0.107[d]	0.003[c,d]	0.107	0.003[c,d]	0.098	0.002[c,d]	0.108[d]	0.003[c,d]	0.122	0.003[c,d]	0.116[d]	0.003[c,d]
Spain	0.041	0.001[c,d]	0.084[d]	0.002[c,d]	0.108[d]	0.003[c,d]	0.107	0.003[c,d]	0.098	0.002[c,d]	0.108[d]	0.003[c,d]	0.122	0.003[c,d]	0.116[d]	0.003[c,d]
Ireland	0.040	0.001[c,d]	0.084[d]	0.002[c,d]	0.108[d]	0.003[c,d]	0.108	0.003[c,d]	0.099[d]	0.002[c,d]	0.109[d]	0.003[c,d]	0.123	0.003[c,d]	0.116[d]	0.003[c,d]
Singapore	0.040	0.001[c,d]	0.084[d]	0.002[c,d]	0.109[d]	0.002[c,d]	0.108[d]	0.002[c,d]	0.100[d]	0.002[c,d]	0.109[d]	0.002[c,d]	0.123	0.003[c,d]	0.117[d]	0.003[c,d]
Mauritius	0.039	0.001[c,d]	0.085[d]	0.002[c,d]	0.109[d]	0.002[c,d]	0.109[d]	0.002[c,d]	0.100[d]	0.002[c,d]	0.110[d]	0.002[c,d]	0.124	0.002[c,d]	0.118[d]	0.002[c,d]
Israel	0.038	0.001[c,d]	0.086[d]	0.002[c,d]	0.110[d]	0.002[c,d]	0.110[d]	0.002[c,d]	0.101[d]	0.002[c,d]	0.111[d]	0.002[c,d]	0.124	0.002[c,d]	0.118[d]	0.002[c,d]
New Zealand	0.037	0.001[c,d]	0.086[d]	0.001[c,d]	0.110[d]	0.002[c,d]	0.110[d]	0.002[c,d]	0.101[d]	0.002[c,d]	0.111[d]	0.002[c,d]	0.124	0.002[c,d]	0.119[d]	0.002[c,d]
Finland	0.037	0.001[c,d]	0.086[d]	0.001[c,d]	0.110[d]	0.002[c,d]	0.110[d]	0.002[c,d]	0.101[d]	0.002[c,d]	0.111[d]	0.002[c,d]	0.124	0.002[c,d]	0.119[d]	0.002[c,d]
Bahamas	0.037	0.001[c,d]	0.086[d]	0.001[c,d]	0.111[d]	0.002[c,d]	0.110[d]	0.002[c,d]	0.102[d]	0.002[c,d]	0.111[d]	0.002[c,d]	0.125	0.002[c,d]	0.119[d]	0.002[c,d]
Sweden	0.035	0.000[c,d]	0.087[d]	0.001[c,d]	0.112[d]	0.001[c,d]	0.112[d]	0.001[c,d]	0.103[d]	0.001[c,d]	0.113[d]	0.001[c,d]	0.126[d]	0.002[c,d]	0.120[d]	0.002[c,d]
Netherlands	0.034	0.000[c,d]	0.088[d]	0.001[c,d]	0.112[d]	0.001[c,d]	0.112[d]	0.001[c,d]	0.103[d]	0.001[c,d]	0.113[d]	0.001[c,d]	0.126[d]	0.002[c,d]	0.120[d]	0.001[c,d]
France	0.032	0.000[c,d]	0.089[d]	0.001[c,d]	0.113[d]	0.001[c,d]	0.113[d]	0.001[c,d]	0.104[d]	0.001[c,d]	0.114[d]	0.001[c,d]	0.127[d]	0.001[c,d]	0.121[d]	0.001[c,d]
United Kingdom	0.032	0.000[c,d]	0.089[d]	0.001[c,d]	0.114[d]	0.001[c,d]	0.113[d]	0.001[c,d]	0.105[d]	0.001[c,d]	0.114[d]	0.001[c,d]	0.127[d]	0.001[c,d]	0.121[d]	0.001[c,d]
Belgium	0.032	0.000[c,d]	0.089[d]	0.001[c,d]	0.114[d]	0.001[c,d]	0.114[d]	0.001[c,d]	0.105[d]	0.001[c,d]	0.115[d]	0.001[c,d]	0.127[d]	0.001[c,d]	0.122[d]	0.001[c,d]
Norway	0.032	0.000[c,d]	0.089[d]	0.001[c,d]	0.114[d]	0.001[c,d]	0.114[d]	0.001[c,d]	0.105[d]	0.001[c,d]	0.115[d]	0.001[c,d]	0.127[d]	0.001[c,d]	0.122[d]	0.001[c,d]

Italy	0.031	0.000[c,d]	0.089[d]	0.001[c,d]	0.114[d]	0.001[c,d]	0.114[d]	0.001[c,d]	0.105[d]	0.001[c,d]	0.115[d]	0.001[c,d]	0.127[d]	0.001[c,d]	0.122[d]	0.001[c,d]
Austria	0.031	0.000[c,d]	0.089[d]	0.001[c,d]	0.114[d]	0.001[c,d]	0.114[d]	0.001[c,d]	0.105[d]	0.001[c,d]	0.115[d]	0.001[c,d]	0.128[d]	0.001[c,d]	0.122[d]	0.001[c,d]
Germany	0.030	0.000[c,d]	0.089[d]	0.001[c,d]	0.114[d]	0.001[c,d]	0.114[d]	0.001[c,d]	0.106[d]	0.001[c,d]	0.115[d]	0.001[c,d]	0.128[d]	0.001[c,d]	0.122[d]	0.001[c,d]
Australia	0.030	0.000[c,d]	0.090[d]	0.001[c,d]	0.115[d]	0.001[c,d]	0.115[d]	0.001[c,d]	0.106[d]	0.001[c,d]	0.116[d]	0.001[c,d]	0.128[d]	0.001[c,d]	0.123[d]	0.001[c,d]
Japan	0.029	0.000[c,d]	0.090[d]	0.001[c,d]	0.115[d]	0.001[c,d]	0.115[d]	0.001[c,d]	0.106[d]	0.001[c,d]	0.116[d]	0.001[c,d]	0.128[d]	0.001[c,d]	0.123[d]	0.001[c,d]
Canada	0.028	0.000[c,d]	0.090[d]	0.000[c,d]	0.115[d]	0.001[c,d]	0.115[d]	0.001[c,d]	0.107[d]	0.001[c,d]	0.116[d]	0.001[c,d]	0.129[d]	0.001[c,d]	0.123[d]	0.001[c,d]
Bermuda	0.027	0.000[c,d]	0.091[d]	0.000[c,d]	0.116[d]	0.000[c,d]	0.116[d]	0.000[c,d]	0.107[d]	0.000[c,d]	0.117[d]	0.000[c,d]	0.129[d]	0.000[c,d]	0.124[d]	0.000[c,d]
Switzerland	0.026	0.000[c,d]	0.091[d]	0.000[c,d]	0.116[d]	0.000[c,d]	0.116[d]	0.000[c,d]	0.108[d]	0.000[c,d]	0.117[d]	0.000[c,d]	0.129[d]	0.000[c,d]	0.124[d]	0.000[c,d]
Barbados	0.026[d]	0.000[c,d]	0.091[d]	0.000[c,d]	0.117[d]	0.000[c,d]	0.116[d]	0.000[c,d]	0.108[d]	0.000[c,d]	0.117[d]	0.000[c,d]	0.129[d]	0.000[c,d]	0.124[d]	0.000[c,d]
Hong Kong	0.026[d]	0.000[c,d]	0.091[d]	0.000[c,d]	0.117[d]	0.000[c,d]	0.116[d]	0.000[c,d]	0.108[d]	0.000[c,d]	0.117[d]	0.000[c,d]	0.130[d]	0.000[c,d]	0.124[d]	0.000[c,d]
Iceland	0.025[d]	0.000[c,d]	0.091[d]	0.000[c,d]	0.117[d]	0.000[c,d]	0.116[d]	0.000[c,d]	0.108[d]	0.000[c,d]	0.117[d]	0.000[c,d]	0.130[d]	0.000[c,d]	0.124[d]	0.000[c,d]
Denmark	0.025[d]	0.000[c,d]	0.091[d]	0.000[c,d]	0.117[d]	0.000[c,d]	0.117[d]	0.000[c,d]	0.108[d]	0.000[c,d]	0.118[d]	0.000[c,d]	0.130[d]	0.000[c,d]	0.125[d]	0.000[c,d]
Luxembourg	0.013[d]	0.000[c,d]	0.094[d]	−0.001[c,d]	0.121[d]	−0.001[c,d]	0.120[d]	−0.001[c,d]	0.112[d]	−0.001[c,d]	0.121[d]	−0.001[c,d]	0.133[d]	−0.001[c,d]	0.128[d]	−0.001[c,d]
United States	0.011	0.000[c]	0.095	−0.001[c]	0.121	−0.001[c]	0.121	−0.001[c]	0.112	−0.001[c,d]	0.122	−0.001[c]	0.133	−0.001[c]	0.128	−0.001[c]
Low-income average	0.039	0.008	0.050	0.010	0.067	0.014	0.067	0.014	0.058	0.012	0.068	0.015	0.114	0.027	0.084	0.019
Middle-income average	0.046	0.004	0.071	0.005	0.092	0.007	0.092	0.007	0.083	0.006	0.093	0.007	0.111	0.008	0.103	0.008
High-income average	0.032	0.000	0.088	0.001	0.113	0.001	0.113	0.001	0.104	0.001	0.114	0.001	0.126	0.001	0.121	0.001

[a]Countries are reported based on ascending per capita real income levels

[b]As the estimated budget share was negative for Tanzania we do not report the elasticity for this country

[c]Elasticity estimate is not significantly different from zero at 0.05 level

[d]Elasticity estimate is not significantly different from the point estimate of the United States at 0.05 level

Table 6.12 Slutsky and Cournot cross-price elasticities with change in education price, 114 countries in 1996[a]

	Food, beverage and tobacco		Clothing and footwear		Gross rent, fuel and power		House furnishing and operations		Medical care		Transport and communication		Recreation[b]		Other	
	Slutsky	Cournot	Slutsky	Cournot	Slutsky	Cournot	Slutsky	Cournot	Slutsky	Cournot	Slutsky	Cournot	Slutsky	Cournot	Slutsky	Cournot
Low-income country																
Tanzania	0.038	−0.005	0.045	−0.006	0.066	−0.009	0.065	−0.009	0.142[c,d]	−0.019[c,d]	0.068[c,d]	−0.009[c,d]			0.126[c,d]	−0.017[c,d]
Nigeria	0.039	−0.005	0.046	−0.006	0.066	−0.009	0.065	−0.009	0.107[c,d]	−0.015	0.067[c,d]	−0.009[c,d]	0.323	−0.044	0.101[c,d]	−0.014[c,d]
Tajikistan	0.039	−0.005	0.046	−0.006	0.066	−0.009	0.065	−0.009	0.099[d]	−0.014	0.067[c,d]	−0.009[c,d]	0.199	−0.027	0.095[c,d]	−0.013[c,d]
Zambia	0.039	−0.005	0.046	−0.006	0.066	−0.009	0.065	−0.009[c]	0.098[d]	−0.014	0.067[c,d]	−0.009[c,d]	0.188	−0.026[c]	0.094[c,d]	−0.013[c,d]
Yemen	0.039	−0.005	0.046	−0.006	0.066	−0.009	0.065	−0.009[c]	0.098[d]	−0.014	0.067[c,d]	−0.009[c,d]	0.187	−0.026[c]	0.094[c,d]	−0.013[c,d]
Malawi	0.039	−0.005	0.047	−0.006	0.066	−0.009	0.065	−0.009[c]	0.095[d]	−0.013	0.067[c,d]	−0.009[c,d]	0.161	−0.022[c]	0.091[c,d]	−0.013[c,d]
Madagascar	0.039	−0.005	0.047	−0.006	0.066	−0.009	0.065	−0.009[c]	0.095[d]	−0.013	0.067[c,d]	−0.009[c,d]	0.160	−0.022[c]	0.091[c,d]	−0.013[c,d]
Mali	0.039	−0.005	0.047	−0.006	0.066	−0.009	0.065	−0.009[c]	0.094[d]	−0.013	0.067[c,d]	−0.009[c,d]	0.155	−0.021[c]	0.091[c,d]	−0.013[c,d]
Mongolia	0.039	−0.005	0.047	−0.007	0.066	−0.009	0.065	−0.009[c]	0.094[d]	−0.013	0.067[c,d]	−0.009[c,d]	0.153	−0.021[c]	0.090[c,d]	−0.013[c,d]
Benin	0.039	−0.005[c]	0.048	−0.007[c]	0.066	−0.009[c]	0.066	−0.009[c]	0.089[d]	−0.012[c]	0.067[d]	−0.009[c,d]	0.124	−0.017[c]	0.086[c,d]	−0.012[c]
Kenya	0.039	−0.006[c]	0.048	−0.007[c]	0.066	−0.009[c]	0.066	−0.009[c]	0.087[d]	−0.012[c]	0.067[d]	−0.009[c]	0.117	−0.016[c]	0.085[c,d]	−0.012[c,d]
Sierra Leone	0.039	−0.006[c]	0.048	−0.007[c]	0.066	−0.009[c]	0.066	−0.009[c]	0.086[d]	−0.012[c]	0.067[d]	−0.010[c]	0.111	−0.016[c]	0.084[d]	−0.012[c]
Nepal	0.039	−0.006[c]	0.048	−0.007[c]	0.066	−0.009[c]	0.066	−0.009[c]	0.086[d]	−0.012[c]	0.067[d]	−0.010[c]	0.111	−0.016[c]	0.084[d]	−0.012[c]
Turkmenistan	0.039	−0.006[c]	0.048	−0.007[c]	0.066	−0.009[c]	0.066	−0.009[c]	0.085[d]	−0.012[c]	0.067[d]	−0.010[c]	0.109	−0.015[c]	0.083[c,d]	−0.012[c]
Congo	0.039	−0.006[c,d]	0.049	−0.007[c]	0.066	−0.009[c]	0.066	−0.009[c]	0.084[d]	−0.012[c]	0.067[d]	−0.010[c]	0.106	−0.015[c]	0.082[c,d]	−0.012[c,d]
Senegal	0.039	−0.006[c,d]	0.049	−0.007[c]	0.066	−0.009[c]	0.066	−0.009[c]	0.083	−0.012[c]	0.068[d]	−0.010[c]	0.103	−0.015[c]	0.082[d]	−0.012[c]

Vietnam	0.039	−0.006[c,d]	0.049	−0.007[c]	0.066	−0.010[c]	0.066	−0.009[c]	0.083	−0.012[c]	0.068[d]	−0.010[c]	0.102	−0.015[c]	0.081[d]	−0.012[c]
Bangladesh	0.039	−0.006[c,d]	0.049	−0.007[c]	0.067	−0.010[c]	0.066	−0.009[c]	0.083	−0.012[c]	0.068[d]	−0.010[c]	0.102	−0.015[c]	0.081[d]	−0.012[c]
Pakistan	0.039	−0.006[c,d]	0.049	−0.007[c]	0.067	−0.010[c]	0.066	−0.010[c]	0.082	−0.012[c]	0.068[d]	−0.010[c]	0.097	−0.014[c]	0.080[d]	−0.012[c]
Azerbaijan	0.039	−0.006[c,d]	0.050	−0.007[c]	0.067	−0.010[c]	0.067	−0.010[c]	0.081	−0.012[c]	0.068[d]	−0.010[c]	0.096	−0.014[c]	0.080[d]	−0.012[c]
Cote d'Ivoire	0.039	−0.006[c,d]	0.050	−0.007[c]	0.067	−0.010[c]	0.067	−0.010[c]	0.081	−0.012[c]	0.068[d]	−0.010[c]	0.095	−0.014[c]	0.080[d]	−0.012[c]
Paraguay	0.039	−0.006[c,d]	0.050	−0.007[c]	0.067	−0.010[c]	0.067	−0.010[c]	0.081	−0.012[c]	0.068[d]	−0.010[c]	0.095	−0.014[c]	0.080[d]	−0.012[c]
Uzbekistan	0.039	−0.006[c,d]	0.050	−0.007[c]	0.067	−0.010[c]	0.067	−0.010[c]	0.081	−0.012[c]	0.068[d]	−0.010[c]	0.094	−0.014[c]	0.079[d]	−0.012[c]
Kyrgyzstan	0.039	−0.006[c,d]	0.050	−0.007[c]	0.067	−0.010[c]	0.067	−0.010[c]	0.081	−0.012[c]	0.068[d]	−0.010[c]	0.094	−0.014[c]	0.079[d]	−0.012[c]
Cameroon	0.039	−0.006[c,d]	0.050	−0.007[c]	0.067	−0.010[c]	0.067	−0.010[c]	0.081	−0.012[c]	0.068[d]	−0.010[c]	0.093	−0.014[c]	0.079[d]	−0.012[c]
Moldova	0.039	−0.006[c,d]	0.050	−0.007[c]	0.067	−0.010[c]	0.067	−0.010[c]	0.081	−0.012[c]	0.068[d]	−0.010[c]	0.093	−0.014[c]	0.079[d]	−0.012[c]
Bolivia	0.038	−0.006[c,d]	0.050	−0.007[c]	0.067	−0.010[c]	0.067	−0.010[c]	0.080	−0.012[c]	0.068[d]	−0.010[c]	0.092	−0.013[c]	0.079[d]	−0.011[c]
Ecuador	0.038	−0.006[c,d]	0.050	−0.007[c]	0.067	−0.010[c]	0.067	−0.010[c]	0.080	−0.012[c]	0.068[d]	−0.010[c]	0.092	−0.013[c]	0.079[d]	−0.011[c]
Armenia	0.038	−0.006[c,d]	0.050	−0.007[c]	0.067	−0.010[c]	0.067	−0.010[c]	0.080	−0.012[c]	0.068[d]	−0.010[c]	0.091	−0.013[c]	0.079[d]	−0.011[c]
Sri Lanka	0.038	−0.006[c,d]	0.050	−0.007[c]	0.067	−0.010[c]	0.067	−0.010[c]	0.080	−0.012[c]	0.068[d]	−0.010[c]	0.091	−0.013[c]	0.079[d]	−0.011[c]
Jordan	0.038	−0.006[c,d]	0.051	−0.007[c]	0.067	−0.010[c]	0.067	−0.010[c]	0.080	−0.012[c]	0.068[d]	−0.010[c]	0.090	−0.013[c]	0.078[d]	−0.011[c]
Albania	0.038	−0.006[c,d]	0.051	−0.007[c]	0.068	−0.010[c]	0.067	−0.010[c]	0.079	−0.012[c]	0.068[d]	−0.010[c]	0.089	−0.013[c]	0.078[d]	−0.011[c]
Indonesia	0.038	−0.006[c,d]	0.051	−0.007[c]	0.068	−0.010[c]	0.067	−0.010[c]	0.079	−0.012[c]	0.068[d]	−0.010[c]	0.089	−0.013[c]	0.078[d]	−0.011[c]
Jamaica	0.038	−0.006[c,d]	0.051	−0.007[c]	0.068	−0.010[c]	0.067	−0.010[c]	0.079	−0.012[c]	0.068[d]	−0.010[c]	0.089	−0.013[c]	0.078[d]	−0.011[c]
Zimbabwe	0.038	−0.006[c,d]	0.051	−0.007[c]	0.068	−0.010[c]	0.067	−0.010[c]	0.079	−0.012[c]	0.068[d]	−0.010[c]	0.089	−0.013[c]	0.078[d]	−0.011[c]
Guinea	0.038	−0.006[c,d]	0.051	−0.007[c]	0.068	−0.010[c]	0.067	−0.010[c]	0.079	−0.012[c]	0.069[d]	−0.010[c]	0.088	−0.013[c]	0.078[d]	−0.011[c]
Syria	0.038	−0.006[c,d]	0.051	−0.008[c]	0.068	−0.010[c]	0.068	−0.010[c]	0.079	−0.012[c]	0.069[d]	−0.010[c]	0.088	−0.013[c]	0.078[d]	−0.011[c]
Georgia	0.038	−0.006[c,d]	0.051	−0.008[c]	0.068	−0.010[c]	0.068	−0.010[c]	0.079	−0.012[c]	0.069[d]	−0.010[c]	0.088	−0.013[c]	0.078[d]	−0.011[c]

(continued)

Table 6.12 (continued)

	Food, beverage and tobacco		Clothing and footwear		Gross rent, fuel and power		House furnishing and operations		Medical care		Transport and communication		Recreation[b]		Other	
	Slutsky	Cournot	Slutsky	Cournot	Slutsky	Cournot	Slutsky	Cournot	Slutsky	Cournot	Slutsky	Cournot	Slutsky	Cournot	Slutsky	Cournot
Middle-income country																
Ukraine	0.037	−0.006[c,d]	0.052	−0.008[c]	0.068	−0.010[c]	0.068	−0.010[c]	0.078	−0.012[c]	0.069[d]	−0.010[c]	0.086	−0.013[c]	0.077[d]	−0.011[c]
Philippines	0.037	−0.006[c,d]	0.052	−0.008[c]	0.068	−0.010[c]	0.068	−0.010[c]	0.078	−0.012[c]	0.069[d]	−0.010[c]	0.086	−0.013[c]	0.077[d]	−0.011[c]
Peru	0.037	−0.006[c,d]	0.052	−0.008[c]	0.068	−0.010[c]	0.068	−0.010[c]	0.078	−0.012[c]	0.069[d]	−0.010[c]	0.086	−0.013[c]	0.077[d]	−0.011[c]
Botswana	0.037	−0.006[c,d]	0.052	−0.008[c]	0.068	−0.010[c]	0.068	−0.010[c]	0.078	−0.012[c]	0.069[d]	−0.010[c]	0.086	−0.013[c]	0.077[d]	−0.011[c]
Thailand	0.037	−0.006[c,d]	0.052	−0.008[c]	0.068	−0.010[c]	0.068	−0.010[c]	0.078	−0.012[c]	0.069[d]	−0.010[c]	0.085	−0.013[c]	0.077[d]	−0.011[c]
Morocco	0.037	−0.005[c,d]	0.052	−0.008[c]	0.068	−0.010[c]	0.068	−0.010[c]	0.078	−0.012[c]	0.069[d]	−0.010[c]	0.085	−0.013[c]	0.077[d]	−0.011[c]
Venezuela	0.037	−0.005[c,d]	0.052	−0.008[c]	0.068	−0.010[c]	0.068	−0.010[c]	0.078	−0.012[c]	0.069[d]	−0.010[c]	0.085	−0.013[c]	0.077[d]	−0.011[c]
Macedonia	0.037	−0.005[c,d]	0.052	−0.008[c]	0.068	−0.010[c]	0.068	−0.010[c]	0.078	−0.012[c]	0.069[d]	−0.010[c]	0.085	−0.013[c]	0.077[d]	−0.012[c]
Belize	0.037	−0.005[c,d]	0.052	−0.008[c]	0.069	−0.010[c]	0.068	−0.010[c]	0.078	−0.012[c]	0.069[d]	−0.010[c]	0.085	−0.013[c]	0.077[d]	−0.012[c]
Egypt	0.037	−0.005[c,d]	0.052	−0.008[c]	0.069	−0.010[c]	0.068	−0.010[c]	0.078	−0.012[c]	0.069[d]	−0.010[c]	0.085	−0.013[c]	0.077[d]	−0.012[c]
St. Vincent and Grenadines	0.037	−0.005[c,d]	0.052	−0.008[c]	0.069	−0.010[c]	0.068	−0.010[c]	0.078	−0.012[c]	0.069[d]	−0.010[c]	0.085	−0.013[c]	0.077[d]	−0.012[c]
Swaziland	0.036	−0.005[c,d]	0.052	−0.008[c]	0.069	−0.010[c]	0.068	−0.010[c]	0.078	−0.012[c]	0.069[d]	−0.010[c]	0.084	−0.013[c]	0.077[d]	−0.012[c]
Lebanon	0.036	−0.005[c,d]	0.052	−0.008[c]	0.069	−0.010[c]	0.069	−0.010[c]	0.078	−0.012[c]	0.069[d]	−0.010[c]	0.084	−0.013[c]	0.077[d]	−0.012[c]
Belarus	0.036	−0.005[c,d]	0.052	−0.008[c]	0.069	−0.010[c]	0.069	−0.010[c]	0.078	−0.012[c]	0.069[d]	−0.010[c]	0.084	−0.013[c]	0.077[d]	−0.012[c]
Kazakhstan	0.036	−0.005[c,d]	0.052	−0.008[c]	0.069	−0.010[c]	0.069	−0.010[c]	0.078	−0.012[c]	0.069[d]	−0.010[c]	0.084	−0.013[c]	0.077[d]	−0.012[c]
Dominica	0.036	−0.005[c,d]	0.052	−0.008[c]	0.069	−0.010[c]	0.069	−0.010[c]	0.078	−0.012[c]	0.069[d]	−0.010[c]	0.084	−0.013[c]	0.077[d]	−0.012[c]
Latvia	0.036	−0.005[c,d]	0.053	−0.008[c]	0.069	−0.010[c]	0.069	−0.010[c]	0.078	−0.012[c]	0.070[d]	−0.010[c]	0.084	−0.013[c]	0.077[d]	−0.012[c]
St. Lucia	0.036	−0.005[c,d]	0.053	−0.008[c]	0.069	−0.010[c]	0.069	−0.010[c]	0.078	−0.012[c]	0.070[d]	−0.010[c]	0.084	−0.013[c]	0.077[d]	−0.012[c]
Brazil	0.036	−0.005[c,d]	0.053	−0.008[c]	0.069	−0.010[c]	0.069	−0.010[c]	0.078	−0.012[c]	0.070[d]	−0.010[c]	0.084	−0.013[c]	0.077[d]	−0.012[c]

Bulgaria	0.036	−0.005[c,d]	0.053	−0.008[c]	0.069	−0.010[c]	0.069	−0.010[c]	0.078	−0.012[c]	0.070[d]	−0.010[c]	0.084	−0.013[c]	0.077[d]	−0.012[c]
Russia	0.036	−0.005[c,d]	0.053	−0.008[c]	0.069	−0.010[c]	0.069	−0.010[c]	0.077	−0.012[c]	0.070[d]	−0.010[c]	0.083	−0.013[c]	0.077[d]	−0.012[c]
Fiji	0.035	−0.005[c,d]	0.053	−0.008[c]	0.069	−0.010[c]	0.069	−0.010[c]	0.077	−0.012[c]	0.070[d]	−0.011[c]	0.083	−0.013[c]	0.077[d]	−0.012[c]
Grenada	0.035	−0.005[c,d]	0.053	−0.008[c]	0.069	−0.010[c]	0.069	−0.010[c]	0.077	−0.012[c]	0.070[d]	−0.011[c]	0.083	−0.013[c]	0.077[d]	−0.012[c]
Turkey	0.035	−0.005[c,d]	0.053	−0.008[c]	0.069	−0.010[c]	0.069	−0.010[c]	0.077	−0.012[c]	0.070[d]	−0.011[c]	0.083	−0.013[c]	0.077[d]	−0.012[c]
Lithuania	0.035	−0.005[c,d]	0.053	−0.008[c]	0.069	−0.010[c]	0.069	−0.010[c]	0.077	−0.012[c]	0.070[d]	−0.011[c]	0.083	−0.013[c]	0.077[d]	−0.012[c]
Romania	0.035	−0.005[c,d]	0.053	−0.008[c]	0.069	−0.010[c]	0.069	−0.010[c]	0.077	−0.012[c]	0.070[d]	−0.011[c]	0.083	−0.013[c]	0.077[d]	−0.012[c]
Iran	0.035	−0.005[c,d]	0.053	−0.008[c]	0.069	−0.010[c]	0.069	−0.010[c]	0.077	−0.012[c]	0.070[d]	−0.011[c]	0.083	−0.013[c]	0.077[d]	−0.012[c]
Mexico	0.035	−0.005 [d]	0.053	−0.008	0.069	−0.011	0.069	−0.010	0.077	−0.012[c]	0.070[d]	−0.011[c]	0.083	−0.013[c]	0.077[d]	−0.012
Bahrain	0.034	−0.005[d]	0.053	−0.008	0.069	−0.011	0.069	−0.010	0.077	−0.012	0.070[d]	−0.011	0.083	−0.013	0.077[d]	−0.012
Chile	0.034	−0.005[d]	0.053	−0.008	0.069	−0.011	0.069	−0.011	0.077	−0.012	0.070[d]	−0.011	0.083	−0.013	0.077[d]	−0.012
Antigua and Barbuda	0.034	−0.005[d]	0.053	−0.008	0.070	−0.011	0.069	−0.011	0.077	−0.012	0.070[d]	−0.011	0.083	−0.013	0.077[d]	−0.012
Poland	0.034	−0.005[d]	0.054	−0.008	0.070	−0.011	0.069	−0.011	0.077[d]	−0.012	0.070[d]	−0.011	0.082	−0.013	0.077[d]	−0.012
Trinidad and Tobago	0.034	−0.005[d]	0.054	−0.008	0.070	−0.011	0.069	−0.011	0.077[d]	−0.012	0.070[d]	−0.011	0.082	−0.013	0.077[d]	−0.012
Estonia	0.034	−0.005[d]	0.054	−0.008	0.070	−0.011	0.070	−0.011	0.077[d]	−0.012	0.070[d]	−0.011	0.082	−0.013	0.077[d]	−0.012
Gabon	0.033	−0.005[d]	0.054	−0.008	0.070	−0.011	0.070	−0.011	0.077[d]	−0.012	0.070[d]	−0.011	0.082	−0.013	0.077[d]	−0.012
Tunisia	0.033	−0.005[d]	0.054	−0.008	0.070	−0.011	0.070	−0.011	0.077[d]	−0.012	0.070[d]	−0.011	0.082	−0.013	0.077[d]	−0.012
St. Kitts and Nevis	0.033	−0.005[d]	0.054	−0.008	0.070	−0.011	0.070	−0.011	0.077[d]	−0.012	0.070[d]	−0.011	0.082	−0.012	0.077[d]	−0.012
Uruguay	0.033	−0.005[d]	0.054	−0.008	0.070	−0.011	0.070	−0.011	0.077[d]	−0.012	0.071[d]	−0.011	0.082	−0.012	0.077[d]	−0.012
Slovakia	0.033	−0.005[d]	0.054	−0.008	0.070	−0.011	0.070	−0.011	0.077[d]	−0.012	0.071[d]	−0.011	0.082	−0.012	0.077[d]	−0.012
Hungary	0.032	−0.005[d]	0.054	−0.008	0.070	−0.011	0.070	−0.011	0.077[d]	−0.012	0.071[d]	−0.011	0.082	−0.012	0.077[d]	−0.012
Argentina	0.031	−0.005[d]	0.054	−0.008	0.070	−0.011	0.070	−0.011	0.077[d]	−0.012	0.071[d]	−0.011	0.081	−0.013	0.077[d]	−0.012
Oman	0.030	−0.005	0.055	−0.008	0.071	−0.011	0.070	−0.011	0.077[d]	−0.012	0.071[d]	−0.011	0.081	−0.013	0.077[d]	−0.012
Qatar	0.030	−0.005	0.055[d]	−0.008	0.071[d]	−0.011	0.071	−0.011	0.077[d]	−0.012	0.071[d]	−0.011	0.081	−0.013	0.077[d]	−0.012
Slovenia	0.029	−0.005	0.055[d]	−0.008	0.071[d]	−0.011	0.071	−0.011	0.077[d]	−0.012	0.071[d]	−0.011[d]	0.081	−0.013	0.077[d]	−0.012

(continued)

Table 6.12 (continued)

	Food, beverage and tobacco		Clothing and footwear		Gross rent, fuel and power		House furnishing and operations		Medical care		Transport and communication		Recreation[b]		Other	
	Slutsky	Cournot	Slutsky	Cournot	Slutsky	Cournot	Slutsky	Cournot	Slutsky	Cournot	Slutsky	Cournot	Slutsky	Cournot	Slutsky	Cournot
High-income country																
Czech Republic	0.029	−0.004	0.055[d]	−0.008	0.071[d]	−0.011	0.071	−0.011	0.077[d]	−0.012[d]	0.071[d]	−0.011[d]	0.081	−0.013	0.077[d]	−0.012[d]
Greece	0.028	−0.004	0.055[d]	−0.009[d]	0.071[d]	−0.011[d]	0.071	−0.011[d]	0.077[d]	−0.012[d]	0.072[d]	−0.011[d]	0.081	−0.013[d]	0.077[d]	−0.012[d]
Korea	0.027	−0.004	0.055[d]	−0.009[d]	0.071[d]	−0.011[d]	0.071	−0.011[d]	0.077[d]	−0.012[d]	0.072[d]	−0.011[d]	0.081	−0.013[d]	0.077[d]	−0.012[d]
Portugal	0.027	−0.004	0.055[d]	−0.009[d]	0.071[d]	−0.011[d]	0.071	−0.011[d]	0.077[d]	−0.012[d]	0.072[d]	−0.011[d]	0.081	−0.013[d]	0.077[d]	−0.012[d]
Spain	0.027	−0.004	0.055[d]	−0.009[d]	0.071[d]	−0.011[d]	0.071[d]	−0.011[d]	0.077[d]	−0.012[d]	0.072[d]	−0.011[d]	0.081	−0.013[d]	0.077[d]	−0.012[d]
Ireland	0.026	−0.004	0.055[d]	−0.009[d]	0.071[d]	−0.011[d]	0.071[d]	−0.011[d]	0.077[d]	−0.012[d]	0.072[d]	−0.011[d]	0.081	−0.013[d]	0.077[d]	−0.012[d]
Singapore	0.026	−0.004	0.056[d]	−0.009[d]	0.071[d]	−0.011[d]	0.071[d]	−0.011[d]	0.077[d]	−0.012[d]	0.072[d]	−0.011[d]	0.081	−0.013[d]	0.077[d]	−0.012[d]
Mauritius	0.025	−0.004	0.056[d]	−0.009[d]	0.072[d]	−0.011[d]	0.071[d]	−0.011[d]	0.077[d]	−0.012[d]	0.072[d]	−0.011[d]	0.081[d]	−0.013[d]	0.077[d]	−0.012[d]
Israel	0.025	−0.004	0.056[d]	−0.009[d]	0.072[d]	−0.011[d]	0.071[d]	−0.011[d]	0.077[d]	−0.012[d]	0.072[d]	−0.011[d]	0.081[d]	−0.013[d]	0.077[d]	−0.012[d]
New Zealand	0.024	−0.004	0.056[d]	−0.009[d]	0.072[d]	−0.011[d]	0.072[d]	−0.011[d]	0.077[d]	−0.012[d]	0.072[d]	−0.011[d]	0.081[d]	−0.013[d]	0.077[d]	−0.012[d]
Finland	0.024	−0.004	0.056[d]	−0.009[d]	0.072[d]	−0.011[d]	0.072[d]	−0.011[d]	0.077[d]	−0.012[d]	0.072[d]	−0.011[d]	0.081[d]	−0.013[d]	0.077[d]	−0.012[d]
Bahamas	0.024	−0.004	0.056[d]	−0.009[d]	0.072[d]	−0.011[d]	0.072[d]	−0.011[d]	0.077[d]	−0.012[d]	0.072[d]	−0.011[d]	0.081[d]	−0.013[d]	0.077[d]	−0.012[d]
Sweden	0.022	−0.003	0.056[d]	−0.009[d]	0.072[d]	−0.011[d]	0.072[d]	−0.011[d]	0.078[d]	−0.012[d]	0.072[d]	−0.011[d]	0.081[d]	−0.013[d]	0.077[d]	−0.012[d]
Netherlands	0.022	−0.003	0.056[d]	−0.009[d]	0.072[d]	−0.011[d]	0.072[d]	−0.011[d]	0.078[d]	−0.012[d]	0.072[d]	−0.011[d]	0.081[d]	−0.013[d]	0.077[d]	−0.012[d]
France	0.021	−0.003	0.056[d]	−0.009[d]	0.072[d]	−0.011[d]	0.072[d]	−0.011[d]	0.078[d]	−0.012[d]	0.073[d]	−0.011[d]	0.081[d]	−0.013[d]	0.077[d]	−0.012[d]
United Kingdom	0.021	−0.003	0.056[d]	−0.009[d]	0.072[d]	−0.011[d]	0.072[d]	−0.011[d]	0.078[d]	−0.012[d]	0.073[d]	−0.011[d]	0.081[d]	−0.013[d]	0.077[d]	−0.012[d]
Belgium	0.020	−0.003	0.056[d]	−0.009[d]	0.072[d]	−0.011[d]	0.072[d]	−0.011[d]	0.078[d]	−0.012[d]	0.073[d]	−0.011[d]	0.081[d]	−0.013[d]	0.077[d]	−0.012[d]
Norway	0.020	−0.003	0.056[d]	−0.009[d]	0.072[d]	−0.011[d]	0.072[d]	−0.011[d]	0.078[d]	−0.012[d]	0.073[d]	−0.011[d]	0.081[d]	−0.013[d]	0.077[d]	−0.012[d]

Italy	0.020	−0.003	0.056[d]	−0.009[d]	0.072[d]	−0.011[d]	0.072[d]	−0.011[d]	0.078[d]	−0.012[d]	0.073[d]	−0.011[d]	0.081[d]	−0.013[d]	0.077[d]	−0.012[d]
Austria	0.019	−0.003	0.056[d]	−0.009[d]	0.072[d]	−0.011[d]	0.072[d]	−0.011[d]	0.078[d]	−0.012[d]	0.073[d]	−0.011[d]	0.081[d]	−0.013[d]	0.077[d]	−0.012[d]
Germany	0.019	−0.003	0.056[d]	−0.009[d]	0.072[d]	−0.011[d]	0.072[d]	−0.011[d]	0.078[d]	−0.012[d]	0.073[d]	−0.011[d]	0.081[d]	−0.013[d]	0.077[d]	−0.012[d]
Australia	0.019	−0.003	0.057[d]	−0.009[d]	0.072[d]	−0.011[d]	0.072[d]	−0.011[d]	0.078[d]	−0.012[d]	0.073[d]	−0.011[d]	0.081[d]	−0.013[d]	0.077[d]	−0.012[d]
Japan	0.018	−0.003	0.057[d]	−0.009[d]	0.072[d]	−0.011[d]	0.072[d]	−0.011[d]	0.078[d]	−0.012[d]	0.073[d]	−0.011[d]	0.081[d]	−0.013[d]	0.077[d]	−0.012[d]
Canada	0.018	−0.003	0.057[d]	−0.009[d]	0.072[d]	−0.011[d]	0.072[d]	−0.011[d]	0.078[d]	−0.012[d]	0.073[d]	−0.011[d]	0.081[d]	−0.013[d]	0.077[d]	−0.012[d]
Bermuda	0.017	−0.003[d]	0.057[d]	−0.009[d]	0.073[d]	−0.011[d]	0.072[d]	−0.011[d]	0.078[d]	−0.012[d]	0.073[d]	−0.011[d]	0.081[d]	−0.013[d]	0.077[d]	−0.012[d]
Switzerland	0.016	−0.003[d]	0.057[d]	−0.009[d]	0.073[d]	−0.011[d]	0.072[d]	−0.011[d]	0.078[d]	−0.012[d]	0.073[d]	−0.012[d]	0.081[d]	−0.013[d]	0.077[d]	−0.012[d]
Barbados	0.016	−0.003[d]	0.057[d]	−0.009[d]	0.073[d]	−0.011[d]	0.072[d]	−0.011[d]	0.078[d]	−0.012[d]	0.073[d]	−0.012[d]	0.081[d]	−0.013[d]	0.077[d]	−0.012[d]
Hong Kong	0.016	−0.003[d]	0.057[d]	−0.009[d]	0.073[d]	−0.011[d]	0.072[d]	−0.011[d]	0.078[d]	−0.012[d]	0.073[d]	−0.012[d]	0.081[d]	−0.013[d]	0.077[d]	−0.012[d]
Iceland	0.016[d]	−0.002[d]	0.057[d]	−0.009[d]	0.073[d]	−0.011[d]	0.073[d]	−0.011[d]	0.078[d]	−0.012[d]	0.073[d]	−0.012[d]	0.081[d]	−0.013[d]	0.077[d]	−0.012[d]
Denmark	0.016[d]	−0.002[d]	0.057[d]	−0.009[d]	0.073[d]	−0.011[d]	0.073[d]	−0.011[d]	0.078[d]	−0.012[d]	0.073[d]	−0.012[d]	0.081[d]	−0.013[d]	0.077[d]	−0.012[d]
Luxembourg	0.008[d]	−0.001[c,d]	0.057[d]	−0.009[d]	0.073[d]	−0.012[d]	0.073[d]	−0.012[d]	0.078[d]	−0.012[d]	0.074[d]	−0.012[d]	0.081[d]	−0.013[d]	0.078[d]	−0.012[d]
United States	0.007	−0.001[c]	0.057	−0.009	0.073	−0.012	0.073	−0.012	0.078	−0.012	0.074	−0.012	0.081	−0.013	0.078	−0.012[d]
Low-income average	0.039	−0.006	0.049	−0.007	0.067	−0.010	0.066	−0.009	0.087	−0.012	0.068	−0.010	0.117	−0.017	0.084	−0.012
Middle-income average	0.035	−0.005	0.053	−0.008	0.069	−0.010	0.069	−0.010	0.078	−0.012	0.070	−0.011	0.083	−0.013	0.077	−0.012
High-income average	0.021	−0.003	0.056	−0.009	0.072	−0.011	0.072	−0.011	0.078	−0.012	0.073	−0.011	0.081	−0.013	0.077	−0.012

[a]Countries are reported based on ascending per capita real income levels
[b]As the estimated budget share was negative for Tanzania we do not report the elasticity for this country
[c]Elasticity estimate is not significantly different from zero at 0.05 level
[d]Elasticity estimate is not significantly different from the point estimate of the United States at 0.05 level

Table 6.13 Slutsky and Cournot cross-price elasticities with change in transport and communication price, 114 countries in 1996[a]

	Food, beverage and tobacco		Clothing and footwear		Gross rent, fuel and power		House furnishing and operations		Medical care		Education		Recreation[b]		Other	
	Slutsky	Cournot	Slutsky	Cournot	Slutsky	Cournot	Slutsky	Cournot	Slutsky	Cournot	Slutsky	Cournot	Slutsky	Cournot	Slutsky	Cournot
Low-income country																
Tanzania	0.047[d]	0.006	0.054	0.007	0.080	0.010	0.079	0.010	0.172[c,d]	0.022[c,d]	0.064	0.008			0.152[c,d]	0.019[c,d]
Nigeria	0.050	0.005	0.059	0.006	0.085	0.008	0.085	0.008	0.139[c]	0.013	0.070	0.006	0.419	0.039	0.131[c,d]	0.012[c,d]
Tajikistan	0.052	0.004	0.062	0.005	0.088	0.007	0.087	0.007	0.133	0.011	0.073	0.006	0.265	0.021	0.126[c,d]	0.010[c,d]
Zambia	0.052	0.004	0.062	0.005	0.088	0.007	0.088	0.007	0.132	0.010	0.073	0.006	0.252	0.020	0.126[c,d]	0.010[c,d]
Yemen	0.052	0.004	0.062	0.005	0.088	0.007	0.088	0.007	0.132	0.010	0.073	0.006	0.251	0.019	0.126[c,d]	0.010[c,d]
Malawi	0.053	0.004	0.064	0.004	0.090	0.006	0.089	0.006	0.129	0.009	0.075	0.005	0.219	0.015	0.124[c,d]	0.009[c,d]
Madagascar	0.053	0.004	0.064	0.004	0.090	0.006	0.089	0.006	0.129	0.009	0.075	0.005	0.218	0.015	0.124[c,d]	0.009[c,d]
Mali	0.053	0.004	0.064	0.004	0.090	0.006	0.090	0.006	0.129	0.009	0.075	0.005	0.212	0.014	0.124[c,d]	0.008[c,d]
Mongolia	0.054	0.004	0.064	0.004	0.090	0.006	0.090	0.006	0.129	0.009	0.075	0.005	0.210	0.014	0.124[c,d]	0.008[c,d]
Benin	0.055	0.003	0.068	0.004	0.094	0.005	0.093	0.005	0.126	0.007	0.079	0.004	0.176	0.009	0.122[c,d]	0.006[c,d]
Kenya	0.056	0.003	0.069	0.003	0.095	0.004	0.095	0.004	0.125	0.006	0.081	0.004	0.168	0.008	0.122[c]	0.006[c,d]
Sierra Leone	0.057	0.002	0.070	0.003	0.096	0.004	0.096	0.004	0.125	0.005	0.082	0.003	0.162	0.007	0.122[c]	0.005
Nepal	0.057	0.002	0.070	0.003	0.096	0.004	0.096	0.004	0.125	0.005	0.082	0.003	0.162	0.007	0.122[c]	0.005
Turkmenistan	0.057	0.002	0.071	0.003	0.097	0.004	0.097	0.004	0.125	0.005	0.083	0.003	0.160	0.006	0.122[c,d]	0.005[c,d]
Congo	0.058	0.002	0.072	0.002	0.098	0.003	0.098	0.003	0.125	0.004	0.085	0.003	0.156	0.005	0.122[c,d]	0.004[c,d]
Senegal	0.058	0.002	0.073	0.002	0.099	0.003	0.099	0.003	0.125	0.004	0.086	0.003	0.154	0.005	0.122	0.004

Vietnam	0.058	0.002	0.073	0.002	0.100	0.003	0.099	0.003	0.125	0.004	0.086	0.002	0.153	0.004	0.122	0.004
Bangladesh	0.058	0.002	0.074	0.002	0.100	0.003	0.099	0.003	0.125	0.004	0.086	0.002	0.153	0.004	0.122	0.003
Pakistan	0.059	0.001	0.076	0.002	0.102	0.002	0.102	0.002	0.125	0.003	0.089	0.002	0.149	0.003	0.123	0.003
Azerbaijan	0.060	0.001	0.077	0.001	0.103	0.002	0.103	0.002	0.125	0.002	0.090	0.002	0.147	0.003	0.123	0.002
Cote d'Ivoire	0.060	0.001	0.077	0.001	0.104	0.002	0.103	0.002	0.125	0.002	0.090	0.001	0.147	0.002	0.123	0.002
Paraguay	0.060	0.001	0.077	0.001	0.104	0.002	0.103	0.002	0.126	0.002	0.091	0.001	0.147	0.002	0.123	0.002
Uzbekistan	0.060	0.001	0.078	0.001	0.105	0.001	0.104	0.001	0.126	0.002	0.091	0.001	0.146	0.002	0.124	0.002
Kyrgyzstan	0.060	0.001	0.078	0.001	0.105	0.001	0.104	0.001	0.126	0.002	0.091	0.001	0.146	0.002	0.124	0.002
Cameroon	0.060	0.001	0.078	0.001	0.105	0.001	0.104	0.001	0.126	0.002	0.092	0.001	0.146	0.002	0.124	0.002
Moldova	0.060	0.001	0.078	0.001	0.105	0.001	0.104	0.001	0.126	0.002	0.092	0.001	0.146	0.002	0.124	0.002
Bolivia	0.060	0.001	0.079	0.001	0.105	0.001	0.105	0.001	0.126	0.001	0.092	0.001	0.145	0.002	0.124	0.001
Ecuador	0.061	0.001	0.079	0.001	0.106	0.001	0.105	0.001	0.126	0.001	0.093	0.001	0.145	0.001	0.124	0.001
Armenia	0.061	0.000	0.080	0.001	0.106	0.001	0.106	0.001	0.126	0.001	0.094	0.001	0.144	0.001	0.125	0.001
Sri Lanka	0.061	0.000	0.080	0.001	0.107	0.001	0.106	0.001	0.127	0.001	0.094	0.001	0.144	0.001	0.125	0.001
Jordan	0.061	0.000	0.081	0.000	0.107	0.000	0.107	0.000	0.127	0.001	0.095	0.000	0.144	0.001	0.125	0.001
Albania	0.061	0.000	0.082	0.000	0.109	0.000	0.108	0.000	0.127	0.000	0.096	0.000	0.143	0.000	0.126	0.000
Indonesia	0.061	0.000	0.082	0.000	0.109	0.000	0.109	0.000	0.128	0.000	0.096	0.000	0.143	0.000	0.126	0.000
Jamaica	0.061	0.000	0.082	0.000	0.109	0.000	0.109	0.000	0.128	0.000	0.096	0.000	0.143	0.000	0.126	0.000
Zimbabwe	0.061	0.000	0.082	0.000	0.109	0.000	0.109	0.000	0.128	0.000	0.097	0.000	0.143	0.000	0.126	0.000
Guinea	0.061	0.000	0.083	0.000	0.110	0.000	0.109	0.000	0.128	0.000	0.097	0.000	0.143	0.000	0.126	0.000
Syria	0.062	0.000	0.083	0.000	0.111	0.000	0.110	0.000	0.128	−0.001	0.098	0.000	0.143	−0.001	0.127	−0.001
Georgia	0.062	0.000	0.084	0.000	0.111	0.000	0.110	0.000	0.128	−0.001	0.098	0.000	0.143	−0.001	0.127	−0.001

(continued)

Table 6.13 (continued)

	Food, beverage and tobacco		Clothing and footwear		Gross rent, fuel and power		House furnishing and operations		Medical care		Education		Recreation[b]		Other	
	Slutsky	Cournot	Slutsky	Cournot	Slutsky	Cournot	Slutsky	Cournot	Slutsky	Cournot	Slutsky	Cournot	Slutsky	Cournot	Slutsky	Cournot
Middle-income country																
Ukraine	0.062	−0.001	0.085	−0.001	0.112	−0.001	0.112	−0.001	0.129	−0.001	0.100	−0.001	0.143	−0.001	0.128	−0.001
Philippines	0.062	−0.001	0.086	−0.001	0.113	−0.001	0.113	−0.001	0.130	−0.001	0.101	−0.001	0.143	−0.002	0.129	−0.001
Peru	0.062	−0.001	0.086	−0.001	0.114	−0.001	0.113	−0.001	0.130	−0.002	0.101	−0.001	0.143	−0.002	0.129	−0.002
Botswana	0.062	−0.001	0.086	−0.001	0.114	−0.001	0.114	−0.001	0.130	−0.002	0.102	−0.001	0.143	−0.002	0.129	−0.002
Thailand	0.062	−0.001	0.087	−0.001	0.114	−0.001	0.114	−0.001	0.130	−0.002	0.102	−0.001	0.143	−0.002	0.129	−0.002
Morocco	0.062	−0.001	0.087	−0.001	0.115	−0.002	0.114	−0.002	0.131	−0.002	0.102	−0.001	0.143	−0.002	0.129	−0.002
Venezuela	0.062	−0.001	0.087	−0.001	0.115	−0.002	0.114	−0.002	0.131	−0.002	0.102	−0.001	0.143	−0.002	0.129	−0.002
Macedonia	0.062	−0.001	0.088	−0.001	0.115	−0.002	0.115	−0.002	0.131	−0.002	0.103	−0.002	0.143	−0.002	0.130	−0.002
Belize	0.062	−0.001	0.088	−0.001	0.116	−0.002	0.115	−0.002	0.131	−0.002	0.103	−0.002	0.143	−0.002	0.130	−0.002
Egypt	0.062	−0.001	0.088	−0.001	0.116	−0.002	0.115	−0.002	0.131	−0.002	0.103	−0.002	0.143	−0.002	0.130	−0.002
St. Vincent and Grenadines	0.062	−0.001	0.088	−0.001	0.116	−0.002	0.115	−0.002	0.131	−0.002	0.103	−0.002	0.143	−0.002	0.130	−0.002
Swaziland	0.062	−0.001	0.089	−0.002	0.116	−0.002	0.116	−0.002	0.132	−0.002	0.104	−0.002	0.143	−0.003	0.131	−0.002
Lebanon	0.062	−0.001	0.089	−0.002	0.117	−0.002	0.116	−0.002	0.132	−0.003	0.105	−0.002	0.143	−0.003	0.131	−0.003
Belarus	0.062	−0.001	0.089	−0.002	0.117	−0.002	0.117	−0.002	0.132	−0.003	0.105	−0.002	0.143	−0.003	0.131	−0.003
Kazakhstan	0.062	−0.001	0.089	−0.002	0.117	−0.002	0.117	−0.002	0.132	−0.003	0.105	−0.002	0.143	−0.003	0.131	−0.003
Dominica	0.062	−0.001	0.089	−0.002	0.117	−0.002	0.117	−0.002	0.132	−0.003	0.105	−0.002	0.143	−0.003	0.131	−0.003
Latvia	0.061	−0.001	0.090	−0.002	0.118	−0.003	0.118	−0.003	0.133	−0.003	0.106	−0.002	0.143	−0.003	0.132	−0.003
St. Lucia	0.061	−0.001	0.090	−0.002	0.118	−0.003	0.118	−0.003	0.133	−0.003	0.106	−0.002	0.143	−0.003	0.132	−0.003
Brazil	0.061	−0.001	0.090	−0.002	0.118	−0.003	0.118	−0.003	0.133	−0.003	0.106	−0.002	0.143	−0.003	0.132	−0.003
Bulgaria	0.061	−0.001	0.090	−0.002	0.118	−0.003	0.118	−0.003	0.133	−0.003	0.106	−0.002	0.144	−0.003	0.132	−0.003

Russia	0.061	−0.001	0.091	−0.002	0.119	−0.003	0.118	−0.003	0.133	−0.003	0.107	−0.003	0.144	−0.003	0.132	−0.003
Fiji	0.061	−0.002	0.091	−0.002	0.119	−0.003	0.119	−0.003	0.134	−0.003	0.107	−0.003	0.144	−0.004	0.133	−0.003
Grenada	0.061	−0.002	0.091	−0.002	0.119	−0.003	0.119	−0.003	0.134	−0.003	0.107	−0.003	0.144	−0.004	0.133	−0.003
Turkey	0.061	−0.002	0.092	−0.002	0.120	−0.003	0.119	−0.003	0.134	−0.003	0.108	−0.003	0.144	−0.004	0.133	−0.003
Lithuania	0.061	−0.002	0.092	−0.002	0.120	−0.003	0.120	−0.003	0.134	−0.004	0.108	−0.003	0.144	−0.004	0.133	−0.004
Romania	0.061	−0.002	0.092	−0.003	0.120	−0.003	0.120	−0.003	0.134	−0.004	0.108	−0.003	0.144	−0.004	0.133	−0.004
Iran	0.060	−0.002	0.093	−0.003	0.121	−0.003	0.121	−0.003	0.135	−0.004	0.109	−0.003	0.144	−0.004	0.134	−0.004
Mexico	0.060	−0.002	0.093	−0.003	0.121	−0.004	0.121	−0.004	0.135	−0.004	0.109	−0.003	0.145	−0.004	0.134	−0.004
Bahrain	0.060	−0.002	0.093	−0.003	0.122	−0.004	0.121	−0.004	0.135	−0.004	0.110	−0.003	0.145	−0.004	0.134	−0.004
Chile	0.060	−0.002	0.094	−0.003	0.122	−0.004	0.122	−0.004	0.136	−0.004	0.110	−0.003	0.145	−0.004	0.134	−0.004
Antigua and Barbuda	0.060	−0.002	0.094	−0.003	0.122	−0.004	0.122	−0.004	0.136	−0.004	0.110	−0.003	0.145	−0.004	0.135	−0.004
Poland	0.060	−0.002	0.094	−0.003	0.123	−0.004	0.122	−0.004	0.136	−0.004	0.111	−0.004	0.145	−0.005	0.135	−0.004
Trinidad and Tobago	0.060	−0.002	0.095	−0.003	0.123	−0.004	0.123	−0.004	0.136	−0.004	0.111	−0.004	0.145	−0.005	0.135	−0.004
Estonia	0.059	−0.002	0.095	−0.003	0.123	−0.004	0.123	−0.004	0.137	−0.005	0.112	−0.004	0.145	−0.005	0.136	−0.005
Gabon	0.059	−0.002	0.095	−0.003	0.124	−0.004	0.123	−0.004	0.137	−0.005	0.112	−0.004	0.145	−0.005	0.136	−0.005
Tunisia	0.059	−0.002	0.095	−0.003	0.124	−0.004	0.124	−0.004	0.137	−0.005	0.112	−0.004	0.146	−0.005	0.136	−0.005
St. Kitts and Nevis	0.059	−0.002	0.096	−0.003	0.124	−0.004	0.124	−0.004	0.137	−0.005	0.112	−0.004	0.146	−0.005	0.136	−0.005
Uruguay	0.059	−0.002	0.096	−0.003	0.124	−0.004	0.124	−0.004	0.137	−0.005	0.113	−0.004	0.146	−0.005	0.136	−0.005
Slovakia	0.059	−0.002	0.096	−0.003	0.125	−0.004	0.124	−0.004	0.137	−0.005	0.113	−0.004	0.146	−0.005	0.136	−0.005
Hungary	0.058	−0.002	0.097	−0.004[d]	0.126	−0.005	0.126	−0.005	0.138	−0.005	0.114	−0.004	0.147	−0.006	0.138	−0.005
Argentina	0.056	−0.002	0.099	−0.004[d]	0.128	−0.005[d]	0.127	−0.005[d]	0.140	−0.006[d]	0.116	−0.005[d]	0.148	−0.006	0.139	−0.006[d]
Oman	0.055	−0.002	0.099	−0.004[d]	0.128	−0.006[d]	0.128	−0.006[d]	0.140	−0.006[d]	0.117	−0.005[d]	0.148	−0.006[d]	0.140	−0.006[d]
Qatar	0.054	−0.002	0.100	−0.004[d]	0.129	−0.006[d]	0.129	−0.006[d]	0.141	−0.006[d]	0.118	−0.005[d]	0.148	−0.007[d]	0.140	−0.006[d]
Slovenia	0.054	−0.002	0.101	−0.005[d]	0.130	−0.006[d]	0.129	−0.006[d]	0.142	−0.006[d]	0.118	−0.005[d]	0.149	−0.007[d]	0.141	−0.006[d]

(continued)

Table 6.13 (continued)

	Food, beverage and tobacco		Clothing and footwear		Gross rent, fuel and power		House furnishing and operations		Medical care		Education		Recreation[b]		Other	
	Slutsky	Cournot	Slutsky	Cournot	Slutsky	Cournot	Slutsky	Cournot	Slutsky	Cournot	Slutsky	Cournot	Slutsky	Cournot	Slutsky	Cournot
High-income country																
Czech Republic	0.053	−0.002	0.101	−0.005[d]	0.130	−0.006[d]	0.130	−0.006[d]	0.142	−0.007[d]	0.119	−0.006[d]	0.149	−0.007[d]	0.141	−0.007[d]
Greece	0.051	−0.002	0.102	−0.005[d]	0.132	−0.006[d]	0.131	−0.006[d]	0.143	−0.007[d]	0.120	−0.006[d]	0.150	−0.007[d]	0.142	−0.007[d]
Korea	0.051	−0.002	0.102	−0.005[d]	0.132	−0.006[d]	0.132	−0.006[d]	0.143	−0.007[d]	0.121	−0.006[d]	0.150	−0.007[d]	0.142	−0.007[d]
Portugal	0.050	−0.002	0.103	−0.005[d]	0.132	−0.007[d]	0.132	−0.007[d]	0.143	−0.007[d]	0.121	−0.006[d]	0.150	−0.007[d]	0.143	−0.007[d]
Spain	0.050	−0.002[c]	0.103	−0.005[d]	0.132	−0.007[d]	0.132	−0.007[d]	0.144	−0.007[d]	0.121	−0.006[d]	0.150	−0.007[d]	0.143	−0.007[d]
Ireland	0.049	−0.002[c]	0.103	−0.005[d]	0.133	−0.007[d]	0.132	−0.007[d]	0.144	−0.007[d]	0.122	−0.006[d]	0.151	−0.008[d]	0.143	−0.007[d]
Singapore	0.048	−0.002[c]	0.104	−0.005[d]	0.133	−0.007[d]	0.133	−0.007[d]	0.144	−0.007[d]	0.122	−0.006[d]	0.151	−0.008[d]	0.143	−0.007[d]
Mauritius	0.047	−0.002[c]	0.104	−0.005[c,d]	0.134	−0.007[c,d]	0.134	−0.007[d]	0.145	−0.008[d]	0.123	−0.006[d]	0.151	−0.008[d]	0.144	−0.008[d]
Israel	0.046	−0.002[c]	0.105	−0.006[c,d]	0.134	−0.007[c,d]	0.134	−0.007[c,d]	0.145	−0.008[c,d]	0.123	−0.007[c,d]	0.152	−0.008[d]	0.144[d]	−0.008[c,d]
New Zealand	0.046	−0.002[c]	0.105	−0.006[c,d]	0.135	−0.007[c,d]	0.134	−0.007[c,d]	0.145	−0.008[c,d]	0.124	−0.007[c,d]	0.152	−0.008[d]	0.145[d]	−0.008[c,d]
Finland	0.045	−0.002[c]	0.105	−0.006[c,d]	0.135	−0.007[c,d]	0.134	−0.007[c,d]	0.146	−0.008[c,d]	0.124	−0.007[c,d]	0.152	−0.008[d]	0.145[d]	−0.008[c,d]
Bahamas	0.045	−0.002[c]	0.105	−0.006[c,d]	0.135	−0.007[c,d]	0.135	−0.007[c,d]	0.146	−0.008[c,d]	0.124	−0.007[c,d]	0.152	−0.008[d]	0.145[d]	−0.008[c,d]
Sweden	0.042	−0.002[c]	0.106[d]	−0.006[c,d]	0.136	−0.008[c,d]	0.136	−0.008[c,d]	0.147[d]	−0.008[c,d]	0.125	−0.007[c,d]	0.153	−0.009[c,d]	0.146[d]	−0.008[c,d]
Netherlands	0.042	−0.002[c]	0.106[d]	−0.006[c,d]	0.136[d]	−0.008[c,d]	0.136	−0.008[c,d]	0.147[d]	−0.008[c,d]	0.125	−0.007[c,d]	0.153	−0.009[c,d]	0.146[d]	−0.008[c,d]
France	0.039	−0.002[c]	0.107[d]	−0.006[c,d]	0.137[d]	−0.008[c,d]	0.137[d]	−0.008[c,d]	0.148[d]	−0.009[c,d]	0.126[d]	−0.007[c,d]	0.154[d]	−0.009[c,d]	0.147[d]	−0.008[c,d]
United Kingdom	0.039	−0.002[c]	0.107[d]	−0.006[c,d]	0.137[d]	−0.008[c,d]	0.137[d]	−0.008[c,d]	0.148[d]	−0.009[c,d]	0.126[d]	−0.007[c,d]	0.154[d]	−0.009[c,d]	0.147[d]	−0.009[c,d]
Belgium	0.039	−0.002[c]	0.107[d]	−0.006[c,d]	0.138[d]	−0.008[c,d]	0.137[d]	−0.008[c,d]	0.148[d]	−0.009[c,d]	0.127[d]	−0.007[c,d]	0.154[d]	−0.009[c,d]	0.147[d]	−0.009[c,d]
Norway	0.038	−0.002[c]	0.107[d]	−0.006[c,d]	0.138[d]	−0.008[c,d]	0.137[d]	−0.008[c,d]	0.148[d]	−0.009[c,d]	0.127[d]	−0.007[c,d]	0.154[d]	−0.009[c,d]	0.147[d]	−0.009[c,d]

Italy	0.038	−0.002[c]	0.107[d]	−0.006[c,d]	0.138[d]	−0.008[c,d]	0.137[d]	−0.008[c,d]	0.148[d]	−0.009[c,d]	0.127[d]	−0.007[c,d]	0.154[d]	−0.009[c,d]	0.147[d]	−0.009[c,d]
Austria	0.037	−0.002[c]	0.108[d]	−0.006[c,d]	0.138[d]	−0.008[c,d]	0.138[d]	−0.008[c,d]	0.148[d]	−0.009[c,d]	0.127[d]	−0.008[c,d]	0.154[d]	−0.009[c,d]	0.148[d]	−0.009[c,d]
Germany	0.037	−0.002[c]	0.108[d]	−0.006[c,d]	0.138[d]	−0.008[c,d]	0.138[d]	−0.008[c,d]	0.148[d]	−0.009[c,d]	0.127[d]	−0.008[c,d]	0.154[d]	−0.009[c,d]	0.148[d]	−0.009[c,d]
Australia	0.036	−0.002[c]	0.108[d]	−0.006[c,d]	0.138[d]	−0.008[c,d]	0.138[d]	−0.008[c,d]	0.149[d]	−0.009[c,d]	0.128[d]	−0.008[c,d]	0.154[d]	−0.009[c,d]	0.148[d]	−0.009[c,d]
Japan	0.035	−0.002[c]	0.108[d]	−0.006[c,d]	0.139[d]	−0.008[c,d]	0.138[d]	−0.008[c,d]	0.149[d]	−0.009[c,d]	0.128[d]	−0.008[c,d]	0.155[d]	−0.009[c,d]	0.148[d]	−0.009[c,d]
Canada	0.034	−0.002[c]	0.109[d]	−0.007[c,d]	0.139[d]	−0.008[c,d]	0.139[d]	−0.008[c,d]	0.149[d]	−0.009[c,d]	0.128[d]	−0.008[c,d]	0.155[d]	−0.009[c,d]	0.148[d]	−0.009[c,d]
Bermuda	0.032	−0.002[c]	0.109[d]	−0.007[c,d]	0.140[d]	−0.009[c,d]	0.139[d]	−0.009[c,d]	0.150[d]	−0.009[c,d]	0.129[d]	−0.008[c,d]	0.155[d]	−0.010[c,d]	0.149[d]	−0.009[c,d]
Switzerland	0.031	−0.002[c]	0.109[d]	−0.007[c,d]	0.140[d]	−0.009[c,d]	0.140[d]	−0.009[c,d]	0.150[d]	−0.009[c,d]	0.129[d]	−0.008[c,d]	0.155[d]	−0.010[c,d]	0.149[d]	−0.009[c,d]
Barbados	0.031	−0.002[c]	0.109[d]	−0.007[c,d]	0.140[d]	−0.009[c,d]	0.140[d]	−0.009[c,d]	0.150[d]	−0.009[c,d]	0.129[d]	−0.008[c,d]	0.155[d]	−0.010[c,d]	0.149[d]	−0.009[c,d]
Hong Kong	0.031	−0.002[c]	0.109[d]	−0.007[c,d]	0.140[d]	−0.009[c,d]	0.140[d]	−0.009[c,d]	0.150[d]	−0.009[c,d]	0.129[d]	−0.008[c,d]	0.155[d]	−0.010[c,d]	0.149[d]	−0.009[c,d]
Iceland	0.030[d]	−0.002[c]	0.109[d]	−0.007[c,d]	0.140[d]	−0.009[c,d]	0.140[d]	−0.009[c,d]	0.150[d]	−0.009[c,d]	0.129[d]	−0.008[c,d]	0.155[d]	−0.010[c,d]	0.149[d]	−0.009[c,d]
Denmark	0.030[d]	−0.002[c]	0.110[d]	−0.007[c,d]	0.140[d]	−0.009[c,d]	0.140[d]	−0.009[c,d]	0.150[d]	−0.009[c,d]	0.129[d]	−0.008[c,d]	0.156[d]	−0.010[c,d]	0.149[d]	−0.009[c,d]
Luxembourg	0.016[c,d]	−0.001[c]	0.112[d]	−0.007[c,d]	0.143[d]	−0.010[c,d]	0.143[d]	−0.010[c,d]	0.153[d]	−0.010[c,d]	0.133[d]	−0.009[c,d]	0.158[d]	−0.010[c,d]	0.152[d]	−0.010[c,d]
United States	0.013[c]	−0.001[c]	0.113	−0.008[c]	0.144	−0.010[c]	0.143	−0.010[c]	0.153	−0.010[c]	0.133	−0.009[c]	0.158	−0.011[c]	0.152	−0.010[c]
Low-income average	0.058	0.002	0.073	0.002	0.100	0.003	0.099	0.003	0.128	0.004	0.086	0.002	0.173	0.006	0.125	0.004
Middle-income average	0.060	−0.002	0.092	−0.002	0.120	−0.003	0.119	−0.003	0.134	−0.003	0.108	−0.003	0.144	−0.004	0.133	−0.003
High-income average	0.039	−0.002	0.107	−0.006	0.137	−0.008	0.136	−0.008	0.147	−0.008	0.126	−0.007	0.153	−0.009	0.146	−0.008

[a]Countries are reported based on ascending per capita real income levels
[b]As the estimated budget share was negative for Tanzania we do not report the elasticity for this country
[c]Elasticity estimate is not significantly different from zero at 0.05 level
[d]Elasticity estimate is not significantly different from the point estimate of the United States at 0.05 level

Table 6.14 Slutsky and Cournot cross-price elasticities with change in recreation price, 114 countries in 1996[a]

	Food, beverage and tobacco		Clothing and footwear		Gross rent, fuel and power		House furnishing and operations		Medical care		Education		Transport and communication		Other	
	Slutsky	Cournot	Slutsky	Cournot	Slutsky	Cournot	Slutsky	Cournot	Slutsky	Cournot	Slutsky	Cournot	Slutsky	Cournot	Slutsky	Cournot
Low-income country																
Tanzania	0.011	0.013[c,d]	0.013[d]	0.016[c,d]	0.018[d]	0.023[c,d]	0.018[d]	0.023[c,d]	0.040[c,d]	0.049[c,d]	0.015[d]	0.018[c,d]	0.019[c,d]	0.024[c,d]	0.035[c,d]	0.044[c,d]
Nigeria	0.015	0.012[c,d]	0.018[d]	0.014[c,d]	0.025[d]	0.020[c,d]	0.025[d]	0.020[c,d]	0.041[d]	0.033[c,d]	0.021[d]	0.017[c,d]	0.026[c,d]	0.021[c,d]	0.039[c,d]	0.031[c,d]
Tajikistan	0.017	0.012[c,d]	0.020[d]	0.014[c,d]	0.028[d]	0.019[c,d]	0.028[d]	0.019[d]	0.043[d]	0.029[c,d]	0.023[d]	0.016[d]	0.029[c,d]	0.020[c,d]	0.041[c,d]	0.028[c,d]
Zambia	0.017	0.011[c,d]	0.020[d]	0.014[c,d]	0.029[d]	0.019[c,d]	0.029[d]	0.019[d]	0.043[d]	0.029[c,d]	0.024[d]	0.016[d]	0.029[c,d]	0.020[c,d]	0.041[c,d]	0.028[c,d]
Yemen	0.017	0.011[c,d]	0.020[d]	0.014[c,d]	0.029[d]	0.019[c,d]	0.029[d]	0.019[d]	0.043[d]	0.029[c,d]	0.024[d]	0.016[d]	0.029[c,d]	0.020[c,d]	0.041[c,d]	0.028[c,d]
Malawi	0.018	0.011[c,d]	0.022[d]	0.013[c,d]	0.031[d]	0.019[c,d]	0.030[d]	0.019[d]	0.044[d]	0.027[c,d]	0.026[d]	0.016[d]	0.031[c,d]	0.019[c,d]	0.042[c,d]	0.026[c,d]
Madagascar	0.018	0.011[c,d]	0.022[d]	0.013[c,d]	0.031[d]	0.019[c,d]	0.030[d]	0.019[d]	0.044[d]	0.027[c,d]	0.026[d]	0.016[d]	0.031[c,d]	0.019[c,d]	0.042[c,d]	0.026[c,d]
Mali	0.018	0.011[d]	0.022[d]	0.013 [cd]	0.031[d]	0.018[c,d]	0.031[d]	0.018[d]	0.045[d]	0.026[d]	0.026[d]	0.015[d]	0.032[c,d]	0.019[c,d]	0.043[c,d]	0.025[c,d]
Mongolia	0.019	0.011[d]	0.022[d]	0.013[c,d]	0.031[d]	0.018[c,d]	0.031[d]	0.018[d]	0.045[d]	0.026[d]	0.026[d]	0.015[d]	0.032[c,d]	0.019[c,d]	0.043[c,d]	0.025[c,d]
Benin	0.021	0.010 [d]	0.025[d]	0.012[d]	0.035[d]	0.017[d]	0.035[d]	0.017[d]	0.047[d]	0.023[d]	0.030[d]	0.015[d]	0.036[d]	0.017[c,d]	0.046[c,d]	0.022[c,d]
Kenya	0.022	0.010[d]	0.027[d]	0.012[d]	0.037[d]	0.017[d]	0.037[d]	0.017[d]	0.049[d]	0.022[d]	0.031[d]	0.014[d]	0.038[d]	0.017[c,d]	0.047[c,d]	0.021[c,d]
Sierra Leone	0.023	0.010[d]	0.028[d]	0.012[d]	0.038[d]	0.016[d]	0.038[d]	0.016[d]	0.050[d]	0.021[d]	0.033[d]	0.014[d]	0.039[d]	0.016[c,d]	0.049[d]	0.020[c,d]
Nepal	0.023	0.010[d]	0.028[d]	0.012[d]	0.038[d]	0.016[d]	0.038[d]	0.016[d]	0.050[d]	0.021[d]	0.033[d]	0.014[d]	0.039[d]	0.016[c,d]	0.049[d]	0.020[c,d]
Turkmenistan	0.023	0.009[d]	0.029[d]	0.012[d]	0.039[d]	0.016[d]	0.039[d]	0.016[d]	0.050[d]	0.020[d]	0.034[d]	0.014[d]	0.040[d]	0.016[c,d]	0.049[c,d]	0.020[c,d]
Congo	0.024	0.009[d]	0.030[d]	0.011[d]	0.040[d]	0.015[d]	0.040[d]	0.015[d]	0.051[d]	0.020[d]	0.035[d]	0.013[d]	0.041[d]	0.016[c,d]	0.050[c,d]	0.019[c,d]
Senegal	0.024	0.009[d]	0.031[d]	0.011[d]	0.042[d]	0.015[d]	0.041[d]	0.015[d]	0.052[d]	0.019[d]	0.036[d]	0.013[d]	0.042[d]	0.015[d]	0.051[d]	0.019[d]
Vietnam	0.025	0.009	0.031[d]	0.011[d]	0.042[d]	0.015[d]	0.042[d]	0.015[d]	0.053[d]	0.019[d]	0.036[d]	0.013[d]	0.043[d]	0.015[d]	0.052[d]	0.018[d]
Bangladesh	0.025	0.009	0.031[d]	0.011[d]	0.042[d]	0.015[d]	0.042[d]	0.015[d]	0.053[d]	0.019[d]	0.036[d]	0.013[d]	0.043[d]	0.015[d]	0.052[d]	0.018[d]

Pakistan	0.026	0.008	0.033[d]	0.011[d]	0.045[d]	0.014[d]	0.044[d]	0.014[d]	0.055[d]	0.017[d]	0.039[d]	0.012[d]	0.045[d]	0.014[d]	0.054[d]	0.017[d]
Azerbaijan	0.027	0.008	0.034[d]	0.010[d]	0.046[d]	0.014[d]	0.046[d]	0.014[d]	0.056[d]	0.017[d]	0.040[d]	0.012[d]	0.046[d]	0.014[d]	0.055[d]	0.017[d]
Cote d'Ivoire	0.027	0.008	0.034[d]	0.010[d]	0.046[d]	0.014[d]	0.046[d]	0.014[d]	0.056[d]	0.017[d]	0.040[d]	0.012[d]	0.047[d]	0.014[d]	0.055[d]	0.016[d]
Paraguay	0.027	0.008	0.035[d]	0.010[d]	0.047[d]	0.014[d]	0.046[d]	0.014[d]	0.056[d]	0.016[d]	0.041[d]	0.012[d]	0.047[d]	0.014[d]	0.055[d]	0.016[d]
Uzbekistan	0.027	0.008	0.035[d]	0.010[d]	0.047[d]	0.013[d]	0.047[d]	0.013[d]	0.057[d]	0.016[d]	0.041[d]	0.012[d]	0.048[d]	0.014[d]	0.056[d]	0.016[d]
Kyrgyzstan	0.027	0.008	0.035[d]	0.010[d]	0.047[d]	0.013[d]	0.047[d]	0.013[d]	0.057[d]	0.016[d]	0.041[d]	0.012[d]	0.048[d]	0.014[d]	0.056[d]	0.016[d]
Cameroon	0.027	0.008	0.035[d]	0.010[d]	0.048[d]	0.013[d]	0.047[d]	0.013[d]	0.057[d]	0.016[d]	0.042[d]	0.012[d]	0.048[d]	0.014[d]	0.056[d]	0.016[d]
Moldova	0.027	0.008	0.035[d]	0.010[d]	0.048[d]	0.013[d]	0.047[d]	0.013[d]	0.057[d]	0.016[d]	0.042[d]	0.012[d]	0.048[d]	0.014[d]	0.056[d]	0.016[d]
Bolivia	0.028	0.008	0.036[d]	0.010[d]	0.048[d]	0.013[d]	0.048[d]	0.013[d]	0.058[d]	0.016[d]	0.042[d]	0.011[d]	0.049[d]	0.013[d]	0.057[d]	0.015[d]
Ecuador	0.028	0.007	0.036[d]	0.010[d]	0.049[d]	0.013[d]	0.048[d]	0.013[d]	0.058[d]	0.016[d]	0.043[d]	0.011[d]	0.049[d]	0.013[d]	0.057[d]	0.015[d]
Armenia	0.028	0.007	0.037[d]	0.010[d]	0.049[d]	0.013[d]	0.049[d]	0.013[d]	0.059[d]	0.015[d]	0.043[d]	0.011[d]	0.050[d]	0.013[d]	0.058[d]	0.015[d]
Sri Lanka	0.028	0.007	0.037[d]	0.010[d]	0.050[d]	0.013[d]	0.049[d]	0.013[d]	0.059[d]	0.015[d]	0.043[d]	0.011[d]	0.050[d]	0.013[d]	0.058[d]	0.015[d]
Jordan	0.029	0.007	0.038[d]	0.009[d]	0.050[d]	0.012[d]	0.050[d]	0.012[d]	0.060[d]	0.015[d]	0.044[d]	0.011[d]	0.051[d]	0.013[d]	0.059[d]	0.015[d]
Albania	0.029	0.007	0.039[d]	0.009[d]	0.052[d]	0.012[d]	0.052[d]	0.012[d]	0.061[d]	0.014[d]	0.046[d]	0.011[d]	0.052[d]	0.012[d]	0.060[d]	0.014[d]
Indonesia	0.029	0.007	0.039[d]	0.009[d]	0.052[d]	0.012[d]	0.052[d]	0.012[d]	0.061[d]	0.014[d]	0.046[d]	0.011[d]	0.053[d]	0.012[d]	0.060[d]	0.014[d]
Jamaica	0.029	0.007	0.039[d]	0.009[d]	0.052[d]	0.012[d]	0.052[d]	0.012[d]	0.061[d]	0.014[d]	0.046[d]	0.011[d]	0.053[d]	0.012[d]	0.060[d]	0.014[d]
Zimbabwe	0.029	0.007	0.039[d]	0.009[d]	0.052[d]	0.012[d]	0.052[d]	0.012[d]	0.061[d]	0.014[d]	0.046[d]	0.011[d]	0.053[d]	0.012[d]	0.060[d]	0.014[d]
Guinea	0.030	0.007	0.040[d]	0.009[d]	0.053[d]	0.012[d]	0.053[d]	0.012[d]	0.062[d]	0.014[d]	0.047[d]	0.010[d]	0.053[d]	0.012[d]	0.061[d]	0.014[d]
Syria	0.030	0.006	0.041[d]	0.009[d]	0.054[d]	0.011[d]	0.054[d]	0.011[d]	0.062[d]	0.013[d]	0.048[d]	0.010[d]	0.054[d]	0.012[d]	0.062[d]	0.013[d]
Georgia	0.030	0.006	0.041[d]	0.009[d]	0.054[d]	0.011[d]	0.054[d]	0.011[d]	0.063[d]	0.013[d]	0.048	0.010[d]	0.055[d]	0.012[d]	0.062[d]	0.013[d]

(continued)

Table 6.14 (continued)

	Food, beverage and tobacco		Clothing and footwear		Gross rent, fuel and power		House furnishing and operations		Medical care		Education		Transport and communication		Other	
	Slutsky	Cournot	Slutsky	Cournot	Slutsky	Cournot	Slutsky	Cournot	Slutsky	Cournot	Slutsky	Cournot	Slutsky	Cournot	Slutsky	Cournot
Middle-income country																
Ukraine	0.031	0.006	0.042[d]	0.008[d]	0.056[d]	0.011[d]	0.055[d]	0.011[d]	0.064[d]	0.013[d]	0.049[d]	0.010[d]	0.056[d]	0.011[d]	0.063[d]	0.012[d]
Philippines	0.031	0.006	0.043[d]	0.008[d]	0.057[d]	0.011[d]	0.057[d]	0.011[d]	0.065[d]	0.012[d]	0.051[d]	0.009[d]	0.057[d]	0.011[d]	0.064[d]	0.012[d]
Peru	0.031	0.006	0.043[d]	0.008[d]	0.057[d]	0.011[d]	0.057[d]	0.010[d]	0.065[d]	0.012[d]	0.051[d]	0.009[d]	0.058[d]	0.011[d]	0.065[d]	0.012[d]
Botswana	0.031	0.006	0.043[d]	0.008[d]	0.057[d]	0.010[d]	0.057[d]	0.010[d]	0.066[d]	0.012[d]	0.051[d]	0.009[d]	0.058[d]	0.011[d]	0.065[d]	0.012[d]
Thailand	0.031	0.006	0.044[d]	0.008[d]	0.057[d]	0.010[d]	0.057[d]	0.010[d]	0.066[d]	0.012[d]	0.051[d]	0.009[d]	0.058[d]	0.011[d]	0.065[d]	0.012[d]
Morocco	0.031	0.006	0.044[d]	0.008[d]	0.058[d]	0.010[d]	0.058[d]	0.010[d]	0.066[d]	0.012[d]	0.052[d]	0.009[d]	0.059[d]	0.010[d]	0.065[d]	0.012[d]
Venezuela	0.031	0.006	0.044[d]	0.008[d]	0.058[d]	0.010[d]	0.058[d]	0.010[d]	0.066[d]	0.012[d]	0.052[d]	0.009[d]	0.059[d]	0.010[d]	0.066[d]	0.012[d]
Macedonia	0.031	0.005	0.045[d]	0.008[d]	0.059[d]	0.010[d]	0.059[d]	0.010[d]	0.067[d]	0.011[d]	0.053[d]	0.009[d]	0.060[d]	0.010[d]	0.066[d]	0.011[d]
Belize	0.032	0.005	0.045[d]	0.008[d]	0.059[d]	0.010[d]	0.059[d]	0.010[d]	0.067[d]	0.011[d]	0.053[d]	0.009[d]	0.060[d]	0.010[d]	0.066[d]	0.011[d]
Egypt	0.032	0.005	0.045[d]	0.008[d]	0.059[d]	0.010[d]	0.059[d]	0.010[d]	0.067[d]	0.011[d]	0.053[d]	0.009[d]	0.060[d]	0.010[d]	0.066[d]	0.011[d]
St. Vincent and Grenadines	0.032	0.005	0.045[d]	0.008[d]	0.059[d]	0.010[d]	0.059[d]	0.010[d]	0.067[d]	0.011[d]	0.053[d]	0.009[d]	0.060[d]	0.010[d]	0.066[d]	0.011[d]
Swaziland	0.032	0.005	0.046[d]	0.007[d]	0.060[d]	0.010[d]	0.060[d]	0.010[d]	0.068[d]	0.011[d]	0.054[d]	0.009[d]	0.061[d]	0.010[d]	0.067[d]	0.011[d]
Lebanon	0.032	0.005	0.046[d]	0.007[d]	0.060[d]	0.010[d]	0.060[d]	0.010[d]	0.068[d]	0.011[d]	0.054[d]	0.009[d]	0.061[d]	0.010[d]	0.068[d]	0.011[d]
Belarus	0.032	0.005	0.046[d]	0.007[d]	0.061[d]	0.010[d]	0.060[d]	0.010[d]	0.068[d]	0.011[d]	0.054[d]	0.009[d]	0.061[d]	0.010[d]	0.068[d]	0.011[d]
Kazakhstan	0.032	0.005	0.046[d]	0.007[d]	0.061[d]	0.010[d]	0.060[d]	0.010[d]	0.068[d]	0.011[d]	0.054[d]	0.009[d]	0.061[d]	0.010[d]	0.068[d]	0.011[d]
Dominica	0.032	0.005	0.046[d]	0.007[d]	0.061[d]	0.010[d]	0.060[d]	0.010[d]	0.068[d]	0.011[d]	0.054[d]	0.009[d]	0.061[d]	0.010[d]	0.068[d]	0.011[d]
Latvia	0.032	0.005	0.047[d]	0.007[d]	0.061[d]	0.009[d]	0.061[d]	0.009[d]	0.069[d]	0.010[d]	0.055[d]	0.008[d]	0.062[d]	0.009[d]	0.069[d]	0.010[d]
St. Lucia	0.032	0.005	0.047[d]	0.007[d]	0.062[d]	0.009[d]	0.061[d]	0.009[d]	0.069[d]	0.010[d]	0.055[d]	0.008[d]	0.062[d]	0.009[d]	0.069[d]	0.010[d]
Brazil	0.032	0.005	0.047[d]	0.007[d]	0.062[d]	0.009[d]	0.062[d]	0.009[d]	0.069[d]	0.010[d]	0.055[d]	0.008[d]	0.062[d]	0.009[d]	0.069[d]	0.010[d]
Bulgaria	0.032	0.005	0.047[d]	0.007[d]	0.062[d]	0.009[d]	0.062[d]	0.009[d]	0.070[d]	0.010[d]	0.055[d]	0.008[d]	0.062[d]	0.009[d]	0.069[d]	0.010[d]

Russia	0.032	0.005	0.048[d]	0.007[d]	0.062[d]	0.009[d]	0.062[d]	0.009[d]	0.070[d]	0.010[d]	0.056[d]	0.008[d]	0.063[d]	0.009[d]	0.069[d]	0.010[d]
Fiji	0.032	0.005	0.048[d]	0.007[d]	0.063[d]	0.009[d]	0.063[d]	0.009[d]	0.071[d]	0.010[d]	0.057[d]	0.008[d]	0.064[d]	0.009[d]	0.070[d]	0.010[d]
Grenada	0.032	0.005	0.048[d]	0.007[d]	0.063[d]	0.009[d]	0.063[d]	0.009[d]	0.071[d]	0.010[d]	0.057[d]	0.008[d]	0.064[d]	0.009[d]	0.070[d]	0.010[d]
Turkey	0.032	0.005	0.048[d]	0.007[d]	0.063[d]	0.009[d]	0.063[d]	0.009[d]	0.071[d]	0.010[d]	0.057[d]	0.008[d]	0.064[d]	0.009[d]	0.070[d]	0.010[d]
Lithuania	0.032	0.004	0.049[d]	0.007[d]	0.064[d]	0.009[d]	0.063[d]	0.009[d]	0.071[d]	0.010[d]	0.057[d]	0.008[d]	0.064[d]	0.009[d]	0.071[d]	0.010[d]
Romania	0.032	0.004	0.049[d]	0.007[d]	0.064[d]	0.009[d]	0.064[d]	0.009[d]	0.072[d]	0.010[d]	0.058[d]	0.008[d]	0.065[d]	0.009[d]	0.071[d]	0.010[d]
Iran	0.032	0.004	0.050[d]	0.006[d]	0.065[d]	0.008[d]	0.065[d]	0.008[d]	0.072[d]	0.009[d]	0.058[d]	0.008[d]	0.065[d]	0.008[d]	0.072[d]	0.009[d]
Mexico	0.032	0.004	0.050[d]	0.006[d]	0.065[d]	0.008[d]	0.065[d]	0.008[d]	0.072[d]	0.009[d]	0.059[d]	0.008[d]	0.066[d]	0.008[d]	0.072[d]	0.009[d]
Bahrain	0.032	0.004	0.050[d]	0.006[d]	0.065[d]	0.008[d]	0.065[d]	0.008[d]	0.073[d]	0.009[d]	0.059[d]	0.007[d]	0.066[d]	0.008[d]	0.072[d]	0.009[d]
Chile	0.032	0.004	0.050[d]	0.006[d]	0.066[d]	0.008[d]	0.065[d]	0.008[d]	0.073[d]	0.009[d]	0.059[d]	0.007[d]	0.066[d]	0.008[d]	0.072[d]	0.009[d]
Antigua and Barbuda	0.032	0.004	0.050[d]	0.006[d]	0.066[d]	0.008[d]	0.066[d]	0.008[d]	0.073[d]	0.009[d]	0.059[d]	0.007[d]	0.066[d]	0.008[d]	0.072[d]	0.009[d]
Poland	0.032	0.004	0.051[d]	0.006[d]	0.066[d]	0.008[d]	0.066[d]	0.008[d]	0.074[d]	0.009[d]	0.060[d]	0.007[d]	0.067[d]	0.008[d]	0.073[d]	0.009[d]
Trinidad and Tobago	0.032	0.004	0.051[d]	0.006[d]	0.067[d]	0.008[d]	0.067[d]	0.008[d]	0.074[d]	0.009[d]	0.060[d]	0.007[d]	0.067[d]	0.008[d]	0.073[d]	0.009[d]
Estonia	0.032	0.004	0.052[d]	0.006[d]	0.067[d]	0.008[d]	0.067[d]	0.008[d]	0.074[d]	0.009[d]	0.061[d]	0.007[d]	0.068[d]	0.008[d]	0.074[d]	0.008[d]
Gabon	0.032	0.004	0.052[d]	0.006[d]	0.067[d]	0.008[d]	0.067[d]	0.008[d]	0.075[d]	0.008[d]	0.061[d]	0.007[d]	0.068[d]	0.008[d]	0.074[d]	0.008[d]
Tunisia	0.032	0.004	0.052[d]	0.006[d]	0.068[d]	0.008[d]	0.068[d]	0.008[d]	0.075[d]	0.008[d]	0.061[d]	0.007[d]	0.068[d]	0.008[d]	0.074[d]	0.008[d]
St. Kitts and Nevis	0.032	0.004	0.052[d]	0.006[d]	0.068[d]	0.008[d]	0.068[d]	0.007[d]	0.075[d]	0.008[d]	0.062[d]	0.007[d]	0.069[d]	0.008[d]	0.074[d]	0.008[d]
Uruguay	0.032	0.004	0.052[d]	0.006[d]	0.068[d]	0.007[d]	0.068[d]	0.007[d]	0.075[d]	0.008[d]	0.062[d]	0.007[d]	0.069[d]	0.008[d]	0.075[d]	0.008[d]
Slovakia	0.032	0.003	0.053[d]	0.006[d]	0.068[d]	0.007[d]	0.068[d]	0.007[d]	0.075[d]	0.008[d]	0.062[d]	0.007[d]	0.069[d]	0.007[d]	0.075[d]	0.008[d]
Hungary	0.032	0.003	0.054[d]	0.005[d]	0.070[d]	0.007[d]	0.070[d]	0.007[d]	0.077[d]	0.008[d]	0.063[d]	0.006[d]	0.070[d]	0.007[d]	0.076[d]	0.008[d]
Argentina	0.031	0.003	0.055[d]	0.005[d]	0.072[d]	0.007[d]	0.071[d]	0.007[d]	0.078[d]	0.007[d]	0.065[d]	0.006[d]	0.072[d]	0.007[d]	0.078[d]	0.007[d]
Oman	0.031	0.003	0.056[d]	0.005[d]	0.072[d]	0.006[d]	0.072[d]	0.006[d]	0.079[d]	0.007[d]	0.066[d]	0.006[d]	0.073[d]	0.006[d]	0.079[d]	0.007[d]
Qatar	0.031	0.003	0.057[d]	0.005[d]	0.073[d]	0.006[d]	0.073[d]	0.006[d]	0.080[d]	0.007[d]	0.067[d]	0.006[d]	0.074[d]	0.006[d]	0.079[d]	0.007[d]
Slovenia	0.030	0.002	0.057[d]	0.005[d]	0.074[d]	0.006[d]	0.074[d]	0.006[d]	0.080[d]	0.006[d]	0.067[d]	0.005[d]	0.074[d]	0.006[d]	0.080[d]	0.006[d]

(continued)

Table 6.14 (continued)

	Food, beverage and tobacco		Clothing and footwear		Gross rent, fuel and power		House furnishing and operations		Medical care		Education		Transport and communication		Other	
	Slutsky	Cournot	Slutsky	Cournot	Slutsky	Cournot	Slutsky	Cournot	Slutsky	Cournot	Slutsky	Cournot	Slutsky	Cournot	Slutsky	Cournot
High-income country																
Czech Republic	0.030	0.002	0.058[d]	0.004[d]	0.074[d]	0.006[d]	0.074[d]	0.006[d]	0.081[d]	0.006[d]	0.068[d]	0.005[d]	0.075[d]	0.006[d]	0.080[d]	0.006[d]
Greece	0.029	0.002	0.059[d]	0.004[d]	0.075[d]	0.005[d]	0.075[d]	0.005[d]	0.082[d]	0.006[d]	0.069[d]	0.005[d]	0.076[d]	0.005[d]	0.082[d]	0.006[d]
Korea	0.029	0.002	0.059[d]	0.004[d]	0.076[d]	0.005[d]	0.076[d]	0.005[d]	0.082[d]	0.006[d]	0.069[d]	0.005[d]	0.076[d]	0.005[d]	0.082[d]	0.006[d]
Portugal	0.029	0.002	0.059[d]	0.004[d]	0.076[d]	0.005[d]	0.076[d]	0.005[d]	0.083[d]	0.006[d]	0.070[d]	0.005[d]	0.077[d]	0.005[d]	0.082[d]	0.006[d]
Spain	0.029	0.002	0.059[d]	0.004[d]	0.076[d]	0.005[d]	0.076[d]	0.005[d]	0.083[d]	0.006[d]	0.070[d]	0.005[d]	0.077[d]	0.005[d]	0.082[d]	0.006[d]
Ireland	0.028	0.002	0.060[d]	0.004[d]	0.077[d]	0.005[d]	0.077[d]	0.005[d]	0.083[d]	0.006[d]	0.070[d]	0.005[d]	0.077[d]	0.005[d]	0.083[d]	0.006[d]
Singapore	0.028	0.002	0.060[d]	0.004[d]	0.077[d]	0.005[d]	0.077[d]	0.005[d]	0.084[d]	0.005[d]	0.071[d]	0.005[d]	0.078[d]	0.005[d]	0.083[d]	0.005[d]
Mauritius	0.027	0.002	0.061[d]	0.004[d]	0.078[d]	0.005[d]	0.078[d]	0.005[d]	0.084[d]	0.005[d]	0.071[d]	0.004[d]	0.078[d]	0.005[d]	0.084[d]	0.005[d]
Israel	0.027	0.002	0.061[d]	0.004[d]	0.078[d]	0.005[d]	0.078[d]	0.005[d]	0.085[d]	0.005[d]	0.072[d]	0.004[d]	0.079[d]	0.005[d]	0.084[d]	0.005[d]
New Zealand	0.027	0.002	0.061[d]	0.004[d]	0.079[d]	0.005[d]	0.078[d]	0.005[d]	0.085[d]	0.005[d]	0.072[d]	0.004[d]	0.079[d]	0.005[d]	0.084[d]	0.005[d]
Finland	0.027	0.002	0.061[d]	0.004[d]	0.079[d]	0.005[d]	0.079[d]	0.005[d]	0.085[d]	0.005[d]	0.072[d]	0.004[d]	0.079[d]	0.005[d]	0.085[d]	0.005[d]
Bahamas	0.026	0.002	0.061[d]	0.004[d]	0.079[d]	0.005[d]	0.079[d]	0.005[d]	0.085[d]	0.005[d]	0.072[d]	0.004[d]	0.079[d]	0.005[d]	0.085[d]	0.005[d]
Sweden	0.025	0.001	0.062[d]	0.003[d]	0.080[d]	0.004[d]	0.080[d]	0.004[d]	0.086[d]	0.005[d]	0.074[d]	0.004[d]	0.081[d]	0.004[d]	0.086[d]	0.004[d]
Netherlands	0.025	0.001	0.063[d]	0.003[d]	0.080[d]	0.004[d]	0.080[d]	0.004[d]	0.087[d]	0.004[d]	0.074[d]	0.004[d]	0.081[d]	0.004[d]	0.086[d]	0.004[d]
France	0.023	0.001	0.063[d]	0.003[d]	0.081[d]	0.004[d]	0.081[d]	0.004[d]	0.087[d]	0.004[d]	0.075[d]	0.004[d]	0.082[d]	0.004[d]	0.087[d]	0.004[d]
United Kingdom	0.023	0.001	0.063[d]	0.003[d]	0.081[d]	0.004[d]	0.081[d]	0.004[d]	0.087[d]	0.004[d]	0.075[d]	0.004[d]	0.082[d]	0.004[d]	0.087[d]	0.004[d]
Belgium	0.023	0.001	0.064[d]	0.003[d]	0.082[d]	0.004[d]	0.081[d]	0.004[d]	0.088[d]	0.004[d]	0.075[d]	0.004[d]	0.082[d]	0.004[d]	0.087[d]	0.004[d]
Norway	0.023	0.001	0.064[d]	0.003[d]	0.082[d]	0.004[d]	0.081[d]	0.004[d]	0.088[d]	0.004[d]	0.075[d]	0.004[d]	0.082[d]	0.004[d]	0.087[d]	0.004[d]

Italy	0.023	0.001	0.064[d]	0.003[d]	0.082[d]	0.004[d]	0.082[d]	0.004[d]	0.088[d]	0.004[d]	0.075[d]	0.003[d]	0.082[d]	0.004[d]	0.087[d]	0.004[d]
Austria	0.022	0.001	0.064[d]	0.003[d]	0.082[d]	0.004[d]	0.082[d]	0.004[d]	0.088[d]	0.004[d]	0.076[d]	0.003[d]	0.083[d]	0.004[d]	0.088[d]	0.004[d]
Germany	0.022	0.001	0.064[d]	0.003[d]	0.082[d]	0.004[d]	0.082[d]	0.004[d]	0.088[d]	0.004[d]	0.076[d]	0.003[d]	0.083[d]	0.004[d]	0.088[d]	0.004[d]
Australia	0.021	0.001	0.064[d]	0.003[d]	0.082[d]	0.004[d]	0.082[d]	0.004[d]	0.088[d]	0.004[d]	0.076[d]	0.003[d]	0.083[d]	0.004[d]	0.088[d]	0.004[d]
Japan	0.021	0.001	0.065[d]	0.003[d]	0.083[d]	0.004[d]	0.082[d]	0.004[d]	0.089[d]	0.004[d]	0.076[d]	0.003[d]	0.083[d]	0.004[d]	0.088[d]	0.004[d]
Canada	0.020	0.001	0.065[d]	0.003[d]	0.083[d]	0.003[d]	0.083[d]	0.003[d]	0.089[d]	0.004[d]	0.076[d]	0.003[d]	0.083[d]	0.003[d]	0.089[d]	0.004[d]
Bermuda	0.019	0.001[d]	0.065[d]	0.003[d]	0.084[d]	0.003[d]	0.083[d]	0.003[d]	0.090[d]	0.004[d]	0.077[d]	0.003[d]	0.084[d]	0.003[d]	0.089[d]	0.004[d]
Switzerland	0.019	0.001[d]	0.065[d]	0.003[d]	0.084[d]	0.003[d]	0.084[d]	0.003[d]	0.090[d]	0.003[d]	0.077[d]	0.003[d]	0.084[d]	0.003[d]	0.089[d]	0.003[d]
Barbados	0.019	0.001[d]	0.066[d]	0.003[d]	0.084[d]	0.003[d]	0.084[d]	0.003[d]	0.090[d]	0.003[d]	0.077[d]	0.003[d]	0.084[d]	0.003[d]	0.089[d]	0.003[d]
Hong Kong	0.018	0.001[d]	0.066[d]	0.002[d]	0.084[d]	0.003[d]	0.084[d]	0.003[d]	0.090[d]	0.003[d]	0.077[d]	0.003[d]	0.084[d]	0.003[d]	0.089[d]	0.003[d]
Iceland	0.018	0.001[d]	0.066[d]	0.002[d]	0.084[d]	0.003[d]	0.084[d]	0.003[d]	0.090[d]	0.003[d]	0.078[d]	0.003[d]	0.084[d]	0.003[d]	0.089[d]	0.003[d]
Denmark	0.018	0.001[d]	0.066[d]	0.002[d]	0.084[d]	0.003[d]	0.084[d]	0.003[d]	0.090[d]	0.003[d]	0.078[d]	0.003[d]	0.085[d]	0.003[d]	0.090[d]	0.003[d]
Luxembourg	0.010[cd]	0.000[cd]	0.068[d]	0.002[d]	0.087[d]	0.002[d]	0.087[d]	0.002[d]	0.093[d]	0.002[d]	0.081[d]	0.002[d]	0.088[d]	0.002[d]	0.093[d]	0.002[d]
United States	0.008[c]	0.000[c]	0.069	0.002	0.088	0.002	0.088	0.002	0.093	0.002	0.081	0.002	0.088	0.002	0.093	0.002
Low-income average	0.024	0.009	0.031	0.011	0.042	0.015	0.042	0.015	0.053	0.020	0.036	0.013	0.043	0.015	0.052	0.019
Middle-income average	0.032	0.004	0.049	0.007	0.063	0.009	0.063	0.009	0.071	0.010	0.057	0.008	0.064	0.009	0.070	0.010
High-income average	0.023	0.001	0.063	0.003	0.081	0.004	0.081	0.004	0.087	0.004	0.074	0.004	0.081	0.004	0.086	0.004

[a]Countries are reported based on ascending per capita real income levels

[b]As the estimated budget share was negative for Tanzania we do not report the elasticity for this country

[c]Elasticity estimate is not significantly different from zero at 0.05 level

[d]Elasticity estimate is not significantly different from the point estimate of the United States at 0.05 level

Table 6.15 Slutsky and Cournot cross-price elasticities with change in other items, 114 countries in 1996[a]

	Food, beverage and tobacco		Clothing and footwear		Gross rent, fuel and power		House furnishing and operations		Medical care		Education		Transport and communication		Recreation[b]	
	Slutsky	Cournot	Slutsky	Cournot	Slutsky	Cournot	Slutsky	Cournot	Slutsky	Cournot	Slutsky	Cournot	Slutsky	Cournot	Slutsky	Cournot
Low-income country																
Tanzania	0.034	0.018	0.039	0.021	0.058	0.031	0.058	0.030	0.125[c,d]	0.066[c,d]	0.046	0.024	0.060[c,d]	0.032[c,d]		
Nigeria	0.041	0.016	0.048	0.019	0.068	0.027	0.068	0.027	0.112[d]	0.044[c,d]	0.056	0.022	0.070[c,d]	0.028[c,d]	0.337	0.133
Tajikistan	0.043	0.015	0.052	0.018	0.073	0.025	0.073	0.025	0.111	0.038	0.061	0.021	0.075[c,d]	0.026[c,d]	0.221	0.077
Zambia	0.044	0.015	0.052	0.018	0.074	0.025	0.073	0.025	0.111	0.038	0.061	0.021	0.076[c,d]	0.026[c,d]	0.211	0.072
Yemen	0.044	0.015	0.052	0.018	0.074	0.025	0.073	0.025	0.111	0.037	0.061	0.021	0.076[c,d]	0.026[c,d]	0.211	0.071
Malawi	0.045	0.014	0.055	0.017	0.077	0.024	0.076	0.024	0.111	0.035	0.064	0.020	0.078[c,d]	0.025[c,d]	0.187	0.059
Madagascar	0.045	0.014	0.055	0.017	0.077	0.024	0.076	0.024	0.111	0.035	0.064	0.020	0.078[c,d]	0.025[c,d]	0.187	0.059
Mali	0.046	0.014	0.055	0.017	0.077	0.024	0.077	0.024	0.111	0.034	0.065	0.020	0.079[c,d]	0.024[c,d]	0.182	0.056
Mongolia	0.046	0.014	0.055	0.017	0.078	0.024	0.077	0.024	0.111	0.034	0.065	0.020	0.079[c,d]	0.024[c,d]	0.181	0.055
Benin	0.050	0.013	0.060	0.016	0.084	0.022	0.083	0.022	0.113	0.029	0.071	0.018	0.085[d]	0.022[c,d]	0.158	0.041
Kenya	0.051	0.012	0.063	0.015	0.086	0.021	0.086	0.021	0.114	0.028	0.074	0.018	0.088[d]	0.021	0.153	0.037
Sierra Leone	0.052	0.012	0.065	0.015	0.089	0.020	0.088	0.020	0.115	0.026	0.076	0.017	0.090[d]	0.021	0.149	0.034
Nepal	0.052	0.012	0.065	0.015	0.089	0.020	0.088	0.020	0.115	0.026	0.076	0.017	0.090[d]	0.021	0.149	0.034
Turkmenistan	0.053	0.012	0.066	0.014	0.090	0.020	0.089	0.020	0.115	0.025	0.077	0.017	0.091[d]	0.020	0.148	0.033
Congo	0.054	0.011	0.067	0.014	0.092	0.019	0.091	0.019	0.117	0.024	0.079	0.016	0.093[d]	0.019	0.146	0.030
Senegal	0.055	0.011	0.069	0.014	0.094	0.019	0.093	0.018	0.118	0.023	0.081	0.016	0.095[d]	0.019	0.145	0.029
Vietnam	0.055	0.011	0.069	0.014	0.094	0.018	0.094	0.018	0.118	0.023	0.081	0.016	0.096[d]	0.019	0.145	0.028
Bangladesh	0.055	0.011	0.070	0.013	0.095	0.018	0.094	0.018	0.118	0.023	0.082	0.016	0.096[d]	0.019	0.145	0.028

Pakistan	0.057	0.010	0.073	0.013	0.098	0.017	0.098	0.017	0.121	0.021	0.086	0.015	0.100[d]	0.017	0.143	0.025
Azerbaijan	0.058	0.010	0.074	0.012	0.100	0.017	0.100	0.017	0.122	0.020	0.087	0.014	0.102	0.017	0.143	0.024
Cote d'Ivoire	0.058	0.009	0.075	0.012	0.101	0.016	0.101	0.016	0.122	0.020	0.088	0.014	0.102	0.017	0.143	0.023
Paraguay	0.059	0.009	0.075	0.012	0.101	0.016	0.101	0.016	0.123	0.020	0.088	0.014	0.103	0.016	0.143	0.023
Uzbekistan	0.059	0.009	0.076	0.012	0.103	0.016	0.102	0.016	0.123	0.019	0.090	0.014	0.104	0.016	0.143	0.022
Kyrgyzstan	0.059	0.009	0.076	0.012	0.103	0.016	0.102	0.016	0.123	0.019	0.090	0.014	0.104	0.016	0.143	0.022
Cameroon	0.059	0.009	0.077	0.012	0.103	0.016	0.102	0.016	0.124	0.019	0.090	0.014	0.104	0.016	0.143	0.022
Moldova	0.059	0.009	0.077	0.012	0.103	0.016	0.102	0.016	0.124	0.019	0.090	0.014	0.104	0.016	0.143	0.022
Bolivia	0.060	0.009	0.078	0.011	0.104	0.015	0.104	0.015	0.125	0.018	0.091	0.013	0.106	0.016	0.143	0.021
Ecuador	0.060	0.009	0.078	0.011	0.105	0.015	0.104	0.015	0.125	0.018	0.092	0.013	0.106	0.015	0.143	0.021
Armenia	0.060	0.008	0.079	0.011	0.106	0.015	0.105	0.015	0.126	0.018	0.093	0.013	0.107	0.015	0.144	0.020
Sri Lanka	0.060	0.008	0.079	0.011	0.106	0.015	0.106	0.015	0.126	0.018	0.093	0.013	0.107	0.015	0.144	0.020
Jordan	0.061	0.008	0.081	0.011	0.107	0.014	0.107	0.014	0.127	0.017	0.095	0.013	0.109	0.015	0.144	0.019
Albania	0.062	0.008	0.082	0.010	0.110	0.014	0.109	0.014	0.128	0.016	0.097	0.012	0.111	0.014	0.145	0.018
Indonesia	0.062	0.008	0.083	0.010	0.110	0.014	0.110	0.014	0.129	0.016	0.097	0.012	0.112	0.014	0.145	0.018
Jamaica	0.062	0.008	0.083	0.010	0.110	0.014	0.110	0.013	0.129	0.016	0.097	0.012	0.112	0.014	0.145	0.018
Zimbabwe	0.062	0.008	0.083	0.010	0.111	0.013	0.110	0.013	0.129	0.016	0.098	0.012	0.112	0.014	0.145	0.018
Guinea	0.062	0.007	0.084	0.010	0.111	0.013	0.111	0.013	0.130	0.016	0.098	0.012	0.113	0.013[c]	0.145	0.017
Syria	0.063	0.007[c]	0.085	0.010[c]	0.113	0.013[c]	0.112	0.013	0.131	0.015[c]	0.100	0.011	0.114	0.013[c]	0.146	0.017
Georgia	0.063	0.007[c]	0.085	0.010[c]	0.113	0.013[c]	0.113	0.013	0.131	0.015[c]	0.100	0.011	0.114	0.013[c]	0.146	0.016

(continued)

Table 6.15 (continued)

	Food, beverage and tobacco		Clothing and footwear		Gross rent, fuel and power		House furnishing and operations		Medical care		Education		Transport and communication		Recreation[b]	
	Slutsky	Cournot	Slutsky	Cournot	Slutsky	Cournot	Slutsky	Cournot	Slutsky	Cournot	Slutsky	Cournot	Slutsky	Cournot	Slutsky	Cournot
Middle-income country																
Ukraine	0.064	0.007[c,d]	0.088	0.00[c]	0.116	0.012[c]	0.115	0.012[c]	0.133	0.014[c]	0.103	0.011[c]	0.117	0.012[c]	0.147	0.015[c]
Philippines	0.064	0.006[c,d]	0.089	0.009[c]	0.117	0.011[c]	0.117	0.011[c]	0.135	0.013[c]	0.105	0.010[c]	0.119	0.012[c]	0.148	0.014[c]
Peru	0.064	0.006[c,d]	0.090	0.009[c]	0.118	0.011[c]	0.118	0.011[c]	0.135	0.013[c]	0.105	0.010[c]	0.120	0.011[c]	0.148	0.014[c]
Botswana	0.064	0.006[c,d]	0.090	0.009[c]	0.118	0.011[c]	0.118	0.011[c]	0.135	0.013[c]	0.105	0.010[c]	0.120	0.011[c]	0.148	0.014[c]
Thailand	0.064	0.006[c,d]	0.090	0.008[c]	0.119	0.011[c]	0.118	0.011[c]	0.136	0.013[c]	0.106	0.010[c]	0.120	0.011[c,d]	0.148	0.014[c]
Morocco	0.064	0.006[c,d]	0.091	0.008[c]	0.119	0.011[c]	0.119	0.011[c]	0.136	0.012[c]	0.107	0.010[c]	0.121	0.011[c,d]	0.149	0.014[c]
Venezuela	0.064	0.006[c,d]	0.091	0.008[c]	0.120	0.011[c]	0.119	0.011[c]	0.136	0.012[c]	0.107	0.010[c]	0.121	0.011[c,d]	0.149	0.013[c]
Macedonia	0.065	0.006[c,d]	0.092	0.008[c,d]	0.121	0.010[c,d]	0.121	0.010[c]	0.137	0.012[c,d]	0.108	0.009[c]	0.122	0.011[c,d]	0.150	0.013[c]
Belize	0.065	0.006[c,d]	0.092	0.008[c,d]	0.121	0.010[c,d]	0.121	0.010[c]	0.137	0.012[c,d]	0.108	0.009[c]	0.122	0.011[c,d]	0.150	0.013[c]
Egypt	0.065	0.006[c,d]	0.092	0.008[c,d]	0.121	0.010[c,d]	0.121	0.010[c]	0.137	0.012[c,d]	0.108	0.009[c]	0.122	0.011[c,d]	0.150	0.013[c]
St. Vincent and Grenadines	0.065	0.006[c,d]	0.092	0.008[c,d]	0.121	0.010[c,d]	0.121	0.010[c]	0.138	0.012[c,d]	0.108	0.009[c]	0.122	0.011[c,d]	0.150	0.013[c]
Swaziland	0.065	0.005[c,d]	0.093	0.008[c,d]	0.123	0.010[c,d]	0.122	0.010[c,d]	0.139	0.011[c,d]	0.110	0.009[c,d]	0.124	0.010[c,d]	0.151	0.012[c,d]
Lebanon	0.065	0.005[c,d]	0.094	0.008[c,d]	0.123	0.010[c,d]	0.123	0.010[c,d]	0.139	0.011[c,d]	0.110	0.009[c,d]	0.124	0.010[c,d]	0.151	0.012[c,d]
Belarus	0.065	0.005[c,d]	0.094	0.007[c,d]	0.123	0.010[c,d]	0.123	0.010[c,d]	0.139	0.011[c,d]	0.111	0.009[c,d]	0.125	0.010[c,d]	0.151	0.012[c,d]
Kazakhstan	0.065	0.005[c,d]	0.094	0.007[c,d]	0.123	0.010[c,d]	0.123	0.010[c,d]	0.139	0.011[c,d]	0.111	0.009[c,d]	0.125	0.010[c,d]	0.151	0.012[c,d]
Dominica	0.065	0.005[c,d]	0.094	0.007[c,d]	0.123	0.010[c,d]	0.123	0.010[c,d]	0.139	0.011[c,d]	0.111	0.009[c,d]	0.125	0.010[c,d]	0.151	0.012[c,d]
Latvia	0.065	0.005[c,d]	0.095	0.007[c,d]	0.125	0.009[c,d]	0.125	0.009[c,d]	0.141	0.011[c,d]	0.112	0.008[c,d]	0.126	0.009[c,d]	0.152	0.011[c,d]

St. Lucia	0.065	0.005[c,d]	0.096	0.007[c,d]	0.125	0.009[c,d]	0.125	0.009[c,d]	0.141	0.010[c,d]	0.112	0.008[c,d]	0.126	0.009[c,d]	0.152	0.011[c,d]
Brazil	0.065	0.005[c,d]	0.096	0.007[c,d]	0.125	0.009[c,d]	0.125	0.009[c,d]	0.141	0.010[c,d]	0.112	0.008[c,d]	0.127	0.009[c,d]	0.152	0.011[c,d]
Bulgaria	0.065	0.005[c,d]	0.096	0.007[c,d]	0.125	0.009[c,d]	0.125	0.009[c,d]	0.141	0.010[c,d]	0.113	0.008[c,d]	0.127	0.009[c,d]	0.152	0.011[c,d]
Iran	0.065	0.004[c,d]	0.100	0.006[c,d]	0.130	0.008[c,d]	0.130	0.008[c,d]	0.145	0.009[c,d]	0.117	0.007[c,d]	0.131[d]	0.008[c,d]	0.155	0.009[c,d]
Mexico	0.065	0.004[c,d]	0.100	0.006[c,d]	0.131	0.008[c,d]	0.130	0.008[c,d]	0.145	0.009[c,d]	0.118	0.007[c,d]	0.132[d]	0.008[c,d]	0.156	0.009[c,d]
Bahrain	0.065	0.004[c,d]	0.101	0.006[c,d]	0.131	0.008[c,d]	0.131	0.008[c,d]	0.146	0.008[c,d]	0.118	0.007[c,d]	0.132[d]	0.008[c,d]	0.156	0.009[c,d]
Chile	0.065	0.004[c,d]	0.101	0.006[c,d]	0.131	0.008[c,d]	0.131	0.007[c,d]	0.146	0.008[c,d]	0.119	0.007[c,d]	0.133[d]	0.008[c,d]	0.156	0.009[c,d]
Antigua and Barbuda	0.065	0.004[c,d]	0.101	0.006[c,d]	0.132	0.007[c,d]	0.131	0.007[c,d]	0.146	0.008[c,d]	0.119	0.007[c,d]	0.133[d]	0.008[c,d]	0.156	0.009[c,d]
Poland	0.065	0.004[c,d]	0.102	0.006[c,d]	0.132	0.007[c,d]	0.132	0.007[c,d]	0.147	0.008[c,d]	0.120	0.007[c,d]	0.134[d]	0.007[c,d]	0.157	0.009[c,d]
Trinidad and Tobago	0.065	0.003[c,d]	0.102	0.005[c,d]	0.133	0.007[c,d]	0.133	0.007[c,d]	0.148	0.008[c,d]	0.121	0.006[c,d]	0.134[d]	0.007[c,d]	0.157	0.008[c,d]
Estonia	0.064	0.003[c,d]	0.103	0.005[c,d]	0.134	0.007[c,d]	0.134	0.007[c,d]	0.148[d]	0.008[c,d]	0.121	0.006[c,d]	0.135[d]	0.007[c,d]	0.158	0.008[c,d]
Gabon	0.064	0.003[c,d]	0.103	0.005[c,d]	0.134	0.007[c,d]	0.134	0.007[c,d]	0.149[d]	0.007[c,d]	0.121	0.006[c,d]	0.135[d]	0.007[c,d]	0.158	0.008[c,d]
Tunisia	0.064	0.003[c,d]	0.104	0.005[c,d]	0.135	0.007[c,d]	0.134	0.007[c,d]	0.149[d]	0.007[c,d]	0.122	0.006[c,d]	0.136[d]	0.007[c,d]	0.158	0.008[c,d]
St. Kitts and Nevis	0.064	0.003[c,d]	0.104	0.005[c,d]	0.135	0.007[c,d]	0.135	0.006[c,d]	0.149[d]	0.007[c,d]	0.122	0.006[c,d]	0.136[d]	0.007[c,d]	0.159	0.008[c,d]
Uruguay	0.064	0.003[c,d]	0.104	0.005[c,d]	0.135	0.006[c,d]	0.135	0.006[c,d]	0.150[d]	0.007[c,d]	0.123	0.006[c,d]	0.137[d]	0.006[c,d]	0.159	0.008[c,d]
Slovakia	0.064	0.003[c,d]	0.105	0.005[c,d]	0.136	0.006[c,d]	0.135	0.006[c,d]	0.150[d]	0.007[c,d]	0.123	0.006[c,d]	0.137[d]	0.006[c,d]	0.159	0.007[c,d]
Hungary	0.063	0.003[c,d]	0.106	0.004[c,d]	0.138	0.006[c,d]	0.138	0.006[c,d]	0.152[d]	0.006[c,d]	0.125	0.005[c,d]	0.139[d]	0.006[c,d]	0.161	0.007[c,d]
Argentina	0.062	0.002[c,d]	0.109	0.004[c,d]	0.141[d]	0.005[c,d]	0.141[d]	0.005[c,d]	0.154[d]	0.005[c,d]	0.128[d]	0.004[c,d]	0.142[d]	0.005[c,d]	0.163[d]	0.006[c,d]
Oman	0.061	0.002[c,d]	0.110[d]	0.004[c,d]	0.142[d]	0.005[c,d]	0.142[d]	0.005[c,d]	0.155[d]	0.005[c,d]	0.130[d]	0.004[c,d]	0.143[d]	0.005[c,d]	0.164[d]	0.005[c,d]
Qatar	0.060	0.002[c,d]	0.111[d]	0.003[c,d]	0.144[d]	0.004[c,d]	0.143[d]	0.004[c,d]	0.157[d]	0.005[c,d]	0.131[d]	0.004[c,d]	0.145[d]	0.004[c,d]	0.165[d]	0.005[c,d]
Slovenia	0.060	0.002[c,d]	0.112[d]	0.003[c,d]	0.144[d]	0.004[c,d]	0.144[d]	0.004[c,d]	0.157[d]	0.004[c,d]	0.132[d]	0.004[c,d]	0.145[d]	0.004[c,d]	0.165[d]	0.005[c,d]

(continued)

Table 6.15 (continued)

	Food, beverage and tobacco		Clothing and footwear		Gross rent, fuel and power		House furnishing and operations		Medical care		Education		Transport and communication		Recreation[b]	
	Slutsky	Cournot	Slutsky	Cournot	Slutsky	Cournot	Slutsky	Cournot	Slutsky	Cournot	Slutsky	Cournot	Slutsky	Cournot	Slutsky	Cournot
High-income country																
Czech Republic	0.059	0.002[c,d]	0.113[d]	0.003[c,d]	0.145[d]	0.004[c,d]	0.145[d]	0.004[c,d]	0.158[d]	0.004[c,d]	0.133[d]	0.003[c,d]	0.146[d]	0.004[c,d]	0.166[d]	0.004[c,d]
Greece	0.057	0.001[c,d]	0.114[d]	0.002[c,d]	0.147[d]	0.003[c,d]	0.147[d]	0.003[c,d]	0.160[d]	0.003[c,d]	0.135[d]	0.003[c,d]	0.148[d]	0.003[c,d]	0.168[d]	0.004[c,d]
Korea	0.057	0.001[c,d]	0.115[d]	0.002[c,d]	0.148[d]	0.003[c,d]	0.147[d]	0.003[c,d]	0.160[d]	0.003[c,d]	0.135[d]	0.003[c,d]	0.149[d]	0.003[c,d]	0.168[d]	0.003[c,d]
Portugal	0.056	0.001[c,d]	0.115[d]	0.002[c,d]	0.148[d]	0.003[c,d]	0.148[d]	0.003[c,d]	0.161[d]	0.003[c,d]	0.136[d]	0.003[c,d]	0.149[d]	0.003[c,d]	0.168[d]	0.003[c,d]
Spain	0.056	0.001[c,d]	0.115[d]	0.002[c,d]	0.148[d]	0.003[c,d]	0.148[d]	0.003[c,d]	0.161[d]	0.003[c,d]	0.136[d]	0.003[c,d]	0.150[d]	0.003[c,d]	0.169[d]	0.003[c,d]
Irelan[d]	0.055	0.001[c,d]	0.116[d]	0.002[c,d]	0.149[d]	0.003[c,d]	0.149[d]	0.003[c,d]	0.162[d]	0.003[c,d]	0.137[d]	0.002[c,d]	0.150[d]	0.003[c,d]	0.169[d]	0.003[c,d]
Singapore	0.055	0.001[c,d]	0.117[d]	0.002[c,d]	0.150[d]	0.002[c,d]	0.150[d]	0.002[c,d]	0.162[d]	0.003[c,d]	0.137[d]	0.002[c,d]	0.151[d]	0.002[c,d]	0.170[d]	0.003[c,d]
Mauritius	0.053	0.001[c,d]	0.117[d]	0.002[c,d]	0.151[d]	0.002[c,d]	0.151[d]	0.002[c,d]	0.163[d]	0.002[c,d]	0.138[d]	0.002[c,d]	0.152[d]	0.002[c,d]	0.171[d]	0.002[c,d]
Israel	0.052	0.001[c,d]	0.118[d]	0.001[c,d]	0.152[d]	0.002[c,d]	0.152[d]	0.002[c,d]	0.164[d]	0.002[c,d]	0.139[d]	0.002[c,d]	0.153[d]	0.002[c,d]	0.171[d]	0.002[c,d]
New Zealand	0.052	0.001[c,d]	0.119[d]	0.001[c,d]	0.152[d]	0.002[c,d]	0.152[d]	0.002[c,d]	0.164[d]	0.002[c,d]	0.140[d]	0.002[c,d]	0.153[d]	0.002[c,d]	0.172[d]	0.002[c,d]
Finland	0.051	0.001[c,d]	0.119[d]	0.001[c,d]	0.152[d]	0.002[c,d]	0.152[d]	0.002[c,d]	0.165[d]	0.002[c,d]	0.140[d]	0.002[c,d]	0.153[d]	0.002[c,d]	0.172[d]	0.002[c,d]
Bahamas	0.051	0.001[c,d]	0.119[d]	0.001[c,d]	0.153[d]	0.002[c,d]	0.152[d]	0.002[c,d]	0.165[d]	0.002[c,d]	0.140[d]	0.002[c,d]	0.154[d]	0.002[c,d]	0.172[d]	0.002[c,d]
Sweden	0.048	0.000[c,d]	0.121[d]	0.001[c,d]	0.155[d]	0.001[c,d]	0.154[d]	0.001[c,d]	0.167[d]	0.001[c,d]	0.142[d]	0.001[c,d]	0.156[d]	0.001[c,d]	0.173[d]	0.001[c,d]
Netherlands	0.047	0.000[c,d]	0.121[d]	0.001[c,d]	0.155[d]	0.001[c,d]	0.155[d]	0.001[c,d]	0.167[d]	0.001[c,d]	0.143[d]	0.001[c,d]	0.156[d]	0.001[c,d]	0.174[d]	0.001[c,d]
France	0.045	0.000[c,d]	0.122[d]	0.001[c,d]	0.156[d]	0.001[c,d]	0.156[d]	0.001[c,d]	0.168[d]	0.001[c,d]	0.144[d]	0.001[c,d]	0.157[d]	0.001[c,d]	0.175[d]	0.001[c,d]
United Kingdom	0.045	0.000[c,d]	0.122[d]	0.001[c,d]	0.157[d]	0.001[c,d]	0.156[d]	0.001[c,d]	0.168[d]	0.001[c,d]	0.144[d]	0.001[c,d]	0.158[d]	0.001[c,d]	0.175[d]	0.001[c,d]
Belgium	0.044	0.000[c,d]	0.122[d]	0.000[c,d]	0.157[d]	0.001[c,d]	0.157[d]	0.001[c,d]	0.169[d]	0.001[c,d]	0.144[d]	0.001[c,d]	0.158[d]	0.001[c,d]	0.175[d]	0.001[c,d]
Norway	0.044	0.000[c,d]	0.122[d]	0.000[c,d]	0.157[d]	0.001[c,d]	0.157[d]	0.001[c,d]	0.169[d]	0.001[c,d]	0.145[d]	0.001[c,d]	0.158[d]	0.001[c,d]	0.175[d]	0.001[c,d]

Italy	0.043	0.000[c,d]	0.123[d]	0.000[c,d]	0.157[d]	0.001[c,d]	0.157[d]	0.001[c,d]	0.169[d]	0.001[c,d]	0.145[d]	0.000[c,d]	0.158[d]	0.001[c,d]	0.176[d]	0.001[c,d]
Austria	0.042	0.000[c,d]	0.123[d]	0.000[c,d]	0.158[d]	0.000[c,d]	0.157[d]	0.000[c,d]	0.169[d]	0.000[c,d]	0.145[d]	0.000[c,d]	0.159[d]	0.000[c,d]	0.176[d]	0.000[c,d]
Germany	0.042	0.000[c,d]	0.123[d]	0.000[c,d]	0.158[d]	0.000[c,d]	0.157[d]	0.000[c,d]	0.169[d]	0.000[c,d]	0.145[d]	0.000[c,d]	0.159[d]	0.000[c,d]	0.176[d]	0.000[c,d]
Australia	0.041	0.000[c,d]	0.124[d]	0.000[c,d]	0.158[d]	0.000[c,d]	0.158[d]	0.000[c,d]	0.170[d]	0.000[c,d]	0.146[d]	0.000[c,d]	0.159[d]	0.000[c,d]	0.177[d]	0.000[c,d]
Japan	0.040	0.000[c,d]	0.124[d]	0.000[c,d]	0.159[d]	0.000[c,d]	0.158[d]	0.000[c,d]	0.170[d]	0.000[c,d]	0.146[d]	0.000[c,d]	0.160[d]	0.000[c,d]	0.177[d]	0.000[c,d]
Canada	0.039	0.000[c,d]	0.124[d]	0.000[c,d]	0.159[d]	0.000[c,d]	0.159[d]	0.000[c,d]	0.171[d]	0.000[c,d]	0.147[d]	0.000[c,d]	0.160[d]	0.000[c,d]	0.177[d]	0.000[c,d]
Bermuda	0.037	0.000[c,d]	0.125[d]	0.000[c,d]	0.160[d]	0.000[c,d]	0.160[d]	0.000[c,d]	0.172[d]	0.000[c,d]	0.148[d]	0.000[c,d]	0.161[d]	0.000[c,d]	0.178[d]	0.000[c,d]
Switzerland	0.036	0.000[c,d]	0.125[d]	0.000[c,d]	0.160[d]	0.000[c,d]	0.160[d]	0.000[c,d]	0.172[d]	0.000[c,d]	0.148[d]	0.000[c,d]	0.162[d]	0.000[c,d]	0.178[d]	0.000[c,d]
Barbados	0.036	0.000[c,d]	0.125[d]	0.000[c,d]	0.161[d]	0.000[c,d]	0.160[d]	0.000[c,d]	0.172[d]	0.000[c,d]	0.148[d]	0.000[c,d]	0.162[d]	0.000[c,d]	0.178[d]	0.000[c,d]
Hong Kong	0.035	0.000[c,d]	0.126[d]	0.000[c,d]	0.161[d]	0.000[c,d]	0.160[d]	0.000[c,d]	0.172[d]	0.000[c,d]	0.148[d]	0.000[c,d]	0.162[d]	0.000[c,d]	0.178[d]	0.000[c,d]
Iceland	0.035	0.000[c,d]	0.126[d]	0.000[c,d]	0.161[d]	0.000[c,d]	0.160[d]	0.000[c,d]	0.172[d]	0.000[c,d]	0.148[d]	0.000[c,d]	0.162[d]	0.000[c,d]	0.179[d]	0.000[c,d]
Denmark	0.034	0.000[c,d]	0.126[d]	0.000[c,d]	0.161[d]	−0.001[c,d]	0.161[d]	−0.001[c,d]	0.172[d]	−0.001[c,d]	0.149[d]	0.000[c,d]	0.162[d]	−0.001[c,d]	0.179[d]	−0.001[c,d]
Luxembourg	0.018[c,d]	0.000[c,d]	0.130[d]	−0.001[c,d]	0.166[d]	−0.002[c,d]	0.166[d]	−0.002[c,d]	0.177[d]	−0.002[c,d]	0.154[d]	−0.002[c,d]	0.167[d]	−0.002[c,d]	0.183[d]	−0.002[c,d]
United States	0.015[c]	0.000[c]	0.131	−0.002[c]	0.167	−0.002[c]	0.166	−0.002[c]	0.178	−0.002[c]	0.154	−0.002[c]	0.168	−0.002[c]	0.184	−0.002[c]
Low-income average	0.055	0.011	0.070	0.014	0.094	0.019	0.094	0.018	0.120	0.025	0.082	0.016	0.096	0.019	0.160	0.035
Middle-income average	0.064	0.004	0.098	0.006	0.128	0.009	0.128	0.008	0.143	0.010	0.115	0.008	0.129	0.009	0.154	0.010
High-income average	0.044	0.000	0.121	0.001	0.155	0.001	0.155	0.001	0.167	0.001	0.143	0.001	0.157	0.001	0.174	0.001

[a]Countries are reported based on ascending per capita real income levels

[b]As the estimated budget share was negative for Tanzania we do not report the elasticity for this country

[c]Elasticity estimate is not significantly different from zero at 0.05 level

[d]Elasticity estimate is not significantly different from the point estimate of the United States at 0.05 level

Price changes of the seven luxury goods do not show any particular pattern. In the case of education which is essentially unitary income elastic, a change in its price results in all Cournot cross-price elasticities being negative for all the other goods for all countries in the sample. However, most of these are not statistically different from zero ($\alpha = .05$) with the exceptions being the poorest countries, except in the case of transport and communications and other, and the richest middle-income and the high-income countries. Also, many of the elasticities are not statistically different from those of the U.S.

The Cournot cross-price elasticities with respect to a change in the price of recreation, the most luxurious good, are all positive for all goods and countries. Most are significantly different than zero ($\alpha = .05$) except in the cases of the poorest countries. Except in the case of food, almost all the elasticities are not statistically different from those of the U.S. Cournot cross-price elasticities with respect to a change in the price of medical care or other items are all positive except for the two (medical care) or three (other items) richest countries in the sample where the cross-price elasticities are negative. While most of the low-income and lower middle-income countries have elasticities with respect to a change in medical care price that are statistically different from zero, the higher middle-income and high-income country elasticities are not. For other, only the low-income countries have elasticities statistically different from zero. Also, few of these elasticities differ statistically from those of the U.S. For the remaining three goods (i.e., gross rent, fuel and power; transportation and communication; and house furnishing and operations), a price change results in positive Cournot cross-price elasticities that eventually turn negative when traveling towards the more affluent countries. However, it should be pointed out that the magnitudes of the cross-price elasticities with respect to changes in a luxury good's price are small and many are not statistically different from zero.

6.6 Conclusions

A simple method for calculating cross-country, cross-price elasticities of demand is articulated in this paper. Using the method, two types of cross-price elasticities, Slutsky and Cournot, are calculated for two-good- and nine-good-demand systems for114 countries. The compensated Slutsky elasticity is calculated holding real income constant, and the uncompensated Cournot elasticity is calculated holding nominal income constant after a price change. The consumption categories of the two-good-demand system are food and nonfood while the categories of the nine-good-demand system are: food, beverage and tobacco; clothing and footwear; education; gross rent, fuel and power; house furnishings and operations; medical care; recreation; transport and communications; and other items.

Comparison of results for the two-good system to those obtained by TCS with 1980 ICP data indicates our elasticities are similar. For countries that witness income growth over this period relative to that of the U.S., cross-price elasticities have become more inelastic over this period. Within both years, Cournot elasticities are more elastic for poor countries than for rich ones.

An important finding is that, for a necessity, the substitution effects (based on Slutsky elasticity estimates) are larger in low- and middle-income countries than in rich ones while the opposite is the case for a price change in the most luxurious goods. The largest substitution effects (consumers switch to a good that becomes relatively less expensive) are from a change in food price in poor countries. The two goods that are most affected by a change in the price of another good are recreation and medical care.

When both the substitution effect and the income effect of a price change are considered (based on Cournot elasticities), a different expenditure pattern emerges. For a price change of a necessity, the cross-price elasticities of all the other goods in all countries are negative, but the negative effects are greater in poor than in rich countries. In comparison, the combined effects on quantity demanded are negligible when the price of a luxury good changes.

Quantity demanded is most affected by a change in food price due to the large income effect associated with a food-price change. When food price increases, due to the income effect, the quantity demanded of all goods falls, particularly in poor countries. Sharp increases in food price therefore have a depressing effect on the overall economy of both rich and poor countries as consumers cut back spending on all goods. The largest cross-price elasticities are those of recreation followed by medical care. Thus food price increases have a detrimental impact on the health of consumers due to reduced purchases of food as well as reduced spending on medical care.

The adverse impacts of food-price hikes on the general economy and the health of poor consumers point to the importance of policy measures which promote market-based means of lowering the costs of producing and distributing food. These can include an improved business environment, lower trade restrictions on food products, a more efficient food supply chain, and greater investment in agricultural research and development. Technological change, resulting from research and innovation, lowers the cost of food production and thereby reduces food prices, in turn positively contributing to the economic well-being of nations.

Finally, the cross-price elasticities and the methodology presented in this paper are potentially important inputs into other research. For example, the estimates in this paper, which represent a larger number of countries and consumption categories than in previous studies, can be used in economic projection models such as USDA's Baseline, the GTAP model, IFPRI's IMPACT model and others (e.g., Hertel et al. 2004; Keeney and Hertel 2005; Winters 2005; Hertel and Ivanic 2006; von Braun 2007; Anderson and Valenzuela 2007; Valenzuela et al. 2008; Hertel 2011). Additionally, the methodology can be used to accommodate other demand systems such as the AIDADS model (Rimmer and Powell 1992, 1996) that has been fit successfully to ICP data (e.g., Reimer and Hertel 2003, 2004; Cranfield et al. 1998b, 2000, 2003, 2004). The methodology may also be generalized to out-of-sample data sets. For example, Cox and Alm (2007) calculate income and own-price elasticities of demand for a set of countries by using the parameter estimates of SRB and applying them to a real income per capita series that links real income in 1996 to that of 2006. In the same way, cross-price elasticities could be estimated as well.

Acknowledgment Partial support for this project is provided by the United States Department of Agriculture under Agreement No. 58-3000-7-0104

Appendix A: Florida Model

TCS develop the Florida model by incorporating prices in Working's (1943) model. TCS began by rewriting Working's model as a cross-country demand system under the assumption that all countries face the same price vector,

$$w_{ic} = \alpha_i + \beta_i \log E_c + \varepsilon_{ic} \tag{6.1}$$

where $w_{ic} = E_{ic}/E_c$ is the budget share of good i ($i = 1, \ldots, n$) in country c ($c = 1, \ldots, N$), E_{ic} is expenditure on good i in c, $E_c = \sum_{i=1}^{n} E_{ic}$ is total nominal consumption expenditure in c, ε_{ic} is a random error term, and α_i and β_i are parameters to be estimated. Summing across all n goods, the sum of the budget shares equals one, $\sum_i w_{ic} = 1$, and the parameter estimates satisfy the adding-up conditions:

$$\sum_{i=1}^{n} \alpha_i = 1 \text{ and } \sum_{i=1}^{n} \beta_i = 0. \tag{6.2}$$

Multiply both sides of Eq. (6.1) by E_c to obtain $w_{ic}E_c = E_{ic}$ on the left side. Differentiating the result, $E_{ic} = \alpha_{ic}E_c + \beta_{ic}E_c \log E_c$, with respect to E_c and using Eq. (6.1), we obtain the marginal (budget) share, θ_{ic}, which exceeds the budget share in country c by β_i,

$$\theta_{ic} = \frac{dE_{ic}}{dE_c} = \alpha_i + \beta_i \left(1 + \log E_c\right) = w_{ic} + \beta_i. \tag{6.3}$$

Both the budget and marginal shares are functions of income such that, when income changes, w_{ic} and θ_{ic} change.[1]

The ratio of the marginal share to the average share equals the income elasticity of demand for good i in country c, η_{ic}, and in the case of Working's model,

$$\eta_{ic} = \frac{\theta_{ic}}{w_{ic}} = \frac{dE_{ic}}{dE_c}\frac{E_c}{E_{ic}} = \frac{d\left(\log E_{ic}\right)}{d\left(\log E_c\right)} = 1 + \frac{\beta_i}{w_{ic}}. \tag{6.4}$$

---

[1]The exception to this is when a good has unitary elasticity; as income increases, expenditure on the good increases in the same proportion and w_{ic} and θ_{ic} are unchanged.

A necessity (luxury) has an income elasticity of demand less than (greater than) one. This result shows that a good is a necessity (luxury) if $\beta_i < 0$ (> 0). If $\beta_i = 0$, the good has unitary elasticity.

Let Q_c represent the real income per capita in country c. TCS substitute Q_c for E_c in Eq. (6.1) and, using Eqs. (6.1) and (6.3), conclude that the budget and marginal shares of good i in c may be written, respectively, as

$$w_{ic} = \alpha_i + \beta_i q_c + \varepsilon_{ic} \quad \text{where } q_c = \log Q_c \tag{6.5}$$

$$\theta_{ic} = \alpha_i + \beta_i q_c^* \quad \text{where } q_c^* = 1 + q_c \tag{6.6}$$

The next step is to incorporate prices into Eq. (6.5). Let p_{ic} and p_{id} represent the domestic-currency price of good *i* in country *c* and in country *d*, respectively, where $c \neq d$. As domestic-currency prices have different dimensions in different countries, the absolute prices p_{ic} and p_{id} from countries *c* and *d* will have different dimensions. However, for cross-country analyses, one needs to have prices for all countries in the same dimension. The solution is to use relative instead of absolute prices. Also note that the price ratio p_{ic}/p_{jc} depends on country c and implies that different countries have different sets of prices. To extend Eq. (6.5) to include prices and still have fixed parameters (i.e., α_i and β_i), one must select a particular set of relative prices. TCS choose to deflate the absolute price of *i* in *c* by the geometric mean price[2] of *i* across all *N* countries, that is:

$$\ln \overline{p}_i = \frac{1}{N}\sum_{c=1}^{N} \log p_{ic}. \tag{6.7}$$

The model that emerges has the budget share on the left and is polynomial in the parameters:

$$w_{ic} = \text{LINEAR} + \text{QUADRATIC} + \text{CUBIC} + \varepsilon_{ic}, \tag{6.8}$$

where

LINEAR = Real-income term,

$$= \alpha_i + \beta_i q_c, \tag{6.8a}$$

QUADRATIC = Pure-price term,

$$= (\alpha_i + \beta_i q_c)\left[\log\frac{p_{ic}}{\overline{p}_i} - \sum\nolimits_{j=1}^{n} (\alpha_j + \beta_j q_c)\log\frac{p_{jc}}{\overline{p}_j}\right], \tag{6.8b}$$

[2]To justify the above choice of converting the absolute prices into relative prices by dividing each absolute price by the geometric mean price, Theil and Seale (1987) prove that the geometric mean price point across countries has a minimum mean-squared distance property.

CUBIC = Substitution term,

$$= \phi \left(\alpha_i + \beta_i q_c^*\right) \left[\log \frac{p_{ic}}{\overline{p}_i} - \sum_{j=1}^{n} \left(\alpha_j + \beta_j q_c^*\right) \log \frac{p_{jc}}{\overline{p}_j} \right], \tag{6.8c}$$

and p_{ic} is the price of good i in c, $\overline{p}_i$ is the geometric mean price of good i across all countries such that $\log \overline{p}_i = \frac{1}{N} \sum_{c=1}^{N} \log p_{ic}$, α_i, β_i, and ϕ (representing income flexibility (the inverse of the income elasticity of the marginal utility of income))[3] are parameters to be estimated, and ε_{ic} is a random error term.

The linear term in the model, Eq. (6.8a), represents the effect of a change in real (per capita) income (i.e., the per capita volume of total consumption expenditure) on the budget share. In the case where all countries face the same set of prices, the quadratic and cubic terms vanish leaving the linear term.[4] It is also the budget share of the Florida model evaluated at geometric mean prices:

$$\overline{w}_{ic} = \alpha_i + \beta_i q_c. \tag{6.9}$$

The quadratic term, Eq. (6.8b), (quadratic because it contains products of α and β) is the pure-price term and shows how an increase in price p_{ic} results in a higher budget share on good i, even if the volume of total expenditure stays the same. The cubic term, Eq. (6.8c), (cubic because it involves the products of α_i, β_i, and ϕ) is the substitution term and recognizes that consumers will not consume the same quantities, but will react to the higher price by substitution away from good i towards other (now) relatively cheaper goods. The expressions in brackets in both (6.8b) and (6.8c) are deflated logarithmic price ratios with the deflators being weighted means of those logarithmic ratios. The weights, however, are different in (6.8b) and (6.8c). In the former, the weights are budget shares ($\overline{w}_{ic} = \alpha_i + \beta_i q_c$) of (6.9) while the latter weights are marginal shares,

$$\overline{\theta}_{ic} = \left(\alpha_i + \beta_i q_c^*\right), \tag{6.10}$$

both evaluated at geometric mean price, $\overline{p}_i$.

The deflators relate to the Divisia price index,

$$DP = \sum_j w_j d \log p_j, \tag{6.11}$$

[3] Frisch (1932, p. 15) refers to the reciprocal of ϕ (i.e., $\phi^{-1} = (d\mu/dE)(E/\mu)$ where μ represents the marginal utility of money and E is total expenditure) as the flexibility of the marginal utility of money, or shorter, as money flexibility.

[4] Deaton and Muellbauer's (1980) model has the same income term as the Florida model, and its price terms also vanish if all countries (households) face the same price vector.

and the Frisch price index,

$$DP* = \sum_j \theta_j d \log p_j, \tag{6.12}$$

by substitution of $\log p_j - \log \overline{p}_j$ for $d \log p_j$ into Eqs. (6.11) and (6.12). The Divisia price index weights the logarithmic price changes by the budget shares while the Frisch price index weights the logarithmic price changes by the marginal shares. The Frisch price index weights luxuries (necessities) more (less) than the Divisia price index since $\theta_j > w_j$ for luxury goods and $\theta_j < w_j$ for necessities.

Homogeneity is imposed by subtracting the nth relative price from all other $n-1$ relative prices, that is, $x_{ic} = \log \frac{p_{ic}}{\overline{p}_i} - \log \frac{p_{nc}}{\overline{p}_n}$, and replacing the relative price terms in Eq. (6.8) with x_{ic}. Under the condition of preference independence, the model has Slutsky price terms as follows:

$$\pi_{ijc} = \phi\theta_{ic}\left(1 - \theta_{ic}\right) \quad i = j \tag{6.13a}$$

$$= -\phi\theta_{ic}\theta_{jc} \quad i \neq j \tag{6.13b}$$

with θ_{ic} defined in Eq. (6.7) and ϕ as defined in footnote 13. Symmetry of the Slutsky coefficients is readily seen as

$$\pi_{ijc} = \pi_{jic} = -\phi\theta_{ic}\theta_{jc} \quad i \neq j. \tag{6.14}$$

Appendix B: Three Types of Price Elasticities

Three prominent types of price elasticities are the Frisch, Slutsky, and Cournot price elasticities. Differences among these are due to the way the consumer is compensated after a price change. For the Frisch (Slutsky) elasticity, the consumer is compensated such that her marginal utility of income (real income) remains constant after a price change while the Cournot elasticity results when nominal income is constrained to remain constant. To calculate any of the elasticities based on the Florida model, one starts with the parameter estimates of the model (αs, βs, ϕ) and real income per capita in all countries relative to the real U.S. per capita income that is normalized to equal one.[5] All elasticities are evaluated at geometric mean prices, $\overline{p}_i$,and the budget and marginal shares of good i in country c, written in terms of the parameters of the Florida model, are, respectively,

$$\overline{w}_{ic} = \alpha_i + \beta_i q_c \tag{6.15}$$

[5]See TCS, pp. 110–111, for the derivation of the three types of own-price elasticities.

and

$$\overline{\theta}_{ic} = \overline{w}_{ic} + \beta_i = \alpha_i + \beta_i q_c^*. \tag{6.16}$$

Using the parameters from the Florida model, the Frisch price elasticity is

$$F_{ijc} = \phi \frac{\overline{\theta}_{ic}}{\overline{w}_{ic}} = \phi \frac{\overline{w}_{ic} + \beta_i}{\overline{w}_{ic}} = \phi \left(\frac{\alpha_i + \beta_i q_c^*}{\alpha_i + \beta_i q_c} \right) \quad i = j \tag{6.17a}$$

$$F_{ijc} = 0 \quad i \neq j \tag{6.17b}$$

The Frisch own-price elasticity, F_{iic},exists but Frisch cross-price elasticities vanish because of the assumption of preference independence (TCS, p. 117). However, one can calculate the Slutsky and Cournot own- and cross-price elasticities of demand in terms of the Frisch own-price elasticities.

The Florida model does not directly estimate Slutsky price parameters when preferences are independent, but one can calculate the Slutsky price parameters with the parameter estimates of the Florida model using Eqs. (6.9a) and (6.16) for each country, that is:

$$\pi_{ijc} = \phi \left(\alpha_i + \beta_i q_c^*\right) \left(1 - \left(\alpha_i + \beta_i q_c^*\right)\right) \quad i = j \tag{6.18a}$$

$$= -\phi \left(\alpha_i + \beta_i q_c^*\right) \left(\alpha_j + \beta_j q_c^*\right) \quad i \neq j \tag{6.18b}$$

The Slutsky price elasticity for good i with respect to a change in the price of good j in country c is the ratio of the coefficient of the Slutsky matrix and the corresponding budget share (Frisch 1959; TCS, p. 155). In terms of the Florida model's parameters and the Frisch own-price elasticity, the Slutsky own-price and cross-price elasticities are

$$S_{ijc} = F_{iic} \left(1 - \overline{\theta}_{ic}\right) = F_{iic} \left(1 - \left(\alpha_i + \beta_i q_c^*\right)\right) \quad i = j \tag{6.19a}$$

$$= -F_{iic} \overline{\theta}_{jc} = -F_{iic} \left(\alpha_j + \beta_j q_c^*\right) \quad i \neq j. \tag{6.19b}$$

The Cournot own-price and cross-price elasticities written in terms of the parameters of the Florida model and the Frisch own-price elasticity are

$$C_{ijc} = F_{iic} \left(1 - \overline{\theta}_{ic}\right) - \overline{\theta}_{ic} = F_{iic} \left(1 - \left(\alpha_i + \beta_i q_c^*\right)\right) - \left(\alpha_i + \beta_i q_c^*\right) \quad i = j \tag{6.20a}$$

$$= -F_{iic} \overline{\theta}_{jc} - \frac{\overline{\theta}_{ic} \overline{w}_{jc}}{\overline{w}_{ic}} = -F_{iic} \left(\alpha_i + \beta_i q_c^*\right) - \frac{\left(\alpha_i + \beta_i q_c^*\right) \left(\alpha_j + \beta_j q_c\right)}{\left(\alpha_i + \beta_i q_c\right)} \quad i \neq j, \tag{6.20b}$$

while, in terms of the Slutsky price elasticities, are

$$= S_{iic} - \left(\alpha_i + \beta_i q_c^*\right) \quad i = j \tag{6.21a}$$

$$= S_{ijc} - \frac{\left(\alpha_i + \beta_i q_c^*\right)\left(\alpha_j + \beta_j q_c\right)}{\left(\alpha_i + \beta_i q_c\right)} \quad i \neq j. \tag{6.21b}$$

As shown in Eqs. (6.21a) and (6.21b), the Cournot price elasticity is equal to the substitution effect of the Slutsky price elasticity minus a positive income term. Under preference independence, all Slutsky cross-price elasticities are positive. If the income effect is greater (smaller) than the substitution effect, the Cournot cross-price elasticities is negative (positive); if the effects are equal, the elasticities are zero.

References

Anderson K, Valenzuela E (2007) Do global trade distortions still harm developing country farmers? Rev World Econ 143(1):108–139

Banks J, Blundell R, Lewbel A (1997) Quadratic Engel curves and consumer demand. Rev Econ Stat 79(4):527–539

Chen D (1994) A demand system for the world. Unpublished working paper, Economic Research Center, department of economics, University of Western Economics, Perth

Chen D (1999a) Empirical regularities in consumption patterns of LDCs. In: Chen D (ed) World consumption economics. World Scientific Publishing Co, Singapore

Chen D (1999b) Income and world food consumption. In: Chen D (ed) World consumption economics. World Scientific Publishing Co, Singapore

Chen D (1999c) A demand system for the world. In: Chen D (ed) World consumption economics. World Scientific Publishing Co, Singapore

Clements KW, Chen D (1996) Fundamental similarities in consumer behavior. Appl Econ 28: 747–757

Clements KW, Chen D (2010) Affluence and food: a simple way to infer incomes. Am J Agric Econ 92(4):909–926

Clements KW, Selvanathan S (1994) Understanding consumption patterns. Empir Econ 19:69–110

Clements KW, Theil H (1979) A cross-country analysis of consumption patterns, Report no. 7924. Center for Mathematical Studies in Business and Economics, University of Chicago, Chicago

Clements KW, Suhm FE, Theil H (1979) A cross-price tabulation of income elasticities of demand. Econ Lett 3:199–202

Clements KW, Wu Y, Zhang J (2006) Comparing international consumption patterns. Empir Econ 31:1–30

Cole W, Gehlhar M, Hertel T, Wang Z, Yu W (1998) Understanding the determinants of structural change in world food markets. Am J Agric Econ 80:1051–1061

Cox WM, Alm R (2007) Opportunity knocks: selling our services to the world. In Federal Reserve Bank of Dallas 2007 annual report. Federal Reserve Bank of Dallas, Dallas

Cranfield JAL, Preckel PV, Hertel TW (2007) Poverty analysis using an international cross-country demand system, policy research working paper 4285. Development Research Group, The World Bank, Washington, D.C.

Cranfield JAL, Preckel PV, Hertel TW (2005) A modified, implicit, directly additive demand system. Unpublished working paper.

Cranfield JAL, Hertel TW, Eales JS, Preckel PV (1998a) Changes in the structure of global food demand, staff paper #98–5. Department of Agricultural Economics, Purdue University, West Lafayette
Cranfield JAL, Hertel TW, Eales JS, Preckel PV (1998b) Changes in the structure of global food demand. Am J Agric Econ 80: 1042–1050
Cranfield JAL, Preckel PV, Eales JS, Hertel TW (2000) On the estimation of 'an implicitly additive demand system'. Appl Econ 32:1907–1915
Cranfield JAL, Eales JS, Hertel TW, Preckel PV (2003) Model selection when estimating and predicting consumer demands using international cross section data. Empir Econ 28:353–364
Cranfield JAL, Preckel PV, Eales JS, Hertel TW (2004) Simultaneous estimation of an implicit directly additive demand system and the distribution of expenditure: an application of maximum entropy. Econ Model 21:361–385
Deaton AS, Muellbauer J (1980) An almost ideal demand system. Am Econ Rev 70:313–326
Faiola A (2008) The new economics of hunger. *The Washington Post*, April 27, 2008
Fiebig DG, Seale JL Jr, Theil H (1987) The demand for energy: evidence from a cross-country demand system. Energy Econ 9:149–153
Fiebig DG, Seale JL Jr, Theil H (1988) Cross–country demand analysis based on three phases of the international comparison project. In: Salazar–Carrillo J, Prosada–Rao DS (eds) World comparison of incomes, prices, and product. Elsevier Science Publishers B.V, Amsterdam, pp 225–235, North–Holland
Finke R, Rosalsky MC, Theil H (1983) A new cross-country tabulation of income elasticities of demand. Econ Lett 12:391–396
Finke R, Lu W-H, Theil H (1984) A cross-country tabulation of own-price elasticities of demand. Econ Lett 14:137–142
Friedman M (1976) Price theory. Aldine Publishing Co., Chicago
Frisch R (1932) New methods of measuring marginal utility. Mohr, Tübingen
Frisch R (1959) A complete scheme for computing all direct and cross demand elasticities in a model with many sectors. Econometrica 27(2):177–196
Gamaletsos T (1973) Further analysis of cross-country comparison of consumer expenditure patters. Eur Econ Rev 4:1–20
Goldberger AS, Gamaletsos T (1970) A cross-country comparison of consumer expenditure patterns. Eur Econ Rev 1:357–400
Harvey A (1990) The econometrics analysis of times series, 2nd edn. The MIT Press, Cambridge, MA
Hertel TW (2011) The global supply and demand for agricultural land in 2050: a perfect storm in the making. Am J Agric Econ 93(2):259–275
Hertel TW, Ivanic M (2006) Assessing the world market impacts of multilateral trade reforms. In: Hertel TW, Winters LA (eds) Poverty and the WTO: impacts of the Doha development agenda. The World Bank/Palgrave Macmillan, Washington, D.C./New York
Hertel TW, Keeney R, Valenzuela E (2004) Global analysis of agricultural trade liberalization: assessing model validity. Paper presented at the American agricultural economics association annual meeting, Denver, http://ageconsearch.umn.edu/bitstream/20199/1/sp04he02.pdf, Accessed 8/29/2013
Houthakker HS (1957) An international comparison of household expenditure patterns, commemorating the centenary of Engel's law. Econometrica 25:532–551
Houthakker HS (1965) New evidence on demand elasticities. Econometrica 33:277–288
Keeney R, Hertel TW (2005) GTAP-AGR: a framework for assessing the implications of multilateral changes in agricultural policies, GTAP technical paper No. 24. Center for global trade analysis, department of agricultural economics, Purdue University, West Lafayette, IN
Keller WJ, van Driel J (1985) Differential consumer demand systems. Eur Econ Rev 27:375–390
Kravis IB, Kenessey Z, Heston AW, Summers R (1975) A system of international comparisons of gross product and purchasing power. Johns Hopkins University Press, Baltimore, for the World Bank

Kravis IB, Heston AW, Summers R (1978) International comparisons of real product and purchasing power. Johns Hopkins University Press, Baltimore, for the World Bank

Kravis IB, Heston AW, Summers R (1982) World product and income: international comparisons of real gross product. Johns Hopkins University Press, Baltimore, for the World Bank

Lluch C, Powell A (1975) International comparisons of expenditure patterns. Eur Econ Rev 5: 275–303

Neves P (1987) Analysis of consumer demand in Portugal, 1958–1981. Memoire de Maitrise en Sciences Economiques, Universite Catholique de Louvain, Louvain-la-Nueve

Parks RW, Barten AP (1973) A cross-country comparison of the effects of prices, income and population composition on consumption patterns. Econ J 83:834–852

Pollack RA, Wales TJ (1987) Pooling international consumption data. Rev Econ Stat 69:90–99

Regmi A, Deepak MS, Seale JL Jr., Bernstein J (2001) Cross-country analysis of food consumption patterns. In Regmi A (ed) Changing structure of global food consumption and trade, WRS-01-1. Market and Trade Economics Division, Economic Research Service, U. S. Department of Agriculture, Washington, D.C

Reimer JJ (2003) Non-homothetic consumer demand and the factor content of trade. Unpublished working paper

Reimer JJ, Hertel TW (2004) Estimation of international demand behavior for use with input–output based data. Econ Syst Res 16(4):347–366

Reimer JJ, Hertel TW (2003) International cross section estimates of demand for use in the GTAP model, GTAP working paper No. 22. Center for global trade analysis, department of agricultural economics, Purdue University, West Lafayette, IN

Rimmer MT, Powell AA (1992) Demand patterns across the development spectrum: estimates for the AIDADS system. Preliminary working paper No. OP-75. Centre of policy studies, Monash University, Monash. Reissued in 2001, http://www.monash.edu.au/policy/ftp/workpapr/op-75.pdf, Accessed 8/21/2013

Rimmer MT, Powell AA (1996) An implicitly directly additive demand system. Appl Econ 28:1613–1622

Seale JL Jr., Regmi A, Bernstein J (2003) International evidence on food consumption patterns, technical bulletin No. 1904. Economic Research Service, U.S. Department of Agriculture, Washington, D.C

Seale JL Jr, Regmi A (2006) Modeling international consumption patterns. Rev Income Wealth 52(4):603–624

Seale JL Jr, Regmi A (2009) International consumption patterns: evidence from the 1996 international comparison project. In: Ghatak S (ed) Macroeconomics of development. Routledge, London/New York

Seale JL Jr, Solano AA (2012) The changing demand for energy in rich and poor countries over 25 years. Energy Econ 34:1834–1844

Seale JL Jr, Theil H (1987) Extending the sample size in cross-country demand analysis. Econ Lett 23:209–212

Seale JL Jr, Theil H (1991a) Income and price sensitivity in demand systems, part I: income sensitivity. In: Kaul TJ, Sengupta JK (eds) Economic models, estimation, and socioeconomic system: essays in honor of Karl A. Fox. Elsevier (North-Holland) Science Publishers, Amsterdam

Seale JL Jr, Theil H (1991b) Income and price sensitivity in demand systems, part II: price sensitivity. In: Kaul TJ, Sengupta JK (eds) Economic models, estimation, and socioeconomic system: essays in honor of Karl A. Fox. Elsevier (North-Holland) Science Publishers, Amsterdam

Seale JL Jr, Walker WE, Kim I-M (1991) The demand for energy: cross-country evidence using the Florida model. Energy Econ 13:33–40

Selvanathan S, Selvanathan EA (1993) A cross-country analysis of consumption patterns. Appl Econ 25:1245–1259

Suhm FE (1979) A cross-country analysis of Divisia covariances of prices and quantities consumed. University of Chicago, Chicago, Manuscript

Theil H (1965) The information approach to demand analysis. Econometrica 33:67–87

Theil H (1987) Evidence on international consumption patterns. In: Theil H, Clements KW (eds) Applied demand analysis. Ballinger Publishing Co., Cambridge, MA, pp 37–100
Theil H (1996) Studies in global econometrics. Kluwer Academic Publishers, Dordrecht
Theil H (1997) The Florida model for demand analysis with cross-country data. In: Antonio J, Salazar–Carrillo J (eds) Price policies and economic growth. Praeger, Westport, pp 227–236
Theil H, Finke R (1985) Income and price elasticities of demand at low levels of real income. Econ Lett 18:1–5
Theil H, Seale JL Jr (1987) Measuring the distance between relative price vectors of different countries. Econ Lett 23:371–374
Theil H, Suhm FE, Meisner JF (1980) Statistical inference in cross-country demand systems. Econ Lett 5:383–387
Theil H, Chung CF, Seale JL Jr (1989) International evidence on consumption patterns. JAI Press, Inc., Greenwich
Timmer CP (1981) Is there curvature in the Slutsky matrix? Rev Econ Stat 63:395–402
United Nations (1986–1987) World comparisons of purchasing power and real product for 1980: phase IV of the international comparison project. Two parts. United Nations Publication, New York
Valenzuela E, Anderson K, Hertel TW (2008) Impacts of trade reform: sensitivity of model results to key assumptions. Int Econ Econ Policy 4:395–420
Von Braun J (2007) The world food situation: new driving forces and required actions, food policy report No. 18. International Food Policy Research Institute, Washington, D.C
Wang HT, Eales HJ, Preckel P (1997) An analysis on international patterns of food demand using the AIDADS demand system. Paper presented at the 1997 American Agricultural Economics Association meeting, Toronto
Winters LA (2005) The European agricultural trade policies and poverty. Eur Rev Agric Econ 32(3):319–346
Working H (1943) Statistical laws of family expenditure. J Am Stat Assoc 38:43–56
World Bank (1993) Purchasing power of currencies: comparing national incomes using ICP data. Socio Economic Data Division, International Economics Department, Washington, D.C.
World Bank (2001) World development indicators. The World Bank, Washington, D.C.
Yu W, Hertel TW, Preckel PV, Eales JS (2003) Projecting world food demand using alternative demand systems. Econ Model 21:99–129

Chapter 7
Large-N and Large-T Properties of Panel Data Estimators and the Hausman Test

Seung Chan Ahn and Hyungsik Roger Moon

7.1 Introduction

Error-components models have been widely used to control for unobservable cross-sectional heterogeneity in panel data with a large number of cross-section units (N) and a small number of time-series observations (T). These models assume that stochastic error terms have two components: an unobservable time-invariant individual effect, which captures the unobservable individual heterogeneity, and the usual random noise. The most popular estimation methods for error-components models are the within and the generalized least squares (GLS) estimators. A merit of the within estimator (least squares on data transformed into deviations from individual means) is that it is consistent even if regressors are correlated with the individual effect (fixed effects). A drawback, however, is that it cannot estimate the coefficients of time-invariant regressors.[1] Among various alternative estimators for

[1]Estimation of the effect of a certain time-invariant variable on a dependent variable could be an important task in a broad range of empirical research. Examples would be the labor studies about the effects of schooling or gender on individual workers' earnings, and the macroeconomic studies about the effect of a country's geographic location (e.g., whether the country is located in Europe or Asia) on its economic growth. The within estimator is inappropriate for such studies.

S.C. Ahn (✉)
Department of Economics, Arizona State University, Tempe, AZ 85287, USA

School of Economics, Sogang University, 35 Baekbeom-ro, Mapo-gu, Seoul, South Korea
e-mail: miniahn@asu.edu; Seung.Ahn@asu.edu

H.R. Moon
Department of Economics, KAP 300, University of Southern California,
Los Angeles, CA 91208, USA

Department of Economics, Yonsei University, 50 Yonsei-Ro, Seodeamun-Gu,
Seoul 120-749, Korea
e-mail: moonr@usc.edu

R.C. Sickles and W.C. Horrace (eds.), *Festschrift in Honor of Peter Schmidt: Econometric Methods and Applications*, DOI 10.1007/978-1-4899-8008-3_7,

the coefficients of time-invariant regressors,[2] the GLS estimator has been popularly used in the literature due to its efficiency. Its consistency, however, requires a strong assumption that no regressor is correlated with the individual effects (random effects). Because of its restrictiveness, the empirical validity of the random effects assumption should be tested to justify the use of the GLS estimator. The Hausman test statistic (1978) has been popularly used for this purpose (e.g., Hausman and Taylor 1981; Cornwell and Rupert 1988; Baltagi and Khanti-Akom 1990; Ahn and Low 1996; or Guggenberger 2010).

This paper studies the asymptotic and finite-sample properties of the within and GLS estimators and the Hausman statistic for a general panel data error-components model with both large N and T. The GLS estimator has been known to be asymptotically equivalent to the within estimator for the cases with infinite N and T (see, for example, Hsiao 1986, Chap. 3; Mátyás and Sevestre 1992, Chap. 4; Baltagi 1995, Chap. 2). This asymptotic equivalence result has been obtained using a sequential limit method ($T \to \infty$ followed by $N \to \infty$) and some strong assumptions such as fixed regressors. This result naturally raises several questions. First, does the equivalence result hold for more general cases? Second, does the equivalence result indicate that the Hausman statistic, which is essentially a distance measure between the within and GLS estimators, should have a degenerating or nonstandard asymptotic distribution under the random effects assumption? Third, does the equivalence result also imply that the Hausman test would have low power to detect any violation of the random effects assumption when T is large? This paper is concerned with answering these questions.

Panel data with a large number of time-series observations have been increasingly more available in recent years in many economic fields such as international finance, finance, industrial organization, and economic growth. Furthermore, popular panel data, such as the Panel Study of Income Dynamics (PSID) and the National Longitudinal Surveys (NLS), contain increasingly more time-series observations as they are updated regularly over the years. Consistent with this trend, some recent studies have examined the large-N and large-T properties of the within and GLS estimators for error-component models.[3] For example, Phillips and Moon (1999) and Kao (1999) establish the asymptotic normality of the within estimator for

---

[2]For example, if only the time-varying regressors are correlated with the individual effects, all of the coefficients of time-varying and time-invariant regressors can be consistently estimated by a two-step estimation procedure. At the first step, the coefficients of time-varying regressors can be consistently estimated by the within estimator. At the second step, the residuals computed with the within estimator are regressed on the time-invariant regressors. The resulting coefficient estimators are consistent as long as the time-invariant regressors are uncorrelated with the individual effects. We thank an anonymous referee for introducing this estimation procedure to us.

[3]Some other studies have considered different panel data models with large N and large T. For example, Levin and Lin (1992, 1993), Quah (1994), Im et al. (2003), and Higgins and Zakrajsek (1999) develop unit-root tests for data with large N and large T. Alvarez and Arellano (2003) and Hahn and Kuersteiner (2002) examine the large-N and large-T properties of generalized method of moments (GMM) and within estimators for stationary dynamic panel data models.

the cases in which regressors follow unit root processes. Extending these studies, Choi (1998) considers a general random effects model which contains both unit-root and covariance-stationary regressors. For this model, he derives the asymptotic distributions of both the within and GLS estimators.

This paper is different from the previous studies in three respects. First, the model we consider contains both time-varying and time-invariant regressors. The time-varying regressors are cross-sectionally heterogeneous or homogeneous. Analyzing this model, we study how cross-sectional heterogeneity and the covariance structure between the time-varying and time-invariant regressors, as well as time trends in regressors, would affect the convergence rates of the panel data estimators. Second, we examine how the large-N and large-T asymptotic equivalence of the within and GLS estimators influences the asymptotic and finite-sample performances of the Hausman test. Ahn and Low (1996) have investigated the size and power properties of the Hausman test for the cases with large N and small T. In this paper, we reexamine the asymptotic and finite-sample properties of the test in more detail. In particular, we study how the power of the Hausman test would depend on the size of T and the covariance structure among regressors. Third, and perhaps less importantly, we use the joint limit approach developed by Phillips and Moon (1999).

The main findings of this paper are as follows. First, consistent with the previous studies, we find that the within and GLS estimators of the coefficients of the time-varying regressors are asymptotically equivalent under quite general conditions. However, the convergence rates of the two estimators depend on (i) whether means of time-varying regressors are cross-sectionally heterogenous or homogenous and (ii) how the time-varying and time-invariant regressors are correlated. Second, if T is large, the GLS estimators of the coefficients of the time-varying regressors are consistent even if the random effect assumption is violated. This finding implies that the choice between within and GLS is irrelevant for the studies focusing on the effects of time-varying regressors. The choice matters for the studies focusing on the effects of time-invariant regressors. Third, despite the equivalence between the GLS and within estimators, the Hausman statistic has well-defined asymptotic distributions under the random effects assumption and under its local alternatives. We also find that the power of the Hausman test crucially depends on the covariance structure between time-varying and time-invariant regressors, the covariance structure between regressors and the individual effects, and the size of T. The Hausman test has good power to detect non-zero correlation between the individual effects and the permanent (individual-specific and time-invariant) components of time-varying regressors, even if T is small. In contrast, the power of the test is somewhat limited when the effects are correlated with the time-invariant regressors and/or they are only correlated with the transitory (time-varying) components of time-varying regressors. For such cases, the size of T could rather decrease the power of the Hausman test.

This paper is organized as follows. Section 7.2 introduces the panel model of interest, and defines the within, between and GLS estimators as well as the Hausman test. For several simple illustrative models, we derive the asymptotic distributions of the panel data estimators and the Hausman test statistic. Section 7.3

reports the results from our Monte Carlo experiments. In Sect. 7.4, we provide our general asymptotic results. Concluding remarks follow in Sect. 7.5. All the technical derivations and proofs are presented in the Appendix and the previous version of this paper.

7.2 Preliminaries

7.2.1 Estimation and Specification Test

The model under discussion here is given:

$$y_{it} = \beta' x_{it} + \gamma' z_i + \zeta + \varepsilon_{it} = \delta' w_{it} + \zeta + \varepsilon_{it}; \varepsilon_{it} = u_i + v_{it}, \tag{7.1}$$

where $i = 1, \ldots, N$ denotes cross-sectional (individual) observations, $t = 1, \ldots, T$ denotes time, $w_{it} = \left(x_{it}', z_i'\right)'$, and $\delta = (\beta', \gamma')'$. In model (7.1), x_{it} is a $k \times 1$ vector of time-varying regressors, z_i is a $g \times 1$ vector of time-invariant regressors, ζ is an overall intercept term, and the error ε_{it} contains a time-invariant individual effect u_i and random noise v_{it}. We consider the cases with both large numbers of individual and time series observations, so asymptotic properties of the estimators and statistics for model (7.1) apply as $N, T \to \infty$. The orders of convergence rates of some estimators can depend on whether or not the model contains an overall intercept term. This problem will be addressed later.

We assume that data are distributed independently (but not necessarily identically) across different i, and that the v_{it} are independently and identically distributed (i.i.d.) with $var(v_{it}) = \sigma_v^2$. We further assume that $u_i, x_{i1}, \ldots, x_{iT}$ and z_i are strictly exogenous with respect to v_{it}; that is, $E(v_{it} \mid u_i, x_{i1}, \ldots, x_{iT}) = 0$, for any i and t. This assumption rules out the cases in which the set of regressors includes lagged dependent variables or predetermined regressors. Detailed assumptions about the regressors $x_{i1}, \ldots, x_{iT}, z_i$ will be introduced later.

For convenience, we adopt the following notational rule: For any $p \times 1$ vector a_{it}, we denote $\overline{a}_i = \frac{1}{T}\sum_t a_{it}$; $\tilde{a}_{it} = a_{it} - \overline{a}_i$; $\overline{a} = \frac{1}{N}\sum_i \overline{a}_i$; $\tilde{a}_i = \overline{a}_i - \overline{a}$. Thus, for example, for $w_{it} = \left(x_{it}', z_i'\right)'$, we have $\overline{w}_i = (\overline{x}_i', z_i')'$; $\tilde{w}_{it} = (\tilde{x}_{it}', 0_{1\times g})'$; $\overline{w} = (\overline{x}', \overline{z})$; $\tilde{w}_i = ((\overline{x}_i - \overline{x})', (z_i - \overline{z})')'$.

When the regressors are correlated with the individual effect, the OLS estimator of δ is biased and inconsistent. This problem has been traditionally addressed by the use of the within estimator (OLS on data transformed into deviations from individual means):

$$\hat{\beta}_w = (\textstyle\sum_{i,t} \tilde{x}_{it}\tilde{x}_{it}')^{-1} \sum_{i,t} \tilde{x}_{it}\tilde{y}_{it}'.$$

Under our assumptions, the variance-covariance matrix of the within estimator is given:

$$Var(\hat{\beta}_w) = \sigma_v^2(\textstyle\sum_{i,t} \tilde{x}_{it}\tilde{x}_{it}')^{-1}. \tag{7.2}$$

Although the within method provides a consistent estimate of β, a serious defect is its inability to identify γ, the impact of time-invariant regressors. A popular treatment of this problem is the random effects (RE) assumption under which the u_i are random and uncorrelated with the regressors:

$$E(u_i \mid x_{i1}, \ldots, x_{iT}, z_i) = 0. \quad (7.3)$$

Under this assumption, all of the parameters in model (7.1) can be consistently estimated. For example, a simple but consistent estimator is the between estimator (OLS on data transformed into individual means):

$$\hat{\delta}_b = (\hat{\beta}_b', \hat{\gamma}_b')' = (\sum_i \tilde{w}_i \tilde{w}_i')^{-1} \sum_i \tilde{w}_i \tilde{y}_i.$$

However, as Balestra and Nerlove (1966) suggest, under the RE assumption, an efficient estimator is the GLS estimator of the following form:

$$\hat{\delta}_g = [\sum_{i,t} \tilde{w}_{it} \tilde{w}_{it}' + T\theta_T^2 \sum_i \tilde{w}_i \tilde{w}_i']^{-1} [\sum_{i,t} \tilde{w}_{it} \tilde{y}_i + T\theta_T^2 \sum_i \tilde{w}_i \tilde{y}_i],$$

where $\theta_T = \sqrt{\sigma_v^2/(T\sigma_u^2 + \sigma_v^2)}$. The variance-covariance matrix of this estimator is given:

$$Var(\hat{\delta}_g) = \sigma_v^2 [\sum_{i,t} \tilde{w}_{it} \tilde{w}_{it}' + T\theta_T^2 \sum_i \tilde{w}_i \tilde{w}_i']^{-1}. \quad (7.4)$$

For notational convenience, we assume that σ_u^2 and σ_v^2 are known, while in practice they must be estimated.[4]

An important advantage of the GLS estimator over the within estimator is that it allows researchers to estimate γ. In addition, the GLS estimator of β is more efficient than the within estimator of β because $[Var(\hat{\beta}_w) - Var(\hat{\beta}_g)]$ is positive definite so long as $\theta_T > 0$. Despite these desirable properties, it is important to notice that the consistency of the GLS estimator crucially depends on the RE assumption (7.3). Accordingly, the legitimacy of the RE assumption should be tested to justify the use of GLS. In the literature, a Hausman test (1978) has been widely used for this purpose. The statistic used for this test is a distance measure between the within and GLS estimators of β:

$$\mathcal{HM}_{NT} \equiv (\hat{\beta}_w - \hat{\beta}_g)' [Var(\hat{\beta}_w) - Var(\hat{\beta}_g)]^{-1} (\hat{\beta}_w - \hat{\beta}_g). \quad (7.5)$$

[4]There are many different ways to consistently estimate σ_v^2 and σ_u^2. One way is to use

$$\hat{\sigma}_v^2 = \sum_{i,t} (\tilde{y}_{it} - \tilde{x}_{it} \hat{\beta}_w)^2 / [N(T-1)]; \hat{\sigma}_u^2 = \sum_{i,t} (\tilde{y}_i - \tilde{w}_i \hat{\delta}_{ols})^2 / NT - \hat{\sigma}_v^2,$$

where $\hat{\delta}_{ols}$ is the OLS estimator of δ.

For the cases in which T is fixed and $N \rightarrow \infty$, the RE assumption warrants that the Hausman statistic $\mathcal{HM}_{NT}$ is asymptotically χ^2-distributed with degrees of freedom equal to k. This result is a direct outcome of the fact that for fixed T, the GLS estimator $\hat{\beta}_g$ is asymptotically more efficient than the within estimator $\hat{\beta}_w$, and that the difference between the two estimators is asymptotically normal; specifically, as $N \rightarrow \infty$,

$$\sqrt{NT}(\hat{\beta}_w - \hat{\beta}_g) \Longrightarrow N(0, plim_{N\rightarrow\infty} NT[Var(\hat{\beta}_w) - Var(\hat{\beta}_g)]), \tag{7.6}$$

where "$\Longrightarrow$" means "converges in distribution."

An important condition that guarantees (7.6) is that $\theta_T > 0$. If $\theta_T = 0$, then $\hat{\beta}_w$ and $\hat{\beta}_g$ become identical and the Hausman statistic is not defined. Observing $\theta_T \rightarrow 0$ as $T \rightarrow \infty$, we can thus easily conjecture that $\hat{\beta}_w$ and $\hat{\beta}_g$ should be asymptotically equivalent as $T \rightarrow \infty$. This observation naturally raises two issues related to the asymptotic properties of the Hausman test as $T \rightarrow \infty$. First, since the Hausman statistic is asymptotically χ^2–distributed for any fixed T under the RE assumption, we can conjecture that it should remain asymptotically χ^2–distributed even if $T \rightarrow \infty$. Thus, we wish to understand the theoretical link between the asymptotic distribution of the Hausman statistic and the equivalence of the within and GLS estimators. Second, it is a well-known fact that the GLS estimator $\hat{\beta}_g$ is a weighted average of the within and between estimators $\hat{\beta}_w$ and $\hat{\beta}_b$ (Maddala 1971). Thus, observing the form of the Hausman statistic, we can conjecture that the Hausman test should have the power to detect any violation of the RE assumption that causes biases in $\hat{\beta}_b$. However, the weight given to $\hat{\beta}_b$ in $\hat{\beta}_g$ decreases with T. Thus, we wish to understand how the power of the Hausman test would be related to the size of T. We will address these two issues in the following sections.

What makes it complex to investigate the asymptotic properties of the Hausman statistic is that its convergence rate crucially depends on data generating processes. The following subsection considers several simple cases to illustrate this point.

7.2.2 *Preliminary Results*

This section considers several simple examples demonstrating that the convergence rate of the Hausman statistic depends on (i) whether or not the time-varying regressors are cross-sectionally heterogeneous and (ii) how the time-varying and time-invariant regressors are correlated.

For model (7.1), we can easily show that

$$\hat{\beta}_w - \beta = A_{NT}^{-1} a_{NT}; \tag{7.7}$$

$$\hat{\beta}_b - \beta = (B_{NT} - C_{NT} H_N^{-1} C_{NT}')^{-1} [b_{NT} - C_{NT} H_N^{-1} c_{NT}]; \tag{7.8}$$

$$\begin{aligned}\hat{\beta}_g - \beta &= [A_{NT} + T\theta_T^2(B_{NT} - C_{NT}H_N^{-1}C_{NT}')]^{-1} \\ &\quad \times [A_{NT}(\hat{\beta}_w - \beta) + T\theta_T^2(B_{NT} - C_{NT}H_N^{-1}C_{NT}')(\hat{\beta}_b - \beta)];\end{aligned} \tag{7.9}$$

$$\begin{aligned}\hat{\beta}_w - \hat{\beta}_g &= [A_{NT} + T\theta_T^2(B_{NT} - C_{NT}H_N^{-1}C_{NT})]^{-1} \\ &\quad \times T\theta_T^2(B_{NT} - C_{NT}H_N^{-1}C_{NT}')[(\hat{\beta}_w - \beta) - (\hat{\beta}_b - \beta)];\end{aligned} \tag{7.10}$$

$$Var(\hat{\beta}_w) - Var(\hat{\beta}_g) = A_{NT}^{-1} - [A_{NT} + T\theta_T^2(B_{NT} - C_{NT}H_N^{-1}C_{NT}')]^{-1}, \tag{7.11}$$

where,

$$A_{NT} = \textstyle\sum_{i,t} \tilde{x}_{it}\tilde{x}_{it}'; B_{NT} = \sum_i \tilde{x}_i\tilde{x}_i'; C_{NT} = \sum_i \tilde{x}_i\tilde{z}_i'; H_N = \sum_i \tilde{z}_i\tilde{z}_i';$$
$$a_{NT} = \textstyle\sum_{i,t} \tilde{x}_{it}v_{it}; b_{NT} = \sum_i \tilde{x}_i(u_i + \overline{v}_i); c_{NT} = \sum_i \tilde{z}_i(u_i + \overline{v}_i).$$

Equation (7.10) provides some insight into the convergence rate of the Hausman test statistic. Note that $(\hat{\beta}_w - \hat{\beta}_g)$ depends on both $(\hat{\beta}_w - \beta)$ and $(\hat{\beta}_b - \beta)$. Apparently, the between estimator $\hat{\beta}_b$ exploits only N between-individual variations, while the within estimator $\hat{\beta}_w$ is computed based on $N(T-1)$ within-individual variations. Accordingly, $(\hat{\beta}_b - \beta)$ converges to a zero vector in probability much slower than $(\hat{\beta}_w - \beta)$ does. Thus, we can conjecture that the convergence rate of $(\hat{\beta}_w - \hat{\beta}_g)$ will depend on that of $(\hat{\beta}_b - \beta)$, not $(\hat{\beta}_w - \beta)$. Indeed, we below justify this conjecture.

In this subsection, we only consider a simple model that has a single time-varying regressor (x_{it}) and a single time-invariant regressor (z_i). Accordingly, all of the terms defined in (7.7)–(7.11) are scalars. The within and GLS estimators and the Hausman test are well defined even if there is no time-invariant regressor. However, we consider the cases with both time-varying and time-invariant regressors because the correlation between the two regressors plays an important role in determining the convergence rate of the Hausman statistic. Asymptotic results for the cases with a single time-varying regressor only can be easily obtained by setting $C_{NT} = 0$.

We consider asymptotics under the RE assumption (7.3). The power property of the Hausman test will be discussed in the following subsection. To save space, we only consider the estimators of β and the Hausman test. The asymptotic distributions of the estimators of γ will be discussed in Sect. 7.4. Throughout the examples below, we assume that the z_i are $i.i.d.$ over different i with $N(0, \sigma_z^2)$. In addition, we introduce a notation e_{it} to denote a white noise component in the time-varying regressor x_{it}. We assume that the e_{it} are i.i.d. over different i and t with $N(0, \sigma_e^2)$, and are uncorrelated with the z_i.

We consider two different cases separately: the cases in which x_{it} and z_i are uncorrelated (CASE A), and the cases in which the regressors are correlated (CASE B).

CASE A: We here consider a case in which the time-varying regressor x_{it} is stationary without trend. Specifically, we assume:

$$x_{it} = \Theta_{a,i} + \Psi_{a,t} + e_{it}, \tag{7.12}$$

where $\Theta_{a,i}$ and $\Psi_{a,t}$ are fixed individual-specific and time-specific effects, respectively. Define $\overline{\Theta}_a = \frac{1}{N}\sum_i \Theta_{a,i}$ and $\overline{\Psi}_a = \frac{1}{N}\sum_i \Psi_i$; and let

$$p_{a,1} = lim_{N\to\infty}\overline{\Theta}_a;\, p_{a,2} = lim_{N\to\infty}\frac{1}{N}\sum_i \left(\Theta_{a,i} - \overline{\Theta}_a\right)^2;$$

$$q_{a,1} = lim_{N\to\infty}\overline{\Psi}_a;\, q_{a,2} = lim_{T\to\infty}\frac{1}{T}\sum_t \left(\Psi_{a,t} - \overline{\Psi}_a\right)^2.$$

We can allow them to be random without changing our results, but at the cost of analytical complexity. We consider two possible cases: one in which the parameters $\Theta_{a,i}$ are heterogeneous, and the other in which they are constant over different individuals. Allowing the $\Theta_{a,i}$ to be different across different individuals, we allow the means of x_{it} to be cross-sectionally heterogeneous. In contrast, if the $\Theta_{a,i}$ are constant over different i, the means of x_{it} become cross-sectionally homogeneous. As we show below, the convergence rates of the between estimator and Hausman test statistic are different in the two cases.

To be more specific, consider the three terms B_{NT}, C_{NT}, and b_{NT} defined below (7.11). Straightforward algebra reveals that

$$B_{NT} = \sum_i(\Theta_{a,i} - \overline{\Theta}_a)^2 + 2\sum_i(\Theta_{a,i} - \overline{\Theta}_a)(\overline{e}_i - \overline{e}) + \sum_i(\overline{e}_i - \overline{e})^2;$$

$$C_{NT} = \sum_i(\Theta_{a,i} - \overline{\Theta}_a)(\overline{z}_i - \overline{z}) + \sum_i(\overline{e}_i - \overline{e})(\overline{z}_i - \overline{z});$$

$$b_{NT} = \sum_i(\Theta_{a,i} - \overline{\Theta}_a)u_i + \sum_i(\overline{e}_i - \overline{e})u_i + \sum_i(\Theta_{a,i} - \overline{\Theta}_a)\overline{v}_i + \sum_i(\overline{e}_i - \overline{e})\overline{v}_i.$$

It can be shown that the terms including $(\Theta_{a,i} - \overline{\Theta}_a)$ will be the dominant factors determining the asymptotic properties of B_{NT}, C_{NT}, and b_{NT}. However, if the parameters $\Theta_{a,i}$ are constant over different individuals so that $\Theta_{a,i} - \overline{\Theta}_a = 0$, none of B_{NT}, C_{NT}, and b_{NT} depend on $(\Theta_{a,i} - \overline{\Theta}_a)$. For this case, the asymptotic properties of the three terms depend on $(\overline{e}_i - \overline{e})$. This result indicates that the asymptotic distribution of the between estimator $\hat{\beta}_b$, which is a function of B_{NT}, C_{NT}, and b_{NT}, will depend on whether the parameters $\Theta_{a,i}$ are cross-sectionally heterogeneous or homogeneous.[5]

We now consider the asymptotic distributions of the within, between, GLS estimators and the Hausman statistic under the two alternative assumptions about the parameters $\Theta_{a,i}$.

[5]Somewhat interestingly, however, the distinction between these two cases becomes unimportant when the model has no intercept term ($\zeta = 0$) and is estimated with this restriction. For such a case, B_{NT}, C_{NT} and b_{NT} depend on $\overline{x}_i$ instead of $\tilde{x}_i$. With $\overline{x}_i$, the terms $(\Theta_{a,i} - \overline{\Theta}_a)$ and $(\overline{e}_i - \overline{e})$ in B_{NT}, C_{NT}, and b_{NT} are replaced by $\Theta_{a,i}$ and $\overline{e}_i$, respectively. Thus, the terms containing the $\Theta_{a,i}$ remain as a dominating factor whether or not the $\Theta_{a,i}$ are heterogenous.

CASE A.1: Assume that the $\Theta_{a,i}$ vary across different i; that is, $p_{a,2} \neq 0$. With this assumption, we can easily show that as $(N, T \to \infty)$[6]:

$$\sqrt{NT}(\hat{\beta}_w - \beta) \Longrightarrow N\left(0, \frac{\sigma_v^2}{(q_{a,2} + \sigma_e^2)}\right); \tag{7.13}$$

$$\sqrt{N}(\hat{\beta}_b - \beta) \Longrightarrow N\left(0, \frac{\sigma_u^2}{p_{a,2}}\right); \tag{7.14}$$

$$\sqrt{NT}(\hat{\beta}_g - \beta) = \sqrt{NT}(\hat{\beta}_w - \beta) + \frac{1}{\sqrt{T}}\frac{\sigma_v^2}{\sigma_u^2}\frac{p_{a,2}}{(q_{a,2} + \sigma_e^2)}\sqrt{N}(\hat{\beta}_b - \beta) + o_p\left(\frac{1}{\sqrt{T}}\right); \tag{7.15}$$

$$plim_{N,T\to\infty} NT^2[Var(\hat{\beta}_w) - Var(\hat{\beta}_g)] = \frac{\sigma_v^4}{\sigma_u^2}\frac{p_{a,2}}{(q_{a,2} + \sigma_e^2)^2}. \tag{7.16}$$

Three remarks follow. First, consistent with previous studies, we find from (7.15) that the within and GLS estimators, $\hat{\beta}_w$ and $\hat{\beta}_g$, are $\sqrt{NT}$-equivalent in the sense that $(\hat{\beta}_w - \hat{\beta}_g)$ is $o_p(\sqrt{NT})$. This is so because the second term in the right-hand side of (7.15) is $O_p(1/\sqrt{T})$. At the same time, (7.15) also implies that $(\hat{\beta}_w - \hat{\beta}_g)$ is $O_p(\sqrt{NT^2})$ and asymptotically normal. These results indicate that the within and GLS estimators are equivalent to each other by the order of $\sqrt{NT}$, but not by the order of $\sqrt{NT^2}$. Second, from (7.15) and (7.16), we can see that the Hausman statistic is asymptotically χ^2-distributed with the convergence rate equal to $\sqrt{NT^2}$.[7] In particular, (7.15) indicates that the asymptotic distribution of the Hausman statistic is closely related to the asymptotic distribution of the between estimator $\hat{\beta}_b$.

Finally, the above asymptotic results imply some simplified GLS and Hausman test procedures. From (7.13) and (7.14), it is clear that

$$\sqrt{N}(\hat{\beta}_b - \hat{\beta}_w) = \sqrt{N}(\hat{\beta}_b - \beta) - \frac{1}{\sqrt{T}}\sqrt{NT}(\hat{\beta}_w - \beta) = \sqrt{N}(\hat{\beta}_b - \beta) + o_p(1).$$

With (7.15), this result indicates that the Hausman test based on the difference between $\hat{\beta}_w$ and $\hat{\beta}_g$ is asymptotically equivalent to the Wald test based on the between estimator $\hat{\beta}_b$ for the hypothesis that the true β equals the within

---

[6]These result are obtained utilizing the fact that limits of $\frac{1}{NT}A_{NT}$, $\frac{1}{N}B_N$, $\frac{1}{N}C_N$, and $\frac{1}{N}H_N$ are finite, while $\frac{1}{\sqrt{NT}}a_{NT}$, $\frac{1}{\sqrt{N}}b_N$, and $\frac{1}{\sqrt{N}}c_{NT}$ are asymptotically normal. More detailed calculations can be found from an earlier version of this paper.

[7]As we can see clearly from (7.15) and (7.16), the Hausman statistic does not depend on $\sqrt{NT^2}$ because it cancels out. Nonetheless, we say that the convergence rate of the Hausman test statistic equals $\sqrt{NT^2}$ because the asymptotic χ^2 result for the statistic is obtained based on the fact that $(\hat{\beta}_w - \hat{\beta}_g)$ is $\sqrt{NT^2}$–consistent.

estimator $\hat{\beta}_w$. We obtain this result because the convergence rate of $\hat{\beta}_w$ is faster than that of $\hat{\beta}_b$. In addition, the GLS estimator of $\hat{\gamma}_g$ can be obtained by the between regression treating $\hat{\beta}_w$ as the true β, that is, the regression on the model $\tilde{y}_i - \tilde{x}_i\hat{\beta}_w = \tilde{z}_i\gamma + error$. An advantage of these alternative procedures is that GLS and Hausman tests can be conducted without estimating θ_T. The alternative procedures would be particularly useful for the analysis of unbalance panel data. For such data, θ_T is different over different cross-sectional units. When T is sufficiently large for individual i's, we do not need to estimate these different θ_T's for GLS. The alternative procedures work out for all of the other cases analyzed below.

CASE A.2: Now, we consider the case in which the $\Theta_{a,i}$ are constant over different i (Θ_a); that is, $p_{a,2} = 0$. It can be shown that the asymptotic distributions of the within and GLS estimators are the same under both CASEs A.1 and A.2. However, the asymptotic distributions of the between estimator $\hat{\beta}_b$ and the Hausman statistic are different under CASEs A.1 and A.2.[8] Specifically, for CASE A.2, we can show that as $(N, T \to \infty)$,

$$\sqrt{\frac{N}{T}}(\hat{\beta}_b - \beta) \Longrightarrow N\left(0, \frac{\sigma_u^2}{\sigma_e^2}\right); \tag{7.17}$$

$$\begin{aligned}\sqrt{NT^3}(\hat{\beta}_w - \hat{\beta}_g) &= -\frac{\sigma_v^2}{\sigma_u^2}\frac{\sigma_e^2}{(q_{a,2} + \sigma_e^2)}\sqrt{\frac{N}{T}}(\hat{\beta}_b - \beta) + o_p(1) \\ &\Longrightarrow N\left(0, \frac{\sigma_v^4}{\sigma_u^2}\frac{\sigma_e^2}{(q_{a,2} + \sigma_e^2)^2}\right);\end{aligned} \tag{7.18}$$

$$plim_{N,T\to\infty} NT^3[Var(\hat{\beta}_w) - Var(\hat{\beta}_g)] = \frac{\sigma_v^4\sigma_e^2}{\sigma_u^2(q_{a,2} + \sigma_e^2)^2}, \tag{7.19}$$

Several comments follow. First, observe that differently from CASE A.1, the between estimator $\hat{\beta}_b$ is now $\sqrt{N/T}$-consistent. An interesting result is obtained when $N/T \to c < \infty$. For this case, the between estimator is inconsistent although it is still asymptotically unbiased. This implies that the between estimator is an inconsistent estimator for the analysis of cross-sectionally homogeneous panel data unless N is substantially larger than T. Second, the convergence rate of $(\hat{\beta}_w - \hat{\beta}_g)$, as well as that of the Hausman statistic, is different between CASEs A.1 and A.2. Notice that the convergence rate of $(\hat{\beta}_w - \hat{\beta}_g)$ is $\sqrt{NT^3}$ for CASE A.2, while it is $\sqrt{NT^2}$ for CASE A.1. Thus, $(\hat{\beta}_w - \hat{\beta}_g)$ converges in probability to zero

[8] If the model contains no intercept term ($\zeta = 0$) and it is estimated with this restriction, all of the results (7.13)–(7.16) are still valid with Θ_a^2 replacing $p_{a,2}$. Thus, the convergence rates of the within, between, GLS estimators and the Hausman statistic are the same under both CASEs A.1 and A.2.

much faster in CASE A.2 than in CASE A.1. Nonetheless, the Hausman statistic is asymptotically χ^2-distributed in both cases, though with different convergence rates.

Even if the time-varying regressor x_{it} contains a time trend, we can obtain the similar results as in CASEs A.1 and A.2. For example, consider a case in which the time-varying regressor x_{it} contains a time trend of order m:

$$x_{it} = \Theta_{b,i} t^m + e_{it}, \tag{7.20}$$

where the parameters $\Theta_{b,i}$ are fixed.[9] Not surprisingly, for this case, we can show that the within and GLS estimators are superconsistent and $T^m\sqrt{NT}$-equivalent. However, the convergence rates of the between estimator $\hat{\beta}_b$ and the Hausman test statistic crucially depend on whether the parameters $\Theta_{b,i}$ are heterogenous or homogeneous. When, the parameters $\Theta_{b,i}$ are heterogeneous over different i, the between estimator $\hat{\beta}_b$ is $T^m\sqrt{N}$-consistent, while the convergence rate of the Hausman statistic equals $T^m\sqrt{NT^2}$. In contrast, somewhat surprisingly, when the parameters $\Theta_{b,i}$ are heterogeneous over different i, the estimator $\hat{\beta}_b$ is no longer superconsistent. Instead, it is $\sqrt{N/T}$-consistent as in CASE A.2. The convergence rate of the Hausman statistic changes to $T^{2m}\sqrt{NT^3}$.[10] This example demonstrates that the convergence rates of the between estimator and the Hausman statistic crucially depend on whether means of time-varying regressors are cross-sectionally heterogenous or not.

CASE B: So far, we have considered the cases in which the time-varying regressor x_{it} and the time-invariant regressor z_i are uncorrelated. We now examine the cases in which this assumption is relaxed. The degree of the correlation between the x_{it} and z_i may vary over time. As we demonstrate below, the asymptotic properties of the panel data estimators and the Hausman test statistic depend on how the correlation varies over time. The basic model we consider here is given by

$$x_{it} = \Pi_i z_i / t^m + e_{it}, \tag{7.21}$$

where the Π_i are individual-specific fixed parameters, and m is a non-negative real number.[11] Observe that because of the presence of the Π_i, the x_{it} are not i.i.d. over

---

[9]We can consider a more general case: for example, $x_{it} = a_i t^m + \Theta_i + \Theta_t + b_i z_i + e_{it}$. However, the same asymptotic results apply to this general model. This is so because the trend term (t^m) dominates asymptotics.

[10]Detailed asymptotic results can be found from an earlier version of this paper.

[11]We can consider a more general model:

$$x_{it} = \Theta_{b,i} + \Psi_{b,t} + \Pi_i z_i / t^m + e_{it},$$

where the $\Theta_{b,i}$ and Ψ_i are individual- and time-specific fixed parameters, respectively. When the parameters $\Theta_{b,i}$ are cross-sectional heterogeneous, the asymptotic results are essentially the same different i.[12] The correlation between x_{it} and z_i decreases over time if $m > 0$. In contrast, $m = 0$ implies that the correlation remains constant over time. For CASE B, the within and GLS estimators are always $\sqrt{NT}$-consistent regardless of the size of m. Thus, we only report the asymptotic results for the between estimator $\hat{\beta}_b$ and the Hausman statistic.

We examine three possible cases: $m \in (0.5, \infty]$, $m = 0.5$, and $m \in [0, 0.5)$. We do so because, depending on the size of m, one (or both) of the two terms e_{it} and $\Pi_i z_i / t^m$ in x_{it} becomes a dominating factor in determining the convergence rates of the between estimator $\hat{\beta}_b$ and the Hausman statistic $\mathcal{HM}_{TN}$.

CASE B.1: Assume that $m \in (0.5, \infty]$. This is the case where the correlation between x_{it} and z_i fades away quickly over time. Thus, one could expect that the correlation between x_{it} and z_i (through the term $\Pi_i z_i / t^m$) would not play any important role in asymptotics. Indeed, straightforward algebra, which is not reported here, justifies this conjecture: The term e_{it} in x_{it} dominates $\Pi_i z_i / t^m$ in asymptotics, and, thus, this is essentially the same case as CASE A.2.[13]

CASE B.2: We now assume $m = 0.5$. For this case, define $\overline{\Pi} = \frac{1}{N}\sum_i \Pi_i$;

$$p_{b,1} = lim_{N\to\infty}\overline{\Pi};\ p_{b,2} = lim_{N\to\infty}\frac{1}{N}\sum_i \left(\Pi_i - \overline{\Pi}\right)^2,$$

and $q_b = lim_{T\to\infty}\frac{1}{T^{1-m}}\int_0^1 r^{-m}dr = \frac{1}{1-m}$ for $m \leq 0.5$. With this notation, a little algebra shows that as $(N, T \to \infty)$,

$$\sqrt{\frac{N}{T}}(\hat{\beta}_b - \beta) \Longrightarrow N\left(0, \frac{\sigma_u^2}{p_{b,2}q_b^2\sigma_z^2 + \sigma_e^2}\right).$$

Observe that the asymptotic variance of the between estimator $\hat{\beta}_b$ depends on both the terms σ_e^2 and $p_{b,2}q_b^2\sigma_z^2$. That is, both the terms e_{it} and $\Pi_i z_i / t^m$ in x_{it} are important in the asymptotics of the between estimator $\hat{\beta}_b$. This implies that the correlation between the x_{it} and z_i, when it decreases reasonably slowly over time, matters for the asymptotic distribution of the between estimator $\hat{\beta}_b$.

---

as those we obtain for CASE A.1. This is so because the terms $\Theta_{b,i}$ dominate and the terms $\Pi_i z_i / t^m$ become irrelevant in asymptotics. Thus, we set $\Theta_{b,i} = 0$ for all i. In addition, we set $\Psi_{b,t} = 0$ for all t, because presence of the time effects is irrelevant for convergence rates of panel data estimators and the Hausman statistic.

[12] We here assume that the Π_i are cross-sectionally heterogeneous. For the cases in which the Π_i are the same for all i, $\hat{\beta}_b$ does not depend on $\Pi_i z_i / t^m$, and we obtain exactly the same asymptotic results as those for CASE A.2. This is due to the fact that the individual mean of the time-varying regressor $\overline{x}_i$ becomes a linear function of the time invariant regressor z_i if the Π_i are the same for all i.

[13] We can obtain this result using the fact that $lim_{T\to\infty}\frac{1}{\sqrt{T}}\sum_t t^{-m} = 0$, if $m > 0.5$.

Nonetheless, the convergence rate of $\hat{\beta}_b$ is the same as that of $\hat{\beta}_b$ for CASEs A.2 and B.1. We can also show

$$\sqrt{NT^3}(\hat{\beta}_w - \hat{\beta}_g) = -\frac{\sigma_v^2}{\sigma_u^2}\frac{p_{b,2}q_b^2\sigma_z^2 + \sigma_e^2}{\sigma_e^2}\sqrt{\frac{N}{T}}(\hat{\beta}_b - \beta) + o_p(1)$$

$$\Longrightarrow N\left(0, \frac{\sigma_v^4}{\sigma_u^2}\frac{p_{b,2}q_b^2\sigma_z^2 + \sigma_e^2}{\sigma_e^4}\right);$$

$$plim_{N,T\to\infty} NT^3[Var(\hat{\beta}_w) - Var(\hat{\beta}_g)] = \frac{\sigma_v^4}{\sigma_u^2}\frac{p_{b,2}q_b^2\sigma_z^2 + \sigma_e^2}{\sigma_e^4},$$

both of which imply that the Hausman statistic is asymptotically χ^2-distributed.

CASE B.3: Finally, we consider the case in which $m \in [0, 0.5)$, where the correlation between x_{it} and z_i decays over time slowly. Note that the correlation remains constant over time if $m = 0$. We can show

$$\sqrt{\frac{N}{T^{2m}}}(\hat{\beta}_b - \beta) \Longrightarrow N\left(0, \frac{\sigma_u^2}{p_{b,2}q_b^2\sigma_z^2}\right).$$

Observe that the asymptotic distribution of $\hat{\beta}_b$ no longer depends on σ_e^2. This implies that the term $\Pi_i z_i/t^m$ in x_{it} dominates e_{it} in the asymptotics for $\hat{\beta}_b$. Furthermore, the convergence rate of $\hat{\beta}_b$ now depends on m. Specifically, so long as $m < 0.5$, the convergence rate increases as m decreases. In particular, when the correlation between x_{it} and z_i remains constant over time ($m = 0$), the between estimator $\hat{\beta}_b$ is $\sqrt{N}$-consistent as in CASE A.1. Finally, the following results indicate that the convergence rate of the Hausman statistic $\mathcal{HM}_{NT}$ also depends on m:

$$\sqrt{NT^{2m+2}}(\hat{\beta}_w - \hat{\beta}_g) = -\frac{\sigma_v^2}{\sigma_u^2}\frac{p_{b,2}q_b^2\sigma_z^2}{\sigma_e^2}\sqrt{\frac{N}{T^{2m}}}(\hat{\beta}_b - \beta) + o_p(1)$$

$$\Longrightarrow N\left(0, \frac{\sigma_v^4}{\sigma_u^2}\frac{p_{b,2}q_b^2\sigma_z^2}{\sigma_e^4}\right);$$

$$plim_{N,T\to\infty} NT^{2m+2}[Var(\hat{\beta}_w) - Var(\hat{\beta}_g)] = \frac{\sigma_v^4}{\sigma_u^2}\frac{p_{b,2}q_b^2\sigma_z^2}{\sigma_e^4}.$$

7.2.3 Asymptotic Power Properties of the Hausman Test

In this section, we consider the asymptotic power properties of the Hausman test for the special cases discussed in the previous subsection. To do so, we need to

Table 7.1 Local alternatives and asymptotic results

Case	Local alternatives	Convergence rate	Noncentral parameter
A.1	$E(u_i \mid \tilde{x}_i, \tilde{z}_i) = \tilde{x}_i \frac{\lambda_x}{\sqrt{N}} + \tilde{z}_i \frac{\lambda_z}{\sqrt{N}}$ [a]	$\sqrt{NT^2}$	$\frac{p_{a,2}\lambda_x^2}{\sigma_u^2}$
A.2	$E(u_i \mid \tilde{x}_i, \tilde{z}_i) = \sqrt{T}\tilde{x}_i \frac{\lambda_x}{\sqrt{N}} + \tilde{z}_i \frac{\lambda_z}{\sqrt{N}}$	$\sqrt{NT^3}$	$\frac{\sigma_e^2\lambda_x^2}{\sigma_u^2}$
B.1	$E(u_i \mid \tilde{x}_i, \tilde{z}_i) = \sqrt{T}\tilde{x}_i \frac{\lambda_x}{\sqrt{N}} + \tilde{z}_i \frac{\lambda_z}{\sqrt{N}}$	$\sqrt{NT^3}$	$\frac{\sigma_e^2\lambda_x^2}{\sigma_u^2}$
B.2	$E(u_i \mid \tilde{x}_i, \tilde{z}_i) = \sqrt{T}\tilde{x}_i \frac{\lambda_x}{\sqrt{N}} + \tilde{z}_i \frac{\lambda_z}{\sqrt{N}}$	$\sqrt{NT^3}$	$\frac{(4p_{b,2}\sigma_z^2 + \sigma_e^2)\lambda_x^2}{\sigma_u^2}$
B.3	$E(u_i \mid \tilde{x}_i, \tilde{z}_i) = T^m\tilde{x}_i \frac{\lambda_x}{\sqrt{N}} + \tilde{z}_i \frac{\lambda_z}{\sqrt{N}}$	$\sqrt{NT^{2m+2}}$	$\frac{\left(\left(\frac{1}{1-m}\right)^2 p_{b,2}\sigma_z^2\right)\lambda_x^2}{\sigma_u^2}$

[a] This sequence of local alternatives can be replaced by

$$E(u_i \mid \overline{x}_i, \overline{z}_i) = \lambda_o + \overline{x}_i \frac{\lambda_x}{\sqrt{N}} + \overline{z}_i \frac{\lambda_z}{\sqrt{N}},$$

where λ_o is any constant scalar. The asymptotic results remain the same with this replacement.

specify a sequence of local alternative hypotheses for each case. Among many, we consider the alternative hypotheses under which the conditional mean of u_i is a linear function of the regressors $\tilde{x}_i$ and $\tilde{z}_i$.

We list in Table 7.1 our local alternatives and asymptotic results for CASEs A.1–B.3. For all of the cases, we assume that $var(u_i \mid \tilde{x}_i, \tilde{z}_i) = \sigma_u^2$ for all i. The parameters λ_x and λ_z are nonzero real numbers. Notice that for CASEs A.2–B.3, we use $\sqrt{T}\tilde{x}_i$ or $T^m\tilde{x}_i$ instead of $\tilde{x}_i$. We do so because, for those cases, $plim_{T\to\infty}\tilde{x}_i = 0$. The third column indicates the convergence rates of the Hausman test, which are the same as those obtained under the RE assumption. Under the local alternatives, the Hausman statistic asymptotically follows a noncentral χ^2 distribution. The noncentral parameters for individual cases are listed in the fourth column of Table 7.1.

A couple of comments follow. First, although the noncentral parameter does not depend on λ_z for any case reported in Table 7.1, it does not mean that the Hausman test has no power to detect nonzero correlation between the effect u_i and the time-invariant regressor z_i. The Hausman test comparing the GLS and within estimators is not designed to directly detect the correlations between the time-invariant regressors and the individual effects. Nonetheless, the test has power as long as the individual effect u_i is correlated with the time-varying regressors conditionally on the time-invariant regressors. To see this, consider a model in which x_{it} and z_i have a common factor f_i; that is, $x_{it} = f_i + e_{it}$ and $z_i = f_i + \eta_i$. (This is the case discussed below in Assumption 5.) Assume $E(u_i \mid f_i, \eta_i, \bar{e}_i) = c\eta_i/\sqrt{N}$. Also assume that f_i, η_i and e_{it} are normal, mutually independent, and i.i.d. over different i and t with zero means, and variances σ_f^2, σ_η^2, and σ_e^2, respectively. Note that x_{it} is not correlated with u_i, while z_i is. For this case, however, we can show that

$$E(u_i \mid \overline{x}_i, \tilde{z}_i) = \overline{x}_i \frac{\lambda_x}{\sqrt{N}} + \tilde{z}_i \frac{\lambda_z}{\sqrt{N}},$$

where $d = (\sigma_f^2 + \sigma_e^2/T)(\sigma_f^2 + \sigma_\eta^2) - \sigma_f^4$, $\lambda_x = -c\sigma_f^2\sigma_\eta^2/d, \lambda_z = c(\sigma_f^2 + \sigma_e^2/T)\sigma_\eta^2/d$. Observe that λ_x is functionally related to λ_z: $\lambda_x = 0$ if and only if $\lambda_z = 0$. For this case, it can be shown that the Hausman test has the power to detect non-zero correlation between u_i and $\tilde{z}_i$.

Second and more importantly, the results for CASE A show that the large-T and large-N power properties of the Hausman test may depend on (i) what components of x_{it} are correlated with the effect u_i and (ii) whether the mean of x_{it} is cross-sectionally heterogeneous. For CASE A, the time-invariant and time-varying parts of x_{it}, $\Theta_{a,i}$ and e_{it}, can be viewed as permanent and transitory components, respectively. For fixed T, it does not matter to the Hausman test which of these two components of x_{it} is correlated with the individual effect u_i. The Hausman test has power to detect any kind of correlations between x_{it} and u_i. In contrast, for the cases with large T, the same test can have power for specific correlations only. To see why, observe that for CASE A.1, the noncentral parameter of the Hausman statistic depends only on the variations of the permanent components Θ_i, not on those of the transitory components e_{it}. This implies that for CASE A.1 (where the permanent components $\Theta_{a,i}$ are cross-sectionally heterogeneous), the Hausman test has power for nonzero correlation between the effect u_i and the permanent component $\Theta_{a,i}$, but no power for nonzero-correlation between the effect and the temporal component e_{it}. In contrast, for CASE A.2 (where the permanent components $\Theta_{a,i}$ are the same for all i), the noncentral parameter depends on the variations in e_{it}. That is, for CASE A.2, the Hausman test does have power to detect nonzero-correlation between the effect and the temporal component of x_{it}.[14]

Similar results are obtained from the analysis of CASE B. The results reported in the fourth column of Table 7.1 show that when the correlation between x_{it} and z_i decays slowly over time ($m \leq 0.5$), the Hausman test has power to detect nonzero-correlation between the individual effect and the transitory component of time-varying regressors, even if T is large. In contrast, when $m > 0.5$, the same test has no power to detect such nonzero correlations if T is large. These results indicate that the asymptotic power of the Hausman test can depend on the size of T. That is, the Hausman test results based on the entire data set with large T could be different from those based on subsamples with small T. These findings will be more elaborated in Sect. 7.3.

[14]This point can be better presented if we choose the following sequence of local alternative hypotheses for CASE A:

$$E(u_i|\tilde{x}_i, \tilde{z}_i) = E(\tilde{x}_i)\frac{\lambda_{x,1}}{\sqrt{N}} + (\tilde{x}_i - E(\tilde{x}_i))\frac{\lambda_{x,2}}{\sqrt{N}} + \tilde{z}_i\frac{\lambda_z}{\sqrt{N}}.$$

Observe that for CASE A, $E(\tilde{x}_i) = \Theta_i$, and $(\tilde{x}_i - E(\tilde{x}_i)) = \tilde{e}_i$. Under the local alternative hypotheses, it can be shown that the noncentral parameter of the Hausman test depends on either $\lambda_{x,1}$ or $\lambda_{x,2}$, but not both. When $E(\tilde{x}_i) \neq 0$ (CASE A.1), the noncentral parameter of the test depends only on $\lambda_{x,1}$. In contrast, when $E(\tilde{x}_i) = 0$, the noncentral parameter depends only on $\lambda_{x,2}$.

7.3 Monte Carlo Experiments

In this section, we investigate the finite-sample properties of the within and GLS estimators, as well as those of the Hausman test. Consistent with the previous section, we consider a model with one time-varying regressor x_{it} and one time-invariant regressor z_i. The foundations of our experiments are CASEs A and B discussed above. For all of our simulations, both the individual effects u_i and random errors v_{it} are drawn from $N(0,1)$.

For the cases in which the two regressors are uncorrelated (CASE A), we generate x_{it} and z_i as follows:

$$x_{it} = \Theta_i + \xi_i \phi_t + e_{it}, \tag{7.22}$$

$$z_i = \rho_{zu} u_i + \sqrt{1-\rho_{zu}^2} f_i, \tag{7.23}$$

where $\Theta_i = \rho_{xu,1} u_i + \sqrt{1-\rho_{xu,1}^2}\Theta_i^c$, $\xi_i = \rho_{xu,2} u_i + \sqrt{1-\rho_{xu,2}^2}\xi_i^c$, the Θ_i^c and ξ_i^c are random variables from $N(0,1)$, the e_{it} and f_i are drawn from a uniform distribution in the range $(-2,2)$. The term $\xi_i\phi_t + e_{it}$ is the transitory component of x_{it}. The term $\xi_i\phi_t$ is introduced to investigate the cases with non-zero correlations between the individual effect and the transitory component of x_{it}. The degrees of correlations between the individual effects and regressors are controlled by $\rho_{xu,1}$, $\rho_{xu,2}$ and ρ_{zu}. For each of the simulation results reported below, 5,000 random samples are used.

Table 7.2 reports the simulation results from CASE A.1. When regressors are uncorrelated with the effect u_i, both the GLS and within estimators have only small biases. The Hausman test is reasonably well sized although it is somewhat oversized when both N and T are small. When the permanent component of x_{it} is correlated with the effect (Panel I), the GLS estimator of β is biased. However, the size of bias decreases with T, as we expected. The bias in the within estimator of β is always small regardless of the sizes of N and T. The Hausman test has great power to detect non-zero correlation between the permanent component of x_{it} and u_i regardless of sample size. The power increases with T while the bias in the GLS estimator of β decreases.

Panel II of Table 7.2 shows the results from the cases in which the effect u_{it} and the transitory component of x_{it} are correlated. Our asymptotic results predict that this type of correlation does not bias the GLS estimates when T is large and is not detected by the Hausman test. The results reported in Panel II are consistent with this prediction. Even if T is small, we do not see substantial biases in the GLS estimates. When T is small, the Hausman test has some limited power to detect the non-zero correlation between the effect and the transitory component of the time-varying regressor. However, the power decreases with T.

Table 7.3 reports the results from the cases in which the time-varying regressor does not have a permanent component (CASE A.2). Similar to those that are

Table 7.2 Monte Carlo simulation results for CASE A.1

		Panel I: $\rho_{xu,2} = 0$					Panel II: $\rho_{xu,1} = 0$				
			Bias					Bias			
			GLS		Within	Hausman rejection		GLS		Within	Hausman rejection
N	T	$\rho_{xu,1}$	β	γ	β	rate	$\rho_{xu,2}$	β	γ	β	rate
50	5	0.0	0.001	0.000	0.001	0.063	0.0	0.001	0.000	0.001	0.063
	50	0.0	0.000	0.001	0.000	0.054	0.0	0.000	0.001	0.000	0.054
	100	0.0	0.000	−0.001	0.000	0.055	0.0	0.000	−0.001	0.000	0.055
100	5	0.0	0.000	0.000	−0.001	0.049	0.0	0.000	0.000	−0.001	0.049
	50	0.0	0.000	−0.002	0.000	0.053	0.0	0.000	−0.002	0.000	0.053
	100	0.0	0.000	−0.002	0.000	0.053	0.0	0.000	−0.002	0.000	0.053
50	5	0.5	0.046	0.000	0.001	0.753	0.5	0.001	0.000	0.000	0.181
	50	0.5	0.005	0.001	0.000	0.960	0.5	0.000	0.001	0.000	0.081
	100	0.5	0.003	−0.001	0.000	0.967	0.5	0.000	−0.001	0.000	0.069
100	5	0.5	0.045	0.000	−0.001	0.956	0.5	0.000	0.000	−0.001	0.286
	50	0.5	0.005	−0.002	0.000	1.000	0.5	0.000	−0.002	0.000	0.111
	100	0.5	0.003	−0.002	0.000	1.000	0.5	0.000	−0.002	0.000	0.080
50	5	1.0	0.110	0.000	0.001	0.999	1.0	0.000	0.000	0.000	0.433
	50	1.0	0.013	0.001	0.000	1.000	1.0	0.000	0.001	0.000	0.163
	100	1.0	0.006	−0.001	0.000	1.000	1.0	0.000	−0.001	0.000	0.112
100	5	1.0	0.109	0.000	−0.001	1.000	1.0	0.000	0.000	−0.001	0.577
	50	1.0	0.012	−0.002	0.000	1.000	1.0	0.000	−0.002	0.000	0.249
	100	1.0	0.006	−0.002	0.000	1.000	1.0	0.000	−0.002	0.000	0.164

reported in Panel II of Table 7.2, there is no sign that non-zero correlation between the effect and the transitory component of x_{it} causes a substantial bias in the GLS estimator. However, differently from the results reported in Panel II of Table 7.2, the Hausman test now has better power to detect non-zero correlation between the effect and the transitory component of x_{it}. The power increases as either N or T increases.

We now consider the cases in which x_{it} and z_i are correlated (CASE B). For these cases, the x_{it} are generated by

$$x_{it} = \pi_i f_i / t^m + \xi_i \phi_t + e_{it}, \tag{7.24}$$

where the π_i are drawn from a uniform distribution in the range (0, 1). As in (7.22), the term $\xi_i \phi_t$ is introduced to investigate the cases with non-zero correlations between the individual effect and the transitory component of x_{it}. Observe that in (7.24), we use f_i, not z_i. As we have discussed in the previous section, the Hausman test would not have any power to detect non-zero correlation between z_i and u_i for the cases with large T if z_i instead of f_i were used for (7.24). We use f_i to investigate the power properties of the Hausman test under more general cases than the cases we have considered in the previous sections. Under (7.24), the Hausman test can have power to detect non-zero correlation between z_i and u_i.

Table 7.3 Monte Carlo simulation results for CASE A.2

			Bias			Hausman rejection rate
			GLS		Within	
N	T	$\rho_{xu,2}$	β	γ	β	
50	5	0.0	0.000	0.001	−0.001	0.052
	50	0.0	0.000	0.001	0.000	0.051
	100	0.0	0.000	0.001	0.000	0.052
100	5	0.0	0.000	0.002	0.000	0.050
	50	0.0	0.000	−0.001	0.000	0.049
	100	0.0	0.000	−0.002	0.000	0.055
50	5	0.5	−0.001	0.001	−0.001	0.396
	50	0.5	0.000	0.001	0.000	0.448
	100	0.5	0.000	0.001	0.000	0.461
100	5	0.5	0.000	0.002	0.000	0.569
	50	0.5	0.000	−0.001	0.000	0.626
	100	0.5	0.000	−0.002	0.000	0.620
50	5	1.0	−0.002	0.001	−0.002	0.999
	50	1.0	0.000	0.001	0.000	1.000
	100	1.0	0.000	0.001	0.000	1.000
100	5	1.0	0.000	0.002	0.000	1.000
	50	1.0	0.000	−0.001	0.000	1.000
	100	1.0	0.000	−0.002	0.000	1.000

Table 7.4 shows our simulation results from the cases in which the time-varying regressor is correlated with the time-invariant regressor. Panel I reports the results when the time-invariant regressor z_i is correlated with the effect u_i. Regardless of how fast the correlation between x_{it} and z_i decays over time, the GLS estimator of γ shows some signs of biases. While the biases reported in Panel I appear only mild, the biases become substantial if we increase the size of ρ_{zu} further. When the correlation between x_{it} and z_i remains constant over time ($m = 0$), the GLS estimator of β is mildly biased. However, the bias becomes smaller as the size of T increases. When the correlation between x_{it} and z_i decays over time ($m \geq 0.5$), no substantial bias is detected in the GLS estimator of β even if T is small. The Hausman test has some power to detect non-zero correlation between the time-invariant regressor z_i and the effect u_i. However, the power appears to be limited in our simulation exercises: Its power never exceeds 61 %. The power increases with T when $m \leq 0.5$, but the power decreases with T if $m > 0.5$.

Panel II of Table 7.4 reports the results for the cases in which the transitory component of x_{it} is correlated with the effect u_i. Similarly to those reported in Table 7.3, both the GLS estimators of β and γ show no signs of significant biases. For the cases in which the correlation between x_{it} and z_i decays only mildly over time ($m < 0.5$), the power of the Hausman test to detect nonzero-correlation

Table 7.4 Monte Carlo simulation results for CASE B

			Panel I: $\rho_{xu,2} = 0$					Panel II: $\rho_{zu} = 0$				
				Bias					Bias			
				GLS		Within	Hausman rejection		GLS		Within	Hausman rejection
m	N	T	ρ_{zu}	β	γ	β	rate	$\rho_{xu,2}$	β	γ	β	rate
0.0	50	5	0.0	0.001	−0.001	0.001	0.059	0.0	0.001	−0.001	0.001	0.059
	50	50	0.0	0.000	−0.001	0.000	0.056	0.0	0.000	−0.001	0.000	0.056
	50	100	0.0	0.000	−0.001	0.000	0.057	0.0	0.000	−0.001	0.000	0.057
	100	5	0.0	−0.001	0.000	−0.001	0.048	0.0	−0.001	0.000	−0.001	0.048
	100	50	0.0	0.000	0.000	0.000	0.051	0.0	0.000	0.000	0.000	0.051
	100	100	0.0	0.000	0.000	0.000	0.052	0.0	0.000	0.000	0.000	0.052
	50	5	0.5	−0.023	0.046	0.001	0.226	0.5	0.001	−0.001	0.000	0.136
	50	50	0.5	−0.002	0.034	0.000	0.344	0.5	0.000	−0.001	0.000	0.067
	50	100	0.5	−0.001	0.033	0.000	0.363	0.5	0.000	−0.001	0.000	0.067
	100	5	0.5	−0.024	0.046	−0.001	0.385	0.5	−0.001	0.000	−0.001	0.226
	100	50	0.5	−0.003	0.034	0.000	0.578	0.5	0.000	0.000	0.000	0.085
	100	100	0.5	−0.001	0.033	0.000	0.596	0.5	0.000	0.000	0.000	0.070
0.5	50	5	0.0	0.000	−0.001	0.000	0.054	0.0	0.000	−0.001	0.000	0.054
	50	50	0.0	0.000	−0.001	0.000	0.047	0.0	0.000	−0.001	0.000	0.047
	50	100	0.0	0.000	−0.001	0.000	0.053	0.0	0.000	−0.001	0.000	0.053
	100	5	0.0	−0.001	0.000	0.000	0.050	0.0	−0.001	0.000	0.000	0.050
	100	50	0.0	0.000	0.000	0.000	0.049	0.0	0.000	0.000	0.000	0.049
	100	100	0.0	0.000	0.000	0.000	0.049	0.0	0.000	0.000	0.000	0.049
	50	5	0.5	−0.014	0.038	0.000	0.199	0.5	0.000	0.000	0.000	0.211
	50	50	0.5	0.000	0.032	0.000	0.258	0.5	0.000	−0.001	0.000	0.214
	50	100	0.5	0.000	0.032	0.000	0.267	0.5	0.000	−0.001	0.000	0.214
	100	5	0.5	−0.015	0.038	0.000	0.348	0.5	−0.001	0.000	0.000	0.350
	100	50	0.5	−0.001	0.033	0.000	0.451	0.5	0.000	0.000	0.000	0.335
	100	100	0.5	0.000	0.033	0.000	0.466	0.5	0.000	0.000	0.000	0.331
2.0	50	5	0.0	0.000	0.000	0.000	0.056	0.0	0.000	0.000	0.000	0.056
	50	50	0.0	0.000	−0.001	0.000	0.054	0.0	0.000	−0.001	0.000	0.054
	50	100	0.0	0.000	−0.001	0.000	0.050	0.0	0.000	−0.001	0.000	0.050
	100	5	0.0	0.000	0.000	0.000	0.052	0.0	0.000	0.000	0.000	0.052
	100	50	0.0	0.000	0.000	0.000	0.048	0.0	0.000	0.000	0.000	0.048
	100	100	0.0	0.000	0.000	0.000	0.051	0.0	0.000	0.000	0.000	0.051
	50	5	0.5	−0.005	0.033	0.000	0.113	0.5	0.000	0.000	0.000	0.323
	50	50	0.5	0.000	0.032	0.000	0.065	0.5	0.000	−0.001	0.000	0.437
	50	100	0.5	0.000	0.032	0.000	0.058	0.5	0.000	−0.001	0.000	0.442
	100	5	0.5	−0.005	0.033	0.000	0.183	0.5	0.000	0.000	0.000	0.512
	100	50	0.5	0.000	0.033	0.000	0.076	0.5	0.000	0.000	0.000	0.603
	100	100	0.5	0.000	0.033	0.000	0.064	0.5	0.000	0.000	0.000	0.604

between the individual effect and the transitory component of the time-varying regressor is extremely low, especially when T is large. In contrast, when $m \geq 0.5$, the power of the Hausman test increases with T. These results are consistent with what the asymptotic results derived in the previous section have predicted.

Our simulation results can be summarized as follows. First, the finite-sample properties of the GLS estimators and the Hausman test are generally consistent with their asymptotic properties. Second, even if time-varying or time-invariant regressors are correlated with the unobservable individual effects, the GLS estimators of the coefficients of the time-varying regressors do not suffer from substantial biases if T is large, although the GLS estimators of the coefficients on time-invariant regressors could be biased regardless of the size of T. Third, the Hausman test has great power to detect non-zero correlation between the unobservable individual effects and the permanent components of time-varying regressors. In contrast, it has only limited power to detect non-zero correlations between the effects and transitory components of the time-varying regressors and between the effects and time-invariant regressors. The power of the Hausman test crucially depends on both the size of T and the covariance structure among regressors and the effects.

Both our asymptotic and Monte Carlo results provide empirical researchers with practical guidance. For the studies that focus on the effects of time-varying regressors on the dependent variable, the choice between the GLS and within estimators is an irrelevant issue when T is as large as N. Both the GLS and within estimators are consistent. For the studies that focus on the effects of time-invariant regressors, some cautions are required for correct interpretations of the Hausman test results. One important reason to prefer GLS over within is that it allows estimation of the effects of time-invariant regressors on dependent variables. For the consistent estimation of the effects of the time-invariant regressors, however, it is important to test endogeneity of the regressors. Our results indicate that large-T data do not necessarily improve the power property of the Hausman test. When the degrees of correlations between time-varying and time-invariant variables decrease quickly over time, the Hausman test generally lacks the power to detect endogeneity of time-invariant regressors. The tests based on subsamples with small T could provide more reliable test results. The different test results from a large-T sample and its small-T subsamples may provide some information about how the individual effect might be correlated with time-varying regressors. The rejection by large-T data but acceptance by small-T data would indicate that the effect is correlated with the permanent components of the time-varying regressor, but the degrees of the correlations are low. In contrast, the acceptance by large-T data but rejection by small-T data may indicate that the effect is correlated with the temporal components of the time-varying regressors.

So far, we have considered several simple cases to demonstrate how the convergence rates of the popular panel data estimators and the Hausman test are sensitive to data generating processes. For these simple cases, all of the relevant asymptotics can be obtained in a straightforward manner. In the following section, we will show that the main results obtained from this section apply to more general cases in which regressors are serially dependent with arbitrary covariance structures.

7.4 General Case

This section derives for the general model (7.1) the asymptotic distributions of the within, between, GLS estimators and the Hausman statistic. In Sect. 7.2, we have considered independently several simple models in which regressors are of particular characteristics. The general model we consider in this section contains all of the different types of regressors analyzed in Sect. 7.2. More detailed assumptions are introduced below.

From now on, the following notation is repeatedly used. The expression "$\rightarrow_p$" means "converges in probability," while "$\Rightarrow$" means "converges in distribution" as in Sect. 7.2.2. For any matrix A, the norm $\|A\|$ signifies $\sqrt{tr(AA')}$. When B is a random matrix with $E\|B\|_p < \infty$, then $\|B\|_p$ denotes $\left(E\|B\|^p\right)^{1/p}$. We use $E_{\mathcal{F}}(\cdot)$ to denote the conditional expectation operator with respect to a sigma field $\mathcal{F}$. We also define $\|B\|_{\mathcal{F},p} = \left(E_{\mathcal{F}}\|B\|^p\right)^{1/p}$. The notation $x_N \sim a_N$ indicates that there exists n and finite constants d_1 and d_2 such that $\inf_{N\geq n}\frac{x_N}{a_N} \geq d_1$ and $\sup_{N\geq n}\frac{x_N}{a_N} \leq d_2$. We also use the following notation for relevant sigma-fields: $\mathcal{F}_{x_i} = \sigma(x_{i1},\ldots,x_{iT})$; $\mathcal{F}_{z_i} = \sigma(z_i)$; $\mathcal{F}_z = \sigma(\mathcal{F}_{z_1},\ldots,\mathcal{F}_{z_N})$; $\mathcal{F}_{w_i} = \sigma(\mathcal{F}_{x_i},\mathcal{F}_{z_i})$; and $\mathcal{F}_w = \sigma(\mathcal{F}_{w_1},\ldots,\mathcal{F}_{w_N})$. The x_{it} and z_i are now $k\times 1$ and $g\times 1$ vectors, respectively.

As in Sect. 7.2, we assume that the regressors $(x'_{i1},\ldots,x'_{iT},z'_i)'$ are independently distributed across different i. In addition, we make the following the assumption about the composite error terms u_i and v_{it}:

Assumption 1 *(about u_i and v_{it}): For some $q > 1$,*

(i) The u_i are independent over different i with $\sup_i E|u_i|^{4q} < \infty$.
(ii) The v_{it} are i.i.d. with mean zero and variance σ_v^2 across different i and t, and are independent of x_{is}, z_i and u_i, for all i, t, and s. Also, $\|v_{it}\|_{4q} \equiv \kappa_v$ is finite.

Assumption 1(i) is a standard regularity condition for error-components models. Assumption 1(ii) indicates that all of the regressors and individual effects are strictly exogenous with respect to the error terms v_{it}.[15]

We now make the assumptions about regressors. We here consider three different types of time-varying regressors: We partition the $k\times 1$ vector x_{it} into three subvectors, $x_{1,it}$, $x_{2,it}$, and $x_{3,it}$, which are $k_1\times 1$, $k_2\times 1$, and $k_3\times 1$, respectively. The vector $x_{1,it}$ consists of the regressors with deterministic trends. We may think of three different types of trends: (i) cross-sectionally heterogeneous nonstochastic trends in mean (but not in variance or covariances); (ii) cross-sectionally homogeneous nonstochastic trends; and (iii) stochastic trends (trends in variance) such as unit-root time series. In Sect. 7.2, we have considered the first two cases while discussing the cases related with (7.20). The latter case is materially similar to CASE A.2, except that the convergence rates of estimators and test statistics are different under these

[15]As discussed in Sect. 7.2.1, this assumption rules out weakly exogenous or predetermined regressors.

two cases. Thus, we here only consider the case (i). We do not cover the cases of stochastic trends (iii), leaving the analysis of such cases to future study.

The two subvectors $x_{2,it}$ and $x_{3,it}$ are random regressors with no trend in mean. The partition of $x_{2,it}$ and $x_{3,it}$ is made based on their correlation with z_i. Specifically, we assume that the $x_{2,it}$ are not correlated with z_i, while the $x_{3,it}$ are. In addition, in order to accommodate CASEs A.1 and A.2, we also partition the subvector $x_{2,it}$ into $x_{21,it}$ and $x_{22,it}$, which are $k_{21} \times 1$ and $k_{22} \times 1$, respectively. Similarly to CASE A.1, the regressor vector $x_{21,it}$ is heterogeneous over different i, as well as different t, with different means $\Theta_{21,it}$. In contrast, $x_{22,it}$ is homogeneous cross-sectionally with means $\Theta_{22,t}$ for all i for given t (Case A.2). We also incorporate CASEs B.1–B.3 into the model by partitioning $x_{3,it}$ into $x_{31,it}$, $x_{32,it}$, and $x_{33,it}$, which are $k_{31} \times 1$, $k_{32} \times 1$, and $k_{33} \times 1$, respectively, depending on how fast their correlations with z_i decay over time. The more detailed assumptions on the regressors x_{it} and z_i follow:

Assumption 2 *(about $x_{1,it}$):*

(i) For some $q > 1$, $\kappa_{x_1} \equiv \sup_{i,t} \|x_{1,it} - Ex_{1,it}\|_{4q} < \infty$.
(ii) Let $x_{h,1,it}$ be the hth element of $x_{1,it}$. Then, $Ex_{h,1,it} \sim t^{m_{h,1}}$ for all i and $h = 1, \ldots, k_1$, where $m_{h,1} > 0$.

Assumption 3 *(about $x_{2,it}$): For some $q > 1$,*

(i) $E(x_{21,it}) = \Theta_{21,it}$ and $E(x_{22,it}) = \Theta_{22,t}$, where $\sup_{i,t} \|\Theta_{21,it}\|$, $\sup_t \|\Theta_{22,t}\| < \infty$, and $\Theta_{21,it} \neq \Theta_{21,jt}$ if $i \neq j$.
(ii) $\kappa_{x_2} \equiv \sup_{i,t} \|x_{2,it} - Ex_{2,it}\|_{4q} < \infty$.

Assumption 4 *(about $x_{3,it}$): For some $q > 1$,*

(i) $E(x_{3,it}) = \Theta_{3,it}$, where $\sup_{i,t} \|\Theta_{3,it}\| < \infty$.
(ii) $E\left(\sup_{i,t} \left\|x_{3,it} - E_{\mathcal{F}_{z_i}} x_{3,it}\right\|_{\mathcal{F}_{z_i},4q}^{8q}\right) < \infty$.
(iii) Let $x_{h,3k,it}$ be the hth element of $x_{3k,it}$, where $k = 1, 2, 3$. Then, conditional on z_i,

(iii.1) $\left(E_{\mathcal{F}_{z_i}} x_{h,31,it} - Ex_{h,31,it}\right) \sim t^{-m_{h,31}}$ *a.s., where $\frac{1}{2} < m_{h,31} \leq \infty$ for $h = 1, \ldots, k_{31}$*
(here, $m_{h,31} = \infty$ implies that $E_{\mathcal{F}_{z_i}} x_{h,31,it} - Ex_{h,31,it} = 0$ a.s.);
(iii.2) $\left(E_{\mathcal{F}_{z_i}} x_{h,32,it} - Ex_{h,32,it}\right) \sim t^{-\frac{1}{2}}$ *a.s. for $h = 1, \ldots, k_{32}$;*
(iii.3) $\left(E_{\mathcal{F}_{z_i}} x_{h,33,it} - Ex_{h,33,it}\right) \sim t^{-m_{h,33}}$ *a.s., where $0 \leq m_{h,33} < \frac{1}{2}$ for $h = 1, \ldots, k_{33}$.*

Assumption 5 *(about z_i): $\{z_i\}_i$ is i.i.d. over i with $E(z_i) = \Theta_z$, and $\|z_i\|_{4q} < \infty$ for some $q > 1$.*

Panel data estimators of individual coefficients have different convergence rates depending on the types of the corresponding regressors. To address these differences, we define:

$$D_{x,T} = diag\left(D_{1T}, D_{2T}, D_{3T}\right);$$
$$D_T = diag\left(D_{x,T}, I_g\right),$$

where

$$D_{1T} = diag\left(T^{-m_1}, \ldots, T^{-m_{k_1}}\right);$$
$$D_{2T} = diag\left(D_{21T}, D_{22T}\right) = diag\left(I_{k_{21}}, \sqrt{T} I_{k_{22}}\right);$$
$$D_{3T} = diag\left(D_{31T}, D_{32T}, D_{33T}\right)$$
$$= diag\left(\sqrt{T} I_{k_{31}}, \sqrt{T} I_{k_{32}}, T^{m_{1,33}}, \ldots, T^{m_{k_{33},33}}\right).$$

Observe that D_{1T}, D_{2T}, and D_{3T} are conformable to regressor vectors $x_{1,it}$, $x_{2,it}$, and $x_{3,it}$, respectively, while D_T and I_g are to x_{it} and z_i, respectively. The diagonal matrix D_T is chosen so that $plim_{N\to\infty}\frac{1}{N}\sum_i D_T\tilde{w}_i\tilde{w}_i' D_T$ is well defined and finite. For future use, we also define

$$G_{x,T} = diag\left(D_{1T}, I_{k_{21}}, I_{k_{22}}, I_{k_3}\right);$$
$$J_{x,T} = diag\left(I_{k_1}, I_{k_{21}}, D_{22T}, D_{3T}\right),$$

so that

$$D_{x,T} = G_{x,T} J_{x,T}.$$

Using this notation, we make the following regularity assumptions on the unconditional and conditional means of regressors:

Assumption 6 *(convergence as $T \to \infty$): Defining $t = [Tr]$, we assume that the following restrictions hold as $T \to \infty$.*

(i) Let $\tau_1(r) = diag\left(r^{m_{1,1}}, \ldots, r^{m_{k_1,1}}\right)$, where $m_{h,1}$ is defined in Assumption 2. Then,

$$D_{1T} E\left(x_{1,it}\right) \to \tau_1(r)\,\Theta_{1,i}$$

uniformly in i and $r \in [0,1]$, for some $\Theta_{1,i} = \left(\Theta_{1,1,i}, \ldots, \Theta_{k_1,1,i}\right)'$ with $\sup_i \|\Theta_{1,i}\| < \infty$.

(ii) $\Theta_{21,it} \to \Theta_{21,i}$ and $\Theta_{3,it} \to \Theta_{3,i}$ uniformly in i with $\sup_i \|\Theta_{21,i}\| < \infty$ and $\sup_i \|\Theta_{3,i}\| < \infty$.

(iii) Uniformly in i and $r \in [0,1]$,

$$D_{31T}\left(E_{\mathcal{F}_{z_i}} x_{31,it} - E x_{31,it}\right) \to 0_{k_{31}\times 1}\ a.s.;$$
$$D_{32T}\left(E_{\mathcal{F}_{z_i}} x_{32,it} - E x_{32,it}\right) \to \frac{1}{\sqrt{r}} I_{k_{32}} g_{32,i}(z_i)\ a.s.;$$
$$D_{33T}\left(E_{\mathcal{F}_{z_i}} x_{33,it} - E x_{33,it}\right) \to \tau_{33}(r)\, g_{33,i}(z_i)\ a.s.,$$

where

$$g_{32,i} = \left(g_{1,32,i}, \ldots, g_{k_{32},32,i}\right)';\ g_{33,i} = \left(g_{1,33,i}, \ldots, g_{k_{33},33,i}\right)',$$

and $g_{32,i}(z_i)$ and $g_{33,i}(z_i)$ are zero-mean functions of z_i with

$$0 < E \sup_i \|g_{3k,i}(z_i)\|^{4q} < \infty, \text{for some} q > 1,$$

and $g_{3k,i} \neq g_{3k,j}$ for $i \neq j$, and $\tau_{33}(r) = diag(r^{-m_{1,33}}, \ldots r^{-m_{k_{33},33}})$.

(iv) *There exist $\tilde{\tau}(r)$ and $\tilde{G}_i(z_i)$ such that*

$$\| D_{3T}\left(E_{\mathcal{F}_{z_i}} x_{3,it} - E x_{3,it}\right) \| \leq \tilde{\tau}(r)\tilde{G}_i(z_i),$$

where $\int \tilde{\tau}(r)^{4q} dr < \infty$ and $E \sup_i \tilde{G}_i(z_i)^{4q} < \infty$ for some $q > 1$.

(v) *Uniformly in (i, j) and $r \in [0, 1]$;*

$$D_{31T}\left(E x_{31,it} - E x_{31,jt}\right) \to 0_{k_{31}\times 1},$$
$$D_{32T}\left(E x_{32,it} - E x_{32,jt}\right) \to \frac{1}{\sqrt{r}} I_{k_{32}}\left(\mu_{g_{32i}} - \mu_{g_{32j}}\right),$$
$$D_{33T}\left(E x_{33,it} - E x_{33,jt}\right) \to \tau_{33}(r)\left(\mu_{g_{33i}} - \mu_{g_{33j}}\right),$$

with $\sup_i \|\mu_{g_{32i}}\|, \sup_i \|\mu_{g_{33i}}\| < \infty$.

Some remarks would be useful to understand Assumption 6. First, to have an intuition about what the assumption implies, we consider, as an illustrative example, the simple model in CASE 3 in Sect. 7.2.2, in which $x_{3,it} = \Pi_i z_i / t^m + e_{it}$, where e_{it} is independent of z_i and $i.i.d.$ across i. For this case,

$$D_{3T}\left(E_{\mathcal{F}_{z_i}} x_{3,it} - E x_{3,it}\right) = D_{3T}\Pi_i\left(z_i - E z_i\right)/t^m;$$
$$D_{3T}\left(E x_{3,it} - E x_{3,jt}\right) = D_{3T}\left(\Pi_i E z_i - \Pi_j E z_j\right)/t^m.$$

Thus,

$$g_{3k,i}(z_i) = \Pi_i(z_i - E z_i);$$
$$\mu_{g_{3k,i}} = \Pi_i E z_i.$$

Second, Assumption 6(iii) makes the restriction that $E \sup_i \|g_{3k,i}(z_i)\|^{4q}$ is strictly positive, for $k = 2, 3$. This restriction is made to warrant that $g_{3k,i}(z_i) \neq 0$ a.s. If $g_{3k,i}(z_i) = 0$ a.s.,[16] then

$$D_{3kT} E_{\mathcal{F}_{z_i}}(x_{3k,it} - E x_{3k,it}) \sim \tau_{3k}(r)\, g_{32,i}(z_i) = 0 \text{a.s.},$$

and the correlations between $x_{3,it}$ and z_i no longer play any important role in asymptotics. Assumption 6(iii) rules out such cases.

[16] An example is the case in which $x_{3,it} = e_{it}\Pi_i z_i / t^m$, where e_{it} is independent of z_i with mean zero.

Assumption 6 is about the asymptotic properties of means of regressors as $T \to \infty$. We also need additional regularity assumptions on the means of regressors that apply as $N \to \infty$. Define

$$H_1 = \int_0^1 \tau_1(r)dr;\ H_{32} = \left(\int_0^1 \frac{1}{\sqrt{r}}dr\right) I_{k_{32}};\ H_{33} = \int_0^1 \tau_{33}(r)dr;$$

and

$$E\left[\begin{pmatrix} H_{32}g_{32,i}(z_i) \\ H_{33}g_{33,i}(z_i) \\ z_i - Ez_i \end{pmatrix}\begin{pmatrix} H_{32}g_{32,i}(z_i) \\ H_{33}g_{33,i}(z_i) \\ z_i - Ez_i \end{pmatrix}'\right] = \begin{pmatrix} \Gamma_{g_{32},g_{32},i} & \Gamma_{g_{32},g_{33},i} & \Gamma_{g_{32},z,i} \\ \Gamma'_{g_{32},g_{33},i} & \Gamma_{g_{33},g_{33},i} & \Gamma_{g_{33},z,i} \\ \Gamma'_{g_{32},z,i} & \Gamma'_{g_{33},z,i} & \Gamma_{zz,i} \end{pmatrix}.$$

With this notation, we assume the followings:

Assumption 7 *(convergence as $N \to \infty$): Define $\tilde{\Theta}_{1,i} = \Theta_{1,i} - \frac{1}{N}\sum_i \Theta_{1,i}$; $\tilde{\Theta}_{21,i} = \Theta_{21,i} - \frac{1}{N}\sum_i \Theta_{21,i}$; $\tilde{\mu}_{g_{32,i}} = \mu_{g_{32,i}} - \frac{1}{N}\sum_i \mu_{g_{32,i}}$; and $\tilde{\mu}_{g_{33,i}} = \mu_{g_{33,i}} - \frac{1}{N}\sum_i \mu_{g_{33,i}}$. As $N \to \infty$,*

$$(i)\ \frac{1}{N}\sum_i \begin{pmatrix} H_1\tilde{\Theta}_{1,i} \\ \tilde{\Theta}_{21,i} \\ H_{32}\tilde{\mu}_{g_{32,i}} \\ H_{33}\tilde{\mu}_{g_{33,i}} \end{pmatrix}\begin{pmatrix} H_1\tilde{\Theta}_{1,i} \\ \tilde{\Theta}_{21,i} \\ H_{32}\tilde{\mu}_{g_{32,i}} \\ H_{33}\tilde{\mu}_{g_{33,i}} \end{pmatrix}' \to \begin{pmatrix} \Gamma_{\Theta_1,\Theta_1} & \Gamma_{\Theta_1,\Theta_{21}} & \Gamma_{\Theta_1,\mu_{32}} & \Gamma_{\Theta_1,\mu_{33}} \\ \Gamma'_{\Theta_1,\Theta_{21}} & \Gamma_{\Theta_{21},\Theta_{21}} & \Gamma_{\Theta_{21},\mu_{32}} & \Gamma_{\Theta_{21},\mu_{33}} \\ \Gamma'_{\Theta_1,\mu_{32}} & \Gamma'_{\Theta_{21},\mu_{32}} & \Gamma_{\mu_{32},\mu_{32}} & \Gamma_{\mu_{32},\mu_{33}} \\ \Gamma'_{\Theta_1,\mu_{33}} & \Gamma'_{\Theta_{21},\mu_{33}} & \Gamma'_{\mu_{32},g_{33}} & \Gamma_{\mu_{33},\mu_{33}} \end{pmatrix}.$$

$$(ii)\ \frac{1}{N}\sum_i \begin{pmatrix} \Gamma_{g_{32},g_{32},i} & \Gamma_{g_{32},g_{33},i} & \Gamma_{g_{32},z,i} \\ \Gamma'_{g_{32},g_{33},i} & \Gamma_{g_{33},g_{33},i} & \Gamma_{g_{33},z,i} \\ \Gamma'_{g_{32},z,i} & \Gamma'_{g_{33},z,i} & \Gamma_{zz,i} \end{pmatrix} \to \begin{pmatrix} \Gamma_{g_{32},g_{32}} & \Gamma_{g_{32},g_{33}} & \Gamma_{g_{32},z} \\ \Gamma'_{g_{32},g_{33}} & \Gamma_{g_{33},g_{33}} & \Gamma_{g_{33},z} \\ \Gamma'_{g_{32},z} & \Gamma'_{g_{33},z} & \Gamma_{z,z} \end{pmatrix}.$$

(iii) The limit of $\frac{1}{N}\sum_i \Theta_{1,i}\Theta'_{1,i}$ exists.

Apparently, by Assumptions 6 and 7, we assume the sequential convergence of the means of regressors as $T \to \infty$ followed by $N \to \infty$. However, this by no means implies that our asymptotic analysis is a sequential one. Instead, the uniformity conditions in Assumption 6 allow us to obtain our asymptotic results using the joint limit approach that applies as $(N, T \to \infty)$ simultaneously.[17] Joint limit results can be obtained under an alternative set of conditions that assume uniform limits of the means of regressors sequentially as $N \to \infty$ followed by $T \to \infty$. Nonetheless, we adopt Assumptions 6 and 7 because they are much more convenient to handle the trends in regressors $x_{1,it}$ and $x_{3,it}$ for asymptotics.

The following notation is for conditional or unconditional covariances among time-varying regressors. Define

$$\Gamma_i(t,s) = [\Gamma_{jl,i}(t,s)]_{jl},$$

[17]For the details on the relationship between the sequential and joint approaches, see Apostol (1974, Theorems 8.39 and 9.16) for the cases of double indexed real number sequences, and Phillips and Moon (1999) for the cases of random sequences.

where $\Gamma_{jl,i}(t,s) = E\left(x_{j,it} - E_{\mathcal{F}_{z_i}} x_{j,it}\right)\left(x_{l,is} - E_{\mathcal{F}_{z_i}} x_{l,is}\right)$, for $j,l = 2,3$. Essentially, the Γ_i is the unconditional mean of the conditional variance-covariance matrix of $(x'_{2,it}, x'_{3,it})'$. We also define the unconditional variance-covariance matrix of $(x'_{1,it}, x'_{2,it}, x'_{3,it})'$ by

$$\tilde{\Gamma}_i(t,s) = [\tilde{\Gamma}_{jl,i}(t,s)]_{jl},$$

where $\tilde{\Gamma}_{jl,i}(t,s) = E\left(x_{j,it} - Ex_{j,it}\right)(x_{l,is} - Ex_{l,is})$, for $j,l = 1,2,3$. Observe that $\Gamma_{22,i}(t,s) = \tilde{\Gamma}_{22,i}(t,s)$, since $x_{2,it}$ and z_i are independent. With this notation, we make the following assumption on the convergence of variances and covariances:

Assumption 8 *(convergence of covariances): As* $(N, T \to \infty)$,

(i) $\frac{1}{N}\sum_i \frac{1}{T}\sum_t \sum_s \begin{pmatrix} \Gamma_{22,i}(t,s) & \Gamma_{23,i}(t,s) \\ \Gamma'_{23,i}(t,s) & \Gamma_{33,i}(t,s) \end{pmatrix} \to \begin{pmatrix} \Gamma_{22} & \Gamma_{23} \\ \Gamma'_{23} & \Gamma_{33} \end{pmatrix}$.

(ii) $\frac{1}{N}\sum_i \frac{1}{T}\sum_t \tilde{\Gamma}_i(t,t) \to \Phi$.

Note that the variance matrix $[\Gamma_{jl}]_{j,l=2,3}$ is the cross section average of the long-run variance-covariance matrix of $\left(x'_{2,it}, x'_{3,it}\right)'$. For future use, we partition the two limits in the assumption conformably to $(x'_{21,it}, x'_{22,it}, x'_{31,it}, x'_{32,it}, x'_{33,it})'$ as follows:

$$\begin{pmatrix} \Gamma_{22} & \Gamma_{23} \\ \Gamma'_{23} & \Gamma_{33} \end{pmatrix} = \begin{pmatrix} \Gamma_{21,21} & \Gamma_{21,22} & \Gamma_{21,31} & \Gamma_{21,32} & \Gamma_{21,33} \\ \Gamma'_{21,22} & \Gamma_{22,22} & \Gamma_{22,31} & \Gamma_{22,32} & \Gamma_{22,33} \\ \Gamma'_{21,31} & \Gamma'_{22,31} & \Gamma_{31,31} & \Gamma_{31,32} & \Gamma_{31,33} \\ \Gamma'_{21,32} & \Gamma'_{22,32} & \Gamma'_{31,32} & \Gamma_{32,32} & \Gamma_{32,33} \\ \Gamma'_{21,33} & \Gamma'_{22,33} & \Gamma'_{31,33} & \Gamma'_{32,33} & \Gamma_{33,33} \end{pmatrix};$$

$$\Phi = \begin{pmatrix} \Phi_{11} & \Phi_{12} & \Phi_{13} \\ \Phi'_{12} & \Phi_{22} & \Phi_{23} \\ \Phi'_{13} & \Phi'_{23} & \Phi_{33} \end{pmatrix}.$$

Assumption 9 *Let* $\mathcal{F}_z^{\infty} = \sigma(z_1, \ldots, z_N, \ldots)$. *For a generic constant M that is independent of N and T, the followings hold:*

(i) $\sup_{i,T} \left\| \frac{1}{T}\sum_t (x_{1,it} - Ex_{1,it}) \right\|_4 < M$,

(ii) $\sup_{i,T} \left\| \frac{1}{\sqrt{T}}\sum_t (x_{2,it} - Ex_{2,it}) \right\|_4 < M$,

(iii) $\sup_{i,T} \left\| \frac{1}{\sqrt{T}}\sum_t \left(x_{3,it} - E_{\mathcal{F}_{z_i}} x_{3,it}\right) \right\|_4 < M$.

Assumption 9 assumes that the fourth moments of the sums of the regressors $x_{1,it}$, $x_{2,it}$, and $x_{3,it}$ are uniformly bounded. This assumption is satisfied under mild restrictions on the moments of x_{it} and on the temporal dependence of $x_{2,it}$ and $x_{3,it}$. For sufficient conditions for Assumption 9, refer to Ahn and Moon (2001).

Finally, we make a formal definition of the random effects assumption, which is a more rigorous version of (7.3).

Assumption 10 *(random effects): Conditional on* $\mathcal{F}_w, \{u_i\}_{i=1,\ldots,N}$ *is i.i.d. with mean zero, variance* σ_u^2 *and finite* $\kappa_u \equiv \|u_i\|_{\mathcal{F}_w,4}$.

To investigate the power property of the Hausman test, we also need to define an alternative hypothesis that states a particular direction of model misspecification. Among many alternatives, we here consider a simpler one. Specifically, we consider an alternative hypothesis under which the conditional mean of u_i is a linear function of $D_T\tilde{w}_i$. Abusing the conventional definition of fixed effects (that indicates nonzero-correlations between $w_i = (x_{it}', z_i')'$ and u_i), we refer to this alternative as the fixed effects assumption:

Assumption 11 *(fixed effects): Conditional on* $\mathcal{F}_w$, *the* $\{u_i\}_{i=1,\ldots,N}$ *is i.i.d. with mean* $\tilde{w}_i' D_T\lambda$ *and variance* σ_u^2, *where* λ *is a* $(k+g)\times 1$ *nonrandom nonzero vector.*

Here, $D_T\tilde{w}_i = [(D_{x,T}\tilde{x}_i)', \tilde{z}_i]$ can be viewed as a vector of detrended regressors. Thus, Assumption 11 indicates non-zero correlations between the effect u_i and detrended regressors. The term $\tilde{w}_i' D_T\lambda$ can be replaced by $\lambda_o + \overline{w}_i' D_T\lambda$, where λ_o is any constant scalar. We use the term $\tilde{w}_i' D_T\lambda$ instead of $\lambda_o + \overline{w}_i' D_T\lambda$ simply for convenience.

A sequence of local versions of the fixed effects hypothesis is given:

Assumption 12 *(local alternatives to random effects): Conditional on* $\mathcal{F}_w$, *the sequence* $\{u_i\}_{i=1,\ldots,N}$ *is i.i.d. with mean* $\tilde{w}_i' D_T\lambda/\sqrt{N}$, *variance* σ_u^2, *and* $\kappa_u^4 = E_{\mathcal{F}_w}(u_i - E_{\mathcal{F}_w}u_i)^4 < \infty$, *where* $\lambda \neq 0_{(k+g)\times 1}$ *is a nonrandom vector in* $\mathbb{R}^{k+g}$.

Under this Assumption, $E(D_T\tilde{w}_i u_i) = \frac{1}{\sqrt{N}} E\left(D_T\tilde{w}_i\tilde{w}_i' D_T\right)\lambda \rightarrow 0_{(k+g)\times 1}$, as $(N, T \rightarrow \infty)$. Observe that these local alternatives are of the forms introduced in Table 7.1

The following assumption is required for identification of the within and between estimators of β and γ.

Assumption 13 *The matrices* Ψ_x *and* Ξ *are positive definite.*

Two remarks on this assumption follow. First, this assumption is also sufficient for identification of the GLS estimation. Second, while the positive definiteness of the matrix Ξ is required for identification of the between estimators, it is not a necessary condition for the asymptotic distribution of the Hausman statistic obtained below. We can obtain the same asymptotic results for the Hausman test even if we alternatively assume that within estimation can identify β (positive definite Ψ_x) and between estimation can identify γ given β (the part of Ξ corresponding to $\tilde{z}_i$ is positive definite).[18] Nonetheless, we assume that Ξ is invertible for convenience.

[18]This claim can be checked with the following simple example. Consider a simple model with one time-varying regressor x_{it} and one time invariant regressor z_i. Assume that $x_{it} = az_i + e_{it}$, where the e_{it} are i.i.d. over different i and t. For this model, it is straightforward to show that the

We now consider the asymptotic distributions of the within, between and GLS estimators of β and γ:

Theorem 1 *(asymptotic distribution of the within estimator): Under Assumptions 1–8 and 13, as* $(N, T \to \infty)$,

$$\sqrt{NT}G_{x,T}^{-1}(\hat{\beta}_w - \beta) \Rightarrow N\left(0, \sigma_v^2 \Psi_x^{-1}\right).$$

Theorem 2 *(asymptotic distribution of the between estimator): Suppose that Assumptions 1–8 and 13 hold. As* $(N, T \to \infty)$,

(a) Under Assumption 10 (random effects),

$$D_T^{-1}\sqrt{N}\begin{pmatrix}\hat{\beta}_b - \beta \\ \hat{\gamma}_b - \gamma\end{pmatrix} = \begin{pmatrix}D_{x,T}^{-1}\sqrt{N}\left(\hat{\beta}_b - \beta\right) \\ \sqrt{N}\left(\hat{\gamma}_b - \gamma\right)\end{pmatrix} \Rightarrow N\left(0, \sigma_u^2 \Xi^{-1}\right);$$

(b) Under Assumption 12 (local alternatives to random effects),

$$D_T^{-1}\sqrt{N}\begin{pmatrix}\hat{\beta}_b - \beta \\ \hat{\gamma}_b - \gamma\end{pmatrix} = \begin{pmatrix}D_{x,T}^{-1}\sqrt{N}\left(\hat{\beta}_b - \beta\right) \\ \sqrt{N}\left(\hat{\gamma}_b - \gamma\right)\end{pmatrix} \Rightarrow N\left(\Xi\lambda, \sigma_u^2 \Xi^{-1}\right).$$

Theorem 3 *(asymptotic distribution of the GLS estimator of* β*): Suppose that Assumptions 1–8 and 13 hold.*

(a) Under Assumption 12 (local alternatives to random effects),

$$\sqrt{NT}G_{x,T}^{-1}\left(\hat{\beta}_g - \beta\right) = \sqrt{NT}G_{x,T}^{-1}\left(\hat{\beta}_w - \beta\right) + o_p(1),$$

as $(N, T \to \infty)$.

(b) Suppose that Assumption 11 (fixed effects) holds. Partition $\lambda = (\lambda_x', \lambda_z')'$ *conformably to the sizes of* x_{it} *and* z_i. *Assume that* $\lambda_x \neq 0_{k\times 1}$. *If* $N/T \to c < \infty$ *and the included regressors are only of the* $x_{22,it}$*- and* $x_{3,it}$*-types (no trends and no cross-sectional heterogeneity in* x_{it}*), then*

$$\sqrt{NT}G_{x,T}^{-1}\left(\hat{\beta}_g - \beta\right) = \sqrt{NT}G_{x,T}^{-1}\left(\hat{\beta}_w - \beta\right) + o_p(1).$$

Theorem 4 *(asymptotic distribution of the GLS estimator of* γ*): Suppose that Assumptions 1–8 and 13 hold. Define* $l_z' = \left(0_{g\times k} \vdots I_g\right)$. *Then, the following statements hold as* $(N, T \to \infty)$.

matrix Ξ fails to be invertible. Nonetheless, under the random effects assumption, the Hausman statistic can be shown to follow a χ^2 distribution with the degree of freedom equal to one.

(a) *Under Assumption 12 (local alternatives to random effects),*

$$\sqrt{N}\left(\hat{\gamma}_g - \gamma\right) = \left(\frac{1}{N}\sum_i \tilde{z}_i \tilde{z}_i'\right)^{-1} \left(\frac{1}{\sqrt{N}}\sum_i \tilde{z}_i \tilde{u}_i\right) + o_p(1)$$

$$\Rightarrow N\left(\left(l_z' \Xi l_z\right)^{-1} l_z' \Xi \lambda, \sigma_u^2 \left(l_z' \Xi l_z\right)^{-1}\right).$$

(b) *Under Assumption 11 (fixed effects),*

$$\left(\hat{\gamma}_g - \gamma\right) \to_p \left(l_z' \Xi l_z\right)^{-1} l_z' \Xi \lambda.$$

Several remarks follow. First, all of the asymptotic results given in Theorems 1–4 except for Theorem 3(b) hold as $(N, T \to \infty)$, without any particular restriction on the convergence rates of N and T. The relative size of N and T does not matter for the results, so long as both N and T are large. Second, one can easily check that the convergence rates of the panel data estimates of individual β coefficients (on the $x_{2,it}$- and $x_{3,it}$-type regressors) reported in Theorems 1–4 are consistent with those from Sect. 7.2.2. Third, Theorem 2 shows that under Assumption 10 (random effects), the between estimator of γ, $\hat{\gamma}_b$, is $\sqrt{N}$-consistent regardless of the characteristics of time-varying regressors. Fourth, both the between estimators of β and γ are asymptotically biased under the sequence of local alternatives (Assumption 12). Fifth, as Theorem 3(a) indicates, the within and GLS estimators of β are asymptotically equivalent not only under the random effects assumption, but also under the local alternatives. Furthermore, the GLS estimator of β is asymptotically unbiased under the local alternatives, while the between estimator of β is not. The asymptotic equivalence between the within and GLS estimation under the random effects assumption is nothing new. Previous studies have shown this equivalence based on a naive sequential limit method ($T \to \infty$ followed by $N \to \infty$) and some strong assumptions such as fixed regressors. Theorem 3(a) and (b) confirm the same equivalence result but with more a rigorous joint limit approach as $(N, T \to \infty)$ simultaneously. It is also intriguing to see that the GLS and within estimators are equivalent even under the local alternative hypotheses.

Sixth, somewhat surprisingly, as Theorem 3(b) indicates, even under the fixed effects assumption (Assumption 11), the GLS estimator of β could be asymptotically unbiased (and consistent) and equivalent to the within counterpart, (i) if the size (N) of the cross section units does not dominate excessively the size (T) of time series in the limit ($N/T \to c < \infty$), and (ii) if the model does not contain trended or cross-sectionally heterogenous time-varying regressors. This result indicates that when the two conditions are satisfied, the biases in GLS caused by fixed effects are generally much smaller than those in the between estimator. If at least one of these two conditions is violated, that is, if $N/T \to \infty$, or if the other types of regressors are included, the limit of $(\hat{\beta}_g - \hat{\beta}_w)$ is determined by how fast $N/T \to \infty$ and how fast the trends in the regressors increase or decrease.[19]

Finally, Theorem 4(a) indicates that under the local alternative hypotheses, the GLS estimator $\hat{\gamma}_g$ is $\sqrt{N}$-consistent and asymptotically normal, but asymptotically biased. The limiting distribution of $\hat{\gamma}_g$, in this case, is equivalent to the limiting distribution of the OLS estimator of γ in the panel model with the known coefficients of the time-varying regressors x_{it} (OLS on $\tilde{y}_{it} - \beta'\tilde{x}_{it} = \gamma'\tilde{z}_i + (u_i + \tilde{v}_{it})$). Clearly, the GLS estimator $\hat{\gamma}_g$ is asymptotically more efficient than the between estimator $\hat{\gamma}_b$. On the other hand, under the fixed effect assumption, unlike the GLS estimator of β, $\hat{\beta}_g$, the GLS estimator $\hat{\gamma}_g$ is not consistent as $(N, T \to \infty)$. The asymptotic bias of $\hat{\gamma}_g$ is given in Theorem 4(b).

Lastly, the following theorem finds the asymptotic distribution of the Hausman test statistic under the random effect assumption and the local alternatives:

Theorem 5 *Suppose that Assumptions 1–8 and 13 hold. Corresponding to the size of $(\overline{x}_i', z_i')'$, partition Ξ and λ, respectively, as follows:*

$$\Xi = \begin{pmatrix} \Xi_{xx} & \Xi_{xz} \\ \Xi_{xz}' & \Xi_{zz} \end{pmatrix}; \lambda = \begin{pmatrix} \lambda_x \\ \lambda_z \end{pmatrix}.$$

Then, as $(N, T \to \infty)$,

(a) Under Assumption 10 (random effects),

$$\mathcal{HM}_{NT} \Rightarrow \chi_k^2;$$

(b) Under Assumption 12 (local alternatives to random effects),

$$\mathcal{HM}_{NT} \Rightarrow \chi_k^2(\eta),$$

where $\eta = \lambda_x'(\Xi_{xx} - \Xi_{xz}\Xi_{zz}^{-1}\Xi_{xz}')\lambda_x/\sigma_u^2$ is the noncentral parameter.

The implications of the theorem are discussed in Sect. 7.2.3.

7.5 Conclusion

This paper has considered the large-N and large-T asymptotic properties of the within, between and random effects GLS estimators, as well as those of the Hausman test statistic. The convergence rates of the between estimator and the

[19]In this case, without specific assumptions on the convergence rates of N/T and the trends, it is hard to generalize the limits of the difference of the within and the GLS estimators.

Hausman test statistic are closely related, and the rates crucially depend on whether regressors are cross-sectionally heterogeneous or homogeneous. Nonetheless, the Hausman test is always asymptotically χ^2-distributed under the random effects assumption. Our simulation results indicate that our asymptotic results are generally consistent with the finite-sample properties of the estimators and the Hausman test even if N and T are small.

Under certain local alternatives (where the conditional means of unobservable individual effects are linear in the regressors), we also have investigated the asymptotic power properties of the Hausman test. Regardless of the size of T, the Hausman test has power to detect non-zero correlations between unobservable individual effects and the permanent components of time-varying regressors. In contrast, the test has no power to detect non-zero correlations between the effects and the transitory components of time-varying-regressors if T is large and if the time-varying regressors do have permanent components. The Hausman test has some (although limited) power to detect non-zero correlations between the effects and time-invariant regressors when the correlations between time-varying and time-invariant regressors remain high over time. However, when the correlations decay quickly over time, the test loses its power.

In this paper, we have restricted our attention to the asymptotic and finite-sample properties of the existing estimators and tests when panel data contain both large numbers of cross section and time series observations. No new estimator or test is introduced. However, this paper makes several contributions to the literature. First, we have shown that the GLS and within estimators, as well as the Hausman test, can be used without any adjustment for the data with large T. Second, for the cases with both large N and T, we provide a theoretical link between the asymptotic equivalence of the within and GLS estimator and the asymptotic distribution of the Hausman test. Third, we have shown that cross-sectional heterogeneity in regressors can play an important role in asymptotics. Previous studies have often assumed that data are cross-sectionally i.i.d. Our findings suggest that future studies should pay attention to cross-sectional heterogeneity. Fourth, we find that the power of the Hausman test depends on T.

Fifth and finally, our results also provide empirical researchers with some useful guidance. Different Hausman test results from large-T and small-T data can provide some information about how the individual effect is correlated with time-varying regressors. The rejection by large-T data but acceptance by small-T data would indicate that the effect is correlated with the permanent components of the time-varying regressor, but the degrees of the correlations are low. In contrast, the acceptance by large-T data but rejection by small-T data may indicate that the effect is correlated with the temporal components of the time-varying regressors. Whether the individual effect is correlated with temporal or permanent components of time-varying regressors is important to determine what instruments should be used to estimate the coefficients of time-invariant regressors when the random effects assumption is rejected. For example, as an anonymous referee pointed out, a key identification requirement of the instrumental variables proposed by Breusch et al. (1989) is that only the permanent components of the time-varying regressors are correlated with the individual effects. If the Hausman test indicates that the individual effects are only temporally correlated with the time-varying regressors, the BMS instruments need not be used.

Needless to say, the model we have considered is a restrictive one. Extensions of our approach to more general models would be useful future research agendas. First, we have not considered the cases with more general errors; e.g., hetroskedastic and/or serially correlated errors. It would be useful to extend our approach to such general cases. Second, we have focused on the large-N and large-T properties of the panel data estimators and tests that are designed for the models with large N and small T. For the models with large N and large T, it may be possible to construct the estimators and test methods based on large-N and large-T asymptotics that may have better properties than the estimators and the tests analyzed here. Developing alternative estimators based on large-T and large-N asymptotics and addressing the issue of unit roots would be important research agendas. Third, another possible extension would be the instrumental variables estimation of Hausman and Taylor (1981), Amemiya and MaCurdy (1986), and Breusch et al. (1989). For an intermediate model between fixed effects and random effects, these studies propose several instrumental variables estimators by which both the coefficients on time-varying and time-invariant regressors can be consistently estimated. It would be interesting to investigate the large-N and large-T properties of these instrumental variables estimators as well as those of the Hausman test and other GMM tests based on these estimators.

Appendix

First, we provide some preliminary lemmas that are useful in proving the main results in Sect. 7.4. Due to space limitation, we omit the proofs of the lemmas.[20]

In this section, notation M denotes a generic constant that is finite. Recall that $w_{it} = \left(x'_{1,it}, x'_{2,it}, x'_{3,it}, z'_i\right)'$. We also repeatedly use the diagonal matrix D_T defined in Sect. 7.4.

Lemma 6 *Under Assumptions 1–8, we obtain the following results as* $(N, T \to \infty)$.

(a) $\frac{1}{N}\sum_i \frac{1}{T}\sum_t G_{x,T}\tilde{x}_{it}\tilde{x}'_{it}G_{x,T} \to_p \Psi_x$;
(b) $\frac{1}{\sqrt{N}}\sum_i \frac{1}{\sqrt{T}}\sum_t G_{x,T}\tilde{x}_{it}\tilde{v}_{it} \Rightarrow N\left(0, \sigma_v^2\Psi_x\right)$,
where

$$\Psi_x = \begin{pmatrix} \int_0^1 \left(\tau_1 - \int \tau_1\right)\left(lim_N \frac{1}{N}\sum_i \Theta_{1,i}\Theta'_{1,i}\right)\left(\tau_1 - \int \tau_1\right)' dr & 0 & 0 \\ 0 & \Phi_{22} & \Phi_{23} \\ 0 & \Phi_{32} & \Phi_{33} \end{pmatrix}.$$

[20] Detailed proofs are available from the authors upon request.

Lemma 7 *Suppose that Assumptions 1–8 hold. Define* $\Xi = \Xi_1 + \Xi_2$, *where*

$$\Xi_1 = diag\left(0_{k_1}, 0_{k_{21}}, \begin{pmatrix} \Gamma_{22,22} & \Gamma_{22,31} & \Gamma_{22,32} \\ \Gamma'_{22,31} & \Gamma_{31,31} & \Gamma_{31,32} \\ \Gamma'_{22,32} & \Gamma'_{31,32} & \Gamma_{32,32} \end{pmatrix}, 0_{k_{33}}, 0_{k_z}\right);$$

$$\Xi_2 = \begin{pmatrix} \Gamma_{\Theta_1,\Theta_1} & \Gamma_{\Theta_1,\Theta_{21}} & 0 & 0 & \Gamma_{\Theta_1,\mu_{32}} & \Gamma_{\Theta_1,\mu_{33}} & 0 \\ \Gamma'_{\Theta_1,\Theta_{21}} & \Gamma_{\Theta_{21},\Theta_{21}} & 0 & 0 & \Gamma_{\Theta_{21},\mu_{32}} & \Gamma_{\Theta_{21},\mu_{33}} & 0 \\ 0 & 0 & 0 & 0 & 0 & 0 & 0 \\ 0 & 0 & 0 & 0 & 0 & 0 & 0 \\ \Gamma'_{\Theta_1,\mu_{32}} & \Gamma'_{\Theta_{21},\mu_{32}} & 0 & 0 & \begin{matrix}\Gamma_{g_{32},g_{32}} \\ +\Gamma_{\mu_{32},\mu_{32}}\end{matrix} & \begin{matrix}\Gamma_{g_{32},g_{33}} \\ +\Gamma_{\mu_{32},\mu_{32}}\end{matrix} & \Gamma_{g_{32},z} \\ \Gamma'_{\Theta_1,\mu_{33}} & \Gamma'_{\Theta_{21},\mu_{33}} & 0 & 0 & \begin{matrix}\Gamma'_{g_{32},g_{33}} \\ +\Gamma'_{\mu_{32},\mu_{32}}\end{matrix} & \begin{matrix}\Gamma_{g_{33},g_{33}} \\ +\Gamma_{\mu_{33},\mu_{33}}\end{matrix} & \Gamma_{g_{33},z} \\ 0 & 0 & 0 & 0 & \Gamma'_{g_{32},z} & \Gamma'_{g_{33},z} & \Gamma_{z,z} \end{pmatrix}.$$

Then, under Assumption 12, as $(N, T \to \infty)$, *the followings hold.*

(a) $\frac{1}{N}\sum_i D_T\tilde{w}_i\tilde{w}_i' D_T \to_p \Xi$.
(b) $\sup_{N,T}\sup_{1\leq i\leq N} E\left\|D_T\tilde{w}_i\right\|^4 < M$, *for some constant* $M < \infty$.
(c) $\frac{1}{\sqrt{N}}\sum_i D_T\tilde{w}_i\tilde{v}_i \to_p 0$.

Lemma 8 *Under Assumptions 1–8 and 12 (local alternatives to random effects), as* $(N, T \to \infty)$,

$$\frac{1}{\sqrt{N}}\sum_i D_T\tilde{w}_i\tilde{u}_i \Rightarrow N\left(\Xi\lambda, \sigma_u^2\Xi\right).$$

Lemma 9 *Under Assumptions 1–8 and 11 (fixed effects),*

$$\frac{1}{N}\sum_i D_T\tilde{w}_i\tilde{u}_i \to_p \Xi\lambda,$$

as $(N, T \to \infty)$.

Proof of Theorem 1

Theorem 1 follows by Lemma 6(a) and (b). ■

Proof of Theorem 2

Theorem 2 holds by Lemmas 7(a), (c) and 8. ■

Before we prove the rest of the theorems given in Sect. 7.4, we introduce the following notation:

$$\begin{array}{c} A_1 = \frac{1}{N}\sum_i \frac{1}{T}\sum_t (x_{it} - \bar{x}_i)(x_{it} - \bar{x}_i)'; \\ A_2 = \frac{1}{N}\sum_i \frac{1}{T}\sum_t (x_{it} - \bar{x}_i)(v_{it} - \bar{v}_i); \\ A_3 = \frac{1}{N}\sum_i \tilde{x}_i\tilde{x}_i'; A_4 = \frac{1}{N}\sum_i \tilde{x}_i\tilde{u}_i; A_5 = \frac{1}{N}\sum_i \tilde{x}_i\tilde{v}_i; \\ B_3 = \frac{1}{N}\sum_i \tilde{z}_i\tilde{z}_i'; B_4 = \frac{1}{N}\sum_i \tilde{z}_i\tilde{u}_i; B_5 = \frac{1}{N}\sum_i \tilde{z}_i\tilde{v}_i; \\ C = \frac{1}{N}\sum_i \tilde{x}_i\tilde{z}_i'; \\ F_1 = A_3 - CB_3^{-1}C'; F_2 = A_4 + A_5 - CB_3^{-1}(B_4 + B_5). \end{array} \tag{7.25}$$

Proof of Theorem 3

Using the notation given in (7.25) , we can express the GLS estimator $\hat{\beta}_g$ by

$$\begin{aligned} &\sqrt{NT}G_{x,T}^{-1}\left(\hat{\beta}_g - \beta\right) \\ &= \left[G_{x,T}A_1G_{x,T} + \theta_T^2 G_{x,T}\left\{A_3 - CB_3^{-1}C'\right\}G_{x,T}\right]^{-1} \\ &\quad \times\sqrt{NT}G_{x,T}\left\{A_2 + \theta_T^2\left[(A_4 + A_5) - CB_3^{-1}(B_4 + B_5)\right]\right\}, \end{aligned} \tag{7.26}$$

where $\theta_T = \sqrt{\sigma_v^2/(T\sigma_u^2 + \sigma_v^2)}$.

Part (a): Using Lemma 7(a), we can show that

$$\theta_T^2 G_{x,T}\left\{A_3 - CB_3^{-1}C'\right\}G_{x,T} = O_p\left(\theta_T^2\right) = o_p(1). \tag{7.27}$$

Next, from Lemmas 7(c) and 8, under the local alternatives to random effects (Assumption 12), it is possible to show that

$$\sqrt{NT}G_{x,T}\left\{\theta_T^2\left[(A_4 + A_5) - CB_3^{-1}(B_4 + B_5)\right]\right\} = O_p\left(\frac{1}{\sqrt{T}}\right) = o_p(1). \tag{7.28}$$

Substituting (7.27) and (7.28) into (7.26), we have

$$\begin{aligned} \sqrt{NT}(\hat{\beta}_g - \beta) &= [G_{x,T}A_1G_{x,T} + o_p(1)]^{-1}[\sqrt{NT}G_{x,T}A_2 + o_p(1)] \\ &= \sqrt{NT}(\hat{\beta}_w - \beta) + o_p(1). \end{aligned}$$

The last equality results from Lemma 6(a), (b) and Theorem 1. ■

Part (b): Similarly to Part (a), we can easily show that under the assumptions given in Part (b), the denominator in (7.26) is

$$\frac{1}{NT}\sum_i\sum_t G_{x,T}(x_{it} - \bar{x}_i)(x_{it} - \bar{x}_i)'G_{x,T} + o_p(1). \tag{7.29}$$

Consider the second term of the numerator of (7.26):

$$\theta^2\sqrt{T}G_{x,T}\left\{\begin{array}{c}\frac{1}{\sqrt{N}}\sum_i\tilde{x}_i(\tilde{u}_i+\tilde{v}_i)\\ -\left(\frac{1}{N}\sum_i\tilde{x}_i\tilde{z}_i'\right)\left(\frac{1}{N}\sum_i\tilde{z}_i\tilde{z}_i'\right)^{-1}\left(\frac{1}{\sqrt{N}}\sum_i\tilde{z}_i\left(\tilde{u}_i+\tilde{v}_i\right)\right)\end{array}\right\}. \tag{7.30}$$

Notice that by Lemmas 6, 7, and 9, under the fixed effect assumption (Assumption 11), the first term of (7.30) is

$$\begin{aligned}\theta^2\sqrt{NT}G_{x,T}\frac{1}{N}\sum_i\tilde{x}_i(\tilde{u}_i+\tilde{v}_i) &= \theta^2\sqrt{NT}G_{x,T}D_{x,T}^{-1}\frac{1}{N}\sum_i D_{x,T}\tilde{x}_i(\tilde{u}_i+\tilde{v}_i)\\ &= \theta^2\sqrt{NT}G_{x,T}D_{x,T}^{-1}\left\{\Xi_x\lambda+o_p(1)\right\},\end{aligned}$$

where we partition $\Xi=\begin{pmatrix}\Xi_{xx} & \Xi_{xz}\\ \Xi_{zx} & \Xi_{zz}\end{pmatrix}$ conformably to the sizes of x_{it} and z_i, and set $\Xi_x=(\Xi_{xx},\Xi_{xz})$. Similarly, by Lemmas 6, 7, and 9, under the fixed effect assumption, the second term of (7.30) is

$$\begin{aligned}&\theta_T^2\sqrt{NT}G_{x,T}D_{x,T}^{-1}\left\{\left(\frac{1}{N}\sum_i D_{x,T}\tilde{x}_i\tilde{z}_i'\right)\left(\frac{1}{N}\sum_i\tilde{z}_i\tilde{z}_i'\right)^{-1}\left(\frac{1}{N}\sum_i\tilde{z}_i\left(\tilde{u}_i+\tilde{v}_i\right)\right)\right\}\\ &=\theta_T^2\sqrt{NT}G_{x,T}D_{x,T}^{-1}\left\{\Xi_{xz}\Xi_{zz}^{-1}\Xi_z\lambda+o_p(1)\right\}.\end{aligned}$$

Therefore, the limit of (7.30) is

$$\left(\theta_T^2\sqrt{NT}G_{x,T}D_{x,T}^{-1}\right)\left[\left(\Xi_{xx}-\Xi_{xz}\Xi_{zz}^{-1}\Xi_{zx}\ \vdots\ 0\right)\lambda+o_p(1)\right].$$

Recall that it is assumed that $\frac{N}{T}\to c<\infty$. Also, recall that under the restrictions given in the theorem, $G_{x,T}=diag\left(I_{k_{22}},I_{k_3}\right)$ and $D_{x,T}=diag\left(\sqrt{T}I_{k_{22}},D_{3T}\right)$. Then, letting $\lambda_{\max}(A)$ denote the maximum eigenvalue of matrix A, we can have

$$\lambda_{\max}\left(\theta_T^2\sqrt{NT}G_{x,T}D_{x,T}^{-1}\right)=O(1)\sqrt{\frac{N}{T}}\lambda_{\max}\left(\frac{1}{\sqrt{T}}I_{k_{22}},D_{3T}^{-1}\right)\to 0.$$

Thus, under the assumptions of Part (b), the probability limit of the numerator of (7.26) is

$$\frac{1}{\sqrt{NT}}\sum_i\sum_t G_{x,T}\tilde{x}_{it}\tilde{v}_{it}+o_p(1). \tag{7.31}$$

Combining (7.29) and (7.31), we can obtain Part (b). ■

Proof of Theorem 4

Using the notation in (7.25), we can express the GLS estimator $\hat{\gamma}_g$ by

$$\hat{\gamma}_g - \gamma = \left[B_3 - C' \left(\frac{1}{\theta_T^2} A_1 + A_3 \right)^{-1} C \right]^{-1}$$
$$\times \left[(B_4 + B_5) - C' \left(\frac{1}{\theta_T^2} A_1 + A_3 \right)^{-1} \left(\frac{1}{\theta_T^2} A_2 + (A_4 + A_5) \right) \right]. \quad (7.32)$$

Part (a): Using Lemmas 6(a) and 7(a), we can show that $C' \left(\frac{1}{\theta_T^2} A_1 + A_3 \right)^{-1} C = o_p(1)$, which implies that, as $(N, T \to \infty)$, the denominator of (7.32) is

$$B_3 + o_p(1). \quad (7.33)$$

Next, under both the random effects assumption (Assumption 10) and the local alternatives (Assumption 12), it follows from Lemmas 6–8 that the second term in the numerator of (7.32) is

$$C' \left(\frac{1}{\theta^2} A_1 + A_3 \right)^{-1} \left(\frac{1}{\theta^2} \sqrt{N} A_2 + \sqrt{N} (A_4 + A_5) \right) = o_p(1).$$

Also, by Lemma 7(c), $\sqrt{N} B_5 = o_p(1)$. Therefore, the numerator of (7.32) is

$$\sqrt{N} B_4 + o_p(1), \quad (7.34)$$

as $(N, T \to \infty)$. In view of (7.32)–(7.34), we have

$$\sqrt{N} (\hat{\gamma}_g - \gamma) = \left(\frac{1}{N} \sum_i \tilde{z}_i \tilde{z}_i' \right)^{-1} \left(\frac{1}{\sqrt{N}} \sum_i \tilde{z}_i \tilde{u}_i \right) + o_p(1),$$

as $(N, T \to \infty)$. Finally, by Lemmas 7(a) and 8, as $(N, T \to \infty)$,

$$\sqrt{N} (\hat{\gamma}_g - \gamma) = \left(\frac{1}{N} \sum_i \tilde{z}_i \tilde{z}_i' \right)^{-1} \left(\frac{1}{\sqrt{N}} \sum_i \tilde{z}_i \tilde{u}_i \right)$$
$$\Rightarrow N \left((l_z' \Xi l_z)^{-1} (l_z' \Xi \lambda), (l_z' \Xi l_z)^{-1} \right),$$

as required. ■

Part (b): Under the assumptions in Part (b), as shown for the denominator of (7.32) ,

$$B_3 - C'\left(\frac{1}{\theta_T^2}A_1 + A_3\right)^{-1} C = \frac{1}{N}\sum_i \tilde{z}_i\tilde{z}_i' + o_p(1) \rightarrow_p l_z'\Xi l_z, \tag{7.35}$$

as $(N, T \to \infty)$. Next, consider the numerator of (7.32) ,

$$\left[(B_4 + B_5) - C'\left(\frac{1}{\theta^2}A_1 + A_3\right)^{-1}\left(\frac{1}{\theta^2}A_2 + (A_4 + A_5)\right)\right]$$

$$= (B_4 + B_5)$$

$$-T\theta^2\left(C'D_{x,T}\right)\frac{J_{x,T}^{-1}}{\sqrt{T}}\left(G_{x,T}A_1G_{x,T} + \frac{J_{x,T}^{-1}}{\sqrt{T}}D_{x,T}A_3D_{x,T}\frac{J_{x,T}^{-1}}{\sqrt{T}}\right)^{-1}$$

$$\times\left(\frac{1}{\sqrt{NT}\theta^2}\sqrt{NT}G_{x,T}A_2 + \frac{J_{x,T}^{-1}}{\sqrt{T}}D_{x,T}\left(A_4 + A_5\right)\right).$$

By Lemmas 6 and 7, $B_5 = o_p(1)$, $\sqrt{NT}G_{x,T}A_2 = O_p(1)$, and $D_{x,T}A_5 = O_p(1)$. Under the fixed effect assumption (Assumption 11), Lemma 9 implies that $D_{x,T}A_4 = O_p(1)$, as $(N, T \to \infty)$. Since $\frac{1}{\sqrt{NT}\theta_T^2} = o(1)$ and $\frac{J_{x,T}^{-1}}{\sqrt{T}} = o(1)$, and

$$T\theta^2\left(C'D_{x,T}\right)\frac{J_{x,T}^{-1}}{\sqrt{T}}\left(G_{x,T}A_1G_{x,T} + \frac{J_{x,T}^{-1}}{\sqrt{T}}D_{x,T}A_3D_{x,T}\frac{J_{x,T}^{-1}}{\sqrt{T}}\right)^{-1} = o_p(1)$$

(as shown in Part (a)), we have

$$(B_4 + B_5) - C'\left(\frac{1}{\theta^2}A_1 + A_3\right)^{-1}\left(\frac{1}{\theta^2}A_2 + (A_4 + A_5)\right) = B_4 + o_p(1). \tag{7.36}$$

But, according to Lemma 9,

$$B_4 = \frac{1}{N}\sum_i \tilde{z}_i\tilde{u}_i \rightarrow_p l_z'\Xi\lambda. \tag{7.37}$$

Therefore, (7.32) and (7.35)–(7.37) imply

$$\hat{\gamma}_g \rightarrow_p \gamma + \left(l_z'\Xi l_z\right)^{-1} l_z'\Xi\lambda,$$

as $(N, T \to \infty)$. ∎

Proof of Theorem 5

Using the notation in (7.25), we can express the Hausman test statistic by

$$\begin{aligned}\mathcal{HM}_{NT} &= \left[\left(A_1+\theta_T^2F_1\right)^{-1}\sqrt{NT}\left(A_2+\theta_T^2F_2\right)-A_1^{-1}\sqrt{NT}A_2\right]' \\ &\times\left[\sigma_v^2A_1^{-1}-\sigma_v^2\left(A_1+\theta_T^2F_1\right)^{-1}\right]^{-1} \\ &\times\left[\left(A_1+\theta_T^2F_1\right)^{-1}\sqrt{NT}\left(A_2+\theta_T^2F_2\right)-A_1^{-1}\sqrt{NT}A_2\right].\end{aligned}$$

Write

$$\left(A_1+\theta_T^2F_1\right)^{-1}-A_1^{-1}=-\theta_T^2A_1^{-1}F_1A_1^{-1}+\theta_T^4R_1, \tag{7.38}$$

where $R_1=\left(A_1+\theta_T^2F_1\right)^{-1}F_1A_1^{-1}F_1A_1^{-1}$. Define $\mathcal{Q}=\left(A_1+\theta_T^2F_1\right)^{-1}\sqrt{NT}$ $\left(A_2+\theta_T^2F_2\right)-A_1^{-1}\sqrt{NT}A_2$. Then, we can deduce that

$$\mathcal{Q}=-\theta_T^2\sqrt{NT}\left[A_1^{-1}F_1A_1^{-1}A_2-A_1^{-1}F_2\right]-\theta_T^4\sqrt{NT}R_2, \tag{7.39}$$

where $R_2=A_1^{-1}F_1A_1^{-1}F_2-R_1\left\{A_2+\theta_T^2F_2\right\}$. Using (7.38) and (7.39), we now can rewrite the Hausman statistic $\mathcal{HM}_{NT}=\mathcal{Q}'\left[\sigma_v^2A_1^{-1}-\sigma_v^2\left(A_1+\theta_T^2F_1\right)^{-1}\right]^{-1}\mathcal{Q}$ as

$$\begin{aligned}&\mathcal{HM}_{NT}\\ &=\theta_T\sqrt{NT}\begin{bmatrix}G_1\left(J_{x,T}^{-1}D_{x,T}F_1D_{x,T}J_{x,T}^{-1}\right)G_1G_{x,T}A_2\\ -G_1J_{x,T}^{-1}D_{x,T}F_2+\theta_T^2G_{x,T}^{-1}R_2\end{bmatrix}'\\ &\times\left[\sigma_v^2G_1\left(J_{x,T}^{-1}D_{x,T}F_1D_{x,T}J_{x,T}^{-1}\right)G_1+\sigma_v^2\theta_T^2\left(G_{x,T}^{-1}R_1G_{x,T}^{-1}\right)\right]^{-1}\\ &\times\theta_T\sqrt{NT}\begin{bmatrix}G_1\left(J_{x,T}^{-1}D_{x,T}F_1D_{x,T}J_{x,T}^{-1}\right)G_1G_{x,T}A_2\\ -G_1J_{x,T}^{-1}D_{x,T}F_2+\theta_T^2G_{x,T}^{-1}R_2\end{bmatrix},\end{aligned}$$

where $G_1=G_{x,T}^{-1}A_1^{-1}G_{x,T}^{-1}$. Using Lemmas 6(a), 7(a), and Assumption 13, we can show that

$$\sigma_v^2\theta_T^2\left(G_{x,T}^{-1}R_1G_{x,T}^{-1}\right)=O_p\left(\theta_T^2\right)=o_p(1). \tag{7.40}$$

Also, under the local alternatives (Assumption 12), from Lemmas 6–8 we may deduce that

$$\theta_T\sqrt{NT}\theta_T^2G_{x,T}^{-1}R_2=O(1)\left[\theta_T^2O_p(1)+o_p(1)\right]=o_p(1). \tag{7.41}$$

From (7.40) and (7.41), we now can approximate the Hausman statistic as follows:

$$\begin{aligned}
&\mathcal{HM}_{NT}\\
&= \frac{\theta_T}{\sigma_v}\sqrt{NT}\left[\left(J_{x,T}^{-1}D_{x,T}F_1D_{x,T}J_{x,T}^{-1}\right)(G_1G_{x,T}A_2) - J_{x,T}^{-1}D_{x,T}F_2 + o_p(1)\right]'\\
&\quad\times\left(J_{x,T}^{-1}D_{x,T}F_1D_{x,T}J_{x,T}^{-1} + o_p(1)\right)^{-1}\\
&\quad\times\frac{\theta_T}{\sigma_v}\sqrt{NT}\left[\left(J_{x,T}^{-1}D_{x,T}F_1D_{x,T}J_{x,T}^{-1}\right)(G_1G_{x,T}A_2) - J_{x,T}^{-1}D_{x,T}F_2 + o_p(1)\right]\\
&= \frac{\theta_T}{\sigma_v}\sqrt{NT}\,(D_{x,T}F_2)'\,(D_{x,T}F_1D_{x,T})^{-1}\,\frac{\theta_T}{\sigma_v}\sqrt{NT}\,(D_{x,T}F_2)\\
&\quad+o_p(1),
\end{aligned}$$

where the last line holds because under the local alternative hypotheses, $J_{x,T}^{-1}D_{x,T}F_1D_{x,T}J_{x,T}^{-1} = O_p(1)$, and $\frac{\theta_T}{\sigma_v}G_1\left(\sqrt{NT}G_{x,T}A_2\right) = O_p(\theta_T) = o_p(1)$ by Lemma 6(a), (b) and Assumption 13. Finally, by Lemma 7(a), as $(N,T\to\infty)$, $D_{x,T}F_1D_{x,T} = D_{x,T}A_3D_{x,T} - D_{x,T}CB_3^{-1}C'D_{x,T} \to_p \Xi_{xx} - \Xi_{xz}\Xi_{zz}^{-1}\Xi_{zx} > 0$. Also, Lemmas 7(c) and 8 imply that under the local alternative hypotheses, as $(N,T\to\infty)$,

$$\begin{aligned}
&\sqrt{N}D_{x,T}F_2\\
&= \sqrt{N}D_{x,T}A_4 + \sqrt{N}D_{x,T}A_5 - D_{x,T}CB_3^{-1}\sqrt{N}\,(B_4+B_5)\\
&= \frac{1}{\sqrt{N}}\sum_{i=1}^{N}D_{x,T}\tilde{x}_i\tilde{u}_i\\
&\quad-\left(\frac{1}{N}\sum_{i=1}^{N}D_{x,T}\tilde{x}_i\tilde{z}_i'\right)\left(\frac{1}{N}\sum_{i=1}^{N}\tilde{z}_i\tilde{z}_i'\right)^{-1}\left(\frac{1}{\sqrt{N}}\sum_{i=1}^{N}\tilde{z}_i\tilde{u}_i\right)+o_p(1)\\
&\Rightarrow \left(I_k - \Xi_{xz}\Xi_{zz}^{-1}\right)N\left(\Xi\lambda,\sigma_u^2\Xi\right).
\end{aligned}$$

As $(N,T\to\infty)$, $\frac{\theta_T}{\sigma_v}\sqrt{T}\to\frac{1}{\sigma_u}$. Therefore, under the hypothesis of random effects, $\mathcal{HM}_{NT}\Rightarrow\chi_k^2$, a χ^2 distribution with the degrees of freedom equal to k. In contrast, under the local alternative hypotheses, $\mathcal{HM}_{NT}\Rightarrow\chi_k^2(\eta)$, where η is the noncentral parameter. ■

Acknowledgements We would like to thank two referees for valuable comments and suggestions and Geert Ridder for helpful discussions. We also appreciate the comments of seminar participants at Arizona State University, the University of British Columbia, and the University of California, Davis.

The first author gratefully acknowledges the financial support of the College of Business and Dean's Council of 100 at Arizona State University, the Economic Club of Phoenix, and the alumni of the College of Business.

The second author gratefully acknowledges the financial supports of USC via FDA and of Yonsei University.

References

Ahn SC, Low S (1996) A reformulation of the Hausman test for regression models with cross-section-time-series data. J Econom 71:291–307

Ahn SC, Moon HR (2001) Large-N and large-T properties of panel data estimators and the Hausman test. CLEO discussion papers, C01-20, University of Southern California

Alvarez J, Arellano M (2003) The time series and cross-section asymptotics of dynamic panel data estimators. Econometrica 71:1121–1159

Amemiya T, MaCurdy TE (1986) Instrumental-variables estimation of an error components model. Econometrica 54:869–880

Apostol T (1974) Mathematical analysis, 2nd edn. Addison-Welsey, Reading

Balestra P, Nerlove M (1966) Pooling cross-section and time-series data in the estimation of a dynamic model: the demand for natural gas. Econometrica 34:585–612

Baltagi B (1995) Econometric analysis of panel data. Wiley, New York

Baltagi B, Khanti-Akom S (1990) On efficient estimation with panel data: an empirical comparison of instrumental variables estimators. J Appl Econom 5:401–406

Breusch TS, Mizon GE, Schmidt P (1989) Efficient estimation using panel data. Econometrica 57:695–700

Choi I (1998) Asymptotic analysis of a nonstationary error component model. Mimeo, Kookmin University, Korea

Cornwell C, Rupert P (1988) Efficient estimation with panel data: an empirical comparison of instrumental variables estimators. J Appl Econom 3:149–155

Guggenberger P (2010) The impact of a Hausman pretest on the asymptotic size of a hypothesis test. Econom Theory 26:369–382

Hahn J, Kuersteiner G (2002) Asymptotically unbiased inference for a dynamic panel model with fixed effects when both n and T are large. Econometrica 70:1639–1657

Hausman JA (1978) Specification tests in econometrics. Econometrica 46:1251–1272

Hausman JA, Taylor WE (1981) Panel data and unobservable individual effects. Econometrica 49:1377–1398

Higgins M, Zakrajsěk E (1999) Purchasing power parity: three stakes through the heart of the unit root null. NBER working paper, Federal Reserve Bank of New York, New York

Hsiao C (1986) Analysis of panel data. Cambridge University Press, New York

Im KS, Pesaran MH, Shin Y (2003) Testing for unit roots in heterogeneous panels. J Econom 115:53–74

Kao C (1999) Spurious regression and residual-based tests for cointegration in panel data. J Econom 90:1–44

Levin A, Lin C-F (1992) Unit root tests in panel data: asymptotic and finite-sample properties. Mimeo, University of California, San Diego

Levin A, Lin C-F (1993) Unit root tests in panel data: new results. Mimeo, University of California, San Diego

Maddala GS (1971) The use of variance components models in pooling cross section and time series data. Econometrica 39:341–358

Mátyás L, Sevestre P (1992) The econometrics of panel data. Kluwer Academic, Dordrecht

Phillips PCB, Moon H (1999) Linear regression limit theory for nonstationary panel data. Econometrica 67:1057–1111

Quah D (1994) Exploiting cross-section variations for unit root inference in dynamic data. Econ Lett 44:9–19

Chapter 8
Comparison of Stochastic Frontier "Effect" Models Using Monte Carlo Simulation

Young Hoon Lee and Jinseok Shin

8.1 Introduction

Since Aigner et al. (1977) and Meeusen and van den Broeck (1977) independently introduced stochastic frontier models, the literature has expanded not only quantitatively but also qualitatively. Stochastic frontier models that examine the technical efficiency of firms can be categorized into two groups: those that analyze production functions with input and output variables (Stevenson 1980; Greene 1990; Pitt and Lee 1981; Schmidt and Sickles 1984; Cornwell et al. 1990; Kumbhakar 1991; Battese and Coelli 1992; Lee and Schmidt 1993; Cuesta 2000; Lee 2006, 2010; Ahn et al. 2007), and those that examine the effects of observable characteristics of a firm on efficiency (so-called stochastic frontier "effect" models, SFEMs) (Reifschneider and Stevenson 1991; Caudill and Ford 1993; Caudill et al. 1995; Kumbhakar et al. 1991; Huang and Liu 1994; Battese and Coelli 1995; Wang 2002; Wang and Schmidt 2002).

This paper focuses on the second group, SFEMs. Although various SFEMs have been proposed, little is known about their comparative performances. This study applied Monte Carlo simulation techniques and compared three types of SFEMs. We focused particularly on the biases of the production function parameters, the marginal effects of exogenous factors on inefficiency, and the technical efficiency estimates in the presence of model misspecifications. Following the

The earlier draft of this paper was based on the second author's thesis. The first author acknowledges that this work is supported by the National Research Foundation of Korea Grant funded by Korean Government (NRF-2013S1A3A2053312).

Y.H. Lee (✉) • J. Shin
Department of Economics, Sogang University, Sinsoo-dong #1, Mapo-gu, Seoul 121-742, South Korea
e-mail: yhnlee@sogang.ac.kr; jinseok.shin820@gmail.com

R.C. Sickles and W.C. Horrace (eds.), *Festschrift in Honor of Peter Schmidt: Econometric Methods and Applications*, DOI 10.1007/978-1-4899-8008-3_8,

recommendation of Wang and Schmidt (2002), this paper uses a one-step approach[1] to examine the models. As explained by Wang and Schmidt (2002), the two-step approach can lead to biased estimates, including severe bias in Monte Carlo simulation results.

Alvarez et al. (2006) compared various SFEMs and categorized them based on the scaling property. This implies that firm characteristics affect the scale of technical inefficiency but not the shape of the inefficiency distribution. To be more specific, let u and z be random variables representing technical inefficiency and observable exogenous variables, respectively, and let u be influenced by z: $u = u(z,\delta)$. Different models specify different distributions of u. Models with the scaling property specify u as $u = s(z,\delta)u*$ where $s(z,\delta)$ is a scaling function and u^* is a random variable with one-sided distribution and is independent of z. Therefore, z influences u only through a deterministic function of $s(z,\delta)$, but does not affect the distribution of u. More specifically, z influences u by changing the variance of u. The model of Reifschneider and Stevenson (1991), Caudill and Ford (1993), and Caudill et al. (1995; hereafter, RSCFG) includes the scaling property, whereas that of Kumbhakar et al. (1991), Huang and Liu (1994), and Battese and Coelli (1995; KGMHLBC) does not. In particular, Battese and Coelli (1995, BC) imposed additive decomposition in the inefficiency function $u = z\delta + w$, where u was assumed to have a normal distribution truncated at zero, $u \sim N^+(z\delta,\sigma_u^2)$. Therefore, z changes the mean of the pre-truncation normal distribution of u and then affects u by changing the shape of the inefficiency distribution. RSCFG and KGMHLBC are identical in the way they require a specific distributional assumption of inefficiency and a normal distribution of a statistical disturbance term and then estimate a production function using a maximum likelihood (ML) method. In addition, both estimate technical inefficiency using the conditional expected value function on residual values originally derived by Jondrow et al. (1982).

Recently, Lee (2012) proposed an SFEM with panel data that estimates a production function and the effects of exogenous factors on inefficiency using the fixed effect (FE) treatment. This model is different from RSCFG and KGMHLBC in that it does not impose a distributional assumption of inefficiency or an uncorrelation assumption between inefficiency and input variables. The assumed additive specification of the inefficiency equation is the same as that of BC, $u = z\delta + w$. In this specification, $w \geq -z\delta$ because $u \geq 0$. Hence, the w values are correlated to z. BC assumed a truncated normal distribution of w to free the model from the endogeneity problem. Lee (2012) took a different approach to escape from the endogeneity problem. In Lee's (2012) model, w was treated as fixed, allowing for the correlation between w and z. Several specifications of w were proposed that were adopted by previous stochastic frontier models, including $w_{it} = \alpha_i$ (Schmidt and Sickles 1984),

[1]The two-step approach estimates a standard stochastic production function first and estimates the inefficiency equation second, whereas the one-step approach substitutes the inefficiency equation for the inefficiency term in the production function and then estimates the production function and the inefficiency equation simultaneously.

$w_{it} = \theta_t \alpha_i$ (Lee and Schmidt 1993), and $w_{it} = \theta_{1t}\delta_{1i} + \theta_{2t}\delta_{2i} + \ldots + \theta_{pt}\delta_{pi}$ (Ahn et al. 2007). The model becomes similar to the conventional panel data model with individual effects or multiplicative individual effects and time effects, and the estimation methods (e.g., the concentrated least squares and the generalized method of moments) are well developed.

Alvarez et al. (2006) compared KGMHLBC and RSCFG and presented several advantages of the scaling property. First, the coefficient of z, δ, can be interpreted independent of the distribution of inefficiency, and the marginal effect (ME) of z on inefficiency is simpler in RSCFG with the scaling property than in KGMHLBC without the property in which the ME equation is complicated and dependent upon the distribution of inefficiency. Second, it is possible for RSCFG to estimate a production function by nonlinear least squares analysis; then, no specific distributional assumption is required. Third, RSCFG may relax the unreasonable assumption that $u|z$ is independent over time by re-specifying $s(z,\delta)$ and u^*. For example, $u_{it} = s(z_{it},\delta)u_i^*$ where u^* is time invariant, can be considered as a general form, as described by Battese and Coelli (1992).[2] Fourth, Alvarez et al. (2006) argued that it is intuitively appealing that the scaling property specifies that firms differ in their mean inefficiency but not in the shape of the inefficiency distribution.

FE also contains the above advantages of RSCFG over KGMHLBC (we will discuss the case of $w_{it} = \alpha_i$, but any other specification will follow the same rationale). The δ itself implies the ME of z on the conditional mean of u, $\delta = \partial E[u_{it}|z_{it}, \alpha_i]/\partial z_{it}$. Therefore, the relationship between z and u is straightforward in the specification of FE, which changes the impact of z on inefficiency in a linear fashion. FE does not require the assumption of uncorrelatedness of inputs and a part of inefficiency (w) or a specific distribution of the one-sided distribution of technical inefficiency. Unlike RSCFG and KGMHLBC, FE does not assume a distribution of statistical noise, v. Instead, it imposes the strict exogeneity assumption for consistency. As the ML estimation is sensitive to the distribution of technical inefficiency, this relaxation in FE is expected to yield robust estimates. Additionally, the independence assumption of u^* in RSCFG or of w in KGMHLBC is practically unreasonable since the efficiency of an individual firm is likely to be more or less consistent over time. However, the inclusion of the time-invariant unobservable inefficiency α_i in FE allows for the time dependence of inefficiency. In other words, this unobservable inefficiency controls for heterogeneity of efficiency across different firms, as is observed in the real world.

However, there are two restrictions in FE: (i) z cannot include all or part of x, and thus input factors can influence output only through a production function. This restriction can be avoided if we specify a nonlinear inefficiency equation; and (ii) the time-invariant variables in z and x cannot be included as regressors because the within-transformation function eliminates all of the time-invariant variables. The second restriction can also be avoided if we adopt a different specification

[2]In Battese and Coelli's model (1992), $s(z_{it},\delta) = \exp[-\delta(t - T)]$. Thus, z is assumed to be individual-invariant.

of w_{it} from $w_{it} = \alpha_i$. For example, the specification of $w_{it} = \theta_t \alpha_i$ presented by Lee and Schmidt (1993) allows for the ability to estimate the effect of a time-invariant regressor on a dependent variable.

The main purpose of this paper is to shed light on the finite sample properties of the aforementioned three models (KGMHLBC, RSCFG, and FE) using Monte Carlo simulations. SFEMs aim to analyze the effects of exogenous factors on efficiency and to precisely estimate technical efficiency based on the characteristics of firms. We used simulations to compare the estimation performances of the three models by examining the accuracy of the ME of z on the mean u as well as the rank correlation between the true inefficiency and inefficiency estimates. The effect parameter δ has different meanings in different models of KGMHLBC, RSCFG, and FE. For example, $\delta = \partial E[u|z, \alpha]/\partial z$ and is then the marginal effect in FE, whereas δ implies the degree of the effect of z on the variance of technical inefficiency in RSCFG. Thus, in our simulation, we compared the estimation performance of ME instead of δ. We extended the comparison of the three models to plausible cases in which (i) the variance of technical inefficiency differs, (ii) the forms of the true structure of inefficiency vary, and (iii) the input factors and environmental factors are allowed to have an arbitrary degree of correlation.

The remainder of this paper is organized as follows. Section 8.2 discusses the three different models. Section 8.3 describes the Monte Carlo simulation design and discusses the simulation results. Finally, Sect. 8.4 presents our conclusions.

8.2 Three Stochastic Frontier Models

The stochastic production frontier model for panel data is defined by

$$y_{it} = \alpha_0 + x_{it}\beta + v_{it} - u_{it}, \tag{8.1}$$

where y_{it} is the dependent variable that represents the logarithm of output at the period t ($t = 1, \ldots, \mathrm{T}$) for firm i ($i = 1, \ldots, \mathrm{N}$), x_{it} is the $1 \times k$ vector of functions of inputs, β is a $k \times 1$ vector of coefficients, and v_{it} is an *i.i.d.* statistical noise term. The variable u_{it} is the non-negative "technical inefficiency" error, and the inefficiency equation is specified as

$$u_{it} = u\left(z_{it}, \delta\right), \tag{8.2}$$

where the $1 \times g$ vector z_{it} is a set of exogenous variables that affect technical inefficiency, and δ is a $g \times 1$ vector of coefficients. The x_{it} and z_{it} can overlap in KGMHLBC and RSCFG but not in FE.

Because both KGMHLBC and RSCFG assume a truncated normal distribution of u_{it}, we note $u_{it} \sim N^{+}(\mu_{it}, \sigma_{it}^2)$ in a general form. Specifically, RSCFG assumes

$\mu_{it} = 0$ and $\sigma_{it}^2 = s(z_{it},\delta)$, whereas KGMHLBC assumes $\mu_{it} = h(z_{it},\delta)$ and $\sigma_{it}^2 = \sigma_u^2$. RSCFG possesses the scaling property, and u_{it} can be expressed as

$$u_{it} = s\left(z_{it}, \delta\right) u_{it}^* \tag{8.3}$$

where the scaling function $s(z_{it}, \delta)$ is positive, and $u_{it}^* \geq 0$ is *i.i.d.*, and then is uncorrelated with z_{it}.

Caudill et al. (1995, CFG) assumed that u_{it}^* follows a half-normal distribution and that $s(z_{it}, \delta) = \exp\ (z_{it}\delta)^{0.5}$. The random variable u_{it}^* represents a firm's intrinsic inefficiency level such as unobservable leadership, and $s(z_{it}, \delta)$ represents a firm's inefficiency that can be explained by observable environmental factors. That is, the scaling property can be seen as a multiplicative decomposition of u_{it} into two independent parts. The *i.i.d.* assumption of u_{it}^* does not seem to be reasonable because a firm's intrinsic efficiency is likely to not be independent. However, the ML estimates are consistent if the model is correctly specified even though u_{it}^* is not independent (Álvarez et al. 2006). The assumption of uncorrelation between the unobservable inefficiency u_{it}^* and the observable efficiency determinants is also not appealing. BC specifies that $\mu_{it} = h(z_{it},\delta)$ and then $u_{it} = z_{it}\delta + w_{it}$, where w_{it} is normally distributed with truncation at $-z_{it}\delta$. Because $w_{it} \geq -z_{it}\delta$, w_{it} and z_{it} must be correlated.

The two different specifications of BC and CFG have different channels for the impact of z_{it} on inefficiency. If δ is positive, both models present a positive ME of z_{it} on inefficiency. An increase in z_{it} in CFG implies larger variance of the pre-truncation normal distribution of inefficiency, and then the half-normal distribution has a smaller density near zero and a larger density at a large value. Therefore, the mean inefficiency level increases. On the other hand, an increase in z_{it} in BC implies a larger mean of the pre-truncation normal distribution of inefficiency, and then the mean inefficiency moves toward the right side in the truncated normal at zero. Specifically, the MEs of the exogenous variable on the mean inefficiency can be summarized as follows for CFG and BC, respectively:

$$\frac{\partial E\left[u_{it}\,\middle|\,z_{it}\right]}{\partial z_{it}} = \delta\frac{\sigma_{it}}{\sqrt{2\pi}} = \delta\frac{\sqrt{\exp\left(z_{it}\delta\right)}}{\sqrt{2\pi}} \tag{8.4}$$

$$\frac{\partial E\left[u_{it}\,\middle|\,z_{it}\right]}{\partial z_{it}} = \delta\left[1 - \lambda_{it}\frac{\phi\left(\lambda_{it}\right)}{\Phi\left(\lambda_{it}\right)} - \left(\frac{\phi\left(\lambda_{it}\right)}{\Phi\left(\lambda_{it}\right)}\right)^2\right], \tag{8.5}$$

where $\lambda_{it} = z_{it}\delta/\sigma_u$ and ϕ and Φ are the probability and cumulative density functions of a standard normal distribution, respectively. Equation (8.4) has the same sign as that of δ. Wang (2002) showed that the second term on the right-hand side of Eq. (8.5) is equal to the second moment of u_{it} divided by the variance of the pre-truncation normal, and then Eq. (8.5) also has the same sign as that of δ. However, the amount of the ME cannot be measured directly from δ.

As mentioned above, Lee (2012) proposed a stochastic frontier model that does not assume any distribution assumption and allows a correlation between inefficiency and input variables. The inefficiency equation is the same as that in BC:

$$u_{it} = z_{it}\delta + w_{it}. \tag{8.6}$$

Equation (8.6) splits the inefficiency into a part influenced by z_{it} and an unobservable random inefficiency. Lee also allowed for correlation between z_{it} and w_{it} by treating w_{it} as fixed. He proposed specifications for w_{it} to transform the model into the forms of previous models (Schmidt and Sickles 1984; Cornwell et al. 1990; Lee and Schmidt 1993; Lee 2006, 2010; Ahn et al. 2007), which are estimated by the FE treatment. The specifications of Kumbhakar (1991), Battese and Coelli (1992), and Cuesta (2000) were also accepted because they can also be estimated by the FE treatment as seen in Han et al. (2005). For example, $w_{it} = \alpha_{1i} + \alpha_{2i}t + \alpha_{3i}t^2$ is assumed, following Cornwell et al. (1990). Then, when substituting Eq. (8.6) for (8.1), the model becomes:

$$y_{it} = \alpha_0 + x_{it}\beta + v_{it} - (z_{it}\delta + w_{it}) = x_{it}\beta - z_{it}\delta - \left(\alpha_{1i}^* + \alpha_{2i}t + \alpha_{3i}t^2\right) + v_{it}, \tag{8.7}$$

where $\alpha_{1i}^* = \alpha_{1i} - \alpha_0$. Following Schmidt and Sickles (1984), another example is $w_{it} = \alpha_i$. This represents unobservable time-invariant firm-specific inefficiency, and Eq. (8.7) is changed to

$$y_{it} = \alpha_0 + x_{it}\beta + v_{it} - (z_{it}\delta + w_{it}) = x_{it}\beta - z_{it}\delta - \alpha_i^* + v_{it}, \tag{8.8}$$

where $\alpha_i^* = \alpha_i - \alpha_0$. In this specification, the strict exogeneity assumption is imposed as $E[v_{it}|x_i, z_i, \alpha_i] = 0,\ t = 1, 2, \ldots, T$ for the consistency of the estimator. Then, the within estimators of β and δ are consistent as $NT \to \infty$. The inefficiency estimation also follows the same method of the maximum operator as the previous models. That is, the best firm in the sample is assumed to be a perfectly efficient one. In the case of $w_{it} = \alpha_i$, the inefficiency and efficiency are measured by

$$\widehat{u}_{it} = \max_{i,t}\left(-z_{it}\widehat{\delta} + \widehat{\alpha}_i^*\right) - \left(-z_{it}\widehat{\delta} + \widehat{\alpha}_i^*\right), \quad \text{and } \widehat{TE}_{it} = \exp\left(-\widehat{u}_{it}\right). \tag{8.9}$$

Unlike CFG and BC, the ME of the exogenous variable on the mean inefficiency is calculated directly by δ because $\delta = \partial E[u_{it}|z_{it}, \alpha_i]/\partial z_{it}$.

Theoretically, FE should be insensitive to the *a priori* distribution of inefficiency and statistical disturbance whereas KGMHLBC and RSCFG are not. However, how sensitive their estimation performances are to misspecification was examined next. We chose BC and CFG as representative models of KGMHLBC and RSCFG, respectively, and compared them to FE.

8.3 Monte Carlo Simulations

To examine the finite sample performance of the ML estimation of BC and CFG and the within estimation of FE, we conducted a series of Monte Carlo experiments for the panel data stochastic frontier model. Our simulations were based on a model with one input factor:

$$y_{it} = \alpha_0 + x_{it}\beta_1 + v_{it} - u_{it}. \tag{8.1}$$

Throughout, we set $\alpha_0 = \beta_1 = 1$. We also had one exogenous factor ($z_{it} = c + \xi_{zi} + s_{zit}$) in which s_{zit} was drawn from a normal distrivution of $N(0,1)$, and one unobservable individual effect. ξ_{zi} was drawn from a uniform distrivution of $U(0,1)$ and $c = 4.0$. The regressor x_{it} was generated in an additive form by the following process: $x_{it} = \alpha_{xz}z_{it} + \xi_{xi} + s_{xit}$, where $\alpha_{xz} = (0, 0.5, 2)$, and the time-invariant components ξ_{xi} and time-varying components s_{xit} were drawn from $U(0,1)$ and $N(0,1)$, respectively.

We generated two error terms of u_{it} and v_{it} using several different data-generating processes (DGPs). The first DGP (DGP1) followed the BC specification. v_{it} was generated by $N(0,\sigma_v^2)$ with $\sigma_v = 1.0$ and the inefficiency term u_{it} was generated by $u_{it} \sim N^+(z_{it}\delta_1, \sigma_u^2)$ where $\delta_1 = 0.5$ and σ_u take several different values of $\left(1, \sqrt{2}, \sqrt{5}\right)$. These standard deviations of the pre-truncation normal imply the standard deviations of u_{it} as $\sqrt{Var(u)} = (0.96, 1.26, 1.78)$. Note that the mean of the pre-truncation normal does not contain a constant. When a constant term is included in z_{it}, the BC estimation results revealed a severe identification problem between a constant coefficient in x_{it} and a constant in z_{it}. DGP2 followed the CFG specification. The inefficiency term u_{it} was generated by $u_{it} \sim N^+(0, \exp(\delta_0 + \delta_1 z_{it}))$ where $\delta_1 = 0.5$ and δ_0 takes several different values (-1, 0, 1) to examine the estimation performance of the three different models as variance of inefficiency changes. The (-1, 0, 1) of δ_0 implies $\sqrt{Var(u)} = (1.13, 1.86, 3.06)$. The error v_{it} followed the same DGP as in DGP1. DGP3 followed the FE specification as $u_{it} = \delta_1 z_{it} + \alpha_i$ where $\delta_1 = 0.5$ and α_i are drawn from a uniform distribution. DGP3 also included several different variances of inefficiency by changing the variance of α_i; specifically, we used different intervals for uniform distribution such as $\sigma_\alpha = (2, 4, 6)$, which implies $\sqrt{Var(u)} = (0.57, 1.15, 1.73)$. Because FE assumes neither an inefficiency distribution nor a statistical disturbance, we chose a uniform distribution of v_{it} instead of a normal distribution. We also generated additional data sets of DGP1-1 and 2-1, which had the same values of the inefficiency term u_{it} as DGP1 and 2, respectively, but v_{it} were generated using uniform distributions. DGP1-2 and 2-2 were generated to examine the estimation performance of BC and CFG when x_{it} and z_{it} overlap. They were the same as DGP1 and 2 but $z_{it}\delta = \delta_1 z_{1it} + \delta_2 x_{it}$ for BC and $z_{it}\delta = \delta_0 + \delta_1 z_{1it} + \delta_2 x_{it}$ for CFG with $\delta_2 = 0.3$.

Each of our experiments consisted of 1,000 independent replications. We considered approximately 50 different DGPs by varying the values of N, T, α_{xz}, and the variance of inefficiency. The basic settings were ($\alpha_0, \beta_1, \delta_1, \sigma_v$,

$\sigma_u, \alpha_{xz}, N, T) = (1, 1, 0.5, 1, \sqrt{2}, 0.5, 100, 10)$ in the BC model, $(\alpha_0, \beta_1, \delta_0, \delta_1, \sigma_v, \alpha_{xz}, N, T) = (1, 1, 1, 0.5, 1, 0.5, 100, 10)$ in CFG, and $(\alpha_0, \beta_1, \delta_1, \sigma_v, \sigma_\alpha, \alpha_{xz}, N, T) = (1, 1, 0.5, 1, 4, 0.5, 100, 10)$ in FE.

We begin by discussing the estimation of production technology and the effect of exogenous factors on efficiency. The results with DGP1, DGP2, and DGP3 are reported in Table 8.1 with different levels of correlation between x_{it} and z_{it}. Each table reports the biases and root mean squared errors (RMSE). The biases are $100 \cdot$(mean bias). So, for example, the first entry in Table 8.1, -2.480, indicates that the mean of $\widehat{\alpha}_0$ is 0.975. Because δ_1 in the three different models do not have the same meaning, the estimates are not comparable. Therefore, we report estimates of all parameters only for a model that is consistent with the true specification. For example, we do not report estimates of δ_1 in CFG or FE when DGP follows the BC specification. Instead, we present the estimation performance for the ME of an exogenous variable on mean inefficiency.

Panel A is relevant to the case that x_{it} and z_{it} are uncorrelated to each other. When the true data follow DGP1, BC is the true specification, and then is expected to produce the most precise estimates. In fact, BC estimates β_1 the most precisely, but the intercept term is relatively inaccurate with a large RMSE, and $\widehat{\sigma}_u$ has a large mean bias of -0.065. CFG has a slightly smaller mean bias of β_1 than does FE, but FE estimates ME quite accurately whereas CFG produces a large bias. Staying with DGP1 and moving to Panels B and C where $\alpha_{xz} = 0.5$ and $\alpha_{xz} = 2$, respectively, the $\widehat{\beta}_1$ in BC is closer to the true value, but the biases of $\widehat{\delta}_1$ and the ME estimator become moderately larger. The bias and RMSE of $\widehat{\beta}_1$ and the ME estimator in CFG begin to snowball as α_{xz} increases. FE shows the second best performance as its biases are slightly larger than those of BC but distinctively smaller than those of CFG. FE is perfectly insensitive to change in α_{xz} with respect to the production function estimation.

When the true data follow DGP2, the true specification is CFG. BC and CFG have a smaller bias of $\widehat{\beta}_1$ than does FE, and $\widehat{\beta}_1$ is slightly more accurate in BC than CFG when $\alpha_{xz} = 0$. However, the estimator of ME has a large mean bias in BC, whereas both CFG and FE have reasonably small values of bias, and CFG is a little more accurate than is FE. As α_{xz} increases, the bias of $\widehat{\beta}_1$ in BC increases rapidly, but $\widehat{\beta}_1$ in FE stays constant. Again, for the model with true specifications, CFG performs the best and FE does the second best in being close to CFG and separating itself from BC. One intriguing finding that we cannot explain is that under correct specifications, CFG produced a relatively large bias compared with BC and FE. As large biases for $\widehat{\delta}_0$ and $\widehat{\delta}_1$ in CFG were also observed, the inaccuracy in estimating ME in CFG may be due to difficulty with the correct identification of $\widehat{\delta}_0$ and $\widehat{\delta}_1$.

In the case of DGP3 where BC and CFG are misspecified, FE performs the best. The bias of $\widehat{\beta}_1$ in FE is unexpectedly larger than that in CFG as shown in Panel A even though the bias gaps are mild, but FE separates itself from BC and CFG with a distinctively small bias of the ME estimator. BC performs better in estimating ME than CFG, possibly because BC and FE share the common additive form of

Table 8.1 The effect of the correlation between x and z

	DGP1			DGP2			DGP3		
	BC	CFG	FE	BC	CFG	FE	BC	CFG	FE
	Panel A: $\alpha_{xz} = 0$								
β_0	−2.480 (0.26)	−164.003 (1.66)		70.093 (0.72)	−0.981 (0.13)		−36.363 (0.44)	−183.523 (1.84)	
β_1	−0.038 (0.05)	−0.146 (0.05)	−0.169 (0.06)	0.163 (0.08)	0.198 (0.08)	0.605 (0.12)	0.185 (0.05)	−0.051 (0.05)	−0.089 (0.03)
δ_0					1.387 (0.24)				
δ_1	−0.592 (0.05)				−0.472 (0.05)				0.014 (0.03)
σ_u	−6.548 (0.37)								
ME	−0.142 (0.05)	−9.816 (0.10)	−0.363 (0.05)	−59.674 (0.60)	−1.328 (0.10)	2.761 (0.13)	−2.422 (0.06)	−20.433 (0.21)	0.014 (0.03)
	Panel B: $\alpha_{xz} = 0.5$								
β_0	−1.285 (0.24)	−154.974 (1.57)		91.033 (0.94)	−0.091 (0.21)		−26.210 (0.47)	−167.414 (1.68)	
β_1	0.009 (0.05)	−3.182 (0.06)	−0.169 (0.06)	−9.435 (0.12)	0.071 (0.07)	0.605 (0.12)	0.077 (0.05)	−6.454 (0.08)	−0.089 (0.03)
δ_0					2.693 (0.24)				
δ_1	−0.418 (0.05)				−0.671 (0.05)				−0.031 (0.04)
σ_u	−3.129 (0.29)								
ME	−0.180 (0.06)	−10.039 (0.11)	−0.447 (0.06)	−62.501 (0.63)	−1.530 (0.10)	3.063 (0.14)	−3.339 (0.07)	−21.499 (0.22)	−0.031 (0.04)
	Panel C: $\alpha_{xz} = 2$								
β_0	−4.120 (0.36)	−74.704 (0.86)		159.100 (1.63)	−4.917 (0.34)		5.083 (0.42)	−89.432 (0.94)	
β_1	0.006 (0.05)	−9.997 (0.11)	−0.169 (0.06)	−11.608 (0.12)	−0.378 (0.07)	0.605 (0.12)	1.516 (0.05)	−14.844 (0.16)	−0.089 (0.03)
δ_0					−11.493 (0.88)				
δ_1	−1.113 (0.12)				−15.930 (1.62)				−0.165 (0.07)
σ_u	−10.764 (0.50)								
ME	−0.213 (0.11)	−25.679 (0.28)	−0.701 (0.12)	−71.387 (0.72)	−0.534 (0.17)	3.970 (0.27)	2.328 (0.13)	−41.994 (0.43)	−0.165 (0.07)

the inefficiency equation. Moving to Panel B and C, the $\widehat{\beta}_1$ in FE is insensitive to change in α_{xz}, but the bias of the ME estimator increases when $\alpha_{xz} - 2$. Again, BC produces relatively reasonable estimates, whereas CFG becomes wildly inaccurate as α_{xz} increases.

The results in Table 8.1 suggest the following. First, FE produces the most robust estimates of ME as well as production technology; this result is not surprising as FE is insensitive to the *a priori* distribution, whereas BC and CFG are very sensitive to misspecification. This implies that it would be good practice to utilize the three different models and compare their estimates to choose the correct specification among BC, CFG, and FE. If BC (or CFG) produces estimates that are similar to those produced by FE, then it is likely that BC (or CFG) is a correct specification. On the other hand, it is likely that neither BC nor CFG is a correct specification if all three models produce different estimates. Second, both BC and CFG estimate ME or the inefficiency equation inaccurately even when they are correctly specified if x_{it} and z_{it} are closely correlated. Therefore, FE is recommended in this case.

Table 8.2 displays how the different models perform in response to changes in the variance of inefficiency when we change σ_u, the variance of the pre-truncation normal for BC, δ_0 for CFG, and σ_α for FE. Panels A and C show the estimation performances using the smallest and the largest variance of the inefficiency term, respectively. (Panel B shows that using an intermediate value). Discussing DGP1 first, we can see that the estimators for production technology parameters, β_0 and β_1, as well as the inefficiency equation parameter δ_1, by BC, the true specification, do not show any particular trend, but the estimator of ME reduces the mean bias as the variance increases, whereas the RMSE remains constant. On the other hand, the other two models (CFG and FE) estimate the production function and ME more precisely as the variance increases. In particular, the performance of FE in both estimating production technology and ME surpasses that of BC in Panel C. Moving to DGP2, CFG with the true specification does not reveal any specific trend in estimating $\beta = (\beta_0, \beta_1)'$ and $\delta = (\delta_0, \delta_1)'$, but both the mean bias and RMSE of the ME estimate expand as the variance of inefficiency increases. Unlike the case of DGP1, where a model with misspecification performs better when the inefficiency variance is large, the other models (BC and FE) perform worse as the inefficiency variance increases. BC in particular deteriorates rapidly. In the case of DGP3, which follows the FE specification, FE apparently performs better in estimating ME than BC and CFG, whereas BC is the next best. In practice, we have to consider the fact that CFG always estimates ME downward in every DGP as found in Tables 8.1 and 8.2, whereas BC also underestimates ME in most cases.

Tables 8.3 and 8.4 show the results of cases with different sample sizes. We first changed the number of cross-sectional observations with a fixed time series (T = 10 and $N = 25$, 100, and 250; Table 8.3), and then we changed T with a fixed N ($N = 100$, T = 5, 25, and 50; Table 8.4). Panel A in Table 8.3 shows the estimation performance when the sample size is the smallest ($N = 25$ and T = 10). When the true data are generated by DGP1, BC is expected to perform the best. However, the $\widehat{\beta}_1$ of BC had a slightly larger bias than that of FE even though BC estimated ME a little more accurately than FE. As the sample became larger by increasing

Table 8.2 The effect of the variance of u

	DGP1			DGP2			DGP3		
	BC	CFG	FE	BC	CFG	FE	BC	CFG	FE
	Panel A: $\sigma_u^2 = 1$ (DGP1), $\delta_0 = -1$ (DGP2), $\sigma_\alpha = 2$ (DGP3)								
β_0	−4.768(0.26)	−143.922(1.45)		82.732(0.85)	0.307(0.16)		3.304(0.24)	−143.453(1.44)	
β_1	0.019(0.04)	−6.021(0.07)	−0.105(0.05)	−1.433(0.05)	0.025(0.04)	0.180 (0.05)	−0.183(0.04)	−8.325(0.09)	−0.089 (0.03)
δ_0					2.786(0.41)				
δ_1	−1.130(0.05)				−0.681(0.07)				−0.031 (0.04)
σ_u	−22.597(0.55)								
ME	−1.097(0.05)	−17.399(0.18)	−1.082(0.05)	−7.113(0.09)	−0.649(0.04)	1.138 (0.06)	−0.333(0.04)	−22.445(0.23)	−0.031 (0.04)
	Panel B: $\sigma_u^2 = 2$ (DGP1), $\delta_0 = 0$ (DGP2), $\sigma_\alpha = 4$ (DGP3)								
β_0	−1.285(0.24)	−154.974(1.57)		91.518(0.94)	−0.855(0.17)		−26.210(0.47)	−167.414(1.68)	
β_1	0.009(0.05)	−3.182(0.06)	−0.169(0.06)	−5.315(0.08)	0.141(0.05)	0.340 (0.08)	0.077(0.05)	−6.454(0.08)	−0.089 (0.03)
δ_0					0.798(0.29)				
δ_1	−0.418(0.05)				−0.397(0.05)				−0.031 (0.04)
σ_u	−3.129(0.29)								
ME	−0.180(0.06)	−10.039(0.11)	−0.447(0.06)	−25.478(0.26)	−0.838(0.06)	1.865 (0.09)	−3.339(0.07)	−21.499(0.22)	−0.031 (0.04)
	Panel C: $\sigma_u^2 = 5$ (DGP1), $\delta_0 = 1$ (DGP2), $\sigma_\alpha = 6$ (DGP3)								
β_0	−4.911(0.34)	−70.178(0.73)		91.033(0.94)	−0.091(0.21)		−38.894(0.66)	−217.930(2.19)	
β_1	−0.032(0.06)	−3.351(0.07)	0.026(0.07)	−9.435(0.12)	0.071(0.07)	0.605 (0.12)	0.322(0.06)	−5.928(0.08)	−0.089 (0.03)
δ_0					2.693(0.24)				
δ_1	−1.122(0.07)				−0.671(0.05)				−0.031 (0.04)
σ_u	−7.694(0.47)								
ME	−0.094(0.06)	−7.344(0.09)	0.006(0.07)	−62.501(0.63)	−1.530(0.10)	3.063 (0.14)	−0.885(0.07)	−20.784(0.21)	−0.031 (0.04)

Table 8.3 The effect of N

	DGP1			DGP2			DGP3		
	BC	CFG	FE	BC	CFG	FE	BC	CFG	FE
	Panel A: $N = 25$, $T = 10$								
β_0	0.931(0.42)	−133.171(1.41)		88.350(0.98)	−0.063(0.42)		−17.853(0.56)	−164.572(1.68)	
β_1	−0.094(0.10)	−4.341(0.10)	−0.056(0.11)	−8.924(0.17)	−0.246(0.13)	0.587 (0.23)	0.811(0.10)	−7.210(0.12)	−0.328 (0.07)
δ_0					4.740(0.45)				
δ_1	−0.588(0.10)				−1.410(0.09)				−0.125 (0.07)
σ_u	−2.040(0.39)								
ME	−0.327(0.10)	−11.459(0.14)	−0.562(0.12)	−64.460(0.66)	−3.656(0.18)	2.136 (0.28)	−2.336(0.10)	−21.982(0.23)	−0.125 (0.07)
	Panel B: $N = 100$, $T = 10$								
β_0	−1.285(0.24)	−154.974(1.57)		91.033(0.94)	−0.091(0.21)		−26.210(0.47)	−167.414(1.68)	
β_1	0.009(0.05)	−3.182(0.06)	−0.169(0.06)	−9.435(0.12)	0.071(0.07)	0.605 (0.12)	0.077(0.05)	−6.454(0.08)	−0.089 (0.03)
δ_0					2.693(0.24)				
δ_1	−0.418(0.05)				−0.671(0.05)				−0.031 (0.04)
σ_u	−3.129(0.29)								
ME	−0.180(0.06)	−10.039(0.11)	−0.447(0.06)	−62.501(0.63)	−1.530(0.10)	3.063 (0.14)	−3.339(0.07)	−21.499(0.22)	−0.031 (0.04)
	Panel C: $N = 250$, $T = 10$								
β_0	−6.564(0.24)	−149.195(1.50)		91.617(0.93)	0.273(0.13)		−27.985(0.43)	−167.792(1.68)	
β_1	0.130(0.03)	−3.397(0.04)	0.159(0.03)	−9.719(0.11)	−0.038(0.04)	0.084 (0.07)	0.068(0.03)	−6.339(0.07)	−0.059 (0.02)
δ_0					0.465(0.15)				
δ_1	−1.014(0.04)				−0.141(0.03)				−0.021 (0.02)
σ_u	−13.491(0.44)								
ME	0.008(0.04)	−10.310(0.11)	−0.195(0.04)	−62.838(0.63)	−0.370(0.06)	2.876 (0.09)	−3.453(0.06)	−21.564(0.22)	−0.021 (0.02)

Table 8.4 The effect of T

	DGP1			DGP2			DGP3		
	BC	CFG	FE	BC	CFG	FE	BC	CFG	FE
	Panel A: $N = 100$, $T = 5$								
β_0	0.220(0.31)	−131.381(1.36)		90.999(0.96)	1.563(0.31)		−14.604(0.46)	−161.047(1.63)	
β_1	0.056(0.07)	−4.044(0.08)	−0.045(0.08)	−9.277(0.14)	−0.461(0.09)	0.273 (0.17)	0.883(0.07)	−5.721(0.09)	−0.141(0.05)
δ_0					6.258(0.33)				
δ_1	−0.260(0.07)				−1.528(0.07)				0.242(0.06)
σ_u	−0.740(0.29)								
ME	−0.170(0.07)	−10.772(0.12)	−0.349(0.09)	−62.677(0.64)	−3.423(0.13)	3.243 (0.21)	−3.292(0.08)	−21.846(0.22)	0.242(0.06)
	Panel B: $N = 100$, $T = 25$								
β_0	−7.188(0.25)	−149.372(1.50)		91.746(0.93)	0.450(0.13)		−40.776(0.51)	−177.023(1.78)	
β_1	−0.040(0.03)	−3.472(0.04)	−0.004(0.03)	−9.855(0.11)	−0.106(0.04)	0.172 (0.07)	−0.097(0.04)	−7.059(0.08)	−0.033(0.02)
δ_0					0.757(0.15)				
δ_1	−1.292(0.05)				−0.203(0.03)				0.000(0.02)
σ_u	−14.061(0.45)								
ME	−0.248(0.04)	−10.332(0.11)	−0.417(0.04)	−62.915(0.63)	−0.491(0.06)	3.000 (0.09)	−2.526(0.05)	−21.597(0.22)	0.000(0.02)
	Panel C: $N = 100$, $T = 50$								
β_0	−10.498(0.27)	−142.901(1.43)		91.750(0.92)	−0.020(0.10)		−51.288(0.58)	−184.514(1.85)	
β_1	−0.067(0.02)	−3.701(0.04)	0.042(0.02)	−9.866(0.10)	0.084(0.03)	0.251 (0.05)	0.069(0.03)	−7.105(0.08)	−0.004(0.01)
δ_0					0.153(0.10)				
δ_1	−1.778(0.05)				−0.053(0.02)				−0.036(0.02)
σ_u	−21.335(0.55)								
ME	−0.232(0.03)	−10.328(0.10)	−0.480(0.03)	−63.028(0.63)	−0.156(0.04)	3.150 (0.06)	−2.387(0.05)	−21.579(0.22)	−0.036(0.02)

N, $\widehat{\beta}_0$ and $\widehat{\sigma}_u$ of BC started to have larger biases, but the core parameter, ME, was estimated more accurately with a smaller RMSE, whereas $\widehat{\beta}_1$ did not have a particular trend in its performance. The overall estimation performances of CFG and FE improved except for $\widehat{\beta}_1$ of FE as N increased. In the case of DGP2, CFG was expected to perform the best among the three models. In the small sample ($N = 25$ and T = 10), the bias of the ME estimator was the least in FE even though CFG had the smallest bias of the production function estimates. However, the performance of CFG improved more rapidly than did that of BC and FE as N increased. In fact, there was no significant improvement in BC and FE. Therefore, CFG had the least bias of ME when N was 250. Regarding DGP3, FE performed the best, and BC did the next best, as expected. As N grew, FE became more accurate, whereas BC and CFG were constant in their estimation performance. The same simulation evidence was found in the case of DGP1 and DGP2 in that the well-specified model performed better with a larger N, whereas the misspecified model performed equally poorly. Comparing the results in Table 8.4, there was not a significant trend in the estimation performances of the three models with DGP1. However, CFG improved in the case of DGP2 as T increased, whereas both BC and FE did not show a particular trend. With DGP3, FE as well as BC improved moderately as T increases, but CFG remained constant. In summary, FE is strongly recommended when the sample size is small given that FE outperformed BC and CFG in small samples independent of a prior distribution.

Table 8.5 compares the estimation performances when DGP1 and 2 were modified in that the statistical noise v_{it} was generated by a uniform distribution instead of a normal distribution (denoted as DGP1-1 and DGP 2-1, respectively). It can be expected that the performances of BC and CFG will deteriorate because both impose a normal distribution assumption for statistical noise in their models, but the extent of deterioration in small samples is not known. First, we discuss the simulation results with DGP1 and DGP1-1. In DGP1-1, BC was no longer the best model. It had the least bias of $\widehat{\beta}_1$ only when $\alpha_{xz} = 0$, but the bias of $\widehat{\delta}_1$ was large, and the mean bias of the ME estimator was about five times as large as that in FE. When the correlation between x_{it} and z_{it} was increased to $\alpha_{xz} = 2$, FE outperformed BC significantly in both production function and ME estimation. Comparing the performances in DGP2 and 2-1, that of CFG was not significantly influenced by change in the distribution of statistical disturbance. We also conducted simulations with non-normal distributions of statistical noise for cases of different variances of inefficiency and different combinations of N and T, as shown in Tables 8.2, 8.3, and 8.4. To save space we will summarize the results (the detailed results are available upon request). The overall results are consistent with those in Table 8.5. As theory suggests, FE and CFG are insensitive to the distribution of v_{it}, but BC becomes worse when the true data of v_{it} do not come from a normal distribution. This property is another advantage of models with scaling properties. RSCFG is relatively insensitive to the *a priori* distribution of statistical noise.

BC and CFG may examine the effects of input factors on technical inefficiency by z_{it} including a part of x_{it}, but z_{it} and x_{it} cannot overlap in FE where input factors can

Table 8.5 The effect of the distribution of v and the correlation between x and z

	DGP1			DGP1-1		
	BC	CFG	FE	BC	CFG	FE
	Panel A: $\alpha_{xz} = 0$					
β_0	−2.480(0.26)	−164.003(1.66)		14.046(0.33)	−162.529(1.65)	
β_1	−0.038(0.05)	−0.146(0.05)	−0.169(0.06)	−0.066(0.05)	−0.137(0.05)	−0.359 (0.05)
δ_0						
δ_1	−0.592(0.05)			2.518(0.07)		
σ_u	−6.548(0.37)			4.992(0.38)		
ME	−0.142(0.05)	−9.816(0.10)	−0.363(0.05)	1.950(0.06)	−9.533(0.10)	−0.425 (0.05)
	Panel B: $\alpha_{xz} = 2$					
β_0	−4.120(0.36)	−74.704(0.86)	58.384(0.67)	9.787(0.36)	−73.352(0.84)	
β_1	0.006(0.05)	−9.997(0.11)	−0.169(0.06)	1.885(0.05)	−10.102(0.11)	−0.359 (0.05)
δ_0						
δ_1	−1.113(0.12)			5.809(0.14)		
σ_u	−10.764(0.50)			6.113(0.43)		
ME	−0.213(0.11)	−25.679(0.28)	−0.701(0.12)	5.995(0.13)	−25.809(0.28)	−1.143 (0.12)

(continued)

Table 8.5 (continued)

	DGP2			DGP2-1		
	BC	CFG	FE	BC	CFG	FE
	Panel A: $\alpha_{xz} = 0$					
β_0	70.093(0.72)	−0.981(0.13)		90.096(0.92)	4.141(0.14)	
β_1	0.163(0.08)	0.198(0.08)	0.605(0.12)	0.126(0.07)	−0.062(0.07)	0.582 (0.12)
δ_0		1.387(0.24)			5.622(0.24)	
δ_1		−0.472(0.05)			−0.958(0.05)	
σ_u						
ME	−59.674(0.60)	−1.328(0.10)	2.761(0.13)	−52.912(0.54)	−1.292(0.10)	2.724 (0.13)
	Panel B: $\alpha_{xz} = 2$					
β_0	159.100(1.63)	−4.917(0.34)		152.705(1.56)	1.300(0.35)	
β_1	−11.608(0.12)	−0.378(0.07)	0.605(0.12)	−8.725(0.10)	−0.405(0.06)	0.582 (0.12)
δ_0		−11.493(0.88)			−3.875(0.56)	
δ_1		−15.93(1.62)			−10.340(0.89)	
σ_u						
ME	−71.387(0.72)	−0.534(0.17)	3.970(0.27)	−63.592(0.64)	−0.616(0.16)	3.889 (0.26)

Table 8.6 The case that *x* and *z* overlaps

	BC	CFG	BC	CFG
	Panel A			
	DGP1		DGP1-2	
β_0	−1.285(0.24)	−154.974(1.57)	−9.158(0.28)	−141.993(1.44)
β_1	0.009(0.05)	−3.182(0.06)	11.183(0.35)	−36.306(0.37)
δ_0				
δ_1	−0.418(0.05)		−2.369(0.07)	
δ_2			11.278(0.35)	
σ_u	−3.129(0.29)		−33.228(0.74)	
ME_z	−0.180(0.06)	−10.039(0.11)	−2.233(0.07)	−13.692(0.14)
ME_x			12.279(0.35)	−32.525(0.33)
	Panel B			
	DGP2		DGP2-2	
β_0	91.033(0.94)	−0.091(0.21)	128.682(1.33)	−2.194(0.30)
β_1	−9.435(0.12)	0.071(0.07)	−25.382(0.28)	−0.234(0.12)
δ_0		2.693(0.24)		−5.063(1.72)
δ_1		−0.671(0.05)		−1.342(0.33)
δ_2				−0.919(0.29)
σ_u				
ME_z	−62.501(0.63)	−1.530(0.10)	−147.563(1.49)	−4.162(0.18)
ME_x			−38.233(0.44)	0.537(0.15)

influence output only through the production process. Therefore, it is a significant advantage of BC and CFG over FE if they are able to produce reasonably accurate estimates of the ME and production technology. Table 8.6 shows the estimation performance of BC and CFG when z_{it} and x_{it} overlap. That is, $z_{it}\delta = \delta_1 z_{1it} + \delta_2 x_{it}$ for BC (DGP1-2) and $z_{it}\delta = \delta_0 + \delta_1 z_{1it} + \delta_2 x_{it}$ for CFG (DGP2-2) with $\delta_2 = 0.3$. Beginning with the true specification of BC (DGP1 and 1-2), not only CFG but also BC produced large biases when an input factor was included as an exogenous efficiency determinant. For example, the mean value of $\widehat{\beta}_1$ in BC was close to the true value of one, and its RMSE was 0.05 when the sample was DGP1, but the bias and RMSE of $\widehat{\beta}_1$ increased to 0.11 and 0.35, respectively. The biases of $\widehat{\delta}_1$ and the ME_z estimator in BC also increased significantly. In particular, $\widehat{\delta}_2$ and the ME_x estimator were extremely inaccurate. The mean value of $\widehat{\delta}_2$ was 0.41 and its RMSE was 0.35 when the true value was 0.3. According to unreported simulation results, these problems were aggravated when z_{it} and x_{it} were more closely correlated. Turning our attention to DGP2 and 2-2, CFG also produced largely biased $\widehat{\beta}_1$ when z_{it} and x_{it} overlapped, even though the degree of aggravation was less severe than BC in DGP1-2. In summary, including some input variables in the environmental variable set does not seem to be an attractive choice for model specification.

Hitherto, we have described the performances of BC, CFG, and FE with respect to the aim of stochastic frontier effect models that analyze the effects of observable environmental factors on technical inefficiency. Another aim is to estimate the level of technical efficiency by utilizing information on environmental factors. Both BC and CFG estimate $\widehat{u}_{it}$ by the conditional expectation of u_{it} on residuals, whereas FE estimates it by the maximum operator. This difference leads the properties of the estimators so that $\widehat{u}_{it}$ in BC and CFG are in absolute values, but $\widehat{u}_{it}$ values in FE are relative. Therefore, we compared the rank correlation between the true rank and the estimated rank; the results are shown in Table 8.7. Overall, FE was outperformed by BC and CFG in estimating the rank of inefficiency level in most DGPs. FE produced very high rank correlations following DGP3, but its inefficiency estimates were not closely correlated to the true rank of inefficiency in other DGPs. On the other hand, the rank correlations in BC and CFG remained constant in the range of [0.60, 0.95] in most DGPs. This may imply an advantage of the conditional expectation over the maximum operator. All three models (BC, CFG, and FE) produced more accurate estimates of inefficiency rank as the variance of inefficiency became larger. Generally, changing the correlation between z_{it} and x_{it} makes little difference in the accuracy of the inefficiency estimates of all three models. However, CFG deteriorated extremely quickly in its estimation performance for technical inefficiency when z_{it} and x_{it} were highly correlated and the inefficiency was misspecified. This result is consistent with our earlier finding in Table 8.1. CFG produced inaccurate estimates of the inefficiency equation parameters (δ_0, δ_1). Therefore, we would recommend against using CFG if z_{it} is closely correlated to x_{it}.

Non-normal distribution of statistical noise caused significant biases in BC estimates of production technology as well as the ME, but the estimation performance of technical inefficiency did not deteriorate significantly in BC. BC and CFG produced more or less equally precise estimates when z_{it} and x_{it} overlapped even though the rank correlation coefficients decreased when the variance of inefficiency was small.

8.4 Conclusion

We examined stochastic frontier models that analyze the effect of observable variables on inefficiency. There are three types of these models: KGMHLBC, RSCFG, and FE. KGMHLBC does not possess the scaling property and is estimated by ML analysis, and we chose BC as a representative of this model. RSCFG includes the scaling property in that environmental factors affect the scale of technical inefficiency but not the shape of the inefficiency distribution, and it is also estimated by ML. CFG was chosen to represent this model. The inefficiency equation specification in FE is similar to that in BC, but FE does not impose a distributional assumption for technical inefficiency or for statistical disturbance. By treating a time-invariant intrinsic inefficiency as fixed, FE did not have to assume correlation between efficiency factors (z) and intrinsic inefficiency (w).

We performed Monte Carlo simulations to examine the performances of the three models. For estimation of the production function and inefficiency equation,

Table 8.7 Average rank correlation coefficients between true and estimated inefficiency

	BC	CFG	FE	BC	CFG	FE	BC	CFG
	DGP1			DGP1-1			DGP1-2	
$\sigma_u^2 = 1$	0.646 (0.15)	0.669 (0.04)	0.445 (0.03)	0.645 (0.13)	0.667 (0.04)	0.443 (0.03)	0.587 (0.10)	0.589 (0.08)
$\sigma_u^2 = 2$	0.778 (0.09)	0.651 (0.08)	0.364 (0.03)	0.767 (0.09)	0.651 (0.07)	0.363 (0.03)	0.700 (0.19)	0.628 (0.09)
$\sigma_u^2 = 5$	0.836 (0.14)	0.864 (0.01)	0.310 (0.03)	0.841 (0.11)	0.859 (0.01)	0.309 (0.03)	0.869 (0.10)	0.875 (0.03)
$\alpha_{xz} = 0$	0.765 (0.12)	0.636 (0.08)	0.365 (0.03)	0.758 (0.11)	0.641 (0.08)	0.364 (0.03)	0.746 (0.15)	0.667 (0.08)
$\alpha_{xz} = 0.5$	0.778 (0.09)	0.651 (0.08)	0.364 (0.03)	0.767 (0.09)	0.651 (0.07)	0.363 (0.03)	0.700 (0.19)	0.628 (0.09)
$\alpha_{xz} = 2$	0.736 (0.16)	0.404 (0.50)	0.359 (0.03)	0.750 (0.13)	0.401 (0.50)	0.358 (0.03)		
	DGP2			DGP2-1			DGP2-2	
$\delta_0 = -1$	0.713 (0.08)	0.729 (0.02)	0.326 (0.03)	0.690 (0.10)	0.718 (0.02)	0.326 (0.03)	0.816 (0.08)	0.846 (0.01)
$\delta_0 = 0$	0.847 (0.07)	0.857 (0.01)	0.355 (0.03)	0.835 (0.10)	0.852 (0.01)	0.355 (0.03)	0.918 (0.01)	0.925 (0.04)
$\delta_0 = 1$	0.933 (0.01)	0.934 (0.01)	0.368 (0.03)	0.932 (0.00)	0.931 (0.04)	0.368 (0.03)	0.965 (0.00)	0.965 (0.06)
$\alpha_{xz} = 0$	0.934 (0.01)	0.934 (0.00)	0.368 (0.03)	0.933 (0.00)	0.933 (0.00)	0.368 (0.03)	0.942 (0.00)	0.907 (0.19)
$\alpha_{xz} = 0.5$	0.933 (0.01)	0.934 (0.01)	0.368 (0.03)	0.932 (0.00)	0.931 (0.04)	0.368 (0.03)	0.965 (0.00)	0.965 (0.06)
$\alpha_{xz} = 2$	0.929 (0.01)	0.913 (0.16)	0.366 (0.03)	0.929 (0.01)	0.914 (0.15)	0.366 (0.03)		
	DGP3							
$\sigma_\alpha = 2$	0.637 (0.03)	0.726 (0.02)	0.922 (0.01)					
$\sigma_\alpha = 4$	0.534 (0.16)	0.644 (0.04)	0.963 (0.01)					
$\sigma_\alpha = 6$	0.703 (0.19)	0.614 (0.06)	0.975 (0.00)					
$\alpha_{xz} = 0$	0.414 (0.06)	0.634 (0.04)	0.963 (0.01)					
$\alpha_{xz} = 0.5$	0.534 (0.16)	0.644 (0.04)	0.963 (0.01)					
$\alpha_{xz} = 2$	0.695 (0.13)	0.035 (0.52)	0.962 (0.01)					

FE is the most robust and insensitive to various specifications. FE estimated the ME of environmental factors on technical inefficiency reasonably accurately in the presence of model misspecifications. On the other hand, BC and CFG are likely sensitive to the *a priori* distribution of technical inefficiency and produce large biases when a model is misspecified. Other notable findings point to practical advantages of FE: (1) FE showed the best estimation performance for ME when the sample size was small, (2) the disadvantage that FE cannot incorporate z to include a part of x was inconsequential because BC and CFG produced inaccurate estimates of the inefficiency equation when x and z overlapped, and (3) BC and CFG were also vulnerable when a statistical disturbance term did not follow a normal distribution. These results are somewhat consistent with those of Gong and Sickles (1989, 1992, GS), who recommended the within estimator as the preferred estimator for the stochastic frontier model. However, GS did not consider efficiency factors and presented only inefficiency estimates.

In the estimation performance of technical inefficiency, FE was the worst, whereas BC and CFG were the best. We may conclude that there is a slight superiority of BC over CFG because CFG deteriorated rapidly when the correlation between x and z was high. This result contrasts with the simulation results of GS. However, GS adopted the max operator proposed by Schmidt and Sickles (1984) for efficiency estimates in the ML estimation. A source of the disparity between our simulation and that of GS with respect to efficiency estimates may be the difference between the conditional expectation and the max operator approaches. In this case, using the conditional expectation as the efficiency estimation appears to produce more accurate estimates than the maximum operator.

We hope that the findings of our Monte Carlo simulation will be informative to applied researchers interested in the choice of legitimate models for efficiency analysis. We recommend FE if the research aim is to analyze production technology or the marginal effects of observable variables on efficiency. However, we recommend the ML estimations of BC and CFG over FE for the estimation of firm efficiency. We also found that models with and without the scaling property did not differ in terms of their estimation performance in our restricted simulation design.

References

Ahn SC, Lee YH, Schmidt P (2007) Stochastic frontier models with multiple time-varying individual effects. J Prod Anal 27(1):1–12

Aigner DJ, Lovell CAK, Schmidt P (1977) Formulation and estimation of stochastic frontier production function models. J Econom 6(1):21–37

Álvarez A, Amsler C, Orea L, Schmidt P (2006) Interpreting and testing the scaling property in models where inefficiency depends on firm characteristics. J Prod Anal 25(3):201–212

Battese GE, Coelli TJ (1992) Frontier production functions, technical efficiency and panel data with application to paddy farmers in India. J Prod Anal 3(2):153–169

Battese GE, Coelli TJ (1995) A model for technical inefficiency effects in a stochastic frontier production function for panel data. Empirical Econ 20(2):325–332

Caudill SB, Ford JM (1993) Biases in frontier estimation due to heteroskedasticity. Econ Lett 41(1):17–20
Caudill SB, Ford JM, Gropper DM (1995) Frontier estimation and firm-specific inefficiency measures in the presence of heteroskedasticity. J Bus Econ Stat 13(1):105–111
Cornwell C, Schmidt P, Sickles R (1990) Production frontiers with cross-sectional and time-series variation in efficiency levels. J Econom 46(1–2):185–200
Cuesta RA (2000) A production model with firm-specific temporal variation in technical inefficiency with application to Spanish dairy farms. J Prod Anal 13(2):139–149
Gong BH, Sickles RC (1989) Finite sample evidence on the performance of stochastic frontier models using panel data. J Prod Anal 1(3):229–261
Gong BH, Sickles RC (1992) Finite sample evidence on the performance of stochastic frontiers and data envelopment analysis using panel data. J Econom 51(1–2):259–284
Greene WH (1990) A gamma-distributed stochastic frontier model. J Econom 46(1–2):141–163
Han C, Orea L, Schmidt P (2005) Estimation of a panel data model with parametric temporal variation in individual effects. J Econom 126(2):241–267
Huang CJ, Liu JT (1994) Estimation of a non-neutral stochastic frontier production function. J Prod Anal 5(2):171–180
Jondrow J, Lovell CAK, Materov IS, Schmidt P (1982) On the estimation of technical inefficiency in the stochastic frontier production function model. J Econom 19(2–3):233–238
Kumbhakar SC (1991) Estimation of technical inefficiency in panel data models with firm-and time-specific effects. Econ Lett 36(1):43–48
Kumbhakar SC, Ghosh S, McGuckin JT (1991) A generalized production approach for estimating determinants of inefficiency in U.S. dairy farms. J Bus Econ Stat 9(3):279–286
Lee YH (2006) A stochastic production frontier model with group-specific temporal variation in technical efficiency. Eur J Oper Res 174(3):1616–1630
Lee YH (2010) Group-specific stochastic production frontier models with parametric specifications. Eur J Oper Res 200(2):508–517
Lee YH (2012) Effects of management practices on productivity evidence from baseball team production. Unpublished working paper, Sogang University
Lee YH, Schmidt P (1993) A production frontier model with flexible temporal variation in technical inefficiency. In: Fried H, Lovell CAK, Schmidt S (eds) The measurement of productive efficiency techniques and applications. Oxford University Press, Oxford
Meeusen W, van den Broeck J (1977) Efficiency estimation from Cobb-Douglas production functions with composed error. Int Econ Rev 18(2):435–444
Pitt MM, Lee LF (1981) The measurement and sources of technical inefficiency in the Indonesian weaving industry. J Dev Econ 9(1):43–64
Reifschneider D, Stevenson R (1991) Systematic departures from the frontier a framework for the analysis of firm inefficiency. Int Econ Rev 32(3):715–723
Schmidt P, Sickles RC (1984) Production frontiers and panel data. J Bus Econ Stat 2(4):367–374
Stevenson RE (1980) Likelihood functions for generalized stochastic frontier estimation. J Econom 13(1):57–66
Wang HJ (2002) Heteroscedasticity and non-monotonic efficiency effects of a stochastic frontier model. J Prod Anal 18(3):241–253
Wang HJ, Schmidt P (2002) One-step and two-step estimation of the effects of exogenous variables on technical efficiency levels. J Prod Anal 18(2):129–144

Chapter 9
Modelling Asymmetric Cointegration and Dynamic Multipliers in a Nonlinear ARDL Framework

Yongcheol Shin, Byungchul Yu, and Matthew Greenwood-Nimmo

JEL Classification: C12, C13, J64.

9.1 Introduction

The nonlinearity of many macroeconomic variables and processes has long been recognised. In a famous remark, Keynes (1936, p. 314) noted that "the substitution of a downward for an upward tendency often takes place suddenly and violently, whereas there is, as a rule, no such sharp turning point when an upward is substituted for a downward tendency". More recently, the joint fields of behavioural finance and economics associated most notably with Daniel Kahneman, Amos Tversky and Robert Shiller (e.g. Kahneman and Tversky 1979; Shiller 1993, 2005) have provided a considerable impetus to the modelling of asymmetry, stressing that nonlinearity is endemic within the social sciences and that asymmetry is fundamental to the human condition.

Y. Shin (✉)
Department of Economics and Related Studies, University of York, Heslington, York, YO10 5DD, UK
e-mail: yongcheol.shin@york.ac.uk

B. Yu
Department of International Trade (BB-1408), School of Management, Dong-A University, Bumin-Dong, 2 Ga-1 Seo-gu, Busan, South Korea
e-mail: bcu@dau.ac.kr

M. Greenwood-Nimmo
Department of Economics, University of Melbourne, 111 Barry Street, Carlton, VIC 3053, Australia
e-mail: matthew.greenwood@unimelb.edu.au

R.C. Sickles and W.C. Horrace (eds.), *Festschrift in Honor of Peter Schmidt: Econometric Methods and Applications*, DOI 10.1007/978-1-4899-8008-3_9,

An expansive literature has developed around the analysis of nonstationary variables following the pioneering work of Dickey and Fuller (1979), Engle and Granger (1987), Johansen (1988), Phillips and Hansen (1990), and Kwiatkowski et al. (1992), to name but a few. Subsequently, since the mid-1990s, a substantial body of work has considered the joint issues of nonstationarity and nonlinearity. This field has been dominated by three regime-switching models: the threshold ECM associated with Balke and Fomby (1997), the Markov-switching ECM of Psaradakis et al. (2004), and the smooth transition regression ECM developed by Kapetanios et al. (2006). The development of this literature reflects the belief that the information revealed by linear models may be insufficiently rich to permit strong inference or to yield reliable forecasts. More generally, it suggests a general concern that the assumption of linear adjustment may be excessively restrictive in a wide range of economically interesting situations, particularly where transaction costs are non-negligible and where policy interventions are observed in-sample.

The majority of these studies, however, maintain the assumption that the long-run relationship may be represented as a symmetric linear combination of nonstationary stochastic regressors. With the notable exceptions of Park and Phillips (2001), Saikkonen and Choi (2004), Escribano et al. (2006) and Bae and de Jong (2007), little research effort has been devoted to the analysis of nonlinear cointegration. Schorderet (2001) has proposed the bivariate asymmetric cointegrating regression of unemployment on output, where output is decomposed into partial sum processes of positive and negative changes. On the basis of this piecewise linear specification, he finds that the impact of recessionary shocks on unemployment is larger in absolute terms than that of cyclical upturns, indicating an hysteretic relationship. Granger and Yoon (2002) further develop the notion that the cointegrating relationship may be defined between the positive and negative components of the underlying variables, an effect that they term 'hidden cointegration'.

Partial sum decompositions have been applied with some success to the analysis of dynamic asymmetry. Examples include Webber's (2000) analysis of the relationship between the exchange rate and import prices, the work of Lee (2000) and Virén (2001) on asymmetries in Okun's Law and the research of Borenstein et al. (1997) and Bachmeier and Griffin (2003) focusing on the asymmetric response of gasoline prices to fluctuations in the oil price. However, most papers modelling short-run asymmetry employ the two step Engle-Granger technique which is inherently less efficient than single-step ECM estimation. Moreover, papers coherently modelling long- and short-run asymmetries jointly are scarce.

Our purpose in this paper is to develop a simple and flexible nonlinear dynamic framework capable of simultaneously and coherently modelling asymmetries both in the underlying long-run relationship and in the patterns of dynamic adjustment. We make four principal contributions. Firstly, we derive the dynamic error correction representation associated with the asymmetric long-run cointegrating regression, resulting in the nonlinear autoregressive distributed lag (NARDL) model. Secondly, following Pesaran and Shin (1998) and Pesaran et al. (2001), we employ a pragmatic bounds-testing procedure for the existence of a stable long-run relationship which is valid irrespective of whether the underlying regressors are $I(0)$, $I(1)$ or mutually cointegrated. Thirdly, we derive asymmetric cumulative dynamic multipliers that allow us to trace out the asymmetric adjustment patterns following positive and negative shocks to the explanatory variables. This has substantial theoretical appeal as it allows us to depict in an intuitive manner the traverse to a new equilibrium following a perturbation to the system. Such is the flexibility of our framework that it can readily accommodate the four general combinations of long- and short-run asymmetry. Finally, we conduct a range of Monte Carlo experiments which largely validate our estimation and inferential framework, revealing little bias in estimation and considerable power of the key test statistics. Moreover, we compute empirical p-values for the cointegration tests and confidence intervals for our dynamic multipliers by means of a non-parametric bootstrap. These exercises highlight a further enviable attribute of our proposed methodology: it is easily estimable by OLS and simple inferential methods provide a straightforward and reliable means of discriminating between the various forms and combinations of asymmetries.

We demonstrate the usefulness of the NARDL framework by applying it to the analysis of the unemployment-output relationship in the US, Canada and Japan over the period 1982m2–2003m11. We find strong evidence of long-run asymmetry consistent with the growing consensus that unemployment is more sensitive to busts than booms. Moreover, particularly in Canada, we find dynamic asymmetries indicating that firms are quick to fire and slow to hire. Finally, the dynamic multipliers reveal a pattern that is often obscured in discussions of persistence – although the half-life of an expansionary shock in the US is smaller than that of an equivalent recessionary shock, the real impact in terms of jobs created/lost is larger in the recessionary case. It follows, therefore, that focusing on the half-life of a shock is insufficient when the long-run relationship is asymmetric as this fails to convey relevant information about the relative magnitude of the economic response to the shock in each regime.

Finally, the flexibility and utility of the NARDL technique is reflected in the growing literature that has adopted our technique for the analysis of a range of economic issues.[1] Van Treeck (2008) has employed the NARDL model in his analysis of asymmetric wealth effects on US consumption, and has found that liquidity constraints and loss-aversion can be reconciled inter-temporally, with the former dominating in the short-run and the latter in the long-run. More recently, Delatte and López-Villavicencio (2012) have applied the NARDL technique in their analysis of long-run asymmetries in the pass-through from exchange rates to

[1]The present version of the paper is a substantially revised version of Shin and Yu (2004), which has benefited greatly from a sequence of incremental improvements and additions arising from the constructive comments of conference and seminar participants and from editorial feedback. Earlier versions of the paper circulated under the titles "*An ARDL Approach to an Analysis of Asymmetric Long-run Cointegrating Relationships*" and "*Modelling Asymmetric Cointegration and Dynamic Multipliers in an ARDL Framework*". By virtue of its wide circulation and prolonged availability as a working paper, our research has informed the development of a subsequent literature that we now discuss. In all cases, however, the development of the NARDL model is properly credited.

consumer prices in developed economies. Nguyen and Shin (2010) have estimated NARDL models on high frequency exchange rate data, revealing interesting patterns of asymmetry in the pricing impacts of order flow. Lastly, Greenwood-Nimmo et al. (2013) have estimated NARDL models of the interest rate pass-through relationship in the USA finding strong evidence of time-varying asymmetry. An important and relatively common finding in this literature is that the direction of asymmetry may switch between the short-run and the long-run. For example, a positive shock may have a larger absolute effect in the short-run while a negative shock has a larger absolute effect in the long-run (or vice-versa). The simplicity and flexibility of NARDL renders it an ideal framework with which to model such complex phenomena.

The paper proceeds as follows. Section 9.2 introduces the asymmetric cointegrating regression model and derives the associated asymptotic theory. On this basis, the NARDL model is derived including expressions for the asymmetric cumulative dynamic multipliers, and the associated testing procedures are developed. Section 9.3 employs a range of Monte Carlo simulations to investigate the finite sample properties of the proposed estimators and test statistics. Section 9.4 presents the results of our empirical illustration. Lastly, Sect. 9.5 offers some concluding remarks, while mathematical proofs are collected in the Appendix.

9.2 Modelling Asymmetries in a Nonlinear ARDL Framework

The increasing popularity of nonlinear modelling in the context of cointegrating long-run relationships has led to the proliferation of regime-switching models. Among existing studies, nonlinearity is typically confined to the error correction mechanism and estimation proceeds on the basis of either the threshold ECM associated with Balke and Fomby (1997), the Markov-Switching ECM of Psaradakis et al. (2004) or the smooth transition regression ECM developed by Kapetanios et al. (2006). However, the common assumption that the underlying cointegrating relationship may be represented as a linear combination of the underlying nonstationary variables may be excessively restrictive. In general, the long-run (cointegrating) relationship may also be subject to asymmetry or nonlinearity.[2] The three regime-switching functional forms mentioned above are equally applicable to the case of long-run asymmetry (Saikkonen and Choi 2004; Escribano et al. 2006).

In principle, it is possible to obtain a unified model capable of combining nonlinearities in the long-run relationship and the error correction mechanism coherently.

[2]The presence of long-run asymmetry will induce a ratchet mechanism if the respective positive and negative regime probabilities are approximately equal and the shocks under each regime are of comparable magnitude. In the more general case in which these conditions are not satisfied, no such simple conclusion may be drawn.

In practice, however, selection of the regime-switching variables and the transition functional forms may be non-trivial.[3] Hence, the development of an operational model of this form is likely to be highly challenging (cf. Saikkonen 2008). We contribute to this literature by developing a nonlinear modelling framework based on the ARDL approach which provides a simple and flexible vehicle for the analysis of joint long- and short-run asymmetries.

9.2.1 Nonlinear Asymmetric Cointegration

Before developing the full representation of the NARDL model, we introduce the following asymmetric long-run regression:

$$y_t = \beta^+ x_t^+ + \beta^- x_t^- + u_t, \tag{9.1}$$

$$\Delta x_t = v_t, \tag{9.2}$$

where y_t and x_t are scalar I(1) variables, and x_t is decomposed as $x_t = x_0 + x_t^+ + x_t^-$ where x_t^+ and x_t^- are partial sum processes of positive and negative changes in x_t:

$$\boldsymbol{x}_t^+ = \sum_{j=1}^{t} \Delta \boldsymbol{x}_j^+ = \sum_{j=1}^{t} \max\left(\Delta \boldsymbol{x}_j, 0\right), \ \boldsymbol{x}_t^- = \sum_{j=1}^{t} \boldsymbol{\Delta} x_j^- = \sum_{j=1}^{t} \min\left(\Delta \boldsymbol{x}_j, 0\right). \tag{9.3}$$

This simple approach to modelling asymmetric cointegration based on partial sum decompositions has been applied by Schorderet (2001) in the context of the nonlinear relationship between unemployment and output.[4]

Granger and Yoon (2002) advance the concept of 'hidden cointegration', where cointegrating relationships may be defined between the positive and negative components of the underlying variables. They demonstrate the relevance of this

[3] Consider the threshold ECM as an example, in which case the choice of the transition variable is of importance both theoretically and empirically. In general, the asymptotic distribution of the test statistic for the null of linearity or symmetry is not only non-standard but also depends on these transition variables.

[4] The concept of asymmetric cointegration is easily conceptualised by use of a simple example. Consider the output-unemployment relationship. In a standard cointegrating regression, one models y_t and x_t subject to a common stochastic trend. As this relationship is assumed to hold in the long-run, it represents the equilibrium to which the system returns after a perturbation (i.e. it acts as a global attractor). However, in our framework, the long-run relationship between y_t and x_t is modelled as piecewise linear subject to the decomposition of x_t. Suppose that $|\beta^+| < |\beta^-|$ in (9.1). This suggests that the long-run effect of a unit negative change in output will increase unemployment by a greater amount than a unit positive change would reduce it. Thus, our model includes a regime-switching cointegrating relationship in which regime transitions are governed by the sign of Δx_t. The economic implication of this line of reasoning is that equilibrium need not be unique in a globally linear sense. The link to the path dependency literature is apparent.

conceptual framework in the context of the linkage between US short- and long-term interest rates and the output-unemployment relationship, both of which are notable for the lack of robust evidence of linear cointegration. Schorderet (2003) generalises this concept and defines the following stationary linear combination of the partial sum components:

$$z_t = \beta_0^+ y_t^+ + \beta_0^- y_t^- + \beta_1^+ x_t^+ + \beta_1^- x_t^- . \tag{9.4}$$

If z_t is stationary, then y_t and x_t are said to be 'asymmetrically cointegrated'. It follows that standard linear (symmetric) cointegration is a special case of (9.4), obtained only if $\beta_0^+ = \beta_0^-$ and $\beta_1^+ = \beta_1^-$. Schorderet modifies (9.4) to analyse hidden cointegration, where only one component of each series appears in (9.4), developing a model of the asymmetric cointegrating relationship between bilateral exchange rates as an illustration. Lardic and Mignon (2008) analyse hidden cointegration between the price of oil and GDP, although they fail to provide any economically meaningful interpretation of the estimated asymmetric coefficients.

Given the difficulty in interpreting the results of hidden cointegration analysis, we will focus on (9.1), imposing the restriction $\beta_0^+ = \beta_0^- = \beta_0$ in (9.4) such that $\beta^+ = -\beta_1^+/\beta_0$ and $\beta^- = -\beta_1^-/\beta_0$. To achieve the greatest possible clarity of exposition, we initially begin with the case of a single regressor decomposed into the relevant partial sum processes.

Assumption 1 *The disturbances u_t and v_t in (9.1) and (9.2) follow iid processes with zero means and finite variances, and they are independently distributed.*

Theorem 1 *Consider the asymmetric cointegrating regression, (9.1) and (9.2). Under Assumption 1, the OLS estimators of β^+ and β^- have the following asymptotic distributions:*

$$T(\hat{\beta}^+ - \beta^+) \Rightarrow -\left(\frac{\mu^- \sigma^u}{\sigma^s}\right) \frac{\frac{1}{3}\int W_{\tilde{s}}(r) dW_{\tilde{u}}(r) - \int r W_{\tilde{s}}(r) dr \left(W_{\tilde{u}}(1) - \int W_{\tilde{u}}(r) dr\right)}{\frac{1}{3}\int W_{\tilde{s}}(r)^2 dr - \left(\int r W_{\tilde{s}}(r) dr\right)^2},$$

$$T(\hat{\beta}^- - \beta^-) \Rightarrow \left(\frac{\mu^+ \sigma^u}{\sigma^s}\right) \frac{\frac{1}{3}\int W_{\tilde{s}}(r) dW_{\tilde{u}}(r) - \int r W_{\tilde{s}}(r) dr \left(W_{\tilde{u}}(1) - \int W_{\tilde{u}}(r) dr\right)}{\frac{1}{3}\int W_{\tilde{s}}(r)^2 dr - \left(\int r W_{\tilde{s}}(r) dr\right)^2},$$

where $\mu^+ := E[\max[0, v_t]]$, $\mu^- := E[\min[0, v_t]]$, $s_t = \mu^+ (\min[0, v_t] - \mu^-) - \mu^- (\max[0, v_t] - \mu^+)$, $\sigma_u^2 := Var(u_t)$, $\sigma_s^2 := Var(s_t)$, and $W_{\tilde{s}}(\cdot)$ and $W_{\tilde{u}}(\cdot)$ are two independent standard Brownian motions defined on $r \in [0, 1]$, and obtained as the weak limit of partial sum processes, $T^{-1/2}\sum_{j=1}^{T(\cdot)} \tilde{s}_t$ and $T^{-1/2}\sum_{j=1}^{T(\cdot)} \tilde{u}_t$, with $\tilde{u}_t := u_t/\sigma_u$ and $\tilde{s}_t := s_t/\sigma_s$. Furthermore,

$$T\{\mu^+(\hat{\beta}^+ - \beta^+) + \mu^-(\hat{\beta}^- - \beta^-)\} = o_p(1).$$

Remark 1 In the special case when v_t follows a symmetric distribution with ${\mu^+}^2 = {\mu^-}^2$ and $Var\ (\max[0, v_t]) = Var\ (\min[0, v_t])$,[5] then we have

$$T(\hat{\beta}^- - \beta^-),\ T(\hat{\beta}^+ - \beta^+)$$
$$\Rightarrow \frac{\frac{1}{3}\int W_{\tilde{s}}(r)dW_{\tilde{u}}(r) - \int rW_{\tilde{s}}(r)dr\left(W_{\tilde{u}}(1) - \int W_{\tilde{u}}(r)dr\right)}{\frac{1}{3}\int W_{\tilde{s}}(r)^2dr - \left(\int rW_{\tilde{s}}(r)dr\right)^2},$$

such that $T\left\{(\hat{\beta}^- - \beta^-) + (\hat{\beta}^+ - \beta^+)\right\} = o_p(1)$.

Remark 2 Let $\boldsymbol{\beta} = (\beta^+, \beta^-)'$, then

$$T\left(\hat{\boldsymbol{\beta}} - \boldsymbol{\beta}\right) \overset{a}{\sim} MN\left(0, \boldsymbol{V}\right), \tag{9.5}$$

where $\boldsymbol{V} = \text{plim}_{T\to\infty}T^2\left(\boldsymbol{X}'\boldsymbol{X}\right)^{-1}\sigma_{\tilde{u}}^2$. Even though x_t^+ and x_t^- are dominated by the deterministic trends by construction, these leading terms cancel off in the derivation of $\left(\boldsymbol{X}'\boldsymbol{X}\right)^{-1}$ such that $\text{plim}_{T\to\infty}T^2\left(\boldsymbol{X}'\boldsymbol{X}\right)^{-1}$ is well-defined and standard inference on $\boldsymbol{\beta}$ remains asymptotically valid.

Remark 3 In a similar manner, when an intercept term is included, we can obtain the asymptotic distributions of the OLS estimator as follows:

$$T(\hat{\beta}^+ - \beta^+) \Rightarrow -\left(\frac{\mu^-\sigma^u}{\sigma^s}\right)$$
$$\times \frac{\frac{1}{12}\int \tilde{W}_{\tilde{s}}(r)dW_{\tilde{u}}(r) - \left(\int(r-\frac{1}{2})\tilde{W}_{\tilde{s}}(r)dr\right)\left(\int(r-\frac{1}{2})dW_{\tilde{u}}(r)\right)}{\frac{1}{12}\int \tilde{W}_{\tilde{s}}(r)^2dr - \left(\int(r-\frac{1}{2}\tilde{W}_{\tilde{s}}(r)\right)^2};$$
$$T(\hat{\beta}^- - \beta^-) \Rightarrow \left(\frac{\mu^+\sigma^u}{\sigma^s}\right)$$
$$\times \frac{\frac{1}{12}\int \tilde{W}_{\tilde{s}}(r)dW_{\tilde{u}}(r) - \left(\int(r-\frac{1}{2})\tilde{W}_{\tilde{s}}(r)dr\right)\left(\int(r-\frac{1}{2})dW_{\tilde{u}}(r)\right)}{\frac{1}{12}\int \tilde{W}_{\tilde{s}}(r)^2dr - \left(\int(r-\frac{1}{2}\tilde{W}_{\tilde{s}}(r)\right)^2};$$

and $T\{\mu^+(\hat{\beta}^+ - \beta^+) + \mu^-(\hat{\beta}^- - \beta^-)\} = o_P(1)$, where $\tilde{W}_{\tilde{s}}(r) := W_{\tilde{s}}(r) - \int W_{\tilde{s}}(r)dr$ for $r \in [0, 1]$.

[5]In the special case where v_t is normally distributed with zero mean and constant variance σ_v^2, it is well-established that the censored normal variates, $v_t^+ = \max[0, v_t]$ and $v_t^- = \min[0, v_t]$, will have $E\left(v_t^+\right) = \frac{\sigma_v}{\sqrt{2\pi}}$, $E\left(v_t^-\right) = -\frac{\sigma_v}{\sqrt{2\pi}}$, and $Var\left(v_t^+\right) = Var\left(v_t^-\right) = \frac{\sigma_v^2}{2}\frac{\pi-1}{\pi}$. We are grateful to Jinseo Cho for pointing this issue out and encouraging us to provide a more general result in Theorem 1.

9.2.2 The Nonlinear ARDL Model

The simple case presented above is useful for exposition and will certainly cover some empirical applications. However, it is too restrictive since it does not allow for weak endogeneity of the regressors and/or serially correlated errors, factors that will significantly affect both the asymptotic and the small sample properties of the estimators. In their presence, the OLS estimator in (9.1) may remain super-consistent but the asymptotic distribution is non-Gaussian. Hence, hypothesis testing cannot be carried out in the usual manner without removing both the serial correlation and the endogeneity of the regressors. In particular, the resulting OLS estimator of the cointegrating parameter will be poorly determined in finite samples.

In the linear cointegration literature, several solutions to these twin problems have been proposed in the context of the static regression model (Phillips and Hansen 1990; Saikkonen 1991) and the dynamic regression model (Pesaran and Shin 1998). Given that our interest is in developing a fully dynamic model, we naturally choose to extend the ARDL approach popularised by Pesaran and Shin (1998) and Pesaran et al. (2001), thereby developing a flexible dynamic parametric framework with which to model relationships that exhibit combined long- and short-run asymmetries.[6]

To this end we consider the following nonlinear ARDL(p, q) model:

$$y_t = \sum_{j=1}^{p} \phi_j y_{t-j} + \sum_{j=0}^{q} \left(\boldsymbol{\theta}_j^{+\prime} \boldsymbol{x}_{t-j}^{+} + \boldsymbol{\theta}_j^{-\prime} \boldsymbol{x}_{t-j}^{-} \right) + \varepsilon_t, \tag{9.6}$$

where $\boldsymbol{x}_t$ is a $k \times 1$ vector of multiple regressors defined such that $\boldsymbol{x}_t = \boldsymbol{x}_0 + \boldsymbol{x}_t^{+} + \boldsymbol{x}_t^{-}$, ϕ_j is the autoregressive parameter, $\boldsymbol{\theta}_j^{+}$ and $\boldsymbol{\theta}_j^{-}$ are the asymmetric distributed-lag parameters, and ε_t is an iid process with zero mean and constant variance, σ_ε^2. Throughout this paper we will focus on the case in which $\boldsymbol{x}_t$ is decomposed into $\boldsymbol{x}_t^{+}$ and $\boldsymbol{x}_t^{-}$ around a threshold of zero, thereby distinguishing between positive and negative changes in the rate of growth of $\boldsymbol{x}_t$. The resulting partial sum processes maintain an intuitively appealing and economically meaningful interpretation in a wide range of applications.[7]

---

[6]Notice that the analysis of short-run dynamic asymmetries is not straightforward in the context of the static regression model employing the semiparametric approach.

[7]In some cases, most notably where the growth rates of the series in $\boldsymbol{x}_t$ are predominantly positive (negative), the use of a zero threshold may result in one regime containing an undesirably low number of effective observations. In such situations, an obvious candidate for an alternative threshold is the mean growth rate. We discuss such issues further in a separate paper (Greenwood-Nimmo et al. 2012).

Following Pesaran et al. (2001), it is straightforward to rewrite (9.6) in the error correction form as

$$\Delta y_t = \rho y_{t-1} + \boldsymbol{\theta}^{+\prime}\boldsymbol{x}_{t-1}^{+} + \boldsymbol{\theta}^{-\prime}\boldsymbol{x}_{t-1}^{-} + \sum_{j=1}^{p-1}\gamma_j \Delta y_{t-j}$$

$$+ \sum_{j=0}^{q-1}\left(\boldsymbol{\varphi}_j^{+\prime}\Delta\boldsymbol{x}_{t-j}^{+} + \boldsymbol{\varphi}_j^{-\prime}\Delta\boldsymbol{x}_{t-j}^{-}\right) + \varepsilon_t$$

$$= \rho\xi_{t-1} + \sum_{j=1}^{p-1}\gamma_j \Delta y_{t-j} + \sum_{j=0}^{q-1}\left(\boldsymbol{\varphi}_j^{+\prime}\Delta\boldsymbol{x}_{t-j}^{+} + \boldsymbol{\varphi}_j^{-\prime}\Delta\boldsymbol{x}_{t-j}^{-}\right) + \varepsilon_t \quad (9.7)$$

where $\rho = \sum_{j=1}^{p}\phi_j - 1$, $\gamma_j = -\sum_{i=j+1}^{p}\phi_i$ for $j = 1,\ldots,p-1$, $\boldsymbol{\theta}^{+} = \sum_{j=0}^{q}\boldsymbol{\theta}_j^{+}$, $\boldsymbol{\theta}^{-} = \sum_{j=0}^{q}\boldsymbol{\theta}_j^{-}$, $\boldsymbol{\varphi}_0^{+} = \boldsymbol{\theta}_0^{+}$, $\boldsymbol{\varphi}_j^{+} = -\sum_{i=j+1}^{q}\theta_j^{+}$ for $j = 1,\ldots,q-1$, $\boldsymbol{\varphi}_0^{-} = \boldsymbol{\theta}_0^{-}$, $\boldsymbol{\varphi}_j^{-} = -\sum_{i=j+1}^{q}\theta_j^{-}$ for $j = 1,\ldots,q-1$, and $\xi_t = y_t - \boldsymbol{\beta}^{+\prime}\boldsymbol{x}_t^{+} - \boldsymbol{\beta}^{-\prime}\boldsymbol{x}_t^{-}$ is the nonlinear error correction term where $\boldsymbol{\beta}^{+} = -\boldsymbol{\theta}^{+}/\rho$ and $\boldsymbol{\beta}^{-} = -\boldsymbol{\theta}^{-}/\rho$ are the associated asymmetric long-run parameters.

To further deal with the possibility of non-zero contemporaneous correlation between the regressors and the residuals in (9.7) we now consider the following reduced form data generating process for $\Delta\boldsymbol{x}_t$[8]:

$$\Delta\boldsymbol{x}_t = \sum_{j=1}^{q-1}\boldsymbol{\Lambda}_j\Delta\boldsymbol{x}_{t-j} + \boldsymbol{v}_t, \quad (9.8)$$

where $\boldsymbol{v}_t \sim iid\,(0, \boldsymbol{\Sigma}_v)$, with $\boldsymbol{\Sigma}_v$ being a $k \times k$ positive definite covariance matrix. Given our focus on conditional modelling, we may express ε_t conditionally in terms of $\boldsymbol{v}_t$ as:

$$\varepsilon_t = \boldsymbol{\omega}'\boldsymbol{v}_t + e_t = \boldsymbol{\omega}'\left(\Delta\boldsymbol{x}_t - \sum_{j=1}^{q-1}\boldsymbol{\Lambda}_j\Delta\boldsymbol{x}_{t-j}\right) + e_t \quad (9.9)$$

where e_t is uncorrelated with $\boldsymbol{v}_t$ by construction. Substituting (9.9) into (9.7) and rearranging it, we finally obtain the following conditional nonlinear ECM:

$$\Delta y_t = \rho\xi_{t-1} + \sum_{j=1}^{p-1}\gamma_j \Delta y_{t-j} + \sum_{j=0}^{q-1}\left(\boldsymbol{\pi}_j^{+\prime}\Delta\boldsymbol{x}_{t-j}^{+} + \boldsymbol{\pi}_j^{-\prime}\Delta\boldsymbol{x}_{t-j}^{-}\right) + e_t \quad (9.10)$$

where $\boldsymbol{\pi}_0^{+} = \boldsymbol{\theta}_0^{+} + \boldsymbol{\omega}$, $\boldsymbol{\pi}_0^{-} = \boldsymbol{\theta}_0^{-} + \boldsymbol{\omega}$, $\boldsymbol{\pi}_j^{+} = \boldsymbol{\varphi}_j^{+} - \boldsymbol{\omega}'\boldsymbol{\Lambda}_j$ and $\boldsymbol{\pi}_j^{-} = \boldsymbol{\varphi}_j^{-} - \boldsymbol{\omega}'\boldsymbol{\Lambda}_j$ for $j = 1,\ldots,q-1$.

[8]For convenience we employ the same lag order, q. One may also allow for feedback effects from the lagged Δy's on Δx_t in (9.8).

It is clear that (9.10) corrects perfectly for the weak endogeneity of any non-stationary explanatory variables and that the choice of an appropriate lag structure will render the model free from residual serial correlation. Our model combines many of the desirable attributes of the fully-modified and the ARDL-based dynamic corrections associated respectively with Phillips and Hansen (1990) and Pesaran and Shin (1998) in a dynamic parametric framework capable of modelling both long- and short-run asymmetries. Moreover, since our model is linear in all the parameters including $\boldsymbol{\theta}^+$, $\boldsymbol{\theta}^-$, $\boldsymbol{\pi}_i^+$ and $\boldsymbol{\pi}_i^-$, reliable estimation of (9.10) can be achieved by standard OLS.

Following the conditions used in the derivations above, we now summarise the following assumption in the context of the NARDL-based ECM, (9.10):

Assumption 2 *(i)* $e_t \sim iid(0, \sigma_e^2)$*; (ii)* $\mathbf{x}_t$ *is a* $k \times 1$ *vector of I(1) regressors given by (9.8); (iii)* e_t *is uncorrelated with* $\mathbf{v}_t$ *through the conditional modelling, (9.9); (iv)* $\rho < 0$ *guarantees that the model is dynamically stable.*

Following Theorems 3.1 and 3.2 in Pesaran and Shin (1998), it is straightforward to show under Assumption 2 that: (i) the OLS estimators of all the short-run dynamic parameters in (9.10) are $\sqrt{T}$-consistent and have the asymptotic normal distribution, and (ii) the OLS estimators of the long-run parameters computed as $\hat{\boldsymbol{\beta}}^+ = -\hat{\boldsymbol{\theta}}^+/\hat{\rho}$ and $\hat{\boldsymbol{\beta}}^- = -\hat{\boldsymbol{\theta}}^-/\hat{\rho}$, are T-consistent and follow the mixture normal distribution as defined in Theorem 1. Hence, the null hypotheses of a symmetric long-run relationship $(\boldsymbol{\beta}^+ = \boldsymbol{\beta}^-)$ or symmetric short-run coefficients can be tested using the Wald statistic following an asymptotic χ^2 distribution. In order to assess the extent to which these theoretical predictions are validated in both large and small samples, we will conduct a series of Monte Carlo experiments in Sect. 9.3.

9.2.3 Bounds-Testing the Asymmetric Long-Run Relationship

We develop two operational testing procedures for the existence of an asymmetric (cointegrating) long-run relationship based on the NARDL ECM, (9.10). If $\rho = 0$, (9.10) reduces to the regression involving only first differences, implying that there is no long-run relationship between the levels of y_t, $\mathbf{x}_t^+$ and $\mathbf{x}_t^-$. We first follow Banerjee et al. (1998) and propose the t-statistic testing $\rho = 0$ against $\rho < 0$ in (9.10). Next, we follow Pesaran et al. (2001) and propose an F-test of the joint null, $\rho = \boldsymbol{\theta}^+ = \boldsymbol{\theta}^- = 0$ in (9.10). We denote these tests, t_{BDM} and F_{PSS}, respectively.

The asymptotic distributions of these test statistics are non-standard under their respective null hypotheses and their exact asymptotic distributions are generally complicated to derive due to the complex dependence structure between $\mathbf{x}_t^+$ and $\mathbf{x}_t^-$, especially when the means of Δy_t and $\Delta \mathbf{x}_t$ are non-zero.[9] In light of

[9]While the associated critical values can be tabulated easily using stochastic simulation, it is impractical to provide a meaningful set of critical values covering all possible combinations.

these difficulties, we propose the use of the pragmatic 'bounds-testing' approach advanced by Pesaran et al. (2001). Two extreme cases can be identified, one in which the level regressors $\boldsymbol{x}_t^+$ and $\boldsymbol{x}_t^-$ in (9.10) are all $I(1)$, and the other in which they are all $I(0)$. It follows that critical values tabulated for these two scenarios provide critical value bounds for all classifications, irrespective of whether the regressors are $I(0)$, $I(1)$ or mutually cointegrated. This is an important property in the current context due to the various dependence structures (including cointegration) that may exist between $\boldsymbol{x}_t^+$ and $\boldsymbol{x}_t^-$. Following Pesaran et al. (2001), we differentiate between five cases of (9.10) for the F_{PSS} statistic: (i) without intercept or linear trend; (ii) with restricted intercept only; (iii) with unrestricted intercept only; (iv) with intercept and restricted linear trend; and (v) with intercept and unrestricted linear trend. Similarly, for the t_{BDM} statistic we differentiate between cases (i), (iii) and (v). Pesaran et al. (2001) tabulate the critical value bounds for both the F_{PSS} and t_{BDM} statistics under each of these cases for a range of values of k, the number of regressors entering the long-run relationship.

In the context of the NARDL model, due to the dependence structure that exists between the partial sum decompositions $\boldsymbol{x}_t^+$ and $\boldsymbol{x}_t^-$, the exact value of k is not clear. In the simplest case where the long-run relationship is defined between y_t, x_t^+ and x_t^-, it follows that the true value of k lies between 1 and 2.[10] In general, we expect that the test will be modestly undersized using $k = 1$ and similarly oversized with $k = 2$. Employing the $k = 1$ critical values results in a more conservative test (a higher critical value) so, at a pragmatic level, rejecting the null of no long-run relationship using these critical values provides strong evidence of the existence of a long-run relationship. The mis-sizing of the test can be readily resolved by bootstrapping, although in practice we find that the pragmatic approach typically leads to the same conclusion. This observation is reinforced below by a series of Monte Carlo simulation experiments designed to evaluate the finite sample properties of the PSS test and the performance of the associated bootstrapping routine.

9.2.4 *Asymmetric Dynamic Multipliers*

It is straightforward to derive the asymmetric dynamic multipliers associated with unit changes in $\boldsymbol{x}_t^+$ and $\boldsymbol{x}_t^-$, respectively, on y_t. Consider the ARDL-in-levels representation of (9.10):

$$\phi(L)\, y_t = \boldsymbol{\theta}^+(L)\, \boldsymbol{x}_t^+ + \boldsymbol{\theta}^-(L)\, \boldsymbol{x}_t^- + e_t, \tag{9.11}$$

It is generally straightforward, however, to compute the appropriate p-values by means of standard bootstrap techniques.

[10]It is straightforward to extend similar reasoning to the more general case with multiple regressors decomposed into partial sum processes.

where $\phi(L) = 1 - \sum_{i=1}^{p-1} \phi_i L^i$, $\boldsymbol{\theta}^+(L) = \sum_{i=0}^{q} \boldsymbol{\theta}_i^+ L^i$, and $\boldsymbol{\theta}^-(L) = \sum_{i=0}^{q} \boldsymbol{\theta}_i^{-1} L^i$.[11] Premultiplying (9.11) by the inverse of $\phi(L)$, we obtain:

$$y_t = \boldsymbol{\lambda}^+(L)\, \boldsymbol{x}_t^+ + \boldsymbol{\lambda}^-(L)\, \boldsymbol{x}_{t-i}^- + [\phi(L)]^{-1} e_t, \tag{9.12}$$

where $\boldsymbol{\lambda}^+(L) \left(= \sum_{j=0}^{\infty} \boldsymbol{\lambda}_j^+\right) = \phi(L)^{-1} \boldsymbol{\theta}^+(L)$ and $\boldsymbol{\lambda}^-(L) \left(= \sum_{j=0}^{\infty} \boldsymbol{\lambda}_j^-\right) = \phi(L)^{-1} \boldsymbol{\theta}^-(L)$.[12] The cumulative dynamic multiplier effects of $\boldsymbol{x}_t^+$ and $\boldsymbol{x}_t^-$ on y_t can be evaluated as follows:

$$\boldsymbol{m}_h^+ = \sum_{j=0}^{h} \frac{\partial y_{t+j}}{\partial \boldsymbol{x}_t^+} = \sum_{j=0}^{h} \boldsymbol{\lambda}_j^+,\ \boldsymbol{m}_h^- = \sum_{j=0}^{h} \frac{\partial y_{t+j}}{\partial \boldsymbol{x}_t^-} = \sum_{j=0}^{h} \boldsymbol{\lambda}_j^-,\ h = 0, 1, 2 \ldots \tag{9.13}$$

Notice that, by construction, as $h \to \infty$, $\boldsymbol{m}_h^+ \to \boldsymbol{\beta}^+$ and $\boldsymbol{m}_h^- \to \boldsymbol{\beta}^-$, where $\boldsymbol{\beta}^+ = -\boldsymbol{\theta}^+/\rho$ and $\boldsymbol{\beta}^- = -\boldsymbol{\theta}^-/\rho$ are the asymmetric long-run coefficients. There is little reason to believe that the dynamic adjustment patterns summarised by $\boldsymbol{m}_h^+$ and $\boldsymbol{m}_h^-$ should generally be symmetric. Therefore, even though we do not directly model asymmetric error correction (i.e. we do not allow for regime-dependency of ρ in (9.10)) we may still observe asymmetric adjustment paths and/or duration of the disequilibrium. This highlights an important feature of the NARDL model. In the interest of clarity, when discussing asymmetry we tend to distinguish only between long- and short-run asymmetries. However, the NARDL model in fact admits *three* general forms of asymmetry: (i) long-run or reaction asymmetry, associated with $\boldsymbol{\beta}^+ \neq \boldsymbol{\beta}^-$; (ii) impact asymmetry, associated with the inequality of the coefficients on the contemporaneous first differences Δx_t^+ and Δx_t^-; (iii) adjustment asymmetry, captured by the patterns of adjustment from initial equilibrium to the new equilibrium following an economic perturbation (i.e. the dynamic multipliers). Adjustment asymmetry derives from the interaction of impact and reaction asymmetries in conjunction with the error correction coefficient, ρ.

In practice, the patterns of dynamic adjustment will depend on the model specification. Four distinct cases can be identified: the unrestricted specification,

[11]The level parameters are obtained as follows:

$$\phi_1 = \rho + 1 + \varphi_1;\ \phi_i = \varphi_i - \varphi_{i-1},\ i = 2, \ldots, p-1;\ \phi_p = -\varphi_{p-1};$$

$$\boldsymbol{\theta}_0^\ell = \boldsymbol{\pi}_0^\ell;\ \boldsymbol{\theta}_1^\ell = \boldsymbol{\theta}^\ell - \boldsymbol{\pi}_0^\ell + \boldsymbol{\pi}_1^\ell;\ \boldsymbol{\theta}_i^\ell = \boldsymbol{\pi}_i^\ell - \boldsymbol{\pi}_{i-1}^\ell,\ i = 2, \ldots, q-1;\ \boldsymbol{\theta}_q^\ell = -\boldsymbol{\pi}_{q-1}^\ell,\ \ell = +, -.$$

[12]The dynamic multipliers, $\boldsymbol{\lambda}_j^+$ and $\boldsymbol{\lambda}_j^-$ for $j = 0, 1, \ldots,$ can be evaluated using the following recursive relationships in which $\boldsymbol{\lambda}_0^\ell = \boldsymbol{\theta}_0^\ell$, $\phi_j = 0$ for $j < 1$ and $\boldsymbol{\lambda}_j^\ell = \mathbf{0}$ for $j < 0$:

$$\boldsymbol{\lambda}_j^\ell = \phi_1 \boldsymbol{\lambda}_{j-1}^\ell + \phi_2 \boldsymbol{\lambda}_{j-2}^\ell + \ldots + \phi_{j-1} \boldsymbol{\lambda}_1^\ell + \phi_j \boldsymbol{\lambda}_0^\ell + \boldsymbol{\theta}_j^\ell,\ \ell = +, -,\ j = 1, 2, \ldots,$$

(9.10), accommodating asymmetries in both the short- and long-run and three restricted specifications obtained by imposing short- and long-run symmetry restrictions in (9.10), either separately or jointly. An early study by Borenstein et al. (1997) investigates short-run dynamic asymmetries in the response of retail gasoline prices to fluctuations in the price of crude oil by implicitly imposing the long-run symmetry restrictions $\boldsymbol{\theta}^{+} = \boldsymbol{\theta}^{-} = \boldsymbol{\theta}$ such that (9.10) simplifies to[13]

$$\Delta y_t = \rho y_{t-1} + \boldsymbol{\theta} \boldsymbol{x}_{t-1} + \sum_{i=1}^{p-1} \gamma_i \Delta y_{t-i} + \sum_{i=0}^{q-1} \left(\boldsymbol{\pi}_i^{+} \Delta \boldsymbol{x}_{t-i}^{+} + \boldsymbol{\pi}_i^{-} \Delta \boldsymbol{x}_{t-i}^{-} \right) + e_t. \quad (9.14)$$

Models of this form have also been employed by Shirvani and Wilbratte (2000) and Apergis and Miller (2006) in their analysis of short-run asymmetric wealth effects on consumption due to liquidity constraints.

Short-run symmetry restrictions can take either of two forms: (i) $\boldsymbol{\pi}_i^{+} = \boldsymbol{\pi}_i^{-}$ for all $i = 0, \ldots, q-1$ or (ii) $\sum_{i=0}^{q-1} \boldsymbol{\pi}_i^{+} = \sum_{i=0}^{q-1} \boldsymbol{\pi}_i^{-}$. When imposing such restrictions in the presence of an asymmetric long-run relationship, we obtain[14]:

$$\Delta y_t = \rho y_{t-1} + \boldsymbol{\theta}^{+} \boldsymbol{x}_{t-1}^{+} + \boldsymbol{\theta}^{-} \boldsymbol{x}_{t-1}^{-} + \sum_{i=1}^{p-1} \gamma_i \Delta y_{t-i} + \sum_{i=0}^{q-1} \boldsymbol{\pi}_i \Delta \boldsymbol{x}_{t-i} + e_t. \quad (9.15)$$

Finally, the most restrictive specification is obtained when assuming linearity of the long-run relationship in conjunction with symmetric short-run adjustment:

$$\Delta y_t = \rho y_{t-1} + \boldsymbol{\theta} \boldsymbol{x}_{t-1} + \sum_{i=1}^{p-1} \gamma_i \Delta y_{t-i} + \sum_{i=0}^{q-1} \boldsymbol{\pi}_i \Delta \boldsymbol{x}_{t-i} + e_t. \quad (9.16)$$

It is clear that (9.14)–(9.16) are special cases of the unrestricted specification described by (9.10) and that the long- and short-run symmetry restrictions can be easily tested in the usual manner following our proposed methodology. Our early experimentation with the model, as well as the results adduced in Van Treeck (2008), Nguyen and Shin (2010) and Greenwood-Nimmo et al. (2013), suggest that the dynamic multipliers obtained from the various cases are generally significantly different from one-another. Moreover, it is generally the case that the results of

[13]The final specification in Borenstein et al. (1997) differs slightly from (9.14) as the lagged Δy_t's on the right hand side are also decomposed into positive and negative changes. However, their derivation is rather ad hoc.

[14]Short-run symmetry restrictions (especially the pair-wise restrictions) may be excessively restrictive in many applications although they may be useful in providing more precise estimation results, particularly when estimating a long-run asymmetric relationship in small samples. The additive symmetry restrictions are somewhat weaker and have been discussed in the literature in terms of assessing the validity of the liquidity constraint where $\sum_{i=0}^{q-1} \boldsymbol{\pi}_i^{+} < \sum_{i=0}^{q-1} \boldsymbol{\pi}_i^{-}$ (e.g. Van Treeck 2008).

linear estimation are profoundly misleading when the underlying relationship is, in fact, asymmetric. This will become apparent during the discussion of our empirical illustration in Sect. 9.4.

A simple and useful addition to the general typology developed above is the extension to the case where a subset of regressors enters the long-run relationship symmetrically[15]:

$$y_t = \boldsymbol{\beta}^{+\prime}\boldsymbol{x}_t^+ + \boldsymbol{\beta}^{-\prime}\boldsymbol{x}_t^- + \boldsymbol{\gamma}'\boldsymbol{w}_t + u_t, \tag{9.17}$$

where $\boldsymbol{x}_t \left(= \boldsymbol{x}_0 + \boldsymbol{x}_t^+ + \boldsymbol{x}_t^-\right)$ is a $k \times 1$ vector of regressors entering the model asymmetrically and $\boldsymbol{w}_t$ is a $g \times 1$ vector of regressors entering symmetrically. Extending the concept of partial asymmetry to both the long- and short-run within our NARDL model, we obtain:

$$\begin{aligned}\Delta y_t &= \rho y_{t-1} + \boldsymbol{\theta}^+\boldsymbol{x}_{t-1}^+ + \boldsymbol{\theta}^-\boldsymbol{x}_{t-1}^- + \boldsymbol{\theta}_w\boldsymbol{w}_{t-1} \\ &\quad + \sum_{i=1}^{p-1}\gamma_i\Delta y_{t-i} + \sum_{i=0}^{q-1}\left(\boldsymbol{\pi}_i^+\Delta\boldsymbol{x}_{t-i}^+ + \boldsymbol{\pi}_i^-\Delta\boldsymbol{x}_{t-i}^- + \boldsymbol{\pi}_{w,i}\Delta\boldsymbol{w}_{t-i}\right) + e_t. \end{aligned} \tag{9.18}$$

In light of the bounds-testing approach employed above, it follows that estimation and inference proceed exactly as before, irrespective of whether $\boldsymbol{x}_t$ and $\boldsymbol{w}_t$ are $I(0)$, $I(1)$ or mutually cointegrated. Furthermore, it is once again clear that this partially asymmetric form represents a special case of (9.10).

9.3 Finite Sample Properties

In order to investigate the finite sample properties of the estimators we conduct a range of Monte Carlo experiments based on the following simple data generating process (DGP):

$$\Delta y_t = a + \rho\left(y_{t-1} - \beta^+ x_{t-1}^+ - \beta^- x_{t-1}^-\right) + \varphi^+\Delta x_t^+ + \varphi^-\Delta x_t^- + u_t, \tag{9.19}$$

where $\Delta x_t = \varepsilon_t$, and (u_t, ε_t) are serially uncorrelated and are generated according to the following bivariate normal distribution:

$$\begin{pmatrix} u_t \\ \varepsilon_t \end{pmatrix} \sim N\left\{\mathbf{0}, \boldsymbol{\Omega} = \begin{pmatrix} 1 & \omega \\ \omega & 1 \end{pmatrix}\right\}. \tag{9.20}$$

[15] Webber (2000) utilises a similar approach in his analysis of the asymmetric pass-through from exchange rates, decomposed as the partial sum processes of appreciations and depreciations, to import prices.

Notice that when $\omega \neq 0$, (9.19) can be estimated by:

$$\Delta y_t = a + \rho y_{t-1} + \theta^+ x_{t-1}^+ + \theta^- x_{t-1}^- + \pi^+ \Delta x_t^+ + \pi^- \Delta x_t^- + e_t, \quad (9.21)$$

where $\pi^+ = \varphi^+ + \omega$ and $\pi^- = \varphi^- + \omega$ and the long run parameters are defined as $\hat{\beta}^+ = -\hat{\theta}^+/\hat{\rho}$ and $\hat{\beta}^- = -\hat{\theta}^-/\hat{\rho}$.

We experiment with a wide variety of parameterisations of (9.19) and (9.20). Specifically, under the assumptions that $a = 0$, $\beta^+ = 0.5$ and $\varphi^+ = 0.5$, and denoting $\beta^- = \beta^+ + \delta_\beta$ and $\varphi^- = \varphi^+ + \delta_\varphi$, we experiment with an array of combinations of the following parameters: $\rho \in (-0.05, -0.1, -0.2)$, $\delta_\beta \in (0.1, 0.2, 0.25, 0.5)$, $\delta_\varphi \in (0.1, 0.2, 0.25, 0.5)$, $\omega \in (-0.5, 0, 0.5)$, and $T \in (100, 200, 400)$. Due to space constraints, we are unable to report the results of all of these simulations herein.[16] Rather, we summarise the key findings that arise across these parameterisations and report in detail the results from a baseline case in which we use $\rho = -0.2$, $\delta_\beta = 0.5$ and $\delta_\varphi = 0.5$, and where ω and T vary over the ranges defined above.

In Table 9.1 we report a range of summary statistics for the parameter estimates based on our simulations using 3,000 replications of our baseline case. We note that the bias and error in the estimation of each of the parameters is largely negligible (this also holds under the other parameterisations of the DGP that we consider). The only exception to this generalisation is the error correction parameter, which shows a modest downward bias especially when $T \leq 100$. However, this observation is not unexpected given the well-documented downward bias associated with the estimation of AR(1) coefficients in time series models.

We also investigate the finite sample size and power of the Wald statistics for the null hypothesis of long-run symmetry $\left(H_{LR}^S : \beta^+ = \beta^-\right)$ and the null of symmetric short-run dynamics $\left(H_{SR}^S : \pi^+ = \pi^-\right)$. To this end, we consider the model for H_{LR}^S:

$$\Delta y_t = a + \rho\left(y_{t-1} - \beta x_{t-1}\right) + \varphi^+ \Delta x_t^+ + \varphi^- \Delta x_t^- + u_t, \quad (9.22)$$

where we set $\beta = \beta^+$, and the model for H_{SR}^S:

$$\Delta y_t = a + \rho\left(y_{t-1} - \beta^+ x_{t-1}^+ - \beta^- x_{t-1}^-\right) + \varphi \Delta x_t + u_t, \quad (9.23)$$

where $\varphi = \varphi^+$. In both cases the alternative model is given by (9.19). Finally, we examine the finite sample size and power of the PSS bounds test of the null hypothesis of no asymmetric cointegration $\left(H_{PSS} : \rho = \beta^+ = \beta^- = 0\right)$. In this case, the restricted model is given by:

$$\Delta y_t = a + \varphi^+ \Delta x_t^+ + \varphi^- \Delta x_t^- + u_t. \quad (9.24)$$

[16] Full results are available on request.

Table 9.1 Monte Carlo simulation results: bias, standard error and RMSE of the OLS estimator

	$T = 100$				$T = 200$				$T = 400$			
	Coef	Bias	STDE	RMSE	Coef	Bias	STDE	RMSE	Coef	Bias	STDE	RMSE
$\omega = -0.5$	α	0.001	0.308	6.932	α	0.001	0.194	3.082	α	0.001	0.130	1.451
	ρ	−0.063	0.070	2.121	ρ	−0.029	0.043	0.825	ρ	−0.014	0.028	0.354
	θ^+	0.019	0.054	1.283	θ^+	0.011	0.028	0.475	θ^+	0.006	0.016	0.195
	θ^-	0.051	0.073	2.001	θ^-	0.026	0.044	0.806	θ^-	0.013	0.029	0.351
	π^+	−0.001	0.179	4.019	π^+	0.000	0.122	1.930	π^+	−0.001	0.085	0.954
	π^-	−0.002	0.178	4.011	π^-	−0.001	0.122	1.937	π^-	0.001	0.085	0.954
	β^+	−0.031	0.205	4.664	β^+	−0.010	0.102	1.628	β^+	−0.003	0.051	0.567
	β^-	−0.031	0.205	4.661	β^-	−0.010	0.102	1.631	β^-	−0.003	0.051	0.567
$\omega = 0$	α	0.002	0.366	8.230	α	0.001	0.229	3.633	α	0.000	0.150	1.681
	ρ	−0.075	0.077	2.427	ρ	−0.037	0.049	0.970	ρ	−0.018	0.033	0.417
	θ^+	0.037	0.072	1.811	θ^+	0.018	0.036	0.647	θ^+	0.009	0.020	0.251
	θ^-	0.075	0.098	2.773	θ^-	0.037	0.056	1.062	θ^-	0.018	0.035	0.441
	π^+	0.002	0.206	4.631	π^+	0.000	0.141	2.228	π^+	0.001	0.098	1.102
	π^-	−0.001	0.205	4.613	π^-	0.000	0.140	2.221	π^-	0.000	0.099	1.104
	β^+	−0.002	0.227	5.104	β^+	0.000	0.114	1.812	β^+	0.000	0.057	0.637
	β^-	−0.001	0.227	5.097	β^-	0.000	0.114	1.813	β^-	0.000	0.057	0.638
$\omega = 0.5$	α	0.005	0.311	7.001	α	0.001	0.195	3.096	α	0.001	0.129	1.441
	ρ	−0.063	0.070	2.121	ρ	−0.029	0.043	0.826	ρ	−0.014	0.028	0.354
	θ^+	0.044	0.074	1.929	θ^+	0.018	0.036	0.634	θ^+	0.008	0.019	0.234
	θ^-	0.075	0.102	2.854	θ^-	0.032	0.054	1.001	θ^-	0.015	0.032	0.396
	π^+	0.002	0.178	4.001	π^+	0.001	0.123	1.948	π^+	0.000	0.085	0.952
	π^-	0.002	0.178	4.002	π^-	0.000	0.122	1.933	π^-	0.000	0.085	0.957
	β^+	0.031	0.207	4.714	β^+	0.010	0.102	1.625	β^+	0.003	0.050	0.565
	β^-	0.032	0.207	4.714	β^-	0.010	0.102	1.621	β^-	0.003	0.050	0.566

Note: Bias $= \hat{\theta}_R - \theta_0$, where θ_0 is the true value of the coefficient θ and $\hat{\theta}_R$ is the mean of the estimates of θ across replications, i.e., $\hat{\theta}_R = \sum_{i=1}^{R} \hat{\theta}_i / R$, where R is the number of replications (we set $R = 3{,}000$ in all cases). STDE θ denotes the standard error of the estimator, $\hat{\theta}_i$, across replications. RMSE denotes the root mean squared error of $\hat{\theta}_i$, defined as $\sqrt{R^{-1} \sum_{i=1}^{R} (\hat{\theta}_i - \theta_0)^2}$

and, as before, the alternative model is given by (9.19). As noted in Sect. 9.2.3, the relevant critical value bounds for the PSS test depend on the number of regressors entering the long-run relationship, k. However, given the dependence between $\boldsymbol{x}_t^+$ and $\boldsymbol{x}_t^-$, the appropriate value of k is unclear. Thus, we propose a pragmatic solution using two sets of critical values, one for which k is defined by counting the partial sums as separate $I(1)$ regressors (here, $k = 2$) and another by counting each set of partial sums collectively as a single $I(1)$ regressor (here, $k = 1$). It follows that the latter approach is the more conservative.

Table 9.2 summarises the simulation results from our baseline case at a nominal size of 5 %. For $T = 100$, the long-run Wald test has very high power and the short-run Wald and PSS tests have moderate power, although this rapidly improves as T increases. Indeed, when $T = 400$ all of the tests achieve close to 100 % power. The short-run Wald test is well-sized regardless of the value of T while W_{LR} is slightly oversized in small samples, although this improves rapidly as T increases. Finally, as expected, we observe some mis-sizing of the PSS F-test dependent on the selection of k. Importantly, however, we find that the power of the test is satisfactory even under the conservative case ($k = 1$).

Table 9.2 also reports the power of the bootstrapped PSS test. For each replication of the simulation routine, using data generated under the alternative hypothesis, we generate 500 bootstrap samples non-parametrically using the resampled residuals from estimation of (9.21) in conjunction with the estimated coefficients from (9.24) under the assumption that the initial values and the $\boldsymbol{x}$'s are known. It is then a simple matter to compute the empirical p-value of the PSS test by estimating (9.21) on the bootstrap samples and calculating the probability that the bootstrapped test statistic exceeds its original value. On this basis, we note that the bootstrapping procedure achieves the desired size correction while retaining admirable power which increases with T.

One important finding that arises from the other parameterisations of the DGP is that the power of the long- and short-run Wald tests is positively associated with the distance between their respective null and alternative hypotheses. Moreover, we find that the long-run Wald test becomes somewhat over-sized especially when the distance of the alternative from the null is small, the error correction parameter is close to zero, and $T \leq 100$. These findings reflect the well known limitations of asymptotic inference under adverse conditions. To overcome these issues, one could adopt the common practice within the literature and compute empirical p-values for the short- and long-run Wald statistics by use of a bootstrap. However, we choose to pursue an alternative and more flexible approach. By computing 95 % bootstrap confidence intervals for the difference between the asymmetric cumulative dynamic multipliers defined for positive and negative shocks, respectively, we are able to convey relevant information about the statistical significance of any observed asymmetries at any horizon, h. Furthermore, in light of our simulations, and given the absence of precise asymptotic critical values for the F_{PSS} and t_{BDM}

Table 9.2 Monte Carlo simulation results: size and power of Wald and PSS tests

	$T=100$			$T=200$			$T=400$		
	Test	Power	Size	Test	Power	Size	Test	Power	Size
$\omega=-0.5$	W_{LR}	0.981	0.089	W_{LR}	1.000	0.067	W_{LR}	1.000	0.059
	W_{SR}	0.425	0.075	W_{SR}	0.675	0.050	W_{SR}	0.935	0.055
	$F_{PSS}^{k=1}$	0.610	0.040	$F_{PSS}^{k=1}$	0.995	0.045	$F_{PSS}^{k=1}$	1.000	0.030
	$F_{PSS}^{k=2}$	0.765	0.090	$F_{PSS}^{k=2}$	1.000	0.100	$F_{PSS}^{k=2}$	1.000	0.070
	$F_{PSS}^{(b)}$	0.720	0.050	$F_{PSS}^{(b)}$	1.000	0.050	$F_{PSS}^{(b)}$	1.000	0.050
$\omega=0$	W_{LR}	0.974	0.100	W_{LR}	1.000	0.075	W_{LR}	1.000	0.062
	W_{SR}	0.308	0.051	W_{SR}	0.548	0.053	W_{SR}	0.870	0.035
	$F_{PSS}^{k=1}$	0.329	0.036	$F_{PSS}^{k=1}$	0.947	0.030	$F_{PSS}^{k=1}$	1.000	0.025
	$F_{PSS}^{k=2}$	0.527	0.080	$F_{PSS}^{k=2}$	0.988	0.072	$F_{PSS}^{k=2}$	1.000	0.070
	$F_{PSS}^{(b)}$	0.422	0.050	$F_{PSS}^{(b)}$	0.976	0.050	$F_{PSS}^{(b)}$	1.000	0.050
$\omega=0.5$	W_{LR}	0.982	0.098	W_{LR}	1.000	0.075	W_{LR}	1.000	0.061
	W_{SR}	0.385	0.075	W_{SR}	0.675	0.025	W_{SR}	0.925	0.055
	$F_{PSS}^{k=1}$	0.540	0.035	$F_{PSS}^{k=1}$	0.985	0.025	$F_{PSS}^{k=1}$	1.000	0.025
	$F_{PSS}^{k=2}$	0.735	0.080	$F_{PSS}^{k=2}$	1.000	0.080	$F_{PSS}^{k=2}$	1.000	0.075
	$F_{PSS}^{(b)}$	0.655	0.050	$F_{PSS}^{(b)}$	0.995	0.050	$F_{PSS}^{(b)}$	1.000	0.050

Note: W_{LR} denotes the Wald test of the null hypothesis of long-run symmetry defined as $\theta^+ = \theta^-$. W_{SR} is the Wald test of the short-run symmetry restrictions $\pi^+ = \pi^-$. $F_{PSS}^{k=n}$ denotes the PSS F-test of the null hypothesis $\rho = \theta^+ = \theta^- = 0$ using the $k = n$ critical values where $n = (1, 2)$ for the case where all regressors follow nonstationary $I(1)$ processes. $F_{PSS}^{(b)}$ refers to the bootstrapped PSS test

test statistics, we choose to provide bootstrapped p-values for these tests in our empirical application.[17]

9.4 An Empirical Application: The Asymmetric Unemployment-Output Relationship

To demonstrate both the simplicity and flexibility of the NARDL approach, we now present an empirical application focusing on the negative relationship between changes in the rate of unemployment and the rate of output growth (Okun's Law). This remains one of the most commonly cited stylized facts in modern macroeconomics and is of fundamental importance in monetary policy transmission, representing the link between unemployment and output which underpins the mechanism by which inflation targeting monetary policy is thought to operate.[18]

However, despite its importance, empirical assessments of Okun's law over the last three decades have been rather disappointing. The majority of this voluminous literature adheres to a linear paradigm, reflecting the assumption that cyclical upturns and downturns have symmetrical effects on unemployment. In general, there is little reason to believe that the labour market should behave in this simplistic fashion. If employers dismiss a given quantity of labour after a negative growth shock, then they may not hire exactly the same amount after a positive shock of equal magnitude (Lang and de Peretti 2009). This may be discussed in terms of labour market hysteresis, the idea that cyclical shocks may permanently affect structural unemployment. In this vein, Blanchard and Summers (1987) explain the persistently high European unemployment of the 1980s using an insider-outsider wage setting model. They argue that adverse shocks that reduce the proportion of insiders (union members) will increase outsider unemployment permanently. There is, therefore, no tendency for the labour market to return to its initial state even after economic growth has recovered (see also Hamermesh and Pfann 1996, on the asymmetric adjustment costs of labour).

In response to these issues, empirical attention is increasingly turning to non-linear modelling. There is a natural complementarity between the asymmetric

---

[17] We employ a non-parametric bootstrapping routine and use 50,000 replications after rejecting those for which $\rho > -1 \times 10^{-4}$. Full details are available on request.

[18] Earlier drafts of the paper include an additional illustration which has subsequently been removed to conserve space. Previously, the NARDL model was used to investigate to the so-called 'rockets-and-feathers' hypothesis associated with Bacon (1991), which describes how retail gasoline prices tend to react asymmetrically to changes in the price of crude oil (an exhaustive survey is provided by Grasso and Manera 2007). Working with Korean data spanning the period 1991q1–2007q2, our results confirm that gasoline prices respond more rapidly to increases in the price of crude oil than to decreases. Furthermore, our results suggest that the gasoline price is more sensitive to exchange rate depreciations than to appreciations and that gasoline price adjustments are approximately symmetric in the long-run. A complete discussion is available from the authors on request.

analyses of Okun's Law, the Phillips curve and the preferences of the central bank which has helped to drive research in the field. Neftci (1984) laid the foundations for this literature with his early study of business cycle effects on the patterns of correlation between major US time series, which revealed that the output-unemployment relationship displays marked asymmetry. Altissimo and Violante (2001) find evidence of nonlinearity between output and unemployment using a nonlinear multivariate VAR model. Their results, which they note are consistent with the majority of existing univariate threshold models, indicate that shocks in the recessionary regime are considerably less persistent than those in the expansionary regime. Similarly, Crespo Cuaresma (2003) develops a regime-dependent specification of Okun's law and finds that the contemporaneous effect of output growth on unemployment is asymmetric and significantly larger in recessions than in expansions, and that shocks to unemployment tend to be more persistent in the expansionary regime.

Attfield and Silverstone (1998) argue that if output and unemployment are cointegrated and potential output and unemployment are defined by the stochastic trend components of the variables constructed from the Beveridge-Nelson decomposition, then Okun's coefficient can be interpreted as the cointegrating coefficient. However, the cointegration test results are ambiguous: the single equation residual based ADF test is unable to reject the null of no cointegration while it is rejected by the Johansen test. Using a static asymmetric regression of the form of (9.1), Schorderet (2001) finds that nonlinearity hinders efforts to detect the stationary relationship between unemployment and output.[19] The contention that the appropriate modelling of nonlinearity strongly affects the cointegration test is one to which we will return shortly.

In this section, we apply the NARDL technique to the simultaneous analysis of both long- and short-run nonlinearities in the relationship between output and unemployment in the US, Canada and Japan.[20] This application demonstrates one of the key strengths of our model: its flexibility and the ease with which it can be applied to each of the four cases of nonlinearity defined above.

Firstly, to establish a reference point, we estimate the static linear regression of unemployment on a constant, a time trend and output (Table 9.3a) and a static asymmetric model of the form of (9.1), the results of which are reported in Table 9.3b.

In keeping with the findings of Attfield and Silverstone (1998), Schorderet (2001) and Granger and Yoon (2002), the EG test finds no evidence of linear cointegration. Moreover, the EG test is unable to reject the null of no cointegration

[19]Further examples of the use of positive/negative decompositions in the modelling of asymmetry in the unemployment-output relationship include Lee (2000) and Virén (2001).

[20]Seasonally-adjusted monthly data for unemployment and industrial production covering the range 1982m2–2003m11 were collected from the OECD's Main Economic Indicators. Although not presented here, ADF testing lends overwhelming support to the hypothesis that all variates are I(1).

Table 9.3 Static estimation of the unemployment-output relationship

	US		Canada		Japan	
Var.	Coeff.	S.E.	Coeff.	S.E.	Coeff.	S.E.
(a) Static linear regression						
Constant	73.16	3.92	74.96	2.94	29.94	1.25
Trend	0.03	0.00	0.03	0.00	0.02	0.00
y_t	−15.66	0.94	−15.19	0.70	−6.38	0.28
R^2	0.77		0.78		0.89	
Adj.R^2	0.77		0.78		0.89	
χ^2_{SC}	250.84[0.000]		233.28[0.000]		235.08[0.000]	
χ^2_H	69.29[0.000]		1.95[0.163]		0.29[0.593]	
χ^2_{FF}	109.11[0.000]		0.21[0.901]		60.72[0.000]	
χ^2_N	3.40[0.183]		6.52[0.011]		21.62[0.000]	
EG_{MAX}	−2.90		−2.42		−2.86	
(b) Static asymmetric regression						
Const.	7.82	0.10	10.56	0.10	2.55	0.62
y_t^+	−10.73	0.51	−13.05	0.48	−4.61	0.28
y_t^-	−25.83	1.81	−20.38	0.92	−7.70	0.33
R^2	0.78		0.81		0.87	
Adj.R^2	0.77		0.81		0.87	
χ^2_{SC}	248.82[0.000]		231.04[0.000]		240.02[0.000]	
χ^2_H	66.99[0.000]		0.31[0.580]		0.16[0.690]	
χ^2_{FF}	110.39[0.000]		0.23[0.892]		57.18[0.000]	
χ^2_N	11.23[0.004]		7.97[0.005]		22.69[0.000]	
$W_{y^+=y^-}$	129.20[0.000]		258.10[0.000]		1607.50[0.000]	
EG_{MAX}	−2.79		−2.60		−2.55	

Note: y_t denotes the natural logarithm of industrial production and y_t^+ and y_t^- the associated positive and negative partial sum processes. Note also that in order to accommodate the strong trending behavior of y_t, we include a deterministic time trend in the symmetric case. χ^2_{SC}, χ^2_H, χ^2_{FF} and χ^2_N denote LM tests for serial correlation, heteroscedasticity, functional form (Ramsey's RESET test) and normality, respectively. Figures in square parentheses are the associated p-values. $W_{y^+=y^-}$ denotes the Wald test of the equality of the coefficients associated with y_t^+ and y_t^-. EG_{MAX} denotes the largest value of the Engle-Granger residual-based ADF test. The 95 % critical values of the EG test are −3.42 (panel (a)) and −3.77 (panel (b))

in the static asymmetric case, highlighting the importance of an appropriate dynamic specification. In all cases, we find a pronounced negative association between output and unemployment, with the results of asymmetric analysis indicating strong non-linearity (the Wald tests of the symmetry restrictions reject the null in all cases). However, the validity of these results is questionable given the evidence of severe model mis-specifications.

Table 9.4 reports estimation results for the restricted symmetric ARDL regression of the form of (9.16). Table 9.5 presents the results of the unrestricted NARDL case allowing for both long- and short-run asymmetry. Notice that the cointegration tests are unable to reject the null hypothesis in the restricted case but that both the t_{BDM} and F_{PSS} statistics resoundingly reject the null when long-run asymmetry

Table 9.4 Dynamic linear estimation of the unemployment-output relationship

US			Canada			Japan		
Var.	Coeff.	S.E.	Var.	Coeff.	S.E.	Var.	Coeff.	S.E.
u_{t-1}	−0.03	0.01	u_{t-1}	−0.02	0.01	u_{t-1}	0.00	0.01
y_{t-1}	−0.04	0.07	y_{t-1}	−0.09	0.10	y_{t-1}	−0.02	0.06
Δu_{t-1}	−0.17	0.06	Δu_{t-2}	−0.12	0.06	Δu_{t-1}	−0.26	0.06
Δu_{t-11}	0.13	0.05	Δy_t	−4.40	1.19	Δu_{t-2}	−0.22	0.06
Δy_t	−8.17	1.61	Δy_{t-2}	−2.83	1.21	Δu_{t-10}	0.16	0.06
Δy_{t-2}	−4.73	1.58	Δy_{t-6}	−3.01	1.16	Δu_{t-12}	−0.18	0.06
Δy_{t-4}	−4.04	1.50	Const.	0.57	0.55	Δy_{t-1}	−1.37	0.42
Const.	0.38	0.35				Δy_{t-2}	−1.27	0.45
						Δy_{t-3}	−1.30	0.43
						Δy_{t-9}	−1.16	0.39
						Const.	0.09	0.27
L_y	−1.66	2.03	L_y	−5.68	3.89	L_y	5.57	20.88
R^2	0.29		R^2	0.13		R^2	0.23	
$\bar{R}^2$	0.27		$\bar{R}^2$	0.11		$\bar{R}^2$	0.20	
χ^2_{SC}	10.75[0.550]		χ^2_{SC}	9.35[0.673]		χ^2_{SC}	11.95[0.450]	
χ^2_{FF}	1.94[0.163]		χ^2_{FF}	0.26[0.609]		χ^2_{FF}	0.03[0.867]	
χ^2_{NOR}	3.72[0.156]		χ^2_{NOR}	12.35[0.002]		χ^2_{NOR}	0.92[0.632]	
χ^2_{HET}	15.19[0.000]		χ^2_{HET}	0.09[0.770]		χ^2_{HET}	0.41[0.521]	
t_{BDM}	−2.34[0.136]		t_{BDM}	−1.27[0.820]		t_{BDM}	0.57[1.000]	
F_{PSS}	4.69[0.081]		F_{PSS}	0.81[0.927]		F_{PSS}	0.18[0.890]	

Note: u_t denotes the rate of unemployment, measured in percentage points. Here we follow the general-to-specific approach to select the final ARDL specification. The preferred specification is chosen by starting with max $p = \max q = 12$ and dropping all insignificant stationary regressors. t_{BDM} is the BDM t-statistic while F_{PSS} denotes the PSS F-statistic testing the null hypothesis $\rho = \theta = 0$. The long-run coefficient L_y is defined by $\hat{\beta} = -\hat{\theta}/\hat{\rho}$. Pesaran et al. (2001) tabulate the 5 % critical values for $k = 1$ as follows: $t_{crit} = -3.22$; $F_{crit} = 5.73$. Empirical p-values are quoted for the BDM t-statistic and the PSS F-statistic

is modelled appropriately. This result underscores the importance of correctly specifying the long-run relationship under scrutiny. Moreover, the finding that the ECM-based tests are able to detect the asymmetric long-run relationship while the EG residual-based approach cannot is generally consistent with the works of Kremers et al. (1992), Hansen (1995), Banerjee et al. (1998) and Pesaran et al. (2001). This reflects the well-established power-dominance of the ECM-based tests resulting from their inclusion of potentially valuable information relating to the correlation between the regressors and the underlying disturbances.

In the restricted symmetric models (Table 9.4), the estimated long-run coefficients for the US, Canada and Japan are −1.66, −5.68 and 5.57, respectively, although none is statistically significant due to the failure to accurately model the long-run relationship. Indeed, the counterintuitive finding of a positive long-run coefficient in the case of Japan reflects the fact that the model misspecification is so severe in this case that the estimated error correction coefficient is positive,

Table 9.5 Dynamic asymmetric estimation of the unemployment-output relationship

US			Canada			Japan		
Var.	Coeff.	S.E.	Var.	Coeff.	S.E.	Var.	Coeff.	S.E.
u_{t-1}	−0.06	0.01	u_{t-1}	−0.07	0.02	u_{t-1}	−0.05	0.01
y_{t-1}^{+}	−0.55	0.17	y_{t-1}^{+}	−1.27	0.28	y_{t-1}^{+}	−0.34	0.10
y_{t-1}^{-}	−1.62	0.50	y_{t-1}^{-}	−2.09	0.46	y_{t-1}^{-}	−0.53	0.14
Δu_{t-1}	−0.19	0.06	Δu_{t-2}	−0.13	0.06	Δu_{t-1}	−0.23	0.06
Δu_{t-11}	0.11	0.05	Δu_{t-12}	−0.12	0.06	Δu_{t-2}	−0.19	0.06
Δy_{t}^{+}	−8.42	2.23	Δy_{t}^{+}	−5.24	1.86	Δu_{t-10}	0.13	0.06
Δy_{t-2}^{+}	−4.82	1.99	Δy_{t-3}^{+}	3.69	1.86	Δu_{t-12}	−0.22	0.06
Δy_{t}^{-}	−8.24	4.28	Δy_{t}^{-}	−5.15	2.60	Δy_{t-1}^{+}	−1.61	0.65
Δy_{t-4}^{-}	−9.74	3.77	Δy_{t-3}^{-}	−5.89	2.64	Δy_{t-9}^{+}	−1.71	0.66
Const.	0.38	0.11	Const.	0.72	0.19	Δy_{t}^{-}	−1.80	0.71
						Const.	0.16	0.04
L_{y^+}	−9.76	1.74	L_{y^+}	−17.26	2.15	L_{y^+}	−7.28	1.64
L_{y^-}	−28.88	6.33	L_{y^-}	−28.48	4.04	L_{y^-}	−11.26	1.97
R^2	0.32		R^2	0.20		R^2	0.24	
$\bar{R}^2$	0.30		$\bar{R}^2$	0.17		$\bar{R}^2$	0.21	
χ_{SC}^2	9.23[0.683]		χ_{SC}^2	8.11[0.777]		χ_{SC}^2	11.85[0.458]	
χ_{FF}^2	0.53[0.466]		χ_{FF}^2	9.74[0.002]		χ_{FF}^2	0.11[0.744]	
χ_{NOR}^2	1.79[0.409]		χ_{NOR}^2	12.62[0.002]		χ_{NOR}^2	0.30[0.861]	
χ_{HET}^2	12.81[0.000]		χ_{HET}^2	0.38[0.537]		χ_{HET}^2	2.77[0.096]	
t_{BDM}	−3.97[0.007]		t_{BDM}	−4.12[0.006]		t_{BDM}	−3.34[0.033]	
F_{PSS}	6.98[0.010]		F_{PSS}	7.13[0.005]		F_{PSS}	5.38[0.038]	
W_{LR}	16.33[0.000]		W_{LR}	32.49[0.000]		W_{LR}	76.69[0.000]	
W_{SR}	0.46[0.498]		W_{SR}	3.65[0.056]		W_{SR}	2.35[0.125]	

Note: L_{y^+} and L_{y^-} denote the long-run coefficients associated with positive and negative changes of output, respectively. W_{LR} refers to the Wald test of long-run symmetry (i.e. $L_{y^+} = L_{y^-}$) while W_{SR} denotes the Wald test of the additive short-run symmetry condition. Pesaran et al. (2001) tabulate the 5 % critical values of t_{BDM} as −3.53 and −3.22 for $k = 2$ and $k = 1$, respectively, while the equivalent values for F_{PSS} are 4.85 and 5.73. Empirical p-values are reported for both tests

indicating explosive instability. By contrast, using the more general unrestricted model of the form (9.10), the F_{PSS} and t_{BDM} tests both reject their respective null hypotheses in all cases, even using the conservative critical values for the PSS test (see Table 9.5). Furthermore, the Wald tests are also able to firmly reject the null hypothesis of long-run symmetry in all cases. In this case, the estimated long-run coefficients on y^+ and y^- are −9.76 and −28.88 for the US, −17.26 and −28.48 for Canada and −7.28 and −11.26 for Japan, respectively. Therefore, we may conclude that an economic upturn of 10.3 % is necessary to reduce unemployment by 1 % in the US while an economic downturn of just 3.5 % achieves the opposite. The associated values for Canada are 5.8 and 3.5 % while in the case of Japan the figures translate to an economic upturn of 13.7 % and a downturn of 8.9 %. The relatively muted response of the labour market to output fluctuations in Japan reflects its

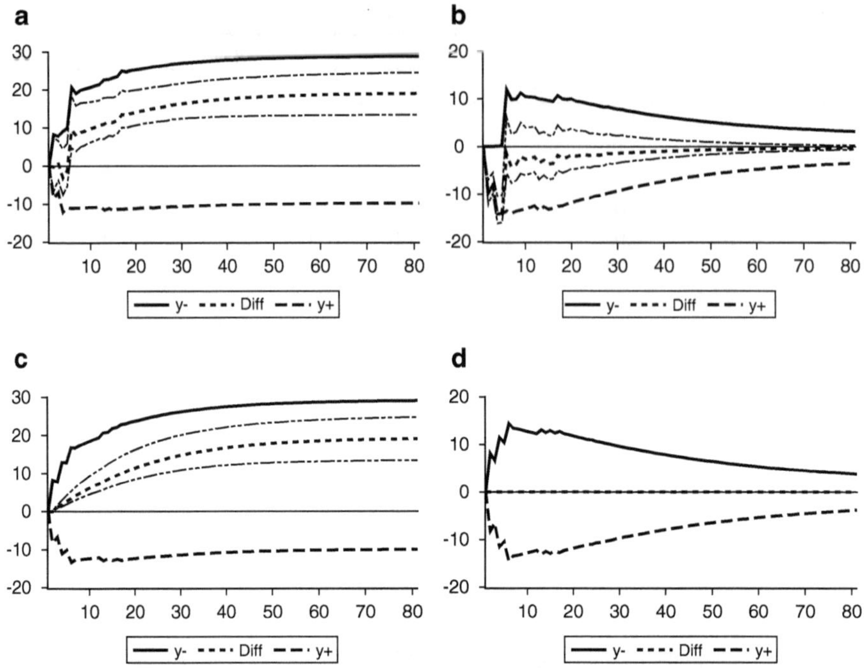

Fig. 9.1 US unemployment-output dynamic multipliers. (**a**) LR & SR asymmetry. (**b**) LR symmetry & SR asymmetry. (**c**) LR asymmetry & SR symmetry. (**d**) LR & SR symmetry

restrictive employment policies and unusually long job tenure (Tanaka 2001), and is comparable to the linear estimation results achieved by Hamanda and Kurosaka (1984).

Turning to the analysis of short-run dynamic asymmetry, we find that the Wald test cannot reject the null of (weak-form) summative symmetric adjustment in the USA or Japan but that it is rejected at the 10 % level in Canada. Consulting the bootstrap confidence intervals for the difference between the asymmetric dynamic multipliers reported in Figs. 9.1–9.3 supports this finding. However, as noted earlier, the pattern of dynamic adjustment depends on a combination of the long-run parameters, the error correction coefficient and the model dynamics. Therefore, although we find little evidence of additive short-run asymmetries, we nevertheless observe apparent asymmetries in the adjustment patterns traced by the dynamic multipliers.

For the benefit of the reader, Fig. 9.1 presents the dynamic multipliers for the US under each of the four combinations of long- and short-run asymmetry. Notice that the imposition of long-run symmetry restrictions fundamentally changes the shape of the dynamic multipliers, resulting in marked overshooting where none was previously observed. In conjunction with the results of a battery of diagnostic tests, we conclude that the imposition of invalid long-run restrictions represents a

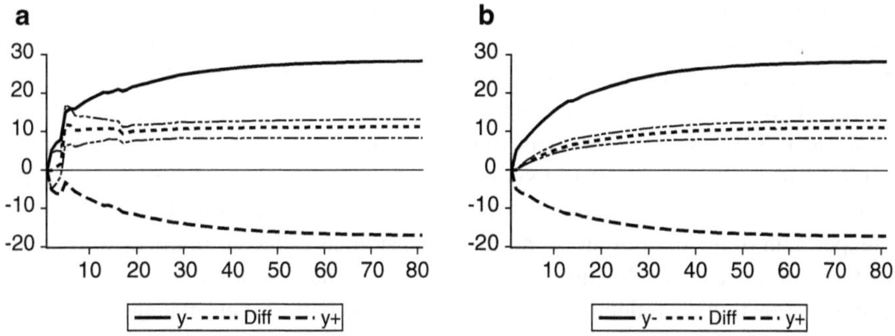

Fig. 9.2 Canadian unemployment-output dynamic multipliers. (**a**) LR & SR asymmetry. (**b**) LR asymmetry & SR symmetry

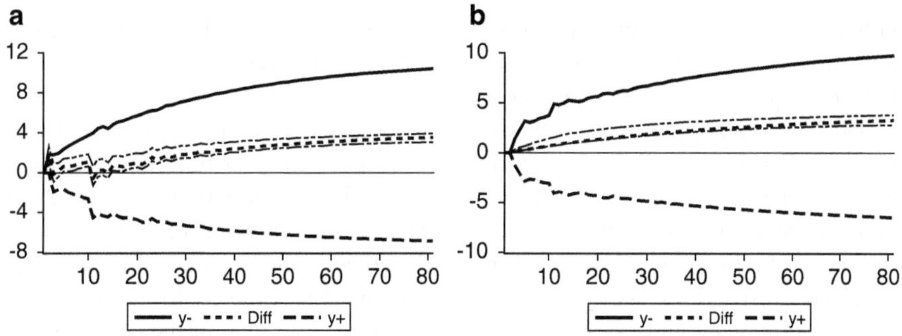

Fig. 9.3 Japanese unemployment-output dynamic multipliers. (**a**) LR & SR asymmetry. (**b**) LR asymmetry & SR symmetry

severe mis-specification of the model. This underscores the importance of correctly accounting for inherent nonlinearities in the long-run relationship and cautions that failure to do so jeopardises the identification of the long-run relationship and compromises the estimation of the model dynamics. In light of the overwhelming rejection of the long-run symmetric models, the associated dynamic multipliers are omitted from Figs. 9.2 and 9.3 to save space.

For the US, the results of both long-run asymmetric models (Fig. 9.1a, c) are remarkably similar, indicating that the labour market responds rapidly and strongly to cyclical downturns in the very short-run (correcting one quarter of disequilibrium within one period) but that full adjustment to the new equilibrium is a relatively prolonged process. By contrast, the labour market responds only mildly to the boom phase but full adjustment is achieved within 6 months. This reflects the flexibility of the US labour market, whereby firms are quick to fire in the short-run in order to cut costs but are also quick to hire in the knowledge that they can easily and quickly release the additional labour should the need arise.

Figure 9.2 reveals that the pattern of dynamic adjustment is considerably richer in the fully asymmetric case in Canada. We again find very rapid labour market adjustment in the immediate wake of a contractionary shock, with more than 50 % of the traverse to equilibrium achieved within 6 months. Again, we find that the remaining disequilibrium error is corrected relatively slowly. By contrast, the labour market response to the cyclical upswing is more gradual, taking 1 year to achieve 50 % of the adjustment toward equilibrium. Furthermore, in panel (b), with the imposition of short-run symmetry, after the initial rapid adjustment to the contractionary shock the gradient of the cumulative dynamic multiplier is noticeably steeper than in the case of an economic expansion, as reflected in the upward slope of the difference curve. In sum, our results suggest that Canadian firms are quick to fire and slow to hire, reflecting conservatism on the part of their management.

Finally, we find little evidence of short-run asymmetry in Japan. Figure 9.3 reveals that the Japanese labour market exhibits very muted responses to both booms and busts when compared to the US and Canada, a finding that reflects the prevalence of restrictive labour market institutions. Focusing on Fig. 9.3b, we note that 50 % of the equilibrium correction occurs within 10–12 months of either a positive or a negative shock, and that after this initial phase, convergence upon long-run equilibrium occurs very slowly.

Despite their superficial differences, a common pattern emerges between Figs. 9.1–9.3. In general, the labour markets in all countries exhibit relatively rapid adjustment in the first year with the absolute effect of an economic contraction being significantly larger than that of an expansion. Following this initial period, the speed of adjustment slows markedly and, subject to the imposition of short-run symmetry restrictions, we find that the labour market response to output shocks remains somewhat more rapid in the contractionary case than in the expansionary environment in both Canada and Japan. The US can be viewed as a special case due to the widely discussed flexibility of its labour market which permits very rapid adjustment to the expansionary shock as firms are eager to hire in the knowledge that subsequent dismissals are neither difficult nor unduly costly.

The subtle patterns revealed by the dynamic multipliers suggest that the focus of the literature on the persistence of shocks (Altissimo and Violante 2001; Crespo Cuaresma 2003) fails to convey important information regarding the magnitude of the implied adjustments to the labour market. Simply put, the impact of a recession in terms of jobs lost is greater in both the short- and the long-run than the job creation associated with an economic expansion of equal magnitude even though the discussion of the half-life of the shocks in the US may indicate the opposite (i.e. 50 % of the long-run effect of a contractionary shock is greater than 100 % of the long-run impact of an expansionary shock of equal magnitude). Focusing on persistence gives an incomplete picture of the phenomenon under study when the long-run relationship is asymmetric. This serves to highlight one of the primary attributes of the asymmetric cumulative dynamic multipliers; they help to shed light on the traverse between the short-run and the long-run, a property whose usefulness and theoretical appeal is difficult to overstate. In a traditional ECM, the speed of adjustment is computed simply as a percentage of the equilibrium error that is corrected in each period. By contrast, NARDL illuminates the dynamic pattern of adjustment in a simple and intuitive manner.

9.5 Concluding Remarks

The investigation of nonstationarity in conjunction with nonlinearity has recently assumed a prominent role in econometric research. This reflects the realisation that asymmetry is pervasive within the social sciences and may be inherent in modern economies. Indeed, the behavioural finance literature can be viewed as an attempt at formalising this observation. In this paper we have proposed a simple method of combining asymmetric cointegration with a dynamically flexible ARDL model and have derived the associated error correction framework. The desirable features of the NARDL model are threefold. Firstly, the estimation of the ECM in one step is likely to improve the performance of the model in small samples, particularly in terms of the power of the cointegration tests. Secondly, the ability to simultaneously estimate both long- and short-run asymmetries in a computationally simple and tractable manner reflects the flexibility of our modelling approach. Moreover, our technique provides a straightforward means of testing both long- and short-run symmetry restrictions. Finally, the use of asymmetric dynamic multipliers provides an intuitive and computationally straightforward means of assessing the traverse between the short- and long-run, a result with significant theoretical appeal. While the dynamic adjustment in most ECMs is discussed in terms of the percentage of the disequilibrium error that is corrected in each period, our approach sheds light on the nature of this dynamic adjustment, mapping the gradual movement of the process under scrutiny from initial equilibrium through the shock and toward the new equilibrium.

These key strengths of the NARDL framework have been demonstrated in the case of the long- and short-run asymmetry of the unemployment-output relationship. The results suggest that the imposition of long-run symmetry where the underlying relationship is nonlinear will confound efforts to test for the existence of a stable long-run relationship and will result in spurious dynamic responses. Similarly, our results stress the importance of correctly capturing short-run asymmetries in order to illuminate potentially important differences in the response of economic agents to positive and negative shocks.

In summary, NARDL represents the simplest method of modelling combined short- and long-run asymmetries yet developed. At this point, it seems appropriate to mention three obvious extensions which present themselves. Firstly, the model can be related to the threshold literature by generalising to the case of one or more unknown non-zero thresholds for use in the construction of the partial sum processes. This is the subject of ongoing research by Greenwood-Nimmo et al. (2012), in which we employ Hansen's (2000) approach to estimation and inference in models with unknown threshold parameters. One could further extend research in this vein by allowing for the state-contingency of the error correction term, ρ (i.e. distinguishing between ρ^+ and ρ^-). Secondly, although highly challenging, the development of a system equivalent of our model capable of dealing with multiple long-run relationships would permit the analysis of a more diverse range of macroeconomic phenomena. Finally, the extension of the model to the dynamic heterogeneous panel context may broaden its appeal further still. The obvious starting point for such developments is the pooled mean group framework advanced by Pesaran et al. (1999), which is readily estimable by FIML under the assumption of long-run homogeneity.

Acknowledgements This is a substantially revised version of an earlier working paper by Shin and Yu (2004). Earlier versions circulated under the titles *"An ARDL Approach to an Analysis of Asymmetric Long-Run Cointegrating Relationships"* and *"Modelling Asymmetric Cointegration and Dynamic Multipliers in an ARDL Framework"*. We are grateful to Badi Baltagi, Jinseo Cho, Ana-Maria Fuertes, Liang Hu, John Hunter, Minjoo Kim, Soyoung Kim, Gary Koop, Kevin Lee, Camilla Mastromarco, Emi Mise, Viet Nguyen, Neville Norman, Hashem Pesaran, Kevin Reilly, Laura Serlenga, Ron Smith, Till van Treeck and participants at the ESEM conference (Vienna 2006), the ICAETE conference (Hyderabad 2009), and research seminars at the IMK, the Bank of Korea, and the Universities of Bari, Lecce, Leeds, Leicester, Korea and Yonsei for their helpful comments. This paper has been widely circulated and the methodology adopted by a number of authors – we are pleased to acknowledge their valuable feedback, comments and discussion. Shin acknowledges partial financial support from the ESRC (Grant No. RES-000-22-3161). Yu is grateful for the hospitality of Leeds University Business School during his visit. The usual disclaimer applies.

Appendix

Proof of Theorem 1

The OLS estimator, $\hat{\boldsymbol{\beta}} := (\hat{\beta}^+, \hat{\beta}^-)'$, in (9.1) is obtained by

$$\hat{\boldsymbol{\beta}} = \begin{bmatrix} \sum_{t=1}^T (x_t^+)^2 & \sum_{t=1}^T x_t^+ x_t^- \\ \sum_{t=1}^T x_t^+ x_t^- & \sum_{t=1}^T (x_t^-)^2 \end{bmatrix}^{-1} \begin{bmatrix} \sum_{t=1}^T x_t^+ y_t \\ \sum_{t=1}^T x_t^- y_t \end{bmatrix},$$

so that

$$\hat{\boldsymbol{\beta}} - \boldsymbol{\beta} = \frac{1}{D_T} \begin{bmatrix} \sum_{t=1}^T (x_t^-)^2 & -\sum_{t=1}^T x_t^+ x_t^- \\ -\sum_{t=1}^T x_t^+ x_t^- & \sum_{t=1}^T (x_t^+)^2 \end{bmatrix} \begin{bmatrix} \sum_{t=1}^T x_t^+ u_t \\ \sum_{t=1}^T x_t^- u_t \end{bmatrix} = \frac{1}{D_T} \begin{bmatrix} A_T \\ B_T \end{bmatrix},$$

where $D_T := \sum_{t=1}^T (x_t^+)^2 \sum_{t=1}^T (x_t^-)^2 - \left(\sum_{t=1}^T x_t^+ x_t^-\right)^2$, $A_T := \sum_{t=1}^T (x_t^-)^2 \sum_{t=1}^T x_t^+ u_t - \sum_{t=1}^T x_t^+ x_t^- \sum_{t=1}^T x_t^- u_t$, and $B_T := -\sum_{t=1}^T x_t^+ x_t^- \sum_{t=1}^T x_t^+ u_t + \sum_{t=1}^T (x_t^+)^2 \sum_{t=1}^T x_t^- u_t$. We now let

$$w_t^+ := \max[0, v_t] - \mu^+, \quad w_t^- := \min[0, v_t] - \mu^-,$$

where $\mu^+ := E[\max[0, v_t]]$ and $\mu^- := E[\min[0, v_t]]$, so that

$$x_t^+ \equiv t\mu^+ + \sum_{j=1}^{t} w_j^+, \quad x_t^- \equiv t\mu^- + \sum_{j=1}^{t} w_j^-$$

Hence, we obtain:

$$\begin{aligned}
D_T = & \left\{\sum_{t=1}^{T} t^2\right\} \left\{\sum_{t=1}^{T}\left[\mu^{+2}\left(\sum_{j=1}^{t} w_j^-\right)^2 + \mu^{-2}\left(\sum_{j=1}^{t} w_j^+\right)^2\right.\right. \\
& \left.\left. -2\mu^+\mu^-\left(\sum_{j=1}^{t} w_j^-\right)\left(\sum_{j=1}^{t} w_j^+\right)\right]\right\} \\
& -\left\{\mu^{+2}\left(\sum_{t=1}^{T} t\sum_{j=1}^{t} w_j^-\right)^2\right. \\
& \left. + \mu^{-2}\left(\sum_{t=1}^{T} t\sum_{j=1}^{t} w_j^+\right)^2 - 2\mu^+\mu^-\left(\sum_{t=1}^{T} t\sum_{j=1}^{t} w_j^-\right)\left(\sum_{t=1}^{T} t\sum_{j=1}^{t} w_j^+\right)\right\} \\
& + o_P(T^5).
\end{aligned}$$

Here, $o_P(T^6)$ terms are canceled off, and the remaining next-order terms are stated as above. We now note that

$$\frac{1}{T^3}\sum_{t=1}^{T} t^2 = \frac{1}{3} + o(1),$$

$$\mu^{+2}\left(\sum_{j=1}^{t} w_j^-\right)^2 + \mu^{-2}\left(\sum_{j=1}^{t} w_j^+\right)^2 - 2\mu^+\mu^-\left(\sum_{j=1}^{t} w_j^-\right)\left(\sum_{j=1}^{t} w_j^+\right) = \left(\sum_{j=1}^{t} s_j\right)^2$$

where $s_j \equiv \mu^+ w_j^- - \mu^- w_j^-$ by the definitions of w_j^- and w_j^+. Hence, by Donsker's FCLT

$$T^{-1/2}\sum_{j=1}^{T(\cdot)} s_t/\sigma_s \Rightarrow W_{\tilde{s}}(\cdot),$$

where $\sigma_s^2 := Var(s_t)$, $\Rightarrow$ indicates weak convergence, and $W_{\tilde{s}}(r)$ is the standard Brownian motions defined on $r \in [0, 1]$. Therefore,

$$T^{-2}\sum_{t=1}^{T}\left(\sum_{j=1}^{t} s_j\right)^2 \Rightarrow \sigma_s^2 \int_0^1 W_{\tilde{s}}(r)^2 dr$$

by the CMT (e.g. Eq. (17.3.22) of Hamilton (1994), p. 486). Also notice that

$$\begin{aligned}
&\mu^{+2}\left(\sum_{t=1}^{T} t\sum_{j=1}^{t} w_j^-\right)^2 + \mu^{-2}\left(\sum_{t=1}^{T} t\sum_{j=1}^{t} w_j^+\right)^2 \\
&- 2\mu^+\mu^-\left(\sum_{t=1}^{T} t\sum_{j=1}^{t} w_j^-\right)\left(\sum_{t=1}^{T} t\sum_{j=1}^{t} w_j^+\right) \\
&= \left(\sum_{t=1}^{T} t\sum_{j=1}^{t}\left(\mu^+ w_j^- - \mu^- w_j^+\right)\right)^2 = \left(\sum_{t=1}^{T} t\sum_{j=1}^{t} s_j\right)^2,
\end{aligned}$$

then it follows that

$$T^{-\frac{5}{2}}\sum_{t=1}^{T} t\sum_{j=1}^{t} s_j \Rightarrow \sigma_s \int_0^1 r W_{\tilde{s}}(r) dr$$

by the CMT. Collecting all these results we obtain:

$$T^{-5} D_T \Rightarrow \sigma_s^2 \left[\frac{1}{3}\int_0^1 W_{\tilde{s}}(r)^2 dr - \left(\int_0^1 r W_{\tilde{s}}(r) dr\right)^2\right]. \tag{9.25}$$

Next, we consider the asymptotic weak limit of the numerator of $\hat{\beta}^+ - \beta^+$. For this, we note that the $O_P(T^{9/2})$ terms cancel off and that the remaining next-order terms are $O_p(T^4)$ so that

$$\begin{aligned}
A_T &:= \sum_{t=1}^{T}(x_t^-)^2\sum_{t=1}^{T} x_t^+ u_t - \sum_{t=1}^{T} x_t^+ x_t^- \sum_{t=1}^{T} x_t^- u_t \\
&= \left\{\mu^{-2}\sum_{t=1}^{T} t^2 \sum_{t=1}^{T} u_t \sum_{j=1}^{t} w_j^+ + 2\mu^-\mu^+ \sum_{t=1}^{T} t u_t \sum_{t=1}^{T}\sum_{j=1}^{t} w_j^-\right\}
\end{aligned}$$

$$-\left\{\mu^+\mu^-\sum_{t=1}^{T}t^2\sum_{t=1}^{T}u_t\sum_{j=1}^{t}w_j^+ + \sum_{t=1}^{T}t\sum_{j=1}^{t}(\mu^+w_j^- + \mu^-w_j^+)\mu^-\sum_{t=1}^{T}tu_t\right\}$$
$$+ o_P(T^4)$$
$$=\mu^-\left\{-\left(\sum_{t=1}^{T}t^2\right)\left(\sum_{t=1}^{T}u_t\sum_{j=1}^{t}s_j\right)+\left(\sum_{t=1}^{T}t\sum_{j=1}^{t}s_j\right)\left(\sum_{t=1}^{T}tu_t\right)\right\}+o_P(T^4) \tag{9.26}$$

where we also employ the definition of $s_j := \mu^+w_j^- - \mu^-w_j^+$. Then, by the CMT (e.g. Eqs. (f) on p. 548 and (17.3.19) on p. 486 of Hamilton (1994), respectively) we have:

$$T^{-1}\sum_{t=1}^{T}u_t\sum_{j=1}^{t}s_j \Rightarrow \sigma_s\sigma_u\int_0^1 W_{\tilde{s}}(r)dW_{\tilde{u}}(r) \tag{9.27}$$

$$T^{-\frac{3}{2}}\sum_{t=1}^{T}tu_t \Rightarrow \sigma_u\left(W_{\tilde{u}}(1)-\int_0^1 W_{\tilde{u}}(r)dr\right) \tag{9.28}$$

where $W_{\tilde{u}}(\cdot)$ is a standard Brownian motion independent of $W_{\tilde{s}}(\cdot)$. Collecting all these results and (9.28) and plugging them into A_T, we obtain by the CMT:

$$T^{-4}A_T \Rightarrow \mu^-\sigma_s\sigma_u$$
$$\times\left\{-\frac{1}{3}\int_0^1 W_{\tilde{s}}(r)dW_{\tilde{u}}(r)+\int_0^1 rW_{\tilde{s}}(r)dr\left(W_{\tilde{u}}(1)-\int_0^1 W_{\tilde{u}}(r)dr\right)\right\} \tag{9.29}$$

We now examine the numerator of $(\hat{\beta}^- - \beta^-)$ in a similar manner. That is,

$$B_T := \mu^+\sigma_s\sigma_u\left\{\left(\sum_{t=1}^{T}t^2\right)\left(\sum_{t=1}^{T}u_t\sum_{j=1}^{t}s_j\right)-\left(\sum_{t=1}^{T}t\sum_{j=1}^{t}s_j\right)\left(\sum_{t=1}^{T}tu_t\right)\right\}+o_P(T^4), \tag{9.30}$$

and

$$T^{-4}B_T\Rightarrow\mu^+\sigma_s\sigma_u\left\{\frac{1}{3}\int_0^1 W_{\tilde{s}}(r)dW_{\tilde{u}}(r)-\int_0^1 rW_{\tilde{s}}(r)dr\left(W_{\tilde{u}}(1)-\int_0^1 W_{\tilde{u}}(r)dr\right)\right\} \tag{9.31}$$

Combining (9.29) and (9.31) respectively with (9.25) we obtain the main results.

Next, from (9.26) and (9.30), it is easily seen that

$$\mu^+ A_T + \mu^- B_T = o_P(T^4),$$

which proves the final result in Theorem 1.

References

Altissimo F, Violante G (2001) The nonlinear dynamics of output and unemployment in the U.S.J Appl Econom 16:461–486

Apergis N, Miller S (2006) Consumption asymmetry and the stock market: empirical evidence. Econ Lett 93:337–342

Attfield CLF, Silverstone B (1998) Okun's law, cointegration and gap variables. J Macroecon 20: 625-637

Bachmeier LJ, Griffin JM (2003) New evidence on asymmetric gasoline price responses. Rev Econ Stat 85:772–776

Bacon RW (1991) Rockets and feathers: the asymmetric speed of adjustment of UK retail gasoline prices to cost changes. Energy Econ 13:211–218

Bae Y, de Jong RM (2007) Money demand function estimation by nonlinear cointegration. J Appl Econom 22:767–793

Balke NS, Fomby TB (1997) Threshold cointegration. Int Econ Rev 38:627–645

Banerjee A, Dolado J, Mestre R (1998) Error-correction mechanism tests for cointegration in a single-equation framework. J Time Ser Anal 19:267–283

Blanchard OJ, Summers LH (1987) Hysteresis and the European unemployment problem. Working paper no. 1950, NBER, Cambridge

Borenstein S, Cameron C, Gilbert R (1997) Do gasoline prices respond asymmetrically to crude oil price changes? Q J Econ 112:305–339

Crespo Cuaresma J (2003) Okun's law revisited. Oxf Bull Econ Stat 65:439–451

Delatte AL, Lopez-Villavicencio A (2012) Asymmetric exchange rate pass-through: Evidence from major countries. J Macroecon 34:833–844

Dickey DA, Fuller WA (1979) Distribution of the estimators for autoregressive time series with a unit root. J Am Stat Assoc 74:427–431

Engle RF, Granger CWJ (1987) Co-integration and error correction: representation, estimation and testing. Econometrica 55:251–276

Escribano A, Sipols AE, Aparicio FM (2006) Nonlinear cointegration and nonlinear error correction: record counting cointegration tests. Commun Stat Simul Comput 35:939–956

Granger CWJ, Yoon G (2002) Hidden cointegration. University of California, Mimeo, San Diego

Grasso M, Manera M (2007) Asymmetric error correction models for the oil-gasoline price relationship. Energy Policy 35:156–177

Greenwood-Nimmo MJ, Shin Y, Van Treeck T, Yu B (2013) The great moderation and the decoupling of monetary policy from long-term rates in the U.S. during the Great Moderation. University of Melbourne, Mimeo

Greenwood-Nimmo MJ, Shin Y, Van Treeck T (2012) The nonlinear ARDL model with multiple unknown threshold decompositions: An application to the Phillips curve in Canada. University of Melbourne, Mimeo

Hamanda K, Kurosaka Y (1984) The relationship between production and unemployment in Japan: Okun's Law in a comparative perspective. Eur Econ Rev 25:71–94

Hamilton JD (1994) Time series analysis. Princeton University Press, Princeton

Hamermesh DS, Pfann GA (1996) Adjustment costs in factor demand. J Econ Lit 34:1264–1292

Hansen BE (1995) Rethinking the univariate approach to unit root tests: how to use covariates to increase power. Econom Theory 11:1148–1171
Hansen BE (2000) Sample splitting and threshold estimation. Econometrica 68:575–603
Johansen S (1988) Statistical analysis of cointegration vectors. J Econ Dyn Control 12:231–254
Kahneman D, Tversky A (1979) Prospect theory: an analysis of decisions under risk. Econometrica 47:263–291
Kapetanios G, Shin Y, Snell A (2006) Testing for cointegration in nonlinear smooth transition error correction models. Econom Theory 22:279–303
Keynes JM (1936) The general theory of employment, interest and money. Macmillan, London
Kremers JJM, Ericsson KR, Dolado JJ (1992) The power of cointegration tests. Oxf Bull Econ Stat 54:325–348
Kwiatkowski D, Phillips PCB, Schmidt P, Shin Y (1992) Testing the null hypothesis of stationarity against the alternative of a unit root. J Econom 54:159–178
Lang D, de Peretti C (2009) A strong hysteretic model for Okun's law: theory and preliminary investigation. Int Rev Appl Econ 23:445–462
Lardic S, Mignon V (2008) Oil prices and economic activity: an asymmetric cointegration approach. Energy Econ 30:847–855
Lee J (2000) The robustness of Okun's Law: evidence from OECD countries. J Macroecon 22: 331–56
Neftci SN (1984) Are economic time series asymmetric over the business cycle? J Pol Econ 92:307–328
Nguyen VH, Shin Y (2010) Asymmetric price impacts of order flow on exchange rate dynamics. Leeds University Business School, Mimeo
Park JY, Phillips PCB (2001) Nonlinear regressions with integrated time series. Econometrica 69:117–161
Pesaran MH, Shin Y (1998) An autoregressive distributed lag modelling approach to cointegration analysis. In: Strom S (ed) Econometrics and economic theory: the Ragnar Frisch centennial symposium. Cambridge University Press, Cambridge
Pesaran MH, Shin Y, Smith RJ (1999) Pooled mean group estimation of dynamic heterogenous panels. J Am Stat Assoc 94:621–634
Pesaran MH, Shin Y, Smith RJ (2001) Bounds testing approaches to the analysis of level relationships. J Appl Econom 16:289–326
Phillips PCB, Hansen B (1990) Statistical inference in instrumental variables regression with I(1) processes. Rev Econ Stud 57:99–125
Psaradakis Z, Sola M, Spagnolo F (2004) On Markov error-correction models with an application to stock prices and dividends. J Appl Econom 19:69–88
Saikkonen P (1991) Asymptotically efficient estimation of cointegrating regressions. Econom Theory 7:1–21
Saikkonen P (2008) Stability of regime switching error correction models under linear cointegration. Econom Theory 24:294–318
Saikkonen P, Choi I (2004) Cointegrating smooth transition regressions. Econom Theory 20:301–340
Schorderet Y (2001) Revisiting Okun's law: an hysteretic perspective. University of California, Mimeo, San Diego
Schorderet Y (2003) Asymmetric cointegration. University of Geneva, Mimeo
Shiller RJ (1993) Macro markets: creating institutions for managing society's largest economic risks. Clarendon Press, Oxford
Shiller RJ (2005) Irrational exuberance, 2nd edn. Princeton University Press, Princeton
Shin Y, Yu B (2004) An ARDL approach to an analysis of asymmetric long-run cointegrating relationships. Leeds University Business School, Mimeo
Shirvani H, Wilbratte B (2000) Does consumption respond more strongly to stock market declines than to increase? Int Econ J 14:41–49
Tanaka Y (2001) Employment tenure, job expectancy and earnings profile in Japan. Appl Econ 33:365–374

Van Treeck T (2008) Asymmetric income and wealth effects in a non-linear error correction model of US consumer spending. Working paper no. 6/2008, Macroeconomic Policy Institute in the Hans-Böckler Foundation, Düsseldorf

Virén M (2001) The Okun curve is non-linear. Econ Lett 70:253–57

Webber AG (2000) Newton's gravity law and import prices in the Asia Pacific. Jpn World Econ 12:71–87

Chapter 10
More Powerful Unit Root Tests with Non-normal Errors

Kyung So Im, Junsoo Lee, and Margie A. Tieslau

JEL Classification: C22, C12, C13

10.1 Introduction

As is well known, traditional unit root tests have relatively low power. As such, the search for more powerful unit root tests has not been a trivial concern. In this paper, we suggest new unit root tests that utilize the information contained in non-normal errors. Our suggested tests show significantly improved power over the traditional tests that do not utilize the information on non-normal errors. It is common practice in the literature of unit root tests to ignore the information on non-normal errors. One of the main reasons might be that the limiting distribution of the usual unit root tests is not affected by ignoring non-normal errors. For example, the limiting distribution of the linear DF tests do not hinge on assumptions regarding the distribution of the error term. However, we argue cautiously that this result does not necessarily imply

K.S. Im
Senior Financial Economist, Division of Insurance and Research, Federal Deposit Insurance Corporation (FDIC), 550 17th Street, NW, Washington, DC 20429, USA
e-mail: kim@fdic.gov

J. Lee
Professor, Department of Economics, Finance and Legal Studies, Culverhouse College of Commerce & Business Administration, The University of Alabama, 263 Alston Hall, Box 870224, Tuscaloosa, AL 35487, USA
e-mail: jlee@cba.ua.edu

M.A. Tieslau (✉)
Associate Professor, Department of Economics, University of North Texas, 1155 Union Circle #311457, Denton, TX 76203, USA
e-mail: tieslau@unt.edu

R.C. Sickles and W.C. Horrace (eds.), *Festschrift in Honor of Peter Schmidt: Econometric Methods and Applications*, DOI 10.1007/978-1-4899-8008-3_10,

that the information embodied in non-normal errors is useless or that it should be ignored. If there is a way to utilize the information, the outcome will be fruitful. This paper clearly shows that utilizing the information on non-normal errors provides an important source for improving the power of unit root tests. The question of interest might be how to utilize the information on non-normal errors.

To begin with, we wish to note that it is not uncommon to find non-normality when dealing with real-world data. Non-normal distributions can occur for a variety of reasons, and they might not be easy to distinguished from some forms of non-linearity. For example, many financial time series variables have fat-tailed or leptokurtic distributions, which often are modeled in a non-linear framework. In addition, some financial variables are characterized by skewed distributions, which can occur when an asymmetric relationship exists in the data. Furthermore, some economic time series variables have a mixture of different distributions, which typically would be modeled as regime switching models. Clearly, these examples illustrate that many cases of non-normality are addressed in terms of non-linearity. If a specific nonlinear form is known, it would be possible to utilize non-linear tests using the specific information. But one potential difficulty of this approach is that such information is not easily available, and there is no convenient test that permits us to choose a proper nonlinear model. Finding a proper density function of the error term also poses a problem.

A key feature of the new tests that we suggest in this paper is that they do not require knowledge of a specific density function or a functional form. Instead, we utilize the non-normality information contained in the higher moments of the residuals in the testing regression. Specifically, we adopt a simple two-step procedure based on the "residual augmented least squares" (RALS) methodology, following the work of Im and Schmidt (2008). While Im and Schmidt (2008) considered a standard regression model under certain conditions, we consider the issue of testing for non-stationarity. There is an important practical advantage in our suggested RALS unit root tests. We do not require nonlinear estimation techniques since the suggested RALS testing procedure is implemented in a *linear* framework that relies on least squares estimation. Our simulation results clearly show significantly improved power of the suggested RALS tests over the DF tests. Since the suggested tests utilize only the moment conditions of the residuals, we may not be able to claim that these new tests can provide improved power in all possible cases of non-normal errors, but the improved power seems substantial in many cases without causing any significant size distortions. This is a very encouraging result.

We first present the theoretical result that the linearized RALS statistics for a unit root are essentially equivalent to the test statistics based on the generalized method of moments (GMM) estimators utilizing nonlinear moment conditions. This result is useful since it permits us to use a simplified testing procedure in a linear model framework. Indeed, the suggested procedure is based on linear least squares estimation, although we utilize non-linear moment conditions in the GMM framework. In short, our RALS-based unit root tests make use of non-linear moment conditions through a computationally simple procedure. It turns out that the limiting distribution of our RALS-based tests is the same as that of Hansen (1995), who suggested augmenting the unit root testing equation with stationary covariates, if available, to gain increased power. In so doing, the error variance of the regression augmented with the stationary covariates will be smaller than that of the usual Dickey-Fuller regression. His result is in line with the work of Wooldridge (1993) and Qian and Schmidt (1999) who also noted that it is possible to increase efficiency of estimation by augmenting the testing equation with variables that are correlated with the error term. The underlying idea of our suggested RALS test is similar. To utilize Hansen's methodology, one needs to find stationary covariates that are correlated with the error term, but uncorrelated with the regressors. Oftentimes, it is not easy to find such "external" variables. The main difference of our RALS tests is that they do not require these external variables but, rather, utilize valuable information contained in non-normal errors, which usually is ignored. Our RALS-based tests are useful since we can make use of information contained in the series itself, rather than having to look for new stationary covariates satisfying the requirement. Still, if such stationary covariates are available, the RALS-based tests can additionally utilize them to further increase their power. The RALS-based unit root tests yield substantial power gains.

The rest of the paper is organized as follows. In next two sections, we propose the RALS-based unit root tests and provide the asymptotic distribution when the errors are non-normal. We show that the asymptotic distribution of the linearized RALS unit root tests is the same as that of the GMM-based unit root tests utilizing nonlinear moment conditions. In Sect. 10.4, we provide simulation results to examine the performance of the RALS-based unit root tests and we compare them with other tests. Section 10.5 provides an empirical example and Sect. 10.6 provides concluding remarks.

10.2 GMM Unit Root Test

Consider a time series that follows

$$y_t = \phi y_{t-1} + \varepsilon_t,\ t = 1, 2, \ldots, T, \tag{10.1}$$

where $\{\varepsilon_t\}_{t=1}^{\infty}$ is a sequence of innovations. For the unit root hypothesis, we are interested in testing $H_0 : \phi = 1$ against the alternative hypothesis $H_A : \phi < 1$. We assume:

Assumption 1. $\varepsilon_t = \sum_{j=1}^{p} a_j \varepsilon_{t-j} + e_t, t = 1, 2, \ldots, T$, where $\{e_t\}_{t=1}^{\infty}$, is an iid sequence with zero mean and a finite second moment σ_e^2, and all roots of $a(z) = 1 - \sum_{j=1}^{p} a_j z^j$ lie outside of the unit circle.

Then, one may consider the augmented Dickey-Fuller testing regression

$$\Delta y_t = \beta y_{t-1} + \sum_{j=1}^{p} \delta_j \Delta y_{t-j} + e_t,\ t = 1, 2, \ldots, T, \tag{10.2}$$

where $\Delta y_t = y_t - y_{t-1}$. Let $\hat{\beta}_{LS}$ be the least squares estimator of β in regression (10.2). We denote t_{LS} as its t-statistic. Then it is well known that under the null hypothesis we have

$$T\hat{\beta}_{LS} \Rightarrow a(1)\left(\int_0^1 W(r)^2 dr\right)^{-1} \int_0^1 W(r)dW(r), \tag{10.3}$$

and

$$t_{LS} \Rightarrow \left(\int_0^1 W(r)^2 dr\right)^{-1/2} \int_0^1 W(r)dW(r) = DF, \tag{10.4}$$

where $a(1) = 1 - \sum_{j=1}^{p} a_j$, and $W(r)$ is the standard Brownian motion on $r \in [0, 1]$.

Let $\xi_t = \left(\Delta y_{t-1}, \Delta y_{t-2}, \ldots, \Delta y_{t-p}\right)'$, and $z_t = (y_{t-1}, \xi_t')'$. Now, we suppose that there are moment conditions:

$$E\left[g(e_t) \otimes z_t\right] = 0, t = 1, 2, \ldots, \tag{10.5}$$

where $g(\cdot)$ is a $J \times 1$ vector that satisfies the following assumption.

Assumption 2. $g(\cdot)$ is differentiable and satisfies the first-order Lipshitz condition $\left|g_j'(x) - g_j'(y)\right| < M\left|x - y\right|$ for some constant M for all j, where $g_j(\cdot)$ is the j-th element of $g(\cdot)$. Also, $E\left[g(e_t)\right] = 0$, the second moment of $g(e_t)$ exists, and $E\left[g'(e_t)\right] < \infty$.

Define $C = E\left[g(e_t)g(e_t)'\right]$ and $D = E\left[\frac{\partial g(e_t)}{\partial e_t}\right]$, and $\psi(e_t) = D'C^{-1}g(e_t)$, for $t = 1, 2, \ldots, T$. Also we define the correlation between e_t and $\psi(e_t)$ as

$$\rho = \frac{\sigma_{\psi e}}{\sigma_\psi \sigma_e} \tag{10.6}$$

where $\sigma_\psi^2 = Var\left[\psi(e_t)\right] = Var\left[D'C^{-1}g(e_t)\right] = D'C^{-1}D$, and $\sigma_{\psi e} = E\left[\psi(e_t)e_t\right] = DC^{-1}E\left[g(e_t)e_t\right]$. Then, we can consider GMM estimators that utilize the moment restrictions in (10.5). We are interested in the asymptotic distributions of the GMM estimators as well as their associated t-statistics. We let $\tilde{\beta}_G$ denote the GMM estimator using the moments conditions (10.5) in the ADF regression (10.2). The asymptotic distributions of $\tilde{\beta}_G$ and its corresponding t-statistic are as given below.

Theorem 1. *Suppose that a time series follows (10.1), and Assumptions 1 and 2 are satisfied. Under the null hypothesis of a unit root,*

$$T\tilde{\beta}_G \Rightarrow \frac{a(1)}{\sigma_e \sigma_\psi}\left(\int_0^1 W_1(r)^2 dr\right)^{-1} \int_0^1 W_1(r)dW_2, \tag{10.7}$$

where $[W_1(r), W_2(r)]'$ *is a bivariate Brownian motion with correlation* ρ. *The corresponding* t*-statistic is given as* $t_G = \tilde{\beta}_G / se(\tilde{\beta}_G)$, *where*

$$se(\tilde{\beta}_G) = \tilde{\sigma}_{\psi}^{-1} \sqrt{\left(\sum_{t=1}^{T} y_{t-1}^2 - \sum_{t=1}^{T} y_{t-1}\xi_t \left(\sum_{t=1}^{T} \xi_t \xi_t' \right)^{-1} \sum_{t=1}^{T} \xi_t' y_{t-1} \right)^{-1}},$$

with $\tilde{\sigma}_{\psi}^2 = \tilde{D}'\tilde{C}^{-1}\tilde{D}$, $\tilde{D} = T^{-1}\sum_{t=1}^{T} g'(\tilde{e}_t)$, and $\tilde{C} = T^{-1}\sum_{t=1}^{T} g(\tilde{e}_t)g(\tilde{e}_t)'$; and where $\tilde{e}_t$ is the residual from GMM estimation of regression (10.2). Then, we have

$$t_G \Rightarrow \rho DF + \sqrt{1-\rho^2}Z, \tag{10.8}$$

where ρ is defined in (10.6), DF denotes the Dickey-Fuller distribution as defined in (10.4), and Z signifies the standard normal distribution.

Proof. See the Appendix.

In the case where an intercept is allowed in the model, we use the regression

$$\Delta y_t = \alpha_1 + \beta y_{t-1} + \sum_{j=1}^{p} \delta_j \Delta y_{t-j} + e_t, t = 1, 2, \ldots, T, \tag{10.9}$$

and we have the additional moment conditions $E\left[g(e_t) \otimes (1, z_t)'\right] = 0$. In view of the expression for the estimator of β in (10.31) of the Appendix, this produces the GMM estimator that is given by

$$T\tilde{\beta}_{G,\mu} = \left(\sigma_{\psi}^2 T^{-2} \sum_{t=1}^{T} \tilde{y}_{t-1}^2 \right)^{-1} T^{-1} \sum_{t=1}^{T} \tilde{y}_{t-1}\psi(e_t) + o_p(1),$$

where $\tilde{y}_{t-1} = y_{t-1} - T^{-1}\sum_{t=1}^{T} y_{t-1}, t = 1, 2, \ldots, T$. Consequently, we have

$$T\tilde{\beta}_{G,\mu} \Rightarrow \frac{a(1)}{\sigma_{\psi}\sigma_e} \int_0^1 \tilde{W}_1(r) dW_2(r) / \int_0^1 \tilde{W}_1(r)^2 dr, \tag{10.10}$$

where $\tilde{W}_1(r)$ is the demeaned Brownian motion: $\tilde{W}_1(r) = W_1(r) - \int_0^1 W_1(r)dr$. Also, by construction, we have

$$t_{G,\mu} \Rightarrow \rho DF_{\mu} + \sqrt{1-\rho^2}Z, \tag{10.11}$$

where DF_μ denotes the limiting distribution of the t-statistic from least squares in regression (10.9).

Similarly, when the model includes a linear time trend and an intercept, we use the regression

$$\Delta y_t = \alpha_1 + \alpha_2 t + \beta y_{t-1} + \sum_{j=1}^{p} \delta_j \Delta y_{t-j} + e_t,\ t = 1, 2, \ldots, T, \tag{10.12}$$

and this will result in the GMM estimator that follows

$$T\tilde{\beta}_{G,\tau} \Rightarrow \frac{a(1)}{\sigma_\psi \sigma_e} \left(\int_0^1 \breve{W}_1(r)^2 dr \right)^{-1} \int_0^1 \breve{W}_1(r) d\breve{W}_2(r), \tag{10.13}$$

where $\breve{W}(r)$ is the detrended Brownian motion. Again, we have

$$t_{G,\tau} \Rightarrow \rho DF_\tau + \sqrt{1-\rho^2} Z, \tag{10.14}$$

where DF_τ denotes the limiting distribution of the t-statistic for the OLS estimator of β in the regression (10.12).

Remark 1. Each of the asymptotic distributions of t_G, $t_{G,\mu}$, and $t_{G,\tau}$ depends on the nuisance parameter ρ. It is interesting to note that the above asymptotic distribution is equivalent to that of Hansen (1995) who suggested using stationary covariates. Hansen (1995) reports the critical values of the asymptotic distribution of these t-statistics for $\rho^2 = 0.1 \sim 1.0$, at increments of 0.1. As such, those critical values can be used for the above GMM based tests.

10.3 RALS Unit Root Test

Now, we wish to consider some useful moment conditions that utilize the information in non-normal errors. We first consider the model with an intercept as in (10.9), and use $x_t = (1, z_t')'$. We let $g(e_t) = \left(e_t, [h(e_t) - K]'\right)'$ and consider the moment condition $E[g(e_t) \otimes x_t] = 0$. We can split this moment condition into two parts. The first part is the usual moment condition of least squares estimation

$$E(e_t \otimes x_t) = 0. \tag{10.15}$$

The second part involves an additional $(J-1)\times(p+2)$ moment conditions given by

$$E[(h(e_t) - K) \otimes x_t] = 0. \tag{10.16}$$

Therefore, we have:

$$C = \begin{bmatrix} \sigma_e^2 & C_{21}' \\ C_{21} & C_{22} \end{bmatrix}, \text{ and } D = \begin{bmatrix} 1 \\ D_2 \end{bmatrix}, \quad (10.17)$$

where $C_{21} = E\left[e_t h(e_t)\right]$, $C_{22} = E\left[h(e_t)h(e_t)'\right]$, and $D_2 = E\left[h'(e_t)\right]$. Then, we define

$$\hat{w}_t = h(\hat{e}_t) - \overline{K} - \hat{e}_t \hat{D}_2, t = 1, 2, \ldots, T, \quad (10.18)$$

where $\hat{e}_t$ is the OLS residual from regression (10.9), $\overline{K} = \frac{1}{T}\sum_{t=1}^{T} h(\hat{e}_t)$, and $\hat{D}_2 = \frac{1}{T}\sum_{t=1}^{T} h'(\hat{e}_t)$. We denote the following equation as the residual augmented least squares (RALS) regression

$$\Delta y_t = \alpha_1 + \beta y_{t-1} + \sum_{j=1}^{p} \delta_j \Delta y_{t-j} + \hat{w}_t' \gamma + v_t, t = 1, 2, \ldots, T. \quad (10.19)$$

where $\hat{w}_t$ augments the DF regression. We denote the resulting estimator the "RALS estimator" since $\hat{w}_t$ is a function of the residuals obtained from the DF regression. The RALS estimator of β is denoted as $\hat{\beta}_{R,\mu}$, and the corresponding t-statistic for $\beta = 0$ is denoted as $t_{R,\mu}$. Note that the RALS estimator is obtained through least squares estimation. Although some moment conditions given in $g(e_t)$ can be nonlinear, we do not require nonlinear optimization procedures. In the following, we show that the RALS estimator is asymptotically identical to the GMM estimator using moment conditions (10.15) and (10.16).

Theorem 2. *Suppose that a time series follows (10.1) with $\phi = 1$. Under Assumptions 1 and 2, the RALS estimator $\hat{\beta}_{R,\mu}$ from (10.19) is asymptotically equivalent to the GMM estimator $\hat{\beta}_{G,\mu}$ using moment conditions (10.15) and (10.16). In addition, the limiting distribution of the RALS-based t-statistic $t_{R,\mu}$ is the same as that of the corresponding GMM t-statistic $t_{G,\mu}$.*

Proof. See the Appendix.

When a linear time trend is included in the regression, we use

$$\Delta y_t = \alpha_1 + \alpha_2 t + \beta y_{t-1} + \sum_{j=1}^{p} \delta_j \Delta y_{t-j} + \hat{w}_t' \gamma + v_t, t = 1, 2, \ldots, T. \quad (10.20)$$

By construction, the RALS estimator $\hat{\beta}_{R,\tau}$ and t-statistic $t_{R,\tau}$ will have the same distributions as the corresponding GMM estimator $\hat{\beta}_{G,\tau}$ and t-statistic $t_{G,\tau}$, which are given in (10.13) and (10.14), respectively. Note in passing that we can obtain similar results for the RALS estimator $\hat{\beta}_R$and t-statistic t_R for the model without a drift or trend.

Thus, to obtain the RALS unit root tests, we first estimate the usual DF testing regression to obtain the residuals from regressions (10.2), (10.9), or (10.12). We then use these residuals to construct $\hat{w}_t$. For example, from (10.9), we have $\hat{e}_t = \Delta y_t - \hat{\alpha}_1 - \hat{\beta} y_{t-1} - \sum_{j=1}^{p} \hat{\delta}_j \Delta y_{t-j}$. Then, in the second step, the t-statistic on $\beta = 0$ is computed using the augmented RALS regression. We wish to provide more guidance on how to apply the RALS procedure in practice.

- ρ^2 is estimated by

$$\hat{\rho}^2 = \hat{\sigma}_A^2/\hat{\sigma}^2,$$

where $\hat{\sigma}^2$ is the usual estimate of the error variance in the standard ADF regression, and $\hat{\sigma}_A^2$ is the estimate of the error variance in the RALS regression in (10.19) and (10.20). See the proof of Theorem 2 [Eqs. (10.38) and (10.41)]. Using the estimated value $\hat{\rho}^2$, we can use the critical values reported in Hansen (1995). Note that our method corresponds to the case where $\rho^2 = R^2$ in Hansen (1995, p. 1151).

- When the sample size is small (e.g. $T \leq 50$), one may impose the restriction of $\beta = 0$ in the first step regression that yields the residuals for the augmented variables in $\hat{w}_t$. According to our simulations, this procedure improves the size property of the test with only minimal effects on power. When the sample is relatively big (e.g., $T = 100$), however, this effect, disappears quickly.
- One may be interested in the asymptotic behavior of the RALS unit root tests under a local alternative. In light of Theorem 2 and Remark 1, one can see that the asymptotic distribution of the RALS unit root tests under a local alternative is the same as that of the unit root tests with stationary covariates. Hansen (1995, Theorem 3) already has shown the distribution of the DF tests with stationary covariates. Since w_t in (10.18) functions just like a stationary covariate for the RALS procedure, the asymptotic distribution and the power function of the RALS tests under a local alternative also would be the same as that of Hansen (1995) under the same situation. Thus, a lower value of ρ^2 will lead to a higher local power function. Then one may consider an extended version of the RALS tests using DF-GLS detrending, as in Elliott and Jansson (2003). It is expected that the DF-GLS approach against a point alternative with $\phi = (1 + c_0/T)$ will lead to further improved power when the errors are not normal. However, the optimal value of the parameter c_0 will need to be determined to avoid the issue of nuisance parameter dependency.
- Alternatively, the LM detrending method of Schmidt and Phillips (1992) can be considered as in Meng et al. (2014). The RALS unit root tests using the LM detrending method also can gain further improved power. While the LM based test can be a little less powerful than the DF-GLS based test, it is free of the nuisance parameter c_0. Moreover, it can be practically more useful in extended models with structural changes.

To implement the RALS unit root tests, we need to choose the moment conditions in (10.16). One plausible option is to utilize the moment conditions that the second and third moments of the errors are not correlated with the lagged dependent variables. Therefore, we let $h(\hat{e}_t) = [\hat{e}_t^2, \hat{e}_t^3]'$ and we call the resulting tests the "RALS(2&3)" test.[1] Letting $m_j = T^{-1}\sum_{t=1}^{T}\hat{e}_t^j$, for $j = 2, 3$, for RALS(2&3) we use

$$\hat{w}_t = \left[\hat{e}_t^2 - m_2, \hat{e}_t^3 - m_3 - 3m_{2t}\hat{e}_t\right]', t = 1, 2, \ldots, T. \qquad (10.21)$$

The first term in $\hat{w}_t$ is associated with the moment condition $E\left[\left(e_t^2 - \sigma_e^2\right) y_{t-1}\right] = 0$ which is the condition of no heteroskedasticity. This condition improves the efficiency of the estimator of β when the errors are not symmetric. The second term in $\hat{w}_t$ improves efficiency unless $\mu_4 = 3\sigma^4$, where $\mu_j = E(e_t^j)$. In general, higher moments μ_{j+1} are uninformative if $\mu_{j+1} = j\sigma^2\mu_{j-1}$. This is the redundancy condition initially identified by MaCurdy (1982) and Breusch et al. (1999). The normal distribution is the only distribution that satisfies the redundancy condition. However, if the distribution of the error term is not normal, this condition is not satisfied. In such cases, we can increase efficiency by augmenting the testing regression with $\hat{w}_t$. As shown in the next section, the increased efficiency will yield higher power for the RALS unit root tests. Note that it is also possible to utilize the moment conditions using higher moments of the residuals, although such a procedure requires the existence of higher moments. Given that the improved power using the second and third moments already is significant, we did not pursue such extended tests in this paper. The key advantage of our tests is that we do not need to specify the functional form or the exact distribution of the error term. By simply utilizing the information contained in the second and third moments of the residuals, our tests provide significant advantages.[2]

10.4 Simulation Results

In this section, we investigate the small sample properties of the RALS unit root tests. We consider two model specifications given in (10.19) or (10.20). We are interested in examining the degree to which the RALS method will improve the power of the DF tests when the former utilizes the information contained in non-normal errors.

---

[1]One might naturally wish to consider a new test, "RALS(2&3&4)," which additionally utilizes the 4th powered residuals. But, the potential power gain would be made at the cost of size. One would need larger samples to make use of higher moments to achieve appropriate size. Further examination might be warranted. We are grateful to an anonymous reviewer for suggesting this.

[2]A relevant question might be: "Why not use different functions of e_t for $g(.)$, other than RALS(2&3), such as $exp(\bullet)$ or $log(\bullet)$?" In such cases, we expect that the GMM based test can differ from the RALS based test. However, it still is possible to consider such nonlinear functions. We relegate this to future research.

In our simulations, we also consider a version of the RALS test that imposes the restrictions that arise from the score of the maximum likelihood procedure when the error density is assumed to be a t-distribution with 5 degrees of freedom. We denote this test as the "RALS(t5)" test. As we assume the error term follows a t-distribution with 5 degrees of freedom, there is a subtle issue on the moments of the error terms. The fifth and higher moments do not exist for the t distribution with 5 degrees of freedom. The new error term $\upsilon_t = e_t - w_t'\gamma$ is a linear function of the augmented term, w_t. As a standard linear regression requires the existence of the second moments of the errors for the validity of inference, we need the existence of the second moments of both υ_t and w_t. But, in practice, w_t is used as a regressor, and the numerical value of the sum of squares of the residuals from RALS is not bigger than that from the original DF regression.

The motivation for choosing the t-distribution with 5 degrees of freedom is that this density function is a popular choice for mimicking a fat-tailed distribution. Thus, the RALS(t5) test would achieve efficiency gains when the distribution of the errors has fat-tails. Although we cannot provide a theoretical justification for using RALS(t5), our simulation results show that the RALS(t5) test performs well.

Another motivation for examining the RALS(t5) test is that we wish to compare our RALS unit root tests with the tests that are based on the assumption that the true density function is known a priori. In this case, we have $h(e_t) = (c+1)\, e_t/(c+e_t^2)$, and $D_2 = (c+1)\left(c - e_t^2\right)/(c+e_t^2)^2$ with $c = 5$. There is no compelling reason behind choosing $c = 5$. However, it seems that the tests are quite robust to the selection of different values of c. For example, our simulations that use $c = 3$, which are not reported here to save space, indicate that the empirical size and power of the tests are almost identical to the case when $c = 5$. Therefore, in this scenario we have

$$\hat{w}_t = \frac{6\hat{e}_t}{5+\hat{e}_t^2} - \frac{1}{T}\sum_{t=1}^{T}\frac{6\hat{e}_t}{5+\hat{e}_t^2} - \hat{e}_t\frac{1}{T}\sum_{t=1}^{T}\frac{6\left(5-\hat{e}_t^2\right)}{(5+\hat{e}_t^2)^2} \tag{10.22}$$

To examine the size property, we report the rejection ratio for $\alpha = 0.05$ when $\phi = 1$ in (10.1). To examine the power, we use $\phi = 0.9$. These results are shown in Tables 10.1 and 10.2. We simulated various cases in small samples with $T = 50$ and 100. The results in larger samples are more promising but they are omitted here. All results are based on 5,000 replications. To compute the size and power of the RALS tests, we used the asymptotic critical values of Hansen (1995), which were obtained with a sample size of $T = 1{,}000$. Thus, we may expect a little size distortion in small samples for the RALS tests. For the DF tests, we have also used the asymptotic critical values (with $T = 1{,}000$) for a fair comparison. We have considered various types of distributions: (i) the standard normal distribution, (ii)–(v) the chi-square distribution with $df = 1, 2, 3$ and 4, (vi)–(ix) t-distribution with $df = 2, 3, 4$ and 8, (x) the double exponential distribution with $df = 1$, symmetric around 0.5, and (xi) the beta distribution, B(2,2).

Table 10.1 Five percent rejection ratio of RALS and DF tests (with drift)

		Size ($\phi = 1$)			Size-adjusted power ($\phi = 0.9$)		
DGP	Model	RALS (2&3)	RALS (t5)	DF	RALS (2&3)	RALS (t5)	DF
		($T = 25$)					
1.	Normal	0.173	0.114	0.064	0.087	0.084	0.036
2.	Chi-square df = 1	0.070	0.044	0.048	0.487	0.114	0.065
3.	Chi-square df = 2	0.094	0.067	0.054	0.268	0.089	0.055
4.	Chi-square df = 3	0.108	0.080	0.056	0.188	0.080	0.050
5.	Chi-square df = 4	0.119	0.086	0.061	0.145	0.080	0.047
6.	t dist. df = 2	0.110	0.086	0.071	0.120	0.105	0.038
7.	t dist. df = 3	0.125	0.084	0.066	0.083	0.080	0.036
8.	t dist. df = 4	0.145	0.098	0.064	0.081	0.075	0.034
9.	t dist. df = 8	0.157	0.105	0.062	0.085	0.075	0.035
10.	Double exponential	0.135	0.092	0.066	0.075	0.073	0.034
11.	Beta (2,2)	0.168	0.116	0.064	0.151	0.132	0.055
		($T = 50$)					
1.	Normal	0.054	0.059	0.058	0.132	0.136	0.041
2.	Chi-square df = 1	0.057	0.038	0.046	0.879	0.337	0.113
3.	Chi-square df = 2	0.067	0.052	0.049	0.679	0.198	0.091
4.	Chi-square df = 3	0.074	0.058	0.052	0.524	0.167	0.077
5.	Chi-square df = 4	0.078	0.064	0.053	0.410	0.145	0.070
6.	t dist. df = 2	0.057	0.065	0.063	0.333	0.397	0.050
7.	t dist. df = 3	0.065	0.059	0.062	0.199	0.237	0.044
8.	t dist. df = 4	0.077	0.067	0.058	0.147	0.164	0.042
9.	t dist. df = 8	0.091	0.070	0.055	0.132	0.133	0.039
10.	Double exponential	0.069	0.063	0.058	0.148	0.175	0.040
11.	Beta (2,2)	0.115	0.087	0.056	0.397	0.331	0.083
		($T = 100$)					
1.	Normal	0.051	0.051	0.053	0.311	0.330	0.106
2.	Chi-square df = 1	0.048	0.038	0.049	0.996	0.791	0.320
3.	Chi-square df = 2	0.055	0.046	0.048	0.971	0.567	0.257
4.	Chi-square df = 3	0.062	0.053	0.054	0.915	0.444	0.213
5.	Chi-square df = 4	0.064	0.054	0.051	0.857	0.407	0.189
6.	t dist. df = 2	0.045	0.055	0.059	0.791	0.886	0.152
7.	t dist. df = 3	0.050	0.052	0.052	0.566	0.642	0.127
8.	t dist. df = 4	0.057	0.057	0.053	0.451	0.503	0.121
9.	t dist. df = 8	0.060	0.056	0.053	0.357	0.380	0.106
10.	Double exponential	0.056	0.056	0.054	0.445	0.533	0.118
11.	Beta (2,2)	0.087	0.071	0.054	0.881	0.801	0.227

Note: For the size of the tests, the asymptotic critical values ($T = 1{,}000$) of Hansen (1995) were used for the RALS tests. Also, for the DF tests, the asymptotic critical values ($T = 1{,}000$) are used throughout

Table 10.2 Five percent rejection ratio of RALS and DF tests (with time trend)

		Size ($\phi = 1$)			Size-adjusted power ($\phi = 0.9$)		
DGP	Model	RALS (2&3)	RALS (t5)	DF	RALS (2&3)	RALS (t5)	DF
		($T = 25$)					
1.	Normal	0.188	0.133	0.071	0.085	0.078	0.045
2.	Chi-square df = 1	0.073	0.051	0.062	0.489	0.120	0.106
3.	Chi-square df = 2	0.100	0.081	0.070	0.254	0.083	0.087
4.	Chi-square df = 3	0.118	0.095	0.065	0.188	0.082	0.075
5.	Chi-square df = 4	0.128	0.102	0.067	0.161	0.081	0.067
6.	t dist. df = 2	0.119	0.097	0.071	0.119	0.100	0.063
7.	t dist. df = 3	0.141	0.100	0.072	0.088	0.080	0.053
8.	t dist. df = 4	0.153	0.106	0.071	0.080	0.073	0.046
9.	t dist. df = 8	0.172	0.123	0.070	0.083	0.076	0.047
10.	Double exponential	0.148	0.103	0.075	0.075	0.073	0.046
11.	Beta (2,2)	0.182	0.130	0.072	0.146	0.133	0.077
		($T = 50$)					
1.	Normal	0.054	0.057	0.058	0.092	0.099	0.038
2.	Chi-square df = 1	0.058	0.034	0.055	0.772	0.224	0.172
3.	Chi-square df = 2	0.071	0.052	0.056	0.515	0.125	0.119
4.	Chi-square df = 3	0.084	0.063	0.058	0.346	0.101	0.093
5.	Chi-square df = 4	0.090	0.070	0.061	0.270	0.099	0.079
6.	t dist. df = 2	0.066	0.072	0.061	0.207	0.256	0.068
7.	t dist. df = 3	0.077	0.068	0.060	0.114	0.136	0.047
8.	t dist. df = 4	0.089	0.072	0.061	0.090	0.109	0.041
9.	t dist. df = 8	0.116	0.090	0.059	0.079	0.081	0.036
10.	Double exponential	0.087	0.072	0.059	0.091	0.109	0.039
11.	Beta (2,2)	0.148	0.105	0.059	0.227	0.184	0.095
		($T = 100$)					
1.	Normal	0.054	0.055	0.052	0.191	0.206	0.069
2.	Chi-square df = 1	0.049	0.035	0.053	0.988	0.650	0.355
3.	Chi-square df = 2	0.059	0.047	0.055	0.927	0.383	0.247
4.	Chi-square df = 3	0.062	0.052	0.052	0.831	0.293	0.195
5.	Chi-square df = 4	0.068	0.056	0.054	0.716	0.260	0.164
6.	t dist. df = 2	0.047	0.058	0.056	0.633	0.786	0.135
7.	t dist. df = 3	0.053	0.056	0.056	0.384	0.463	0.093
8.	t dist. df = 4	0.056	0.056	0.054	0.292	0.334	0.080
9.	t dist. df = 8	0.069	0.064	0.054	0.199	0.208	0.067
10.	Double exponential	0.056	0.058	0.054	0.271	0.353	0.079
11.	Beta (2,2)	0.102	0.080	0.053	0.737	0.632	0.204

Note: For the size of the tests, the asymptotic critical values ($T = 1{,}000$) of Hansen (1995) were used for the RALS tests. Also, for the DF tests, the asymptotic critical values ($T = 1{,}000$) are used throughout

Table 10.1 reports the simulation results for various cases with 11 different distributions for the model specification with a constant term but without a linear trend. As is seen throughout Table 10.1, the sizes of all of the DF, RALS(2&3) and RALS(t5) tests are quite close to the nominal 5 % size, except for a few cases in small samples when $T = 25$ or 50. This outcome is expected since the limiting distribution of the linear based tests using the DF and RALS regressions will not be affected by the presence of non-normal errors. We observe non-negligible size distortions in finite samples with $T = 25$ or 50, since we used the asymptotic critical values (which were derived with $T = 1{,}000$) throughout. However, in practice, we often encounter time series with about 25 data points such as annual exchange rates. Thus, it would be helpful to obtain the finite sample critical values. As such, we have simulated new critical values using the distributions given in (10.11) and (10.14) for finite samples of $T = 25$, 50 and 100, and we report them in the Appendix. These new critical values can be also used for Hansen's unit root tests with covariates in finite samples.[3] As such, the second panel of Table 10.1 reports the results for $T = 25$ when the finite sample critical values are used. As expected, the size distortions can be reduced compared to the results in the first panel. For the remaining simulations for size properties, we have used the asymptotic critical values.

When the error has a normal distribution (DGP 1), the size-adjusted power of both RALS tests is close to that of the DF test. However, when the error term follows a non-normal distribution (DGP 2–11), it is clear that both RALS tests become much more powerful than the DF test. The improvement in power is highly significant for both RALS tests especially with skewed distributions when the degrees of freedom for the chi-square distribution or t-distribution takes on relatively low values. For example, when the error term follows the chi-square distribution with $df = 1$ and $T = 100$, the power of the RALS(2&3) and RALTS(t5) tests is 0.988 and 0.650, respectively, while the power of the DF test is 0.172. When the error term follows a t-distribution with $df = 2$, the power of the RALS(2&3) and the RALTS(t5) tests is 0.633 and 0.786, respectively, while the power of the DF test is 0.146. In other cases with non-normal errors, the RALS tests are still more powerful than the DF tests. We note that the RALS(2&3) tests are usually more powerful than the RALS(t5) tests except for the case of a t-distribution. It seems encouraging that the RALS(t5) test still achieves improved power when the degrees of freedom is not equal to 5. The RALS(t5) test shows improved power with fat-tailed distributions when the degrees of freedom for the t-distribution is relatively low. However, the RALS(t5) tests are less powerful than the RALS(2&3) tests under various types of chi-square distributions. In general, the RALS(t5) test is marginally better than the RALS(2&3) test when the density is symmetric. As we can see for the case when the density is chi-square with 1 degree of freedom, the RALS(2&3) test is generally

[3]We are grateful to an anonymous reviewer who suggested using the finite critical values since the size distortions would not be trivial otherwise, as shown in Hansen (1995).

better than the RALS(t5) test when the error density is skewed. The difference in power is quite substantial in some cases.

On the other hand, we observe that the power of the DF test decreases slightly in the presence of various non-normal errors (DGPs 2–11), but we do not see any significant loss of power. Note that the critical values of the DF tests are driven by the data following the normal distribution of the error term. Although the DF tests can remain fairly robust to non-normal errors even under the alternative hypothesis, the DF tests fail to utilize the valuable information contained in non-normal errors. Our RALS tests are quite different. The RALS tests remain robust under the null without inducing any significant size distortions in almost all cases, and they become much more powerful by utilizing the information in non-normal errors. The overall pattern of improved power of the RALS tests over the DF test is similar in the model with a linear trend, as shown in Table 10.2. Both the RALS(2&3) and the RALS(t5) tests are much more powerful than the DF test.

Next, we examine the performance of the RALS tests when the errors are serially correlated. There are no particular reasons to believe that autocorrelated errors will affect the RALS tests differently from the ADF tests. We report the results in Tables 10.3 and 10.4 for the model with a constant term, when using a fixed augmentation lag as well as using the Schwarz criteria. For these results, we continue to use the asymptotic critical values for the RALS tests but we used the finite sample critical values for the ADF tests. Again, the overall pattern of the results under non-normal errors is similar. Indeed, the net effects of the autocorrelation structure on the RALS tests are not much different from those of the ADF tests when we considered two cases with AR(1) errors and MA(1) errors, where $\varepsilon_t = 0.5\varepsilon_{t-1} + e_t$, or $\varepsilon_t = e_t - 0.5e_{t-1}$. The results for the model with a linear time trend are similar and they are reported in Tables 10.5 and 10.6. The sizes of all three tests are close to the 5 % nominal size, even when the errors are generated from a t-distribution with 2 degrees of freedom. Except for the case where the errors follow a normal distribution, the RALS-based tests are substantially more powerful than the OLS-based ADF tests, and the RALS(2&3) test compares favorably with the RALS(t5) test.

One interesting question is how the RALS tests can be compared with the tests that are based on a specific non-normal distribution. If the true density function of the error term were known, it is possible to utilize this information to develop new tests using maximum likelihood estimation or other nonlinear estimation methods. For example, Cox and Llatas (1991), Lucas (1995) and Shin and So (1999) examined unit root tests based on nonlinear optimization procedures for some specific cases where the true density is assumed to be known. This information is generally unknown a priori. Nonetheless, we are interested in comparing our RALS tests with those tests. There are a few existing tests that would be interesting to include in this comparison. We consider the test based on the M-estimate assuming that the true density is the student-t density with 5 degrees of freedom (denoted as the "M5" test), as studied by Lucas (1995). We also examine the tests based on adaptive estimation (denoted as the "AD" test) as examined by Beelder (1996) and Shin and So (1999). These results are reported in Table 10.7. The overall power

Table 10.3 Five percent rejection ratio of the tests with AR(1) error (with drift, AR coefficient 0.5)

		(T = 50)								
		ADF			RALS(2&3)			RALS(t5)		
Distributions		p = 2	p = 4	SC	p = 2	p = 4	SC	p = 2	p = 4	SC
Normal	$\phi = 1$	0.056	0.055	0.071	0.053	0.054	0.061	0.054	0.053	0.067
	$\phi = 0.9$	0.100	0.080	0.116	0.087	0.074	0.097	0.093	0.073	0.110
Cauchy	$\phi = 1$	0.075	0.079	0.055	0.046	0.053	0.063	0.048	0.059	0.051
	$\phi = 0.9$	0.074	0.074	0.088	0.664	0.599	0.698	0.567	0.504	0.568
Student t	$\phi = 1$	0.063	0.060	0.056	0.050	0.054	0.064	0.049	0.056	0.055
df = 2	$\phi = 0.9$	0.080	0.069	0.089	0.300	0.252	0.326	0.343	0.281	0.341
Double	$\phi = 1$	0.051	0.053	0.059	0.048	0.050	0.057	0.049	0.051	0.058
Exponential	$\phi = 0.9$	0.091	0.084	0.109	0.131	0.110	0.150	0.151	0.120	0.161
Chi-square	$\phi = 1$	0.051	0.058	0.061	0.050	0.045	0.032	0.052	0.051	0.061
4 df	$\phi = 0.9$	0.094	0.080	0.110	0.260	0.202	0.191	0.091	0.081	0.106
Beta(2,2)	$\phi = 1$	0.060	0.055	0.073	0.057	0.050	0.059	0.053	0.047	0.060
	$\phi = 0.9$	0.100	0.087	0.121	0.126	0.101	0.133	0.131	0.103	0.149
		(T = 100)								
		ADF			RALS(2&3)			RALS(t5)		
Distributions		p = 3	p = 6	SC	p = 3	p = 6	SC	p = 3	p = 6	SC
Normal	$\phi = 1$	0.055	0.053	0.061	0.056	0.048	0.052	0.055	0.051	0.056
	$\phi = 0.9$	0.217	0.163	0.243	0.196	0.142	0.217	0.207	0.145	0.230
Cauchy	$\phi = 1$	0.080	0.076	0.055	0.040	0.042	0.055	0.045	0.050	0.042
	$\phi = 0.9$	0.144	0.125	0.181	0.907	0.852	0.943	0.796	0.775	0.803
Student t	$\phi = 1$	0.053	0.053	0.050	0.049	0.052	0.067	0.050	0.047	0.049
df = 2	$\phi = 0.9$	0.190	0.134	0.220	0.610	0.512	0.678	0.716	0.616	0.740
Double	$\phi = 1$	0.059	0.053	0.062	0.055	0.050	0.063	0.055	0.047	0.056
Exponential	$\phi = 0.9$	0.216	0.155	0.246	0.321	0.231	0.362	0.377	0.273	0.400
Chi-square	$\phi = 1$	0.052	0.048	0.052	0.046	0.048	0.025	0.050	0.045	0.047
df = 4	$\phi = 0.9$	0.224	0.156	0.242	0.629	0.480	0.556	0.217	0.157	0.237
Beta(2,2)	$\phi = 1$	0.057	0.053	0.063	0.048	0.048	0.052	0.050	0.046	0.054
	$\phi = 0.9$	0.216	0.155	0.246	0.324	0.225	0.355	0.343	0.235	0.376

of the AD or M5 tests is fairly comparable to the power of the RALS(2&3) and RALS(t5) tests. This is an encouraging result. The performance of the RALS(t5) and M5 tests is similar when the true density is student-t with 3 degrees of freedom, which is a special case where higher moments do not exist, but RALS still can be examined via simulations. RALS(t5) is seen as more powerful when the density is mixture normal. When the true density is a chi-square distribution with 1 degree of freedom, both the AD and M5 tests are dominated by the RALS(2&3) test. The bottom line is that the RALS tests perform reasonably well when compared to the tests that are based on the true distribution. Moreover, the RALS tests achieve much improved power in the presence of other non-normal errors and yet the RALS tests

Table 10.4 Five percent rejection ratio of the tests with MA(1) error (with drift, MA coefficient −0.5)

		($T = 50$)								
		ADF			RALS(2&3)			RALS(t5)		
Distributions		p = 2	p = 4	SC	p = 2	p = 4	SC	p = 2	p = 4	SC
Normal	$\phi = 1$	0.088	0.054	0.095	0.079	0.051	0.079	0.085	0.052	0.091
	$\phi = 0.9$	0.227	0.109	0.231	0.19	0.091	0.182	0.205	0.097	0.208
Cauchy	$\phi = 1$	0.102	0.077	0.079	0.180	0.092	0.194	0.109	0.068	0.108
	$\phi = 0.9$	0.163	0.087	0.177	0.853	0.712	0.867	0.625	0.557	0.622
Student t	$\phi = 1$	0.091	0.060	0.079	0.109	0.06	0.123	0.102	0.059	0.101
df = 2	$\phi = 0.9$	0.198	0.089	0.199	0.538	0.347	0.547	0.553	0.379	0.539
Double	$\phi = 1$	0.083	0.053	0.085	0.088	0.050	0.094	0.087	0.054	0.09
Exponential	$\phi = 0.9$	0.219	0.104	0.216	0.285	0.149	0.289	0.32	0.168	0.313
Chi-square	$\phi = 1$	0.085	0.050	0.088	0.108	0.054	0.07	0.079	0.051	0.082
df = 4	$\phi = 0.9$	0.223	0.102	0.227	0.522	0.282	0.425	0.209	0.098	0.212
Beta(2,2)	$\phi = 1$	0.095	0.054	0.101	0.086	0.051	0.084	0.087	0.05	0.09
	$\phi = 0.9$	0.237	0.112	0.241	0.259	0.135	0.250	0.276	0.140	0.277
		($T = 100$)								
		ADF			RALS(2&3)			RALS(t5)		
Distributions		p = 3	p = 6	SC	p = 3	p = 6	SC	p = 3	p = 6	SC
Normal	$\phi = 1$	0.05	0.049	0.057	0.052	0.046	0.053	0.05	0.046	0.056
	$\phi = 0.9$	0.26	0.187	0.287	0.23	0.172	0.257	0.246	0.176	0.269
Cauchy	$\phi = 1$	0.078	0.073	0.049	0.041	0.044	0.057	0.04	0.042	0.036
	$\phi = 0.9$	0.171	0.134	0.207	0.938	0.889	0.962	0.785	0.776	0.796
Student t	$\phi = 1$	0.053	0.048	0.048	0.05	0.047	0.065	0.048	0.046	0.05
df = 2	$\phi = 0.9$	0.235	0.159	0.266	0.682	0.57	0.745	0.771	0.666	0.798
Double	$\phi = 1$	0.058	0.051	0.059	0.052	0.05	0.058	0.053	0.048	0.054
Exponential	$\phi = 0.9$	0.263	0.187	0.303	0.379	0.28	0.444	0.44	0.321	0.486
Chi-square	$\phi = 1$	0.047	0.044	0.05	0.046	0.045	0.027	0.041	0.043	0.045
df = 4	$\phi = 0.9$	0.254	0.183	0.293	0.705	0.543	0.65	0.248	0.174	0.286
Beta(2,2)	$\phi = 1$	0.051	0.047	0.059	0.047	0.046	0.053	0.049	0.045	0.052
	$\phi = 0.9$	0.253	0.186	0.296	0.372	0.265	0.407	0.391	0.28	0.438

do not require knowledge of a specific the density function. Overall, our simulation results show that the RALS-based unit root tests show significantly improved power under various forms of non-normal errors.

10.5 An Application of the RALS Unit Root Test

We now present an empirical application of our RALS(2&3) test applied to the CPI inflation rate series of several member-countries of the Organization for Economic Co-operation and Development (OECD). Knowledge of the long-run properties of the inflation rate (or the aggregate price level) is a key issue for policy makers, applied econometricians and financial analysts who seek to understand or affect

Table 10.5 Five percent rejection ratio of the tests with AR(1) error (with time trend, AR coefficient 0.5)

		(T = 50)								
		ADF			RALS(2&3)			RALS(t5)		
Distributions		p = 2	p = 4	SC	p = 2	p = 4	SC	p = 2	p = 4	SC
Normal	$\phi = 1$	0.053	0.048	0.074	0.049	0.044	0.06	0.05	0.044	0.07
	$\phi = 0.9$	0.08	0.069	0.106	0.069	0.056	0.081	0.077	0.059	0.097
Cauchy	$\phi = 1$	0.06	0.058	0.055	0.064	0.066	0.078	0.099	0.103	0.094
	$\phi = 0.9$	0.073	0.067	0.067	0.591	0.516	0.631	0.37	0.319	0.383
Student t	$\phi = 1$	0.057	0.049	0.06	0.054	0.06	0.073	0.058	0.055	0.063
df = 2	$\phi = 0.9$	0.078	0.062	0.081	0.252	0.201	0.281	0.248	0.195	0.255
Double	$\phi = 1$	0.058	0.053	0.075	0.055	0.048	0.074	0.056	0.049	0.071
Exponential	$\phi = 0.9$	0.083	0.064	0.098	0.106	0.085	0.13	0.115	0.099	0.135
Chi-square	$\phi = 1$	0.058	0.053	0.073	0.053	0.049	0.032	0.053	0.049	0.065
df = 4	$\phi = 0.9$	0.074	0.066	0.094	0.204	0.133	0.128	0.074	0.064	0.091
Beta(2,2)	$\phi = 1$	0.059	0.05	0.08	0.05	0.044	0.058	0.052	0.044	0.066
	$\phi = 0.9$	0.082	0.065	0.111	0.09	0.072	0.095	0.092	0.072	0.112
		(T = 100)								
		ADF			RALS(2&3)			RALS(t5)		
		p = 3	p = 6	SC	p = 3	p = 6	SC	p = 3	p = 6	SC
Normal	$\phi = 1$	0.055	0.053	0.061	0.053	0.048	0.057	0.053	0.053	0.058
	$\phi = 0.9$	0.155	0.109	0.175	0.136	0.094	0.153	0.139	0.101	0.167
Cauchy	$\phi = 1$	0.061	0.055	0.031	0.05	0.057	0.074	0.12	0.12	0.108
	$\phi = 0.9$	0.11	0.1	0.115	0.867	0.8	0.925	0.652	0.627	0.675
Student t	$\phi = 1$	0.055	0.045	0.042	0.049	0.047	0.071	0.05	0.05	0.051
df = 2	$\phi = 0.9$	0.133	0.09	0.145	0.525	0.411	0.608	0.61	0.495	0.644
Double	$\phi = 1$	0.059	0.049	0.061	0.049	0.045	0.066	0.051	0.044	0.059
Exponential	$\phi = 0.9$	0.15	0.105	0.177	0.223	0.164	0.276	0.277	0.196	0.305
Chi-square	$\phi = 1$	0.06	0.049	0.059	0.05	0.046	0.021	0.053	0.044	0.056
df = 4	$\phi = 0.9$	0.149	0.102	0.174	0.524	0.37	0.414	0.147	0.1	0.168
Beta(2,2)	$\phi = 1$	0.052	0.046	0.064	0.042	0.036	0.044	0.043	0.039	0.047
	$\phi = 0.9$	0.157	0.106	0.185	0.235	0.155	0.259	0.239	0.159	0.281

the behavior of the macroeconomy. For example, forecasters who seek to project expected or future inflation rates must know whether or not inflation rates are stationary when building their models. Similarly, officials who seek to use monetary policy to affect the behavior of macroeconomic variables also must have knowledge of the long-run properties of inflation when constructing optimal commodity price rules or when engaging in inflation rate targeting. In addition, financial planners who, for example, rely on the capital asset pricing model also must understand the long-run behavior of inflation.

Yet the question of whether or not the inflation rate is stationary still is widely disputed in the literature. Numerous researchers employing various methodologies applied to the inflation rates of several different countries have found this series

Table 10.6 Five percent rejection ratio of the tests with MA(1) error (with time trend, MA coefficient −0.5)

Distributions		ADF			RALS(2&3)			RALS(t5)		
		$(T = 50)$								
		p=2	p=4	SC	p=2	p=4	SC	p=2	p=4	SC
Normal	$\phi = 1$	0.111	0.054	0.127	0.091	0.046	0.096	0.096	0.051	0.108
	$\phi = 0.9$	0.176	0.076	0.191	0.145	0.067	0.148	0.157	0.072	0.170
Cauchy	$\phi = 1$	0.102	0.061	0.085	0.262	0.125	0.270	0.130	0.094	0.126
	$\phi = 0.9$	0.138	0.080	0.126	0.784	0.608	0.801	0.423	0.346	0.424
Student t	$\phi = 1$	0.101	0.055	0.099	0.147	0.076	0.166	0.115	0.066	0.120
df=2	$\phi = 0.9$	0.158	0.071	0.157	0.441	0.263	0.467	0.401	0.245	0.397
Double	$\phi = 1$	0.114	0.059	0.119	0.116	0.057	0.124	0.120	0.061	0.125
Exponential	$\phi = 0.9$	0.177	0.082	0.184	0.226	0.109	0.237	0.250	0.122	0.248
Chi-square	$\phi = 1$	0.111	0.059	0.118	0.144	0.059	0.087	0.102	0.052	0.108
df=4	$\phi = 0.9$	0.168	0.071	0.171	0.420	0.183	0.295	0.153	0.071	0.154
Beta(2,2)	$\phi = 1$	0.121	0.055	0.135	0.101	0.052	0.099	0.101	0.051	0.108
	$\phi = 0.9$	0.181	0.076	0.199	0.186	0.086	0.179	0.201	0.091	0.211
		$(T = 100)$								
		ADF			RALS(2&3)			RALS(t5)		
		p=3	p=6	SC	p=3	p=6	SC	p=3	p=6	SC
Normal	$\phi = 1$	0.089	0.052	0.134	0.080	0.048	0.122	0.083	0.051	0.130
	$\phi = 0.9$	0.260	0.123	0.396	0.230	0.112	0.336	0.243	0.119	0.359
Cauchy	$\phi = 1$	0.081	0.056	0.067	0.156	0.075	0.310	0.134	0.111	0.144
	$\phi = 0.9$	0.188	0.111	0.306	0.934	0.839	0.972	0.658	0.620	0.680
Student t	$\phi = 1$	0.079	0.044	0.105	0.098	0.050	0.195	0.090	0.052	0.133
df=2	$\phi = 0.9$	0.233	0.106	0.360	0.684	0.473	0.823	0.745	0.556	0.820
Double	$\phi = 1$	0.093	0.052	0.135	0.084	0.048	0.152	0.086	0.048	0.136
Exponential	$\phi = 0.9$	0.261	0.125	0.396	0.371	0.185	0.533	0.436	0.228	0.570
Chi-square	$\phi = 1$	0.085	0.049	0.127	0.095	0.048	0.091	0.080	0.049	0.120
df=4	$\phi = 0.9$	0.268	0.128	0.397	0.708	0.429	0.725	0.253	0.121	0.373
Beta(2,2)	$\phi = 1$	0.084	0.048	0.136	0.077	0.040	0.113	0.078	0.040	0.125
	$\phi = 0.9$	0.265	0.135	0.400	0.362	0.189	0.483	0.377	0.192	0.519

to be non-stationary (see, for example, Crowder and Hoffman 1996; Rapach and Weber 2004; Crowder and Phengpis 2007). At the same time, several authors have concluded that inflation is stationary (see, for example, Baillie et al. 1996; Costantini and Lupi 2007). This contradiction in the empirical results on the inflation rate might be due, in part, to the low power of traditional unit root tests. We wish to examine whether or not accounting for non-normality in the series will make a difference. Since our test will be more powerful in the face of departures from normality or apparent non-linearities, we seek to shed light on the issue of whether or not inflation is stationary through the application of our more powerful tests.

Table 10.7 Five percent rejection ratio of adaptive estimation and M-tests

	Size ($\phi = 1$)		Power ($\phi = 0.9$)	
Model	*AD*	*M5*	*AD*	*M5*
	With drift ($T = 50$)			
Normal	0.043	0.094	0.091	0.198
Chi-square df = 1	0.048	0.058	0.360	0.332
t dist. df = 3	0.045	0.052	0.197	0.291
Mixture normal	0.040	0.178	0.790	0.217
	($T = 100$)			
Normal	0.049	0.069	0.263	0.346
Chi-square df = 1	0.047	0.036	0.796	0.666
t dist.df = 3	0.067	0.037	0.535	0.649
Mixture normal	0.049	0.130	0.991	0.281
	With time trend ($T = 50$)			
Normal	0.025	0.148	0.049	0.204
Chi-square df = 1	0.026	0.064	0.251	0.277
t dist. df = 3	0.026	0.062	0.120	0.231
Mixture normal	0.024	0.292	0.628	0.258
	($T = 100$)			
Normal	0.035	0.078	0.129	0.251
Chi-square df = 1	0.038	0.048	0.647	0.506
t dist. df = 3	0.039	0.036	0.386	0.495
Mixture normal	0.027	0.192	0.981	0.255

Note: The 5 % significance level was used. AD denotes the test based on the adaptive MLE of Shin and So (1999) and M5 is the test of Lucas (1995) using the M-estimate assuming that the error density is the student-*t* with 5 degrees of freedom
Note: Mixture normal is 0.5N(−3,1) + 0.5N(3,1). This case was not considered in Tables 10.1 and 10.2. Our simulation results for the DF and RALS tests are as follows

		Size ($\phi = 1$)			Power ($\phi = 0.9$)		
Model		RALS(23)	RALS(t5)	DF	RALS(23)	RALS(t5)	DF
No trend	$T = 50$	0.044	0.045	0.055	0.850	0.916	0.145
	$T = 100$	0.045	0.044	0.058	0.995	0.998	0.361
Time trend	$T = 50$	0.042	0.044	0.054	0.669	0.784	0.097
	$T = 100$	0.042	0.043	0.053	0.981	0.996	0.219

The series used in our analysis are the first-differences of the log of the monthly consumer price index series (all items) for 12 OECD countries.[4] The data were taken from the International Monetary Fund's "International Financial Statistics" CD rom

[4]The countries are: Belgium, Canada, Finland, France, Italy, Japan, Luxembourg, the Netherlands, Norway, Spain, the UK and the USA.

(July 2009), and span the period from January of 1957 through April of 2009. We analyze these inflation rates applying the RALS(2&3) test to both (10.19) and (10.20). The first step of the procedure begins by conducting the traditional Dickey-Fuller unit root test while choosing the optimal number of augmentation terms to ensure non-correlated errors in the testing equation.[5] The OLS residuals from this equation are then retained for use in the second step. The second step involves estimation of the RALS unit root testing equation, which is an augmented version of the original Dickey-Fuller equation.

The results of the RALS unit root test are presented in Table 10.8. In the case where the testing equation includes only an intercept, the RALS unit root test rejects the null of a unit root in 8 out of 12 cases, while the Dickey-Fuller unit root test rejects the null in only 3 of 12 cases. Similarly, when allowing for both a constant and a trend in the testing equation, the RALS unit root test rejects the null in 7 of 12 cases, while the Dickey-Fuller test rejects the null in only 2 cases. The ability of the RALS unit root test to reject the null in more cases may lend support to the notion that our test is better able to distinguish non-normality from non-stationarity. However, as is shown in Kim et al. (2012) and others, the effects of time varying persistence and time varying volatility, such as the period of the great moderation, may need to be taken into account when testing for unit root in inflation rates. We might conjecture that the null could be rejected for more series if the RALS tests could be modified further to control these nonlinear effects. We relegate this issue to further study.[6] The estimated values of $\hat{\rho}^2$ are somewhat higher than we expected. We might expect more rejections of the null if these values are lower. When $\hat{\rho}^2$ is close to 1, the RALS test becomes the usual DF test and no power gain is expected. In general, the efficiency gain of RALS will be large, at least asymptotically, when $\hat{\rho}^2$ is lower.

10.6 Summary and Concluding Remarks

This paper proposes new unit root tests that are more powerful when the error term follows a non-normal distribution. The improved power is gained by utilizing more moment conditions through a computationally simple procedure. Specifically,

[5]One may choose the optimal lag length following the usual practice. For example, one can determine the optimal number of augmentation terms using the sequential t-test, following Ng and Perron (1995), or through use of the traditional Akaike Information Criteria or Schwarz Criteria, or other similar methods. In our application, we followed the procedure of Ng and Perron (1995) with a maximum of 12 lags.

[6]We thank an anonymous referee who brought to our attention the influence of the great moderation on unit root tests applied to inflation rates. In addition, we expect that the null could be rejected for more cases if the RALS procedure could be modified to account for conditional heteroskedasticity.

Table 10.8 Empirical application: inflation rates

Country	RALS (2&3)	$\hat{\rho}^2$	RALS 5 % cv	ADF
With drift				
Belgium	−2.967[a]	0.90	−2.810	−2.642
Canada	−2.167	0.92	−2.817	−2.013
Finland	−3.161[a]	0.78	−2.745	−2.240
France	−3.303[a]	0.76	−2.740	−3.296[a]
Italy	−4.544[a]	0.77	−2.741	−1.943
Japan	−6.346[a]	0.81	−2.758	−2.430
Luxembourg	−2.331	0.80	−2.752	−2.482
Netherlands	−3.140	0.59	−2.637	−3.201[a]
Norway	−3.359[a]	0.77	−42.745	−3.261[a]
Spain	−3.527[a]	0.83	−2.772	−2.311
UK	−3.746[a]	0.80	−2.754	−2.305
USA	−2.326	0.82	−2.764	−2.330
With linear trend				
Belgium	−3.160	0.91	−3.338	−2.838
Canada	−2.324	0.92	−3.348	−2.189
Finland	−3.099	0.78	−3.246	−2.578
France	−3.328[a]	0.76	−3.235	−3.255
Italy	−4.424[a]	0.77	−3.244	−2.100
Japan	−6.329[a]	0.83	−3.287	−3.350
Luxembourg	−2.365	0.80	−3.268	−2.599
Netherlands	−3.867[a]	0.59	−3.079	−3.466[a]
Norway	−3.540[a]	0.77	−3.245	−3.594[a]
Spain	−3.774[a]	0.83	−3.290	−2.582
UK	−3.974[a]	0.80	−3.266	−2.528
USA	−2.302	0.82	−3.282	−2.401

[a]Significant at 5 %. The critical value for the ADF test is −2.87

we adopt the residual augmented least squares (RALS) estimator suggested by Im and Schmidt (2008) in order to use the information implied by non-normal errors when testing for a unit root. We show that the asymptotic distribution of our simple RALS-based estimator is the same as that of the GMM estimator as well as the test of Hansen (1995) who suggested including stationary covariates. Our Monte Carlo simulation results show that the size of the RALS-based unit root tests is quite close to the asymptotic size, and the power is improved significantly over the usual Dickey-Fuller tests when the error is not normal. As such, our findings show significant efficiency gains, although this information is ignored in traditional unit root tests. It seems promising to consider some extensions of our tests using different detrending methods, as in Meng et al. (2014). Also, our suggested tests can be applied to more general models including panel data and cointegration models. We leave this work for future research.

Appendix

Lemma 1. *We let* $z_t = (y_{t-1}, \xi_t')'$, *as defined previously in Eq. (10.5). We define a* $(p+1) \times (p+1)$ *matrix,* $\Upsilon_T = diag\left(T, \sqrt{T}, \ldots, \sqrt{T}\right)$. *Assume that Assumptions 1 and 2 hold. Then, we have under the null hypothesis*

$$\sum_{t=1}^{T} \left[g'(e_t) \otimes \Upsilon_T^{-1} z_t z_t' \Upsilon_T^{-1}\right] \Rightarrow D \otimes \int zz', \tag{10.23}$$

$$\sum_{t=1}^{T} g(e_t) g(e_t)' \otimes \Upsilon_T^{-1} z_t z_t' \Upsilon_T^{-1} \Rightarrow C \otimes \int zz', \tag{10.24}$$

where $\int zz' = diag\left(a(1)^{-2} \sigma_e^2 \int_0^1 W_1(r)^2 dr, E\left(\xi_t \xi_t'\right)\right)$, *and C and D are defined in (10.17). Also, we have*

$$\sum_{t=1}^{T} \psi(e_t) \Upsilon_T^{-1} z_t = \begin{bmatrix} T^{-1} \sum_{t=1}^{T} \psi(e_t) y_{t-1} \\ T^{-1/2} \sum_{t=1}^{T} \psi(e_t) \xi_t \end{bmatrix} \Rightarrow \begin{bmatrix} \frac{\sigma_\psi \sigma_e}{a(1)} \int_0^1 W_1(r) d W_2(r) \\ \Gamma \end{bmatrix}, \tag{10.25}$$

where Γ *is a* $p \times p$ *multivariate normal variable with covariance matrix* $\sigma_\psi^2 E\left(\xi_t \xi_t'\right)$.

Proof. Lucas (1995, Lemma 1 in Appendix). See also Hansen (1995, Lemma).

Lemma 2. ρ *is defined as in Eq. (10.6). Then,*

$$\rho = \frac{1}{\sigma_e \sigma_\psi}. \tag{10.26}$$

Also,

$$\frac{1}{\sigma_\psi^2} = \sigma_e^2 - \left(C_{21} - \sigma_e^2 D_2\right)' \left(C_{22} + \sigma_e^2 D_2 D_2' - C_{21} D_2' - D_2 C_{21}'\right)^{-1} \left(C_{21} - \sigma_e^2 D_2\right). \tag{10.27}$$

Proof. The first result follows from routine matrix algebra using the partitioned inverse lemma. For the second result, straightforward algebra gives

$$\left(D' C^{-1} D\right)^{-1} = \sigma_e^2 \left(1 + \left(C_{21} - \sigma_e^2 D_2\right)' \left(\sigma_e^2 C_{22} - C_{21} C_{21}'\right)^{-1} \left(C_{21} - \sigma_e^2 D_2\right)\right)^{-1},$$

which is the same as $1/\sigma_\psi^2$; see Amemiya (1985, p. 461, Lemma 20).

Proof of Theorem 1: We note that the entire proof follows immediately from Lucas (1995, Theorem 1) since the GMM estimator is obtained by solving the score $\sum_{t=1}^{T} \left[D C^{-1} g(e_t) z_t\right] = \sum_{t=1}^{T} \left[\psi(e_t) z_t\right] = 0$, and this score could be viewed as that of the M-estimate. Here, we provide more details. Let $\theta = \left(\beta, \delta_1, \delta_2, \ldots, \delta_p\right)'$. The GMM estimator is obtained by solving

$$\min_{\theta} \sum_{t=1}^{T} \left[g(e_t) \otimes z_t\right]' \tilde{\Lambda}^{-1} \sum_{t=1}^{T} \left[g(e_t) \otimes z_t\right], \tag{10.28}$$

where $\tilde{\Lambda} = \left(\sum_{t=1}^{T} g(\tilde{e}_t) g(\tilde{e}_t)' \otimes z_t z_t'\right)$, and $\tilde{e}_t$ is the residual from an initial consistent estimator of θ. Taking the derivative with respect to θ, we obtain the score

$$\sum_{t=1}^{T} \left[g'(\tilde{e}_t) \otimes z_t z_t'\right]' \tilde{\Lambda}^{-1} \sum_{t=1}^{T} \left[g(\tilde{e}_t) \otimes z_t\right] = 0, \tag{10.29}$$

where $\tilde{e}_t = \Delta y_t - z_t \tilde{\theta}$, and $\tilde{\theta}$ is the GMM estimator. The Taylor series expansion of the term $\sum_{t=1}^{T} \left[g(\tilde{e}_t) \otimes z_t\right]$ with respect to the true disturbance e_t and premultiplication of $I_J \otimes \Upsilon_T^{-1}$ yields

$$\begin{aligned} &\sum_{t=1}^{T} \left[g(\tilde{e}_t) \otimes \Upsilon_T^{-1} z_t\right] \\ &= \sum_{t=1}^{T} \left[g(e_t) \otimes \Upsilon_T^{-1} z_t - g'(e_t) \otimes \Upsilon_T^{-1} z_t z_t' \Upsilon_T^{-1} \Upsilon_T \left(\tilde{\theta} - \theta\right)\right] + o_p(1). \end{aligned} \tag{10.30}$$

Solving (10.29) with respect to $\Upsilon_T \left(\tilde{\theta} - \theta\right)$, after substituting (10.30) into (10.29), we obtain

$$\begin{aligned} \Upsilon_T(\tilde{\theta} - \theta) = &\left\{ \sum_{t=1}^{T} \left[g'(\tilde{e}_t) \otimes \Upsilon_T^{-1} z_t z_t' \Upsilon_T^{-1}\right]' \left[\sum_{t=1}^{T} g(\tilde{e}_t) g(\tilde{e}_t)' \otimes \Upsilon_T^{-1} z_t z_t' \Upsilon_T^{-1}\right]^{-1} \right. \\ &\left. \sum_{t=1}^{T} \left[g'(\tilde{e}_t) \otimes \Upsilon_T^{-1} z_t z_t' \Upsilon_T^{-1}\right] \right\}^{-1} \\ &\times \left\{ \sum_{t=1}^{T} \left[g'(\tilde{e}_t) \otimes \Upsilon_T^{-1} z_t z_t' \Upsilon_T^{-1}\right]' \left[\sum_{t=1}^{T} g(\tilde{e}_t) g(\tilde{e}_t)' \otimes \Upsilon_T^{-1} z_t z_t' \Upsilon_T^{-1}\right]^{-1} \right. \\ &\left. \sum_{t=1}^{T} \left[g(e_t) \otimes \Upsilon_T^{-1} z_t\right] \right\} + o_p(1). \end{aligned} \tag{10.31}$$

Noting that

$$\sum_{t=1}^{T}\{[g'(\tilde{e}_t)-g'(e_t)]\otimes \Upsilon_T^{-1}z_t z_t'\Upsilon_T^{-1}\}=o_p(1),$$

and

$$\sum_{t=1}^{T}\{[g(\tilde{e}_t)g(\tilde{e}_t)'-g(e_t)g(e_t)']\otimes \Upsilon_T^{-1}z_t z_t'\Upsilon_T^{-1}\}=o_p(1),$$

we have, from Lemma 1

$$T\tilde{\beta}_G \Rightarrow \frac{a(1)}{\sigma_\psi \sigma_e}\left(\int_0^1 W_1(r)^2 dr\right)^{-1}\int_0^1 W_1(r)dW_2(r), \tag{10.32}$$

where $[W_1(r), W_2(r)]$ is a bivariate Brownian motion with correlation ρ. Then, we have for the t-statistic

$$t_G \Rightarrow \left(\int_0^1 W_1(r)^2 dr\right)^{-1/2}\int_0^1 W_1(r)dW_2(r), \tag{10.33}$$

which is a mixture of the Dickey-Fuller and the standard normal distribution as described in (10.8). To see this, note

$$T^{-1/2}\sum_{t=1}^{[rT]}\begin{bmatrix} e_t \\ \psi(e_t)\end{bmatrix} \Rightarrow \begin{bmatrix}\sigma_e W_1(r) \\ \sigma_\psi W_2(r)\end{bmatrix}, \tag{10.34}$$

where $[rT]$ denotes the integer part of rT. Noting that $W_1(r)$ and $W_2(r)$ are standard normal variables with correlation ρ, we may define a new standard normal variable, $W_3(r)$, which is independent of $W_1(r)$, such that

$$W_2(r) = \rho W_1(r) + \sqrt{1-\rho^2}W_3(r), \tag{10.35}$$

This result follows if we note that

$$\left(\int_0^1 W_1(r)^2 d(r)\right)^{-1/2}\int_0^1 W_1(r)dW_3(r)$$

is standard normal.

Proof of Theorem 2: Define a variable as a function of true disturbances

$$w_t = h(e_t) - K - e_t D_2,\ t = 1, 2, \ldots, T,$$

where $K = E(h(e_t))$. The variables in w_t are not observable, but we momentarily assume that they are observed. Then we show that the augmentation of w_t or $\hat{w}_t$ asymptotically yields the same estimator of β. Consider a regression

$$\Delta y_t = \alpha_1 + \beta y_{t-1} + \sum_{j=1}^{p} \delta_j \Delta y_{t-j} + w_t'\gamma + v_t,\ t = 1, 2, \ldots, T. \tag{10.36}$$

Therefore,

$$e_t = w_t'\gamma + v_t,\ t = 1, 2, \ldots, T. \tag{10.37}$$

Let $\hat{\beta}_A^*$ be the least squares estimator of β from regression (10.36), $\sigma_v^2 = Var(v_t)$, and

$$\lambda = \frac{\sigma_{ev}}{\sigma_e \sigma_v} = \frac{\sigma_v}{\sigma_e}, \tag{10.38}$$

where $\sigma_{ev} = E(e_t v_t)$. The second equality of (10.38) follows since w_t and v_t are not correlated, so that $\sigma_{ev} = \sigma_v^2$. From Hansen (1995, Theorems 2 and 3), we have

$$T\hat{\beta}_A^* \Rightarrow \frac{\sigma_v}{\sigma_e}\left(\int_0^1 W_4(r)^2\right)^{-1} \int_0^1 W_4(r) d W_5(r), \tag{10.39}$$

and for the t-statistic

$$t_A^* = \lambda DF_\mu + \sqrt{1 - \lambda^2} N(0, 1), \tag{10.40}$$

where $[W_4(r), W_5(r)]'$ is the bivariate Brownian motion with correlation λ. Next, we will show that

$$\rho = \lambda. \tag{10.41}$$

Note that $\gamma = E(w_t w_t')^{-1} E(w_t e_t)$, so we have

$$\sigma_v^2 = \sigma_e^2 - E(e_t w_t') E(w_t w_t')^{-1} E(w_t' e_t). \tag{10.42}$$

Also, $E(w_t' e_t) = C_{21} - \sigma_e^2 D_2$ and $E(w_t w_t') = C_{22} + \sigma_\varepsilon^2 D_2 D_2' - C_{21} D_2' - D_2 C_{21}'$. Therefore,

$$\sigma_v^2 = \sigma_e^2 - \left(C_{21} - \sigma_e^2 D_2\right)' \left(C_{22} + \sigma_e^2 D_2 D_2' - C_{21} D_2' - D_2 C_{21}'\right)^{-1} \left(C_{21} - \sigma_e^2 D_2\right),$$

which becomes $1/\sigma_\psi^2$ from Lemma 1. Therefore, we have $\rho = \lambda$.

Now we let $\hat{\beta}_A$ be the OLS estimator of β in the regression (10.19). The proof is complete if we show that $T\hat{\beta}_A$ and $T\hat{\beta}_A^*$ are identical asymptotically. Let $\hat{\zeta}_t = \left(\hat{\xi}_t', \hat{w}_t'\right)'$, where $\hat{\xi}_t = \xi_t - T^{-1}\sum_{t=1}^{T}\xi_t$. Also, we let $\hat{y}_{t-1}$ be the demeaned or detrended series for the model with drift or trend, respectively. Then we have

$$T\hat{\beta}_A = \frac{T^{-1}\left(\sum_{t=1}^{T}\hat{y}_{t-1}e_t - \sum_{t=1}^{T}\hat{y}_{t-1}\zeta_t'\left(\sum_{t=1}^{T}\hat{\xi}_t\hat{\xi}_t'\right)^{-1}\sum_{t=1}^{T}\zeta_t e_t\right)}{T^{-2}\left(\sum_{t=1}^{T}\hat{y}_{t-1}^2 - \sum_{t=1}^{T}\hat{y}_{t-1}\zeta_t'\left(\sum_{t=1}^{T}\hat{\xi}_t\hat{\xi}_t'\right)^{-1}\sum_{t=1}^{T}\zeta_t\hat{y}_{t-1}\right)},$$

Since $T^{-1}\sum_{t=1}^{T}\hat{w}_t\xi_t' = o_p(1)$, and $T^{-1}\sum_{t=1}^{T}\hat{\xi}_t e_t = o_p(1)$, we have

$$T\hat{\beta}_A = \frac{T^{-1}\left(\sum_{t=1}^{T}\hat{y}_{t-1}e_t - \sum_{t=1}^{T}\hat{y}_{t-1}\hat{w}_t'\left(\sum_{t=1}^{T}\hat{w}_t\hat{w}_t'\right)^{-1}\sum_{t=1}^{T}\hat{w}_t' e_t\right)}{T^{-2}\left(\sum_{t=1}^{T}\hat{y}_{t-1}^2\right)} + o_p(1).$$

Similarly,

$$T\hat{\beta}_A^* = \frac{T^{-1}\left(\sum_{t=1}^{T}\hat{y}_{t-1}e_t - \sum_{t=1}^{T}\hat{y}_{t-1}w_t'\left(\sum_{t=1}^{T}\hat{w}_t\hat{w}_t'\right)^{-1}\sum_{t=1}^{T}\hat{w}_t' e_t\right)}{T^{-2}\left(\sum_{t=1}^{T}\hat{y}_{t-1}^2\right)} + o_p(1).$$

$T\hat{\beta}_A$ and $T\hat{\beta}_A^*$ are asymptotically identical if $T^{-1}\sum\hat{y}_{t-1}\left(\hat{w}_t - w_t\right) = o_p(1)$. However, using a Taylor expansion, one can see

$$\begin{aligned} T^{-1}\sum\hat{y}_{t-1}\hat{w}_t &= T^{-1}\sum\hat{y}_{t-1}\left[h(\hat{e}_t) - \overline{K} - \hat{e}_t\hat{D}_2\right] \\ &= T^{-1}\sum\hat{y}_{t-1}\left[h(e_t) + (\hat{e}_t - e_t)h'(e_t) - \overline{K} - \hat{e}_t\hat{D}_2\right] + o_p(1). \end{aligned}$$

and

$$T^{-1}\sum\hat{y}_{t-1}w_t = T^{-1}\sum\hat{y}_{t-1}\left[h(e_t) - K - e_t D_2\right].$$

Therefore,

$$\begin{aligned} &T^{-1}\sum\hat{y}_{t-1}\left(\hat{w}_t - w_t\right) \qquad (10.43)\\ &= T^{-1}\sum\hat{y}_{t-1}\left[(\hat{e}_t - e_t)h'(e_t) - (\hat{e}_t - e_t)\hat{D}_2 - e_t\left(\hat{D}_2 - D_2\right)\right] + o_p(1) \end{aligned}$$

Table 10.9 Critical values of the RALS unit root tests in finite samples

		Drift			Trend		
T	ρ^2	1 %	5 %	10 %	1 %	5 %	10 %
25	0.1	−2.909	−2.256	−1.912	−2.974	−2.304	−1.938
	0.2	−3.091	−2.469	−2.146	−3.256	−2.565	−2.211
	0.3	−3.194	−2.616	−2.291	−3.422	−2.770	−2.413
	0.4	−3.254	−2.706	−2.411	−3.585	−2.919	−2.581
	0.5	−3.301	−2.775	−2.511	−3.764	−3.078	−2.724
	0.6	−3.279	−2.828	−2.579	−3.901	−3.191	−2.846
	0.7	−3.246	−2.846	−2.619	−4.041	−3.316	−2.961
	0.8	−3.213	−2.851	−2.657	−4.166	−3.423	−3.067
	0.9	−3.099	−2.816	−2.663	−4.256	−3.527	−3.159
50	0.1	−2.989	−2.312	−1.966	−2.970	−2.297	−1.949
	0.2	−3.217	−2.570	−2.228	−3.223	−2.564	−2.205
	0.3	−3.353	−2.732	−2.412	−3.375	−2.748	−2.391
	0.4	−3.447	−2.879	−2.556	−3.506	−2.887	−2.547
	0.5	−3.564	−2.985	−2.686	−3.686	−3.027	−2.688
	0.6	−3.633	−3.079	−2.792	−3.797	−3.136	−2.813
	0.7	−3.680	−3.174	−2.897	−3.883	−3.236	−2.913
	0.8	−3.737	−3.244	−2.980	−3.970	−3.341	−3.018
	0.9	−3.750	−3.303	−3.053	−4.037	−3.423	−3.102
100	0.1	−2.774	−2.100	−1.746	−2.950	−2.295	−1.947
	0.2	−2.957	−2.289	−1.933	−3.224	−2.547	−2.208
	0.3	−3.061	−2.402	−2.060	−3.377	−2.727	−2.384
	0.4	−3.177	−2.516	−2.175	−3.523	−2.881	−2.545
	0.5	−3.247	−2.596	−2.266	−3.632	−3.005	−2.682
	0.6	−3.279	−2.662	−2.337	−3.734	−3.112	−2.791
	0.7	−3.344	−2.732	−2.419	−3.832	−3.215	−2.903
	0.8	−3.391	−2.781	−2.465	−3.898	−3.304	−2.991
	0.9	−3.444	−2.845	−2.529	−3.979	−3.384	−3.076

Note: These critical values can be used in finite samples for the RALS-DF tests. They can be also for the unit root tests with covariates of Hansen (1995) in finite samples

but,

$$T^{-1}\sum \hat{y}_{t-1}(\hat{e}_t - e_t)h'(e_t) = T\left(\hat{\beta} - \beta\right)T^{-2}\sum \tilde{y}_{t-1}^2 h'(e_t) + o_p(1), \quad (10.44)$$

$$T^{-1}\sum \hat{y}_{t-1}(\hat{e}_t - e_t)\hat{D}_2 = \hat{D}_2 T\left(\hat{\beta} - \beta\right)T^{-2}\sum \hat{y}_{t-1}^2 + o_p(1), \quad (10.45)$$

and

$$T^{-1}\sum \hat{y}_{t-1}e_t\left(\hat{D}_2 - D_2\right) = o_p(1). \quad (10.46)$$

The two terms (10.44) and (10.45) cancel each other in the limit in (10.43), so the proof is complete.

References

Amemiya T (1985) Advanced econometrics. Basil Blackwell, Oxford
Baillie RT, Chung CF, Tieslau MA (1996) Analyzing inflation by the fractionally integrated ARFIMA-GARCH model. J Appl Econom 11:23–40
Beelder O (1996) Adaptive estimation and unit root tests. Manuscript, Department of Economics, Rochester University
Breusch T, Qian H, Schmidt P, Wyhowski DJ (1999) Redundancy of moment conditions. J Econom 91:89–112
Costantini M, Lupi C (2007) An analysis of inflation and interest rates. New panel unit root results in the presence of structural breaks. Econ Lett 95:408–414
Cox DD, Llatas I (1991) Maximum likelihood type estimation for nearly nonstationary autoregressive time series. Ann Stat 19:1109–1128
Crowder WJ, Hoffman DL (1996) The long-run relationship between nominal interest rates and inflation: the Fisher equation revisited. J Money Credit Bank 28:102–118
Crowder WJ, Phengpis C (2007) A re-examination of international inflation convergence over the modern float. J Int Financ Mark Inst Money 17:125–139
Elliott G, Jansson M (2003) Testing for unit roots with stationary covariates. J Econom 115:75–89
Hansen BE (1995) Rethinking the univariate approach to unit root testing: using covariates to increase the power. Econom Theory 11:1148–1171
Im KS, Schmidt P (2008) More efficient estimation under non-normality when higher moments do not depend on the regressors, using residual-augmented least squares. J Econom 144:219–233
Kim C, Manpimoke P, Nelson C (2012) Trend inflation and the nature of structural breaks in the New Keynesian Phillips curve. Working paper, University of Washington
Lucas A (1995) Unit root tests based on M-estimators. Econom Theory 11:331–346
MaCurdy TE (1982) Using information on the moments of disturbances to increase the efficiency of estimation. In: NBER technical paper 22, Cambridge
Meng M, Im KS, Lee J, Tieslau M (2014) More powerful LM unit root tests with non-normal errors. Chapter 11, this book
Ng S, Perron P (1995) Unit root tests in ARMA models with data-dependent methods for the selection of the truncation lag. J Am Stat Assoc 90:268–281
Qian H, Schmidt P (1999) Improved instrumental variables and generalized method of moments estimators. J Econom 91:145–170
Rapach DE, Weber CE (2004) Are real interest rates really nonstationary? New evidence from tests with good size and power. J Macroecon 26:409–430
Schmidt P, Phillips PCB (1992) LM tests for a unit root in the presence of deterministic trends. Oxf Bull Econ Stat 54:257–285
Shin DW, So BS (1999) Unit root tests based on adaptive maximum likelihood estimation. Econom Theory 15:1–23
Wooldridge JM (1993) Efficient estimation with orthogonal regressors. Econom Theory 9:687

Chapter 11
More Powerful LM Unit Root Tests with Non-normal Errors

Ming Meng, Kyung So Im, Junsoo Lee, and Margie A. Tieslau

11.1 Introduction

A recent paper of Im et al. (2014) adopts the Residual Augmented Least Squares (RALS) estimation procedure of Im and Schmidt (2008) in order to improve the power of the traditional Dickey and Fuller (1979, DF) unit root tests. We refer to this test as the RALS-DF unit root test since it is an extension of the traditional DF test. The RALS procedure utilizes the information that exists when the errors in the testing equation exhibit any departures from normality, such as non-linearity, asymmetry, or fat-tailed distributions. The underlying idea of the RALS procedure is appealing because it is intuitive and easy to implement. If the errors are non-normal, the higher moments of the residuals contain the information on the nature of the non-normality. The RALS procedure conveniently utilizes these moments in a linear testing equation without the need for a priori information on the nature of

M. Meng
Department of Economics, Temple University, 879 Ritter Hall Annex, 1301 Cecil B Moore Avenue, Philadelphia, PA 19122, USA
e-mail: ming.meng@temple.edu

K.S. Im
Division of Insurance and Research, Federal Deposit Insurance Corporation, 550 17th Street, NW, Washington, DC 20429–0002, USA
e-mail: kim@fdic.gov

J. Lee
Department of Economics, Finance, & Legal Studies, Culverhouse College of Commerce & Business Administration, University of Alabama, Tuscaloosa, AL 35487, USA
e-mail: jlee@cba.ua.edu

M.A. Tieslau (✉)
Department of Economics, University of North Texas, 1155 Union Circle 311457, Denton, TX 76203, USA
e-mail: tieslau@unt.edu

R.C. Sickles and W.C. Horrace (eds.), *Festschrift in Honor of Peter Schmidt: Econometric Methods and Applications*, DOI 10.1007/978-1-4899-8008-3_11,

the non-normality, such as the density function or the precise functional form of any non-linearity. The power gain over the usual DF tests is considerable when the error term is asymmetric or has a fat-tailed distribution.

This paper extends the work of Im et al. (2014), and considers the Lagrange Multiplier (LM) version of the RALS unit root tests. We refer to them as the RALS-LM tests. We provide the relevant asymptotic distribution of these new tests and their corresponding critical values. The LM unit toot tests were initially suggested by Schmidt and Phillips (1992, SP). To begin with, consider an unobserved components model,

$$y_t = \psi + \xi t + x_t, x_t = \beta x_{t-1} + e_t. \tag{11.1}$$

The unit root null hypothesis implies $\beta = 1$, against the alternative that $\beta < 1$. Here, the parameters ψ and ξ will denote level and deterministic trend, respectively, regardless of whether y_t contains a unit root ($\beta = 1$) or not. The key difference between the LM and the DF procedures is found in the detrending method. For the LM version tests, the coefficients of the deterministic trend components are estimated from the regression in differences of Δy_t on Δz_t with $z_t = [1,t]'$. Denoting the ML estimates from the LM procedure as $\tilde{\psi}$ and $\tilde{\xi}$, SP (1992) suggest using the detrended form of y_t,

$$\tilde{y}_t = y_t - \tilde{\psi} - \tilde{\xi} t. \tag{11.2}$$

On the other hand, the DF test is based on the estimates of the coefficients from the regression of y_t in levels on $(1,t)$.[1] The LM tests show improved power over the DF tests. This paper shows that the same feature will carry-over to the RALS version tests; the RALS-LM tests show improved power over the RALS-DF tests.

The main advantage of the LM tests of SP (1992) is that they are less sensitive to the parameters related to structural changes. In particular, they are free of nuisance parameters in models with level shift, as we will explain in more detail in the next section. However, the DF version tests do not have this property. As such, there are operating advantages of using the LM version of the unit root test for models with structural changes, and the same feature can be utilized in the RALS-LM tests with level-shifts, although it would be difficult to consider the RALS-DF tests with breaks. The rest of the paper is organized as follows. In Sect. 11.2, we discuss the

[1]We note that the GLS tests of Hwang and Schmidt (1996), and the DF-GLS tests of Elliott et al. (1996) adopt a detrending method similar to that of the LM test. For the GLS tests, the coefficients of the deterministic trend components are estimated from the regression in quasi-differences of $\Delta y_t^* \; (= y_t - (1 - c/T)y_{t-1})$ on $\Delta z_t^* \; (= z_t - (1 - c/T)z_{t-1})$, where c is a nuisance parameter that takes on some small value. The GLS tests of Hwang and Schmidt (1996) use a fixed value c/T which is given a priori as a small value, such that $c/T = 0.02$ and $\Delta y_t^* = y_t - 0.98y_{t-1}$. The DF-GLS tests search for the optimal small value of c/T that maximizes the power under the local alternative. When c/T is zero, these GLS-based tests are identical to the LM tests of SP (1992). In reality, the difference in the power of the LM tests and the GLS tests is not significant. The main source of the power gain for the GLS tests is its use of the LM type detrending procedure, although searching for the optimal value of c/T can lead to a marginal improvement in power.

LM procedure and propose the RALS-LM tests. In Sect. 11.3, we examine the size and power properties and compare them with those of the RALS-DF tests. Section 11.4 provides concluding remarks.

11.2 LM and RALS-LM Tests

We are interested in testing the unit root null hypothesis $H_0 : \beta = 1$ against the stationary alternative hypothesis $H_a : \beta < 1$. We let z_t denote the deterministic terms, including structural changes, and rewrite the data generating process (DGP) in (11.1) as

$$y_t = z_t'\delta + x_t, x_t = \beta x_{t-1} + e_t. \tag{11.3}$$

For example, if $z_t = [1,t]'$, we have the usual no-break LM test of SP (1992). To consider a model with level shift where a break occurs at $t = T_B$, we may add a dummy variable, D_t, where $D_t = 1$ if $t \geq T_B + 1$ and $D_t = 0$ if $t \leq T_B$. Then, we have

$$y_t = \psi + \xi t + dD_t + x_t, x_t = \beta x_{t-1} + e_t. \tag{11.4}$$

Again, the parameter d is estimated from the regression in differences of Δy_t on Δz_t, where $z_t = [1,t,D_t]'$. Here, the estimated value of d will denote the magnitude of the level shift in a consistent manner, regardless of whether y_t contains a unit root or not. We do not need to assume that $d = 0$ under the null, and the critical values of the test will not change for different values of d. More importantly, the LM tests will not depend on the nuisance parameter, $\lambda(=T_B/T)$, which denotes the location of the break, as shown in Amsler and Lee (1995). As such, the same critical values of the usual LM test (without breaks) can be used even in the presence of multiple level shifts. By contrast, Perron's (1989) tests with level shifts depend on λ, and different critical values need to be obtained for all different combinations of the break locations in the case of multiple level shifts.

While the dependency on λ might be matter of minor inconvenience for the exogenous tests of Perron (1989), the issue becomes complicated in the case of endogenous-break unit root tests for which the location of the break is determined from the data where the t-statistic on the unit root hypothesis is minimized, or the F-statistic on the dummy coefficients is maximized. The popular endogenous-break unit root tests based on the DF version models can exhibit spurious rejections unless the parameters in d, which denote the magnitude of the structural breaks (either in level-shifts or trend-shifts), take on zero values. Such an approach leads to a conceptual difficulty of not allowing for breaks under the null of a unit root. Therefore, rejections of the unit root null hypothesis will not necessarily imply trend-stationarity since the possibility of a unit root with break(s) still remains; see

Nunes et al. (1997) and Lee and Strazicich (2001) for details. The LM-based tests, on the other hand, are free of this problem in models with level-shift. In light of this, the LM tests with two endogenous breaks are considered in Lee and Strazicich (2003) who allow for breaks both under the null and alternative hypotheses in a consistent manner.

It also is possible to allow for multiple breaks by employing additional dummy variables for multiple level shifts with $z_t = [1, t, D_{1t} \ldots, D_{Rt}]$, where $D_{jt} = 1$ for $t \geq T_{Bj} + 1, j = 1, \ldots, R$, and zero otherwise; R is the number of structural breaks. The invariance feature of the LM tests with level-shifts is useful for extending the univariate LM tests to a panel setting. To that end, Im et al. (2005) suggest panel LM unit root tests with level breaks. Without the invariance feature of the LM tests, the panel test statistic would not be feasible since the test would depend on the nuisance parameters indicating the location of the breaks. This is particularly true when each cross-section unit is likely to experience a different number and location of breaks.

This paper shows that the same invariance feature in the LM tests also will hold in the RALS-LM tests with level-shifts. In this case, the RALS-LM tests with multiple level-shifts will have the same distribution as the RALS-LM tests without breaks.[2] This is one main advantage of the RALS-LM tests. Without the invariance feature of the LM tests, it would be difficult to construct valid critical values for RALS-based tests, since the RALS procedure will induce an additional nuisance parameter. Thus, it would be extremely difficult to construct valid RALS-DF tests with breaks.

We now explain details of the RALS-LM procedure. In general, following the LM (score) principle, the LM unit root test statistic can be obtained from the following regression:

$$\Delta y_t = \delta' \Delta z_t + \phi \tilde{y}_{t-1} + e_t \tag{11.5}$$

where $\tilde{y}_t = y_t - \tilde{\psi} - z_t \tilde{\delta}$, $t = 2, \ldots, T$; $\tilde{\delta}$ is the vector of coefficients in the regression of Δy_t on Δz_t, and $\tilde{\psi}$ is the restricted MLE of ψ given by $y_1 - z_1 \tilde{\delta}$; and, y_1 and z_1 denote the first observation of y_1 and z_t, respectively. To control for autocorrelated errors, one can include the terms $\Delta \tilde{y}_{t-j}, j = 1,..,p$ in (11.5), and the testing regression is given as:

$$\Delta y_t = \delta' \Delta z_t + \phi \tilde{y}_{t-1} + \sum_{j=1}^{p} c_j \Delta \tilde{y}_{t-j} + e_t \tag{11.6}$$

[2]The invariance property of the LM tests does not hold in models with trend-shifts where $z_t = [1, t, D_t, tD_t]'$ is used. However, the LM based tests are much less sensitive to the parameters of trend-breaks than the DF version tests. For example, Nunes (2004) found that the critical values do not change much in the models with trend-shifts and considered a method using the same critical values regardless of different values of λ; see also Nunes and Rodrigues (2011). However, the LM tests still depend on the nuisance parameter in these models, and using the same critical values can lead to mild size distortions.

Then, the LM test statistic is given by:

$\tilde{\tau}_{LM} = t$ -statistic testing the null hypothesis $\phi = 0$.

Next, we explain how to utilize the information on non-normal errors in order to improve upon the power of the unit root test, making use of the RALS estimation procedure as suggested in Im and Schmidt (2008), and Im et al. (2014). To begin with, we define $\xi_t = (\Delta\tilde{y}_{t-1}, \Delta\tilde{y}_{t-2}, \ldots, \Delta\tilde{y}_{t-p})'$, $f_t = (\tilde{y}_{t-1}, \xi_t')'$ and $F_t = (\Delta z_t', f_t')'$. Suppose we have the following moment conditions:

$$E\left[g\left(e_t\right) \otimes F_t\right] = 0, t = 1, 2, \ldots., T \tag{11.7}$$

where $g(e_t)$ is a function defined as $g(e_t) = (e_t, [h(e_t) - K]')'$ with $K = E(e_t)$, and $h(e_t)$ is a nonlinear function of the error term e_t. Then the moment condition becomes:

$$E\left[e_t \otimes F_t\right] = 0 \tag{11.8}$$

$$E\ \left[\left(h\left(e_t\right) - K\right) \otimes F_t\right] = 0 \tag{11.9}$$

The first part is the usual moment condition of least squares estimation and the second part involves an additional moment conditions based on nonlinear functions of e_t. We let $\widehat{e}_t$ denote the residuals from the usual LM regression (11.6). Following Im and Schmidt (2008), we define the following term

$$\widehat{w}_t = h\left(\widehat{e}_t\right) - \widehat{K} - \widehat{e}_t \widehat{D}_2 \tag{11.10}$$

where $h\left(\widehat{e}_t\right) = \left[\widehat{e}_t^2, \widehat{e}_t^3\right]'$, $\widehat{K} = \frac{1}{T}\sum_{t=1}^{T} h\left(\widehat{e}_t\right)$, and $\widehat{D}_2 = \frac{1}{T}\sum_{t=1}^{T} h'\left(\widehat{e}_t\right)$. Using $m_j = T^{-1}\sum_{t=1}^{T} \widehat{e}_t^j$, we define the augmented terms

$$\widehat{w}_t = \left[\widehat{e}_t^2 - m_2, \widehat{e}_t^3 - m_3 - 3m_2\widehat{e}_t\right]' \tag{11.11}$$

The RALS-LM procedure involves augmenting the testing regression (11.6) with $\widehat{w}_t$. The first term in $\widehat{w}_t$ is associated with the moment condition $E\left[\left(e_t^2 - \sigma_e^2\right)\tilde{y}_{t-1}\right] = 0$, which is the condition of no heteroskedasticity. This condition improves the efficiency of the estimator of ϕ when the error terms are not symmetric. The second term in $\widehat{w}_t$ improves efficiency unless $m_4 = 3\sigma^4$. It is possible to use higher moments using $h\left(\widehat{e}_t\right) = \left[\widehat{e}_t^2, \widehat{e}_t^3, \widehat{e}_t^4, \ldots, \widehat{e}_t^k\right]'$ with $k > 3$, and the properly defined $\widehat{w}_t$ in (11.11) that corresponds to the higher moments. The additional efficiency gain is expected, unless $m_{k+1} = k\sigma^2 m_{k-1}$ which holds only for the normal distribution.[3] Thus, when the distribution of the error term is not normal, one may increase efficiency by augmenting the testing regression with $\widehat{w}_t$, as follows.

$$\Delta y_t = \delta' \Delta z_t + \phi \tilde{y}_{t-1} + \sum_{j=1}^{p} g_j \Delta \tilde{y}_{t-j} + \widehat{w}_t' \gamma + e_t \tag{11.12}$$

The RALS-LM statistic is obtained through the usual least squares estimation procedure applied to (11.12). We denote the corresponding t-statistic for $\phi = 0$ as τ_{RLM}. We adopt Assumption 1 and Assumption 2 of Im et al. (2014) for the error term e_t, and $g(e_t)$ in (11.7), respectively. Then it can be shown that the asymptotic distribution of τ_{RLM} is given as follows.

Lemma 1 *Suppose that we consider the usual t-statistic on* $\phi = 0$ *in* Eq. (11.12). *Then, under the null, the limiting distribution of the RALS-LM t-statistic* τ_{RLM} *can be derived as*

$$\tau_{RLM} \rightarrow \rho \tau_{LM} + \sqrt{1-\rho^2}\, N(0,1) \tag{11.13}$$

where τ_{LM} *denotes the limiting distribution of the t-statistic for the usual LM estimator in regression* (11.6), *and* ρ *is the correlation between* e_t *and* $\psi(e_t)$

$$\rho = \frac{\sigma_{\psi e}}{\sigma_\psi \sigma_e} \tag{11.14}$$

Where $\psi(e_t) = D'C^{-1}g(e_t)$, $\sigma_\psi^2 = Var[\psi(e_t)] = Var[D'C^{-1}g(e_t)] = D'C^{-1}D$, *and* $\sigma_{\psi e} = E[\psi(e_t)e_t] = DC^{-1}E[g(e_t)e_t]$.

Proof See the Appendix.

These results are essentially similar to those given in Im et al. (2012). Also, the RALS-LM tests are asymptotically identical to the GMM estimators using the same moment conditions in (11.8) and (11.9). It is interesting to see that the limiting distribution of τ_{LM} is similar to that of the unit root tests with stationary covariates, as advocated by Hansen (1995).[4] The difference is how the parameter ρ^2 is estimated. We have a special case of Hansen's models and ρ^2 can be estimated by

$$\widehat{\rho}^2 = \widehat{\sigma}_A^2 / \widehat{\sigma}^2, \tag{11.15}$$

where $\widehat{\sigma}^2$ is the usual estimate of the error variance in the LM regression (11.6), and $\widehat{\sigma}_A^2$ is the estimate of the error variance in the RALS-LM regression in (11.12).

[3]However, we do not pursue this direction further and leave it as future research. This extension requires the assumption that the higher moments exist. In any case, the power gain is already significant enough when using the augmented terms in (11.11).

[4]A similar asymptotic result also is advocated in Guo and Phillips (1998, 2001).

Note that the asymptotic distribution of the RALS-LM test statistic τ_{RLM} does not depend on the break location parameter λ_j in the model with level-shifts, following the results of Amsler and Lee (1995). Thus, we do not need to simulate new critical values, regardless of the number of level-shifts and all possible different combinations of break locations. From a practical perspective, it likely would be infeasible to obtain all possible different critical values corresponding to different break locations and values of ρ^2. For a finite number of level-shifts, we only need one set of critical values since they are asymptotically invariant to both the break magnitude and location.

Note that when $\rho^2=1$, we have $\tau_{RLM} = \tau_{LM}$, so that the critical value for the usual LM test can be used. In Table 11.1, we report the asymptotic critical values of the RALS-LM tests, for different values of $\rho^2 = 0, 0.1, \ldots, 1.0$ and $T = 50$, 100, 300 and 1,000, respectively. All of these critical values are obtained via Monte Carlo simulations using 100,000 replications. These critical values can be used even when multiple level breaks occur in the data. To see this we provide the empirical critical values of the RALS-LM tests when the number of level-shifts is 1 and 2. The results in Table 11.2 are virtually identical to the critical values of the RALS-LM tests without breaks, as reported in Table 11.1.

11.3 Simulations

In this section, we investigate the finite small sample properties of the RALS-LM unit root tests. Our goal is to verify the theoretical results presented above and examine the performance of the tests. Pseudo-iid $N(0,1)$ random numbers were generated using the RATS procedure $\%RAN(1)$ and all results were obtained via simulations in WinRATS. The DGP was given in (11.4), and the initial values x_0 and e_0 are assumed to be random. In order to examine the power when non-normal error exists, we consider seven types of non-normal errors which include (i) a chi-square distribution with $df = 1, 2, 3, 4$, and (ii) a t-distribution with $df = 2, 3, 4$. For purposes of comparison, we also examined the case when the error term follows a standard normal distribution. The size and power properties are examined with two different DGPs; (a) no break with $z_t = [1,t]'$ and $\delta' = (0,1)$, and (b) one level shift with $z_t = [1,t,D_t]'$ and $\delta' = (0,1,5)$. We also let $\lambda = T_B/T$ denote the fraction of the series before the break occurs at $t = T_B + 1$. For all of these cases, we have used the same critical values in Table 11.1 of the usual RALS-LM tests without breaks. All simulation results are calculated using 10,000 replications for the sample size, $T = 100$ by using the 5% significance level.[5]

In Table 11.3, we report the size and power properties of the RALS-LM tests, and compare them with the usual LM tests, the DF tests and the RALS-DF tests. We begin by examining the model with no breaks. From Panel A in Table 11.3, we

[5]Results for the larger sample sizes with $T = 300$ and 1,000 are omitted. They show a similar pattern with greatly improved power properties. They are available with upon request.

Table 11.1 Critical values of the RALS-LM test with no breaks

		ρ^2										
T	%	0	0.1	0.2	0.3	0.4	0.5	0.6	0.7	0.8	0.9	1
50	1	−2.333	−2.882	−3.089	−3.213	−3.314	−3.401	−3.477	−3.543	−3.599	−3.650	−3.707
	5	−1.640	−2.216	−2.426	−2.572	−2.689	−2.783	−2.862	−2.928	−2.992	−3.045	−3.089
	10	−1.286	−1.864	−2.081	−2.235	−2.358	−2.459	−2.545	−2.619	−2.684	−2.740	−2.793
100	1	−2.322	−2.875	−3.069	−3.200	−3.301	−3.378	−3.446	−3.499	−3.551	−3.595	−3.625
	5	−1.646	−2.216	−2.422	−2.562	−2.672	−2.764	−2.840	−2.903	−2.958	−3.010	−3.062
	10	−1.283	−1.861	−2.075	−2.230	−2.352	−2.450	−2.535	−2.606	−2.665	−2.719	−2.772
300	1	−2.332	−2.874	−3.057	−3.175	−3.265	−3.347	−3.403	−3.455	−3.509	−3.553	−3.596
	5	−1.642	−2.211	−2.413	−2.554	−2.664	−2.755	−2.830	−2.893	−2.944	−2.992	−3.028
	10	−1.276	−1.856	−2.071	−2.231	−2.351	−2.450	−2.532	−2.603	−2.664	−2.711	−2.758
1,000	1	−2.345	−2.892	−3.080	−3.205	−3.299	−3.374	−3.428	−3.474	−3.510	−3.538	−3.570
	5	−1.652	−2.223	−2.428	−2.568	−2.677	−2.761	−2.836	−2.897	−2.947	−2.990	−3.031
	10	−1.291	−1.871	−2.083	−2.234	−2.352	−2.451	−2.535	−2.605	−2.667	−2.715	−2.755

Table 11.2 Critical values of RALS-LM test with level break

			ρ^2										
T	*R*	%	0	0.1	0.2	0.3	0.4	0.5	0.6	0.7	0.8	0.9	1
50	1	1	−2.333	−2.886	−3.077	−3.208	−3.309	−3.398	−3.478	−3.543	−3.605	−3.653	−3.711
		5	−1.640	−2.216	−2.422	−2.570	−2.688	−2.784	−2.862	−2.932	−2.990	−3.044	−3.094
		10	−1.286	−1.863	−2.081	−2.237	−2.358	−2.461	−2.546	−2.619	−2.683	−2.742	−2.794
	2	1	−2.333	−2.891	−3.078	−3.209	−3.309	−3.398	−3.467	−3.532	−3.587	−3.646	−3.695
		5	−1.640	−2.220	−2.427	−2.575	−2.696	−2.791	−2.867	−2.933	−2.991	−3.044	−3.100
		10	−1.286	−1.866	−2.080	−2.235	−2.358	−2.460	−2.546	−2.622	−2.687	−2.743	−2.794
100	1	1	−2.322	−2.876	−3.066	−3.203	−3.307	−3.383	−3.456	−3.515	−3.560	−3.609	−3.637
		5	−1.646	−2.218	−2.421	−2.563	−2.675	−2.761	−2.839	−2.903	−2.963	−3.011	−3.062
		10	−1.283	−1.861	−2.076	−2.228	−2.351	−2.451	−2.535	−2.607	−2.667	−2.720	−2.771
	2	1	−2.322	−2.877	−3.066	−3.204	−3.295	−3.372	−3.444	−3.497	−3.554	−3.583	−3.636
		5	−1.646	−2.220	−2.422	−2.566	−2.677	−2.767	−2.842	−2.908	−2.962	−3.013	−3.056
		10	−1.283	−1.862	−2.076	−2.231	−2.349	−2.450	−2.533	−2.604	−2.662	−2.717	−2.771
300	1	1	−2.332	−2.875	−3.055	−3.175	−3.270	−3.344	−3.402	−3.458	−3.505	−3.545	−3.588
		5	−1.642	−2.213	−2.413	−2.557	−2.666	−2.757	−2.833	−2.892	−2.944	−2.991	−3.028
		10	−1.276	−1.856	−2.070	−2.229	−2.349	−2.450	−2.531	−2.601	−2.660	−2.711	−2.757
	2	1	−2.332	−2.875	−3.057	−3.175	−3.273	−3.353	−3.410	−3.457	−3.506	−3.554	−3.593
		5	−1.642	−2.212	−2.414	−2.556	−2.664	−2.754	−2.831	−2.894	−2.945	−2.990	−3.023
		10	−1.276	−1.856	−2.072	−2.229	−2.349	−2.449	−2.532	−2.604	−2.664	−2.709	−2.756
1,000	1	1	−2.345	−2.895	−3.080	−3.204	−3.296	−3.376	−3.427	−3.470	−3.504	−3.536	−3.565
		5	−1.652	−2.223	−2.428	−2.570	−2.677	−2.763	−2.836	−2.896	−2.948	−2.993	−3.029
		10	−1.291	−1.870	−2.082	−2.234	−2.352	−2.452	−2.534	−2.607	−2.667	−2.715	−2.755
	2	1	−2.345	−2.895	−3.077	−3.202	−3.300	−3.375	−3.427	−3.470	−3.510	−3.544	−3.571
		5	−1.652	−2.221	−2.427	−2.567	−2.675	−2.762	−2.836	−2.897	−2.950	−2.990	−3.031
		10	−1.291	−1.870	−2.082	−2.234	−2.353	−2.452	−2.536	−2.606	−2.665	−2.715	−2.756

Table 11.3 Size, power and size-adjusted power with no break ($T = 100$)

β	Tests	Distribution of the error term χ_1^2	χ_2^2	χ_3^2	χ_4^2	t_2	t_3	t_4	$N(0,1)$
		Panel A. Size							
1	RALS-LM	0.057	0.059	0.060	0.064	0.045	0.042	0.052	0.086
	LM	0.038	0.042	0.044	0.047	0.037	0.043	0.046	0.052
	DF	0.046	0.051	0.046	0.049	0.053	0.049	0.052	0.051
		Panel B. Power							
0.8	RALS-LM	0.997	0.995	0.991	0.985	0.948	0.887	0.856	0.780
	LM	0.770	0.757	0.763	0.765	0.789	0.755	0.762	0.754
	DF	0.656	0.648	0.654	0.650	0.637	0.651	0.645	0.643
0.9	RALS-LM	0.977	0.929	0.870	0.809	0.664	0.474	0.393	0.341
	LM	0.244	0.254	0.255	0.254	0.236	0.253	0.248	0.268
	DF	0.170	0.181	0.180	0.182	0.161	0.180	0.183	0.193
		Panel C. Size-adjusted power							
0.8	RALS-LM	0.998	0.996	0.992	0.985	0.962	0.918	0.864	0.659
	LM	0.817	0.789	0.787	0.776	0.848	0.787	0.779	0.745
	DF	0.688	0.645	0.670	0.654	0.609	0.657	0.635	0.638
0.9	RALS-LM	0.976	0.925	0.858	0.784	0.705	0.515	0.389	0.227
	LM	0.294	0.286	0.282	0.266	0.296	0.282	0.265	0.260
	DF	0.187	0.178	0.190	0.185	0.150	0.183	0.177	0.190
		Panel D. Size and size-adjusted power of RALS-DF tests							
1.0	RALS-DF	0.049	0.059	0.062	0.068	0.047	0.053	0.056	0.054
0.9	RALS-DF	0.988	0.927	0.831	0.716	0.633	0.384	0.292	0.191

observe that, in all cases, none of the three tests shows any serious size distortions. The RALS-LM tests show significantly improved power over the usual LM tests when the errors are non-normal with either a chi-square or t-distribution. The results in Panel C for the size-adjusted power are more relevant. The gain in power of the RALS-LM tests is greater when the degrees of freedom of the chi-square distribution is smaller, implying more asymmetric patterns of the error distribution. For example, when $\beta = 0.9$ and the error term follows a $\chi^2(1)$ distribution, the size-adjusted power of the RALS-LM test is 0.976, while the power of the usual LM test is 0.294 (and 0.187 for the DF test). Also, the gain is larger when the degrees of freedom of the t-distribution is smaller, implying fatter-tails of the error term.[6] In Fig. 11.1, we have provided a graph to show these results.

[6]The question of interest is the effect of using the estimated values of $\widehat{\rho}^2 = \widehat{\sigma}_A^2/\widehat{\sigma}^2$ in (11.15) on the size and power property of the tests. The true value of ρ^2 is unknown, but it depends on the type and degree of non-normal errors. It seems clear that the size property is fair in all cases that we examined. The power gain would be larger when the value of ρ^2 is small. This occurs when the degrees of freedom of the chi-square distribution is smaller, implying more asymmetric patterns, and when the degrees of freedom of the t-distribution is smaller, implying fatter-tails. Our simulation results are consistent with our expectations.

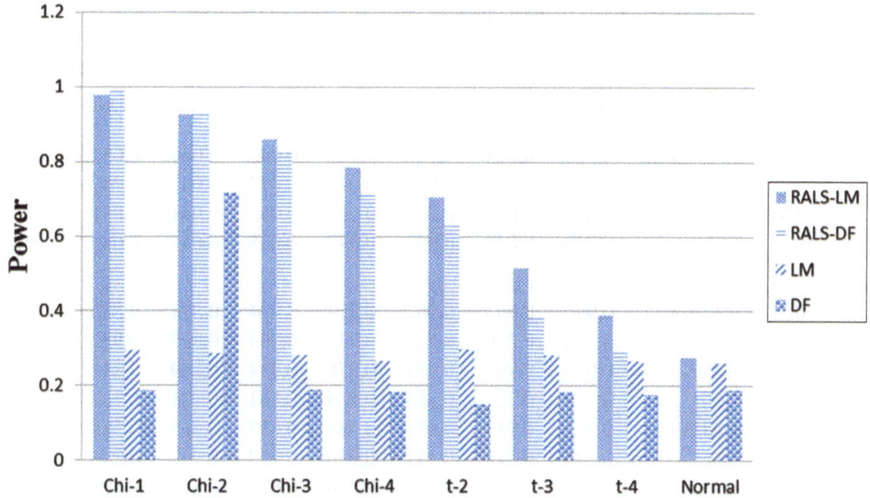

Fig. 11.1 Size-adjusted power, T = 100

When the error term follows a normal distribution, the LM tests are more powerful than the RALS-LM tests. However, the difference in power is rather small. These results prove that the RALS-LM tests have good size and power properties even when the sample size is relatively small. In Panel D of Table 11.3, we report the size and size-adjusted power of the RALS-DF tests of Im et al. (2014). It seems clear that the RALS-LM tests are generally more powerful than the RALS-DF tests. The difference is as expected since the LM tests are usually more powerful than the DF tests.

Next, we examine the property of these tests when the DGP includes a structural break where the size and power properties are examined for $\lambda = 0.25$ and $\lambda = 0.5$. In this case, it is not useful to consider the RALS-DF test since the distribution of the test depends on λ. The results for the RALS-LM and traditional LM tests are presented in Table 11.4. Note that we use the same critical values for the traditional LM tests without breaks and the RALS-LM tests without breaks. Again, we do not observe any significant size distortions under the null, even when the critical values of the tests without breaks are used for the models with breaks. Regardless of the locations of breaks with either $\lambda = 0.25$, or $\lambda = 0.5$, the results on the size, power and size-adjusted power do not change appreciably. This outcome clearly shows the invariance results for both the LM and the RALS-LM tests. Also, we observe significant power gains for the RALS-LM tests when the error term follows a non-normal distribution.

Table 11.4 Size, power, and size-adjusted power with level break ($T = 100$)

β	λ	Tests	Distribution of the error term							
			χ_1^2	χ_2^2	χ_3^2	χ_4^2	t_2	t_3	t_4	$N(0,1)$
			Panel A. Size							
1	0.25	RALS-LM	0.056	0.054	0.057	0.062	0.046	0.044	0.051	0.083
		LM	0.040	0.046	0.045	0.046	0.037	0.043	0.047	0.053
	0.50	RALS-LM	0.055	0.056	0.057	0.062	0.046	0.041	0.051	0.083
		LM	0.040	0.045	0.043	0.047	0.035	0.041	0.049	0.052
			Panel B. Power							
0.8	0.25	RALS-LM	0.996	0.993	0.987	0.979	0.934	0.871	0.833	0.753
		LM	0.743	0.730	0.735	0.733	0.764	0.727	0.732	0.724
	0.50	RALS-LM	0.996	0.993	0.987	0.978	0.934	0.869	0.832	0.755
		LM	0.739	0.727	0.738	0.739	0.761	0.731	0.732	0.726
0.9	0.25	RALS-LM	0.971	0.919	0.851	0.788	0.653	0.463	0.385	0.327
		LM	0.235	0.248	0.251	0.250	0.227	0.247	0.246	0.260
	0.50	RALS-LM	0.971	0.918	0.853	0.786	0.653	0.462	0.389	0.329
		LM	0.235	0.249	0.251	0.249	0.231	0.243	0.246	0.256
			Panel C. Size-adjusted power							
0.8	0.25	RALS-LM	0.997	0.994	0.989	0.979	0.951	0.898	0.839	0.643
		LM	0.785	0.748	0.758	0.752	0.822	0.760	0.744	0.715
	0.50	RALS-LM	0.996	0.994	0.988	0.978	0.950	0.901	0.843	0.645
		LM	0.788	0.758	0.768	0.758	0.829	0.770	0.737	0.719
0.9	0.25	RALS-LM	0.971	0.918	0.842	0.766	0.688	0.498	0.379	0.228
		LM	0.281	0.266	0.272	0.266	0.285	0.275	0.257	0.252
	0.50	RALS-LM	0.970	0.915	0.842	0.761	0.689	0.508	0.388	0.235
		LM	0.275	0.273	0.277	0.262	0.293	0.283	0.251	0.250

11.4 Concluding Remarks

This paper develops new RALS based LM unit root tests. These new RALS-LM tests show improved power gains over the corresponding RALS-DF tests, and the power of both RALS-DF and RALS-LM tests can increase drastically when the error term is highly asymmetric or has fat-tails with unknown forms of non-normal distributions. Also, the RALS-LM tests have the feature that they are invariant to the nuisance parameter in the models with multiple level shifts, and it is expected that they can be more useful in extended models with other types of structural changes.

Overall, we conclude that the RALS-LM tests show improved performance over the corresponding RALS-DF tests. However, we should note that the power gain of the LM version tests (and also the DF-GLS version tests) will disappear when the initial value is large. In such cases, the RALS-DF version tests are more powerful than the RALS-LM version tests. As such, one may consider a fair balance between the RALS-LM and the RALS-DF tests in the presence of non-normal errors; it is incorrect to say that one version would dominate uniformly over the other. Clearly, the main advantage of the RALS-LM tests lies in the invariance feature that the distribution does not depend on the nuisance parameter in the presence of level-breaks, and that they are less sensitive in other extended break models. On the other hand, the RALS-DF version tests can be more useful in standard models without breaks, especially when the initial value is large.

Appendix

Proof of Lemma 1. Consider the regression (11.12). We let $\widehat{\zeta}_t = \left(\tilde{\xi}_t', \widehat{w}_t'\right)'$, where $\tilde{\xi}_t = \xi_t - T^{-1}\sum_{t=1}^{T}\xi_t$, and $\xi_t = (\Delta\tilde{y}_{t-1}, \Delta\tilde{y}_{t-2}, \ldots, \Delta\tilde{y}_{t-p})'$. Following Theorem 2 in Hansen (1995), we have

$$T\left(\widehat{\phi}-\phi\right) = \frac{T^{-1}\left(\sum_{t=2}^{T}\tilde{y}_{t-1}^{*}\, e_t - \sum_{t=2}^{T}\tilde{y}_{t-1}^{*}\,\tilde{\zeta}_t'\left(\sum_{t=2}^{T}\tilde{\zeta}_t\,\tilde{\zeta}_t'\right)^{-1}\sum_{t=2}^{T}\tilde{\zeta}_t\, e_t\right)}{T^{-2}\left(\sum_{t=2}^{T}\tilde{y}_{t-1}^{*2} - \sum_{t=2}^{T}\tilde{y}_{t-1}^{*}\,\tilde{\zeta}_t'\left(\sum_{t=2}^{T}\tilde{\zeta}_t\,\tilde{\zeta}_t'\right)^{-1}\sum_{t=2}^{T}\zeta_t\,\tilde{S}_{t-1}^{*}\right)},$$

From the moment condition $T^{-1}\sum_{t=1}^{T}\widehat{w}_t\,\xi_t' = o_p(1)$, and $T^{-1}\sum_{t=1}^{T}\tilde{\xi}_t\, e_t = o_p(1)$, we have

$$T\left(\widehat{\phi}-\phi\right) = \frac{T^{-1}\left(\sum_{t=2}^{T}\tilde{y}_{t-1}^{*} e_t - \sum_{t=2}^{T}\tilde{y}_{t-1}^{*}\,\widehat{w}_t'\left(\sum_{t=2}^{T}\widehat{w}_t\widehat{w}_t'\right)^{-1}\sum_{t=2}^{T}\widehat{w}_t'\, e_t\right)}{T^{-2}\left(\sum_{t=2}^{T}\tilde{y}_{t-1}^{*2}\right)}$$

$$+\, o_p(1).$$

Since $1/T\sum_{t=2}^{T}\tilde{y}_{t-1}^{*}\,\widehat{w}_t = O_p(1)$, $1/T\sum_{t=2}^{T}\widehat{w}_t\widehat{w}_t' \to_p M > 0$, $1/T\sum_{t=2}^{T}\widehat{w}_t e_t = o_p(1)$, then we have

$$T\left(\widehat{\phi}-\phi\right) = \frac{T^{-1}\sum_{t=2}^{T}\tilde{y}_{t-1}^{*} e_t}{T^{-2}\left(\sum_{t=2}^{T}\tilde{y}_{t-1}^{*2}\right)} + o_p(1).$$

Apply the lemma from Hansen (1995),

$$T\left(\widehat{\phi}-\phi\right)=a(1)R\left(\rho\frac{\int_0^1 W_1^c dW_1}{\int_0^1 \left(W_1^c\right)^2}+\left(1-\rho^2\right)^{1/2}\frac{\int_0^1 W_1^c dW_2}{\int_0^1 \left(W_1^c\right)^2}\right),$$

where $R=\sigma_u/\sigma_e$. Additionally, we have

$$\begin{aligned}
t\left(\widehat{\phi}\right) &= \widehat{\psi}\sigma_u{}^{-1}T\left(1/T^2\sum_{t=2}^{T}\tilde{y}_{t-1}^{*2}-1/T^2\sum_{t=2}^{T}\tilde{y}_{t-1}^{*}\,\widehat{\zeta}_t'\left(\sum_{t=2}^{T}\widehat{\zeta}_t\widehat{\zeta}_t'\right)^{-1}\sum_{t=2}^{T}\widehat{\zeta}_t\,\tilde{y}_{t-1}^{*}\right)^{1/2}\\
&= T\widehat{\phi}\sigma_u^{-1}\left(1/T^2\sum_{t=2}^{T}\tilde{y}_{t-1}^{*2}-1/T^2\sum_{t=2}^{T}\tilde{y}_{t-1}^{*}\,\widehat{w}_t'\left(\sum_{t=2}^{T}\widehat{w}_t\widehat{w}_t'\right)^{-1}\sum_{t=2}^{T}\widehat{w}_t\,\tilde{y}_{t-1}^{*}\right)^{1/2}\\
&= \sigma_u^{-1}\left(1/T^2\sum_{t=2}^{T}\tilde{y}_{t-1}^{*2}\right)^{1/2}T\widehat{\phi}+o_p(1),
\end{aligned}$$

and $T\phi=-ca(1)$. The test statistics under the null of $\phi=0$ can be obtained as

$$\begin{aligned}
t\left(\widehat{\phi}\right) &= \sigma_u{}^{-1}\left(a(1)^{-2}\sigma_e{}^2\int_0^1 (W_1{}^c)^2\right)^{1/2}\cdot\\
&\quad\left[-ca(1)+a(1)R\left(\rho\frac{\int_0^1 W_1{}^c dW_1}{\int_0^1 (W_1{}^c)^2}+\left(1-\rho^2\right)^{1/2}\frac{\int_0^1 W_1{}^c dW_2}{\int_0^1 (W_1{}^c)^2}\right)\right]\\
&= -\tfrac{c}{R}\left(\int_0^1 (W_1{}^c)^2\right)(1/2)+\rho\frac{\int_0^1 W_1{}^c dW_1}{\left((W_1{}^c)^2\right)^{1/2}}+\left(1-\rho^2\right)\frac{\int_0^1 W_1{}^c dW_1}{\left((W_1{}^c)^2\right)^{1/2}}
\end{aligned}$$

The null holds when $c=0$. Then we obtain

$$t\left(\widehat{\phi}\right)=\rho t_\phi+\sqrt{(1-\rho^2)}\,N\ (0,1)\,.$$

References

Amsler C, Lee J (1995) An LM test for a unit root in the presence of a structural change. Econom Theory 11(2):359–368

Dickey DA, Fuller W (1979) Distribution of the estimators of autoregressive time series with a unit root. J Am Stat Assoc 70:427–431

Elliott G, Rothenberg TJ, Stock J (1996) Efficient tests for an autoregressive unit root. Econometrica 64(4):813–836

Guo B, Phillips PCB (1998) Efficient estimation of second moment parameters. In ARCH models'. Working paper, Yale University
Guo B, Phillips PCB (2001) Testing for autocorrelation and unit roots in the presence of conditional heteroskedasticity. Working paper, University of California, Santa Cruz
Hansen BE (1995) Rethinking the univariate approach to unit root testing: using covariates to increase power. Econom Theory 11:1148–1171
Hwang J, Schmidt P (1996) Alternative methods of detrending and the power of unit root tests. J Econom 71:227–248
Im KS, Schmidt P (2008) More efficient estimation under non-normality when higher moments do not depend on the regressors, using residual-augmented least squares. J Econom 144:219–233
Im KS, Lee J, Tieslau M (2005) Panel LM unit root tests with level shifts. Oxford Bull Econ Stat 67(3):393–419
Im KS, Lee J, Tieslau M (2014) More powerful unit root tests with nonnormal errors, this book chapter 10
Lee J, Strazicich M (2001) Break point estimation and spurious rejections with endogenous unit root tests. Oxford Bull Econ Stat 63(5):535–558
Lee J, Strazicich M (2003) Minimum LM unit root test with two structural breaks. Rev Econ Stat 85:1082–1089
Nunes L (2004) LM-type tests for a unit root allowing for a break in trend. Working paper, Universidade Nova de Lisboa
Nunes L, Rodrigues P (2011) LM-type tests for seasonal unit roots in the presence of a break in trend, 2011. J Time Ser Anal 32(2):108–134
Nunes L, Newbold P, Kuan C-M (1997) Testing for unit roots with breaks: evidence on the great crash and the unit root hypothesis reconsidered. Oxford Bull Econ Stat 59(4):435–448
Perron P (1989) The great crash, the oil price shock, and the unit root hypothesis. Econometrica 57(6):1361–1401
Schmidt P, Phillips PCB (1992) LM tests for a unit root in the presence of deterministic trends. Oxford Bull Econ Stat 54(3):257–285

Chapter 12
Efficiency Selection Procedures for Capacity Utilization Estimation

William C. Horrace and Kurt E. Schnier

12.1 Introduction

A critical aspect of fisheries management is the ability to understand the performance of fishing vessels within managed waters. Since overcapacity is cited as one of the primary causes of over-fishing (Food and Agriculture Organization 1998), estimating the productive capacity and capacity utilization of fishing vessels has become an important policy initiative. Capacity utilization in fisheries is traditionally estimated using data envelop analysis (Pascoe et al. 2001; Felthoven 2002; Kirkley et al. 2003; Tingley and Pascoe 2005) or stochastic production frontier modeling (Kirkley et al. 2002, 2004). It is defined as the ratio of observed total output to the maximal or potential output that could be produced (Kirkley et al. 2002, 2004). All the estimation complexity is in obtaining appropriate measures of maximal or potential output. If observed total output (production) for a fishery is y, then *maximal output* ($y^{\max}$) is the production resulting from maximal utilization of some or all variable inputs (labor, time at sea, etc.) for each vessel in the fishery. *Potential output* is defined as the technically efficient production level (y^{TE}) and is often called *efficiency adjusted production* (Kirkley et al. 2002, 2004). Calculating potential output is typically an exercise in imputing maximal efficiency to *all* vessels

W.C. Horrace (✉)
Department of Economics, Syracuse University,
426 Eggers Hall, Syracuse, NY 13244, USA
e-mail: whorrace@maxwell.syr.edu

K.E. Schnier
Department of Economics, Andrew Young School of Policy Studies, Georgia State University,
438 Andrew Yong School, 14 Marietta St NW, Atlanta, GA 30303, USA
e-mail: kschnier@gsu.edu

R.C. Sickles and W.C. Horrace (eds.), *Festschrift in Honor of Peter Schmidt: Econometric Methods and Applications*, DOI 10.1007/978-1-4899-8008-3_12,

in the fishery regardless of how inefficient they may be.[1] However, how realistic is it that highly inefficient vessels will actually attain efficiency? Perhaps, all things being equal, there are subsets of vessels that would almost never attain maximal efficiency. If so, what levels of efficiency might they reasonably attain, and how can we adjust our estimate of potential output to account for this? These are multivariate statistical inference questions, which we propose to answer at the cost of requiring an inferential error rate. Low error tolerance returns the usual efficiency adjusted estimate of potential output, while larger tolerances return estimates based on classes of vessels at sub-maximal levels. The results have immediate implications for U.S. fishery policy.

We use selection theory (Gupta 1956, 1965) to estimate efficiency subsets (tiers) for $n = 12$ vessels in the U.S. Bering Sea flat fish fishery over a 9-year period, $T = 9$. That is, we calculate the Gupta subset of efficient vessels at a pre-specific error rate to construct a first-best efficiency subset. The first-best subset contains the most efficient vessel with probability equal to one minus the error rate. Then, from the remaining inefficient vessels, a second-best Gupta subset is constructed. This procedure is continued until the set of vessels is exhausted, and $J \leq n$ subsets are constructed. Then, rather than impute maximal efficiency to *all* vessels, we impute maximal efficiency *within* each efficiency subset. Therefore, only the vessels in the first-best efficient subset are imputed maximal efficiency in the calculation of potential output, because their efficiency estimates cannot be distinguished in a statistical sense from the (unknown) most efficient vessel in the fishery. The potential output of vessels in the lower efficiency subsets are calculated based on lower values of maximal efficiency within each tier. Notice, that this procedure nests the traditional practice of imputing the maximal efficiency to all vessels, because the first-best efficiency subset may contain all vessels in the fleet. Thus, the pre-specified error rate is an important policy variable, because it controls the cardinality of the subsets and, if set low enough, produces a single subset containing all vessels in the fishery. In the sequel, it is shown that the error rate can be interpreted as a measure of policy-maker risk preference or as a sensitivity parameter that a policy-maker could use to analyze alternative harvesting strategy scenarios.

Since vessel-level production efficiency is estimated from a regression model of production, the efficiency estimates are necessarily correlated through input correlations (regressor correlations). The lack of independence necessitates calculation of critical values from an 11-dimensional probability integral which we ultimately simulate using the algorithm in Horrace (1998). It has been argued that *simulation* of critical values in political economy applications is acceptable in the sense that

[1] This presumes the existence of technical inefficiency, where different vessels employing the same inputs, technology, and 'luck' may have different output.

economic experiments need not be exactly reproducible to be meaningful (Horrace and Schmidt 2000, p. 5).[2] We control the overall error rate of the sequential subset procedure with the Bonferroni inequality.

The proposed technique is a unique application of Gupta's selection procedures, which have received limited attention in the political economy literature. The technique has immediate policy implications for fisheries managers who estimate capacity utilization. The next section is a brief explanation of the methodology. Section 12.3 is the data description and the analysis. Section 12.4 summarizes and concludes.

12.2 Methodology

What follows is a brief explanation of production estimation for panel data in the style of Schmidt and Sickles (1984). It is not intended to serve as a comprehensive survey, nor is it intended to be a complete discussion of the nuances and difficulties associated with production function estimation in general. Therefore, we take the ability to specify and estimate a production function as given, and ultimately focus our attention on the application of selection theory to the production function estimates. Suppose that fishery production can be modeled as a linear fixed-effect model for panel data,

$$y_{it} = \alpha + x_{it}\beta + v_{it} - u_i = \alpha_i + x_{it}\beta + v_{it}, \tag{12.1}$$

where $i = 1, \ldots, n$ indexes vessels in the fleet, and $t = 1, \ldots, T$ indicates any appropriate time period (years in our case). If inputs and outputs are in logarithms, then the linear specification may represent a Cobb-Douglas or a translog production function. Scalar y_{it} represents catch (fish landed), x_{it} is a row vector of fixed and variable inputs of production such as vessel net-tonnage, horsepower, crew size, or time at sea. The parameters, α_i, are individual effects that embody unobserved, time-invariant technical efficiency (see Schmidt and Sickles 1984). The larger the value of α_i, the more efficient is vessel i. In Eq. (12.1), all production heterogeneity is captured in the vessel-level fixed-effect, α_i.[3] An alternative specification might allow marginal products, β, to vary across vessels. Flores-Lagunes et al. (2007) estimate a latent class regression in a maximum likelihood setting to identify a

[2]Numerical approximation of critical values is also an option. See Hsu 1996, Sect. 7.2.1 and Appendix A.

[3]Since the differences in the fixed-effects are the usual measure of inefficiencies (see Schmidt and Sickles 1984), inefficiency in the sole source of production heterogeneity in this simple model.

separate β for different groups of vessels. Alternative methods of incorporating heterogeneity are within the realm of possibilities, depending on what one is willing to assume about production.[4]

Under a weak exogeneity assumption on scalar error v_{it}, unbiased and consistent estimation of β proceeds by the "within transformation" and ordinary least-squares. That is,

$$\widehat{\beta} = \left(\sum_{i}^{N}\sum_{t}^{T} x_{it}^{*\prime} x_{it}^{*}\right)^{-1} \left(\sum_{i}^{N}\sum_{t}^{T} x_{it}^{*\prime} y_{it}^{*}\right)$$

$$y_{it}^{*} = y_{it} - T^{-1}\sum_{t=1}^{T} y_{it},\quad x_{it}^{*} = x_{it} - T^{-1}\sum_{t=1}^{T} x_{it},\quad v_{it}^{*} = v_{it} - T^{-1}\sum_{t=1}^{T} v_{it},$$

is unbiased and consistent ($n \to \infty$ or $T \to \infty$) for β. Define the residuals $\widehat{v}_{it} = y_{it} - x_{it}\widehat{\beta}$, then $\widehat{\alpha}_i = T^{-1}\sum_t \widehat{v}_{it}$ is unbiased and consistent ($T \to \infty$) for α_i. Let the set of vessel indices be $N = \{1, \ldots, n\}$. Per Schmidt and Sickles (1984), an estimate of technical inefficiency is $\widehat{u}_i = \max_{s\in N}\widehat{\alpha}_s - \widehat{\alpha}_i$, and a normalized vessel efficiency estimate is $\exp\{-\widehat{u}_i\} \in (0, 1]$, $i \in N$. The reader is referred to Schmidt and Sickles (1984) and Feng and Horrace (2012) for this and alternative measures of technical efficiency for panel data. In the environmental and resource economics literature, vessel efficiency is often referred to as "unobserved heterogeneity in *skipper skill*" and is associated with "the good captain hypothesis," which posits that a fleet may have captains that systematically outperform all other captains, *ceteris paribus* (Kirkley et al. 1998; Pascoe and Coglan 2002; Sharma and Leung 1998; Squires and Kirkley 1999; Viswanathan et al. 2002).

Maximal output estimation is a fishery-wide forecast of production based on maximal variable input for each vessel (assuming that output is increasing in each input). That is, let x_{it}^{max} be the vector of variable inputs for each vessel i in year t, such that one or several variable inputs are at their maximal sample values over all t. Then maximal output for vessel i in year t is $\widehat{y}_{it}^{\max} = \widehat{\alpha}_i + x_{it}^{\max}\widehat{\beta}$, and maximal production for the fleet in year t is $\widehat{y}_t^{\max} = \sum_i \widehat{y}_{it}^{\max}$. If observed production in year t is $y_t = \sum_i y_{it}$, then capacity utilization in year t is $y_t/\widehat{y}_t^{\max}$.[5] This estimate assumes that vessel-specific output is maximized through maximal use of inputs. *Efficiency adjusted production* or *potential output* for the fleet imputes the maximal $\widehat{\alpha}_i$ to each vessel: $\widehat{y}_t^{TE} = \sum_i \left(\max_{s\in N}\widehat{\alpha}_s + x_{it}\widehat{\beta}\right)$. This production estimate

[4]Our purpose here is not to discuss specification issues, but to demonstrate a unique application of selection procedures, so for parsimony we consider only the most restrictive specification in Eq. (12.1).

[5]It is also possible to calculate aggregate or average maximal output over the entire period, but the annual calculation seems more intuitive, particularly if interest centers on how capacity utilization changes over time.

assumes each vessel is operating at maximal relative efficiency (inefficiency equal to zero). It is as if all vessels are being piloted by the best skipper in the fleet or that each vessel's captain obtains the skill and knowledge of the best captain in the fleet. Then capacity utilization in year t is $y_t/\widehat{y}_t^{TE}$. This is the current state-of-the-art for capacity utilization based on potential output.

We now propose an alternative *potential output* estimate based on Gupta subsets that allows for heterogeneous risk preferences for policy-makers (through a preselected error rate). Assume that $\widehat{\alpha}_i,\ i \in N$ are normally distributed with ranked means $\alpha_{[n]} > \alpha_{[n-1]} > \ldots > \alpha_{[1]}$.[6] Then for error rate $\gamma \in [0, 0.5)$, the first-best efficient subset of vessel indices, $S_1 \subseteq N$, satisfies the probability statement:

$$\Pr\{[n] \in S_1\} \geq 1 - \gamma. \tag{12.2}$$

Subset S_1 can be constructed using Gupta (1956, 1965) for the multivariate normal distribution (details are in the next section). Once S_1 is formed, let $N - S_1$ be the set of remaining indices with cardinality n_1. Let the ranked means associated with the indices in $N - S_1$ be: $\alpha_{[n_1*]} > \alpha_{[n_1-1*]} > \cdots > \alpha_{[1*]}$. Then, the second-best efficient subset, $S_2 \subseteq N - S_1$, satisfies the probability statement:

$$\Pr\left\{\left[n_1{}^*\right] \in S_2\right\} \geq 1 - \gamma,$$

with remaining indices in $N - (S_1 \cup S_2)$. This process can be repeated J times until the subsets $S_1, S_2, \ldots, S_J$ partition N. For small J the Bonferroni inequality controls for the overall error rate of the iterative procedure. In our examples $J = 2$, so the overall error rate is no more than 2γ.[7] Let the maximal estimate of $\widehat{\alpha}_i$ associated with each subset be $\widehat{\alpha}_{(j)}^{\max} = \max_{s \in S_j} \widehat{\alpha}_s, j = 1, \ldots, J$. Then, $\widehat{\alpha}_{(1)}^{\max} > \widehat{\alpha}_{(2)}^{\max} > \cdots > \widehat{\alpha}_{(J)}^{\max}$, and proposed potential output is:

$$\widehat{y}_t(\gamma) = \sum_{j=1}^{J} \sum_{i \in S_j} \left(\widehat{\alpha}_{(j)}^{\max} + x_{it}\widehat{\beta}\right).$$

Notice that potential output is now a function of the error rate and $\widehat{y}_t(\gamma) \leq \widehat{y}_t^{TE}$. It is through our estimates $\widehat{\alpha}_{(1)}^{\max} > \widehat{\alpha}_{(2)}^{\max} > \cdots > \widehat{\alpha}_{(J)}^{\max}$ that our model generates the alternative estimate. By allowing vessels to be grouped together based on the efficient subsets, we are defining the frontier for each subset by the maximal $\widehat{\alpha}_i$

[6] This will be true if, say, the errors v_{it} are normal. Relaxing this assumption is not beyond the realm of possibilities. In particular bootstrapping the procedure seems like a promising alternative. However, we leave that for future research.

[7] It would be useful to develop a procedure that automatically controls for the error rate. For large J the Bonferroni inequality will be too conservative and the procedure will not work well.

within each subset.[8] Also, notice that for sufficiently small γ or $\gamma = 0$, Eq. (12.2) implies that $S_1 = N$, $J = 1$, and $\widehat{y}_t(\gamma) = \widehat{y}_t(0) = \widehat{y}_t^{TE}$. Therefore, the traditional estimate of potential output is a special case of the proposed estimate. Also, $\widehat{y}_t(\gamma)$ is decreasing in γ, and capacity utilization $y_t/\widehat{y}_t(\gamma) \in (0, 1]$ is increasing in γ. As such, the error rate (or risk tolerance) is an important policy variable that can be interpreted as a policy-maker risk preference or sensitivity parameter. For example, if a policy-maker is risk-averse, then she has a low tolerance for errors and selects a small γ. Therefore, J is small, and $\widehat{y}_t(\gamma) \cong \widehat{y}_t^{TE}$. Also, capacity utilization is small, so for a risk-averse policy-maker the fishery is far from full-utilization, and the potential for heavy depletion in fish stocks is large. Hence, fishery policy might be aimed at conservation efforts. A risk-loving policy-maker will have a high tolerance for errors and selects a large γ, causing $\widehat{y}_t(\gamma)$ to be small (not close to upper-bound $\widehat{y}_t^{TE}$), and capacity utilization will be close to 100 %. For a risk-loving policy-maker the fishery is close to full-utilization, so the potential for heavy stock depletion is small. Therefore, resource conservation policy may not be justified.

In practice, risk preferences are unknown, so an alternative interpretation of γ is that it represents a "sensitivity parameter" that allows policy-makers to estimate a range of capacity estimates based on the level of conservatism they exhibit for the resource.[9] By changing the value of γ a policy-maker is in essence defining the upper and lower bound on their capacity estimates. This notion of upper and lower bounds is consistent with how policy-makers project future biomass levels conditional on different harvesting strategies. Examples of future harvesting strategies are harvesting at maximum allowable biological catch or not harvesting at all. Much as these estimates provide bounds on expected future population levels, a policy maker's selection of γ provides bounds on their estimates of capacity.

12.3 Example

Data are compiled from weekly production reports for vessels operating in the flatfish fishery collected by the National Marine Fisheries Service (NMFS). Weekly production reports contain information on the complete composition of fish landed within a week, vessel characteristics, crew sizes, number of gear deployments (*hauls*), and length of time the gear is in the water over the course of the week. To ensure a balanced panel, weekly data were aggregated to the year; this was done simply for computational convenience.[10] Further, we limit attention only to vessels

[8] Note that this is not an exercise in modeling and estimating heterogeneous frontiers for a single fishery; we are simply proposing an alternative estimator of potential output that incorporates statistical noise though the error rate and that nests the usual estimate.

[9] We would like to thank an anonymous referee for pointing out this alternative interpretation of γ.

[10] An unbalanced panel has $t = 1,..,T_i$ for every i, and introduces estimation computational complexities that are beyond the scope of this exercise.

Table 12.1 Production estimation

Variable	Coefficient (t-statistics)
Net − tons	−0.0729
	(−1.32)
Crew	1.1369
	(6.48)
Duration	0.2363
	(1.87)
R^2	0.335

using identical production technology (bottom-trawlers) and only those vessels with 100 % of their production activities observed by the NMFS (some smaller vessels are not always required to report catch). This was done to ensure a reasonable level of *ex ante* homogeneity in the analysis. The final sample is 12 vessels observed over 9 years (1995–2003).[11]

To identify α_i in our 'within' estimation exercise, all variables were divided by the time-varying annual *hauls* variable, making them time-varying rates. This identification strategy is in the spirit of Wooldridge (2002, p. 269) and is employed in the fishery production literature by Horrace and Schnier (2010). Output is the aggregation of all species caught (and retained) per haul.[12] The inputs (regressors) are the vessel's net-tonnage per haul (*Net-tons*), the average crew-size per haul (*crew*), and the average amount of time the nets were deployed during the year per haul (*duration*). Therefore, output is a catch rate, and inputs are rates of input utilization. All variables (input and output) are log transformed.

Table 12.1 contains the results for within estimation of Eq. (12.1), which indicate that variable inputs (*crew* and *duration*) are the most important inputs to production. The negative coefficient on vessel *net-tons* is a theoretical curvature violation, but it is not statistically significant and, hence, has a neutral effect on production.[13] Again, a more sophisticated production function could have been estimated, however our focus is on the selection procedures that follow and how they may be used to calculate potential output.

Table 12.2 contains the estimates of $\widehat{\alpha}_i$ and their standard errors. All parameters are significantly different from zero. It also contains the results of the first iteration of the subset selection procedure. Using the estimated variance-covariance matrix and a multivariate normality assumption on $\widehat{\alpha}_i$, one-sided multivariate critical values at $\gamma = 0.05$ and $\gamma = 0.10$ were simulated using the algorithm in Horrace (1998), but with a general covariance structure. These are in the last two columns of Table 12.2.

[11]In practice a capacity utilization exercise might include all vessels, but then specification of the production function becomes difficult. This is beyond the scope of this exercise.

[12]An alternative specification would explicitly account for different species. See, for example Orea et al. (2005) or Felthoven (2002).

[13]For maximal and potential output estimation, the net-tons coefficient is set to zero.

Table 12.2 First iteration of selection procedure

$\widehat{\alpha}_i$	Estimate	Standard error	Gupta critical value $\gamma = 0.05$	Gupta critical value $\gamma = 0.10$
α_1	2.272	0.302	2.361[a]	2.065[a]
α_2	2.329	0.256	2.469	2.179
α_3	1.950	0.264	2.478[a]	2.201[a]
α_4	2.546	0.297	2.283	1.960
α_5	2.617	0.372	2.196	1.850
α_6	2.312	0.250	2.471	2.179
α_7	2.319	0.251	2.481	2.183
α_8	2.482	0.280	2.367	2.089
α_9	2.242	0.257	2.478	2.183
α_{10}	2.356	0.266	2.462	2.164
α_{11}	2.323	0.296	2.304	1.992[a]
α_{12}	2.188	0.244	2.474	2.182[a]

[a]Indicates a negative "multiple comparison with a control" upper bound and exclusion from S_1
For $\gamma = 0.05$, $S_1 = \{2, 4, 5, 6, 7, 8, 9, 10, 11, 12\}$
For $\gamma = 0.10$, $S_1 = \{2, 4, 5, 6, 7, 8, 9, 10\}$

Using these critical values and the covariance structure of the $\widehat{\alpha}_i$, upper-bounds for *multiple comparisons with a control* (MCC) were calculated for each vessel (see Dunnett 1955). That is, let $k \in N$ be a control index. Then simultaneous upper-bounds were calculated for $\alpha_k - \alpha_i$, for all $i \neq k$. The rule for subset membership is: $k \in S_1$ if all MCC upper-bounds are non-negative. In Table 12.2, vessels that violate the selection rule are indicated with an a for each error rate. Therefore, the index $[n] \in N$ associated with the largest α_i is in the first-best subset: {2, 4, 5, 6, 7, 8, 9, 10, 11, 12} with probability at least 95 %. With probability at least 90 %, the index associated with the largest α_i is in first-best subset: {2, 4, 5, 6, 7, 8, 9, 10}.

Table 12.3 contains the results of the second and final iteration of the selection procedure. Using the same procedure as the first iteration (but with smaller dimensionality), critical values and MCC upper-bounds were calculated at each error rate, $\gamma = 0.05$ and $\gamma = 0.10$. At both error rates only vessel 3 violates the selection rule of no non-negative MCC upper-bounds, so it is the only index in S_3. The inference suggests that $[n_1{}^*] = 1$ with probability at least 95 %. With probability at least 90 %, the index $[n_1{}^*]$ associated with the largest α_i, $i \in N - S_1$, is in second-best subset: {1, 11, 12}. Based on the three subsets and the Bonferroni inequality, the conclusion is that $\alpha_{(1)}^{max} = \alpha_5 = 2.617$, $\alpha_{(2)}^{max} = \alpha_1 = 2.272$, and $\alpha_{(3)}^{max} = \alpha_3 = 1.950$ with probability at least 90 %. (Since $J = 2$, the overall error rate is at most 2γ.) Alternatively, $\alpha_{(1)}^{max} = \alpha_5 = 2.617$, $\alpha_{(2)}^{max} = \alpha_{11} = 2.323$, and $\alpha_{(3)}^{max} = \alpha_3 = 1.950$ with probability at least 80 %. From an efficiency frontier perspective, the values of $\alpha_{(j)}^{max}$ for each error rate represent different efficiency tiers within the fishery: the first-best tier, the second-best tier, and the third-best tier.

Table 12.3 Second (final) iteration of selection procedure

$\widehat{\alpha}_i$	Estimate	Standard error	Gupta critical value $\gamma = 0.05$	Gupta critical value $\gamma = 0.10$
α_1	2.272	0.302	1.646	1.693
α_3	1.950	0.264	1.647[a]	1.716[a]
α_{11}	2.322	0.296	–	1.673
α_{12}	2.188	0.244	–	1.687

[a]Indicates a negative "multiple comparison with a control" upper bound and exclusion from S_2
For $\gamma = 0.05$, $S_2 = \{1\}$; $S_3 = \{3\}$
For $\gamma = 0.10$, $S_2 = \{1, 11, 12\}$; $S_3 = \{3\}$

Table 12.4 2003 capacity utilization estimates in metric tons of fish

Error rate γ	Potential output S_1	Potential output S_2	Potential output S_3	Potential output $\widehat{y}_T(\gamma)$	Capacity utilization $y_T/\widehat{y}_T(\gamma)$
0.00	90,551	–	–	90,551	0.856
0.05	72,884	4,311	5,941	83,136	0.933
0.10	58,638	15,145	5,941	79,723	0.973

Total observed output in 2003 = 77,555 metric tons

Table 12.4 contains capacity utilization based on the proposed potential output $\widehat{y}_T(0.05)$ and $\widehat{y}_T(0.10)$, where $T = 2003$ is the last year in the sample.[14] The traditional estimates $\widehat{y}_T(0) = \widehat{y}_T^{TE}$ are also in the table for comparison purposes. It is worth repeating that if $\gamma = 0$, then $J = 1$, and $S_1 = N$, so that all vessels are in a single efficiency subset. We couch our discussion in terms of policy-maker risk preference. For $\gamma = 0$, the largest $\alpha_5 = 2.617$ is imputed to all vessels for nominal inputs in year 2003 (the coefficient on *Net-tons* is set to 0 in this exercise). This yields potential output of 90,551 metric tons of fish and conservative capacity utilization of 85.6 %. The potential output increase in a worst case scenario is 90,551–77,555 = 12,996 metric tons, a relatively large increase in production. For $\gamma = 0.05$ the most efficient subset of vessels, S_1, has the potential for 72,884 tons of fish, the second most efficient subset, S_2, has the potential for 4,311 tons of fish, and the least efficient subset, consisting of only vessel 3, will stay at its predicted nominal level of 5,941 tons of output. This yields a less conservative potential output of $83{,}136 < 90{,}551$ tons of fish, a less conservative capacity utilization of $93.3\,\% > 85.6\,\%$, and a worst case scenario output increase of only 83,136–77,555 = 5,581 tons. The $\gamma = 0.10$ case has a capacity utilization of close to one: 97.3 %. Hence, the capacity for increased output is close to zero (2.7 %).

[14]Maximal output results are available from the authors. Standard errors on the capacity measures could be bootstrapped without much complication, but we do not attempt that here.

12.4 Conclusions

The proposed potential output and capacity utilization measures account for differences in fisheries managers' risk behavior through selection of the inferential error rate. One motivation for fisheries managers to be conservative in selection of this rate is dynamic stock uncertainty. Some fisheries exhibit cyclical dynamics that make it particularly difficult to predict future stock levels and, more importantly, spawning stock biomass. Therefore, managers may wish to adopt smaller error rates to hedge this uncertainty. This being the case, one could also view the error rate as a proxy for stock predictability. Although a more comprehensive analysis is required before the proposed techniques could be used to directly influence fishery policy, our results are informative and illustrate the empirical benefits of using selection procedures in this setting. The selection technique could prove useful in guiding policies that focus on vessel buybacks or input restrictions to manage the natural resource.

References

Dunnett CW (1955) A multiple comparison procedure for comparing several treatments with a control. J Am Stat Assoc 50:1096–1121

Felthoven RG (2002) Effects of the American Fisheries Act on capacity, utilization and technical efficiency. Mar Resour Econ 17(3):181–205

Feng Q, Horrace WC (2012) Alternate technical efficiency measures: skew, bias and scale. J Appl Econom 27:253–268

Flores-Lagunes A, Horrace WC, Schnier KE (2007) Identifying technically efficient fishing vessels: a non-empty, minimal subset approach. J Appl Econom 22:729–745

Food and Agriculture Organization (1998) Report of the technical working group on the management of fishing capacity, FAO fisheries report number 586. Food and Agriculture Organization, Rome

Gupta SS (1956) On a decision rule for a problem of ranking means, Institute of statistics mimeo series no. 150. University of North Carolina, Chapel Hill, NC

Gupta SS (1965) On some multiple decision (selection and ranking) rules. Technometrics 7:225–245

Horrace WC (1998) Tables of percentage points of the k-variate normal distribution for large values of k. Commun Stat Simulat Comput 27:823–831

Horrace WC, Schmidt P (2000) Multiple comparisons with the best, with economic applications. J Appl Econom 15:1–26

Horrace WC, Schnier KE (2010) Fixed effect estimation of highly-mobile production technologies. Am J Agr Econ 92:1432–1445

Hsu JC (1996) Multiple comparisons: theory and methods. Chapman and Hall, London

Kirkley J, Squires D, Strand IE (1998) Characterizing managerial skill and technical efficiency in a fishery. J Prod Anal 9:145–160

Kirkley J, Morrison Paul CJ, Squires D (2002) Capacity and capacity utilization in common-pool resource industries. Environ Resour Econ 22:71–97

Kirkley JE, Squires D, Alam MF, Ishak HO (2003) Excess capacity and asymmetric information in developing country fisheries: the Malaysian purse seine fishery. Am J Agr Econ 85(3):647–662

Kirkley J, Morrison Paul CJ, Squires D (2004) Deterministic and stochastic capacity estimation for fishery capacity reduction. Mar Resour Econ 19(3):271–294

Orea L, Alvarez A, Morrison Paul CJ (2005) Modeling and measuring production processes for a multi-species fishery: alternative technical efficiency estimates for the northern Spain hake fishery. Nat Resour Model 18(2):183–213

Pascoe S, Coglan L (2002) The contribution of unmeasurable inputs to fisheries production: an analysis of technical efficiency of fishing vessels in the English Channel. Am J Agr Econ 84(3):585–597

Pascoe S, Coglan L, Mardle S (2001) Physical versus harvest based measures of capacity: the case of the UK vessel capacity unit system. ICES J Mar Sci 58(6):1243–1252

Schmidt P, Sickles R (1984) Production frontiers and panel data. J Bus Econ Stat 2:367–374

Sharma KR, Leung PS (1998) Technical efficiency of Hawaii's longline fishery. Mar Resour Econ 13(4):259–274

Squires D, Kirkley J (1999) Skipper skill and panel data in fishing industries. Can J Fish Aquat Sci 56:2011–2018

Tingley D, Pascoe S (2005) Eliminating excess capacity: implications for the Scottish fishing industry. Mar Resour Econ 20(4):407–424

Viswanathan KK, Omar IH, Jeon Y, Kirkley J, Squires D, Susilowati I (2002) Fishing skill in developing country fisheries: the Kedah, Malaysia Trawl Fishery. Mar Resour Econ 16:293–314

Wooldridge JM (2002) Econometric analysis of cross section and panel data. MIT Press, Cambridge

Chapter 13
Bartlett-Type Correction of Distance Metric Test

Wanling Huang and Artem Prokhorov

JEL Classification: C12

13.1 Introduction

The Distance Metric (DM) test of Newey and West (1987) is commonly used in econometrics to assess competing specifications. This is a simple test – the DM test statistic is usually calculated as the sample size times the difference in the criterion function evaluated at the restricted and the unrestricted estimate. At the same time, the test has several advantages over other classical tests. It is invariant to different but equivalent formulations of the restriction unlike, e.g., the Wald test (see, e.g., Breusch and Schmidt 1988), and robust to autocorrelation and heteroskedasticity of unknown form provided that the criterion function uses a heteroskedasticity-consistent estimate of the covariance matrix (see, e.g., Newey and McFadden 1994). This makes the test popular among applied researchers. For example, this test has been widely used in covariance structure analysis in the context of asymptotic distribution-free estimation (see, e.g., Browne 1984; Satorra and Bentler 2001, for the theory of ADF estimation).

W. Huang
Department of Economics & Finance, College of Business Administration, The University of Texas – Pan American, 1201 West University Drive, Edinburg, TX 78539, USA
e-mail: huangw@utpa.edu

A. Prokhorov (✉)
Business School, University of Sydney, Sydney, NSW 2006, Australia

Faculty of Economics, St.Petersburg State University, St.Petersburg 191194, Russia
e-mail: artem.prokhorov@sydney.edu.au

R.C. Sickles and W.C. Horrace (eds.), *Festschrift in Honor of Peter Schmidt: Econometric Methods and Applications*, DOI 10.1007/978-1-4899-8008-3_13,

It is well known that the DM test statistic asymptotically has the chi-square distribution with r degrees of freedom, where r is the number of restrictions (see, e.g., Newey and McFadden 1994). However, the sampling distribution of the test statistic is poorly approximated by the asymptotic distribution if samples are small (see, e.g., Clark 1996). Edgeworth expansions can deal with this problem by expanding the sampling density of test statistics around the asymptotic density in decreasing powers of $N^{-\frac{1}{2}}$, with N being the sample size. This may improve the accuracy of the asymptotic approximation. Surveys of Edgeworth expansion methods, including the theory of their validity, are provided by Phillips (1977, 1978), Kallenberg (1993), Rothenberg (1984), Reid (1991), and Sargan and Satchell (1986), among others.

However, Edgeworth expansion methods have not yet been applied to the most general version of the DM test. Most of known results concern the LR, Wald and the score test (see, e.g., Cribari-Neto and Cordeiro 1996; Phillips and Park 1988; Magee 1989; Linton 2002; Hausman and Kuersteiner 2008). Hansen (2006) is the only application (known to us) of the Edgeworth correction to the DM test but it is restricted to the setting of a normal linear regression with a single constraint. Moreover, it is well known that Edgeworth expansions do not always improve the quality of first-order asymptotic approximations (see, e.g., Phillips 1983). The main contribution of the paper is that we derive the Edgeworth correction, also known as the Bartlett-type correction, for the DM test in its general form and illustrate in simulations that this corrected approximation does work better, often surprisingly better, than the uncorrected test.

We do not consider alternative ways to remedy the inaccuracy of first-order asymptotic approximations. Such alternatives include resampling techniques and other types of asymptotic approximations, e.g., saddle-point (tilted Edgeworth) or Cornish-Fisher expansions. Validity of the former is usually based on existence of an asymptotic approximation in the first place (see, e.g., Hall 1992) and the various forms of the latter are substantially more complicated than the classical Edgeworth expansion (see, e.g., Barndorff-Nielsen and Cox 1979).

The paper can be viewed as a generalization of the results by Hansen (2006), who obtained the DM test correction in the setting of linear regressions with one restriction, to most of the extremum and minimum distance estimators and to multiple linear and nonlinear restrictions. We also draw on the results by Phillips and Park (1988) and Kollo and Rosen (2005). Phillips and Park (1988) investigate how higher-order terms in the asymptotic approximation of the Wald test are affected by various formulations of the null hypothesis. The DM test is invariant to such reformulations. However, their theorem on asymptotic expansion of the distribution provides a useful shortcut that substantially facilitates our proof. Kollo and Rosen (2005) provide general forms of Taylor series expansions for vector-valued functions, applicable in our setting.

In the application section, we consider a covariance structure model of Abowd and Card (1989). We address the question at what sample sizes would the proposed asymptotic correction make a difference for the empirical conclusions of that paper.

It turns out that this happens at sample sizes as large as 900–1,000 observations. An interesting by-product of the application is that it explains the old puzzle in labor economics that longer panels reverse the original inference.

The DM test statistic is defined in Sect. 13.2. In Sect. 13.3 we derive the asymptotic expansion to order $O_p(N^{-1})$ of the DM test statistic, and in Sect. 13.4 we give the higher-order approximation of its distribution. Simple simulations are provided in Sect. 13.5, and an empirical illustration is presented in Sect. 13.6. Section 13.7 contains brief concluding remarks.

13.2 Distance Metric Test

For a family of distributions $\{P_\theta, \theta \in \Theta \subset \mathbb{R}^p\}$, Θ compact, consider the test

$$H_0 : g(\theta) = 0,$$
$$H_1 : g(\theta) \neq 0,$$

where $g : R^p \to R^r$ is a continuously differentiable function with the first derivative defined by

$$\underset{p\times r}{A(\theta)} \equiv \frac{dg(\theta)}{d\theta}.$$

Let $A(\theta_o)$ be denoted by A.

We assume that underlying the test is a parametric model that can be written in terms of the moment condition

$$\mathbb{E}m(Z_i, \theta) = 0 \qquad \text{iff } \theta = \theta_0, \tag{13.1}$$

where $m(\cdot,\cdot)$ is a continuous k-valued function, Z_i is a vector of data, independently distributed over $i = 1, \ldots, N$, and θ_0 is the true value of the parameter vector. We assume that the moments identify θ_0. In covariance structure models, for example, $m(Z_i, \theta) = vech Z_i Z_i' - vech \Sigma(\theta)$, where $vech$ denotes vertical vectorization of the lower triangle of a matrix and $\Sigma(\theta)$ is a model for the covariance matrix, in which $k \geq p$.

For some positive definite weighting matrix W_N, define the criterion function

$$-Q_N(\theta) \equiv \frac{1}{2} m_N'(\theta) W_N m_N(\theta), \tag{13.2}$$

where $\underset{k\times 1}{m_N(\theta)} \equiv \frac{1}{N}\sum_{i=1}^{N} m(Z_i, \theta)$. The estimator that minimizes this function is known in econometrics as the Generalized Method of Moments (GMM) estimator (see, e.g., Hansen 1982). In psychometric literature this estimator is also known as the asymptotically distribution free (ADF) or weighted least squared (WLS) estimator (see, e.g., Browne 1984). It is well known that efficient weighting of $m(\cdot,\cdot)$ requires that

$$\underset{k\times k}{W_N} \xrightarrow{p} W \equiv \left\{\mathbb{E}[m(Z_i,\theta_0)m'(Z_i,\theta_0)]\right\}^{-1}.$$

We assume efficient weighting. What this means for our expansions will be clarified below.

The independence assumption on Z_i can be relaxed to the weak dependence assumption. This would mean that W would need to be replaced with the inverse of the so called long run variance matrix of $m(Z_i,\theta_0)$. As long as we assume efficient weighting this would have no influence on the results that follow.

The test statistic we consider is based on the value of $Q_N(\theta)$ for two competing models, one that satisfies H_0 and the other that is unrestricted. Let $\bar{\theta}$ and $\hat{\theta}$ denote the corresponding estimators:

$$\bar{\theta} = \arg\max_{\theta\in\Theta} Q_N(\theta), \text{ subject to } g(\theta) = 0;$$

$$\hat{\theta} = \arg\max_{\theta\in\Theta} Q_N(\theta).$$

Then, the DM test statistic is defined (see, e.g., Newey and McFadden 1994, p. 2222) as

$$DM \equiv -2N[Q_N(\bar{\theta}_N) - Q_N(\hat{\theta}_N)]. \tag{13.3}$$

Throughout, we assume that the standard regularity conditions are satisfied (see, e.g., Newey and McFadden 1994, conditions of Theorems 2.6, 3.4, 4.5, and 9.1).

13.3 Stochastic Expansion of DM Test Statistic

Let

$$\mathbb{M}_N(\theta) = W_N^{1/2} m_N(\theta).$$

Assume that $\mathbb{M}_N(\theta)$ is three-times continuously differentiable. We follow Kollo and Rosen (2005, Definition 1.4.1) and define the derivative matrices recursively as follows

$$\underset{p\times p}{G_N(\theta)} \equiv \frac{\partial \mathbb{M}'_N(\theta)}{\partial\theta},$$

$$\underset{p\times p^2}{D_N(\theta)} \equiv \frac{\partial vec' G_N(\theta)}{\partial\theta},$$

$$\underset{p\times p^3}{C_N(\theta)} \equiv \frac{\partial vec' D_N(\theta)}{\partial\theta}.$$

Let $G = \mathbb{E}[G_N(\theta_0)]$, $D = \mathbb{E}[D_N(\theta_0)]$, and $C = \mathbb{E}[C_N(\theta_0)]$. In simulations, our focus is on covariance structure models for which the moment conditions have the form $m(Z_i, \theta) = r(Z_i) + h(\theta)$, for some functions $r(\cdot)$ and $h(\cdot)$. In this case, $G_N(\theta_0)$, $D_N(\theta_0)$, and $C_N(\theta_0)$ are nonrandom matrices.

The quadratic form in (13.2) becomes

$$-Q_N(\theta) = \frac{1}{2}\mathbb{M}_N'(\theta)\mathbb{M}_N(\theta),$$

and the DM test statistic in (13.3) can be written as follows

$$DM = N[\mathbb{M}_N'(\bar{\theta})\mathbb{M}_N(\bar{\theta}) - \mathbb{M}_N'(\hat{\theta})\mathbb{M}_N(\hat{\theta})]. \tag{13.4}$$

Note that, due to the efficient weighting,

$$-\sqrt{N}\mathbb{M}_N(\theta_0) \equiv q_N \xrightarrow{d} \underset{k\times 1}{\bar{q}} \sim N(0, \mathbb{I}). \tag{13.5}$$

Following Hansen (2006) and Phillips and Park (1988), we derive higher order expansions of the DM test under the stronger assumption that we have carried out the standardizing transformation and that

$$-\sqrt{N}\mathbb{M}_N(\theta_o) \equiv \bar{q} \sim N(0, \mathbb{I}). \tag{13.6}$$

We further assume that

$$\sqrt{N}(\hat{\theta}_N - \theta_0) \equiv \tilde{q} \sim N(0, \Omega_1), \tag{13.7}$$

$$\sqrt{N}(\bar{\theta}_N - \hat{\theta}_N) \equiv \hat{q} \sim N(0, \Omega_2). \tag{13.8}$$

The usual first order asymptotic expansions of the constrained and unconstrained GMM (Newey and McFadden 1994, p. 2219) imply that

$$\tilde{q} = B^{-1}G\bar{q},$$

$$\hat{q} = -\mathbb{H}G\bar{q},$$

where $\underset{p\times p}{\mathbb{H}} \equiv B^{-1}A(A'B^{-1}A)^{-1}A'B^{-1}$ and $B^{-1} = (GG')^{-1}$. So $\Omega_1 = B^{-1}$ and $\Omega_2 = \mathbb{H}$.

Assumptions (13.6)–(13.8) substantially simplify derivations by disregarding possibly important higher order terms of $\bar{q}$, $\tilde{q}$ and $\hat{q}$. In the OLS setting, this would correspond to Hansen's (2006) assumption that the regression error is homoskedastic and has exact normal distribution. As noted by Hansen (2006), this places focus on nonlinearity. In our setting, this is the nonlinearity of the test statistic as a function of moment conditions and of parameter estimates.

It is in principle possible to generalize our results as in Phillips and Park (1988, Appendix B) to the more general case of only (13.5), by carrying additional higher order terms involved in $\bar{q}$ and in the transformations using W_N, B, G and $\mathbb{H}$. That is, it is possible in principle that $\bar{q}$, $\tilde{q}$ and $\hat{q}$ come from any distribution that admits a valid Edgeworth expansion, not only normal. Aside from allowing for non-normality in finite samples, this would correct for the difference between the sample and population versions of the weighting matrices W, B, G and $\mathbb{H}$ and would allow for the optimal weighting matrix W to depend explicitly on θ as in the CU-GMM estimator of Hansen et al. (1996) or in a two-step GMM procedure. However, for reasons to be discussed next we do not pursue such a generalization here.

We follow Hansen (2006) and Phillips and Park (1988) and disregard the approximation inherent in the first order asymptotic result (13.5). We do so for several reasons. First, we wish to focus on the nonlinearity of the test statistic as a function of moment conditions. This type of nonlinearity distinguishes this test from, e.g., the Wald test statistic, which depends on the nonlinearity of the restrictions.

Second, for the class of models we focus on, the derivatives of the moment functions with respect to the parameters are not random functions. That is, they are fixed functions of θ and so, given θ, there is no difference between the sample and population version of these matrices. In other words, given θ, estimation of weights B, G and $\mathbb{H}$ does not add estimation error for this class of models.

Third, our setup implicitly allows for W to depend on θ. We achieve this by using the weighted function $\mathbb{M}_N(\theta)$ instead of $m_N(\theta)$ – if W depends on θ in a known manner then the derivatives G, D, C will be different and this will change our correction factor. This does not explicitly account for the estimation error inherent in replacing W by W_N but this *does* account for the estimation error inherent in replacing θ_0 in W by an estimate and for the nonlinearity of $\mathbb{M}_N(\theta)$ as a function of parameter estimates.[1]

Finally, the expansions for the general case quickly become hard to manage using matrix notation. As an alternative we study the effect of non-normality and nonlinearity by simulations and find that, at least for the models we consider, our correction works very well. We argue that the correction works for non-normal distributions, inspite of the limitations imposed by assuming (13.6)–(13.8), when the deviations of the sampling distribution of the test statistics from the first-order

[1]As noted by a referee this means that we ignore the estimation error in W_N, or more precisely, that we assume that estimation error, coupled with some nonlinearities we disregard, has, in some sense, no bigger effect than the estimation error in $\hat{\theta}$ and the nonlinearities we focus on.

asymptotics remain relatively small. This feature of Edgeworth corrections has been noted in previous literature (see, e.g., Phillips and Park 1988).

Using the above notation and Theorem 3.1.1 of Kollo and Rosen (2005, p. 280), which we provide in Appendix 1 for reference, the Taylor expansion of $\mathbb{M}_N(\bar{\theta}_N)$ about $\hat{\theta}_N$ can be written as follows

$$\begin{aligned}\mathbb{M}_N(\bar{\theta}_N) = \; & \mathbb{M}_N(\hat{\theta}_N) + G_N'(\hat{\theta}_N)(\bar{\theta}_N - \hat{\theta}_N) \\ & + \frac{1}{2}[I_k \otimes (\bar{\theta}_N - \hat{\theta}_N)']D_N'(\hat{\theta}_N)(\bar{\theta}_N - \hat{\theta}_N) + o_p(N^{-1}).\end{aligned} \tag{13.9}$$

Substituting (13.9) into (13.4), we obtain

$$\begin{aligned}DM = \; & \bar{q}'G'\mathbb{H}G_N(\hat{\theta}_N)G_N'(\hat{\theta}_N)\mathbb{H}G\bar{q} \\ & + \mathbb{M}_N'(\hat{\theta}_N)(I_k \otimes \bar{q}'G'\mathbb{H})D_N'(\hat{\theta}_N)\mathbb{H}G\bar{q} \\ & - N^{-1/2}\bar{q}'G'\mathbb{H}G_N(\hat{\theta}_N)(I_k \otimes \bar{q}'G'\mathbb{H})D_N'(\hat{\theta}_N)\mathbb{H}G\bar{q} \\ & + \frac{1}{4}N^{-1}\bar{q}'G'\mathbb{H}D_N(\hat{\theta}_N)(I_k \otimes \mathbb{H}G\bar{q})(I_k \otimes \bar{q}'G'\mathbb{H})D_N'(\hat{\theta}_N)\mathbb{H}G\bar{q} + o_p(N^{-2}).\end{aligned} \tag{13.10}$$

We will now expand at θ_0 all functions of $\hat{\theta}_N$ contained in (13.10). We wish to use Theorem 3.1.1 of Kollo and Rosen (2005) to do that. So we will transform the current representation into the one based on vector functions. Specifically, we need the vectorized versions of matrices $G_N(\hat{\theta}_N)$ and $D_N(\hat{\theta}_N)$. Using the facts that

$$\begin{aligned} & vec(ABC) = (C' \otimes A)vecB, \\ & (A \otimes B)' = A' \otimes B', \end{aligned}$$

we obtain the following equations

$$\begin{aligned}\bar{q}'G'\mathbb{H}G_N(\hat{\theta}_N) &= vec'G_N(\hat{\theta}_N)(I_k \otimes \mathbb{H}G\bar{q}), \\ D_N'(\hat{\theta}_N)\mathbb{H}G\bar{q} &= (I_{pk} \otimes \bar{q}'G'\mathbb{H})vecD_N(\hat{\theta}_N).\end{aligned}$$

Equation (13.10) can now be rewritten as

$$\begin{aligned}DM = \; & vec'G_N(\hat{\theta}_N)M_1 vecG_N(\hat{\theta}_N) \\ & + \mathbb{M}_N'(\hat{\theta}_N)M_2 vecD_N(\hat{\theta}_N) \\ & - N^{-1/2}vec'G_N(\hat{\theta}_N)M_3 vecD_N(\hat{\theta}_N) \\ & + N^{-1}\frac{1}{4}vec'D_N(\hat{\theta}_N)M_4 vecD_N(\hat{\theta}_N) + o_p,\end{aligned} \tag{13.11}$$

where

$$M_1 = (I_k \otimes \mathbb{H}G\bar{q})(I_k \otimes \bar{q}'G'\mathbb{H}),$$
$$M_2 = I_k \otimes \bar{q}'G'\mathbb{H} \otimes \bar{q}'G'\mathbb{H},$$
$$M_3 = (I_k \otimes \mathbb{H}G\bar{q})(I_k \otimes \bar{q}'G'\mathbb{H} \otimes \bar{q}'G'\mathbb{H}),$$
$$M_4 = I_k \otimes \mathbb{H}G\bar{q}\bar{q}'G'\mathbb{H} \otimes \mathbb{H}G\bar{q}\bar{q}'G'\mathbb{H}.$$

Substituting the Taylor expansions at θ_0 of $\mathbb{M}_N(\hat{\theta}_N)$, $vec\,G_N(\hat{\theta}_N)$ and $vec\,D_N(\hat{\theta}_N)$ into (13.11) gives the asymptotic expansion of the DM test statistic, which is summarized in the following theorem.

Theorem 1. *The asymptotic expansion of the DM test statistic is given by*

$$DM = \bar{q}'P\bar{q} + N^{-1/2}u(\bar{q}) + N^{-1}v(\bar{q}) + o_p, \tag{13.12}$$

where

$$\underset{k\times k}{P} \equiv G'\mathbb{H}G,$$
$$u(\bar{q}) = u_1(\bar{q}) + u_2(\bar{q}) + u_3(\bar{q}),$$
$$v(\bar{q}) = v_1(\bar{q}) + v_2(\bar{q}) + v_3(\bar{q}) + v_4(\bar{q}), \tag{13.13}$$

with $u_i(\bar{q})$ $(i = 1, 2, 3)$ and $v_i(\bar{q})$ $(i = 1, 2, 3, 4)$ specified by

$$u_1(\bar{q}) = 2\bar{q}'G'B^{-1}DM_1 vec\,G, \tag{13.14}$$
$$u_2(\bar{q}) = \bar{q}'(G'B^{-1}G - I_k)M_2 vec\,D, \tag{13.15}$$
$$u_3(\bar{q}) = -vec'GM_3 vec\,D; \tag{13.16}$$

$$v_1(\bar{q}) = \bar{q}'G'B^{-1}DM_1D'B^{-1}G\bar{q} + \bar{q}'G'B^{-1}C(I_{pk} \otimes B^{-1}G\bar{q})M_1 vec\,G, \tag{13.17}$$

$$v_2(\bar{q}) = \bar{q}'(G'B^{-1}G - I_k)M_2C'B^{-1}G\bar{q} + \frac{1}{2}\bar{q}'G'B^{-1}D(I_k \otimes B^{-1}G\bar{q})M_2 vec\,D, \tag{13.18}$$

$$v_3(\bar{q}) = -\bar{q}'G'B^{-1}CM_3' vec\,G - \bar{q}'G'B^{-1}DM_3 vec\,D, \tag{13.19}$$

$$v_4(\bar{q}) = \frac{1}{4}vec'DM_4 vec\,D. \tag{13.20}$$

Proof. See Appendix 2 for all proofs.

13.4 Distribution of DM Test Statistic

In this section we follow Phillips and Park (1988) and use the Taylor expansion of DM to derive the Edgeworth expansion of its distribution to order $O(N^{-1})$. Theorem 2.4 of Phillips and Park (1988) allows us to skip intermediate steps in deriving the expansion for the distribution from the expansion of the test statistics. Hansen (2006) used this approach for a single restriction DM test in a normal linear regression with known error variance.

In order to use Phillips and Park's results, we first show that $u(\bar{q})$ and $v(\bar{q})$ can be written in terms of Kronecker products of $\bar{q}$ and $\bar{q}\bar{q}'$. This is done in the following lemma.

Lemma 1. *$u(\bar{q})$ and $v(\bar{q})$ in Theorem 1 can be written as*

$$u(\bar{q}) = vec'J(\bar{q} \otimes \bar{q} \otimes \bar{q}),$$
$$v(\bar{q}) = tr[L(\bar{q}\bar{q}' \otimes \bar{q}\bar{q}')],$$

where $vecJ = vecJ_1 + vecJ_2 + vecJ_3$ with

$$vecJ_1 = 2(G'\mathbb{H}G \otimes G'\mathbb{H} \otimes G'B^{-1})vecD,$$
$$vecJ_2 = [(G'B^{-1}G - I_k) \otimes G'\mathbb{H} \otimes G'\mathbb{H}]vecD,$$
$$vecJ_3 = -(G'\mathbb{H}G \otimes G'\mathbb{H} \otimes G'\mathbb{H})vecD;$$

and

$$L = L_1 + L_2 + L_3 + L_4, \tag{13.21}$$

with

$$L_1 = (G'\mathbb{H}\otimes G'B^{-1})V_D(\mathbb{H}G\otimes B^{-1}G)+(G'\mathbb{H}\otimes G'B^{-1})M_V(I_k\otimes\mathbb{H}G), \tag{13.22}$$

$$L_2 = (G'\mathbb{H} \otimes G'\mathbb{H})M_{VI} + \frac{1}{2}(G'\mathbb{H} \otimes G'\mathbb{H})V_D(B^{-1}G \otimes B^{-1}G), \tag{13.23}$$

$$L_3 = -(G'\mathbb{H} \otimes G'\mathbb{H})M_V(I_k \otimes \mathbb{H}G) - (G'\mathbb{H} \otimes G'\mathbb{H})V_D(\mathbb{H}G \otimes B^{-1}G), \tag{13.24}$$

$$L_4 = \frac{1}{4}(G'\mathbb{H} \otimes G'\mathbb{H})V_D(\mathbb{H}G \otimes \mathbb{H}G), \tag{13.25}$$

where V_D, M_V and M_{VI} are given in Appendix 2.

We can now follow Hansen (2006, Theorem 3) and apply the result of Phillips and Park (1988, pp. 1069–1072). Specifically, we can obtain the characteristic function of the DM test statistic:

$$C_{DM}(t) = (1-2it)^{-r/2}\{1 + \frac{1}{N}[(a_0 - \frac{1}{4}b_1)it$$
$$+ (a_1 + \frac{1}{4}b_1 - \frac{1}{4}b_2)it(1-2it)^{-1}$$
$$+ (a_2 + \frac{1}{4}b_2 - \frac{1}{4}b_3)(1-2it)^{-2}$$
$$+ \frac{1}{4}b_3 it(1-2it)^{-3}]\} + o_p(N^{-1}),$$

where a_i, $i = 0, 1, 2$, and b_j, $j = 1, 2, 3$, are defined in Appendix 2. Note that the first term $(1-2it)^{-r/2}$ is the characteristic function for a χ^2_r variate, reflecting the first order asymptotics. Then, using the Fourier transform, we can derive the distribution of the DM test statistic. This is done in Theorem 2.

Theorem 2. *The asymptotic expansion to $O(N^{-1})$ of the distribution function of DM is given by*

$$F_{DM}(x) = F_r\left(x - N^{-1}(\alpha_1 x + \alpha_2 x^2 + \alpha_3 x^3)\right) + o(N^{-1}) \tag{13.26}$$

where F_r denotes the distribution function of a χ^2_r variate and

$$\alpha_1 = (4a_1 - b_2)/4r,$$
$$\alpha_2 = (4a_2 + b_2 - b_3)/4r(r+2),$$
$$\alpha_3 = b_3/4r(r+2)(r+4),$$

with a_i $(i = 1, 2)$ and b_i $(i = 1, 2, 3)$ defined in Appendix 2.

The Edgeworth correction factor that follows from (13.26) can be written as

$$1 - N^{-1}(\alpha_1 + \alpha_2 DM + \alpha_3 DM^2) \tag{13.27}$$

where DM is the original (uncorrected) DM test statistic. If multiplied by the correction factor, the DM test statistic should be better approximated by the χ^2_r distribution than the uncorrected statistic. Strictly speaking, the correction cannot be called "Bartlett" because it depends on the uncorrected statistic DM. However, it is common to call such corrections Bartlett-type due to their similarity to the classical (Bartlett 1937) correction (see, e.g., Cribari-Neto and Cordeiro 1996, for a review of Bartlett and Bartlett-type corrections of common tests).

The unknown α's ultimately depend on the number of restrictions r and on the expected derivative matrices G, D, C, evaluated at θ_0. Since the DM test is invariant to alternative formulations of the restriction $g(\theta) = 0$, so are the α's (see, e.g., Hansen 2006, p. 15). It is standard to estimate the unknown quantities using a consistent estimate of θ_0 and, if needed, sample averages in place of expected values.

Note that increasing the number of restrictions r does not necessarily result in a bigger correction factor because α_i $(i = 1, 2, 3)$ may be negative. Moreover, it is important to note that, even if the restrictions are linear, the Bartlett-type correction factor in (13.27) will be different from one so long as $\mathbb{M}_N(\theta)$ is nonlinear in parameters. The theorem imposes no constraint on the number of restrictions tested or on the specific estimator represented by the moment condition (13.1).

Edgeworth expansions do not always improve the quality of asymptotic approximations. It has been documented that their performance is parameter dependent and that they fail when deviations of the sampling distribution from the first order asymptotic distribution are large (see, e.g., Phillips 1983). We cannot expect the correction in (13.27) to work in all circumstances but when it does work, the quality of the correction can be expected to depend on nonlinearities (through matrices J and L), the size of the model (through the number of restrictions r), the sample size N and the true distribution (through $\bar{q}$). We now demonstrate the behavior of the correction along some of these dimensions.

13.5 Illustrative Simulations

In this section, we use simulations to illustrate the theoretical results obtained in Sect. 13.4 in the settings of a simple covariance structure model. Consider a random vector $Z \in \mathcal{Z} \subset \mathbb{R}^q$ from P_{θ_0}, $\theta_0 \in \Theta \subset \mathbb{R}^p$. Assume that $\mathbb{E}[Z] = 0$, $\mathbb{E}\{\|Z\|^4\} < \infty$ and $\mathbb{E}[ZZ'] = \Sigma(\theta_0)$. The matrix function $\Sigma(\theta)$ may come from a variety of models, e.g., LISREL, MIMIC, factor model, random effects or simultaneous equations model. For a random sample $(Z_1, \cdots, Z_N)$, let

$$S_i \equiv Z_i Z_i'$$

and

$$S \equiv \frac{1}{N} \sum_{i=1}^{N} S_i .$$

Then, S satisfies a central limit theorem:

$$\sqrt{N}(vechS - vech\Sigma(\theta_0)) \to N(0, \Delta(\theta_0)),$$

where

$$\Delta(\theta_0) = \mathbb{V}(vechS_i) = \mathbb{E}[vechS_i vech' S_i] - vech\Sigma(\theta_0) vech'\Sigma(\theta_0).$$

Assume $p \leq \frac{1}{2}q(q+1)$. Then, in terminology of covariance structure literature, the degrees of freedom of the model are equal to $\frac{q(q+1)}{2} - p$, and they will be increased by one for each independent restriction imposed on $\Sigma(\theta)$ by the model. We can write all distinct sample moment functions as follows

$$\underset{\frac{1}{2}q(q+1)\times 1}{m_N(\theta)} \equiv \frac{1}{N} \sum_{i=1}^{N} m(Z_i, \theta) = vechS - vech\Sigma(\theta)$$

where

$$\underset{\frac{1}{2}q(q+1)\times 1}{m(Z_i,\theta)} = vechS_i - vech\Sigma(\theta).$$

The sample covariance matrix of the moments is

$$\begin{aligned}\underset{\frac{1}{2}q(q+1)\times\frac{1}{2}q(q+1)}{W_N^{-1}(\theta)} &= \frac{1}{N}\sum_{i=1}^{N}[m(Z_i,\theta)m'(Z_i,\theta)]\\ &= \frac{1}{N}\sum_{i=1}^{N}[vechS_i vech'S_i - vechS_i vech'\Sigma(\theta)\\ &\qquad - vech\Sigma(\theta)vech'S_i + vech\Sigma(\theta)vech'\Sigma(\theta)].\end{aligned}$$

In practice, either the restricted or the unrestricted estimate of θ will be used in these infeasible expressions.

We are interested in testing $H_0 : \Sigma(\theta_o) = \Sigma(c)$ against $H_1 : \Sigma(\theta_o) \neq \Sigma(c)$, where c is a constant vector. This type of test is fundamental in covariance structure analysis. Known as the ADF test in the covariance structure literature, it has been studied by Korin (1968), Sugiura (1969), Nagarsenker and Pillai (1973), Browne (1984), Chou et al. (1991), Muthen and Kaplan (1992), Yuan and Bentler (1997), Satorra and Bentler (2001), Yanagihara et al. (2004), among others. Ogasawara (2009) provides an asymptotic expansion similar to ours for the ADF test statistic in the setting of covariance structure models. The literature has focused on three dimensions of the test behavior: (1) what is the effect of the sample size; (2) how the sample size requirements change for different nonnormal distributions; (3) how the sample size requirements change for models of different size. We wish to apply our Bartlett-type correction to the DM test of this restriction and study its behavior along the same dimensions.

For simplicity, we consider a bivariate problem (i.e. $q = 2$) in which

$$\Sigma(\theta) = \begin{bmatrix}\sigma_1^2 & \sigma_{12}\\ \sigma_{12} & \sigma_2^2\end{bmatrix},$$

$\theta' = (\sigma_1, \sigma_{12}, \sigma_2)$, $c' = (1, 0, 1)$ and $p = k = r = 3$. So the parameter vector is completely specified under the null and there are no parameters to estimate in the restricted model. Write the null hypothesis as

$$H_0 : \underset{3\times 1}{g(\theta)} = 0, \quad \text{where} \quad g(\theta) = vech\Sigma(\theta) - vech\Sigma(c) = \begin{bmatrix}\sigma_1^2 - 1\\ \sigma_{12} - 0\\ \sigma_2^2 - 1\end{bmatrix}.$$

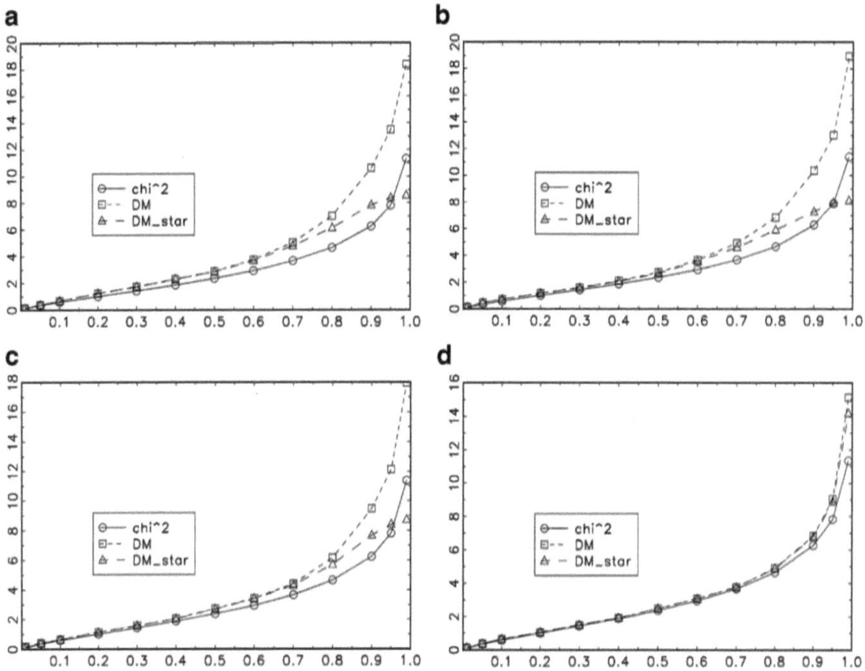

Fig. 13.1 Quantiles of chi-square and bootstrap distribution of uncorrected and corrected DM test statistics for various sample sizes; $q = 2$. (**a**) $N = 25$ (**b**) $N = 35$ (**c**) $N = 65$ (**d**) $N = 200$

In order to demonstrate the effect of the Bartlett-type correction, we generate samples of varying size from normal, Student-t and uniform distributions and compute the uncorrected and corrected versions of the DM test statistic. This is done 1,000 times. Then we plot the quantiles of the resulting bootstrap distributions. These are displayed on Figs. 13.1–13.3. The quantile curve of the chi-square distribution, marked "chi^2", is drawn as a reference. The uncorrected and corrected versions of the DM test statistic are marked "DM" and "DM_star," respectively.

All figures show severe over-rejection of the uncorrected DM test statistic. The fact that the size of the DM test is substantially greater in small samples than the asymptotic size is well documented (see, e.g., Clark 1996), and our results agree with that. Our corrected statistic performs much better for all distributions and all sample sizes. Of course, the corrected distribution is not identical to the chi-square distribution and the corrected test exhibits over- and under-rejection at times, but the deviations are substantially smaller than for the uncorrected test. It is notable how much improvement one can obtain using the corrected statistic in the area close to the 95th percentile, which corresponds to the commonly used 5 % significance level. At that level, the correction is almost perfect.

Figure 13.1 shows the quantiles for various sample sizes from $\mathcal{N}(0, 1)$. One can clearly see from the figure how the uncorrected curve deviates from the chi-square

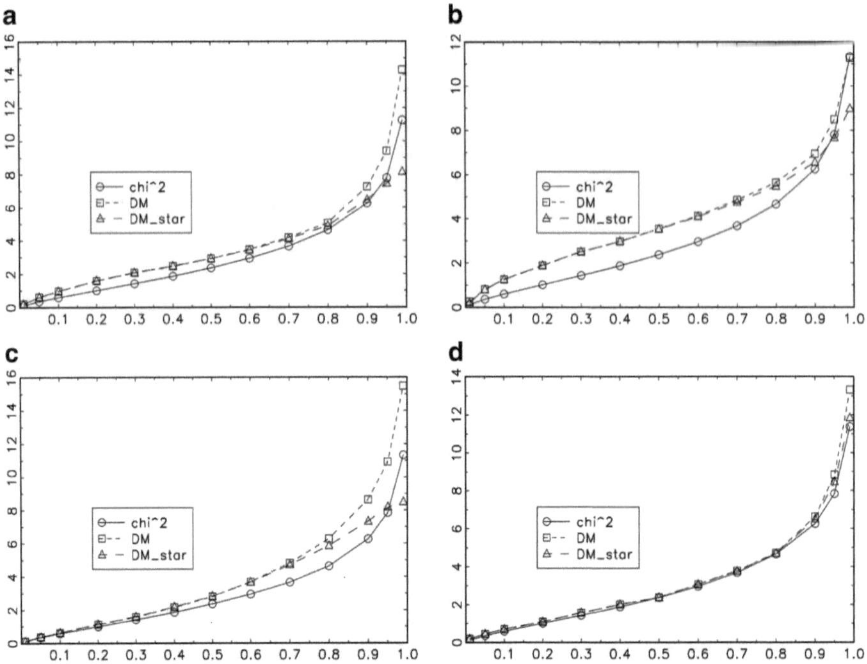

Fig. 13.2 Quantiles of chi-square and bootstrap distribution of uncorrected and corrected DM test statistics for two data distributions and two sample sizes; $q = 2$. (**a**) $N = 25$, Student-t with 9 df. (**b**) $N = 65$, Student-t with 9 df. (**c**) $N = 25$, Uniform (**d**) $N = 65$, Uniform

quantiles as the sample size decreases while the degree of model complexity does not change ($q = 2$). At the same time, the corrected curve consistently provides a great deal of improvement.

In Fig. 13.2 we show the behavior of the corrected and uncorrected test statistics for two distributions, Student-t and uniform, and two sample sizes, $N = 25$ and $N = 65$. As expected, the test, being distribution-free, exhibits similar behavior under the two distributions. The correction works very well for the non-normal distributions. The figures also show that the benefit of a larger sample size varies for the two distributions. For other distributions (not reported here), the sample size needed to obtain a similar level of approximation accuracy as in panel (d) was several hundred observations. For some distributions, the correction may be trivial even when samples are small while for others it may produce a large correction even when samples are large.

In Fig. 13.3, in addition to the bivariate case, we consider a univariate ($q = 1$) model in which $\Sigma(\theta) = \sigma^2$. The null is $\sigma = c$, and the restricted model has one degree of freedom. This is done to show how model size (as measured by the degrees of freedom of the model) affects the performance of the test statistics. In the larger model ($q = 2$), the gap between the sampling and asymptotic χ^2_3 distribution is much larger than between the sampling and the asymptotic χ^2_1 distribution in the smaller model. It is interesting to note that the model size plays as important a

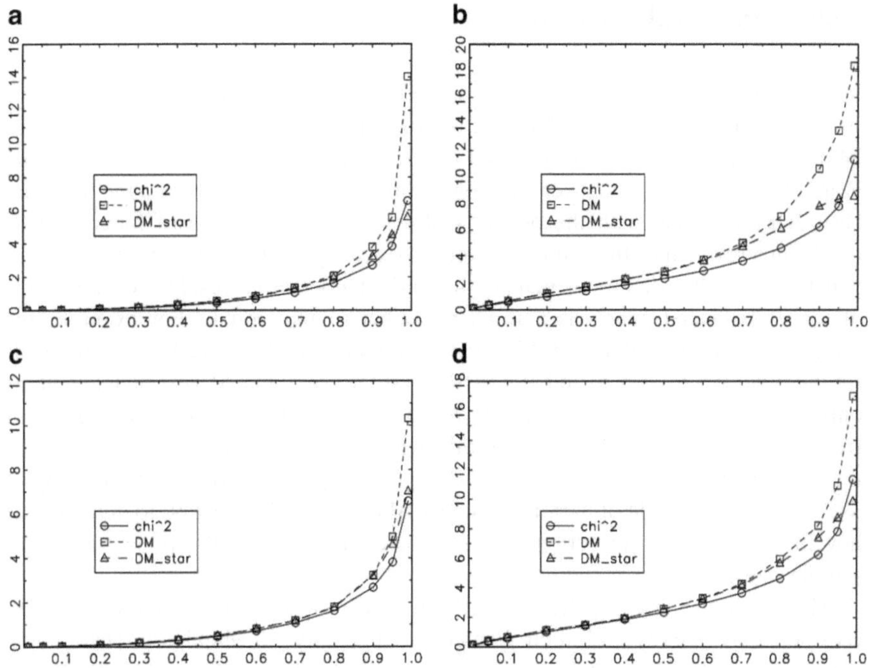

Fig. 13.3 Quantiles of chi-square and bootstrap distribution of uncorrected and corrected DM test statistics for two values of q and two sample sizes. (**a**) $q = 1$, $N = 25$ (**b**) $q = 2$, $N = 25$ (**c**) $q = 1$, $N = 65$ (**d**) $q = 2$, $N = 65$

role in accuracy of asymptotic approximations as the sample size: we more than double the sample size between panel (b) and panel (d), and this has a similar effect on the larger model accuracy as replacing it by a model with 2 fewer degrees of freedom. This is consistent with the findings of Hoogland and Boomsma (1998) that the chi-square statistics are sensitive to model size (as measured by the degrees of freedom of the model). A bigger model requires a larger sample size to ensure good behavior of the statistics. At the same time, for the smaller models (panels (a) and (c)), larger sample sizes do not improve the asymptotic approximation by much – the approximation error is small to start with. The corrected statistic displays an improved behavior for both model sizes and both sample sizes.

The sampling distributions we see in the simulations are all farely close to the asymptotic limits. We have not discovered any cases in our simulations when the corrected distribution was farther away from the asymptotic distribution than the sampling distribution, at least visually. It is difficult to predict how the correction will behave in cases when the sampling distribution drastically deviates from the asymptotics or when the models are very large. Yet, based on the presented simulations we should expect the correction to work well for small models as measured by the degrees of freedom and for standard “well behaved” non-normal distributions.

13.6 Empirical Illustration

In this section, we study applicability of the Bartlett-type correction to a covariance structure model of earnings. This type of model has been a focus of many papers in labor economics (see, e.g., MaCurdy 1982; Abowd and Card 1987, 1989; Topel and Ward 1992; Baker 1997; Baker and Solon 2003). Among other things, the literature has been concerned with the puzzling observation that the use of longer panels results in a reversal of the original inference (see, e.g., Baker 1997, p. 358). Longer panels are usually used to estimate higher-order autocovariances. However, the cost of longer balanced panels is a smaller number of individuals. For example, the sample sizes used by Baker (1997) in 10-year panels are 992 and 1,331 individuals for the periods 1967–1976 and 1977–1986, respectively; his 20-year panel contains only 534. On the other hand, as the panel gets longer (q increases), degrees of freedom grow. As mentioned earlier, this generally requires larger sample sizes for the DM statistic to remain close to the asymptotic approximation. In this section, we use parts of the sample of earnings used by Abowd and Card (1989) to demonstrate how the Bartlett-type correction affects the outcomes of a hypothesis test for various sample sizes.

The earnings data are from the Panel Study of Income Dynamics (PSID), conducted by Survey Research Center at University of Michigan. The sample consists of male heads of household, who were between the ages of 21 and 64 in the period 1969 to 1974 and who reported positive earnings in each year. The sample we use – a subsample of the data used by Abowd and Card (1989) – contains 1,578 individuals. Individuals with average hourly earnings greater than $100 or those who reported annual hours worked greater than 4,680 were excluded. A detailed description of the PSID variables is given in Appendix 3. Covariances and correlations between demeaned changes in log of real annual earnings (in 1967 dollars) are displayed in Table 13.1. Covariances are presented below the diagonal, while correlations and their two-tailed p-values are presented above the diagonal.

Table 13.1 Covariances (below diagonal) and correlations (above diagonal) between changes in log-earnings: PSID Males 1967–1974

Covariance/correlation(with two-tailed p-value) of:					
With:	$\Delta \ln e$ 69–70	$\Delta \ln e$ 70–71	$\Delta \ln e$ 71–72	$\Delta \ln e$ 72–73	$\Delta \ln e$ 73–74
$\Delta \ln e$ 69–70	0.228	−0.204	−0.006	0.018	−0.006
		(0)	(0.827)	(0.463)	(0.823)
$\Delta \ln e$ 70–71	−0.04418	0.205	−0.415	−0.082	0
			(0)	(0.001)	(0.994)
$\Delta \ln e$ 71–72	−0.00117	−0.08345	0.197	−0.347	−0.041
				(0)	(0.101)
$\Delta \ln e$ 72–73	0.003442	−0.01447	−0.06	0.152	−0.305
					(0)
$\Delta \ln e$ 73–74	−0.00102	−0.0000303	−0.00697	−0.04518	0.144

A generic population covariance matrix for Table 13.1 can be written as

$$\Sigma(\theta) = \begin{bmatrix} \sigma_1^2 & \sigma_{12} & \sigma_{13} & \sigma_{14} & \sigma_{15} \\ \sigma_{21} & \sigma_2^2 & \sigma_{23} & \sigma_{24} & \sigma_{25} \\ \sigma_{31} & \sigma_{32} & \sigma_3^2 & \sigma_{34} & \sigma_{35} \\ \sigma_{41} & \sigma_{42} & \sigma_{43} & \sigma_4^2 & \sigma_{45} \\ \sigma_{51} & \sigma_{52} & \sigma_{53} & \sigma_{54} & \sigma_5^2 \end{bmatrix}, \qquad (13.28)$$

where $\theta = (\sigma_1, \sigma_{21}, \sigma_{31}, \sigma_{41}, \sigma_{51}, \sigma_2, \sigma_{32}, \sigma_{42}, \sigma_{52}, \sigma_3, \sigma_{43}, \sigma_{53}, \sigma_4, \sigma_{54}, \sigma_5)'$.

The question Abowd and Card (1989) ask is whether the information in the covariance matrix in Table 13.1 could be adequately summarized by some relatively simple statistical model. Specifically, they ask whether an MA(2) process (possibly nonstationary) can serve as the model. Indeed, there are very few covariances (correlations) that are large or statistically significant at lags greater than two. In order to address this concern, two tests were performed using the DM test statistic.

The first one is to test for a nonstationary MA(2) representation of the changes in earnings. The changes in earnings have a nonstationary MA(2) representation if the covariances at lags greater than two are zero. The null is H_0: changes in earnings are nonstationary MA(2), and the alternative is H_1: changes in earnings are not nonstationary MA(2). Equivalently, the null can be rewritten as

$$H_0 : \begin{bmatrix} \sigma_{41} \\ \sigma_{51} \\ \sigma_{52} \end{bmatrix} = \underset{3\times 1}{0}. \qquad (13.29)$$

The second one is to test for a stationary MA(2) representation of the changes in earnings. By a stationary MA(2) representation, we mean (i) $cov(\Delta \ln e_t, \Delta \ln e_{t-j})$ depends only on j and does not change over t, and (ii) $cov(\Delta \ln e_t, \Delta \ln e_{t-j})$ is zero for $|j| > 2$. The null is H_0: changes in earnings are stationary MA(2), and the alternative is H_1: changes in earnings are not stationary MA(2). Equivalently, the null can be rewritten as

$$\begin{aligned} H_0 : \begin{bmatrix} \sigma_{41} \\ \sigma_{51} \\ \sigma_{52} \end{bmatrix} &= \underset{3\times 1}{0}, \\ \sigma_1 = \sigma_2 = \sigma_3 &= \sigma_4 = \sigma_5, \\ \sigma_{21} = \sigma_{32} &= \sigma_{43} = \sigma_{54}, \\ \sigma_{31} = \sigma_{42} &= \sigma_{53}. \end{aligned} \qquad (13.30)$$

The test results are presented in Table 13.2. The values of the uncorrected and corrected DM test statistic (and the corresponding p-values) are very close for both tests. Not surprisingly, the corrections for this relatively large sample are minor to none. We now demonstrate the effect of the Bartlett-type correction as the sample size becomes smaller.

Table 13.2 Goodness-of-fit tests for changes in earnings: PSID males 1967–1974

Goodness-of-fit test	DM test statistic		Asy. p-value	
N = 1,578	Uncorrected	Corrected	Uncorrected	Corrected
I. Nonstationary MA(2) ($df = 3$)	0.3325	0.3320	0.9538	0.9539
II. Stationary MA(2) ($df = 12$)	19.9889	19.6262	0.0673	0.0745

Table 13.3 Testing stationary MA(2) for changes in earnings: PSID males 1967–1974

	DM test statistic		Asy. p-value	
Sample size	Uncorrected	Corrected	Uncorrected	Corrected
N = 1,400	22.21	21.64	0.035	0.042
N = 1,200	24.15	22.83	0.019	0.029
N = 1,000	25.46	22.12	0.012	0.036
N = 900	25.99	20.35	0.010	0.061

As expected, when the sample size becomes smaller the Bartlett-type correction becomes more important. Consider the second test as an example. The results for that test are presented in Table 13.3. We randomly select increasingly smaller subsamples of data. As the sample size decreases from $N = 1{,}400$ to 900, the correction becomes larger to the point at which the outcome of the test is reversed at conventional significance levels. For example, if $N = 900$, the corrected test does not reject at the 5 % level while the uncorrected test does.

We conclude from this table that, for the current number of degrees of freedom, cross sections as large as 900 are not large enough to justify application of the uncorrected first-order asymptotic approximation to this covariance structure model. If used against the asymptotic critical values, the uncorrected DM test severely over-rejects.

This conclusion is based on the assumption that the corrected DM statistic approximates the asymptotic distribution better than the uncorrected one. We have no way of verifying this assumption. However, even though this model features a larger covariance matrix than considered in simulations, the model has three degrees of freedom – a model size which is not much larger than that used in simulations. We assume the correction works for models of this size.

13.7 Concluding Remarks

This paper provides a Bartlett-type correction of the DM test statistic. Our setting covers linear and nonlinear restrictions and all extremum and minimum distance estimators that can be stated in terms of moment conditions, although we focus on covariance structure models. The expansions used to obtained the correction are based on several normality assumptions that can be relaxed using methods similar to Phillips and Park (1988, Appendix B). The correction may work better if we do so but we leave this general case for future work.

We also provide some simulation evidence about the behavior of the corrected test statistic in a fairly general class of covariance structure models. Given the poor performance of Edgeworth approximations documented in settings when the error in the first order asymptotics is large, we present simulations where the errors are relatively small. We find that the correction works extremely well in such settings.

In practice, it is often necessary to consider a very large (as measured by the degrees of freedom of the model) covariance structure model (see, e.g., Herzog et al. 2007; Kenny and McCoach 2003), which makes it difficult to maintain good properties of the DM test and of our correction even in large samples. Moreover, the available data are often very non-normal. In such cases, the correction may perform worse and larger samples may be needed before the correction performs better.

We illustrate using an example from labor economics how in a setting where our correction is likely to work well, the initial inference is reversed after the correction.

Acknowledgements Helpful comments from Gordon Fisher, Nikolay Gospodinov, Jorgen Hansen, Lynda Khalaf, Eric Renault, Paul Rilstone, seminar participants at University of Manitoba (Department of Economics) and Ryerson University (Department of Economics) and participants of the 26th annual meeting of Canadian Econometric Study Group (CESG), the 43rd Conference of the Canadian Economics Association (CEA), and 17th International Panel Data Conference are gratefully acknowledged. Research for this paper was supported by the FQRSC Doctoral Scholarship (Huang), the J. W. McConnell Memorial Graduate Fellowship (Huang) and an FQRSC Research Grant (Prokhorov).

Appendix 1

Theorem 3.1.1 of Kollo and Rosen (2005)

Let $\{x_n\}$ and $\{\varepsilon_n\}$ be sequences of random p-vectors and positive numbers, respectively, and let $x_n - x_0 = o_p(\varepsilon_n)$, where $\varepsilon_n \to 0$ as $n \to \infty$. If the function $f(x)$ from $\mathbb{R}^p$ to $\mathbb{R}^s$ has continuous partial derivatives up to the order $(\mathcal{M}+1)$ in a neighborhood $\mathcal{D}$ of a point x_0, then the function $f(x)$ can be expanded at the point x_0 into the Taylor series

$$f(x) = f(x_0)+\sum_{k=1}^{\mathcal{M}} \frac{1}{k!}\left(I_s \otimes (x-x_0)^{\otimes(k-1)}\right)'\left(\frac{d^k f(x)}{dx^k}\right)'_{x=x_0}(x-x_0)+o(\rho^{\mathcal{M}}(x,x_0)),$$

where the Kroneckerian power $A^{\otimes k}$ for any matrix A is given by $A^{\otimes k} = \underbrace{A \otimes \cdots \otimes A}_{\text{k times}}$ with $A^{\otimes 0} = 1$, $\rho(.,.)$ is the Euclidean distance in $\mathbb{R}^p$, and the matrix derivative for any matrices Y and X is given by $\frac{d^kY}{dX^k} = \frac{d}{dX}\left(\frac{d^{k-1}Y}{dX^{k-1}}\right)$ with $\frac{dY}{dX} \equiv \frac{d\,vec'Y}{d\,vecX}$; and

$$f(x_n) = f(x_0) + \sum_{k=1}^{\mathcal{M}} \frac{1}{k!}\left(I_s \otimes (x_n - x_0)^{\otimes(k-1)}\right)' \times \left(\frac{d^k f(x_n)}{dx_n^k}\right)'_{x_n=x_0} (x_n - x_0) + o_p(\varepsilon_n^{\mathcal{M}}).$$

Appendix 2

Proofs

Proof of Theorem 1: Write (13.11) as

$$DM \cong 1_{DM} + 2_{DM} + 3_{DM} + 4_{DM}, \tag{13.31}$$

where,

$$\begin{aligned} 1_{DM} &= vec'G_N(\hat{\theta}_N)M_1 vecG_N(\hat{\theta}_N), \\ 2_{DM} &= \mathbb{M}'_N(\hat{\theta}_N)M_2 vecD_N(\hat{\theta}_N), \\ 3_{DM} &= -N^{-1/2}vec'G_N(\hat{\theta}_N)M_3 vecD_N(\hat{\theta}_N), \\ 4_{DM} &= N^{-1}\frac{1}{4}vec'D_N(\hat{\theta}_N)M_4 vecD_N(\hat{\theta}_N). \end{aligned}$$

Taking Taylor expansions of $\mathbb{M}_N(\hat{\theta}_N)$, $vec\ G_N(\hat{\theta}_N)$ and $vec\ D_N(\hat{\theta}_N)$ about θ_0 and using (13.5) and (13.7), we have

$$\begin{aligned} \underset{k\times 1}{\mathbb{M}_N(\hat{\theta}_N)} &= \mathbb{M}_N(\theta_0) + G'(\hat{\theta}_N - \theta_0) + \frac{1}{2}[I_k \otimes (\hat{\theta}_N - \theta_0)']D'(\hat{\theta}_N - \theta_0) + o_p(N^{-1}) \\ &= -N^{-1/2}\bar{q} + N^{-1/2}G'B^{-1}G\bar{q} + N^{-1}\frac{1}{2}(I_k \otimes \bar{q}'G'B^{-1})D'B^{-1}G\bar{q} + o_p(N^{-1}), \end{aligned}$$

$$\begin{aligned} \underset{pk\times 1}{vec\ G_N(\hat{\theta}_N)} &= vecG + D'(\hat{\theta}_N - \theta_0) + \frac{1}{2}[I_{pk} \otimes (\hat{\theta}_N - \theta_0)']C'(\hat{\theta}_N - \theta_0) + o_p(N^{-1}) \\ &= vecG + N^{-1/2}D'B^{-1}G\bar{q} + N^{-1}\frac{1}{2}(I_{pk} \otimes \bar{q}'G'B^{-1})C'B^{-1}G\bar{q} + o_p(N^{-1}), \end{aligned}$$

$$\begin{aligned} \underset{p^2k\times 1}{vec\ D_N(\hat{\theta}_N)} &= vecD + C'(\hat{\theta}_N - \theta_0) + o_p(N^{-1/2}) \\ &= vecD + N^{-1/2}C'B^{-1}G\bar{q} + o_p(N^{-1/2}). \end{aligned}$$

Note that we do not need to expand $vecD_N(\hat{\theta}_N)$ further for our purpose. Substituting these expressions into the terms of (13.31) gives:

$$\begin{aligned}
1_{DM} &= vec'G_N(\hat{\theta}_N)M_1vecG_N(\hat{\theta}_N) \\
&= vec'GM_1vecG + N^{-1/2}2\bar{q}'G'B^{-1}DM_1vecG \\
&\quad + N^{-1}[\bar{q}'G'B^{-1}DM_1D'B^{-1}G\bar{q} + \bar{q}'G'B^{-1}C(I_{pk} \otimes B^{-1}G\bar{q})M_1vecG] \\
&\quad + o_p(N^{-1}) \\
&= \bar{q}'P\bar{q} + N^{-1/2}u_1(\bar{q}) + N^{-1}v_1(\bar{q}) + o_p(N^{-1}),
\end{aligned} \tag{13.32}$$

where

$$\underset{k\times k}{P} \equiv G'\mathbb{H}G$$

is a projection matrix, and

$$\begin{aligned}
u_1(\bar{q}) &= 2\bar{q}'G'B^{-1}DM_1vecG, \\
v_1(\bar{q}) &= \bar{q}'G'B^{-1}DM_1D'B^{-1}G\bar{q} + \bar{q}'G'B^{-1}C(I_{pk} \otimes B^{-1}G\bar{q})M_1vecG;
\end{aligned}$$

$$\begin{aligned}
2_{DM} &= \mathbb{M}_N'(\hat{\theta}_N)M_2vecD_N(\hat{\theta}_N) \\
&= -N^{-1/2}\bar{q}'M_2vecD - N^{-1}\bar{q}'M_2C'B^{-1}G\bar{q} \\
&\quad + N^{-1/2}\bar{q}'G'B^{-1}GM_2vecD + N^{-1}\bar{q}'G'B^{-1}GM_2C'B^{-1}G\bar{q} \\
&\quad + N^{-1}\frac{1}{2}\bar{q}'G'B^{-1}D(I_k \otimes B^{-1}G\bar{q})M_2vecD + o_p(N^{-1}) \\
&= N^{-1/2}(\bar{q}'G'B^{-1}M_2vecD - \bar{q}'M_2vecD) \\
&\quad + N^{-1}[\bar{q}'G'B^{-1}GM_2C'B^{-1}G\bar{q} - \bar{q}'M_2C'B^{-1}G\bar{q} \\
&\qquad + \frac{1}{2}\bar{q}'G'B^{-1}D(I_k \otimes B^{-1}G\bar{q})M_2vecD] + o_p(N^{-1}) \\
&= N^{-1/2}u_2(\bar{q}) + N^{-1}v_2(\bar{q}) + o_p(N^{-1}),
\end{aligned} \tag{13.33}$$

where

$$\begin{aligned}
u_2(\bar{q}) &= \bar{q}'G'B^{-1}GM_2vecD - \bar{q}'M_2vecD \\
&= \bar{q}'(G'B^{-1}G - I_k)M_2vecD, \\
v_2(\bar{q}) &= \bar{q}'G'B^{-1}GM_2C'B^{-1}G\bar{q} - \bar{q}'M_2C'B^{-1}G\bar{q} \\
&\quad + \frac{1}{2}\bar{q}'G'B^{-1}D(I_k \otimes B^{-1}G\bar{q})M_2vecD \\
&= \bar{q}'(G'B^{-1}G - I_k)M_2C'B^{-1}G\bar{q} + \frac{1}{2}\bar{q}'G'B^{-1}D(I_k \otimes B^{-1}G\bar{q})M_2vecD;
\end{aligned}$$

$$\begin{aligned}
3_{DM} &= -N^{-1/2} vec' G_N(\hat{\theta}_N) M_3 vec D_N(\hat{\theta}_N) \\
&= -N^{-1/2} vec' G M_3 vec D - N^{-1} vec' G M_3 C' B^{-1} G \bar{q} \\
&\quad - N^{-1} \bar{q}' G' B^{-1} D M_3 vec D + o_p(N^{-1}) \\
&= N^{-1/2} u_3(\bar{q}) + N^{-1} v_3(\bar{q}) + o_p(N^{-1}), \qquad (13.34)
\end{aligned}$$

and

$$\begin{aligned}
u_3(\bar{q}) &= -vec' G M_3 vec D, \\
v_3(\bar{q}) &= -vec' G M_3 C' B^{-1} G \bar{q} - \bar{q}' G' B^{-1} D M_3 vec D \\
&= -\bar{q}' G' B^{-1} C M_3' vec G - \bar{q}' G' B^{-1} D M_3 vec D;
\end{aligned}$$

$$\begin{aligned}
4_{DM} &= N^{-1} \frac{1}{4} vec' D_N(\hat{\theta}_N) M_4 vec D_N(\hat{\theta}_N) \\
&= N^{-1} \frac{1}{4} vec' D M_4 vec D + o_p(N^{-1}) \\
&= N^{-1} v_4(\bar{q}) + o_p(N^{-1}), \qquad (13.35)
\end{aligned}$$

where

$$v_4(\bar{q}) = \frac{1}{4} vec' D M_4 vec D.$$

Finally, collecting the terms (13.32)–(13.35) gives Eq. (13.12). □

Proof of Lemma 1: From Theorem 1, if $u_i(\bar{q})$ $(i = 1, 2, 3)$ and $v_i(\bar{q})$ $(i = 1, 2, 3, 4)$ could be rewritten as

$$u_i(\bar{q}) = vec' J_i (\bar{q} \otimes \bar{q} \otimes \bar{q}), \qquad (13.36)$$

$$v_i(\bar{q}) = tr[L_i(\bar{q}\bar{q}' \otimes \bar{q}\bar{q}')], \qquad (13.37)$$

then,

$$u(\bar{q}) = vec' J (\bar{q} \otimes \bar{q} \otimes \bar{q}),$$

$$v(\bar{q}) = tr[L(\bar{q}\bar{q}' \otimes \bar{q}\bar{q}')],$$

where

$$vec J = vec J_1 + vec J_2 + vec J_3,$$

and

$$L = L_1 + L_2 + L_3 + L_4.$$

Therefore, the proof is reduced to showing (13.36) and (13.37).

Using

$$(A \otimes C)(B \otimes D) = (AB) \otimes (CD),$$
$$K_{p,q} vecA = vec(A'),$$
$$A \otimes B = K_{p,r}(B \otimes A)K_{s,q},$$

for $A : p \times q$ and $B : r \times s$ where K is the commutation matrix, we can rewrite (13.14):

$$\begin{aligned} u_1(\bar{q}) &= 2\bar{q}'G'B^{-1}D(I_k \otimes \mathbb{H}G\bar{q})vec(\bar{q}'G'\mathbb{H}G) \\ &= 2\bar{q}'G'\mathbb{H}G(I_k \otimes \bar{q}'G'\mathbb{H})(\bar{q}'G'B^{-1} \otimes I_{pk})vec(D') \\ &= 2\bar{q}'G'\mathbb{H}G(I_k \otimes \bar{q}'G'\mathbb{H})(I_{pk} \otimes \bar{q}'G'B^{-1})vecD \\ &= 2(\bar{q}'G'\mathbb{H}G \otimes \bar{q}'G'\mathbb{H} \otimes \bar{q}'G'B^{-1})vecD \\ &= 2(\bar{q}' \otimes \bar{q}' \otimes \bar{q}')(G'\mathbb{H}G \otimes G'\mathbb{H} \otimes G'B^{-1})vecD \\ &= vec'J_1(\bar{q} \otimes \bar{q} \otimes \bar{q}), \end{aligned} \tag{13.38}$$

where

$$vecJ_1 = 2(G'\mathbb{H}G \otimes G'\mathbb{H} \otimes G'B^{-1})vecD. \tag{13.39}$$

Let

$$R_1 = (\mathbb{H}G \otimes B^{-1}G)(\bar{q}\bar{q}' \otimes \bar{q}\bar{q}')(G'\mathbb{H} \otimes G'B^{-1}), \tag{13.40}$$

partition $vecD$ as

$$\underset{p^2k \times 1}{vecD} = \begin{bmatrix} V_{D1} \\ V_{D2} \\ \vdots \\ V_{Dk} \end{bmatrix} \tag{13.41}$$

where each subvector V_{Di} is $p^2 \times 1$, and let

$$V_D = V_{D1}V'_{D1} + V_{D2}V'_{D2} + \cdots + V_{Dk}V'_{Dk}. \tag{13.42}$$

Then, since

$$\begin{aligned} (I_k \otimes \bar{q}'G'\mathbb{H})D'B^{-1}G\bar{q} &= (I_k \otimes \bar{q}'G'\mathbb{H})(\bar{q}'G'B^{-1} \otimes I_{pk})vec(D') \\ &= (I_k \otimes \bar{q}'G'\mathbb{H})(I_{pk} \otimes \bar{q}'G'B^{-1})vecD \\ &= (I_k \otimes \bar{q}'G'\mathbb{H} \otimes \bar{q}'G'B^{-1})vecD, \end{aligned}$$

the first term of $v_1(\bar{q})$ in (13.17) becomes

$$\begin{aligned}
&\bar{q}'G'B^{-1}D(I_k\otimes \mathbb{H}G\bar{q})(I_k\otimes \bar{q}'G'\mathbb{H})D'B^{-1}G\bar{q}\\
&\quad= vec'D(I_k\otimes \mathbb{H}G\bar{q}\otimes B^{-1}G\bar{q})(I_k\otimes \bar{q}'G'\mathbb{H}\otimes \bar{q}'G'B^{-1})vecD\\
&\quad= vec'D(I_k\otimes R_1)vecD\\
&\quad= \begin{bmatrix} V'_{D1} & V'_{D2} & \cdots & V'_{Dk}\end{bmatrix}\begin{bmatrix} R_1 & & & 0\\ & R_1 & & \\ & & \ddots & \\ 0 & & & R_1\end{bmatrix}\begin{bmatrix} V_{D1}\\ V_{D2}\\ \vdots \\ V_{Dk}\end{bmatrix}\\
&\quad= V'_{D1}R_1V_{D1}+V'_{D2}R_1V_{D2}+\cdots+V'_{Dk}R_1V_{Dk}\\
&\quad= tr[(V_{D1}V'_{D1}+V_{D2}V'_{D2}+\cdots+V_{Dk}V'_{Dk})R_1]\\
&\quad= tr[V_D(\mathbb{H}G\otimes B^{-1}G)(\bar{q}\bar{q}'\otimes \bar{q}\bar{q}')(G'\mathbb{H}\otimes G'B^{-1})]\\
&\quad= tr[(G'\mathbb{H}\otimes G'B^{-1})V_D(\mathbb{H}G\otimes B^{-1}G)(\bar{q}\bar{q}'\otimes \bar{q}\bar{q}')]. \qquad (13.43)
\end{aligned}$$

Similarly, let

$$R_2 = (\mathbb{H}G\otimes B^{-1}G)(\bar{q}\otimes \bar{q}), \qquad (13.44)$$

$$R_3 = \bar{q}'G'\mathbb{H}, \qquad (13.45)$$

partition $G'B^{-1}C$ and $vecG$ as

$$\underset{k\times p^2k}{G'B^{-1}C} = \begin{bmatrix} M_{GC1} & M_{GC2} & \cdots & M_{GCk}\end{bmatrix}, \qquad (13.46)$$

$$\underset{pk\times 1}{vecG} = \begin{bmatrix} V_{G1}\\ V_{G2}\\ \vdots \\ V_{Gk}\end{bmatrix}, \qquad (13.47)$$

where M_{GCi} and V_{Gi} are $k\times p^2$ and $p\times 1$ respectively, and let

$$M_V = M'_{GC1}\otimes V'_{G1}+M'_{GC2}\otimes V'_{G2}+\cdots+M'_{GCk}\otimes V'_{Gk}. \qquad (13.48)$$

Then, since

$$\begin{aligned}
\bar{q}'m\bar{q}'M(\bar{q}\otimes\bar{q}) &= m'\bar{q}\bar{q}'M(\bar{q}\otimes\bar{q})\\
&= [(\bar{q}\otimes\bar{q})'M'\otimes m']vec(\bar{q}\bar{q}')\\
&= (\bar{q}\otimes\bar{q})'(M'\otimes m')(\bar{q}\otimes\bar{q})\\
&= tr[(M'\otimes m')(\bar{q}\bar{q}'\otimes\bar{q}\bar{q}')]
\end{aligned}$$

for some vector m and matrix M of appropriate sizes, the second term of $v_1(\bar{q})$ in (13.17) becomes

$$\begin{aligned}
&\bar{q}'G'B^{-1}C(I_{pk} \otimes B^{-1}G\bar{q})(I_k \otimes \mathbb{H}G\bar{q})(I_k \otimes \bar{q}'G'\mathbb{H})vecG \\
&\quad = \bar{q}'G'B^{-1}C(I_k \otimes R_2)(I_k \otimes R_3)vecG \\
&\quad = \bar{q}'\left[M_{GC1}\ M_{GC2} \cdots M_{GCk}\right]\begin{bmatrix} R_2 & & 0 \\ & R_2 & \\ & & \ddots & \\ 0 & & & R_2 \end{bmatrix}\begin{bmatrix} R_3 & & 0 \\ & R_3 & \\ & & \ddots & \\ 0 & & & R_3 \end{bmatrix}\begin{bmatrix} V_{G1} \\ V_{G2} \\ \vdots \\ V_{Gk} \end{bmatrix} \\
&\quad = \sum_{i=1}^{k}(\bar{q}'M_{GCi}R_2R_3V_{Gi}) \\
&\quad = tr\sum_{i=1}^{k}[\bar{q}'M_{GCi}(\mathbb{H}G \otimes B^{-1}G)(\bar{q} \otimes \bar{q})\bar{q}'G'\mathbb{H}V_{Gi}] \\
&\quad = tr\sum_{i=1}^{k}[\bar{q}'G'\mathbb{H}V_{Gi}\bar{q}'M_{GCi}(\mathbb{H}G \otimes B^{-1}G)(\bar{q} \otimes \bar{q})] \\
&\quad = tr\sum_{i=1}^{k}\{\{[(G'\mathbb{H} \otimes G'B^{-1})M'_{GCi}] \otimes V'_{Gi}\mathbb{H}G\}(\bar{q}\bar{q}' \otimes \bar{q}\bar{q}')\} \\
&\quad = tr\sum_{i=1}^{k}[(G'\mathbb{H} \otimes G'B^{-1})(M'_{GCi} \otimes V'_{Gi})(I_k \otimes \mathbb{H}G)(\bar{q}\bar{q}' \otimes \bar{q}\bar{q}')] \\
&\quad = tr[(G'\mathbb{H} \otimes G'B^{-1})M_V(I_k \otimes \mathbb{H}G)(\bar{q}\bar{q}' \otimes \bar{q}\bar{q}')]. \qquad (13.49)
\end{aligned}$$

From (13.43) and (13.49), (13.17) can be rewritten as

$$v_1(\bar{q}) = tr[L_1(\bar{q}\bar{q}' \otimes \bar{q}\bar{q}')], \qquad (13.50)$$

where

$$L_1 = (G'\mathbb{H} \otimes G'B^{-1})V_D(\mathbb{H}G \otimes B^{-1}G) + (G'\mathbb{H} \otimes G'B^{-1})M_V(I_k \otimes \mathbb{H}G). \qquad (13.51)$$

Similar to $u_1(\bar{q})$, $u_2(\bar{q})$ in (13.15) can be rewritten as

$$\begin{aligned}
u_2(\bar{q}) &= \bar{q}'(G'B^{-1}G - I_k)(I_k \otimes \bar{q}'G'\mathbb{H} \otimes \bar{q}'G'\mathbb{H})vecD \\
&= (\bar{q}' \otimes \bar{q}' \otimes \bar{q}')[(G'B^{-1}G - I_k) \otimes G'\mathbb{H} \otimes G'\mathbb{H}]vecD \\
&= vec'J_2(\bar{q} \otimes \bar{q} \otimes \bar{q}), \qquad (13.52)
\end{aligned}$$

where

$$vecJ_2 = [(G'B^{-1}G - I_k) \otimes G'\mathbb{H} \otimes G'\mathbb{H}]vecD. \tag{13.53}$$

The first term of $v_2(\bar{q})$ in (13.18) can be written as

$$\bar{q}'G'B^{-1}C(I_k \otimes \mathbb{H}G\bar{q} \otimes \mathbb{H}G\bar{q})(G'B^{-1}G - I_k)\bar{q}.$$

Since

$$\begin{aligned}(G'B^{-1}G - I_k)\bar{q} &= vec[\bar{q}'(G'B^{-1}G - I_k)] \\ &= (I_k \otimes \bar{q}')vec(G'B^{-1}G - I_k),\end{aligned}$$

and $vec(G'B^{-1}G - I_k)$ can be partitioned as

$$vec(G'B^{-1}G - I_k) = \begin{bmatrix} V_{GI1} \\ V_{GI2} \\ \vdots \\ V_{GIk} \end{bmatrix} \tag{13.54}$$

where V_{GIi} is $k \times 1$, we may mimic the second term of $v_1(\bar{q})$ and rewrite the first term of $v_2(\bar{q})$ further as

$$\begin{aligned} tr\sum_{i=1}^{k}&[\bar{q}'M_{GCi}(\mathbb{H}G \otimes \mathbb{H}G)(\bar{q} \otimes \bar{q})\bar{q}'V_{GIi}] \\ &= tr[(G'\mathbb{H} \otimes G'\mathbb{H})M_{VI}(\bar{q}\bar{q}' \otimes \bar{q}\bar{q}')], \end{aligned} \tag{13.55}$$

where

$$M_{VI} = M'_{GC1} \otimes V'_{GI1} + M'_{GC2} \otimes V'_{GI2} + \cdots + M'_{GCk} \otimes V'_{GIk}. \tag{13.56}$$

Similar to the first term of $v_1(\bar{q})$, since

$$\bar{q}'G'B^{-1}D = vec'(\bar{q}'G'B^{-1}D) = vec'D(I_{pk} \otimes B^{-1}G\bar{q}),$$

the second term of $v_2(\bar{q})$ in (13.18) can be rewritten as

$$\begin{aligned} &\frac{1}{2}vec'D(I_k \otimes B^{-1}G\bar{q} \otimes B^{-1}G\bar{q})(I_k \otimes \bar{q}'G'\mathbb{H} \otimes \bar{q}'G'\mathbb{H})vecD \\ &= \frac{1}{2}tr[V_D(B^{-1}G \otimes B^{-1}G)(\bar{q}\bar{q}' \otimes \bar{q}\bar{q}')(G'\mathbb{H} \otimes G'\mathbb{H})] \\ &= tr[\frac{1}{2}(G'\mathbb{H} \otimes G'\mathbb{H})V_D(B^{-1}G \otimes B^{-1}G)(\bar{q}\bar{q}' \otimes \bar{q}\bar{q}')]. \end{aligned} \tag{13.57}$$

From (13.55) and (13.57), we have

$$v_2(\bar{q}) = tr[L_2(\bar{q}\bar{q}' \otimes \bar{q}\bar{q}')], \tag{13.58}$$

where

$$L_2 = (G'\mathbb{H} \otimes G'\mathbb{H})M_{VI} + \frac{1}{2}(G'\mathbb{H} \otimes G'\mathbb{H})V_D(B^{-1}G \otimes B^{-1}G). \tag{13.59}$$

Since

$$\begin{aligned} &vec'G(I_k \otimes \mathbb{H}G\bar{q}) \\ &= [(I_k \otimes \bar{q}'G'\mathbb{H})vecG]' \\ &= \bar{q}'G'\mathbb{H}G, \end{aligned}$$

(13.16) becomes

$$\begin{aligned} u_3(\bar{q}) &= -\bar{q}'G'\mathbb{H}G(I_k \otimes \bar{q}'G'\mathbb{H} \otimes \bar{q}'G'\mathbb{H})vecD \\ &= -(\bar{q}' \otimes \bar{q}' \otimes \bar{q}')(G'\mathbb{H}G \otimes G'\mathbb{H} \otimes G'\mathbb{H})vecD \\ &= vec'J_3(\bar{q} \otimes \bar{q} \otimes \bar{q}), \end{aligned} \tag{13.60}$$

where

$$vecJ_3 = -(G'\mathbb{H}G \otimes G'\mathbb{H} \otimes G'\mathbb{H})vecD. \tag{13.61}$$

Similar to the second term of $v_1(\bar{q})$, the first term of $v_3(\bar{q})$ in (13.19) can be rewritten as

$$\begin{aligned} &-\bar{q}'G'B^{-1}C(I_k \otimes \mathbb{H}G\bar{q} \otimes \mathbb{H}G\bar{q})(I_k \otimes \bar{q}'G'\mathbb{H})vecG \\ &= tr\sum_{i=1}^{k}[-\bar{q}'M_{GCi}(\mathbb{H}G \otimes \mathbb{H}G)(\bar{q} \otimes \bar{q})\bar{q}'G'\mathbb{H}V_{Gi}] \\ &= tr[-(G'\mathbb{H} \otimes G'\mathbb{H})M_V(I_k \otimes \mathbb{H}G)(\bar{q}\bar{q}' \otimes \bar{q}\bar{q}')]. \end{aligned} \tag{13.62}$$

Similar to the second term of $v_2(\bar{q})$, the second term of $v_3(\bar{q})$ in (13.19) can be rewritten as

$$\begin{aligned} &-\bar{q}'G'B^{-1}D(I_k \otimes \mathbb{H}G\bar{q})(I_k \otimes \bar{q}'G'\mathbb{H} \otimes \bar{q}'G'\mathbb{H})vecD \\ &= -vec'D(I_{pk} \otimes B^{-1}G\bar{q})(I_k \otimes \mathbb{H}G\bar{q})(I_k \otimes \bar{q}'G'\mathbb{H} \otimes \bar{q}'G'\mathbb{H})vecD \\ &= -vec'D(I_k \otimes \mathbb{H}G\bar{q} \otimes B^{-1}G\bar{q})(I_k \otimes \bar{q}'G'\mathbb{H} \otimes \bar{q}'G'\mathbb{H})vecD \\ &= tr[-V_D(\mathbb{H}G \otimes B^{-1}G)(\bar{q}\bar{q}' \otimes \bar{q}\bar{q}')(G'\mathbb{H} \otimes G'\mathbb{H})] \\ &= tr[-(G'\mathbb{H} \otimes G'\mathbb{H})V_D(\mathbb{H}G \otimes B^{-1}G)(\bar{q}\bar{q}' \otimes \bar{q}\bar{q}')]. \end{aligned} \tag{13.63}$$

From (13.62) and (13.63), we have

$$v_3(\bar{q}) = tr[L_3(\bar{q}\bar{q}' \otimes \bar{q}\bar{q}')], \tag{13.64}$$

where

$$L_3 = -(G'\mathbb{H} \otimes G'\mathbb{H})M_V(I_k \otimes \mathbb{H}G) - (G'\mathbb{H} \otimes G'\mathbb{H})V_D(\mathbb{H}G \otimes B^{-1}G). \tag{13.65}$$

Similar to the first term of $v_1(\bar{q})$, $v_4(\bar{q})$ in (13.20) can be easily rewritten as

$$\begin{aligned} v_4(\bar{q}) &= \frac{1}{4}tr[V_D(\mathbb{H}G \otimes \mathbb{H}G)(\bar{q}\bar{q}' \otimes \bar{q}\bar{q}')(G'\mathbb{H} \otimes G'\mathbb{H})] \\ &= tr[\frac{1}{4}(G'\mathbb{H} \otimes G'\mathbb{H})V_D(\mathbb{H}G \otimes \mathbb{H}G)(\bar{q}\bar{q}' \otimes \bar{q}\bar{q}')] \\ &= tr[L_4(\bar{q}\bar{q}' \otimes \bar{q}\bar{q})], \end{aligned} \tag{13.66}$$

where

$$L_4 = \frac{1}{4}(G'\mathbb{H} \otimes G'\mathbb{H})V_D(\mathbb{H}G \otimes \mathbb{H}G). \tag{13.67}$$

By using (13.38), (13.50), (13.52), (13.58), (13.60), (13.64) and (13.66), we obtain (13.36) and (13.37), thus finishing the proof. □

Proof of Theorem 2: First, a_i and b_i are defined (Phillips and Park 1988) as

$$a_i = tr(A_i) \quad (i = 0, 1, 2), \tag{13.68}$$

where

$$\begin{aligned} A_0 &= L[(I + K_{k,k})(\bar{P} \otimes \bar{P}) + vec\bar{P}vec'\bar{P}], \\ A_1 &= L[(I + K_{k,k})(\bar{P} \otimes P + P \otimes \bar{P}) + vec\bar{P}vec'P + vecPvec'\bar{P}], \\ A_2 &= L[(I + K_{k,k})(P \otimes P) + vecPvec'P]; \end{aligned}$$

$$b_i = vec'JB_ivecJ \quad (i = 1, 2, 3), \tag{13.69}$$

where

$$\begin{aligned} B_0 = {} & H(\bar{P} \otimes \bar{P} \otimes \bar{P}) + H(\bar{P} \otimes vec\bar{P}vec'\bar{P})H \\ & + \bar{P} \otimes K_{k,k}(\bar{P} \otimes \bar{P}) + K_{k,k}(\bar{P} \otimes \bar{P}) \otimes \bar{P} \\ & + K_{k,k^2}[\bar{P} \otimes K_{k,k}(\bar{P} \otimes \bar{P})]K_{k^2,k} = C_0(\bar{P}),\ say, \end{aligned}$$

$$
\begin{aligned}
B_1 &= H(P \otimes \bar{P} \otimes \bar{P})H \\
&\quad + H(P \otimes vec\bar{P}vec'\bar{P} + \bar{P} \otimes vecPvec'\bar{P} + \bar{P} \otimes vec\bar{P}vec'P)H \\
&\quad + P \otimes K_{k,k}(\bar{P} \otimes \bar{P}) + \bar{P} \otimes K_{k,k}(P \otimes \bar{P}) \\
&\quad + \bar{P} \otimes K_{k,k}(\bar{P} \otimes P) + K_{k,k}(P \otimes \bar{P}) \otimes \bar{P} \\
&\quad + K_{k,k}(\bar{P} \otimes \bar{P}) \otimes \bar{P} + K_{k,k}(\bar{P} \otimes \bar{P}) \otimes P \\
&\quad + K_{k,k^2}\{[P \otimes K_{k,k}(\bar{P} \otimes \bar{P})] + [\bar{P} \otimes K_{k,k}(P \otimes \bar{P})] \\
&\qquad + [\bar{P} \otimes K_{k,k}(\bar{P} \otimes P)]\}K_{k^2,k} = C_1(\bar{P}, P), \ say, \\
B_2 &= C_1(P, \bar{P}), \\
B_3 &= C_0(P),
\end{aligned}
$$

with

$$
\begin{aligned}
H &= I + K_{k,k^2} + K_{k^2,k}, \\
\bar{P} &\equiv I - P.
\end{aligned}
$$

Secondly, from (13.68),

$$
\begin{aligned}
a_0 = tr(A_0) &= tr\{L[(I + K_{k,k})(\bar{P} \otimes \bar{P}) + vec\bar{P}vec'\bar{P}]\} \\
&= tr[(\bar{P} \otimes \bar{P})L(I + K_{k,k}) + vec'\bar{P}Lvec\bar{P}] \\
&= tr[(\bar{P} \otimes \bar{P})L(I + K_{k,k})] + tr(vec'\bar{P}Lvec\bar{P}). \qquad (13.70)
\end{aligned}
$$

Using (13.13) and $\bar{P} \equiv I - P$, we have

$$(A'B^{-1}G)\bar{P} = 0, \qquad (13.71)$$

$$\bar{P}(G'B^{-1}A) = 0. \qquad (13.72)$$

Therefore, by (13.21)–(13.25),

$$(\bar{P} \otimes \bar{P})L = 0, \qquad (13.73)$$

and

$$(\mathbb{H}G \otimes B^{-1}G)vec\bar{P} = vec(B^{-1}G\bar{P}G\mathbb{H}) = 0, \qquad (13.74)$$

$$(I_k \otimes \mathbb{H}G)vec\bar{P} = vec(\mathbb{H}G\bar{P}) = 0. \qquad (13.75)$$

Combining (13.74) and (13.75) with (13.22) yields

$$L_1 vec\bar{P} = 0. \qquad (13.76)$$

Similarly,

$$L_3 vec\bar{P} = 0, \tag{13.77}$$

$$L_4 vec\bar{P} = 0, \tag{13.78}$$

and

$$vec'\bar{P}L_2 = (L_2' vec\bar{P})' = 0. \tag{13.79}$$

From (13.76)–(13.79),

$$tr(vec'\bar{P}Lvec\bar{P}) = 0. \tag{13.80}$$

Substituting (13.73) and (13.80) into (13.70) gives

$$a_0 = 0. \tag{13.81}$$

Also, from (13.69),

$$\begin{aligned} b_1 &= vec'JB_1vecJ \\ &= vec'JH(P \otimes \bar{P} \otimes \bar{P})HvecJ \\ &\quad + vec'JH(P \otimes vec\bar{P}vec'\bar{P} + \bar{P} \otimes vecPvec'\bar{P} + \bar{P} \otimes vec\bar{P}vec'P)HvecJ \\ &\quad + vec'J[P \otimes K_{k,k}(\bar{P} \otimes \bar{P}) + \bar{P} \otimes K_{k,k}(P \otimes \bar{P})]vecJ \\ &\quad + vec'J[\bar{P} \otimes K_{k,k}(\bar{P} \otimes P) + K_{k,k}(P \otimes \bar{P}) \otimes \bar{P}]vecJ \\ &\quad + vec'J[K_{k,k}(\bar{P} \otimes \bar{P}) \otimes \bar{P} + K_{k,k}(\bar{P} \otimes \bar{P}) \otimes P]vecJ \\ &\quad + vec'JK_{k,k^2}\{[P \otimes K_{k,k}(\bar{P} \otimes \bar{P})] + [\bar{P} \otimes K_{k,k}(P \otimes \bar{P})] \\ &\qquad + [\bar{P} \otimes K_{k,k}(\bar{P} \otimes P)]\}K_{k^2,k}vecJ. \end{aligned} \tag{13.82}$$

Using

$$\begin{aligned} K_{p,q}vecA &= vec(A'), \\ A \otimes B &= K_{p,r}(B \otimes A)K_{s,q}, \end{aligned}$$

for $A : p \times q$ and $B : r \times s$ where K is the commutation matrix, the following equations are obtained:

$$K_{k,k^2}vecJ_1 = 2(G'B^{-1} \otimes G'\mathbb{H}G \otimes G'\mathbb{H})vec(D'), \tag{13.83}$$

$$K_{k,k^2}vecJ_2 = [G'\mathbb{H} \otimes (G'B^{-1}G - I_k) \otimes G'\mathbb{H}]vec(D'), \tag{13.84}$$

$$K_{k,k^2}vecJ_3 = -(G'\mathbb{H} \otimes G'\mathbb{H}G \otimes G'\mathbb{H})vec(D'); \tag{13.85}$$

$$K_{k^2,k}vecJ_1 = 2(G'\mathbb{H} \otimes G'B^{-1} \otimes G'\mathbb{H}G)K_{p^2,k}vecD, \tag{13.86}$$

$$K_{k^2,k}vecJ_2 = [G'\mathbb{H} \otimes G'\mathbb{H} \otimes (G'B^{-1}G - I_k)]K_{p^2,k}vecD, \tag{13.87}$$

$$K_{k^2,k}vecJ_3 = -(G'\mathbb{H} \otimes G'\mathbb{H} \otimes G'\mathbb{H}G)K_{p^2,k}vecD. \tag{13.88}$$

Then, substituting (13.83)–(13.88) into (13.82), and using

$$vec(ABC) = (C' \otimes A)vecB,$$

$$(A \otimes B)' = A' \otimes B',$$

$$(A \otimes C)(B \otimes D) = (AB) \otimes (CD),$$

together with (13.71) and (13.72) yield

$$b_1 = 0. \tag{13.89}$$

Given (13.81) and (13.89), the proof of Theorem 2.4 in Phillips and Park (1988) establishes the conclusion of Theorem 2. □

Appendix 3

Data Description

The earnings data used are drawn from the Panel Study of Income Dynamics (PSID), available at http://psidonline.isr.umich.edu/

The sample consists of men who were heads of household from 1969 to 1974, between the ages of 21 (not inclusive) and 64 (not inclusive), and who reported positive earnings in each year. Individuals with average hourly earnings greater than \$100 or reported annual hours greater than 4680 were excluded.

Variables V7492, V7490, V0313, V0794, V7460, V7476, V7491 listed on p.443 of Abowd and Card (1989) are not available now on the PSID website. The variables for sex listed on that page are not consistent with those on the PSID website. The following are the PSID variables used here:

- ANNUAL EARNINGS: V1196, V1897, V2498, V3051, V3463, V3863;
- ANNUAL HOURS: V1138, V1839, V2439, V3027, V3423, V3823;
- SEX: ER32000;
- AGE: ER30046.

References

Abowd JM, Card D (1987) Intertemporal labor supply and long-term employment contracts. Am Econ Rev 77:50–68

Abowd JM, Card D (1989) On the Covariance structure of earnings and hours changes. Econometrica 57:411–445

Baker M (1997) Growth-rate heterogeneity and the covariance structure of life-cycle earnings. J Labor Econ 15:338–375

Baker M, Solon G (2003) Earnings dynamics and inequality among Canadian men, 1976–1992: evidence from longitudinal income tax records. J Labor Econ 21:289–321

Barndorff-Nielsen O, Cox DR (1979) Edgeworth and saddle-point approximations with statistical applications. J R Stat Soc B (Methodol) 41:279–312

Bartlett MS (1937) Properties of sufficiency and statistical tests. Proc R Soc Lond A Math Phys Sci 160:268–282

Breusch TS, Schmidt P (1988) Alternative forms of the Wald test: how long is a piece of string? Commun Stat Theory Methods 17:2789–2795

Browne MW (1984) Asymptotically distribution-free methods for the analysis of covariance structures. Br J Math Stat Psychol 37:62–83

Chou C-P, Bentler PM, Satorra A (1991) Scaled test statistics and robust standard errors for non-normal data in covariance structure analysis: a Monte Carlo study. Br J Math Stat Psychol 44:347–357

Clark TE (1996) Small-sample properties of estimators of nonlinear models of covariance structure. J Bus Econ Stat 14:367–373

Cribari-Neto F, Cordeiro GM (1996) On Bartlett and Bartlett-type corrections. Econ Rev 15:339–367

Hall P (1992) The bootstrap and the edgeworth expansion. Springer, New York

Hansen LP (1982) Large sample properties of generalized method of moments estimators. Econometrica 50:1029–1054

Hansen BE (2006) Edgeworth Expansions for the Wald and GMM statistics for nonlinear restrictions. In: Corbae D, Durlauf SN, Hansen BE (eds) Econometric theory and practice: frontiers of analysis and applied research. Cambridge University Press, Cambridge/New York, pp 9–35

Hansen L, Heaton J, Yaron A (1996) Finite-sample properties of some alternative GMM estimators. J Bus Econ Stat 14:262–280

Hausman J, Kuersteiner G (2008) Difference in difference meets generalized least squares: higher order properties of hypotheses tests. J Econ 144:371–391

Herzog W, Boomsma A, Reinecke S (2007) The model-size effect on traditional and modified tests of covariance structures. Struct Equ Model Multidisciplinary J 14:361–390

Hoogland JJ, Boomsma A (1998) Robustness studies in covariance structure modeling: an overview and a meta-analysis. Sociol Methods Res 26:329–367

Kallenberg WCM (1993) Interpretation and manipulation of Edgeworth expansions. Ann Inst Stat Math 45:341–351

Kenny DA, McCoach DB (2003) Effect of the number of variables on measures of fit in structural equation modeling. Struct Equ Model Multidisciplinary J 10:333–351

Kollo T, von Rosen D (2005) Advanced multivariate statistics with matrices. Springer, Dordrecht

Korin BP (1968) On the distribution of a statistic used for testing a covariance matrix. Biometrika 55:171–178

Linton O (2002) Edgeworth approximations for semiparametric instrumental variable estimators and test statistics. J Econom 106:325–368

MaCurdy TE (1982) The use of time series processes to model the error structure of earnings in a longitudinal data analysis. J Econom 18:83–114

Magee L (1989) An Edgeworth test size correction for the linear model with AR(1) errors. Econometrica 57:661–674

Muthen B, Kaplan D (1992) A comparison of some methodologies for the factor analysis of non-normal Likert variables: a note on the size of the model. Br J Math Stat Psychol 45:19–30
Nagarsenker BN, Pillai KCS (1973) Distribution of the likelihood ratio criterion for testing a hypothesis specifying a covariance matrix. Biometrika 60:359–364
Newey W, McFadden D (1994) Large sample estimation and hypothesis testing. In: Handbook of econometrics, vol IV. North-Holland, Amsterdam, pp 2113–2241
Newey WK, West KD (1987) Hypothesis testing with efficient method of moments estimation. Int Econ Rev 28:777–787
Ogasawara H (2009) Asymptotic expansions of the distributions of the chi-square statistic based on the asymptotically distribution-free theory in covariance structures. J Stat Plan Inference 139:3246–3261
Phillips PCB (1977) A general theorem in the theory of asymptotic expansions as approximations to the finite sample distributions of econometric estimators. Econometrica 45:1517–1534
Phillips PCB (1978) Edgeworth and saddlepoint approximations in the first-order noncircular autoregression. Biometrika 65:91–98
Phillips PCB (1983) ERA's: a new approach to small sample theory. Econometrica 51:1505–1525
Phillips PCB, Park JY (1988) On the formulation of Wald tests of nonlinear restrictions. Econometrica 56:1065–1083
Reid N (1991) Approximations and asymptotics. In: Hinkley D, Reid N, Snell E (eds) Statistical theory and modeling: in honour of Sir David Cox, FRS. Chapman and Hall, London
Rothenberg T (1984) Approximating the distributions of econometric estimators and test statistics. In: Griliches Z, Intriligator MD (eds) Handbook of econometrics, vol II. North-Holland, Amsterdam, pp 881–935
Sargan JD, Satchell SE (1986) A theorem of validity for edgeworth expansions. Econometrica 54:189–213
Satorra A, Bentler P (2001) A scaled difference chi-square test statistic for moment structure analysis. Psychometrika 66:507–514
Sugiura N (1969) Asymptotic expansions of the distributions of the likelihood ratio criteria for covariance matrix. Ann Math Stat 40:2051–2063
Topel RH, Ward MP (1992) Job mobility and the careers of young men. Q J Econ 107:439–479
Yanagihara H, Matsumoto C, Tonda T (2004) Asymptotic expansion of the null distribution of the modified normal likelihood ratio criterion for testing $\Sigma = \Sigma_0$ under nonnormality. Hiroshima Math J 34:81–100
Yuan K-H, Bentler PM (1997) Mean and covariance structure analysis: theoretical and practical improvements. J Am Stat Assoc 92:767–774

Index

R.C. Sickles and W.C. Horrace (eds.), *Festschrift in Honor of Peter Schmidt: Econometric Methods and Applications*, DOI 10.1007/978-1-4899-8008-3,

MIX
Papier aus verantwortungsvollen Quellen
Paper from responsible sources
FSC® C105338

If you have any concerns about our products,
you can contact us on
ProductSafety@springernature.com

In case Publisher is established outside the EU,
the EU authorized representative is:
Springer Nature Customer Service Center GmbH
Europaplatz 3, 69115 Heidelberg, Germany

Printed by Libri Plureos GmbH
in Hamburg, Germany